Understanding Financial Accounts

EDITED BY PETER VAN DE VEN
AND DANIELE FANO

OECD
BETTER POLICIES FOR BETTER LIVES

This work is published under the responsibility of the Secretary-General of the OECD. The opinions expressed and arguments employed herein do not necessarily reflect the official views of OECD member countries.

This document, as well as any data and any map included herein are without prejudice to the status of or sovereignty over any territory, to the delimitation of international frontiers and boundaries and to the name of any territory, city or area.

Please cite this publication as:
OECD (2017), *Understanding Financial Accounts*, OECD Publishing, Paris.
http://dx.doi.org/10.1787/9789264281288-en

ISBN 978-92-64-28125-7 (print)
ISBN 978-92-64-28128-8 (PDF)
ISBN 978-92-64-28129-5 (ePub)

The statistical data for Israel are supplied by and under the responsibility of the relevant Israeli authorities. The use of such data by the OECD is without prejudice to the status of the Golan Heights, East Jerusalem and Israeli settlements in the West Bank under the terms of international law.

Corrigenda to OECD publications may be found on line at: *www.oecd.org/about/publishing/corrigenda.htm*.
© OECD 2017

You can copy, download or print OECD content for your own use, and you can include excerpts from OECD publications, databases and multimedia products in your own documents, presentations, blogs, websites and teaching materials, provided that suitable acknowledgment of the source and copyright owner is given. All requests for public or commercial use and translation rights should be submitted to *rights@oecd.org*. Requests for permission to photocopy portions of this material for public or commercial use shall be addressed directly to the Copyright Clearance Center (CCC) at *info@copyright.com* or the Centre français d'exploitation du droit de copie (CFC) at *contact@cfcopies.com*.

Foreword

The 2007-09 financial and economic crisis started with a collapse in the US housing market which triggered defaults on subprime mortgages. The trouble quickly spread to other financial markets, leading to great financial instability and multiple defaults of financial corporations, not only in the United States but throughout the world. This in turn ushered in the deepest recession since the 1930s. Economic growth turned significantly negative in many countries and unemployment rates increased sharply, especially among younger people. An important indirect impact was the sovereign debt crisis in Europe, with Greece as the most prominent example.

All these developments underlined once again, and more forcefully, the importance of financial accounts and balance sheets to timely, reliable and comprehensive monitoring of financial and economic developments, including their interconnections across sectors and countries. The framework of financial accounts and balance sheets, which is part of the system of national accounts, brings coherence to hundreds of statistical sources available in countries. It delivers essential macro economic information to monitor financial risks and vulnerabilities, and analyse links between the world of finance and the "real" economy. As such, it can make an important contribution to policy making.

This publication aims to show the richness of the information contained in the financial accounts and balance sheets – and the system of national accounts more generally – and to demonstrate their usefulness for economic research, analysis, and policy formulation. It also explains the concepts and statistical sources underpinning the financial accounts and balance sheets, and the complexities involved in compiling a fully consistent set of statistics on finance and wealth. The overall objective is to offer a better understanding of the framework of financial accounts and balance sheets in an accessible, yet rigorous, format.

Understanding Financial Accounts extends and deepens the analysis in Chapter 8 of the publication *Understanding National Accounts*. It responds to the renewed interest in monetary and financial stability issues, and in monitoring financial risks and vulnerabilities, including their impact on growth and employment. It therefore places special emphasis on the links between the financial accounts and balance sheets and the non-financial accounts section of the system of national accounts which deals with the "real" economy. Often these are treated as separate systems, partly because they are compiled by different national statistical authorities.

But while Understanding National Accounts *was primarily an OECD product, with some outside contributions, this publication is a fully co-operative effort with colleagues from the OECD and the Bank for International Settlements (BIS), the European Central Bank (ECB), Fondazione AIB, the International Monetary Fund (IMF), National Central Banks (Austria, Italy and Portugal) and National Statistical Offices (Australia and Canada) and the Treasury of Canada.*

We recommend this guide to young statisticians, students, journalists, economists, policy makers and all citizens who want to know more about the statistics at the heart of the analysis of financial developments in OECD economies.

Table of contents

Acknowledgements 9

Executive summary 11

A brief overview of financial accounts and balance sheets 15
    1. Financial accounts and balance sheets: a lively and pertinent matter 16
    2. A rich and stimulating history 19
    3. Common misconceptions and interpretation errors 20
    4. Overview of this book 21
    References 22

Chapter 1. **Financial accounts and balance sheets within the System of National Accounts** 23
    1. Introduction 24
    2. Overview of financial accounts and balance sheets within the System of National Accounts 24
    3. Institutional sectors 37
    4. Financial instruments 43
    5. Accounting rules 46
    6. Statistical guidance, data sources and compilation methodology . . . 54
    Key points 58
    Notes 60
    References 60

Chapter 2. **The role of financial markets** 61
    1. Introduction 62
    2. Financial markets in the 2008 SNA 62
    3. Financial intermediation 78
    4. Interconnectedness between sectors 80
    5. Risk elements within the financial system 83
    Key points 89
    Notes 90
    References 90

Chapter 3. **The role of financial corporations in the financial system** . . . 91
    1. Short overview 92

TABLE OF CONTENTS

    2. The Central Bank 96
    3. Deposit-taking corporations apart from the central bank 103
    4. Money market funds 112
    5. The increasing role of other financial institutions (OFIs)......... 117
    6. Insurance corporations and pension funds 122
    7. Analysing the financial corporation sector 129
    Key points 133

    Notes 134
    References 136

Chapter 4. **Households and their financial behaviour** 139
    1. Households as consumers, entrepreneurs, investors and net lenders . 140
    2. The interlinkages between income, saving, financial
       and non-financial investments, and debt..................... 151
    3. Distributional aspects of wealth and going beyond households'
       economic well-being 165
    Key points 170
    Going further... 171

    Notes 174
    References 174

Chapter 5. **The financing of non-financial corporations** 177
    1. The role of non-financial corporations in the economy
       and in financial markets..................................... 178
    2. Sources and uses of funds for non-financial corporations 183
    3. Capital gains in the non-financial corporations' sector 197
    4. The financial position of non-financial corporations:
       balance sheets 198
    5. Globalisation, foreign direct investment and non-financial
       corporations 210
    Key points 213
    Going further... 215

    Notes 218
    References 218

Chapter 6. **Deficit and debt of general government and public sector** ... 219
    1. Delineating the government sector 220
    2. Key financial accounts indicators for general government/
       public sector 226
    3. Going into more detail..................................... 239
    Key Points 247

    Notes 249
    References 249

Chapter 7. **The financial relationships with the Rest of the World** 251
   1. A general overview 252
   2. The balance of payments and its relationship with national
      accounts 254
   3. The underlying components of non-financial and financial accounts .. 261
   Key points 274
   Going further 275

   Notes 277
   References 277

Chapter 8. **A full accounting for wealth: Including non-financial assets** ... 279
   1. General introduction to financial and non-financial wealth 280
   2. Specificities of non-financial assets, including their measurement .. 284
   3. Who owns wealth: distribution across institutional sectors 289
   4. Accumulation and de-accumulation of wealth 296
   5. Macro and micro: extending the system of national accounts 298
   Key points 301

   References 302

Chapter 9. **Accounting for the financial consequences of demographic
     changes** 303
   1. The effect of demographic changes on household saving
      and wealth 304
   2. Demographic changes and government finances 309
   3. Demographic changes and pension schemes 313
   Key points 327

   Notes 328
   References 328

Chapter 10. **Globalisation, financial innovation and crises** 331
   1. Introduction 332
   2. Countries' fragilities and international crises 332
   3. Assessing the build-up of financial risks in a globalised world 344
   4. Analysing the impacts of leverage and financial innovation
      on economic growth and policy 351
   5. Integrating micro information in the financial accounts
      perspective 361
   6. Addressing the information gaps highlighted by the 2007-09
      economic and financial crisis 367
   Key points 372
   Going further 373

   Notes 377
   References 377

TABLE OF CONTENTS

Chapter 11. **Financial accounts uses** 381
   1. Annual versus quarterly financial accounts and balance sheets .. 382
   2. The use of financial accounts to assess financial stability 392
   3. Uses of financial accounts and balance sheets in economic
      research 407
   Key points 415

   Notes 416
   References 416

Follow OECD Publications on:

http://twitter.com/OECD_Pubs

http://www.facebook.com/OECDPublications

http://www.linkedin.com/groups/OECD-Publications-4645871

http://www.youtube.com/oecdilibrary

http://www.oecd.org/oecddirect/

This book has...

StatLinks
A service that delivers Excel® files from the printed page!

Look for the *StatLinks* at the bottom of the tables or graphs in this book. To download the matching Excel® spreadsheet, just type the link into your Internet browser, starting with the *http://dx.doi.org* prefix, or click on the link from the e-book edition.

Acknowledgements

The main editor of this publication is Peter van de Ven (OECD). However, this publication would not have been possible without the active involvement of Daniel Fano (Fondazione AIB) who had the idea to compile a publication on financial accounts and balance sheets. His perseverance made *Understanding Financial Accounts* happen. Daniele also participated actively in drafting, editing and reviewing various chapters.

The editors would like to thank, first, the authors and co-authors of the chapters, for their excellent input, and their willingness and patience to address the continuous stream of comments, suggestions and proposals for further additions: Michael Andreasch (Oesterreichische Nationalbank), João Cadete de Matos (Banco de Portugal), Julia Catz (ECB), Derick Cullen (Australian Bureau of Statistics), Riccardo De Bonis (Banca d'Italia), Robert Dippelsman (IMF), Celestino Giron (ECB), Paul Goebel (Treasury Board of Canada Secretariat), Andreas Hertkorn (ECB), Luigi Infante (Banca d'Italia), Filipa Lima (Banco de Portugal), Antonio Matas-Mir (ECB), Patrick O'Hagan (Statistics Canada), Gabriel Quirós (IMF), Gabriele Semeraro (Banca d'Italia), Amanda Seneviratne (Australian Bureau of Statistics), James Tebrake (Statistics Canada), Bruno Tissot (BIS), and Jorrit Zwijnenburg (OECD).

Many thanks also go to Sarah Geisman and Maja Kunstelj, two interns at the OECD, and Leonie Beisemann (OECD), who did a marvellous job in reviewing all chapters, introducing many improvements, making excellent proposals for redrafting, and working on the tables and graphs. Without them, this publication would not have happened. Thanks also go to Matthew De Queljoe for taking care of the final editorial changes and all other requests related to the finalisation of this publication.

Special thanks for their thorough review of the manuscript to Michaela Bello, Esther Bolton, Matthew De Queljoe, Rachida Dkhissi, Federico Giovannelli, Haukur Gudjonsson, Jennifer Ribarsky, Elena Van Eck, Bettina Wistrom, Florence Wolff, Isabelle Ynesta and Jorrit Zwijnenburg, all from the OECD Statistics Directorate.

Also many thanks to Tom Lay, Grace Kim and Michael Davies (from the Australian Bureau of Statistics), and João Abreu, Sérgio Branco, Inês Câncio Pinto, Ângela Coelho, Teresa Crespo, Gonçalo Duarte, João Falcão, André Guerreiro,

ACKNOWLEDGEMENTS

Filipe Morais, Sónia Mota, Rita Pisco, Rita Poiares, Ana Margarida Ribeiro and Vítor Silveira (from Banco de Portugal), Hans Olsson (from ECB), and Sonia Primot (OECD) for providing support in completing Chapters 1, 2, 3, 6 and 7.

Finally, thanks to the OECD Public Affairs and Communication Directorate for their support, and in particular, to Julia Stockdale-Otarola and Carmen Fernandez-Biezma for their valuable contributions, and to Martine Zaïda from the OECD Statistics Directorate for her coordinating role.

Executive summary

Understanding Financial Accounts provides a non-technical explanation of all aspects of financial accounts and balance sheets, allowing users of these statistics to gain a good understanding of the topic. Each chapter uses practical examples to explain key concepts in the framework of financial accounts and balance sheets in a clear and accessible way.

The publication begins, in Chapter 1, by situating financial accounts and balance sheets within the broader System of National Accounts reporting system. In Chapter 2, it subsequently identifies the various financial markets for which financial accounts and balance sheets provide a tool for monitoring, analysis and policy making.

The publication continues, in Chapters 3 to 7, with providing an overview of each of the sectors included in the framework of financial accounts and balance sheets: financial corporations, households (including non-profit institutions serving households), non-financial corporations, general government, and the rest of the world (i.e. the financial transactions and positions between the residents of an economy and non-residents).

Chapter 3 on financial corporations provides more details on the roles and functions of these corporations which are in the centre of the financial system, channelling funds from lenders/savers to borrowers/investors. The chapter also discusses the transformation of the financial system in the run-up to the 2007-09 economic and financial crisis, from the "originate-to-keep" to the "originate-to-distribute" model, and the accompanying emergence of securitisation companies and other financial intermediaries.

Chapter 4 focuses on the financial behaviour of households, as consumers, investors in financial and non-financial assets (dwellings), and owners of unincorporated enterprises. It shows that the creation and the structure of households' financial wealth depends on several factors, such as the level of and change in disposable income and saving, the financial system, market conditions, and regulation related to pensions and taxes.

The importance of non-financial corporations in the "real" economy is evident in nearly every economic activity. Chapter 5 dwells upon non-financial corporations' interactions within the financial system, both as borrowers and as lenders. Their investments of available funds across instruments provides important insights into their strategies and their propensity towards risk, while different sources of funding shed light on their key choices, such as the choice of debt or equity or the mix of long-term versus short-term debt.

General government, or more broadly the public sector, plays an important role in the economy. When it comes to finance, they are major borrowers, issuers of securities, and funders of other entities. Chapter 6 gives examples of statistics and indicators for monitoring and analysing government financial behaviour, such as net lending/net borrowing and the composition of government financial assets and liabilities.

The financial relationships with non-residents, the "Rest of the World", are described in Chapter 7. The external balance of the current and capital accounts are linked to issues such as productivity, costs of production factors, product/market diversification, tariff regimes, development of the financial system, as well as other factors such as the ageing of population, the propensity to save and the trade openness of the country. The chapter shows, for example, how persistent imbalances with the Rest of the World may lead to growing international indebtedness, which, sooner or later, needs to be addressed. Standard criteria developed to test external debt sustainability, or thresholds to assess the impact of consistent surpluses, are presented.

Non-financial assets play a crucial role in balance sheets, in addition to financial assets and liabilities. For an economy as a whole, non-financial assets are the most important determinant of net worth, or net wealth, of an economy. Chapter 8 describes the place of non-financial assets in the system of national accounts, and their delineation, ownership and valuation. Attention is also paid to the distribution of non-financial assets and net worth across institutional sectors, and their evolution over time.

Chapter 9 to 11 describe some broader themes related to financial accounts and balance sheets. First, Chapter 9 deals with the impact of demographic changes on the financial behaviour of the various agents in an economy. They directly affect household saving and wealth accumulation. Government deficit may also be affected as expenditures and revenues often have a close relationship with the demographic structure of a society. The changing ratio between the retired population and the working population may have an impact on the balance sheets of pension funds and may also distort the sustainability of pension schemes, both occupational and social security schemes.

Chapter 10 highlights the usefulness of the framework of financial accounts and balance sheets for understanding financial globalisation, innovation and crises. A more in-depth analysis is provided of countries' fragilities related to external financial exposures. Furthermore, the build-up of financial risks over time and the contributing roles of international finance and globalisation are analysed in a broader perspective. The chapter also shows how the financial accounts and balance sheets can be mobilised to analyse financial crises, drawing in particular on recent episodes of stress and considering the impact of leverage and financial innovation. The importance of integrating a micro, entity-level perspective in the macro approach of the financial accounts and balance sheets is shortly dwelt upon, including international efforts to enhance countries' statistical frameworks in response to 2007-09 economic and financial crisis.

Finally, Chapter 11 takes the perspective of users of financial accounts and balance sheets, both quarterly and annual. It shows that the interest in financial accounts and balance sheets, both from the perspective of financial stability analysis and the perspective of monetary policy, is a function of specific events and times, with the 2007-09 economic and financial crisis as the most prominent example. The chapter also highlights the use of financial accounts and balance sheets by famous economists, from the early 1950s to today.

A brief overview of financial accounts and balance sheets

Daniele Fano (Fondazione AIB)

Concepts from financial accounts and balance sheets are part of everyday policy debates as well as academic research. This chapter introduces financial accounts and balance sheets by placing these concepts within the framework of the System of National Accounts (SNA), and also offers a short account of the origins and developments of the SNA, up to 1952, when the OECD (then the OEEC) took the lead in establishing international standards for macroeconomic statistics within the United Nations statistics framework. Finally, this chapter provides an overview of the key questions this book attempts to answer.

1. Financial accounts and balance sheets: a lively and pertinent matter

"Asset price inflation", "sustained current account surplus", "sovereign external debt", "household net lending", "corporate leverage", "financial sector balance sheets" – these are just a few financial terms that we, not only as specialists, but also as concerned citizens, hear on the radio and TV, and read in newspapers, books and blogs. They are all part of the System of National Accounts, more specifically the financial accounts and balance sheets. The use of these technical concepts has become much more widespread since the 2007-09 economic and financial crisis, although their importance was already well-established before.

In a nutshell, financial accounts and balance sheets provide a systematic overview, by economic sector, of assets and liabilities of those economic sectors at a certain point in time. The following main sectors are included: non-financial corporations, financial corporations, government, households, and non profit institutions serving households. In addition, data on foreign exposures, for example foreign assets owned by the residents of an economy, or the liabilities that residents have incurred towards non-residents, are recorded in the balance sheets of the so-called "Rest of the World". Assets and liabilities are typically broken down into various "financial instruments", such as currency and deposits, debt securities and loans, and equity. In addition to providing an overview of the stocks of the various financial instruments, the balance sheets, financial accounts and other "accumulation accounts" show a complete picture of the acquisitions and purchases of financial assets and liabilities, or the changes in stocks due to, for example, holding gains and losses.

There are a wealth of examples of central bankers, government officials, financial and academic experts and others discussing the numerous uses and advantages of the System of National Accounts, and financial accounts and balance sheets.

In the words of Michael Palumbo and Jonathan Parker:

"The implementation of the System of National Accounts (SNA) ... has two significant advantages ... First, the SNA are organized according to sectors of the economy defined by economic agents: firms, financial institutions, consumers, governments and the rest of the world. Second, the accounts integrate real and financial information, so that one can track not only production of, income from, and use of output, but also net lending, net borrowing, and net worth by sector" (Palumbo and Parker, 2009).

Financial accounts and balance sheets allow for reality checks. In 2009, the Financial Stability Board under Mario Draghi issued a report stating that "… data gaps are an inevitable consequence of the ongoing development of markets and institutions … Indeed, the recent crisis has reaffirmed an old lesson – good data and good analysis are the lifeblood of effective surveillance and policy responses at both the national and international levels" (IMF, 2009). In response to the document by the Financial Stability Board, the G-20 decided to pursue a strong focus on the systematic implementation of the financial accounts and balance sheets, with the goal of offering a more cohesive and complete set of financial statistics at the macro level (OECD, 2015).

Financial accounts and balance sheets have provided powerful insights that lead to key policy decisions. When explaining why the Federal Reserve engaged in radically new monetary policies, Ben Bernanke explained that "…financial institutions [had] seen their capital depleted by losses and write-downs and their balance sheets clogged" (Bernanke, 2009).

Through financial stability reports regularly published by the IMF and national central banks, the financial accounts and balance sheets provide a way to understand prospective financial risks and measures to be taken to address them. The Bank of England, for example, described how the current account can provide warnings about a country's financial stability: "A persistent current account deficit could lead to a sudden adjustment in capital flows or depreciation of the exchange rate, with adverse consequences for … financial stability … the composition of capital flows can change over time and vulnerabilities can build quickly, particularly when the deficit is persistently large" (Bank of England, 2015). Another example is the IMF describing their concerns about developments in balance sheets: "But balance sheets have become stretched thinner in many…companies and banks. These firms have become more susceptible to financial stress, economic downturn, and capital outflows. Deteriorating corporate health runs the risk of deepening the sovereign-corporate and the corporate-bank nexus in some key…markets" (IMF, 2015).

In fact, financial accounts and balance sheets not only allow a reader to understand short-term risks, but also more structural and longer term features of economic and financial systems, as shown, for example, in Paoli and Küçük (2016):

"The world has gone through a process of financial globalization over the past decades, with countries increasing their holdings of foreign assets and liabilities. At the same time, countries have started to have a more positive foreign currency exposure by reducing their bias toward holding assets in domestic currency instead of foreign currency."

Financial accounts and balance sheets can also put events in a broader historical perspective:

"The costs imposed by the financial crises that hit western economies in 2007 have been enormous ... [and] include huge rises in public debt ... This is the fourth most costly fiscal event of the past 225 years, after the wars with post-revolutionary France and the first and second world wars. Mismanaged finance imposes fiscal costs that are not far short of world wars" (Wolf, 2015).

Figure 1. **Gross general government debt**
Percentage of GDP

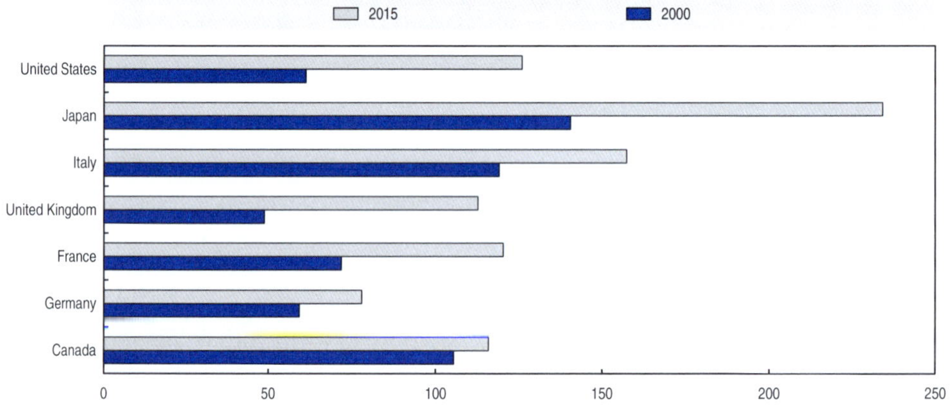

OECD (2017), "Financial Balance Sheets, SNA 2008 (or SNA 1993): Consolidated stocks, annual", *OECD National Accounts Statistics* (database), http://dx.doi.org/10.1787/data-00719-en.
StatLink ⟶ http://dx.doi.org/10.1787/888933587832

The importance of national accounts in understanding major economic events is best captured in the bestseller book titled *This Time is Different* (Reinhart and Rogoff, 2009), which offers an in-depth historical perspective based on empirical investigation of financial crises in the past centuries with special reference to debt.

Last but not least, financial accounts and balance sheets may trigger thoughts on new intellectual challenges and highlight the need for fresh thinking:

"Failure to foresee either the crisis or the length of the subsequent recession reflects an intellectual failure within mainstream economics – an inadequate focus on the links between financial stability and macroeconomic stability, and on the crucial role that leverage levels and cycles play in macroeconomic developments" (Turner, 2003).

2. A rich and stimulating history

The fact that the interpretation of financial accounts and balance sheets can be difficult and complicated, and focuses on unpleasant numbers such as deficit and debt, likely explains why the accounts are not more popular. But are financial accounts and balance sheets really that complicated or abstruse? Back in 1777, David Hume started his *Essays on Commerce and Trade* with a surprising warning that can apply to the intricacies (and importance) of financial accounts: "The greater part of mankind may be divided in two classes, that of shallow thinkers who fall short of the truth; and that of abstruse thinkers who go beyond it. The latter class are by far the most rare and, I may add, the most useful and valuable."

When David Hume was writing his critical essay, rudimentary national accounts figures such as sovereign wealth and international trade estimates had been around for a couple of centuries. Then, as now, such figures gave rise to economic debates and theories. Bullionism, focusing on monetary policy, was superseded by Mercantilism, which had a broader perspective. David Hume, Adam Smith and the French and Italian "laissez-faire" school of economics developed the Classical Economy criticism and fostered an even more complete framework. Further developments in economic thought led to better definitions of economic agents, their interactions, and their grouping into sectors.

The current version of the System of National Accounts, based on international shared principles and standards, is relatively recent. In fact, it was developed during the past century, following the Great Depression and the accompanying urgent need for data to offer support to the US government in crafting economic policies that would steer the economy towards recovery. In the absence of comprehensive national income and output measures, the US Department of Commerce commissioned Simon Kuznets of the National Bureau of Economic Research (NBER) to produce a series on National Income accounts. His research was published in 1934 and the original set of accounts was presented in a report to Congress in 1937, marking the start of the development of comprehensive national income accounts.

World conflict and economic downturns brought policy making to the forefront, and the new "tool box" of national accounts for monitoring economic developments gradually became part of the required information set. While initially used for "back of the envelope" estimates of the impact of alternative policy decisions, national accounts were soon used in ever-more sophisticated models. In his 1940 book *How to Pay for the War,* John Maynard Keynes used macro accounting to craft an economic policy proposal for addressing the challenge of non-inflationary financing of the war effort. His then-assistant, young researcher and statistician Richard Stone, later became a founding father of the modern System of National Accounts and went on to receive the Nobel Memorial Prize in Economic Sciences for his work on developing an accounting model to track economic activities on both the national and international scale.

Morris Copeland should also be mentioned here; through his analysis of money flows in the six-year period encompassing the recovery from the Depression and the outbreak of World War II, Copeland pioneered the so-called "Flow of Funds Accounts". His research addressed key theoretical questions pertaining to national accounting: "When total purchases of our national product increase, where does the money come from to finance them? When purchases of our national product decline, what becomes of the money that is not spent? What part do cash balances, other liquid holdings, and debts play in the cyclical expansion of money flow?" (Copeland, 1949). The Flow of Funds reports have since 1952 been published quarterly by the US Federal Reserve and are considered an important element to understanding national accounts.

All of this led up to the current System of National Accounts. As far back as 1952, the OECD (then the OEEC) took the lead in establishing a standardised System of National Accounts within the United Nations Statistics framework (Ward, 2004). Since then, successive waves of improvements under a group of international organisations (OECD, IMF, United Nations, World Bank, and more recently the European Commission) have followed. The latest version is the 2008 System of National Accounts (the "2008 SNA"), which was implemented in most developed countries in 2014. The last decade has also shown a significant improvement in the availability of annual and quarterly national accounts figures for a whole range of countries on a common rigorous basis.

3. Common misconceptions and interpretation errors

The reader should be warned that intuition may be deceiving when analysing financial accounts figures. There are frequent confusions about, for example, the distinction between "stocks" and "flows" or the composition of different parts of the saving balancing item. These distinctions may appear to many as cumbersome refinements, but they are important and will be further addressed in this book.

Misplaced intuition may be reinforced by the fact that, when thinking about figures, we may be looking for confirmation of existing ideas. Often the effort of taking a fresh look at the numbers can be rewarding. For example, one concept that has traditionally been prevalent in economics is that households are net lenders and that corporations are net borrowers, while the other sectors are more or less balanced. The truth is that in many countries, corporations have, in the recent past, acted as net lenders for many years in a row, while governments have been major borrowers and, in the period just before the 2007-09 economic and financial crisis, even households became net borrowers (Fano and Trovato, 2013).

4. Overview of this book

Financial accounts and balance sheets allow us to answer some key questions that are, amongst others, addressed in the various chapters of this book:

- What are the financial linkages between the various sectors of the economy? How does it all come together in the complete set of accounts? Which financial instruments are distinguished, and what are the main accounting rules? (Chapter 1).
- Which financial markets can be distinguished? What is the role of the various economic actors? How does the connectedness between sectors and countries play a role in the spread of financial risks? Which risks are involved in investing and borrowing? (Chapter 2).
- What is the role of banks and other financial corporations, and how do they interact with the rest of the economy? Has their role increased over time? What is "shadow banking", and what types of new financial corporations have emerged? (Chapter 3).
- How do we assess households' ability to accumulate wealth and to incur debt? How is this distributed across household groups? (Chapter 4).
- What are the sources and uses of funds for non-financial corporations in the era of globalisation? How has the financial behaviour of companies changed over time? (Chapter 5).
- What are the key indicators for assessing the financial situation of a government? How can government debt be defined and measured? (Chapter 6).
- How is a national economy connected to the rest of world? How can one evaluate the opportunities and risks of foreign exposures? (Chapter 7).
- What are the differences between financial and non-financial wealth? Who owns the wealth, and how is it (de)accumulated? How can one arrive at a complete set of balance sheets for the various sectors? (Chapter 8).
- Why is demography so relevant for understanding financial accounts? What is the role of pension funds and governments in providing retirement resources? (Chapter 9).
- What lessons can we draw from recent financial crises? How can we monitor and assess the build-up of risks and transmission channels, and what type of statistics do we need to do this? What is the role of, and risks related to, "globally systemically important financial institutions"? (Chapter 10).

- Which statistics related to the financial accounts and balance sheets are typically compiled and disseminated? What are the uses of financial accounts and balance sheets? What has the academic literature contributed in this area? (Chapter 11).

References

Bank of England (2015), *Financial Stability Report, December 2015*, Bank of England, London, *www.bankofengland.co.uk/publications/Documents/fsr/2015/dec.pdf*.

Bernanke, B. (2009), *The Crisis and the Policy Response*, the Stamp Lecture, 13 January, London School of Economics, London.

Copeland, M. (1949), "Social Accounting for Money Flows", *Accounting Review*, Vol. 24/3, pp. 254-264.

De Paoli, B. and H. Küçük (6 January 2016), "Hedging income fluctuations with foreign currency assets", Liberty Street Economics blog, *http://libertystreeteconomics. newyorkfed.org/2016/01/hedging-income-fluctuations-with-foreign-currency-assets. html?utm_source=feedburner&utm_medium=feed&utm_campaign= Feed%3A+Liberty StreetEconomics+%28Liberty+Street+Economics%29*.

Fano D. and G. Trovato (2013), "Patterns in financial flows? A longer-term perspective on intersectoral relationships", in *Public Debt, Global Governance and Economic Dynamism*, Springer Verlag, Milan.

IMF (2015), *Global Stability Report, October 2015*, IMF, Washington, DC, *www.imf.org/en/ Publications/GFSR/Issues/2016/12/31/Vulnerabilities-Legacies-and-Policy-Challenges*.

IMF and Financial Stability Board (2009), *Financial Crisis and Information Gaps: Report to the G20 Finance Ministers and to the Central Bank Governors*, *www.imf.org/external/np/ g20/pdf/102909.pdf*.

OECD (2017), "Financial Balance Sheets, SNA 2008 (or SNA 1993): Consolidated stocks, annual", *OECD National Accounts Statistics* (database), *http://dx.doi.org/10.1787/data-00719-en*.

OECD (2015), "G20 Data Gaps Initiative (DGI)", *OECD Statistics Newsletter*, Issue 63, OECD, Paris, pp. 3-7, *www.oecd.org/std/OECD-Statistics-Newsletter-September-2015.pdf*.

Palumbo, M.G. and J.A. Parker (2009), "The integrated financial and real System of National Accounts for the United States: Does it presage the financial crisis?", *NBER Working Paper*, No. 14663, National Bureau of Economic Research, Cambridge, *www.nber.org/papers/w14663.pdf*.

Reinhart, C.M. and K.S. Rogoff (2009), *This Time is Different*, Princeton University Press, Princeton.

Turner, A. (2003), "Debt, money, and Mephistopheles: How do we get out of this mess?", *Occasional Papers (Group of Thirty)*, No. 87, Washington, DC, *http:// group30.org/images/uploads/publications/G30_DebtMoney Mephistopheles.pdf*.

Ward, M. (2004), *Quantifying the World: UN Ideas and Statistics*, Indiana University Press, Bloomington.

Wolf, M. (2015), "Indispensable banks need a sturdy ringfence", *The Financial Times*, 25 June 2015.

Chapter 1

Financial accounts and balance sheets within the System of National Accounts

Derick Cullen (Australian Bureau of Statistics),
Peter van de Ven (OECD) and Jorrit Zwijnenburg (OECD)

> *Financial accounts and balance sheets play an important role in the system of national accounts, focusing on the accumulation and stocks/ positions of financial assets and liabilities. This chapter starts with an overview of how the financial accounts and balance sheets are embedded in the system of national accounts, how they are an intrinsic part of a comprehensive and fully consistent accounting system, governed by various accounting identities. It also explains how this results in a set of interrelated accounts which show how different sectors in a country interact with each other, and how the balances of assets and liabilities change over time. The chapter also includes some further guidance on the definitions of sectors and financial instruments, and accounting rules which guide the recognition and valuation of assets and liabilities.*

1. Introduction

The 2008 System of National Accounts (2008 SNA) sets out a framework of accounts that enables the recording of all relevant elements of an economy's production, income, final consumption, accumulation of assets and liabilities, and its wealth, in a comprehensive and consistent way. Economic flows and stocks are recorded according to specified accounting rules and presented in a set of accounts for the economy as a whole and broken down into institutional sectors and subsectors. The sectors and subsectors comprise groups of "institutional units" with the same economic role, such as non-financial and financial corporations, the government sector and households. In addition to having full balance sheets, the national accounts distinguish a number of accounts, which group together flows of a similar nature, such as production, generation and (re)distribution of income or accumulation of wealth.

This chapter focuses on elements within the national accounts that enable the measurement of the accumulation and resulting positions of financial assets and liabilities, as recorded in the financial accounts and balance sheets. Discussion will include the role of financial accounts and balance sheets in the accounting framework of the national accounts (Section 2), a presentation of the sectors and instruments that are distinguished in the accounts with their main characteristics (Sections 3 and 4 respectively), the accounting rules that are at the basis of the financial accounts and balance sheets (Section 5), and an overview of the main aspects of the compilation process including data sources and main guidance (Section 6).

2. Overview of financial accounts and balance sheets within the System of National Accounts

The sequence of accounts

The 2008 SNA framework of accounts is presented as a sequence of interconnected accounts representing different types of economic activity occurring within a period of time, including balance sheets that record stocks of assets and liabilities held by each institutional sector at the start and end of that period. This complete sequence of accounts is referred to as "institutional sector accounts". Figure 1.1 provides a simplified overview of the sequence of accounts.

The sequence of accounts can be broken down into current and accumulation accounts. The current accounts provide information on

1. FINANCIAL ACCOUNTS AND BALANCE SHEETS WITHIN THE SYSTEM OF NATIONAL ACCOUNTS

Figure 1.1. **Sequence of accounts in the 2008 SNA**

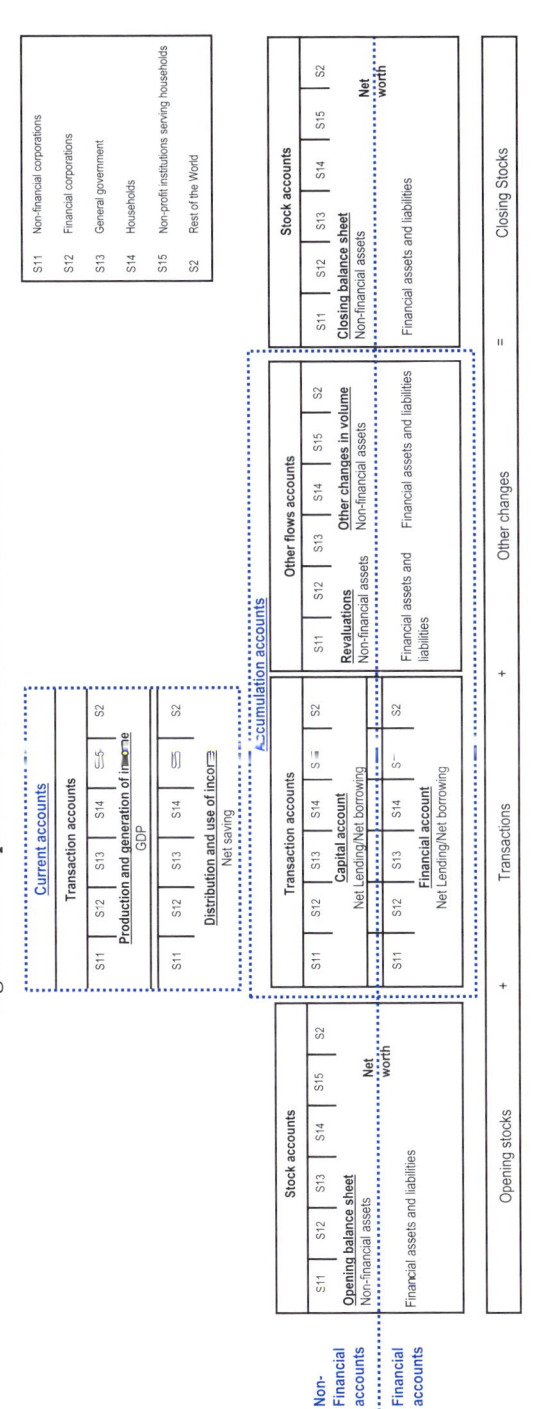

production, income generated by production, the subsequent distribution and redistribution of incomes, and the use of income for consumption and saving purposes. These relate to the upper part of Figure 1.1. The accumulation accounts record flows that affect the balance sheets and consist of the capital and financial account, which primarily record transactions (purchases less disposals of assets and net incurrence of liabilities), and the other changes in assets account, which consists of a separate account for revaluations and one for other changes in the volume of assets. Together these accounts represent the changes in the stock accounts or balance sheets. All of this is presented in the lower part of Figure 1.1.

The balance sheets show the values of the stocks of assets and liabilities at the start and the end of the recording period. They also provide insight into the financial status of a sector by illustrating how that sector finances its activities or invests its funds. On the balance sheets, a clear distinction can be made between non-financial assets on the one hand, and financial assets and liabilities on the other hand. Examples of non-financial assets include produced assets like houses, infrastructure, machinery and equipment, and inventories, but they also comprise non-produced assets such as land, mineral and energy resources and water resources. Deposits, shares, loans and bonds are examples of financial assets (and liabilities). The value of the assets and liabilities at the start of a period is referred to as "opening stock" and at the end of the period as "closing stock".

Transactions are defined in the SNA as economic flows that are interactions "between institutional units by mutual agreement" (SNA 2008, paragraph 3.51). All types of purchases and sales of goods and services and assets qualify as transactions. The same is true for various income receipts and payments, such as interest, dividends, and income transfers.

Transactions can be clearly distinguished from the "other flows", which comprise revaluations (holding gains or losses) and other changes in the volume of assets (for example, discoveries of natural resources, losses due to catastrophic events, and uncompensated seizures). As the examples show, these "other flows", which are recorded in the other changes in assets accounts, are different from transactions in the sense that they do not represent a transaction between two economic agents. In theory, the other changes in assets account is broken down into the revaluation account and the other changes in the volume of assets accounts, although in practice many countries are not able to do so.

Balancing items

Each account ends with a balancing item which is usually the starting item for the subsequent account. The balancing item typically represents the net result of the flows (or positions) recorded in the account in question, and is calculated as the difference between the total resources and total uses recorded. Examples of balancing items are gross value added on the production account and saving on the use of income account. The national totals of these balancing items often represent important macro-economic aggregates. For example, the sum of gross value added generated in the various domestic sectors equals Gross Domestic Product (GDP), while the sum of (gross/net) primary income, the balancing item of the primary distribution of income account, represents (Gross/Net) National Income.

The current accounts and the accumulation accounts are linked through saving. When the current accounts show negative saving, the excess of consumption over disposable income must be financed by disposing of financial or non-financial assets or by incurring liabilities. Conversely, when the current accounts show positive saving, this will lead to an accumulation of assets or redemption of liabilities.

The capital account constitutes the first part of the accumulation accounts. From the perspective of balance sheets, it provides two important pieces of information in linking current and capital accounts. First of all, it shows, for each sector, the balancing item "changes in net worth due to saving and capital transfers", which equals saving *plus* net capital transfers received. The latter transfers often relate to lump sum payments by governments to corporations (e.g. investment grants and payments to cover losses in financial distress). It may also include, for example, capital taxes or legacies. The balancing item "changes in net worth due to saving and capital transfers" is a crucial link in the system of national accounts. It represents not only the excess available for investing in non-financial or financial assets, or, in the case of a negative balance, the need to borrow funds, it also equals – as the term already suggests – the change in net wealth due to receiving incomes that exceeds expenditures. The other changes in net wealth are due to revaluations and other changes in the volume of assets.

The second piece of information that can be derived from the capital accounts concerns the purchases, less disposals, of non-financial assets. The resulting balancing item is called "net lending/net borrowing". If this balancing item is positive, i.e. the sum of saving and net capital transfers exceeds the net accumulation of non-financial assets, the remaining funds are available to purchase financial assets, which *ceteris paribus* lead to an increase of the financial wealth of the relevant unit or sector. This is recorded as net lending. If it falls short, it is recorded as net borrowing. In the latter case, the unit or sector would need to borrow funds to cover the shortfall.

The net lending/net borrowing amount from the capital account has its counterpart in the balancing item of the financial account, in which the transactions in financial assets and liabilities are recorded. Conceptually the two balancing items are the same; see also the quadruple accounting principle below. In practice, however, due to the different data sources and methods used to compile the production, income and capital accounts versus those used for the compilation of financial accounts, the items often differ from each other. These differences are referred to as 'statistical discrepancies'.

As noted before, balance sheet items are also affected by revaluations and other changes in the volume of assets. The relevant "flows" are recorded on two separate accumulation accounts, where the balancing item of the revaluations account is called "changes in net worth due to revaluations", and the balance of the other changes in the volume of assets account is called the "changes in net worth due to other changes in the volume of assets". These two balancing items, together with the "changes in net worth due to saving and capital transfers", add up to the changes in "net worth" as recorded on the balance sheet.

Net worth, the balancing item from the balance sheet, is defined as the value of all assets owned by an institutional unit or sector less the value of all its outstanding liabilities, and it provides insight into the financial health of a unit or sector. It is recorded, together with the liabilities, on the right-hand side of the balance sheet. Figure 1.2 presents an example of a balance sheet of the non-financial corporations' sector. It should be noted here that equity is also considered as a liability in the national accounts. It is, however, excluded from the various definitions of "debt".

Figure 1.2. **Balance sheet example for the non-financial corporations' sector**

Assets		Liabilities	
Non-financial assets	100		
Fixed assets	90		
Inventories	10		
Financial assets	200	Financial liabilities	230
Deposits	25	Debt securities	60
Loans	55	Loans	35
Equity	100	Equity	120
Other accounts receivable	20	Other accounts payable	15
		Net worth	70

StatLink ⇒ http://dx.doi.org/10.1787/888933587851

Recording flows and stocks

Quadruple accounting principle

The accounting principle underlying the national accounts is that of quadruple-entry bookkeeping. This means that for a single transaction, four simultaneous entries are recorded in the national accounts. First of all, the national accounts respect the double entry system, as applied in traditional business accounting. From an accounting system's perspective, one can look upon national accounts as a further extension of business accounting; see e.g. Gleeson-White (2011). In national accounts terminology, each income or capital transaction recorded on the current or capital account has a counterpart entry in the financial account. In the case of the purchase/sale of a financial asset, or in the case of the incurrence of a liability, both entries appear in the financial account.

However, the goal of national accounts is to arrive at exhaustive estimates for all economic agents on the domestic territory of a country, including the engagements of residents with non-residents. As such, the national accounts do not only record the transactions of a particular unit, but also the transactions of the counterparty unit. As a result, each transaction leads to four entries, the quadruple entry bookkeeping system. A few examples, as presented in Figures 1.3-1.5, illustrate this systematic approach. These figures are necessarily simplified and only include the recording directly related to the transactions that are being illustrated.

Figure 1.3 illustrates the recording of payment of wages ("compensation of employees") from a non-financial corporation to its employees. In the accounts of the non-financial corporations' sector, an expense would be recorded in the generation of income account, to reflect the payment of the wage by the corporation, accompanied by a decrease in deposits in the financial account. In the accounts of the households' sector, the receipt of the wage would be recorded as a resource in the allocation of primary income account, with an accompanying increase in deposits in the financial account.

Figure 1.3. **Receipt of wages by the employees of a non-financial corporation**

Non-financial corporations		Households	
Generation of income account		Allocation of primary income account	
Uses	Resources	Uses	Resources
Compensation of employees 80			Compensation of employees 80
Financial account		Financial account	
Assets	Liabilities	Assets	Liabilities
Deposits -80		Deposits 80	

Figure 1.4 shows how the purchase of debt securities by a household from a financial corporation would be recorded in the national accounts. The sale would be reflected in the financial accounts of the financial corporation via a decrease in debt securities and an accompanying increase in deposits. This would be mirrored in the financial accounts of the households' sector, where the purchase would be reflected via an increase in debt securities and a

decrease in deposits. This purchase would not affect the financial accounts of the issuer of the debt securities. For the issuer, the transaction would only change the counterpart of the debt security, which is reflected in a from-whom-to-whom (FWTW) table (see the discussion of these tables later in this chapter).

Figure 1.4. **Purchase of a debt security by a household**

Financial corporations

Financial account		
Assets		Liabilities
Debt securities	-20	
Deposits	20	

Households

Financial account		
Assets		Liabilities
Debt securities	20	
Deposits	-20	

Finally, Figure 1.5 illustrates the transactions that would be recorded when a household purchases a newly-built dwelling, and finances that purchase by taking out a mortgage loan. In this case, there are three different parties involved in the transactions: the non-financial corporation that constructed and sold the dwelling, the individual purchasing the dwelling and taking out the mortgage loan, and the financial corporation providing the loan. As a result, in the accounts of the non-financial corporations sector, the construction and the sale of the house are recorded as "output" in the production account, with an accompanying increase in deposits in the financial account reflecting the payment for the dwelling. In the accounts of the households, the purchase of the dwelling is recorded as investment ("gross fixed capital formation") in the capital account, while the loan appears as a liability in the financial account, to reflect that the purchase of the dwelling is financed by a mortgage. Finally, in the accounts of the financial corporations' sector, the mortgage loan will show up as a financial asset. The use of this mortgage loan by the household to pay for the dwelling will initially show up as an increase in the deposits of households' sector and a corresponding increase in the liabilities of the financial corporations' sector. But these funds are immediately used for the purchase of the dwelling and lead to an increase of the deposits of the non-financial corporations' sector, and therefore do not affect the balance sheets of the households. All in all, there are eight entries in total, reflecting two transactions: i) the purchase of the dwelling and ii) the incurrence of a mortgage debt.

The quadruple entry bookkeeping system provides a powerful tool for checking the quality of the data, by looking at the consistency of the estimates in two ways. First of all, one can see whether the numbers for a unit or sector are internally consistent by checking whether they respect the traditional double entry rules. In the national accounts, this consistency can be checked by comparing the balancing item from the capital account with the balancing item of the financial account. The other check concerns the consistency

Figure 1.5. **Purchase of a newly-built dwelling with a mortgage loan by a household**

Non-financial corporations

Production account	
Uses	Resources
	Output 120

Financial account	
Assets	Liabilities
Deposits 120	

Financial corporations

Financial account	
Assets	Liabilities
Loans 120	Deposits 120

Households

Capital account	
Uses	Resources
Gross fixed capital formation 120	

Financial account	
Assets	Liabilities
Deposits 120	Loans 120
Deposits -120	

between total payments and total receipts, for each of the transactions (and positions), as each receipt/payment should have an equivalent counterparty entry. In the compilation of national accounts, usually the latter consistency is accomplished by changing the original source data which are considered to be lowest-quality. As said before, the consistency between capital accounts and financial accounts for some or all sectors is not always realised in practice.

Asset boundary

To distinguish what flows and stocks should be included in the national accounts, the 2008 SNA applies specific "boundaries". For example, the "production boundary" is an important boundary which describes which activities are considered as productive and income generating. It therefore directly defines what is included, or not included, in GDP. However, as this boundary is of lesser importance for financial accounts and balance sheets, it will not be further dwelt upon, and reference is made to paragraphs 6.23-6.48 of the 2008 SNA. The "asset boundary", on the other hand, is of direct relevance to the financial accounts and balance sheets, as it provides a definition to determine which items should be included as assets in national accounts. The 2008 SNA states that "assets […] are entities that must be owned by some unit, or units, and from which economic benefits are derived by their owner(s) by holding them or using them over a period of time" (SNA 2008, paragraph 1.46).

From the definition of an asset, a financial liability can also be defined. Paragraph 3.33 of the 2008 SNA explains that a liability is established when a unit (the debtor) is obliged under specific circumstances to provide a payment to another unit (the creditor). The most common way a liability is established is through a legally binding contract that specifies terms and conditions of payments which are unconditional. However, a liability may also arise from a long and well-recognised custom that is not easily refuted from which a creditor has a valid expectation of payment. These liabilities are called "constructive liabilities". The delineation between explicit liabilities (and financial assets) that are recognised as such in the central framework of the national accounts, and contingent liabilities which are not recorded in the central framework is a tricky one. If the payment is related to the occurrence of a certain specified condition in the future, then the liability is considered to be contingent. However, standardised guarantees "where, although each individual arrangement involves a contingent liability, the number of similar guarantees is such that an actual liability is established for the proportion of guarantees likely to be called" (SNA 2008, paragraph 3.40) are not considered to be contingent liabilities, and are recorded as explicit liabilities. Classic examples of such standardised guarantees are export credit guarantees and student loan guarantees. Furthermore, provisions set aside by corporations to cover, for example, unexpected events or to cover default by their customers, are not considered to fall within the asset boundary. Finally, it should be noted that the 2008 SNA recognises non-financial assets, but does not recognise non-financial liabilities.

Time of recording

Another important principle in national accounts is that flows and stocks are recorded on the basis of accrual accounting. This means that they are recorded at the time that the economic value is created, transformed, exchanged, transferred or extinguished (SNA 2008, paragraph 3.166). This is in line with business accounting. With regard to financial flows and stocks this means that the flow is recorded when the change of ownership occurs. This may in some cases differ from cash accounting, in which transactions are recorded when the cash movement takes place. Two examples can help to explain the difference between accrual accounting and cash accounting. The first example concerns the delivery of a product, which is paid for some time after delivery. The 2008 SNA requires recording the sale/purchase of the product at the time of delivery, not when the cash payment takes place. As long as the cash payment is still outstanding, the delayed payment leads to the creation of an "accounts receivable" asset for the seller of the product, and a concomitant "accounts payable" liability for the purchaser of the product. The other example relates to the receipt of interest on a saving deposit. Usually, the accumulated interest is paid out at the end of the year. However, in national accounts, the interest receipts are recorded when they accrue over time. The accrued interest which is not yet paid is added to the value of the saving deposit.

Valuation

Finally, an important accounting rule of national accounts is that, in general, flows and stocks are recorded at the prices at which they could be acquired or disposed of at the reporting date. With regard to financial assets and liabilities this means that they should, in principle, be valued as if they were acquired on the market at the reporting date. However, exceptions are made for deposits and loans, which are typically recorded at nominal value, i.e. the amount the debtor owes to the creditor, which consists of the outstanding principle and any accrued interest. For financial instruments that are valued at market prices, it is relatively easy to determine their value if they are traded on markets, such as securities which are traded on the stock market. However, for other financial items like equity in small and medium enterprises, it may not be so straightforward. Market-equivalent values may have to be determined for these instruments, for instance on the basis of the net present value of future earnings, or using the intrinsic value of a corporation as a starting point. Valuation will be discussed in more detail in Section 5.

Alternative presentations

Flow of funds and from-whom-to-whom matrices

The term "flow of funds" is often used in the area of financial accounts and balance sheets. However, the term also often creates confusion, as it is used for different purposes. Sometimes, people use the term to simply refer to the standard overview of financial accounts and balance sheets. In other cases, it refers to a combination of all accumulation accounts (and the resulting balance sheets). In this publication, we use the term to refer to the description of the relationships between debtor and creditor sectors for a particular financial instrument, or for the sum of financial instruments. A "flow of funds" analysis shows which sectors are providing financing to which other sectors, by providing a breakdown of financing by holder and counterparty sector. It may show, for example, the bonds held by the investment fund sector, broken down by issuing sector. Another term that is frequently used for these overviews is "from-whom-to-whom" (FWTW) matrices, a term that is used throughout the rest of this publication. These FWTW presentations can be applied to the transaction accounts, to the other changes in assets accounts, and to the balance sheet positions. An example is provided in Table 1.1 below.

The main advantage of a FWTW presentation is that it provides insight into the sources and destinations of financial funds. A by-product of this disaggregation is that it supports the analysis of implicit risks. For example, holdings of bonds issued by securitisation companies may be considered riskier than holdings of bonds issued by central governments, and a FWTW presentation makes the split of types of investment very clear. Furthermore, a FWTW presentation can provide insight into which sectors may be affected by certain economic events, because of their linkages to other sectors. This became especially important during the 2007-09 economic and financial crisis, where it was evidenced how easily defaults due to the collapse of the housing market in the United States spilled over to other sectors in the economy and to other countries. Furthermore, policy makers can use FWTW information to better assess the impact of specific policies, such as the potential rescue of a defaulting bank.

Another illustration of the analytical benefits of the FWTW presentation is shown in the following diagram (Figure 1.6) that reveals the aggregate net lending transactions and the direction of flows between the main five sectors of the Australian economy during the fourth quarter of 2016. For example, households repaid in aggregate (across all financial instruments) AUD 4.2 billion (Australian dollars) to financial corporations. A similar picture can be constructed for the net financial positions of each of the five sectors on the basis of the information contained in a FWTW presentation.

Presenting data in a FWTW framework is significantly more data-intensive than the presentation required for the standard financial accounts and balance sheets, and therefore requires more detailed data collection. However, compiling FWTW matrices can actually help to improve the financial accounts and balance sheets, as it typically uses the maximum amount of available source information. For example, a country may not have good quality data on total loans borrowed by households. However, for financial corporations, total lending broken down by counterparty sector, including households, might be available. By bringing together all this information in a FWTW matrix, one can make a first assessment of borrowing by households, using counterparty information. Of course, this matching is done by implementing a hierarchy of sources for the different pieces of information, usually by identifying priority sectors for which the information is considered to be of higher quality (e.g. data coming from banks might be considered more accurate and should not be changed). The hierarchy of sources ensures horizontal consistency and allows for completion of the FWTW matrix.

More generally, one can state that, from a statistical point of view, the construction of the accounts on a FWTW basis is an important compilation tool for enhancing the quality and consistency of the data, since it allows for cross-checking the information from both debtor and creditor sides, thus ensuring full consistency in terms of the values and the time of recording of all transactions, other changes in stocks, and related stocks. When, after using all the available data for the identification of counterparts, there are still parts of the FWTW matrix that remain unfilled, assumptions are made to arrive at a

1. FINANCIAL ACCOUNTS AND BALANCE SHEETS WITHIN THE SYSTEM OF NATIONAL ACCOUNTS

Table 1.1. **From-whom-to-whom matrix for long-term loans, Netherlands, 2014**
EUR, millions

Sectors (assets)	Total domestic sectors	Non-financial corporations	Financial corporations	Monetary financial institutions	Other financial institutions	Non-MMF investment funds	Other fin. inst. excl. investment funds	Insurance corporations and pension funds	Insurance corporations	Pension funds	General government	Central government	Local government	Social security funds	Households including NPISHs	Rest of the world
Total domestic sectors	1 307 208	298 576	236 110	41 593	189 272	554	183 724	5 245	3 255	1 990	56 351	4 352	51 996	3	716 171	1 073 802
The non-financial corporations sector	33 796	17 816	6 411	1 238	4 216	54	4 162	957	274	683	712	249	463	-	8 857	127 498
Financial corporations	1 211 269	261 216	224 146	35 855	184 855	548	179 372	3 436	2 909	527	48 860	1 834	47 026	-	677 047	927 660
Monetary financial institutions	851 317	219 902	168 000	6 764	160 706	4 263	156 443	530	529	1	47 441	1 145	46 296	-	415 974	109 639
Other financial institutions	271 526	36 553	28 562	10 224	16 460	711	15 749	1 878	1 353	525	73	73	-	-	206 338	813 425
Non-MMF investment funds	11 074	3 083	1 100	1	1 097	423	674	2	-	2	-	-	-	-	6 891	12 840
Other fin. inst. excl. investment funds	260 452	33 470	27 462	10 223	15 363	288	15 075	1 876	1 353	523	73	73	-	-	199 447	800 585
Insurance corporations and pension funds	88 426	4 761	27 584	18 867	7 689	509	7 180	1 028	1 027	1	1 346	616	730	-	54 735	4 596
Insurance corporations	74 594	3 516	24 349	16 550	6 774	9	6 765	1 025	1 025	-	272	272	-	-	46 457	2 941
Pension funds	13 832	1 245	3 235	2 317	915	500	415	3	2	1	1 074	344	730	-	8 278	1 655
General government	54 332	17 500	5 180	4 210	186	-	186	784	4	780	6 638	2 128	4 507	3	25 014	18 644
Central government	41 523	9 705	4 470	3 626	60	-	60	784	4	780	3 368	2 054	1 311	3	23 980	16 570
Local government	12 809	7 795	710	584	126	-	126	-	-	-	3 270	74	3 196	-	1 034	2 074
Social security funds	-	-	-	-	-	-	-	-	-	-	-	-	-	-	-	-
Households including NPISHs	7 811	2 044	373	290	15	-	4	68	68	-	141	141	-	-	5 253	-
Rest of the world	729 383	162 924	547 276	14 428	532 661	3 076	529 585	187	184	3	16 107	15 127	980	-	3 076	-

Source: Statistics Netherlands (2017), Financial Instruments: From-whom-to-whom matrices; National Accounts (database), http://statline.cbs.nl/Statweb/publication/?DM=SLEN&PA=83205ENG&D1=4&D2=a&D3=a&D4=l&D5=79&LA=EN&HDR=T,G2&STB=G1,G3,G4&VW=T.

StatLink ⇒ http://dx.doi.org/10.1787/888933589694

UNDERSTANDING FINANCIAL ACCOUNTS © OECD 2017

Figure 1.6. **From-whom-to-whom information for net lending transactions, Australia, fourth quarter 2016**
Billions of AUD

Fourth quarter 2016

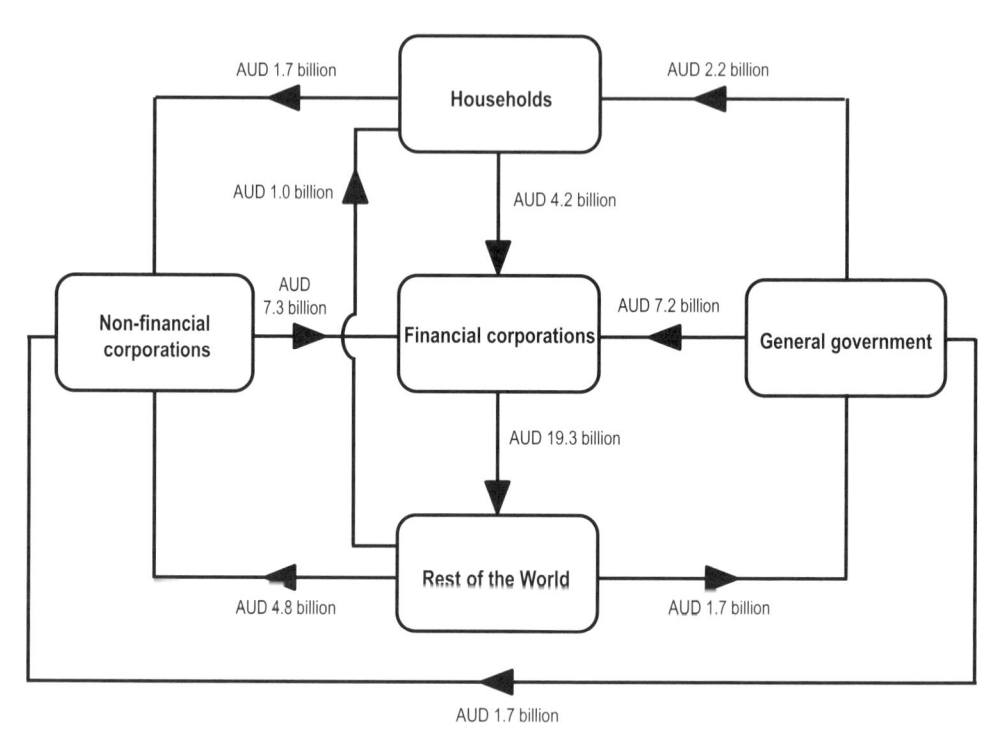

```
                    AUD 1.7 billion                  AUD 2.2 billion
              ◄──────────────── Households ◄────────────────┐
              │                      │                       │
              │  AUD 1.0 billion     │ AUD 4.2 billion      │
              │         ▲            ▼                       │
              │         │                                    │
    ┌─────────────┐  AUD 7.3   ┌──────────────┐  AUD 7.2   ┌──────────────┐
    │ Non-financial│ billion   │  Financial   │  billion   │   General    │
    │ corporations │──────────►│ corporations │◄───────────│  government  │
    └─────────────┘            └──────────────┘            └──────────────┘
              │                        │                         │
              │                        │ AUD 19.3 billion        │
              │                        ▼                         │
              │                 ┌──────────────┐                 │
              │                 │ Rest of the  │                 │
              │◄────────────────│    World     │────────────────►│
              │  AUD 4.8 billion└──────────────┘  AUD 1.7 billion│
              │                        ▲                         │
              └────────────────────────┴─────────────────────────┘
                              AUD 1.7 billion
```

Source: Australian Bureau of Statistics (2017), 5232.0 – Australian National Accounts: Finance and Wealth (database), www.abs.gov.au/ausstats/abs@.nsf/mf/5232.0

complete matrix. These assumptions typically involve the use of additional information allowing the application of structures, or simple rules of thumb. Taking into account the above information, some statisticians therefore argue that it is preferable to start with the compilation of FWTW matrices in the compilation of financial accounts and balance sheets, even (more so) in the case of fragmented source information. Chapter 2 provides an illustration of FWTW data for Portugal.

Alternative measures of income and saving

The financial accounts and balance sheets can be used to produce alternative measures of income and saving which can aid financial analyses. In particular, items from the other changes in assets account relating to holding gains and losses on assets and liabilities have been added to the traditional national accounts measures of income and saving. The resulting alternative measures of income and saving may support the analysis of consumption and saving behaviour, as they take a broader measure of perceived income with more explanatory power for consumption patterns. They are also consistent with concepts of income and saving, as defined by, for example, Hicks (1983).

Figure 1.7 shows two alternative concepts of household disposable income. The first calculates disposable income according to the traditional national accounts definition. In the second, other changes in real net worth, i.e. changes in net worth adjusted for general inflation, have been added. It shows that the addition of AUD 219.1 billion in other changes in real net worth

Figure 1.7. **Alternative measures of household disposable income, Australia, 2006-16**
AUD, billions

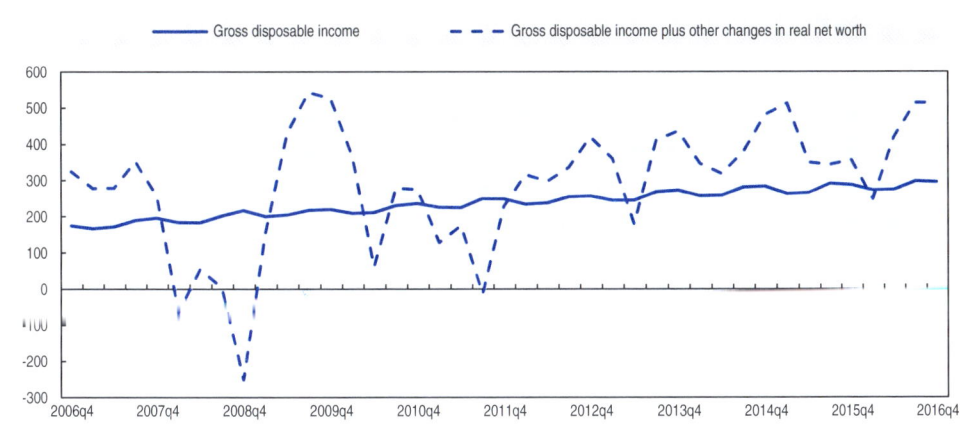

Source: Australian Bureau of Statistics (2017), 5204.0 – Australian System of National Accounts, 2015-16 (database), www.abs.gov.au/AUSSTATS/abs@.nsf/DetailsPage/5204.02015-16?OpenDocument.
StatLink ⟶ http://dx.doi.org/10.1787/888933587927

increased Australia's gross disposable income from AUD 296.7 billion to AUD 515.8 billion in the fourth quarter of 2016. On the other hand, at the peak of the financial crisis in the fourth quarter of 2008 the addition of inflation-adjusted holding gains and losses had a large negative impact on household income, decreasing it by AUD 467.9 billion to minus AUD 249.9 billion. This shows that including holding gains and losses may significantly alter the income measure and may in some periods better explain trends that can be observed with regard to consumption and saving.

3. Institutional sectors

In the national accounts, the economy is viewed as comprising many transactors engaging in economic activity (such as production, income, expenditure, capital accumulation, lending and borrowing, etc.). These transactors are clustered into statistical units on the basis of "uniformity of behaviour and decision-making autonomy in the exercise of its principal function". For instance, a household is an institutional unit in the sense that income is often pooled and decisions are usually made at the level of the household, for instance with regard to consumption of food and housing. For legal units, like corporations, non-profit institutions and government units, to qualify as separate institutional units, it is important that they are able to take economic decisions (i.e. they have autonomy in decision-making), and engage in economic activities for which they are themselves held to be directly responsible and accountable by law. They should also be entitled to own assets in their own right, and to incur liabilities on their own behalf. In practice, an important indicator is whether the unit is able to provide a complete set of accounts.

In the institutional sector accounts, statistical units are clustered into institutional sectors and subsectors on the basis of their principal function, behaviour and objectives. The sector accounts describe the activities and positions of these (sub)sectors according to the sequence of accounts as was described in the previous section. The 2008 SNA groups institutional units with similar functions into five resident institutional sectors. These are introduced briefly below. They are discussed in more detail in Chapters 3 to 6.

Non-financial corporations

The non-financial corporations' sector consists of all resident corporations that are principally engaged in the production of market goods and/or non-financial services. This sector may comprise public corporations, national private corporations, and foreign controlled corporations. It does not include unincorporated enterprises and sole proprietorships, which are typically recorded in the households' sector. The sector also does not include non-market producers, such as most government units. The delineation between the corporations' sectors and the government, based on the distinction between market and non-market, is an important but difficult one. For more details, please refer to Chapter 6.

Financial corporations

The financial corporations' sector consists of all resident corporations that are principally engaged in financial intermediation or in auxiliary financial activities. Financial corporations are distinguished from non-financial corporations because of the inherent differences in their respective functions and activity. Financial corporations are mainly engaged in financial services, such as borrowing and lending money, providing life, health or other insurance, financial leasing, investing in financial assets, and related activities. These corporations are often not acting as agents, but rather place themselves at risk by trading in financial markets on their own account. The financial corporations' sector may be further broken down into more detailed subsectors, such as monetary financial institutions, other financial institutions, insurance corporations and pension funds.

General government

The general government sector consists of government units and non-profit institutions (NPIs) controlled by the government that produce non-market services. The general government sector thus includes all government departments, offices and other bodies mainly engaged in the production of goods and services outside the normal market mechanism, for collective consumption by government itself (e.g., public administration, defense, police, etc.) and for individual consumption by the general public (e.g., health and education). The government sector may be further broken down into central government, state government, local government, and social security funds.

Households

The households' sector consists of all resident households, defined as small groups of persons who share accommodation, pool some or all of their income and wealth, and collectively consume goods and services, principally housing and food. Although households are primarily consumers of goods and services, they also engage in other forms of economic activity such as producing goods and services within unincorporated enterprises. These are enterprises like partnerships and sole proprietorships for which it is often difficult to distinguish between business and personal transactions, and for which it may not be possible to derive separate sets of accounts for the part that relates to the business activity. For those reasons, unincorporated enterprises are generally included in the households' sector. However, some of these unincorporated enterprises may be quite large and likely to behave as if they were corporations. Examples are large family companies, or unincorporated legal, accounting or architectural firms. Where this is the case, and complete sets of accounts are available, these units are classified in the corporations' sector.

Non-profit institutions serving households (NPISH)

The non-profit institutions serving households' (NPISH) sector includes units that produce non-market goods and services provided for free (or at prices that are not economically significant), and that are not controlled by the government. Examples of units belonging to this sector are trade unions, consumers' associations, political parties, churches, sports clubs, charities, and aid organisations.

Total economy

Within the national accounts framework, the "total economy" is the aggregate of the five main resident institutional sectors. For each transaction (or financial position), total receipts (and total stocks of financial assets) equals total payments (and total stocks of liabilities) by definition. Therefore, the total net transactions (positions) of the domestic sectors must have a counterpart in the net transactions (positions) of non-residents with residents. The latter are recorded in the accounts for the Rest of the World (see below). Given the above equality, net lending of the domestic economy, which represents the balancing item of all non-financial transactions and also the balancing item of all financial transactions, is equal to net lending of the Rest of the World, but with an opposite sign. The same holds for net financial wealth, the balance of all financial assets and liabilities. Here too, net financial wealth of the domestic economy is the mirror image of net financial wealth of non-residents towards residents. These balancing items are important macro-economic indicators in themselves.

Rest of the World

The Rest of the World consists of all non-resident institutional units, be it non-resident governments, corporations or persons, that enter into transactions with resident units, or that have other economic links with resident units. It is not a sector for which complete sets of accounts have to be compiled, as only the links with the domestic economy are relevant. However, it is often convenient to describe the Rest of the World as if it were another sector.

Alternative sectoring

One of the major strengths of the national accounts framework is the ability to compile accounts for whole sectors, individual units, or some intermediate levels and to aggregate the accounts in different ways. Disaggregating the economy into various sectors and subsectors makes it possible to derive aggregates and balancing items for sectors which may be more relevant for purposes of policymaking. In doing so, one may also better observe and analyse the interactions between the different parts of the economy. Some alternative sector classifications are often applied.

General government versus public sector

The accounts of the general government sector show how goods and services are provided to the community that are mainly financed by taxes or compulsory transfers, i.e., non-market production. Furthermore, the general government accounts show the government's role in the distribution of income and wealth. The range of goods and services that the government provides and the prices it charges are largely based on political and social considerations rather than on profit-maximisation considerations. However, governments often fulfil their public policy objectives through public corporations (for example, railways, airlines, public utilities and public financial corporations) which are not part of the government sector in the national accounts, because they are considered as engaging in market production. Although these market producers can be regarded as separate institutional units, they are often still controlled by the government. Furthermore, public corporations may be required to provide services to areas of the economy that would not be covered otherwise and/or at subsidised prices. As a consequence, it often operates with a reduced profit or at a loss, and is dependent on government funds.

In order to analyse the full impact of government on the economy, it is useful to form a sector consisting of all the units of general government and all public corporations. This alternative sector is referred to as the public sector. Presenting the sequence of accounts, including balancing items, in this way can be more useful for government finance analysts and policy makers. Public sector accounts can be used, for example, to assess the use of resources to produce individual and collective services, the need to collect taxes and other revenues, the ability of government to borrow and repay debt, and the sustainability of the desired level of government operations.

Breakdown of foreign-controlled corporations

A breakdown that becomes increasingly relevant in the present-day globalised economy is the breakdown of domestic corporations that are owned and controlled by non-resident multinational enterprises (MNEs). For policy purposes, one may want to know how much value added and employment is generated by these MNEs, how much an economy depends on these activities, and how much the domestic economy is integrated in global value chains. More generally, one may want to know the total of MNE activities, i.e. not only the domestic activities of foreign-based MNEs, but also the activities of domestically headquartered MNEs. An important (implicit) policy concern behind this user demand is the fear that these activities may be more easily relocated from one country to another. However, when looking at net financial exposures towards the Rest of the World and the related financial risks, it also matters whether the asset-liability relationship is between two affiliated enterprises within the same MNE or with a third party.

Treatment of unincorporated enterprises

As noted earlier, unincorporated enterprises are generally included in the household sector. However, some users prefer to group together all enterprises that are engaged in the production of market goods and services to arrive at a complete overview of the "business sector". This is done, for example, in the

National Income and Production Accounts, as published by the US Bureau of Economic Analysis (US BEA). Applying this alternative sectoring in a consistent way throughout the whole sequence of accounts can be quite problematic. It may not be possible to disaggregate income transactions and financial transactions into those belonging to the unincorporated enterprise and those belonging to the household as a consumer. For this reason, the business sector is only compiled for the production account and the capital account, while for the other accounts the unincorporated enterprises are consolidated with the households owning them. Most countries, however, compile the household sector according to the 2008 SNA, and unincorporated businesses are therefore usually classified in the household sector. For reasons of international comparison, the US BEA also produces data according to the 2008 SNA when providing data to international organisations.

Regional accounts

In the case that there are important disparities between the economic and social developments of the various regions in a country, regional accounts are usually compiled to provide more insight into these differences. In regional accounts, each region is treated as a different economic entity, implying that transactions with other regions are recorded as if they were external transactions. For example, a purchase of a good or service from another region would be treated as an import.

Compiling regional accounts poses a number of practical issues in the financial context. For example, it is not straightforward to assign financial transactions and positions of a multiregional unit with a centre of economic interest in various regions. Most large banks will usually have a head office within one region along with local branch offices across several regions. If a bank issues a loan to a household, the practical issue to overcome is whether to assign the loan to the head office of the respective bank or the local branch which conducts the application and assessment of the loan. The same issue will arise for other multiregional enterprises with various establishments across the country, such as chain stores, or manufacturers which have spread their production across regions.

This problem is further exacerbated with national units where the centre of economic interest is not located geographically at all. This is particularly the case for central governments and national public corporations which provide services to a whole country. For example, the central government borrowing through issuance of debt securities simply cannot be assigned to a geographical location. For these reasons, financial accounts and balance sheets are usually not produced by region. An exception may be the compilation of regional accounts for households.

4. Financial instruments

Financial assets and liabilities

Financial assets, for the most part, represent a claim on another institutional unit and entitle the holder to receive an agreed sum at an agreed date. The only exception is equity, which is treated as a financial asset even though the financial claim their holders have on the corporation is not a fixed or predetermined monetary amount. A liability is established when one unit (the debtor) is obliged, under specific circumstances, to provide a payment or series of payments to another unit (the creditor) (SNA 2008, paragraph 11.5). Due to the symmetry of financial claims and liabilities, the same classification is used for financial assets and liabilities. With a few clearly defined exceptions, every financial instrument is both an asset and a liability, depending on the perspective from which it is analysed. There are many different ways to classify assets and liabilities; the 2008 SNA uses a classification that groups together instruments with similar properties and characteristics. The various financial instruments that are distinguished within the 2008 SNA are listed below, in Table 1.2. More details can be found in chapters 11 and 13 of the 2008 SNA.

Table 1.2. **Detailed descriptions of financial instruments**

Type of financial instrument	Description
Monetary gold (F11)	Monetary gold is gold that is held as reserve asset by the monetary authorities (either the central bank or the government). These assets can be used for exchange rate policies, for maintaining confidence in the currency and the economy, and as a basis for foreign borrowing. It can take the form of gold bullion or unallocated gold accounts with non-residents that entitle the holder to claim the delivery of gold. Gold bullion held as reserve asset is the only financial asset with no corresponding liability in the 2008 SNA.
Special Drawing Rights (SDRs) (F12)	SDRs are international reserve assets created by the International Monetary Fund (IMF) and allocated to its members to supplement their reserve assets (see monetary gold). They are held exclusively by official holders (central banks and other international organisations) and represent claims on the participants collectively (and not on the IMF).
Currency (F21)	Currency consists of notes and coins that are of fixed nominal values and that are issued by the monetary authority of a country (either the central bank or government). It may consist of domestic and of foreign currencies. Domestic currency is the liability of the resident monetary authority (or in case of a monetary union the central bank of this union), whereas foreign currencies are liabilities of non-resident authorities, such as foreign central banks and governments.
Transferable deposits (F22) Other deposits (F29)	There are two categories of deposits; transferable deposits and other deposits: i) Transferable deposits are deposits that are exchangeable for currency on demand at par and without penalty or restriction. They are directly usable for making payments by cheque, draft, direct debit/credit, or any other direct payment facility. It has to be noted that a transferable deposit cannot have a negative value. In case of an overdraft, the related amount is treated as a loan. ii) Other deposits comprise all other types of deposits, such as saving deposits and fixed-term deposits. They are characterised by the fact that they have limited transferability, for instance by restrictions on number of third party payments over a given period, no direct access to funds held in the deposit and/or penalty payments associated with the withdrawal of funds.

1. FINANCIAL ACCOUNTS AND BALANCE SHEETS WITHIN THE SYSTEM OF NATIONAL ACCOUNTS

Table 1.2. **Detailed descriptions of financial instruments** (cont.)

Type of financial instrument	Description
Debt securities (F3)	A debt security is a negotiable instrument serving as evidence of debt, such as bills, bonds, commercial paper and asset-backed securities. In the 2008 SNA they are broken down by original date to maturity: i) Short-term debt securities (F31) are those with an original term to maturity of one year or less, such as bills of exchange, negotiable certificates of deposits and commercial paper. ii) Long-term debt securities (F32) include those securities that have an original maturity of more than one year, such as government bonds, asset-backed securities, covered bonds and convertible notes prior to conversion. Another optional supplementary breakdown that may be applied is into remaining maturity. This may be more relevant for the analysis of maturity and liquidity risk, as it provides more insight into which debt securities are going to expire within a short time period.
Loans (F4)	Loans are direct borrowings between a debtor and a creditor which are not evidenced by the issue of debt securities. They are usually not traded. Loans to be recorded on the balance sheets of both creditors and debtors are recorded at their nominal values, i.e. the amounts of the principal outstanding and the amount of interest earned but not yet paid. As is the case with debt securities, loans are classified by their original date to maturity: i) Short-term loans (F41) comprise loans that have an original maturity of one year or less. Loans repayable on the demand of the creditor should be classified as short-term even when these loans are expected to be outstanding for more than one year. Examples of short-term loans include debt related to credit cards and other forms of revolving credit. Furthermore, overdrafts on transferable deposits should also be recorded as short-term loans. ii) Long-term loans (F42) comprise loans that have an original maturity of more than one year. As for debt securities, an optional supplementary breakdown may be provided regarding remaining maturity.
Equity and investment fund shares (F5)	Equity and investment fund shares differ from all other assets and liabilities in the sense that they do not provide the owner with a right to a predetermined amount, but only to a residual claim on the assets of the issuer of these instruments. These instruments are therefore not regarded as part of debt. However, in the 2008 SNA they are still treated as financial assets and liabilities. The 2008 SNA classifies equity and investment fund shares into two distinct classes: i) Equity (F51) represents the owner's funds in the institutional unit and usually takes the form of shares, stocks or participations. Equity can be further subdivided into a) listed shares which are equity securities listed on an exchange, b) unlisted shares which are not listed on an exchange (also known as private equity); and c) other equity which is equity that is not issued in the form of securities, such as participations or limited liability in quasi-corporations. ii) Investment fund shares (F52) are shares issued by collective investment vehicles that pool funds for investment in financial and non-financial assets, such as bond funds, hedge funds, and real estate funds. These investment fund shares are divided into a) money market fund shares which are shares in investment funds that invest primarily in short-term money market securities such as treasury bills, certificate of deposits and commercial paper; and b) non-money market fund shares which are shares in funds that primarily invest in long-term financial assets and non-financial assets, such as real estate.
Insurance, pension and standardised guarantee schemes (F6)	Insurance, pension and standardised guarantee schemes mainly function as a redistribution of income or wealth, mainly mediated by insurance corporations and pension funds. Units participating in these schemes contribute to them and may receive benefits in the same or later period, dependent on the occurrence of specific events, such as reaching the retirement age (related to pension and life insurance schemes), or damage to goods or property, harm to persons, or financial losses due to events such as sickness or unemployment (in the case of non-life insurance schemes). The most relevant items recorded in this category are non-life insurance technical reserves (F61), which represent prepayments of premiums and reserves to meet

Table 1.2. **Detailed descriptions of financial instruments** *(cont.)*

Type of financial instrument	Description
	outstanding claims, and – more substantially – life insurance and annuity entitlements (F62) and pension entitlements (F63), which represent the accumulated assets in the life insurance scheme (in the case of defined contribution schemes) or the net present value of future entitlements (in the case of defined benefit schemes; see also Table 1.4).
Financial derivatives (F71)	Financial derivatives are financial instruments that are linked to a specific financial instrument or indicator or commodity, through which specific financial risks can be traded in financial markets in their own right. They are categorised into two groups, i.e. option contracts (F711) in which the holder has the option to buy or sell an underlying instrument or commodity (e.g. shares or oil) at a predetermined price within a given time span or on a given date, and forward contracts in which two parties agree to exchange financial assets or products at an agreed price on a specified date. An example of the latter is an interest rate swap in which a fixed interest rate may be exchanged for a variable interest rate plus a premium. Through the use of financial derivatives, units may "hedge" certain risky positions in their portfolio and exchange uncertain future flows for known results or the other way around. Their use has increased over the last couple of decades, sometimes leading to very complex combinations of different types of derivatives.
Employee Stock Options (F72)	An employee stock option is an agreement made on a given date (the "grant" date) under which an employee may purchase a given number of shares of the employer's stock at a stated price either at a stated time (the "vesting" date) or within a period of time immediately following the vesting date.
Other accounts receivable or payable (F8)	Other accounts receivable or payable comprise trade credit for goods and services, and advances for work that is in progress or is to be undertaken. This basically relates to timing differences between the delivery of a good or service and the actual payment. Other accounts receivable/payable also contain other amounts that are still to be paid or received, such as wages and salaries, taxes, or rents. These differences are all due to using accrual recording instead of cash recording in the 2008 SNA.

Limitations of the financial instrument classification

The financial instrument classification allows analysts to understand the types of financial assets and liabilities held on balance sheets. However, this classification does not allow for full inference of risks. First of all, analysis of risk is dependent on underlying financial instruments as well as on the source and destination sectors. For example, investing in government bonds may be less risky than investing in corporate bonds. A deposit at a foreign bank may be liable to change in value due to exchange rate changes; this is not the case for a deposit in national currency at a domestic bank. As discussed in Section 2 of this chapter, FWTW matrices may provide more insight into the interlinkages between the various sectors in an economy and consequently are helpful in assessing risks and possible spillover effects.

Another reason that the 2008 SNA financial instrument classification may not provide a perfect overview of all related risks is that, for certain types of risk, additional disaggregations would be needed. For example, to have more insight into exchange rate risk, financial instruments should be broken down into denomination in domestic and foreign currencies. Moreover, as noted in Table 1.2, information may be needed on the remaining maturity of instruments instead of on their original maturity, in order to analyse, for example, liquidity risk.

Furthermore, risks may be hedged through the use of financial derivatives. For example, even if a unit seems to be liable to maturity risk as a consequence of having long-term obligations combined with short-term assets, the unit may have "hedged" this mismatch by using interest rate swaps to either convert the interest on the long-term liabilities into a short-term rate or to obtain a long-term interest rate on the short-term assets. Derivatives may also be used to create positions which may lead to increased risk exposure. In that regard, more information on the various types of financial derivatives that are used, their main purpose and their main characteristics would assist in better capturing their impact on the financial position and risk exposures.

Finally, the aggregated presentation of the results per sector may conceal risky positions of individual units that may partly cancel out at an aggregated level. For example, zero holding gains for the category investment fund shares for a specific sector may actually consist of various positive and negative holding gains of similar size that may affect different units within the sector. Furthermore, consolidation may conceal many inter-linkages that may exist within a sector or subsector which may lead to increased systemic risk.

5. Accounting rules

The 2008 SNA contains some specific guidance on how to record and classify information on financial flows and stocks in national accounts. This section provides insight into the recognition of assets and liabilities and borderline cases such as contingent liabilities, provisions, leasing constructions and public-private partnerships. Furthermore, it discusses issues regarding the valuation of the various instruments and the impact of consolidation.

Recognition of assets and liabilities

As was already mentioned in Section 2, the asset boundary determines what should be included in national accounts. It states that balance sheets "record the value of the assets [institutional units or sectors] own or the liabilities they have incurred" (SNA 2008 paragraph 1.46). This is further specified in the definition of a liability where it is explained that a liability is most commonly established by a legally binding contract that specifies the terms and conditions of the payment(s) that must be made, but that a liability, and a concomitant asset, may also be established "by long and well-recognised custom that is not easily refuted". In the latter case, the creditor must have "a valid expectation of payment, despite the lack of a legally binding contract". These liabilities are called "constructive liabilities" and may apply to some payments by the government sector, for instance those relating to social security schemes (SNA 2008 paragraph 3.34). Work is still ongoing in developing more guidance on how to clearly interpret and delineate these constructive liabilities.

In addition to legally binding obligations and constructive obligations, it is possible to distinguish some other type of liabilities, which are not covered by the asset boundary. A framework that was developed by Polackova (1999) may be helpful to distinguish between different types of liabilities and to understand which should be included in the financial accounts and balance sheets, and which should not. In relation to the sustainability of government finances, Polackova developed a fiscal matrix distinguishing between direct and contingent liabilities, and between explicit and implicit liabilities. Direct liabilities are obligations that constitute a liability in any event, whereas contingent liabilities are dependent on specific events to occur. On the other hand, one can also make a distinction between implicit and explicit liabilities. Explicit liabilities are liabilities that are recognised by a law or contract. Implicit liabilities on the other hand are derived from a long and well-recognised custom, and relate to the constructive obligations as discussed above. Table 1.3 provides an overview of these two distinctions and the various types of liabilities that may relate to them.

Table 1.3. **Various sources of government obligations**

Sources of obligations	Direct liabilities	Contingent liabilities
Explicit	• Sovereign debt (loans contracted and securities issued) • Expenditures legally binding in the long-term (consumptional spending)	• Guarantees, such as deposit insurance and export credit guarantees
Implicit	• Social security pensions • Future health care financing	• Failure of the banking system which requires support beyond government insurance • Environmental recovery, disaster relief

Direct explicit liabilities will always satisfy the asset boundary of the 2008 SNA and will always be recorded within the financial accounts and balance sheets. As was discussed before, direct implicit liabilities may qualify as constructive obligations as defined in the 2008 SNA and also be recorded in the financial accounts and balance sheets. However, this depends on whether it meets the relevant criteria that still need to be developed. Contingent liabilities are currently only recorded in national accounts when the qualifying events have occurred. In that case, the occurrence of the contingency leads to the initial contingent liability becoming a direct liability. However, when the contingency has not occurred, most of these guarantees will not be recognised in the system. The only case in which these contingencies are recognised is in the case of so-called standardised guarantees where, although each individual arrangement involves a contingent liability, the number of similar guarantees is such that an actual liability is established for the proportion of guarantees that is likely to be called.

Provisions

While corporations often set aside funds to cover unexpected events or to cover default by their customers on their balance sheet, such provisions are not treated as liabilities in the national accounts. The main reason is that these provisions are not the subject of the sort of contract, legal or constructive, associated with a liability. Furthermore, no other entity would have a claim to these provisions, except the unit setting aside the funds itself. These provisions therefore remain part of the net worth of the corporations, as recorded in the national accounts. Though financial institutions may regularly write off bad debts, for example, it would not be appropriate to regard the provisions set aside for this as assets of the borrowers. It is, however, recommended to identify loans that have not been serviced for some time as a memorandum item for the creditor under the heading "non-performing loans".

Leasing arrangements

A leasing arrangement is one in which it is not always clear which party is the economic owner of an asset. In this kind of arrangements the actual user of the asset may be different from the legal owner. There are two types of leasing arrangements. The first one is a financial lease in which the legal owner (lessor) contracts with another unit to shift the use, benefits and related risks related to the use of the asset to that other unit (lessee) in exchange for an agreed fee. In this case, legal and economic ownership no longer coincide as the lessee becomes the economic owner of the asset, instead of the lessor who is the legal owner. According to the 2008 SNA, the leased assets are to be recorded on the balance sheet of the lessee, with an accompanying loan on the liability side of its balance sheet towards the lessor. A lease can also be set up as operational lease. In that case, the legal owner rents out the asset, but still accepts the operating risks and rewards related to the use of it, and remains the economic owner of the asset. Consequently, the asset is to be recorded on the balance sheet of the lessor, although it is used by the lessee.

Public-private partnerships

Another legal construction in which ownership is not always straightforward is in case of public-private partnership (PPP) schemes. These are long-term contracts between two units, whereby one unit acquires or builds an asset, operates it for a period and then hands the asset over to a second unit after a period of time. Although various units may be involved, it often concerns a private enterprise and a government unit. Units may engage in PPPs for various reasons, but mostly it is due to the expectation that private management may lead to a more efficient production, and may have easier access to a broad range of financial sources.

In PPPs it is not always clear which unit is the owner during the contract period and how the change in economic ownership should be recorded. In order to determine the economic ownership, there is usually an assessment of which unit bears the majority of the risks and is expected to receive the majority of the rewards. As the recording of these types of constructions may affect important indicators such as government debt, more specific guidance has been developed to clearly prescribe how to record these constructions; see, for example, EPEC and Eurostat (2016).

Reverse transactions

Finally, some transactions include a commitment to reverse the specific transaction on a specified date in the future (or on demand). In many of these cases the legal ownership changes for that period of time, whereas many of the risks and benefits related to the underlying asset remain with the original owner. Examples of these kinds of transactions are repurchase agreements and securities lending. The funds that are provided under such arrangements are treated as either loans or deposits (the latter if the transaction concerns the provision of cash by a deposit-taking corporation) and the securities that are provided as collateral are treated as not having changed ownership, as the cash receiver is still subject to the risks or benefits of any change in the price of the security.

Valuation

There are different types of valuations that may be applied to financial instruments, such as historic cost, face value, nominal value, book value or market value. Historic cost refers to the price at which the asset was bought; face value is the undiscounted amount of principal to be repaid, for instance the value on a debt security as stated by the issuer; nominal price reflects the amount the debtor owes to the creditor, which usually comprises the outstanding principal amount including any accrued interest; book value generally refers to the value recorded in the enterprise's records; finally, market value is equal to the price at which the instrument could be sold on the market at the day of valuation. For some items, such as currency and deposits, the valuation method chosen makes little difference. However, for some other items, particularly those that are sold on financial markets, such as debt securities and shares, the valuation method chosen can have a significant impact. Box 1.1 shows how differences in valuation may affect important macro-economic indicators such as government debt.

In the 2008 SNA it is recommended to value assets and liabilities at "current values" at the balance sheet date. It is elaborated that this is the value at which the instruments might be bought in markets or the amount that a debtor must pay the creditor to extinguish the claim. For tradeable assets and liabilities this will be rather straightforward; observable market prices can be used for their

Box 1.1. **Impact of different valuations on government debt measures**

Differences in valuation may give rise to different debt measures. Whereas market value may fluctuate over time because of changes in creditworthiness, interest rates, or investor preferences, nominal value is determined by the principal amount and the accrued but unpaid interest. In times with large fluctuations in market interest rates, the market value and the nominal value of specific instruments may differ significantly. Figure 1.8 shows an example of the market value and the nominal value for government debt securities of some OECD countries at the end of the years 2007 and 2013. While, for many countries, these valuations differed only slightly in 2007, the gaps had widened for several countries by 2013. In most countries, the market value of the securities exceeded the nominal value, mainly due to significant decreases in interest rates during this period.

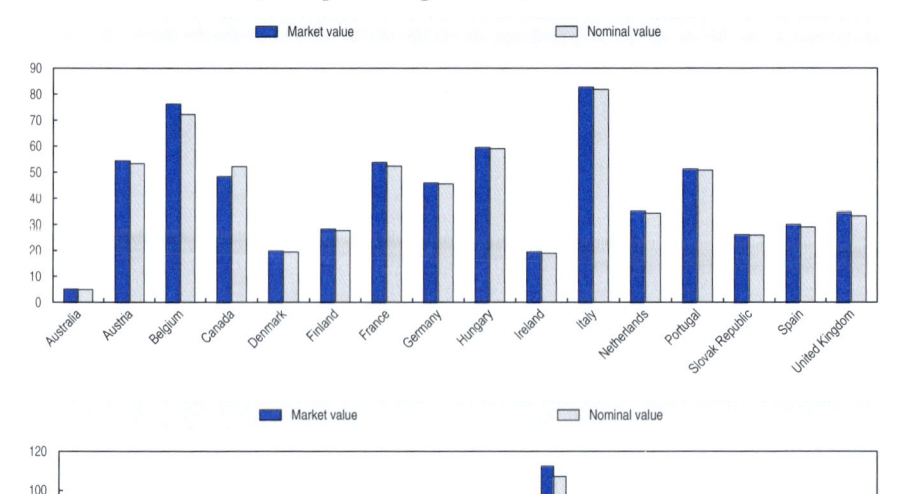

Figure 1.8. **General government debt securities: market value versus nominal value, as a percentage of GDP, 2007 and 2013***

* Nominal value data from public sector debt statistics, and market value data from financial balance sheets statistics.
Source: OECD (2017), "Public Sector Debt: Public sector debt – consolidated", OECD National Accounts Statistics (database), http://dx.doi.org/10.1787/data-00620-en.

StatLink http://dx.doi.org/10.1787/888933587946

valuation. However, when market prices are not available, it will be more difficult to arrive at an appropriate market equivalent price. In that case, the 2008 SNA prescribes two methods to value the relevant assets (see paragraph 13.23-24). The first method consists of accumulating past purchases (appropriately adjusted for possible depreciation), and revaluing the accumulated assets to the price level of the current year. This method is usually applied to value non-financial assets. The second method consists of estimating the discounted present value of future returns expected from a given asset. This method is applied to financial assets for which a market value is lacking. It is sometimes also referred to as the nominal value, derived on the basis of the net present value of the principal and interest payments that are due to maturity.

As explained above, the 2008 SNA recommends valuing assets and liabilities at current values at balance sheet date. For tradeable instruments this will be the market value, and for non-tradable instruments current value will be reflected by a market-equivalent price. As valuation may vary across instruments, Table 1.4 below provides an overview of the valuation that should be applied for the various financial instruments. As a consequence of the quadruple entry accounting principle, all transactions and stocks are recorded at the same value throughout the accounts, that is, for the various sectors involved and for both assets and liabilities.

Consolidation

An important principle that is sometimes applied in presenting results from financial accounts and balance sheets is the principle of consolidation. The principle of consolidation means that transactions and positions between units within the same sector or subsector are eliminated in the presentation of financial accounts. The standard according to the 2008 SNA is to present financial accounts and balance sheets on an unconsolidated basis to have a comprehensive overview of all transactions and positions within an economy. However, for specific purposes, it may be preferable to eliminate flows and positions within sectors. This may, for example, be the case for the government sector, so users can focus on the net relations between the government and the rest of the economy. Especially when the government sector contains many financial links between the central government and local governments and social security funds, unconsolidated reports may hamper a proper comparison of gross government debt data across countries. A sustainability analysis of the financial situation of the government as a whole may be advisable on the basis of consolidated data. Consolidation may also be relevant for other sectors and subsectors.

Even though consolidation may be preferable for some purposes, it may also conceal relevant information on positions within a sector or subsector. The 2007-09 economic and financial crisis, for example, showed the importance of the increased interconnectedness between financial entities in

1. FINANCIAL ACCOUNTS AND BALANCE SHEETS WITHIN THE SYSTEM OF NATIONAL ACCOUNTS

Table 1.4. **Valuation principles according to the 2008 SNA, by financial instrument**

Type of financial instrument	Valuation
Monetary gold (F11)	At the price established in organised markets or in bilateral arrangements between central banks.
Special Drawing Rights (SDRs) (F12)	At the price determined daily by the IMF on the basis of a basket of currencies.
Currency (F21)	At nominal or face value of the currency, applying the current exchange rate in case of foreign currency to denominate it in domestic currency.
Deposits (F22, F29)	At nominal value, including any interest due that the debtors are contractually obliged to repay the creditors.
Debt securities (F3)	At market value, for both short and long-term debt securities.
Loans (F4)	At nominal value, including any interest due that the debtors are contractually obliged to repay the creditors.
Equity and investment fund shares (F5)	Listed shares should be valued at market value. For unlisted shares an estimate is required, for example on the basis of recent transaction prices, net asset values, or reported book values. Other equity should be valued as equal to the value of total assets minus the value of total debt liabilities of the relevant unit. These valuation principles apply to both equity and investment fund shares.
Insurance, pension and standardised guarantee schemes (F6)	For non-life insurance technical reserves the valuation should equal the premiums paid but not earned at the balance sheet date plus the net present value of the amounts expected to be paid out in settlement claims on the basis of current policies. Life insurance entitlements (including annuities) are valued at the net present value of all expected future claims. Pension entitlements' valuation depends on the type of pension scheme. For defined benefit pension schemes (for which the amount of the future pension is agreed in advance), the valuation is derived on the basis of the net present value of future claims (usually on the basis of actuarial estimations). For defined contribution schemes (for which the amount of the pension depends on the performance of the assets accumulated in the scheme), the valuation is equal to the market value of the financial assets held by the pension fund on behalf of future beneficiaries.
Financial derivatives (F71)	Listed derivatives should be valued at market value. Unlisted derivatives should be valued at market equivalent prices, for example based on option pricing models or net present value of expected flows.
Employee Stock Option (F72)	At values related to the market value of the equity instruments granted (F5) or equivalent traded options (F71). If market prices are not available, the value should be obtained using option pricing models.
Other accounts receivable or payable (F8)	At nominal value, including any interest due, that the debtors are contractually obliged to repay the creditors.

creating systemic risk and spreading shocks throughout the economy. In that regard, unconsolidated data would show this increased interconnectedness which would be eliminated in case of consolidation. Whatever the case, it is always important to be aware of the consolidation status when analysing financial accounts and balance sheets.

International accounting standards

Recently, international accounting standards have become increasingly important in commercial and public sector accounting. The International

Accounting Standards Board (IASB) and the International Public Sector Accounting Standards Board (IPSASB) have developed several standards in this respect, the former relating to commercial accounting and the latter to public sector accounting. In these international accounting standards, the boards prescribe how corporations and government bodies should record various transactions and positions, and how they should address specific reporting issues, to arrive at transparent and comparable information in financial statements. The standards that are developed by the IASB are called International Financial Reporting Standards (IFRS) which are applied by many large private companies, especially multinationals, in more than 100 countries. The standards that are developed by the IPSASB are known as International Public Sector Accounting Standards (IPSAS) and these are increasingly adopted by many governments around the world.

The principles underlying these international accounting standards are broadly in line with the principles of the 2008 SNA. Both try to arrive at standards that are correct from a conceptual point of view, but that are also feasible to apply from a practical point of view. As they share the same underlying principles, the guidance from international accounting standards is generally in line with 2008 SNA guidance. This is important as company and government accounts are relevant inputs in the compilation process of the national accounts. The closer the alignment between the two, the easier it will be to obtain the correct input data, which will improve the quality of the national accounts, while at the same time will reduce the reporting burden on corporations and government entities.

However, even though there is a general alignment between the accounting standards and the 2008 SNA, there are some specific differences. One important difference is the treatment of holding gains and losses. Whereas in the 2008 SNA these are treated as revaluations, they are recorded, at least partly, as income according to the accounting standards. Another significant difference relates to the boundaries for the recognition of non-financial assets. Generally, one can state that the asset boundary of the 2008 SNA is larger than the one applied in business accounting. This mainly concerns the recognition of intellectual property products, such as those resulting from research and development, as assets in 2008 SNA. The accounting standards also apply different rules with regard to contingent liabilities and provisions, in that they generally recommend including the expected value related to these two items on the balance sheet, whereas they will only be included in the central framework of the national accounts once they become explicit liabilities (except for standardised guarantees).

Moreover, international accounting standards may be applied to entities that do not qualify as statistical units as distinguished in the 2008 SNA. This will mainly be the case for multinational corporations. Whereas in the national accounts information is needed on the national parts of these corporations, international accounting standards may only be applied to create accounts for the multinational group as a whole, consolidating relationships between the entities located in different countries. In that case, the applied standards may still be the same, but additional work is needed to break down the relevant amounts into their national components. In most cases, such information is often available, if only because of reporting requirements to national tax authorities.

Because of the importance of correspondence between accounting standards and statistical requirements, a close co-operation between the standard setters and national accountants is very important. For that reason, recent years have seen an increased co-operation between the accounting world and the statistical world in further aligning existing accounting rules and in developing new standards.

6. Statistical guidance, data sources and compilation methodology

Statistical standards and guidance manuals

In addition to the 2008 SNA, the international standards for compiling national accounts, there are multiple other standards and sources of guidance for the compilation of financial accounts and balance sheets. These may focus on specific sectors, such as the public or government sector in the Public Sector Debt Statistics (PSDS) Guide and the IMF Government Finance Statistics (GFS) Manual; the Rest of the World in the Balance of Payments Manual (BPM6) and the External Debt Statistics Guide; or specific regions, such as on the European Union in the European System of Accounts (ESA 2010). In general the guidance provided by these sources is in line with the 2008 SNA, but may provide more detailed information with regard to specific sectors or issues. They generally deviate from the 2008 SNA only in a few specific cases. Table 1.5 provides a short overview.

Data sources

The compilation of financial accounts and balance sheets usually involves the combination of information from various data sources, as the framework encompasses a complete and exhaustive overview of all economic agents, flows and stocks involved. The type and quality of information available will depend on the country, but countries typically use data derived from specific statistics, administrative data sources, surveys and financial reports. These data sources may relate to specific units or sectors, or may relate to specific instruments. The source information available may be quite different depending on the frequency (e.g., quarterly versus annual) and the timeliness of the financial accounts and balance sheets.

Table 1.5. **Summary of statistical standards and guidance manuals**

Manual[1]	Focus	Differences from 2008 SNA
Public Sector Debt Statistics Guide (PSDS Guide 2013)	Guidance on compiling and presenting gross and net debt figures for the public sector and subsectors	1) Focus is on public instead of government sector. 2) It recommends presenting debt instruments at nominal value, in addition to market value for tradeable securities.
Government Finance Statistics Manual (GFSM 2014)	Principles and guidelines for compiling and presenting government statistics to support the analysis and evaluation of fiscal policies	1) More detailed breakdowns to better focus on government-specific issues. 2) Slightly different treatment of specific transactions, such as own-account capital formation.
Balance of Payments Manual (BPM6) (2009)	Guidance on compiling and presenting balance of payments and statistics on international investment positions	1) Results are presented from the viewpoint of the domestic economy instead of that of the Rest of the World. 2) More detailed guidance on specific cross-border issues and data presentation, e.g. relating to foreign direct investment.
External Debt Statistics Guide (2014)	Guidance on compiling and presenting the external debt position of a country	1) Results are presented from the viewpoint of the domestic economy instead of that of the Rest of the World. 2) More detailed guidance on specific issues relating to cross-border liabilities.
Monetary and Financial Statistics Manual (2000) and Compilation Guide (2008)	Guidance on compiling and presenting balance sheet data for depository corporations (including the central bank) for financial stability assessment	1) More detailed guidance on specific monetary and financial issues. 2) The Manual and Guide still have to be updated to 2008 SNA.
European System of Accounts (ESA 2010)	Presents the national accounting framework for member states of the European Union	1) Deviating guidance on a few quite specific issues tuned to specific EU needs. 2) More detailed guidance on specific transactions to obtain better comparability across European countries.

Specific financial statistics usually provide important input for the financial accounts and balance sheets. These statistical outputs are usually compiled for rather specific purposes other than national accounts, but can provide valuable information on specific sectors. For example, balance of payments and international investment position statistics provide information on flows and stocks with the Rest of the World, and government finance statistics provide financial information on the various governments units. Moreover, statistics are typically available for the various subsectors within the financial corporations' sector (such as banks, institutional investors and pension funds), for non-financial corporations, and in some cases also for the household sector. As these statistics usually serve a different purpose than the financial accounts and balance sheets, they may not cover all instruments, differ in sector coverage and in valuation, but – as stated before – they may still provide valuable input in the compilation process.

In addition to the above statistics, useful information can also be derived from administrative data sources, such as tax records and regulatory information. Tax records may contain information on the value of various assets and liabilities of households and corporations, whereas regulators may collect supervisory information on various financial and/or public units. Again, adjustments may be needed to arrive at the coverage, the definitions and the valuation according to the 2008 SNA. Another source of administrative data that has become increasingly important over the last couple of years is the databases that contain information on the issuance and holdings of securities, such as the Centralised Securities Database as operated jointly by the members of the European System of Central Banks (ESCB). This database contains consistent and up-to-date information on all individual securities issued in member states and provides, among other things, the market value, issuer and holder for each security. As a result, the database can serve as a very useful input for the compilation of stock and flow data, and FWTW information, for listed shares and debt securities.

Thirdly, survey data may also provide an important input in the compilation process of financial accounts and balance sheets. Survey data is especially useful for (sub)sectors for which information is otherwise lacking from other data sources. This is especially true when it comes to very timely and high frequency data for non-financial corporations and the household sector. In some cases information may be available using counterparty information from other data sources (for example counterparty information from banking statistics that provide detailed information on the counterpart sectors of deposits and loans). However, this is not the case for all instruments, and in particular information on transactions and positions between households and/or non-financial corporations will be lacking. Surveys may in those cases provide some input, although it is not always possible to obtain information according to the exact definitions of the 2008 SNA. On the other hand, due to the increased alignment between the 2008 SNA and international accounting standards, it becomes easier to obtain relevant information from corporations' financial reports.

Compilation process

As the data sources that are used as input for the compilation of the financial accounts and balance sheets are usually not fully in line with the 2008 SNA standards, some adjustments usually need to be made first, before integrating the results in the framework of national accounts. This may relate to differences in sector coverage, conceptual differences with regard to the recording and valuation of the flows and stocks for the various instruments, and items that may be missing from the data sources. The latter may relate to specific instruments but also to breakdowns of the change in stock data into underlying flows (i.e. transactions, revaluations and other changes in the volume of assets). In some cases these adjustments can be made on the basis of counterpart information available from other data sources, but sometimes assumptions have to be made to fill these gaps.

Subsequently, the information has to be integrated in the system of national accounts. This means that the data sources have to be confronted and balanced within the framework of the national accounts in order to ensure consistency at the instrument level (changes in assets have to equal changes in liabilities) and at the sector level (net lending/borrowing from the capital account should equal net lending/borrowing from the financial account for each sector). Moreover, the opening stock plus the transactions plus the revaluations plus the other changes in the volume of assets must equal the value in the closing balance sheet.

As the various data sources usually contain different types of information (with regard to the level of instrument detail, counterparty information, stock versus flow data, etc.), have undergone different types of adjustments, and differ in quality, the balancing process is often very complex. The balancing process often involves weighting the various data sources, discussing possible reasons for any differences, making decisions on which information to use and simultaneously adjusting the information in the framework to arrive at full consistency. In this process many countries apply a so-called building block approach to be able to start from information on specific sectors and/or instruments that are deemed most reliable, such as the government sector, the Rest of the World, monetary financial institutions and securities statistics, and then supplement this information with counterparty information and information from financial reports and surveys to complete the accounts. The specific compilation approach to take will depend on the amount and quality of information available.

1. FINANCIAL ACCOUNTS AND BALANCE SHEETS WITHIN THE SYSTEM OF NATIONAL ACCOUNTS

Key points

- The financial accounts and balance sheets play an important role in the system of national accounts and are presented as a sequence of interconnected accounts showing the changes that occur in a country during a period of time, including how stocks of assets and liabilities change during that period.

- The system of national accounts, including financial accounts and balance sheets, is a fully consistent and closed accounting system guided by the quadruple-entry bookkeeping principle. As a consequence, from a conceptual point of view, all transactions and positions of a unit/sector add up, and for all transactions (stocks) total receipts (stocks of financial assets) of all agents are equal to total payments (stocks of liabilities).

- Financial accounts and balance sheets may include flow-of-funds information or FWTW matrices, which show the relationships between sectors for certain types of financial instruments, or transactions, or groupings thereof. The financial accounts and balance sheets can also be used to produce alternative measures of income and saving, which can aid financial analyses.

- Financial accounts and balance sheets are compiled and presented for institutional sectors, where statistical units are clustered into sectors on the basis of their principal function, behaviour and objectives. There are five main resident institutional sectors: non-financial corporations, financial corporations, general government, households, and non-profit institutions serving households. Together, these comprise the "total economy" of a country. Financial accounts and balance sheets also contain information about a country's financial transactions and positions with non-resident institutional units, called the "Rest of the World".

- Financial accounts and balance sheets also disaggregate information on the basis of the type of assets and liabilities that are involved in transactions and stocks. In terms of financial instruments, in particular, the 2008 SNA provides detailed guidance on the classification of different types of financial instruments. These types include monetary gold and SDRs; currency and deposits; debt securities; loans; equity and investment fund shares; insurance, pension and standardised guarantee schemes; financial derivatives; and other accounts receivable/payable.

- The 2008 SNA also contains specific accounting rules providing guidance on things like the definition, recognition and valuation of assets and liabilities. These rules are very important because they determine what is presented in the financial accounts and balance sheets, and at what amount. While the 2008 SNA is not fully consistent with international business accounting standards, they are generally well aligned, and there is close co-operation between standard setters and national accountants.

- In compiling national accounts, many sources of data are used, including administrative data sources (like tax records and regulatory information), surveys and financial reports. Moreover, there are several statistical standards and guidance manuals that provide detailed guidance on specific sectors, transactions or regions.

Notes

1. These manuals can be found at the following sites:
   - PSDS Guide 2013: *www.tffs.org/pdf/method/2013/psds2013.pdf*.
   - GFSM 2014: *www.imf.org/external/Pubs/FT/GFS/Manual/2014/gfsfinal.pdf*.
   - BPM6: *www.imf.org/external/pubs/ft/bop/2007/pdf/bpm6.pdf*.
   - External Debt Statistics: *www.tffs.org/pdf/edsg/ft2014.pdf*.
   - Monetary and Financial Statistics Manual: *www.imf.org/external/pubs/ft/mfs/manual/pdf/mmfsFT.pdf*.
   - Monetary and Financial Statistics Compilation guide: *hww.imf.org/external/pubs/ft/cgmfs/eng/pdf/cgmfs.pdf*.
   - ESA 2010: *http://ec.europa.eu/eurostat/cache/metadata/Annexes/nasa_10_f_esms_an1.pdf*.

References

Australian Bureau of Statistics (2017), 5204.0 – *Australian System of National Accounts*, Australian Bureau of Statistics, Canberra, *www.abs.gov.au/ausstats/abs@.nsf/mf/5204.0*.

Australian Bureau of Statistics (2017), 5232.0 – *Australian National Accounts: Finance and Wealth*, Australian Bureau of Statistics, Canberra, *www.abs.gov.au/ausstats/abs@.nsf/mf/5232.0*.

European PPP Expertise Centre (EPEC) and Eurostat (2016), *A Guide to the Statistical Treatment of PPPs: September 2016*, European Investment Bank, Luxembourg, *www.eib.org/epec/resources/publications/epec_eurostat_guide* ppp.

Gleeson-White, J. (2011), *Double Entry: How the Merchants of Venice Created Modern Finance*, W.W. Norton & Company, New York City.

Hicks, J.R. (1983), *Classics and Moderns, Collected Papers*, Vol. 3, Blackwell, Oxford.

OECD (2017), "Public Sector Debt: Public sector debt – consolidated", *OECD National Accounts Statistics* (database), *http://dx.doi.org/10.1787/data-00620-en*.

Polackova, H. (1999), "Contingent government Liabilities: A hidden fiscal risk", *Finance & Development*, Vol 36/1, IMF, Washington, DC, *www.imf.org/external/pubs/ft/fandd/1999/03/pdf/polackov.pdf*.

Statistics Netherlands (2017), *Financial Instruments: From-whom-to-whom matrices; National Accounts*, Statistics Netherlands, the Hague, *http://statline.cbs.nl/Statweb/publication/?DM=SLEN&PA=83205ENG&D1=4&D2=a&D3=a&D4=l&D5=79&LA=EN&HDR=T,G2&STB=G1,G3,G4&VW=T)*.

Chapter 2

The role of financial markets

João Cadete de Matos (Banco de Portugal), Daniele Fano
(Fondazione AIB), Filipa Lima (Banco de Portugal)
and Amanda Seneviratne (Australian Bureau of Statistics)

> This chapter describes the financial markets as a key to understanding financial systems: capital markets for shares and bonds, money markets, foreign exchange markets, derivatives markets, and other markets related to deposits, loans and pooled investment. For each of these markets, the focus is on their purpose and major players, and on financial intermediation activities. The chapter also describes the construction of tables that illustrate the interconnectedness between institutional sectors, and provides a brief description of the risk elements within the financial system and the ability of the financial accounts and balance sheets to capture such information.

1. Introduction

Financial accounts and balance sheets are often presented by showing an overview of all transactions and positions, disaggregated by institutional sectors (non-financial corporations, financial corporations, households, government, etc.). Another way of presenting financial developments is by showing overviews of the various financial markets.

The financial system of a nation can be thought of as having three overlapping components:

- The financial institutions (such as banks), which are described in the 2008 System of National Accounts (2008 SNA) as belonging to the financial corporations sector (see Chapter 3).
- The financial markets, such as the stock exchange; their participants, the issuers of shares on the exchange; and the investors in these shares, such as households. The 2008 SNA captures these financial markets by describing the financial instruments that make up the market, and grouping participants in the markets by institutional sectors.
- The payment system (e.g. electronic means by which payments are effected) and its participants (e.g. banks and other enterprises).

The interaction of the three components of the financial system, through mechanisms of financial intermediation and financial markets, enables funds from saving in some parts of the economy to become available for investment or consumption in other parts of the economy. In addition to describing this interaction, the chapter also focuses on the mechanism of financial intermediation, and the structure and activities of the financial markets within the overall financial system.

2. Financial markets in the 2008 SNA

The 2008 SNA describes financial intermediation as an activity undertaken by financial institutions (financial intermediaries) of matching the needs of borrowers with the desires of lenders. There are many ways in which money can be borrowed and lent. The act of financial intermediation is one of devising financial instruments that encourage those with saving to commit to lend to financial institutions on the conditions inherent in the instruments, so that these financial institutions, in a second round, can then lend the same funds to others as another set of instruments with different conditions. This activity encompasses financial risk management and liquidity transformation.

A financial market may be defined narrowly as a market in which trading of financial instruments such as equities (e.g. shares), debt securities (e.g. bonds) and currencies occur at competitive transaction costs and at prices that reflect supply and demand, with no intervention of financial intermediaries (or the need for a "middle man"). An example is trading on stock exchanges in many countries. Alternatively, financial markets may be thought of more broadly to include the interaction of financial intermediaries with financial markets. Below are examples of financial markets which include financial intermediation:

- organisations that facilitate trade in securities, e.g. a stock exchange in a physical location like the New York Stock Exchange, or an electronic system like the NASDAQ;
- banks offering services to households such as loans or accounts;
- trade in foreign currency, which often concerns direct transactions between two parties (over-the-counter), but is nonetheless described as the foreign exchange market;
- corporate mergers and acquisitions, activities which include the sale of equities and the underwriting activity of investment bankers to organise the deal;
- delisting of equities from a stock exchange and transferring to a private equity (unlisted equity) market, and vice versa;
- the privatisation of government owned enterprises; and
- investments by households into mutual funds (pooled investment).

Figure 2.1 below shows how financial markets and financial intermediaries move funds from lenders to borrowers across sectors and the Rest of the World. The movement of funds can be between: lenders and financial intermediaries; lenders and markets; markets and the financial intermediaries and vice versa; markets and borrowers; and financial intermediaries and borrowers. In this chapter, financial markets will be discussed with this broad definition in mind.

Types of financial markets

The global financial system is comprised of the following financial markets: the capital market, consisting of the share market and the bond market; the money market; the foreign exchange (Forex) market; and the market for derivatives. Figure 2.2 provides a short overview.

Financial markets can be either primary or secondary. Primary markets are used to describe new lending and borrowing arrangements that are raising

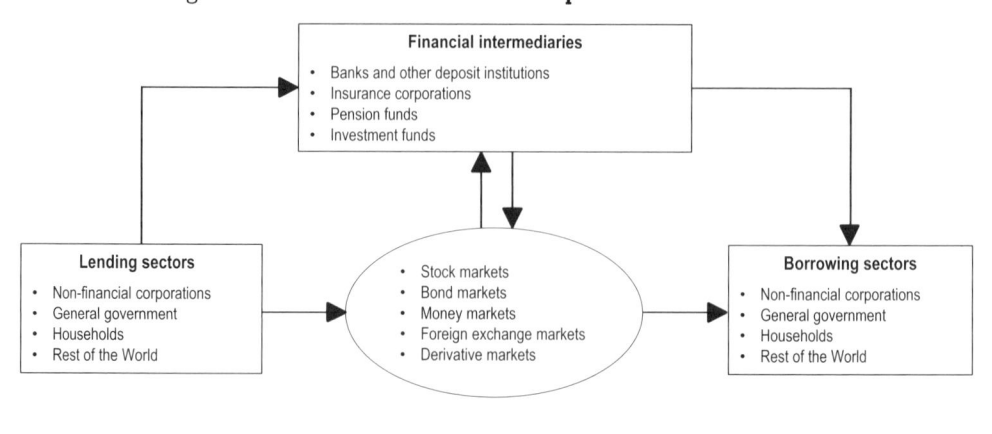

Figure 2.1. **Illustration of relationships in financial markets**

Financial intermediaries
- Banks and other deposit institutions
- Insurance corporations
- Pension funds
- Investment funds

Lending sectors
- Non-financial corporations
- General government
- Households
- Rest of the World

- Stock markets
- Bond markets
- Money markets
- Foreign exchange markets
- Derivative markets

Borrowing sectors
- Non-financial corporations
- General government
- Households
- Rest of the World

Figure 2.2. **Types of financial markets**

Capital market	Money market	Forex market	Derivative market
Financial instruments: • Listed shares • Unlisted shares • Bonds	*Financial instruments:* • Certificate of deposits • Treasury notes • Promissory notes • Commercial paper	*Financial instruments:* • US dollars • Euros • UK pounds • Other currencies	*Financial instruments:* • Futures • Forwards • Options • Swaps
Participants: • Non-financial corporations • Banks and depository corporations • Institutional investors • Brokers and dealers • Governments • Households • Foreign investors	*Participants:* • Non-financial corporations • Banks and depository corporations • Institutional investors • Brokers and dealers • Governments • Households • Foreign investors	*Participants:* • Non-financial corporations • Banks and depository corporations • Institutional investors • Brokers and dealers • Governments • Households • Foreign investors	*Participants:* • Non-financial corporations • Banks and depository corporations • Institutional investors • Brokers and dealers • Governments • Foreign investors

funds for new investment. For example, a primary market activity is the issue of a new set of treasury bonds by government or the flotation of new shares, rights issues, and dividend reinvestment schemes on the equity market. These transactions occur between issuers and investors. Secondary markets are used to describe the subsequent buying and selling of securities that have already been issued. Transactions in the secondary market occur between investors, and the market allows investors to reduce or increase their holdings of financial assets. The primary market cannot operate effectively unless there is an efficiently operating secondary market. Investors are less likely to invest their funds if they cannot retrieve or reallocate their funds at any given time. This illustrates the importance of liquidity in a secondary market. Liquidity refers to the ease with which a security can be sold without the loss of value.

Capital markets

Capital markets are markets for financial assets which have a maturity period above one year or indefinite maturity. A distinction is typically made between the share market and the bond market.

a) Share market. The share (or equity) market operates the issuance and trading of a share in the ownership of corporate enterprises. The share market includes trading of shares listed on a stock exchange as well as unlisted shares traded privately (private equity) or over-the-counter (OTC) through a dealer network. The stock exchange provides an important way for enterprises to raise money publicly by selling shares of ownership of the company in a public market. The stock exchange also acts as the clearing house for each transaction by collecting and delivering shares and guaranteeing the payment to the seller of the security, therefore eliminating the risk of an individual buyer or seller defaulting. Exchanges may be physical locations where transactions are carried out on the trading floor (New York Stock Exchange) or a virtual market composed of networks of computers (NASDAQ) where trades are made electronically.

In general, shares of small companies are traded over-the-counter because the relative size of the company makes it difficult to meet exchange listing requirements. The unlisted shares are traded by broker-dealers who negotiate directly with one another using computer networks and by phone. Broker-dealers are generally part of large financial institutions such as investment banks. By contrast, private equity consists of investors that invest directly into private companies or conduct buyouts of public companies that result in a delisting of the publicly listed shares. These types of activities involve the purchase and sale of equities, underwritten by investment bankers.

Participants in the share market range from individual retail investors (households), institutional investors (pension funds, insurance companies, mutual funds, hedge funds and banks) and companies trading in their own shares. The term institutional investor refers to the fact that over time markets (including the share market) have become dominated by buyers and sellers from institutions, a move away from wealthy businessmen with long family histories in particular corporations who have historically dominated investing. For example, the majority of private equity investment consists of investment from institutional investors who can commit large sums of money for long period of times, as private equity investment often demands long holding periods.

This chapter will contain a number of tables using figures from Australia as a way to illustrate the concepts discussed in this chapter. Table 2.1 shows some details of the Australian total equity market, classified by issuing and holding sectors, from the *Australian National Accounts: Finance and Wealth* publication.

2. THE ROLE OF FINANCIAL MARKETS

Table 2.1. **Australian equity market**
Millions of AUD, amounts outstanding on 31 December

	ISSUED BY			HELD BY		
	2014	2015	2016	2014	2015	2016
Total equity and investment fund shares	4 323 752	4 575 436	4 820 364	4 323 752	4 575 436	4 820 364
Listed	1 580 331	1 627 506	1 757 818			
Unlisted	2 743 421	2 947 930	3 062 546			
Non-Financial corporations	1 856 872	1 958 358	2 174 751	312 296	307 684	305 887
Financial corporations	1 458 406	1 564 270	1 535 332	1 919 343	2 054 943	2 125 939
Banks and other depository corporations	583 943	606 529	613 140	148 099	156 823	155 942
Pension funds	0	0	0	1 009 608	1 104 074	1 267 415
Insurance corporations	114 345	113 448	118 239	298 916	312 140	242 186
Investment funds	695 750	768 766	723 007	322 984	338 793	314 557
Other financial corporations	64 368	768 766	723 007	322 984	338 793	314 557
General government	0	0	0	424 727	449 362	481 527
Households	0	0	0	720 440	772 083	798 174
Rest of the World	1 008 474	1 052 808	1 110 281	946 946	991 364	1 108 837

Source: Australian Bureau of Statistics (2017), 5232.0-*Australian National Accounts: Finance and Wealth* (database), www.abs.gov.au/ausstats/abs@.nsf/mf/5232.0/.

StatLink ⟶ http://dx.doi.org/10.1787/888933589713

The table includes the share market as described above and also the ownership of public sector corporations (unlisted equities) by the government sectors, and the foreign direct investment in subsidiaries (unlisted equities).

Table 2.1 shows that the Australian equity market increased by 6% and 5% in 2015 and 2016, respectively. Australian non-financial corporations had just over 45% of the total equity issuance at the end of 2016, and the Australian pension fund sector was the largest investor in the market with 26% of the total equity held, followed by overseas investors and Australian households.

b) Bond market. Bonds are issued on the bond market with original term to maturity of one or more years. The investors are usually paid a set periodic interest, called a coupon, for the life of the bond and receive their initial investment back at maturity. Some bonds have variable interest rates, some have indexed principal repayments, and some bonds are zero-couponed or deep discount bonds that are issued at a discount to face value.

Governments and large trading enterprises issue bonds to finance long-term funding for government deficit financing and for business investment requirements, and financial institutions such as banks issue bonds to fund their loan assets. Private enterprises raise medium to long-term funding by issuing corporate bonds, debentures and notes. For these entities, the bond market generally provides an alternative source of funds than borrowing directly from banks and other financial institutions. An important part of the bond market is the government bond market; due to its size and liquidity, government bonds are often used to compare other bonds and their credit risk. Another reason why the government bonds are important is related to their role in borrowing and lending to other governments. Governments often purchase debt from other countries; for example, Japan is major holder of US government debt. The bond market in many countries is bigger in terms of the value of securities issued than the listed share market (the most popular financial market quoted in the media) This is the case for Australia, as illustrated when comparing the numbers in Table 2.2 with those in Table 2.1.

Table 2.2. **Total bond market, Australia**
Millions of AUD, amounts outstanding on 31 December

	ISSUED BY			HELD BY		
	2014	2015	2016	2014	2015	2016
Total bonds	**1 895 969**	**2 124 833**	**2 301 953**	**1 895 969**	**2 124 833**	**2 301 953**
Issued in Australia	1 255 367	1 468 310	1 559 488			
of which non-resident bonds	133 440	150 091	157 966			
Issued offshore	640 602	656 523	742 465			
of which resident bonds	529 240	547 214	618 103			
of which non-resident bonds, held by residents				111 362	109 309	124 362
Non-financial corporations	242 582	243 784	285 855	81 081	10 180	11 111
Financial corporations	1 091 173	1 227 460	1 288 647	880 256	1 049 984	1 135 165
Banks and other depository corporations	503 511	535 675	581 044	577 977	708 606	768 548
Pension funds	0	0	0	147 961	170 441	182 032
Insurance corporations	8 098	6 888	6 656	73 941	77 125	77 619
Central borrowing authorities*	242 243	269 507	267 127	12 278	14 190	17 176
Other financial corporations	337 321	415 390	433 820	68 099	79 622	89 778
General government	317 411	394 189	445 123	30 191	23 227	23 384
Households	0	0	0	3 769	3 845	4 175
Rest of the World	244 802	259 400	282 328	957 679	1 037 649	1 127 112
of which non-resident bonds issued in Australia				66 721	75 045	78 983

* Central borrowing authorities are financial institutions of regional governments in Australia.
Source: Australian Bureau of Statistics (2017), 5232.0-Australian National Accounts: Finance and Wealth (database), www.abs.gov.au/ausstats/abs@.nsf/mf/5232.0/.

StatLink http://dx.doi.org/10.1787/888933589732

The majority of the trading in the bond market occurs over-the-counter between broker-dealers and large institutional investors through organised electronic trading networks. Only a small number of bonds, mainly corporate bonds, are listed on exchanges. Table 2.2 shows the details of the Australian bond market from the *Australian National Accounts: Finance and Wealth* publication. The table presents two views of the Australian bond market, which consists of both resident and non-resident bond issuers and holders. The first view shows where the bonds were issued, that is in Australia or in offshore markets. In the second view, the issuance of resident and non-resident bonds in Australia and the offshore markets are presented by sector of issuance and the holding sectors.

Table 2.2 shows that at the end of 2016, just over 28% of Australian domestic bonds were issued offshore and 10% of bond issued in Australia were non-resident bonds. The largest issuers of bonds were the banks and other depository corporations, followed by the general government sector (mainly made up of the central government) and non-residents. The largest investors in the Australian bond market with just over 47% of the total bond issuance were non-resident investors; the pension fund sector held only 9% of the bond market, compared to 26% of the total equity market (see Table 2.1).

Money markets

The money market is where financial instruments with high liquidity and very short maturities are traded. This market brings together individuals and institutions with temporary surpluses of funds and temporary shortage of funds. Money market securities are short-term, that is, they have an original term to maturity of less than one year, often 30, 90 or 180 days. They are issued by borrowers at a discount to face value and carry no payments other than repayments of face value at maturity.

Money market securities consist of negotiable certificates of deposits, bankers' acceptance (bills of exchange), treasury bills (notes) and commercial paper (promissory notes). The securities are typically issued by government, financial institutions and large corporations. The majority of trading in the money market is undertaken over-the-counter through organised electronic trading networks, between brokers-dealers and large institutional investors.

An important segment of the money market is interbank lending, banks borrowing and lending to each other using short-term securities and repurchase agreements for specified terms. Most interbank lending is for maturities of one week or less, the majority being overnight. Banks borrow and lend money in the interbank lending market in order to manage liquidity and satisfy regulations such as reserve requirements set by central banks. The US federal funds rate and the London Interbank Offered Rate (LIBOR) are published interbank interest rates which are used widely to determine short-term interest rates across the world. Figure 2.3 shows the details of the holding sectors of the Australian money market securities issued by banks as at 31 December 2016.

In the Australian money market, banks are the most significant issuer of these securities, issuing just over 75 % of the total securities in the market at the end of 31 December 2016. Non-residents hold the majority of the Australian

2. THE ROLE OF FINANCIAL MARKETS

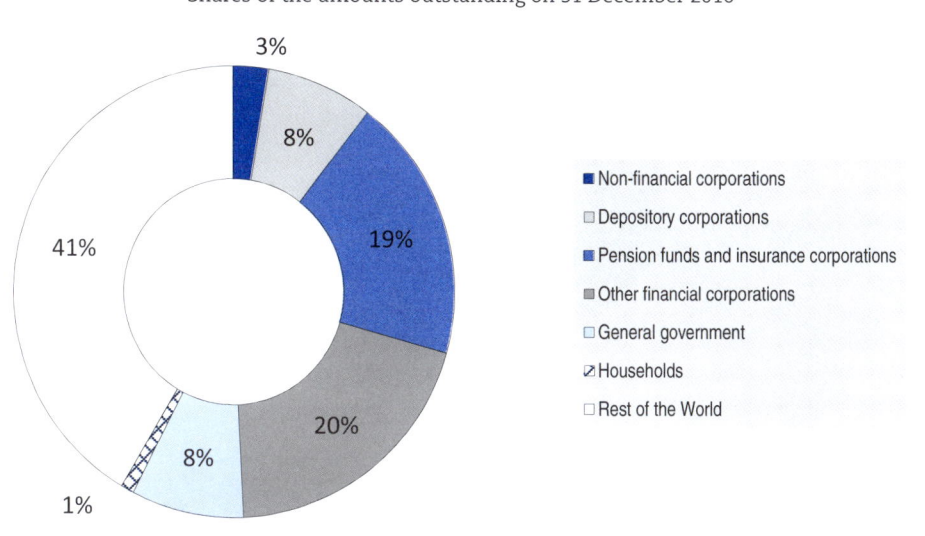

Figure 2.3. **Holding sectors of the Australian bank money market securities**
Shares of the amounts outstanding on 31 December 2016

- 3%
- 8%
- 19%
- 20%
- 8%
- 1%
- 41%

■ Non-financial corporations
□ Depository corporations
■ Pension funds and insurance corporations
■ Other financial corporations
□ General government
▨ Households
□ Rest of the World

Source: Australian Bureau of Statistics (2017), 5232.0-Australian National Accounts: Finance and Wealth (database), www.abs.gov.au/ausstats/abs@.nsf/mf/5232.0/.
StatLink ⟶ http://dx.doi.org/10.1787/888933587965

bank money market securities, at 41%, followed by pension funds and insurance corporations at 19%.

Foreign exchange markets

The foreign exchange market is the means whereby currencies of different countries can be bought and sold. It sets the current market price of the value of one currency as demanded against another. It is the most liquid market in the world, with participation by nearly all sectors of the economy. The market is a global over-the-counter market where broker-dealers negotiate directly with each other. In terms of trading volume it is also the largest market in the world, with the United Kingdom geographically having the largest share of the volume, followed by the United States (Figure 2.4). The large volume of trade through the United Kingdom makes it the most important centre for foreign exchange, and consequently a particular currency's quoted price is more than likely to be the London market price.

The foreign exchange market assists international trade and investment by enabling currency conversions to pay for goods and services. It also facilitates investment in foreign securities, is integral in derivative contracts that try to minimise risk in currency fluctuations, and supports direct and indirect speculative activity on the movement of currencies. The majority of the transactions in the foreign exchange market occur between large banks

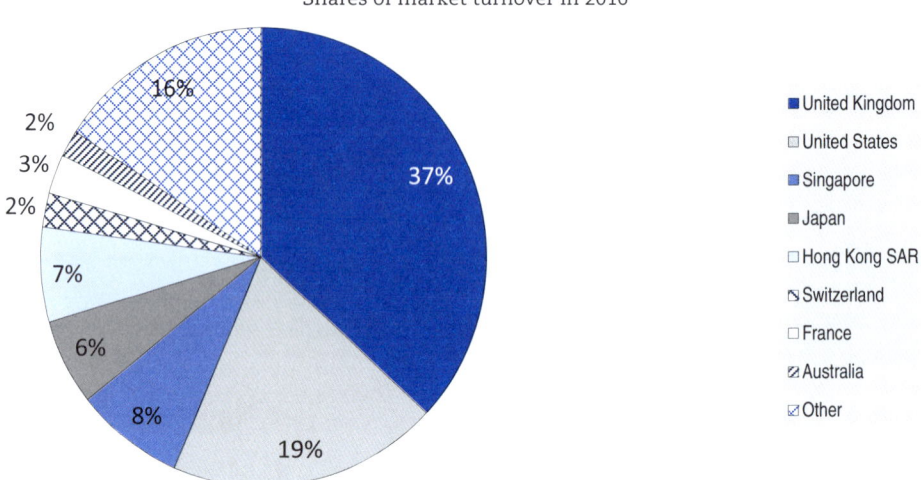

Figure 2.4. **Geographical distribution of global foreign exchange market turnover**
Shares of market turnover in 2016

- United Kingdom: 37%
- United States: 19%
- Singapore: 8%
- Japan: 6%
- Hong Kong SAR: 7%
- Switzerland: 2%
- France: 3%
- Australia: 2%
- Other: 16%

Source: Bank for International Settlements (2016), *Triennial Central Bank Survey: Foreign exchange turnover in April 2016*, www.bis.org/publ/rpfx16fx.pdf.

StatLink ⟶ http://dx.doi.org/10.1787/888933587984

and broker-dealers from major financial institutions, followed by smaller banks, large corporations and hedge funds. Pension funds, insurance corporations and mutual funds have increased their participation in these markets in the last 20 years. Central banks also play an important role in the market by controlling the money supply, inflation and/or interest rates, often having official and unofficial target rates for their currencies.

Derivative markets

As explained in Chapter 1, derivatives are financial instruments that are linked to another financial instrument (bonds, shares), an indicator (interest rates, market indices) or a commodity, that isolate specific financial risks associated with those instruments, indicators or commodities, and transform them into financial instruments that can be traded in the financial markets in their own right. The value of the derivative is derived from the price of the underlying item (the "reference price"). Derivatives are not issued for the purpose of raising new capital or transferring ownership of assets; instead, they are used to manage financial risks, and perform arbitrage between markets to increase profits, sometimes for speculative reasons.

There are two broad types of derivatives: options and forward-type contracts. The major difference between the two is that a buyer of an option contract acquires an asset, and the option writer incurs a liability, whereas for forward-type contracts, either party is a potential debtor. There are large assortments of derivatives in the two broad categories. Forward type contracts include futures (which are traded on exchanges), swaps (such as interest rate, foreign currency and equity) and forward rate agreements. Options include call and put options, warrants and more exotic variations.

Derivative trading most commonly takes place over-the-counter (OTC) but can also occur on specialised or other exchanges, such as the Chicago Mercantile Exchange. The main participants in the derivative market include large trading and financial corporations (banks, mutual funds, and insurance corporations). Exchange traded derivatives are traded via specialised derivative exchanges (future exchanges) or other exchanges. At the exchanges, the parties enter into standardised contracts that are defined by the exchange, and the exchange acts as the intermediary to the related transactions. The exchange facilitates liquidity, mitigates all credit risk concerning the default of one party in the transaction, provides transparency and maintains the current market price. In contrast, OTC derivatives are privately negotiated between two parties, and include both common derivative products such as swaps as well as more exotic derivatives (exchange-traded derivatives only comprise common derivative products). The OTC market is the largest market for derivatives and is generally unregulated in relation to required disclosures. The main players in the OTC market are large financial institutions such as banks and hedge funds, and broker dealers in usually form large financial institutions that arrange transactions for their customers.

The compilation of high quality derivatives estimates presents one of the more difficult challenges for national statisticians. Derivatives comprise quite a heterogeneous set of financial instruments, many of which are complex and difficult to understand. The 2008 SNA requires survey respondents to compile and report information that is often not routinely generated for internal management reporting purposes. At the time of writing this publication, the Australian national accounts publishes a derivative market table with inputs from a simple domestic derivatives model and non-resident derivatives data collected in a quarterly survey of international investment. Australia, along with other countries, is planning to improve the compilation of the statistics on derivatives over the medium to longer term. In doing so, they plan to utilise, for example, information from repositories on OTC derivative trading data. These data repositories were set up globally as a response to the 2007-09 economic and financial crisis to provide some transparency around the significant OTC derivative market to financial market regulators. It has proven to be quite difficult to account for these heterogeneous financial products within the framework of the 2008 SNA, as new "innovative constructs" are being developed almost continuously.

Other financial markets

The broad definition of financial markets includes the interaction of financial intermediaries with the financial markets. It therefore also comprises the deposit market, the loan market, and the pooled investment market. Applying the broad definition makes it possible to present all transactions and positions included in the financial accounts and positions in the form of markets, with supply (the issuers) and demand (the holders) of the relevant financial instruments included.

a) Deposit market. The 2008 SNA does not provide a precise definition of a deposit. Therefore, the distinction between deposits and loans is somewhat blurred, and differs between countries' national accounts. For example, the Australian national accounts added additional criteria to the definition of deposits, such that deposit liabilities can only be incurred by institutions which are included in the calculation of the central bank's definition of "broad money". In Australia these institutions are: the central bank; banks; credit unions; building societies; and registered financial corporations. In most countries, deposit-taking institutions are regulated by prudential authorities.

The deposit market provides households and businesses a place to keep funds to purchase goods and services, pay and receive wages and salaries, and earn interest income from interest-bearing accounts. Moreover, bank deposits in many developed countries, including Australia, are a major source of funding of the bank loan asset market. All sectors of an economy participate in the banking deposit market. Building societies and credit unions can, for example, be major deposit taking institutions for households and smaller businesses, while the central bank is the major deposit taking institution for banks, government sector and non-resident central banks. Table 2.3 shows the detail of the Australian bank deposit market, using the 2008 SNA categories of transferable and other deposits.

In Australia, the banks are the most significant deposit taking institution, holding respectively 87 per cent and 89 per cent of the total transferable and other deposit markets as at 31 December 2016. Within the bank deposit market, households are the largest contributor, holding 46 per cent and 45 per cent of the banks' transferable and other deposit market. In Australia, during the three year period up to 31 December 2016, households' transferable deposit grew 36 per cent, while households' other deposits grew 13 per cent. The larger growth rate in transferable deposits is related to the significant growth during this period of deposit accounts that households use to offset the interest charges of their home loan accounts.

b) Loan market. The loan market referenced here consists mostly of secured loans, where the borrower pledges an asset such as residential property, or

Table 2.3. **Australian bank deposit market**
Millions of AUD, amounts outstanding on 31 December

	2014		2015		2016	
	Transferable	Other	Transferable	Other	Transferable	Other
Total bank deposits	553 216	1 226 270	631 721	1 300 654	704 315	1 407 476
Non-financial corporations	156 156	206 712	178 942	192 869	200 337	208 473
Financial corporations	94 983	261 004	98 153	276 158	104 042	304 587
Depository corporations	18 635	15 803	17 548	23 952	16 286	23 849
Pension funds	47 179	199 833	50 585	203 475	56 670	223 338
Insurance corporations	16 248	9 814	15 112	9 419	14 397	8 786
Investment funds	8 590	17 932	9 916	20 199	11 132	20 733
Other financial corporations	4 331	17 622	4 992	19 113	5 557	27 881
General government	28 957	36 634	29 072	43 063	32 529	45 502
Households	239 264	556 890	294 774	579 863	324 729	627 751
Rest of the World	33 856	165 030	30 780	208 701	42 678	220 736
Total deposit market	645 920	1 388 118	736 279	1 453 252	809 581	1 585 631

Source: Australian Bureau of Statistics (2017), 5232.0-Australian National Accounts: Finance and Wealth (database), www.abs.gov.au/ausstats/abs@.nsf/mf/5232.0/.

StatLink http://dx.doi.org/10.1787/888933589751

plant and equipment of a business as collateral, and unsecured loans, where the loans are not secured against the borrower's assets. In essence, the loan market in this context implies that actual issue of debt securities does not occur and the relevant instruments are usually not traded. In this sense, it is quite different from the bond market and the money market. Unsecured loans typically include credit card debt, personal loans and bank overdrafts. A further breakdown of the loan market is often made into personal loans (if the borrower is a household) and business loans. For both personal and business loans, secured loans will generally attract a lower rate of interest to unsecured loans. Loan markets, for example, serve households to purchase residential property or vehicles, and small and large businesses to raise funds for capital investments in non-financial assets.

The major providers of loans in the market are banks, followed by other deposit taking institutions and securitisation companies. The latter organisations are financial intermediaries that pool various types of assets such as residential mortgages, commercial property loans and/or credit card debt, and package them as collateral to issue debt securities, referred to as asset backed securities. The loan market also contains significant loan transactions between parent companies and their subsidiaries. Table 2.4 offers a breakdown of the Australian loans market.

The 2007-09 economic and financial crisis significantly impacted the securitisation sector, and Australia was not an exception. At the end of 2007, the market for securitised loans was AUD 218 095 million. By 31 December 2012,

Table 2.4. **Australian loan market**
Millions of AUD, amounts outstanding on 31 December

	Borrowed by:					
	2007		2012		2016	
	Banks	Securitiser	Banks	Securitiser	Banks	Securitiser
Loan market	1 314 742	218 095	1 917 529	115 153	2 667 384	115 326
Non-financial corporations	335 511	19 687	387 962	14 371	543 176	16 740
Financial corporations	46 072	2 328	30 219	543	37 038	1 014
General government	1 098	0	5 540	0	6 656	0
Households	838 884	196 080	1 317 227	100 239	1 738 951	97 572
Rest of the World	93 177	0	176 581	0	341 563	0

Source: Australian Bureau of Statistics (2017), 5232.0-Australian National Accounts: Finance and Wealth (database), www.abs.gov.au/ausstats/abs@.nsf/mf/5232.0/.
StatLink http://dx.doi.org/10.1787/888933589770

it had declined by 47 per cent of the value on 31 December 2007. Since then the securitised loan market has struggled to recover, and by 31 December 2016, total securitised loans were AUD 115 326 million. During the same period, the total bank loan market doubled in value from 31 December 2007 to 31 December 2016.

c) Pooled investment market. The pooled investment market consists of investment funds through which investors indirectly invest in shares, bonds, money market instruments, and real estate assets. The main advantage of investing in such funds is that these funds give investors access to professionally managed, diversified portfolios, even at small amounts of capital. Mutual funds and exchange-traded investment funds are examples of investment funds that are open to the public, while hedge funds and private equity funds are typically limited to private placements (non-public offerings) to chosen investors.

The 2008 SNA categorises investment fund units between i) money market fund (MMF) shares/units; and ii) non-money market fund (NMMF) shares/units. The difference between these funds is that MMFs typically invest in money market instruments with a residual maturity of less than one year, while NMMF investment funds invest in longer-term financial assets and in non-financial assets such as real estate. The major investors in investment funds are pension funds, insurance corporations, households and other investments funds. Table 2.5 shows investment details about Australian investment funds.

The investment fund sector has grown significantly in Australia in the last 25 years, and this is especially the case for NMMFs, where the equity outstanding grew 950% from December 1988 to December 2002, and then a further 182% from December 2002 to December 2016. NMMFs may be broken further down

Table 2.5. **Total equity, Australian investment fund market**
Millions of AUD, amounts outstanding on 31 December

	HELD BY					
	1988		2002		2016	
	MMF	NMMF	MMF	NMMF	MMF	NMMF
Total equity	6 889	23 075	35 542	242 338	37 677	685 330
Non-financial corporations	0	437	0	170	198	2 179
Financial corporations						
Depository corporations	0	42	0	628	0	644
Pension funds	264	4 460	2 182	66 591	12 870	203 950
Insurance corporations	1 863	8 354	1 898	68 454	7 505	174 567
Investment funds	1 021	3 097	4 389	67 974	1 703	111 912
Other financial corporations	0	407	0	2 318	0	48 582
General government	0	0	0	12 621	0	19 459
Households	3 741	3 294	27 073	9 598	15 401	30 254
Rest of the World	0	2 984	0	13 984	0	93 783

Source: Australian Bureau of Statistics (2017), 5232.0-Australian National Accounts: Finance and Wealth (database), www.abs.gov.au/ausstats/abs@.nsf/mf/5232.0/.

StatLink ⟶ http://dx.doi.org/10.1787/888933589789

in specific sub-categories, such as bond funds, equity funds, balanced funds and others targeted to specific securities and investment styles. Pension funds and insurance corporations are the major investors in the NMMFs, together holding 55% of the equity in these funds as at 31 December 2016.

Demand for credit

To provide an overall view on borrowing and lending in an economy, data are often summarised in statistics on the demand for credit. Credit may be defined broadly as all funds provided to those seeking to borrow. Since financial corporations mainly act as intermediaries, meaning they borrow in order to lend, analytical measures of credit usually exclude the lending between these corporations. Furthermore, lending and borrowing between enterprises that have special relationships, such as between companies in the same group or between government agencies, is often excluded from credit measures because these transactions are frequently of a non-market nature. Similarly, some types of financial instruments, such as accounts payable, are not considered to be part of an organised financial market. Table 2.6 and Figure 2.5 present a summary of the demand for credit and credit outstanding in Australia by the non-financial sectors.

Demand for credit in the fourth quarter of 2016 was AUD 92.9 billion. Households borrowed an additional amount of AUD 28.6 billion, while private non-financial corporations raised a net AUD 64.0 billion, and general government

Table 2.6. **Australian demand for credit and credit outstanding by non-financial sectors**
Billions of AUD

	Credit market outstanding at end	Demand for credit during	Other changes during	Credit market outstanding at end
	Q3 2016	Q4 2016	Q4 2016	Q4 2016
Non-financial corporations	3 063.2	49.5	17.3	3 129.9
Private	2 926.7	64.0	17.3	3 008.0
Public	136.5	-14.5	0.0	121.9
General government	670.0	14.8	-24.8	660.0
National	514.8	23.3	-24.7	513.4
State and local	155.2	-8.5	-0.1	146.6
Households	2 052.0	28.6	2.7	2 083.3
Total	5 785.2	92.9	-4.8	5 873.2

Source: Australian Bureau of Statistics (2017), 5232.0-Australian National Accounts: Finance and Wealth (database), www.abs.gov.au/ausstats/abs@.nsf/mf/5232.0/.
StatLink ⟶ http://dx.doi.org/10.1787/888933589808

Figure 2.5. **Australian demand for credit by non-financial sectors**
Billions of AUD

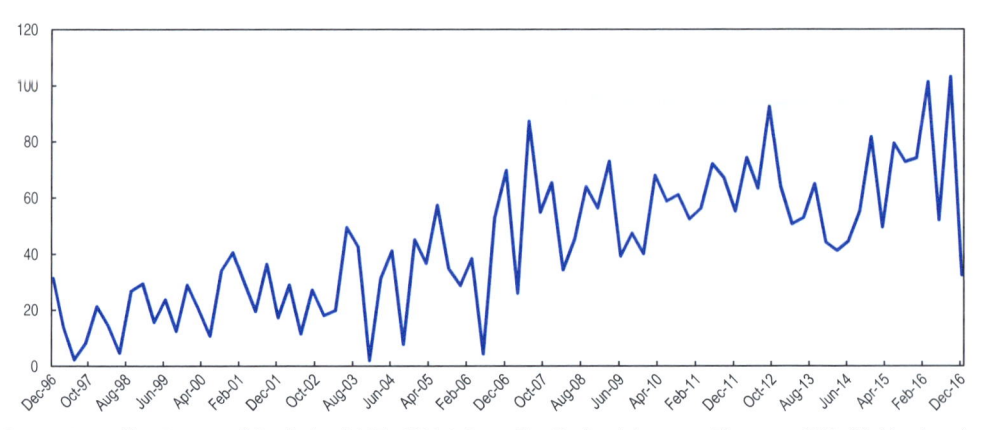

Source: Australian Bureau of Statistics (2017), 5232.0-Australian National Accounts: Finance and Wealth (database), www.abs.gov.au/AUSSTATS/abs@.nsf/Lookup/5232.0Main+Features1Dec%202016?OpenDocument.
StatLink ⟶ http://dx.doi.org/10.1787/888933588003

raised a net AUD 14.8 billion. Australian households raised credit primarily through the loans market. Other private non-financial corporations raised credit through a variety of channels or markets: loan borrowings, issuance of shares and other equity, and issuance of bonds. General government raised credit through issuances of government bonds.

As can be derived from Figure 2.5, a significant amount of short-term volatility exists in the demand for credit by non-financial sectors. However, the long-term trend in Australia in the last 20 years has been a steady growth in the demand for credit.

The credit market presented above may be narrowed in scope for alternative analytical requirements. For example, Australia's central bank, the Reserve Bank of Australia, publishes monthly credit market aggregates of private and public enterprises, and households, which includes only the financial instruments of loans, short-term securities, and bank acceptances. The lenders included are banks, non-bank financial institutions, and securitisation companies. These credit aggregates for households and businesses are utilised by the central bank in formulating Australia's monetary policy.

Box 2.1. **Australian financial markets – data sources**

Section 2 above illustrated financial markets using data from the Australian National Accounts, Finance and Wealth quarterly publication. On a quarterly basis, the publication produces:

- for each sector and subsector, financial accounts and balance sheets by financial instrument;
- twelve financial instrument market tables, each with a breakdown into nineteen sectors and subsectors issuing/accepting/borrowing by counterparty (sub)sector; the tables are presented within a from-whom-to-whom framework (see Section 3); and
- quarterly household balance sheets.

The data within the publication is mainly based on administrative data collected by the Australian Prudential Regulatory Authority (APRA) and Australian Bureau of Statistics (ABS) statistical surveys. Of particular importance are the ABS *Survey of Financial Information* (SFI) and the *Survey of International Investment* (SII), both of which are conducted quarterly. Other data sources are used to supplement the ABS and APRA sources, such as market capitalisation for different sector and subsector share issuance from the Australian Securities Exchange data; information on central government from ledgers obtained from Government Finance Statistics (GFS); debt issuance data from Austraclear (an Australian debt registration service); and bond price indices from private financial market analysts.

All in all, detailed information on the balance sheets for depository corporations, pension funds and insurance corporations is provided by the APRA administrative data. Data for the non-regulated financial corporations in Australia, such as investment funds and securitisation companies, are gathered from the ABS SFI surveys. For the government sector and subsectors, data is collected through Government Finance Statistics (GFS) plus ABS SFI collection, while the ABS SII collection provides the data for the transactions and positions between residents and non-residents. Data for the household sector is mainly derived from counterparty information collected via APRA administrative data and ABS surveys.

Source: Australian Bureau of Statistics.

3. Financial intermediation

Role of financial intermediation and intermediaries in financial markets

As discussed in Section 2 of this chapter, financial markets may be defined narrowly to mean a market in which trading of financial instruments occur with no intervention of financial intermediaries. They can also be defined more broadly to include the interaction of financial intermediaries with financial markets. While this is a simple way to present the various financial markets, it should be noted that even the financial institutions that are participants in the narrow definition of financial markets perform the activity of financial intermediation, which is defined in paragraph 17.228 of the 2008 SNA as follows: "devising financial instruments that encourage those with saving to commit to lend to the financial institutions on the conditions inherent in the instruments, so that the financial institutions can then lend the same funds to others as another set of instruments with different conditions". As such, the issuance of debt securities and equity by banks, which is part of the narrowly defined financial markets, cannot be distinguished from the banks' role as financial intermediaries.

In all the financial markets presented in Section 2, the role of financial intermediation is evident. In the case of banks, deposits, bonds, equities and money market instruments are devised and then channelled to fund borrowers such as households in the form of loans. In the case of pension funds, the reserves from accumulating the contributions from households, the so-called insurance technical reserves, are channelled to fund borrowers such as non-financial corporations in the form of bonds and equities. Similarly, investment fund equity shares/units are channelled to fund borrowers such as non-financial corporations and banks in the form of bonds and equities.

However, for other participants in the narrowly defined markets (e.g. capital markets) that are not financial corporations, such as non-financial corporations, government and households, financial instruments such as debt are devised (or packaged), but the role is not considered financial intermediation, as the funds are generally not used to channel funds from lenders to borrowers. Instead they are used to invest in, for example, machinery and equipment, or to finance a shortfall of income. In this sense, non-financial corporations, government and households can be considered as the ultimate borrowers (or lenders).

For the financial markets presented in Section 2 which were more broadly defined, such as loan, deposit and pooled investment markets, the important distinction here is that in general all of these markets include the interaction of financial intermediaries and therefore the activity of financial intermediation as defined in the SNA occurs within these financial markets.

Expansion of the "core" financial intermediation in financial markets

While not all intermediation takes place within the financial sector, the vast majority does so in most economies. Intermediation can occur explicitly through subsidiaries in the financial sector and sub-sectors, or implicitly through "captive" financial companies, all of which may be included on the books of the parents. For example, a wholly-owned subsidiary that is consolidated in the books of its parent, may exist to provide a specific stream of financial services to the parent – ancillary services in support of the parent's operations.

This gives rise to two financial statistics issues. First, these captive companies may not be directly observable and therefore cannot be separately distinguished and sectored within the financial corporations' sector. Second, captive companies can also be found within non-financial corporations outside of the financial corporations' sector, while the associated services can be exclusively financial in nature. This second case is of interest, since it underlines that some financial activity can take place outside purely financial corporations.

Non-financial corporations may thus be engaged in financial intermediation as secondary or tertiary activities. This type of intermediation usually revolves around lending and (financial) leasing (and obtaining the required sources of funds), in support of their primary activities (e.g. vehicle manufacturing). In other words, these units provide financing to customers that are buying or acquiring the parent company's product. Another example may relate to holding companies of large, often multinational operating, enterprises whose sole activity is to raise funds from the financial markets in order to finance the activities of related companies. These captive companies often will not have decision-making autonomy. A separate set of books for these captive companies may not be available, as they are consolidated within the books of the operating enterprise in the non-financial corporations' sector. As a consequence, they are not considered as separate institutional units (unless they are resident in another country than the rest of the enterprise group). Therefore, there may be no direct measure of these intermediation services and the related financial instruments in the financial statistics for an economy. This intermediation activity thus falls outside the financial corporations' sector and may not be visible to analysts using the statistics that can be derived from financial accounts and balance sheets.

Notwithstanding the above, for analytical purposes, it may be useful to treat these captive companies as a separate establishment of their parent enterprises. This would enhance the understanding of financial intermediation in different economies, and broaden the notion of "shadow banking" in the process. That said, this objective may be difficult to accomplish, as separate sets of books may not be kept for captive finance/leasing companies. However, these type of activities are often related to specific financial instruments, such as, in the case of leasing and finance companies, loans and leases on the asset side and a source of funds (typically, short-term paper and bonds) on the liability side. Therefore, for completeness and analytical purposes, it is possible to present this information (for those specific instruments) on intermediation activity as a supplement to the standard delineations of the financial corporations' sector and the financial markets, in a pseudo-sector entitled "intermediation activities of non-financial corporations". This would enhance the usefulness of the financial accounts and balance sheets in terms of the accounting for the sources and uses of funds in the relevant markets.

4. Interconnectedness between sectors

National accounts provide an integrated framework for developing financial flows and stocks. Its underlying principles ensure that the linkages of the economic and financial activities within an economy are fully captured and consistent. The exhaustiveness of national accounts means that all financial assets have a counterpart in liabilities. If someone has provided a loan to someone else, the lender will have a financial asset on its balance sheet, while the borrower has an equivalent amount of debt on its balance sheets. As a consequence, one can construct so-called "from-whom-to-whom tables" (FWTW tables, or matrices), which show the interconnectedness between (institutional) sectors. They present, for a given financial instrument (or groups of instruments), the assets of the owning sectors (or creditor sectors) broken down by counterparty sectors (the debtor sectors which have incurred the liabilities) with the respective values of the transactions during a certain period of time and/or the stocks at the end of the period. The diagonal of the FWTW table shows the intra-sector transactions and stocks, i.e. claims/liabilities between entities belonging to the same sector. These amounts are cancelled out in so-called "consolidated" overviews of financial assets and liabilities of a sector. For more details, please refer to Chapter 1.

Tables 2.7 and 2.8, and Figure 2.6 contain fictional data meant to illustrate FWTW tables. In the example of Table 2.7, it is possible to observe that, in the period under analysis, non-financial corporations (NFC), as debtors, issued a net amount of debt securities of 120, with an intra-sector transaction of 50. The household sector (HH) was the other major counterpart/creditor, with a change of 50 in claims towards NFC. On the asset side, the NFC, as creditors, acquired a total net amount of 50, by increasing their holdings of securities issued by the Rest of the World (RoW) by 30, and increasing their intra-sector claims by 50 (exactly the same as in the debtor side of the analysis), while reducing their claims on the other resident sectors (financial corporations (FC) by -10, and general government (GG) by -20).

Table 2.8, showing the relevant FWTW table for stocks, allows the users to have a measure of the exposure of each institutional sector vis-à-vis the other domestic sectors and the rest of the word for a certain moment in time. It can be

Table 2.7. **FWTW table for transactions in debt securities**

		Debtor					
		NFC	FC	GG	HH	RoW	Total
Creditor	NFC	50	-10	-20	0	30	50
	FC	10	-10	10	0	-50	-40
	GG	0	45	-25	0	-10	10
	HH	50	-10	50	0	-20	70
	RoW	10	-10	90	0	-	90
	Total	120	5	105	0	-50	180

StatLink http://dx.doi.org/10.1787/888933589827

Table 2.8. **FWTW table for stocks of debt securities**

		Debtor					
		NFC	FC	GG	HH	RoW	Total
Creditor	NFC	500	200	300	0	1 000	2 000
	FC	1 000	7 500	6 000	0	2 000	16 500
	GG	100	2 000	4 000	0	100	6 200
	HH	2 000	3 500	100	0	500	6 100
	RoW	2 500	3 000	6 000	0	-	11 500
	Total	6 100	16 200	16 400	0	3 600	42 300

StatLink http://dx.doi.org/10.1787/888933589846

seen that the NFC sector had a net liability position for debt securities of 4 100[1], and that the main net financing sectors of the NFC sector are HH (2 000) and RoW (1 500).[2] This is also shown in the first graph of Figure 2.6. In the case of the RoW, a net asset position can be derived for debt securities vis-à-vis all domestic sectors, except HH. Regarding the HH sector, their holdings of debt securities are mainly vis-à-vis the corporate sectors of the domestic economy (FC and NFC).

The FWTW tables may also be shown as flow of funds charts, which display the net flows, for the period under analysis, between the institutional sectors including the Rest of the World. In this type of chart, circles are used to represent the sectors. The area of the circle is proportional to the net flows (or positions) of each sector, for a given financial instrument (or groups of instruments), filled in grey when positive and in blue when negative. Arrows are used to show the flows from the creditors to the debtor (on a net basis), with the width of the arrow proportional to the magnitude of transactions (or positions) between the relevant sectors. The scheme may be adapted to other instruments or to the total of transactions in all financial instruments. Figure 2.7 shows the net flows of debt securities presented in Table 2.7, as a flow of funds scheme.

These FWTW tables and flow of funds charts thus enable a comprehensive tracking of the relationships between the different sectors of an economy. As

2. THE ROLE OF FINANCIAL MARKETS

Figure 2.6. **Debt securities: exposure to the other institutional sectors**

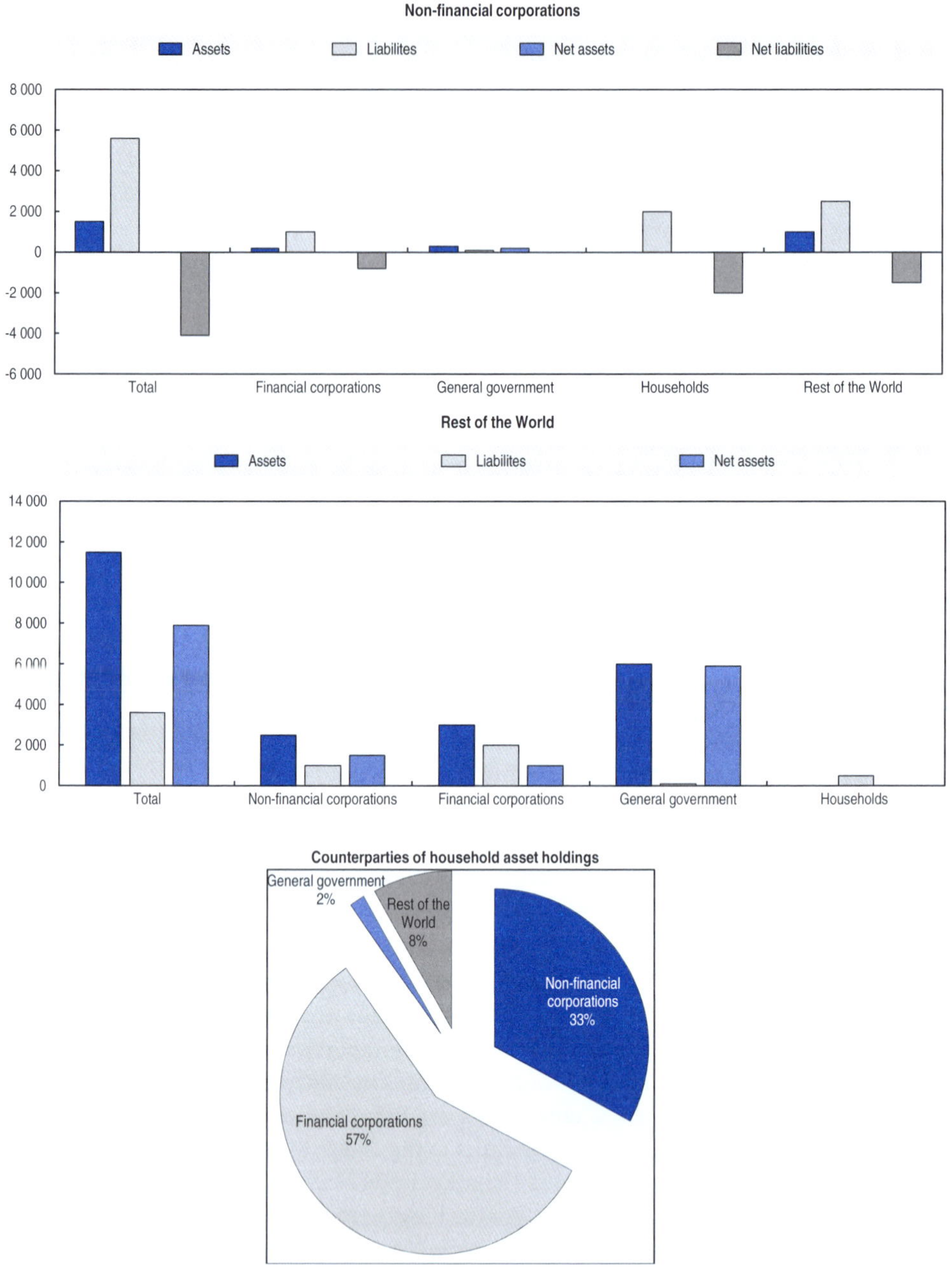

StatLink ⟶ http://dx.doi.org/10.1787/888933588022

2. THE ROLE OF FINANCIAL MARKETS

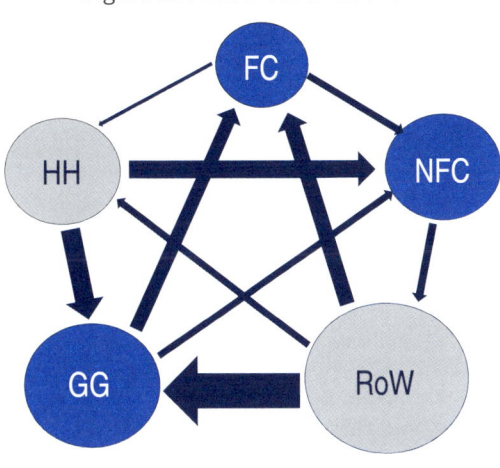

Figure 2.7. **Flow of funds chart**

Net flows

	NFC	FC	GG	HH	RoW	Total
NFC	-	-20	-20	-50	20	**-70**
FC	20	-	-35	10	-40	**-45**
GG	20	35	-	-50	-100	**-95**
HH	50	-10	50	-	-20	**70**
RoW	-20	10	100	20		**140**

StatLink ⧉ http://dx.doi.org/10.1787/888933588041

such, they are an important analytical tool for macroeconomic and financial stability analysis, in a world characterized by an increasing financial interconnectedness between economies and ever increasing financial positions of the different sectors.

The national accounts framework of the FWTW tables thus provides an important tool to capture and illustrate the interconnectedness between the different sectors. It also enables a comprehensive tracking of the relationships between the different sectors of an economy and the identification of the exposure of each institutional sector vis-à-vis the other sectors.

5. Risk elements within the financial system

Financing and investment involves risks and may create vulnerabilities, which are discussed in this section. First the main risks related to financial intermediation as such are addressed. Subsequently, a broader overview of the various types of risks related to the engagement in the financial markets is presented in slightly more detail.

2. THE ROLE OF FINANCIAL MARKETS

> Box 2.2. **Changing economic patterns through the flow of funds – example for Portugal**
>
> The flow of funds representation provides a picture of inter-sectoral patterns of an economy. In this box, four different phases of the evolution of the Portuguese economy are shown using the financial accounts compiled by Portugal's central bank, Banco de Portugal.
>
> **a) 2000-07**
>
> The period of 2000-07 roughly comprises the period between Portugal joining the Euro Area up to the initial tensions in global financial markets on the wake of the 2007-09 economic and financial crisis. During this period, the financial sector was carrying out its typical intermediary role, raising funds mainly from the Rest of the World, and channelling these funds to non-financial corporations. There was a significant asymmetry between domestic and foreign financing sources, as domestic saving and lending were clearly insufficient to finance the needs of the domestic sectors. Hence, the vast majority of the funding was coming from abroad. Another important trademark of this period was the relatively contained funding needs of the general government.
>
> **b) 2008-10**
>
> The second period covers the international financial turmoil up to 2010, when the Greek sovereign debt crisis broke out. As compared with the previous period, the overall financing needs of the country were larger than before, with those of the general government reaching around 10% of GDP. At the same time, the government ceased to be able to access international funding. To cover the financing gap, the financial sector stepped in and most of the funding provided by financial corporations was channelled to government instead of to corporations. In other words, there was a crowding out effect of domestic credit being diverted to the public sector away from the private sector.

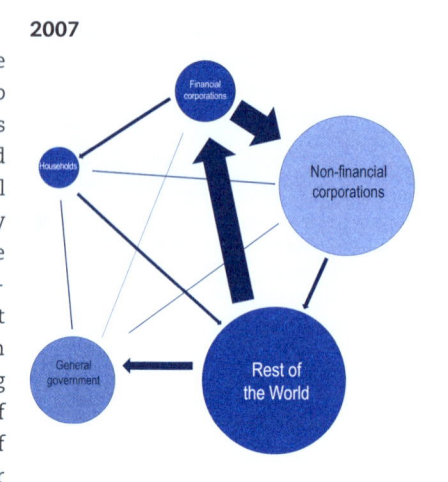

84 UNDERSTANDING FINANCIAL ACCOUNTS © OECD 2017

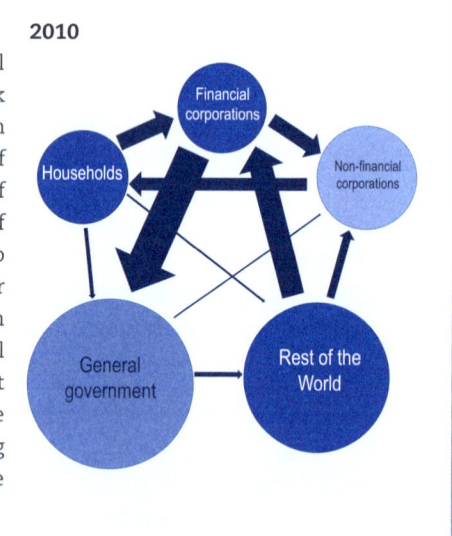

Box 2.2. **Changing economic patterns through the flow of funds – example for Portugal** (cont.)

c) 2011 and 2012

The third period started in 2011 with the beginning of the Economic and Financial Assistance Programme to Portugal. The main consequence of the Assistance Programme was the replacement of the funding of the government sector from the domestic financial sector to foreign international institutions (European Union, International Monetary Fund and European Central Bank). Also due to the Programme, the general government became a net lender to the financial sector by granting financial support to banks.

2011

d) 2013 and 2014

The Assistance Programme to Portugal ended in 2014. The flow of funds of the Portuguese economy in this period was very different from the beginning of the 2010s. Portugal became a net lender in 2012, the government deficit decreased, and non-financial corporations became net lenders, as a consequence of a sharp decline in non-financial investments. Moreover, households increased their saving rate as a result of a contraction in private consumption.

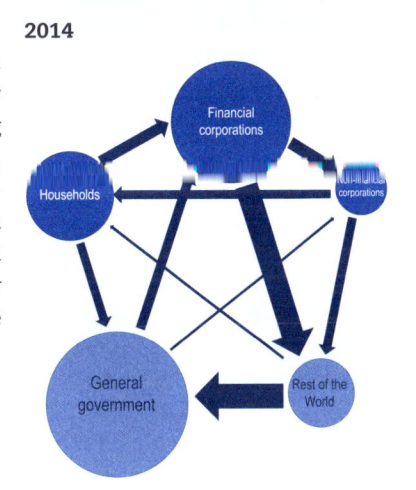

2014

Source: Banco de Portugal (2015), *Financial Accounts*, www.bportugal.pt/EstatisticasWeb/(S(vejoqt45bzga0v55jov0hj3x))/SeriesCronologicas.aspx.

Financial intermediaries – risk and maturity transformation

Financial intermediaries have a primary role of channelling funds from savers to borrowers, but they also undertake the crucial role of transforming risk and maturity. In general, financial intermediaries hold assets with higher risk of default than their own liabilities. To minimise this risk, financial intermediaries undertake risk transformation by the processes of diversification, screening and monitoring of assets, and the formation of reserves. There are two ways to undertake diversification: by spreading risk and by pooling risk. Financial intermediaries spread risk by bearing the risk of their investors (household bank deposits), and investing these household funds across various financial instruments and sectors, for example by issuing loans to households and purchasing government bonds. Secondly, financial intermediaries pool risk, for example by ensuring that their loan assets are large enough to contain the risk of any loans that may default and the loss due to the default is spread among all investors. The process of diversification allows financial intermediaries to allocate assets and bear risk more efficiently.

The role of financial intermediaries in maturity transformation is related to the fact that investors and borrowers have differing maturity needs – savers typically want to lend funds at short maturity and borrowers want to borrow for long maturities. The financial intermediary finances the needs of borrowers with long-term maturity preferences by pooling the investor funds (i.e. deposits) that have short-term maturity. This role of the financial intermediary ensures that investors and borrowers have more choice concerning the maturity of their investments and borrowings.

Types of financial risks and strategies for the mitigation of risks

There are multiple types of financial risk faced by financial market participants and financial intermediaries associated with their functions they undertake in the financial system. Listed below are some of these risks and strategies that are undertaken for mitigation.

Credit default risk is the risk associated with borrowers failing to make the required debt payments. The loss to the lender could include the principle and the interest. The risk is likely to impact loans, bonds and derivatives. Examples are a household unable to make payments due on a mortgage loan to a bank, or a corporate bond issuer not making coupon or principle payments to the holder. In the case of a bank loan, the bank may mitigate credit default risk by requiring borrowers to provide collateral, taking out insurance, such as mortgage insurance, or undertaking credit assessments on customers to rank the potential risk. With unsecured loans, the banks will charge a higher price for higher risk customers, and with revolving products such as credit cards, risk is controlled through setting credit limits. For default risk related to bonds and derivatives, financial intermediaries or other counterparties may hedge using derivative products such as swaps or credit derivatives, such as credit default swaps.

Interest rate risk is the risk associated with interest bearing investment earnings fluctuating with changes in interest rates. A change in interest rates has an inverse impact on the value of investments. For example, an increase in interest will decrease the value of debt securities with a fixed coupon rate. The impact of the interest rate change is dependent on the time to maturity and the coupon rate of the securities. The impact on the value of short-term securities is much smaller than on long-term securities. For financial intermediaries, interest rate risk can be split into two components: traded and non-traded interest rate risk, the latter often referred to as interest rate risk on the balance sheet. Traded interest rate risk impacts the market value of banks' traded securities such as government securities and interest rate swaps. The interest rate risk on the balance sheet arises from the bank's core activities, and the main source of the interest rate risk is the maturity mismatch or re-pricing risk, reflecting the fact that banks' assets and liabilities are of different maturities and are priced at different interest rates.

To minimise interest rate risk associated with bond assets, investors may hedge using derivative products, such as forwards, options and interest rate swaps. To manage maturity mismatches between the assets and liabilities on bank balance sheets, banks have adopted tools such as the asset liability management framework. The framework undertakes sophisticated modelling that allows the measurement of the mismatch of the assets and liabilities maturity patterns, and recommends strategies such as direct restructuring of balance sheets or adoption of financial instruments such as swaps, futures, options and other customised agreements to alter the balance sheet interest risk exposure. Furthermore, in most countries banks are regulated, and some national banking regulatory have demand banks to hold extra capital against both interest rate risks associated with the trading positions and the balance sheet.

Foreign exchange risk is the potential risk of loss from fluctuating foreign exchange rates when an investor has exposure to foreign currency or to foreign currency traded investments. For example, holders of foreign bonds face currency risk, when bonds make interest and principle payment in a foreign currency. Foreign exchange risk may impact exporting and importing businesses, investors in foreign financial assets, and foreign direct investment in a company. To minimise foreign exchange risk, a variety of foreign exchange derivatives are available such as forward contracts, future contracts, options and swaps.

Risks such as credit default risk and interest rate risk may be indirectly captured in national accounts. For example, an indirect measure of credit default risk may be ascertained by comparing, for example, loans at market value with the same loans at nominal values, where the market values would typically adjust the valuation of loans by deducting the value of specific provisions for bad and doubtful debt. The exposure of the interest rate risk on the banks' balance sheets may be broadly ascertained by comparing the value of short- and long-term liabilities and assets. The 2008 SNA disaggregates both loans and, to a lesser extent, deposits into short- and long-term maturities, along with a split of debt securities into short- and long-term.

New international reporting requirements since the 2007-09 economic and financial crisis have requested countries to collect data on debt securities both on an original and a residual term to maturity. The latter measure should assist in highlighting interest rate risk both from a trading and a balance sheet perspective. Similarly, the new reporting standards dictate that assets and liabilities issued in foreign currency should be reported separately by financial institutions, assisting in exposing any vulnerability to foreign currency risks.

The balance sheets, presented in a FWTW framework at a given point in time and over time, can also be useful in providing an assessment of the overall health of resident and non-resident sectors, by providing:

- the household sector's exposure to real estate assets in times of asset price decreases;
- pension funds', investments funds' and life insurance corporations' exposure to debt securities during times of liquidity risks in the security market;
- so-called "leverage measures", such as debt-to-equity measures in the non-financial corporations sector; during periods of buoyant income and stable and low interest rates, a leveraged corporation, i.e. a corporation with substantial debt as compared to equity and reserves, stands to make a substantial return on equity compared with an un leveraged corporation However, during more uncertain times a leveraged corporation is at risk from fluctuations in earnings and/or rising interest rates, such that debt servicing costs may not be met;
- probable measures of increasing or declining cost of funds for banks assets by showing proportion of deposits, equity and debt funding over time;
- overall debt and type of debt by financial instrument for households, government and non- financial corporations, either direct comparison or to their disposable income;
- households' debt-to-assets ratio, or more specifically debt-to-residential assets ratio, whereby an increase in the ratio over time is indicative that (mortgage) debt grew faster than the value of (residential) assets owned by households;
- debt-to-liquidity asset ratio, illustrating a sector's ability to extinguish debt;
- holding gains or losses over time by asset type; and
- shifts in short- to long-term debt financing, potentially indicating a decline in cost pressures in the capital markets.

2. THE ROLE OF FINANCIAL MARKETS

Key points

- The financial system of a nation can be thought of as having three overlapping components: financial corporations; the financial markets; and the payment system. The interaction of the three components, through mechanisms of financial intermediation and financial markets, enables the channelling of funds from savers to borrowers.

- Financial markets may be defined narrowly to mean a market in which trading of financial instruments such as securities and currencies occur at low transaction costs and at prices that reflect supply and demand, with no intervention of financial intermediaries (or the need for a "middle man"). Within the global financial system the following financial markets fall into the narrow definition: capital markets (which consist of share markets and bond markets); money markets; derivatives markets; and foreign exchange markets.

- The broad definition of financial markets includes the interaction of financial intermediaries with the financial market. The following markets additionally fall into this broad definition: the deposit market, the loan market, and the pooled investment market.

- The role of financial intermediation, or the devising of a financial instrument (debt securities, equities, derivatives, loans and deposits) by financial intermediaries (banks, investment funds, or pension funds) and to channel monies from lenders to borrowers, is evident in a majority of the financial markets described.

- Data on the interconnectedness between sectors (FWTW tables and flow of funds schemes) enable a full knowledge of the financial linkages between the various actors in the economy, by capturing the flows between the different sectors of the economy and revealing the level of exposure of each institutional sector vis-à-vis the other sectors. As such, they are a relevant analytical tool in the fields of macroeconomic and financial stability analysis.

- Financial intermediaries undertake the crucial role of transforming risk and maturity. There are multiple types of financial risk faced by financial market participants and financial intermediaries associated with functions they undertake in the financial system, including credit default risk, interest rate risk and foreign exchange risk. The financial accounts and balance sheets indirectly capture some of these risks.

Notes

1. The net liability position of the NFC sector in the instrument debt securities is obtained from the difference between the debtor position of the NFC sector in this instrument (6 100), and the creditor position in the same instrument (2 000).

2. The RoW is a net creditor of the NFC sector (for the instrument debt securities). This value is obtained considering the creditor position minus the debtor position of the RoW sector vis-à-vis the NFC sector (2 500 *minus* 1 000).

References

ABS (2017), *5232.0-Australian National Accounts: Finance and Wealth* (database), *www.abs.gov.au/ausstats/abs@.nsf/mf/5232.0/*.

Banco de Portugal (2015), Financial Accounts, Banco de Portugal, Lisbon, *www.bportugal.pt/EstatisticasWeb/(S(vejoqt45bzga0v55jov0hj3x))/SeriesCronologicas.aspx*.

BIS (2016), Triennial Central Bank Survey: Foreign Exchange Turnover in April 2016, Bank for International Settlements, Basel, *www.bis.org/publ/rpfx16fx.pdf*.

Chapter 3

The role of financial corporations in the financial system

Andreas Hertkorn (ECB), Antonio Matas-Mir (ECB),
Gabriel Quirós (IMF), João Cadete de Matos (Banco de Portugal)
and Filipa Lima (Banco de Portugal)

> Financial corporations are at the centre of the financial system, channelling funds from lenders/savers to borrowers/investors. Although a large part of the funds is channelled through financial corporations, savers can also finance investment directly (for example, households granting loans to an enterprise). Savers may place their funds with a bank in order to benefit from the higher liquidity of a deposit, or purchase investment fund shares as a convenient way to diversify their assets. Even if savers buy securities on the stock market, they typically make use of a security broker or other so called "financial auxiliaries". This chapter explains the role of the different types of financial corporations in the economy, how they are evolving and how they can be analysed.

1. Short overview

The financial corporations' sector is defined in the 2008 System of National Accounts (2008 SNA) as all institutional units whose principal activity is the production of financial services which are "the result of financial intermediation, financial risk management, liquidity transformation or auxiliary financial activities" (SNA 2008, paragraph 4.98). This definition does not only include financial intermediaries, such as banks, insurance companies and pension funds, but also financial auxiliaries as well as captive financial institutions; see Table 3.1.[1]

Table 3.1. **The financial corporations' sector and its subsectors**

Financial corporations
    Monetary financial institutions (MFIs)
        Central bank
        Deposit-taking corporations except the central bank – "banks"
        Money market funds (MMFs)
    Other financial institutions (OFIs, i.e. financial corporations except MFIs, insurance corporations and pension funds)
        Non-MMF investment funds
        OFIs excluding investment funds
            Other financial intermediaries
                Financial corporations engaged in securitisation of assets
                Securities and derivatives dealers
                Financial corporations engaged in lending
                Specialised financial corporations
            Financial auxiliaries
            Captive financial institutions and money lenders
    Insurance corporations
    Pension funds

StatLink ⇒ http://dx.doi.org/10.1787/888933589865

Financial intermediaries play an important role in monetary and economic analysis, because of their role in channelling funds from savers to investors. They are further broken down into subsectors on the basis of their function and their main type of financing. Monetary financial institutions (MFIs) comprise the central bank, which issues currency and deposits, and exercises control over the financial system; deposit-taking institutions, which engage in financial intermediation via incurring liabilities in the form of deposits (or close substitutes); and money market funds (MMFs). MMFs consist of investment schemes that raise funds by issuing shares (or units), and invest primarily in short-term funds. MMFs belong to the MFI sector, as their shares are considered close substitutes for bank deposits. Because of their important role in the supply of money, they are usually closely monitored and subject to specific regulations.

Non-monetary financial institutions are characterised by the fact they cannot issue deposits or money market shares. As they do not offer deposits (or close substitutes) to the public they are not subject to the same regulations as MFIs. Three non-monetary financial subsectors can easily be distinguished by their main liabilities: non-MMF investment funds, insurance corporations and pension funds. While non-MMF funds also raise funds by issuing shares (or units), similar to MMFs, they typically invest in longer-term investments, such as shares, debt securities and real estate. Insurance corporations and pension funds have quite different objectives, in that their main function is related to the provision of life insurance, insurance against accidents, sickness, fire, etc., or to provide and organise (collective) pension schemes for employees and self-employed. Because of this distinct function, they are usually grouped separately.

The final group, the so-called "other financial intermediaries", is very heterogeneous and comprises, for example, financial vehicle corporations (FVCs) engaged in securitisation transactions, security and derivative dealers, financial corporations engaged in lending, and other specialised financial corporations. Due to the lack of harmonised data sources in many OECD countries, which would allow separate identification of these subsectors, other financial intermediaries are frequently grouped together with financial auxiliaries and "captives", and referred to as "other financial institutions". Depending on data availability, other financial institutions are, in some countries, grouped together with non-MMF investment funds.

Figure 3.1 shows that in terms of size of the balance sheets, MFIs are the largest group of financial institutions in most OECD countries, typically followed by OFIs (other financial institutions – that is, financial corporations except MFIs, insurance corporations and pension funds) and then insurance corporations and pension funds. However, in some countries, like the United States, the combined balance sheets of OFIs are larger than those of MFIs. In other countries like Iceland, Ireland, Luxembourg and the Netherlands, more than 50% of the balance sheets total concerns OFIs. This is related to country-specific circumstances, such as the massive presence of holdings of multinational operating enterprises in OFIs in the latter two countries. Generally, the relative size of the OFI sector has increased in more than 75% of OECD countries over the last decade.

3. THE ROLE OF FINANCIAL CORPORATIONS IN THE FINANCIAL SYSTEM

Figure 3.1. **Relative size of financial corporations by subsector, 2016**
Financial corporations' liabilities by subsector, percentage % of total

* Separation between non-MMF IFs and OFIs excluding IFs is not available for the United Kingdom.
Source: OECD (2017), "Financial Balance Sheets, SNA 2008 (or SNA 1993): Non-consolidated stocks, annual", OECD National Accounts Statistics (database), http://dx.doi.org/10.1787/data-00720-en.
StatLink ▶ http://dx.doi.org/10.1787/888933588060

The importance of the financial sector for the channelling of funds from savers/lenders to investors/borrowers is evident in the financial accounts. The financial sector's share of financial assets and liabilities is about 60% of the total outstanding amount in the economy of the Euro Area (see Figure 3.2) which broadly means that the majority of funds are channelled through financial institutions.

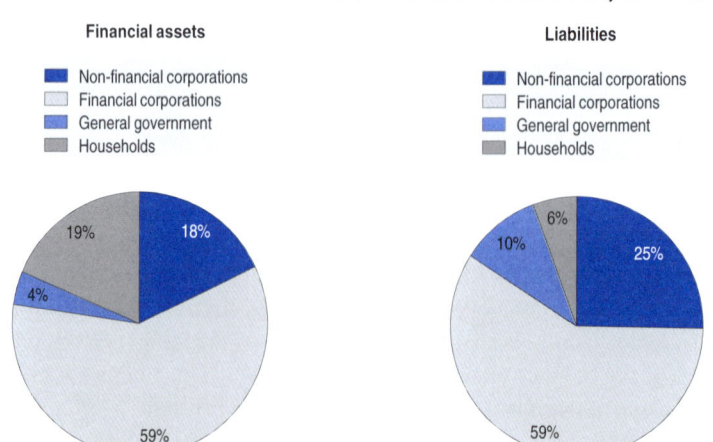

Figure 3.2. **Sector shares in total financial assets and liabilities, Euro Area, 2016**

Financial assets: Non-financial corporations 18%, Financial corporations 59%, General government 4%, Households 19%

Liabilities: Non-financial corporations 25%, Financial corporations 59%, General government 10%, Households 6%

Source: Eurostat (2017), National Accounts (including GDP) (database), http://ec.europa.eu/eurostat/web/national-accounts/data/database.

94 UNDERSTANDING FINANCIAL ACCOUNTS © OECD 2017

The direct contributions of the financial sector to the production of goods and services in terms of valued added and compensation of employees is generally much smaller; for example, it is about 5% in the Euro Area (see Figure 3.3).

Figure 3.3. **Sector shares in total value added and total compensation of employees, Euro Area, 2016**

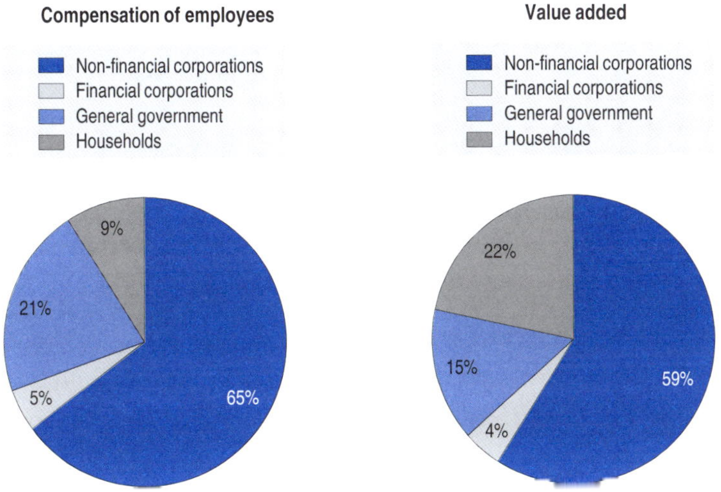

Compensation of employees
- Non-financial corporations
- Financial corporations
- General government
- Households

9%, 21%, 5%, 65%

Value added
- Non-financial corporations
- Financial corporations
- General government
- Households

22%, 15%, 4%, 59%

Source: Eurostat (2017), *National Accounts (including GDP)* (database), http://ec.europa.eu/eurostat/web/national-accounts/data/database.

Value added generated by financial corporations can, to a large extent, only be measured indirectly. Financial corporations sell some of their services by charging explicit service fees for certain financial transactions (for example, brokerage fees). However, the core activities of financial intermediaries are typically not covered by explicit fees. A financial institution like a bank accepts deposits from creditors wishing to receive interest on funds and lends them to debtors whose funds are insufficient to meet their financial needs. The bank thus provides a mechanism to allow the first unit to lend to the second. Each of the two parties implicitly pays a fee to the bank for the service provided: the depositor pays by accepting a rate of interest lower than a "reference rate" of interest, while the debtor pays by accepting a rate of interest higher than the "reference rate" of interest. The exact methods to be used for this indirect measurement of financial intermediation services have been debated for decades, and raised renewed concerns after the 2007-09 economic and financial crisis, when output and value added of financial corporations increased because of the larger spread between the interest rate on loans and the interest rate on deposits.[2]

Given these measurement issues and the apparent low direct contributions of the financial sector to the real economy, the financial sector was for a long time neglected in economic analysis. Macroeconomic models typically just assumed that financial markets and financial intermediaries efficiently channelled funds from savers to investors. However, the outbreak of the 2007-09 economic and financial crisis highlighted the importance of financial intermediation for the functioning of the economy, and it became evident that a better understanding of the financial sector was needed. Furthermore, the activities of issuers of asset-backed securities, hedge funds and other so-called shadow banks are thought to have contributed to obfuscating the build-up of risks in the financial sector (see Box 3.2 for more details). However, little information on these other financial institutions was available, and interest increased in particular in these financial institutions outside the traditional banking sector. With the implementation of the revised international statistical standards (SNA 2008, BPM6, ESA 2010) between 2012 and 2014, more detailed and internationally comparable data on financial institutions outside the deposit taking corporations' subsector became available. This chapter uses this newly developed information, amongst other things, to provide an introduction to the different financial institutions and how they interact with other sectors of the economy.

2. The Central Bank

A central bank is "the national financial institution that exercises control over key aspects of the financial system" (SNA 2008, paragraph 4.104). Among these key aspects are the issuance and management of the currency of a country or – in the case of a monetary union – a group of countries; the maintenance of the internal and external value of the currency; and holding of all, or part, of the international reserves of the country. The primary objective of most central banks is to maintain price stability, which generally means setting a target for inflation. Some central banks also have the responsibility of acting in support of full employment and economic growth.

Central banks typically enjoy a large degree of independence and autonomy when exercising their main activities. David Ricardo identifies three pillars through which such independence is guaranteed:[3]

- institutional separation between the powers to create and to spend money;
- inhibition of monetary funding to governments; and
- an obligation to justify the central bank's monetary policy measures.

However, over time, essentially during the period of the Great Depression and in the aftermath of the collapse of the gold standard, several countries did not apply these principles and their central banks primarily acted in response to fiscal requirements, providing funds to the government. Only later in the 20th century did governments prioritise the independence of central banks to guarantee the fulfilment of central banks' main objective of price stability. Nowadays, the majority of countries have central banks that are designed to be independent from governments.

Overall, the objectives and functional roles of central banks have evolved over different periods, in response to changing economic and financial situations of countries.[4] The main functions of a modern central bank are: creating money and conducting monetary policy; lender of last resort; bank of the government; and centre of the payments system. Examples of other relevant functions for some central banks are supervision and financial stability functions. Each one of the main functions is briefly discussed below.

Figure 3.4. **Summary of central banks' functions**

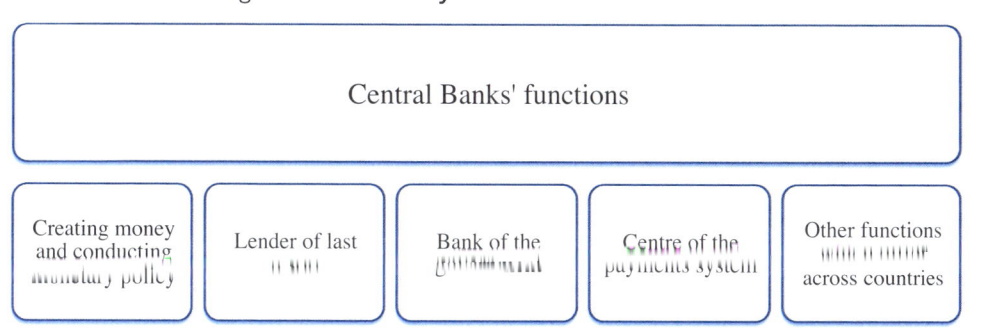

Central Banks' functions

- Creating money and conducting monetary policy
- Lender of last resort
- Bank of the government
- Centre of the payments system
- Other functions across countries

Creating money and conducting monetary policy

In most countries, the central bank is responsible for controlling the flow of money to commercial banks and controlling the "cost of money" through determining the money supply. Central banks are the only suppliers of banknotes and bank reserves. By controlling the amount of money in circulation, central banks can influence economic activity and pursue the goal of price stability. This is evidenced by the Quantitative Theory of Money, which shows that inflation corresponds to the difference between the growth of nominal money stock and economic growth. This relationship is illustrated in the following equations:

$$M \times V = P \times T \Leftrightarrow m + v = \pi + y$$

Given $v = 0$, $\quad \pi = m - y$

Where:
- M is the nominal stock of money
- V is the velocity of money
- P is the price level
- T is the volume of economic transactions
- m is the growth in the nominal stock of money

v is the growth in the velocity of money
π is the inflation rate
y is economic growth

To achieve their goal of price stability central banks may also use the Fisher Principle that expresses the relation between the behaviour of nominal and real interest rates:

$i = r + \pi^e$

Where: i is the (nominal) interest rate
r is the real interest rate (i.e. the interest rate adjusted for inflation)
π^e is the expected inflation rate

In this context, the monetary policy can influence the real inflation rate by controlling the growth of the nominal money stock or by controlling the nominal interest rate.

In pursuing their monetary policy goals, the majority of central banks have the following tools: defining the reference interest rates; conducting open market operations; and defining minimum reserve requirements. The central bank can influence key interest rates by setting the reference rate at which the domestic banks can borrow from the central bank. These rates determine the domestic banks' cost of borrowing and indirectly influence the interest rates charged to borrowers, which encourages or discourages the economic agents from borrowing. Such actions affect the money supply in the economy, which should be compliant with the objective of maintaining price stability. This process represents the more traditional mechanism of monetary policy transmission.

In order to pursue the objective of price stability, central banks can also perform open market operations, which involve the central bank buying or selling debt securities in the market. In some countries, these operations only involve government debt, but in general it can involve any kind of securities. In specific situations, central banks may also adopt non-standard measures of monetary policy, such as the purchase of government debt in secondary markets. By buying securities the central bank can increase the money supply. Selling securities will have an opposite effect and will lead to a decrease of the money supply. See Box 3.1 for more details on these non-standard measures adopted by central banks.

Moreover, commercial banks are often subject to minimum reserve requirements, which are set by the central bank and thus can serve as another monetary policy instrument. This reserve ratio, defined as a percentage of the liabilities, has a direct impact on the amount of reserves to be held by each commercial bank in deposit at their central bank accounts, and consequently also affects the amount of money supply.

> Box 3.1. **Non-standard measures adopted by central banks**
>
> As a consequence of the 2007-09 economic and financial crisis and the ensuing low inflation levels, central banks faced extra challenges in meeting their respective price stability objectives. In fact, in order to achieve the desired core objectives of financial stability and targeted inflation, central banks had to resort to non-standard measures. These measures, which constituted unconventional ways of boosting inflation, consisted of the purchase of assets by central banks, mainly government bonds, leading to an increase in the amount of money in the financial system, thus fostering an improvement in the lending conditions in the real economy. The rationale underlying this action is that lowering banks' funding costs and credit spreads will translate into looser financing conditions for final borrowers in the economy. This is also referred to as quantitative easing (QE).
>
> In spite of the aforementioned benefits, these non-standard measures bear some risks for the central banks who adopt them, namely the possibility of the existence of potential losses on the purchased securities and the potential creation of conditions for high inflation, due to the injection of money in the economy. Nevertheless, the measures have been implemented by the Bank of Japan (in the 1990s), the Bank of England, the US Federal Reserve (both in 2008), and the European Central Bank (in 2009).
>
> In the case of Japan, it faced a financial crisis during the 1990s and had to use the monetary policy channel to provide assistance to financial institutions and financial markets, and to act as lender of last resort. However, the monetary policy of the Bank of Japan was often criticised for not being aggressive enough, thus leading to a long term financial crisis.
>
> In order to give a quick response to the economic and financial crisis that affected Europe in 2007-09, the ECB decided to complement its regular monetary policy operations and gradually implement a wide range of unconventional measures. The main objectives of these measures were to inject liquidity in the markets and in financial institutions, in order to stimulate new lending to the real economy and enhance the functioning of the monetary policy transmission mechanism, to create conditions for ensuring market liquidity, and to avoid a deflationary period in the Euro Area. Chronologically and concisely, the ECB took the following measures:
>
> - 2008: increased the frequency and size of its longer-term refinancing operations (LTRO);
> - 2009: implemented the first programme of covered bonds purchase (CBPP1);
> - 2010: introduced the securities markets programme (SMP);
> - 2011: implemented the second programme of covered bonds purchase (CBPP2);

> Box 3.1. **Non-standard measures adopted by central banks** *(cont.)*
>
> - 2014: created the longer-term refinancing operations (TLTRO), the third programme of covered bonds purchase (CBPP3), and the asset-backed securities purchase programme (ABSPP);
> - 2015: increased the scope of purchases of government debt with the Public Sector Purchase Programme (PSPP); and
> - 2016: purchased corporate bonds within the corporate sector purchase programme (CSPP).

Lender of last resort

The central bank also has the role of assisting commercial banks with emergency liquidity assistance in case of immediate liquidity problems. Due to this function, central banks are often referred to as "lenders of last resort". With this function, central banks can safeguard liquidity and provide financial accommodation to banks, also preventing a possible collapse of the banking system. The latter is important in order to prevent a bank run, caused by liquidity problems in one bank, which could lead to loss of confidence in the banking system as a whole. Nevertheless, this role can create a conflict of interest between the central bank's policies and the safeguarding of financial markets, and may also lead to moral hazard with banks assuming that their deposits will be guaranteed by the central bank. Emergency liquidity assistance is usually provided in exchange for eligible securities or bills as a guarantee.

Bank of the government

In some countries the central bank has the function of being the bank of the government, which means that the central bank carries out the banking business of the government, such as managing the government's accounts with their cash balances, providing loans and advances to governments, accepting receipts and making payments on behalf of the government, and acting as a consultant on specific government issues.

Moreover, within their responsibilities, central banks can directly purchase government debt in order to support government policies. This process, also referred to as the monetisation of debt, aims to provide funding to the government and, consequently, causing an increase of money supply in the economy. However, often central banks are prohibited by law from directly financing their governments.

Centre of the payments system

Since the central bank is the monetary authority and the entity responsible for currency issuance, it is at the centre of payment systems, which means that the central bank is responsible for providing and overseeing mechanisms for the payment, clearing and settlement of monetary transactions in the economy. Generally, the term "payment system" includes the set of instruments, intermediaries, procedures, rules, processes and interbank fund transfer systems responsible for facilitating the circulation of money in a country or between countries with the same currency. The central bank must keep economic agents confident about the safety and reliability of the payment systems in order to ensure a regular functioning of the financial system and the maintenance of financial stability.

Central bank's integration within the financial accounts and balance sheets

The balance sheets of a central bank follow the conventional structure of financial accounts and balance sheets, being divided into assets and liabilities and distinguishing the same types of financial instruments. Compared to commercial banks, the main differences concern the holding of monetary gold and the issuance of currency. Although the structure of a central bank balance sheet may differ across countries, it is possible to generalise the structure, as shown in Figure 3.5.

Figure 3.5. **Stylised central bank balance sheet**

Assets	Liabilities
Monetary gold and SDRs	Currency
Deposits	Deposits
Debt securities	Equity
Other assets	

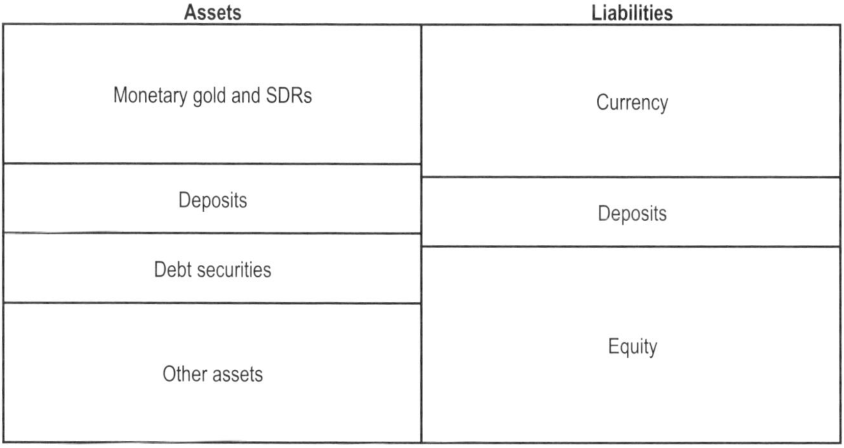

The main components on the asset side of a central bank's balance sheet include deposits with banks, first and foremost related to the liquidity-providing operations of the central bank to the financial system, as well as the debt securities, held for monetary policy purposes. The remaining significant elements on the asset side are monetary gold, defined as the gold to which monetary authorities have title and which is held as a reserve asset, and special drawing rights (SDRs), defined as reserve assets created by the IMF that are held by central banks and certain international agencies. On the liability side, currency (banknotes issued by the central banks that are in circulation) and deposits (mainly related to commercial bank reserves and general government deposits) represent the main items, while the equity component completes the typical structure.

An analysis of a central bank's balance sheet can provide very useful insights on the central bank's monetary policy stance. This is particularly evident by observing the impact of the 2007-09 economic and financial crisis on the balance sheets of the central banks (see Figure 3.6). In response to the crisis, some central banks engaged in large-scale asset purchase programmes (see Box 3.1), showing an increase in the share of debt securities and also an increase in the overall size of the balance sheets. The assets of the US Federal Reserve, for example, increased by around 25% of GDP from 2007 to 2014. The ECB's total of assets also increased, due to the acquisitions of securities under the asset-purchase programmes and the enlargement of liquidity-providing monetary policy operations. These policies allowed central banks to ease credit conditions and inject liquidity into the financial system.

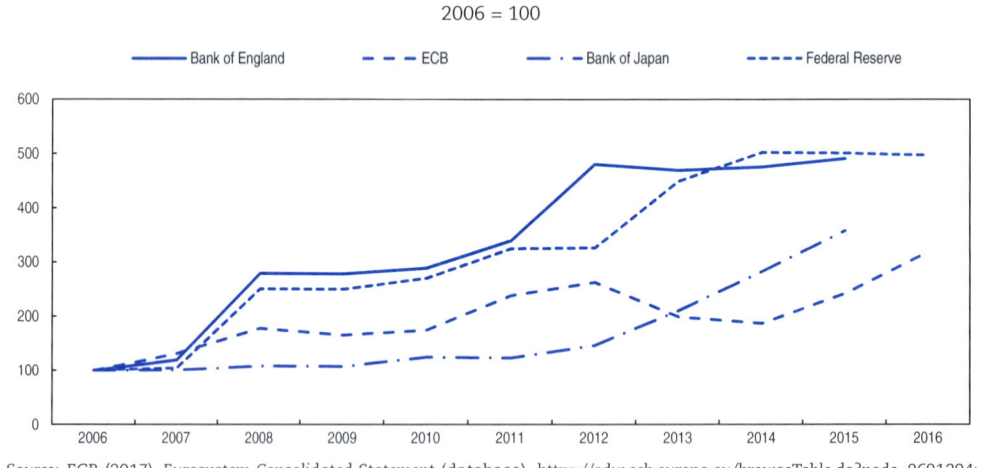

Figure 3.6. **Central bank balance sheets – total assets**
2006 = 100

Source: ECB (2017), *Eurosystem Consolidated Statement* (database), https://sdw.ecb.europa.eu/browseTable.do?node=9691294; OECD (2017a), "Financial Balance Sheets, SNA 2008 (or SNA 1993): Consolidated stocks, annual", *OECD National Accounts Statistics* (database). http://dx.doi.org/10.1787/data-00719-en; and Bank of England (2017), *Bankstats (Monetary and Fiscal Statistics)* (database), www.bankofengland.co.uk/statistics/Pages/bankstats/2017/may.aspx.

StatLink http://dx.doi.org/10.1787/888933588174

Finally, a central bank is obviously treated as a resident unit of the relevant country. However, some particularities arise when it comes to monetary unions. For example, in the case of the European Monetary Union, the ECB is not treated as a resident in any of the member countries of the monetary union, but is treated as a resident of the monetary union as a whole. Additionally, the currency issued by the Eurosystem is only considered as a liability of the resident national central bank to the extent of its notional share in the total issue. The latter share is calculated based on the population and GDP of the respective countries.

3. Deposit-taking corporations apart from the central bank

Deposit-taking corporations apart from the central bank (hereafter referred to as deposit-taking corporations) are by far the most important type of financial intermediaries in almost any financial system. The defining feature of deposit-taking corporations is their engagement in financial intermediation by accepting deposits (or other financial instruments that are a close substitute for deposits) as their main funding source. Deposit-taking corporations also issue other types of financial liabilities, but these will typically play a lesser role as a percentage of total liabilities.

Deposit-taking corporations coincide to a large degree with what are commonly known as "banks". The traditional business of banks is to take deposits from the public, provide loans to households and businesses, and intermediate the making of payments between economic agents. Entities with a traditional banking business model are typically known as "commercial banks". Depending on local regulations, a wider set of intermediation activities may be undertaken by commercial banks. Some larger banks, for instance, have a strong presence in capital markets, including market-making and investment banking activities such as helping to raise funds in those markets for their clients. These banks are typically referred to as "universal banks".

Commercial banks and universal banks are the most predominant form of deposit-taking corporations in most countries. Other more specialised entities which are also deposit-taking corporations are merchant banks (specialised in trade finance), mortgage banks (specialised in real estate finance), rural banks (providing banking services in remote or agricultural areas), and credit unions (a model of banking whereby placing funds with the union entitles the fundholder to become a member and partial owner), among others. All these entities, however, are still characterised by being mainly funded by deposits, or close substitutes of deposits.

The institutional setting of deposit-taking corporations

Deposit-taking corporations are very different from other financial corporations. On the liability side, they issue a large proportion of instruments perceived to be both liquid and capital certain, such as short-term bank deposits. However, their asset side is dominated by more risky, largely illiquid assets, such as loans to customers. Their ability to perform such large-scale maturity and risk transformation owes to some key features of their institutional framework. The most important of these are a strict regulatory and supervisory regime, the existence of deposit insurance schemes, access to central bank refinancing and implicit government guarantees.

Deposit-taking corporations are subject to a strict regulatory regime compared to other financial intermediaries, including stronger capital and liquidity requirements. They are also subject to strict oversight by supervisory authorities, to whom they regularly report data much more comprehensive than ordinary financial reporting. The supervision often includes on-site inspections. As key actors in the payment system and, especially, as the main issuers of most money-like liabilities in the economy, banks also pose systemic risks that justify close scrutiny by authorities. Conversely, bank deposits are perceived to be as capital certain as currency to a large degree due to such strict regulation. In a sense, bank regulation could be viewed as a co-ordinating device that, together with deposit insurance, ensures that bank deposits are accepted as money by the public notwithstanding the asset structure backing those liabilities.

Regulations for banks are the object of international co-ordination efforts under the auspices of the Basel Committee on Banking Supervision (BCBS). International co-ordination is required because jurisdictions could obtain an unfair advantage in attracting international banking business by being too lax on the amount of capital required from banks, as equity is typically the most costly form of liability for banks.[5] The BCBS sets international standards on bank supervision (known as the "Basel Accords") that regulate the minimum amount of capital and other requirements needed for an entity to operate as a bank.[6]

Trust by the public in bank deposits is further reinforced by means of deposit insurance schemes. Historically, deposit insurance was introduced mainly to reduce the possibility of bank runs. In a bank run, a cascade of deposit withdrawals occurs due to adverse news about a bank in particular or the health of the banking system as a whole. Bank runs are self-reinforcing as more depositors demand to be reimbursed before the bank's small fraction of assets kept as liquid reserves runs out. The highly interconnected nature of the banking system may quickly promote contagion from one institution to the next, making many bank-runs systemic.

Deposit insurance breaks the self-reinforcing cycle of bank runs by preventing them to take hold in the first place. Deposit insurance guarantees that depositors will be reimbursed, usually up to a maximum amount per depositor and bank, even in the case of bank failure. The maximum amount is usually set up so as to cover most retail deposits. Since most depositors perceive that their money is not at risk, the incentive for panic withdrawals is reduced or altogether eliminated.

Deposit-taking institutions are also often privileged by having direct access to central bank refinancing. In fiat money systems, i.e. money systems in which the intrinsic value of currency is not equal to the denoted value of the currency (or the denoted value is not exchangeable to an equivalent amount of a commodity such as gold), the central bank does not face any limit on the amount of currency or bank reserves it may create, and it is therefore always able to provide funding to banks that are short on liquidity so long as they are considered solvent (see also Section 2, "Lender of last resort"). Having access to central bank funding further strengthens a deposit-taking institution's promise of par redemption (redemption at face value), even under tight conditions in private money markets.

Finally, deposit-taking institutions often benefit from an implicit government guarantee. A guarantee is implicit when there is no formal commitment on the part of the government to repay the bank's creditors in case of its failure, but these creditors perceive that the institution will not be allowed to fail because it is too large or systemically important. Implicit guarantees, real or perceived, may provide a further measure of stability to the financial system. However they might also constitute an unwanted subsidy by taxpayers to banks, which then face a lower cost of funding than would otherwise be the case, thereby distorting an efficient allocation of capital. In addition, implicit guarantees may in some cases be destabilising when the government itself is not in a strong financial position and the weakness of banks and the weakness of the sovereign end up reinforcing each other.

Deposit-taking corporations as issuers of monetary liabilities

Deposit-taking corporations supply the reference financial asset in the economy: money. Money is defined as including currency in circulation (coins and banknotes, typically issued by the central bank), short-term bank deposits (issued by deposit-taking corporations), and often also other short-term instruments similar to deposits. Currency in circulation typically represents only a small proportion of total money holdings, so that quantitatively most money in an economy is issued by deposit-taking corporations in the form of bank deposits.[7] A more precise definition of monetary aggregates and their relationship to the corresponding items in the financial accounts and balance sheets can be found later in this section.

In supplying bank deposits, deposit-taking corporations respond to the demand for money arising from economic agents. One important source for this demand is a deposit-taking corporation's ability to make payments and manage cash flows efficiently and securely by holding transferable deposits. Economic theory often refers to this demand as emanating from a "transactions motive". Depository corporations are typically the sole suppliers of transferable deposits. These are central to the smooth operation of the payment system, as most payments in a modern economy operate by way of a transfer of funds, or equivalent operations such as direct debit, cheque or draft, between transferable deposits.

Perhaps counterintuitively, customers' transferable deposits are one of the most stable sources of funding for banks. Individual transferable deposits are immediately redeemable on demand, but in aggregate, the overall quantity tends to be quite stable. This is because one agent's withdrawal is typically another agent's receipt from/into transferable deposits. Thus, the need to be able to effect payments efficiently yields a fairly stable demand for transferable deposits, at least in the medium run.

Many economic agents also prefer to hold at least part of their financial wealth in liquid, safe assets that can be redeemed at par on demand, or within a reasonably short period of time. For instance, agents may expect interest rates to rise in the future, and therefore postpone investment in bonds or other interest-rate sensitive assets ("speculative demand"), or they may have a degree of risk aversion that limits their desire to hold riskier and/or less liquid assets ("portfolio demand", "precautionary demand"). This demand is often satisfied by holding more bank deposits than what is required for making payments.

Both for transactions and for other reasons, a large part of money demand is effectively captive to the supply of deposits by deposit-taking corporations. This stems to a large degree from the institutional setting in which banks operate, in which the ability to issue liabilities with all the desired characteristics of liquidity and capital certainty is typically restricted to banks.

To reflect the role of deposit-taking corporations as the main suppliers of monetary liabilities, many countries define monetary aggregates as encompassing only liabilities issued by this sector, together with currency in circulation which is a liability of the central bank. Table 3.2 below shows the definition of monetary aggregates for the Euro Area, together with the link to instruments distinguished in the financial accounts and balance sheets, which – in all cases but currency in circulation and money market fund share/units – are liabilities of deposit-taking corporations.

Monetary aggregates measure the money in circulation in the economy, and are defined according to different degrees of closeness to the most liquid monetary liability, i.e. currency in circulation. The narrowest of money measures, M1, includes currency itself plus overnight deposits, as the latter can typically be converted into currency on sight. M2 also encompasses certain forms of bank deposits (such as term deposits and deposits redeemable after a

Table 3.2. **Monetary aggregates and financial instruments in the financial accounts and balance sheets in the Euro Area**

Liability	Subsector	Financial accounts item	M1	M2	M3
Currency in circulation	Central bank	Currency	X	X	X
Overnight deposits	Deposit-taking corporations (in the EU, monetary financial institutions other than the central bank and MMFs)	Mostly transferable deposits	X	X	X
Deposits redeemable at notice of up to 3 months		Other deposits		X	X
Deposits with an agreed maturity of up to 2 years		Other deposits		X	X
Repurchase agreements		Other deposits			X
Debt securities issued with a maturity of up to 2 years		Short-term debt securites and long-term debt securities with original maturity of less than 2 years			X
Money market fund shares/units	Money market funds	Money market fund shares			X

StatLink ᕱᔕᕗ http://dx.doi.org/10.1787/888933589884

particular period of notice) that, although not immediately convertible into currency, can be liquidated within a reasonable period of time (usually defined as within two years). M3 is the broadest measure of money and includes financial products that, although they are not strictly speaking short-term bank deposits, function as close substitutes to these. For instance, according to the ECB definition, these include money market fund shares/units, repurchase agreements that are a liability of an MFI, and debt securities issued by banks with a maturity of less than two years.

Deposit taking corporations as main suppliers of credit and core to the transmission mechanism of monetary policy

Deposit-taking corporations are also central to the financial system as the main providers of credit to households and businesses. This is inextricably linked to their ability to raise large amounts of funds in the form of deposits. The deposit and loan business of commercial banks reinforce each other, making banks key for the flow of funds from those with excess saving to those seeking funds to finance investment projects. Mechanistically, one could think that any addition to bank deposits allows banks to grant new loans. But it is equally true that a decision to grant credit on the part of a bank automatically creates a new bank deposit. Thus, economists have long argued, in different forms, over whether the provision of credit creates money, or whether, inversely, the availability of money leads to additional supply of credit.

The canonical illustration of a "money first" interpretation is the so-called "money multiplier" model. The money multiplier quantifies how any exogenous addition to base money (e.g. an increase in bank reserves due to a central bank open market operation) is multiplied up by the banking system to a much larger amount of new broad money (such as deposits in commercial banks). Specifically, the model postulates a multiplying factor of $1/r$, where r represents the reserve ratio (see Section 2). Thus, for a reserve ratio of 10%, an addition to central bank money will lead to a growth in banks deposits ten times as large.[8] Money comes first in this view because the initial trigger leading to a cascade of money creation is assumed to be an increase in the money base.

A "credit first" view would contend that the money multiplier model is misleading because it assumes that banks face a binding restriction to lending explained by the reserve ratio. In reality, banks may first face many other restrictions before insufficient central bank reserves. For instance, a lack of profitable lending opportunities, insufficient capital, the stance of macro-prudential policy, willingness and ability to take out loans by borrowers, collateral valuations, and others, are more likely to play a role in determining the amount of credit in equilibrium. The amount of bank deposits created by the economy follows more or less passively from such an equilibrium in the credit market,[9] regardless of increases in base money.

Irrespective of which view is a better description of reality, the transmission of monetary policy to the real economy typically requires that bank balance sheets are in a healthy state. A weak capital position, for instance, might make banks unwilling to make new loans even to solvent customers with profitable investment projects. A reduction of short-term rates by the central bank may well increase the amount of such projects, but these may not be undertaken due to lack of funding by banks. Asset purchase programmes by the central bank may be more successful in bypassing an impaired banking system. Nevertheless, they also have much less than their desired effect if bank balance sheets are compromised, especially when credit to small businesses and households is key for monetary policy transmission. Economists speak often of an "impaired transmission mechanism" in these situations. The unwillingness or inability of banks to provide credit to solvent customers is often referred to as a "credit crunch".[10]

Deposit-taking corporations from the perspective of the financial accounts

In this section we examine some of the features of deposit-taking institutions from the perspective of the financial accounts and balance sheets for the sector. Table 3.3 presents summarised figures for the balance sheets of other depository corporations in OECD countries. Loans, representing 53% of total assets, are by far the main item on the asset side of banks' balance sheets. Bank loans are made to businesses, households, and, less importantly, local and state governments. Some loans may also be made to non-bank financial intermediaries. Loans granted by banks are typically illiquid, since the bank cannot in most cases require repayment from the borrower at short notice. In addition, unlike debt securities, loans are not easily tradeable on secondary markets – quite often not tradeable at all.[11] Loans, therefore, contribute most significantly to the maturity mismatch between assets and liabilities inherent to the banking business – the mismatch of illiquid assets mostly funded through the issuance of monetary liabilities.

Table 3.3. **Financial account balance sheets of other depository corporations in OECD countries*, 2015**

Median percentage of the balance sheet total

	Assets	Liabilities
Financial net worth		0.9
Financial instruments	100	99.1
Currency and deposits	20.3	66.3
Currency	0.4	0.0
Transferable deposits	4.9	29.5
Other deposits	11.4	42.4
Debt securities	14.3	11.1
Short-term debt securities	9.4	1.6
Long-term debt securities	15.1	9.0
Loans	53.4	2.8
Short-term loans	9.4	0.0
Long-term loans	37.2	0.4
Equity and investment fund shares/units	3.1	7.4
Equity	2.6	6.0
Listed shares	0.6	2.2
Unlisted shares	2.2	1.9
Other equity	0.4	0.7
Investment fund shares/units	0.2	0.0
Financial derivatives and employee stock options	0.8	1.0
Other accounts	2.4	2.2

* Data analysed correspond to 20 OECD countries for which complete financial account balance sheet of the sector was available. It should also be noted that the details do not necessarily add up to the (sub)totals, because median shares have been used for each separate line.
Source: OECD (2017a), "Financial Balance Sheets, SNA 2008 (or SNA 1993): Non-consolidated stocks, annual", OECD National Accounts Statistics (database), http://dx.doi.org/10.1787/data-00720-en.

StatLink http://dx.doi.org/10.1787/888933589903

As illustrated in Table 3.3, currency and deposits, comprising 20.3% of total assets, follow as a distant second to loans within the asset portfolio of banks. Transferable deposits, which allow banks to effect payments without delay, make up 4.9% of total assets. Banks keep transferable deposits as a liquidity buffer, e.g. to satisfy withdrawals from clients, as well as any imbalances between payments made and received by the banks' customers. Transferable deposits held by banks are typically deposits with other banks, including those with the central bank. Since both central bank reserves and inter-bank deposits receive a smaller remuneration compared to other investments, banks will normally minimise these to an amount compatible with prudential liquidity management and supervisory regulations. Other deposits (11.4% of total assets) comprise deposits that are not considered transferable because they are not immediately available to make payments. This may include reverse repurchase agreements, margin payments related to derivative positions, and non-negotiable certificates of deposit. The counterparty of these positions is often another bank. Banks also keep small amounts of currency in the form of coins and banknotes (0.4% of total assets) to satisfy the needs of their clients, for instance withdrawals from ATMs, or banknotes deposited by businesses that receive payments from customers in this form.

Deposit-taking corporations also invest in long-term debt securities, representing 15.1% of total assets. In many countries these will be issued primarily by the central government and by other banks, with a smaller role for corporate securities and asset-backed securities. Some of these securities are tradeable in reasonably liquid markets. In addition, certain securities can also be pledged as collateral in private repurchase agreements and/or in refinancing operations with the central bank, in both cases giving access to liquid funds. However, the amount that can be obtained immediately by the bank from liquidating a security varies according to market circumstances. In other words, liquidity comes at the expense of capital certainty.[12]

On the liability side, the main source of funding for deposit-taking corporations are overwhelmingly deposits, comprising 66.3% of the balance sheet total. Most of these are deposits placed by customers, followed by interbank deposits and, depending on the operational framework for monetary policy, deposits resulting from central bank refinancing operations. A substantial part of deposit liabilities (29.5% of the balance sheet total) are transferable deposits. This means that more than a quarter of all bank liabilities are withdrawable on demand, compared to only 4.9% of assets being redeemable on the same terms. In addition, other deposits, comprising 42.4% of the balance sheet total, will typically include a substantial amount of deposits which, though not redeemable on demand, have much shorter maturities than most of the claims within the banks' loan portfolio.

Long-term debt securities also play a significant role, comprising around 9% of the balance sheet total. These are typically purchased by other banks and by institutional investors such as investment funds, insurance corporations and pension funds. Depending on regulations, banks may also reserve special tranches or specific issues to place directly with retail clients, including households. This permits banks to offer these clients a better remuneration than through an insured deposit. In return, the customer assumes an increased risk, as bank debt liabilities are not covered by deposit insurance.

Equity and net worth, jointly considered, represent 8.3% of the balance sheet total of deposit-taking corporations. Equity and net worth are considered here jointly because they provide a measure more directly related with bank capital than equity alone. Although there are many different ways of defining bank capital, from the financial accounts' perspective, both equity and net worth represent the ability of deposit-taking corporations to absorb losses under adverse scenarios.

Figure 3.7 depicts recent trends in some key ratios in deposit-taking institutions in OECD countries. The left part (a) shows the evolution of the ratio of loans to total financial assets over time. Contrary to what could be expected after the lending boom that took place in many OECD countries from approximately 2003 to 2007, loans as a percentage of total assets tended to increase rather than decrease in its aftermath (2007-11). One possible explanation is that banks' customers made ample use of lending commitments established prior to the 2007-09 economic and financial crisis, drawing down facilities such as credit lines in anticipation of an expected tightening in the supply of bank loans. Another potential driver in some jurisdictions was a tighter supervisory enforcement of the rules regulating asset de-recognition. As a result, securitised loans that were recorded off-balance sheet within the shadow banking system were brought back onto banks' financial statements unless the respective securitisations met strict criteria.

Figure 3.7. **Some key ratios of deposit-taking institutions across OECD countries, 2007-14**

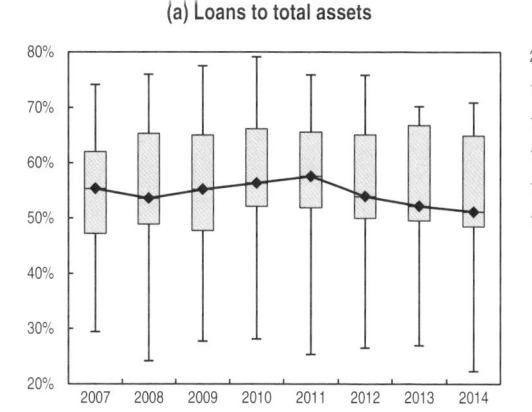

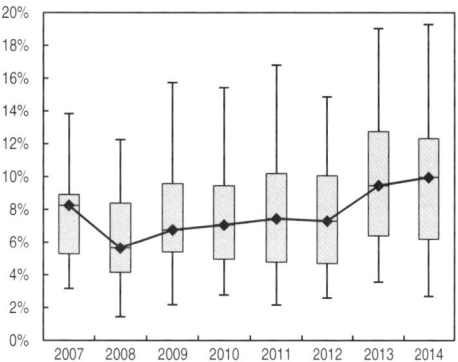

Note: Based on the set of all OECD countries for which all required data were available. The graph indicates: black line – median of the ratio; lower and upper edges of the grey boxes, first and third quartiles; edges of the grey lines, maximum and minimum ratio observed. The equity ratio is defined as the sum of equity and net financial worth over total assets.
Source: OECD (2017a), "Financial Balance Sheets, SNA 2008 (or SNA 1993): Non-consolidated stocks, annual", OECD National Accounts Statistics (database), http://dx.doi.org/10.1787/data-00720-en.
StatLink ⟶ http://dx.doi.org/10.1787/888933588193

In turn, between 2011 and 2013, deleveraging pressures on banks' balance sheets became more apparent. Special vehicles were set up in many jurisdictions to help banks wind-down bad loan portfolios from their balance sheets. Although often referred to as "bad banks", these vehicles are usually not classified in the deposit-taking corporations' sector. Instead, given their unique constructions, they are recorded as part of the other financial intermediaries or the government sector, depending on the level of government support received by the vehicle. As a result, significant amounts of loans were transferred out of the deposit-taking corporations and into the other financial intermediaries or the general government sectors.

The right part of Figure 3.7(b) plots the equity plus financial net worth ratios of deposit-taking corporations across OECD countries from 2007 to 2015. The effect of the 2007-09 economic and financial crisis at its height on bank capital can be seen clearly in 2008, where the median ratio was reduced by more than 200 basis points. Emergency recapitalisations followed in many countries, with ratios partly recovering over the period 2009-11, albeit with larger dispersion across countries. In the second phase of the crisis in 2012, with attention increasingly focused on banks and sovereigns in the Euro Area, bank capital suffered further setbacks. Over 2013-14, a new wave of recapitalisations allowed banks to increase their equity capital. At the same time, positive developments in financial asset prices led to a growth in bank profits, allowing banks to further cushion their capital position by increasing retained earnings. A significant recovery of the ratios over 2013-14 can be observed as a result of these additions to equity and financial net worth.

Finally, a commercial bank will typically use financial derivatives to hedge unwanted risks in the course of running its business. For instance, a mortgage bank that primarily invests in loans paying a fixed interest rate may be funded by liabilities paying mostly floating rates. In order to better balance receipts and outlays, the bank may wish to swap some of its fixed-interest receipts in exchange for floating-interest flows. In addition to hedging their own portfolios, banks may also offer derivative contracts to corporate and government customers. In doing that, banks will usually try to hedge these positions in order to avoid a short or long position that poses too much risk. The outstanding market value of derivatives at a typical bank is not particularly large. Nevertheless, the presence of large banks acting as international derivatives dealers in few countries creates a significantly skewed distribution of the value of banks' positions in derivatives across OECD countries.[13]

4. Money market funds

Money market funds (MMFs) are collective investment institutions whose purpose is to invest in short-term liquid assets, such as bank deposits, repurchase agreements, short-term debt securities and/or securities close to maturity, as well as securities issued by other money market funds. Their main liabilities are investment fund shares (or units) that represent a participation in the collective investment.

The fund shares issued by MMFs are considered to be close substitutes for deposits because the investment strategy of the fund is to repay the shares on request at a value that approximates the yield offered by a short-term deposit. Unlike deposits, however, money market fund shares are not usually issued with a guarantee of capital certainty. Potential capital losses are, however, generally small due to the limited exposure of the fund to interest rate and credit risk.

As they are not bank deposits, money market fund shares are not covered by deposit insurance schemes. This also implies that issuers do not face the costs of contributing to the (potential) expenses of such schemes, potentially offering a yield advantage to investors, especially in an environment of high short-term interest rates. Partly due to this, corporate treasurers have often been keen investors in money market funds. In addition, money market funds allow large corporations to diversify the counterparty risk associated with large cash holdings.[14]

Since the 2007-09 economic and financial crisis, money market funds have received some attention from a financial stability perspective as potential amplifiers or initiators of runs on money markets. Money market funds are important providers of funding in these markets, yet their reaction to market events may be very different to that of other players such as banks. Although not explicitly capital-certain, the funds are typically seen by investors as ensuring at least par redemption. This expectation might make the funds too reactive, being more likely to liquidate a significant amount of assets at the smallest hint of a disturbance in money markets. Frequent disclosure obligations also play a role by making investors immediately aware of any problems in a fund's portfolio before they can be addressed – in opposition to a bank where these would only be known to supervisors.[15] As a result, investors may also be more likely to initiate a run on the fund's shares. A run on large MMFs may propagate in the form of mounting difficulties for the issuers of commercial paper and other money market instruments, because the funds are unable or unwilling to renew their investments.

> Box 3.2. **The transformation of the banking sector and the 2007-09 economic and financial crisis**
>
> Financial crises are unavoidable. They have happened since the start of economic and financial history. The reason is that a key function of financial institutions is to deal with risks, and risks come with the possibility of financial failures. The current financial system started in the mid-17th century, when London goldsmiths transformed their business from purely safekeeping excess gold, silver or money for wealthy people, to issuing payable bills accepted as a means of exchange, under the promise of being redeemed at short notice. With this transformation, the goldsmiths widened their business opportunities

Box 3.2. **The transformation of the banking sector and the 2007-09 economic and financial crisis** (cont.)

enormously, but they also assumed higher risks. In fact as soon as there was a rumour that any of the goldsmiths (or the people to whom the goldsmiths lent money) was in financial difficulty, there was the possibility of "a run on the goldsmith" by people demanding their deposited valuables back.

Trust and financial soundness of banks and other institutions is, therefore, very important for a financial system. Similar to what happened from time to time in London's Lombard Street in the mid-17th century, bank runs may happen when depositors lose their trust in the safety of the banks where they have deposited their money. A distinctive cause of the 2007-09 economic and financial crisis is related to lending to "sub-prime borrowers", particularly in the US housing market. Doubts about the creditworthiness of these loans and the corresponding risk exposures (sometimes via asset backed securities, as discussed below) led to mistrust, or as a minimum to a lack of clarity, around the financial situation of banks. As a consequence of this situation, banks and other institutions stopped rolling over short-term lending, and all banks had to turn to the central bank to borrow the liquidity they needed. This made central banks to become the only lender in the market.

More generally, risks in the financial systems are of very different types. In addition to solvency risk, the two most important risks are credit and liquidity risk, which were also at the heart of the 2007-09 crisis. Credit risk refers to the possibility that the lender does not get back what he lends. In February 2014, for example, the Spanish banking system owned non-performing loans amounting to 13.6% of total outstanding loans. This presented high solvency risks for the relevant banks. Similar high risk exposures were also evident in the United States and many other countries. The second form of risk, liquidity risk, refers to a situation where a financial institution cannot pay out to its customers, because there are no lenders in the market willing to lend them the additional resources needed for payouts, irrespective of the solvency of the borrower.

The government, often via the central bank, attempts to control and manage the above risks for the financial sector and the economy at large with financial regulation. While key for a well-functioning financial sector, financial regulation can, however, give rise to additional costs for financial institutions, for example, when banks have to maintain additional reserves to meet regulations designed to mitigate credit risk. This was a main reason behind the rapid development of less regulated institutions in the 1990s and 2000s, when the belief in "market efficiency" became popular. The deregulatory trend allowed new players in the financial markets, e.g. investment banks or hedge funds. These institutions were lightly regulated, mainly because they did not issue deposits. However, as these institutions offered close substitutes for

Box 3.2. **The transformation of the banking sector
and the 2007-09 economic and financial crisis** *(cont.)*

deposits, they exerted additional competition on traditional banks. These and other forms of "shadow banking" have consequently increased tremendously, in particular in the United States where they nowadays represent more than half of the financial system. In Europe the size of the shadow banking sector is slightly smaller, representing one-third of the financial system.

In the late 20th and early 21st century, not only did new financial institutions come into the market, but new financial products were also designed and introduced. In fact, financial innovation accelerated enormously during the 1990s and the 2000s. Some of the most important financial innovations fall within the general phenomenon of securitisation. Securitisation describes the transformation of bank loans into securities, after having being split and bundled into tranches, allowing banks to finance loans via those securities, not just by deposits. Securitisation also allows banks to eliminate the credit risk that they had with the particular debtor whose loan has been securitised. The resulting securities are called asset-backed securities (ABS), or mortgage-backed securities (MBS) if the securitised loan is a mortgage. The holders of these securities face the credit risk of non-payment of the loan, which originates from a bank lending money to a household, e.g. for buying a house or a car.

The appearance of new financial players and new financial products triggered the transformation of the traditional banking business from the "originate-to-keep" model to the "originate-to-distribute" model. In the traditional model, banks had to control both credit and liquidity risk on their long-term loans portfolio. The new originate-to-distribute model, however, is formed in a way that eliminates the incentives to monitor the underlying loans which back ABS/MBS securities. Apart from banks, many others institutions are involved in this "originate-to-distribute" model; mainly institutions from the shadow banking system, like money market funds, investment funds, hedge funds, and investment banks.

Credit agencies also played an important role in the 2007-09 economic and financial crisis as they had the responsibility to assess (with strict independence) the credit risk of the ABS/MBS securities. Final investors in these types of assets were other financial institutions, investment funds, insurance companies and pension funds, households and non-financial corporations. In the case of the US, most of the investors were non-resident. As ABS/MBS were often re-securitised into new asset-backed securities, and as many investors were involved in the process of financing these types of securities, it could easily occur that ultimately a risk-averse final investor would unintentionally lend to a "subprime-borrower" in another country, certainly in a situation where credit agencies provided an artificially inflated credit rating of the relevant financial products (as discussed below).

> Box 3.2. **The transformation of the banking sector
> and the 2007-09 economic and financial crisis** (cont.)
>
> Some blame the new "originate to distribute" banking model as a key source of the crisis. They argue that the traditional banking system was well regulated with respect to the assets, liabilities and own reserves banks had on their balance sheets, while the operations the very same banks were doing off-balance sheet were poorly regulated. They argue that, when a bank shifts a loan off its balance sheet through securitisation, the risks introduced by that loan shift away from the eye of regulators and supervisors, as the ABS move to the de-regulated part of the financial system, that is, the shadow banking system. Timothy Geithner, at the time the President of the US Federal Reserve Bank of New York, declared in 2008 that by 2007 shadow banking had reached in the United States an estimated USD 10.5 trillion in assets/liabilities, while the regulated banking system's assets/liabilities totalled USD 10 trillion. At that time, the main types of shadow banks were hedge funds and investment banks (which included the "big five investment banks": Lehman Brothers, Bearn Sterns, Goldman Sachs, Morgan Stanley and Merrill Lynch).
>
> In the new "originate-to-distribute" model, self-regulation by the agents involved was more important than ever. This role was expected to be played by credit agencies, i.e. Moody's, Standard and Poor's, and Fitch, which together covered 95% of the credit rating market. However, these credit agencies failed to assess the actual credit risk borne by securities related to sub-prime mortgages. A key problem was related to the rating of products produced by the "originate-to-distribute" agencies, who were also the credit agencies' customers. It can be argued that the credit agencies had a vested interest to underestimate the credit and liquidity risk of such financial instruments, as they relied upon those who wanted to sell the relevant securities, thereby undermining their supposed independence.
>
> Finally, it may be argued that the "originate-to-distribute" model has heightened the excessive dependence of the whole financial system on the wholesale or inter-bank money market. All types of institutions (but prominently hedge funds) finance their acquisition of assets, which include long-term non-liquid loans, by short-term borrowing that needs to be rolled over. For example, to finance a five-year bond, a financial institution depending on a one month interbank borrowing needs to roll over that borrowing sixty times. However, if the money market becomes unstable, the roll-over may not take place, forcing the bondholder to sell the bond in a situation where many others will also start to sell. Strong falls in prices will follow (known as a "fire sale"), which will generate high losses, and may turn an initial liquidity crisis into a solvency crisis.

5. The increasing role of other financial institutions (OFIs)

The strong growth of financing prior to the 2007-09 economic and financial crisis through less regulated financial institutions outside the banking sector is generally linked to the move to the so-called "originate-to-distribute" model (see Box 3.2), as evolved in particular in the United States. In this model, a large part of the loans portfolio of banks was securitised. Already in the 1980s in the United States other financial institutions (OFIs) became the largest net investor in loans ahead of banks. In the Euro Area, banks remained the main lenders until 2009, when monetary financial institutions (MFIs) started to reduce their loan portfolios; see Figure 3.8. To better understand these developments it is important to know what types of institutions are grouped under the OFI heading, and why some of them have played such an important role, in particular in the run up to the 2007-09 economic and financial crisis.

Figure 3.8. **Net transactions in loans for MFIs and OFIs in the United States and the Euro Area, 1999-2016**

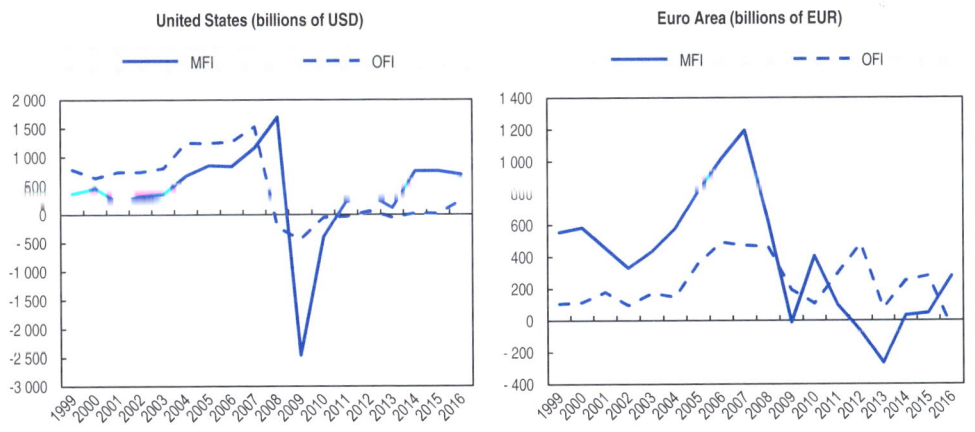

Source: US Federal Reserve (2017), *National Accounts* (database), www.federalreserve.gov/apps/fof/FOFTables.aspx; and ECB (2017), *National Accounts* (database), http://sdw.ecb.europa.eu/browse.do?node=9691262.
StatLink ⟹ http://dx.doi.org/10.1787/888933588212

Other financial institutions (OFIs) are defined as financial institutions other than MFIs, insurance corporations and pension funds in the 2008 SNA. As discussed in Section 1, in most OECD countries, OFIs are the second largest group of financial corporations, typically after MFIs and before insurance corporations and pension funds (ICPFs). In some countries, e.g. the United States,[16] OFIs' combined balance sheets are even larger than those of MFIs; see Figure 3.9. OFIs can generally be further divided into Non-MMF investment funds (IFs) and OFIs excluding IFs. OFIs excluding IFs are a very heterogeneous group of institutions. An overview of the types of institutions is provided in Table 3.1. For the OECD as a whole, the available data shows that OFIs grew faster than MFIs since the 2007-09 economic and financial crisis, more in particular since mid-2011. This faster growth was mainly driven by investment funds, although other OFIs grew faster as well; see Figure 3.9.[17]

Figure 3.9. **OFI balance sheet developments compared to MFIs and ICPFs, OECD countries,* 2007-15**
Total liabilities, 2007 = 100

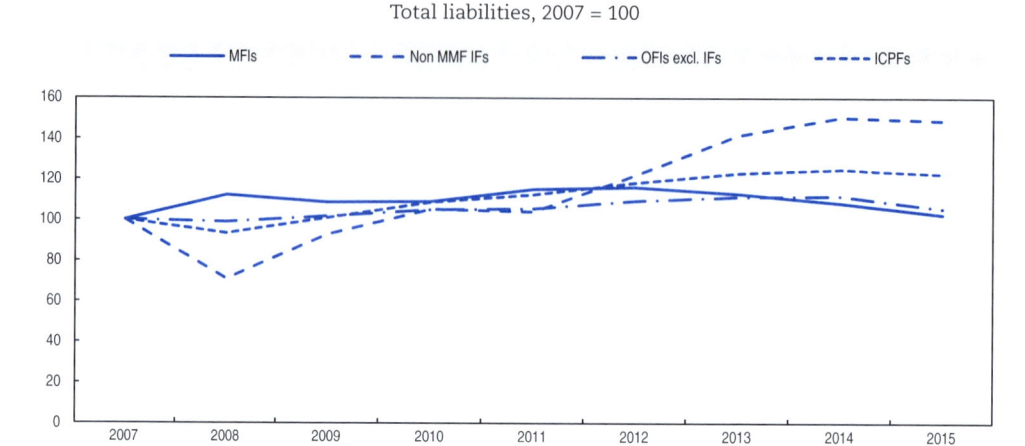

* This figure only includes OECD countries for which data are available for all subsectors and years.
Source: OECD (2017a), "Financial Balance Sheets, SNA 2008 (or SNA 1993): Non-consolidated stocks, annual", OECD National Accounts Statistics (database), http://dx.doi.org/10.1787/data-00720-en.

StatLink ⇒ http://dx.doi.org/10.1787/888933588231

Non-MMF investment funds (IFs)

The continued growth of the OFI sector can be broadly explained by the increasing specialisation of the financial industry. This is most evident in the large variety of Non-MMF investment funds (IFs) which offer a myriad of investment products for all types of investors, from individual savers to large institutional investors. Investment funds are collective investment schemes that raise funds by issuing investment fund shares (or units), and invest these funds in the financial markets or in real estate. This model allows an investor to invest in predefined sets of assets of their choosing, such as debt securities, shares of a particular sector, or "trackers" that follow the developments of a particular stock market index. Investors can choose between actively managed investment portfolios or passive funds following a specific market.

Most IFs raise funds exclusively by issuing investment fund shares. In the case of so-called "open-end" funds the value of the investment fund shares reflects on a one-to-one basis the value of the funds' investments, i.e. the IF is not "leveraged". In the case of closed-end funds, a limited number of shares are being issued which are subsequently traded on the stock market, as a consequence of which there may be a difference between the fund's assets and the value of the shares issues by the fund. Exceptions from this simple IF financing model are hedge funds which may incur substantial amounts of other liabilities such as loans. This additional financing allows hedge funds to purchase more assets – the fund gets "leveraged". As a consequence, the value of hedge fund shares reacts more than 1:1 to the value of the funds' investments. Leverage can be further increased by taking positions in financial derivative contracts, as they require small initial investments compared to the potential gains and losses. This is called synthetic leverage.

The names and definitions for the various types of investment funds differ across countries. Generally the more leveraged ("riskier") funds are called hedge funds, in particular if they involve high minimum investments, de facto restricting them to institutional investors and very wealthy individuals. As hedge funds are not marketed to the public at large, they tend to be less regulated than other investment funds. In many countries, the more regulated non-leveraged investment funds are called mutual funds. In the financial accounts of the United States, this term is restricted to open-end funds, while closed end funds and exchange traded funds (ETFs) are shown separately.

Other financial intermediaries

The OFIs excluding IFs include, amongst others, "other financial intermediaries", consisting of specialised branches. They typically raise funds from savers and lend these funds to the public or invest them in markets, but they are not deposit-taking institutions, investment funds, insurance corporations, or pension funds. Other financial intermediaries include, for example, financial corporations engaged in the securitisation of assets, security and derivative dealers, financial corporations engaged in lending, and other specialised financial corporations. Generally, these institutions are less regulated and their economic and financial importance differs widely between countries. Data sources for these institutions also tend to be less developed and less harmonised, as a consequence of which statistics are often based on indirect information from, for example, security markets or counterpart sector information (e.g. loans by monetary financial institutions). For most OECD countries, other financial intermediaries are grouped together with financial auxiliaries and captives (as discussed below), and referred to as other financial institutions excluding investment funds.

The financial corporations engaged in asset securitisation were particularly linked to the rapid growth of financing outside the regulated banking sector. Securitisation companies are created to purchase assets, such as portfolios of loans originated by an MFI or another lender. They finance the purchase of these assets by issuing asset backed securities (ABS). In doing so, they increase the liquidity of the original holders of the assets, and they allow the purchasers of the ABS to invest in a specified pool of assets. The practice of banks to move loans off their balance sheets via securitisation, in particular in the United States, led to the rapid growth of securitisation companies. The US Federal Reserve classifies these institutions into two separate sectors: Issuers of Asset-Backed Securities (ABS) and Agency- and Government Sponsored Enterprises (GSE)-Backed Mortgage Pools.[18] In the Euro Area, financial vehicle corporations (FVCs) engaged in securitisation transactions were less important in the lead-up to the 2007-09 economic and financial crisis. Since the crisis the importance of FVCs has further decreased; see Figure 3.10.

Apart from financial corporations engaged in asset securitisation, in many countries little information currently exists on the other types of financial intermediaries. This gap in data availability was recognised by the G-20, and was the reason why a recommendation was included on "shadow banking" in the G-20 Data Gaps Initiative;[19] see also Chapter 10. Because of their increased importance, it is understood that more information is needed on the various subgroups within the other financial intermediaries sector and it is expected that more detailed information will become available in the future. Preliminary findings for the Euro Area indicate that security and derivative dealers are the largest subgroup of other financial intermediaries excluding FVCs. In the United States, the main types of other financial intermediaries are finance companies, security brokers and dealers, and funding corporations.

Figure 3.10. **Balance sheet developments of other financial intermediaries, investment funds (IFs) and financial vehicle companies (FVCs) in the Euro Area, 1999-2016**
Total liabilities, Billions of EUR

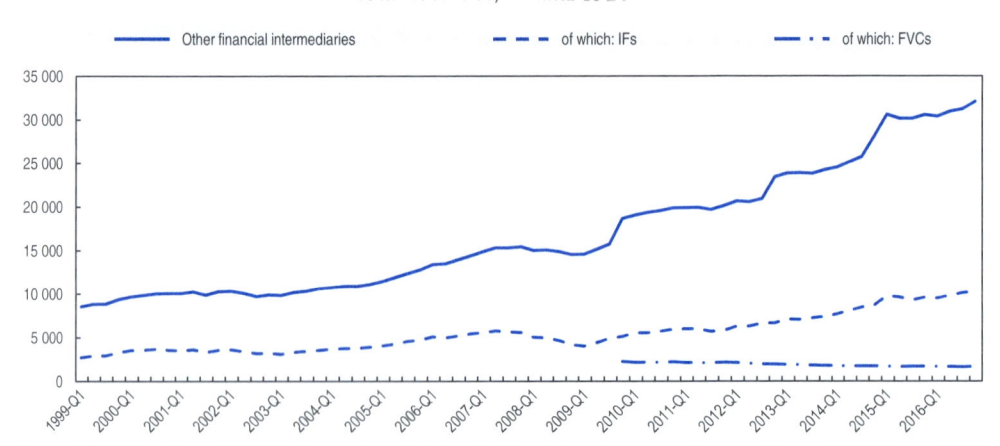

Source: ECB (2017), *Financial Vehicle Corporations* (database), https://sdw.ecb.europa.eu/browse.do?node=9691119; and OECD (2017a), "Financial Balance Sheets, SNA 2008 (or SNA 1993): Non-consolidated stocks, annual", *OECD National Accounts Statistics* (database), http://dx.doi.org/10.1787/data-00720-en.

StatLink ⟶ http://dx.doi.org/10.1787/888933588079

Captive financial institutions and money lenders

Captive financial institutions and money lenders are defined as institutional units, for which most of either their assets or liabilities are not transacted on open markets. They do not channel funds from one part of the public to another part of the public, and are thus not considered as financial intermediaries. They either raise funds from the public but only channel them to an enterprise group, or they receive funds from one individual household, enterprise, or enterprise group and invest the funds in the financial markets on their behalf. Examples of the latter are trusts and money lenders. Trusts receive funds from individual households or families and invest the funds in the financial markets. Similarly, money lenders use their own funds, i.e. they do not raise funds from the public to lend to creditors.

An example of units whose assets are not transacted on open markets are Special Purpose Entities (SPEs, also referred to as conduits) that raise funds in open markets – e.g. by issuing debt securities – but which lend exclusively to a parent corporation or an enterprise group. If such entities are resident in the same country as their parent corporations they are generally not considered as a separate institutional unit, but as an artificial subsidiary which is consolidated with the parent company. However, SPEs are often concentrated in a few financial centres in the world and are thus often not resident in the same country as their parent. In this case, they are recorded as separate institutional units in the country where they are located. For the countries in which they reside, often for tax reasons, the balance sheet totals of these entities may be very significant, whereas in most other countries they will be negligible. Similarly to SPEs, holding companies issue shares and their assets consist mainly of the equity of a group of subsidiary corporations.[20] Holding companies are generally treated as separate institutional units, as they are generally owned by multiple shareholders.[21]

The recording of non-resident SPEs and holding companies as separate financial institutions was introduced with the change-over to the new international statistical standards (notably the 2008 SNA and BPM6) to have a clearer separation between financial and non-financial corporations, allowing for a better analysis of the financing and investments of these sectors. This separation implies, for example, that financing raised by SPEs or holding companies is allocated to the financial corporations' sector. Such a recording is particularly important for countries that host financial centres attractive to SPEs and holding companies, such as Ireland, Luxembourg and the Netherlands. However, the financing raised by these institutions often has little connection to their resident economy.

Financial auxiliaries

Financial auxiliaries facilitate financial transactions between third parties without becoming the legal counterpart, for example as brokers or consultants. They therefore do not put themselves at risk and their financial

6. Insurance corporations and pension funds

Insurance corporations and pension funds provide financial services associated with five types of activities: non-life insurance, life insurance and annuities, reinsurance, social insurance schemes, and standardised guarantee schemes. This subsector, however, does not include obligatory insurance schemes, like protection against unemployment, illness and invalidity, medical expenses and retirement, which are provided and controlled by the government. These social security schemes, and the funds operating them, are treated as part of the general government.

Paragraph 6.176 of the 2008 SNA provides the following guidance regarding insurance corporations and pension funds:

"All these schemes lead to redistribution of funds, which are recorded in either the secondary distribution of income account or the financial account. For non-life insurance and standardised guarantee schemes, most of the redistribution takes place between different units in the same period. Many client units pay relatively small policy premiums or fees and a small number of them receive relatively large claims or payments. For life insurance, annuities and pension schemes, the redistribution is primarily, though not entirely, between different periods for a single client. In fulfilling their responsibilities as managers of these funds, insurance companies and pension funds are involved in both risk management and liquidity transformation, the prime functions of financial institutions."

The activities carried out by insurance corporations are mainly related to the pooling of risk, but life insurance and pension schemes are also related to long-term investment, as discussed below.

Insurance corporations

In exchange for a periodic payment, known as a "premium" or "contribution", the policyholder buys protection against the occurrence of certain negative events or, as in the case of some life insurance products similar to long-term saving, the right to a payment of either a lump sum or a monthly income in a given future period of time. With products related to risk events, the premium is calculated according to the risks involved (i.e. the larger the underlying risk, the higher the premium) and a certain profit for the insurance corporation. Nevertheless, the premium is usually smaller than the financial risk of possible future losses that may occur to the policyholder from the materialisation of such an event. Insurance companies are able to engage in such practices due to the pooling of risks, consisting of aggregating a diversified and uncorrelated group of insurances, mitigating each other's risk through dispersion and the so-called law of large numbers.

From a broader perspective, insurance has a significant social and economic role, as it allows a generally risk adverse society to take on some risks due to the fact that they know any negative events will be fully or partially covered. For the insurance companies, the meticulous calculation of insurance premiums is crucial for the success of its business. According to the nature of the covered risks, insurance can be split in two large types: non-life insurance (including re-insurance) and life insurance. In life insurance the risks are related to death or life events like retirement, while the other risks are covered by non-life insurance.

Non-life insurance including reinsurance

Risks covered by non-life insurance include motor vehicles accident protection, income protection against certain events such as invalidity, medical expenses, credit default and suretyship, financial loss and others. Due to the nature of the covered risks, non-life insurance and economic activity are highly interconnected. First of all, insurance boosts economic activity, allowing entrepreneurs to develop by calming fears of negative sudden events that might ultimately damage the business activity and by permitting a shift of financial funds held against potential losses to new projects and investments, hence promoting the business' growth. By being insured, businesses are also more likely to get better conditions when seeking credit and other sort of financial support, because the insurance protection mitigates some of the risks involved in the businesses' activities. Similarly, households will not need to set aside funds to protect themselves against uncertain future events that may seriously affect their assets or their future income.

From the perspective of financial accounts and balance sheets, non-life insurance corporations are not very significant. On the liability side, the prepayments of premiums and reservations made to meet outstanding insurance claims are recorded under "non-life insurance technical provisions", which is considered an asset of the policy holders. The counterpart for transactions and positions in this instrument is not that easy to asses, since the collected information does not have the required detail on the exact counterparts of prepaid premiums and the outstanding claims. Usually, it is assumed that this is more or less proportional to the stratification of the policy holders. Other transactions and positions relate to "provisions for calls under standardised guarantees". One example of such activity is export credit guarantees, where the insurer acts as the guarantor.

A special type of insurance is reinsurance, through which the insurance business itself can get coverage and protection for the risk of loss. Figure 3.11 shows how direct insurance and reinsurance are connected within the insurance business. As illustrated, insurance companies cover the risks of the original policyholders, through what is commonly called direct insurance, regardless of their line of business (life, non-life or composite). However, insurance companies may transfer part of the risk taken via reinsurance, which can be done through either reinsurance companies (the risk is transferred in exchange for a fee, similar to the payment of a premium), or Special Purpose Vehicles via securitisation (see Section 5 above). Reinsurance is also applicable to reinsurers, but in this case it is called retrocession. The activity of reinsurance is heavily concentrated in a few countries, such as Switzerland and the United Kingdom.

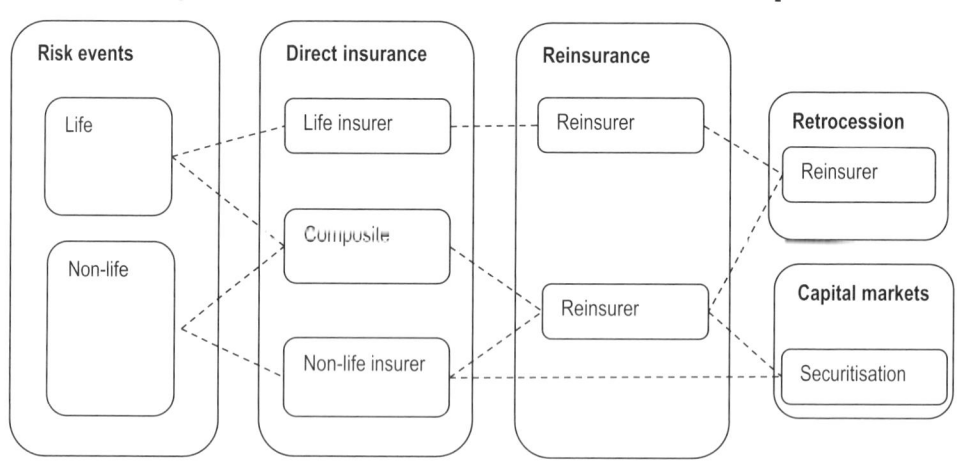

Figure 3.11. **The insurance business – a workflow example**

Life insurance

As stated previously, life insurance covers risks related to death and certain life events such as retirement. Different from pension schemes and social security schemes provided by government, life insurance is taken out on an individual basis. The policy holder periodically pays a premium, which – after the insured event occurs – leads to a stream of future benefits (annuities) or a lump sum. The insurance corporation invests the premiums received to cover the future payments. As such, life insurance offers financial investment products, competing hand in hand with more or less similar products offered by other financial corporations, such as banks and investment funds. Good examples of products similar to financial investments offered by life insurers are unit-linked products, in which there is a full or partial transfer of the investment risk from the insurer to the policyholder. The investment is done through the purchase of units and the investor is able to choose the level of investment risk by selecting the underlying investments which compose the unit-linked policy, ultimately determining its future cash value. This type of investment product is closer to collective investment vehicles than to conventional insurance policies.

Given the similarity with other investment products, the payments of premiums are not recorded as expenditures for the policy holders in the current accounts. Instead, these payments, after a deduction of the costs (and profit margin) made by the insurer, are treated as a financial transaction leading to the building up of entitlements, which are recorded as an asset of the policy holder and as a liability of the insurance corporation, under the heading "life insurance and annuity entitlements". Investment income that the insurance corporations earn on the assets accumulated through the investment of the premiums and that they allocate to the policy holder, is recorded as an income of the policy holder, under "investment income attributable to life insurance policy holders". This income is subsequently added to the entitlements as well. Correspondingly, benefits are not treated as income, but as a run-down of entitlements.

Figure 3.12 presents the life insurance business in a number of OECD countries. The density of life insurance, as shown in Figure 3.12, is measured as the average (life) insurance spending per capita in a given country. Countries where the density is higher are countries where life insurance products are more used as alternative investment products. Often, the differences in density may be related to certain income tax regulations for these products, or the

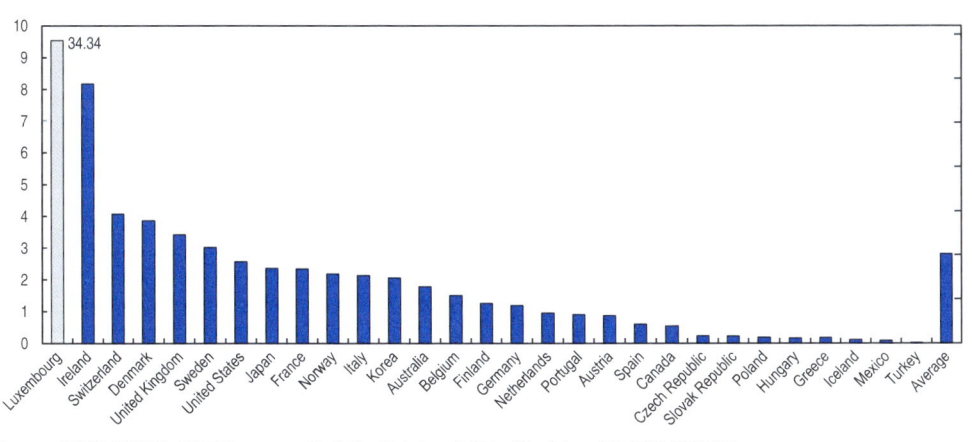

Figure 3.12. **Density of life insurance in OECD countries, 2015**
Average life insurance spending per capita (in thousands of USD)

Source: OECD (2017b), OECD Insurance Statistics (database), http://dx.doi.org/10.1787/2307843x.
StatLink http://dx.doi.org/10.1787/888933588117

presence/absence of collective insurance, either through government or pension funds.

Life insurance products and pension schemes have become increasingly important over the past years; this is partly related to an ageing society. In OECD countries, life expectancy increased 5.2 years from 1993 to 2013 (OECD, 2016a) and, within the same period, fertility ratios have decreased from 1.81 to 1.67 (OECD, 2016b). As a consequence of these developments, the old-age-dependency ratio, i.e. the number of persons aged 65 and more relative to the number of individuals aged 20 to 64, will increase, thus jeopardising the sustainability of pay-as-you-go social security pension systems. In this context both individual life insurance and pension funds become a relevant and highly encouraged alternative to complement retirement income. More discussion on the relationship between the ageing society and financial accounts and balance sheets is presented in Chapter 9.

Pension funds

Similarly to (individual) life insurance, pension schemes also aim to provide income and financial relief, mainly in the event of retirement, complemented by other benefits in the case of death and/or disability. However, different from (individual) life insurance, pension funds relate to so-called "social insurance schemes" in which i) participation is obligatory, either by law or under the terms and conditions of employment; ii) the scheme is a collective one for the benefit of a designated group of workers; and/or iii) an employer makes a contribution to the scheme. As noted before, if these schemes are operated by government, they are considered as social security and recorded as part of the transactions and positions of government, unless they relate to (partially) funded employment-related pension schemes. However, if they are arranged by, for example, employers for their employees, usually designated pension funds are set up, which are then recorded in the financial corporations' sector. In some countries, these pension funds also include separated schemes for government employees. Because of the ageing society, these funds are growing in importance.

Pension funds basically pool assets which are accumulated by investing the premiums or contributions paid by the employees, and/or on behalf of them, by the employers, with the purpose of financing future pension benefits. There are two main types of pension schemes, based on the guarantees they provide to their members: defined benefit schemes and defined contribution schemes. But there are also hybrid types, somewhere in between defined benefit and defined contribution schemes. In a defined benefit scheme, the benefit is determined in advance, for example as a fixed percentage of salary, and the contributions are calculated in order to ensure this benefit. Implicitly this means that the risk falls upon the pension manager/sponsor (often the employer), who is responsible to ensure that the accumulated assets are sufficient to cover the future payments of benefits, although in some countries this responsibility is shared between the employer, the employees and the retirees. In a defined contribution scheme, only the contributions made to the fund are determined up front. The benefits arising from these contributions will depend on the performance of the accumulated assets, so that the entitlements are fully matched with the underlying assets' performance, hence transferring the risk from the pension sponsor to the contributor. This is an important difference. If, for example, life expectancy increases, in the case of defined benefit schemes, the contributions would have to increase to pay for the extra years in retirement. However, in the case of defined contribution schemes, contributions would not change and less money per year in retirement will be available.

Nowadays, the trend in pensions' activity is tilted towards defined contribution schemes, thus transferring the risk to the employee. Many factors can be identified as contributors to this shift: the problems related to an adequate accounting for and prediction of the pension liabilities; increased workforce mobility; demographic changes; and financial markets' behaviour, especially in periods of low long-term interest rates.

The above distinction of pension schemes is also very relevant in terms of recording in the national accounts. In a defined benefit scheme, the entitlements due to the employee at a certain point in time are based on the net present value of the estimated future stream of pension benefits (calculated according to actuarial information), using a certain discount rate. In a defined contribution scheme, the entitlements are calculated as the amount of contributions made to the scheme plus any gains or losses incurred from the pension fund's investment of these contributions. The total claims of households related to these pensions are recorded under the financial instrument "pension entitlements". In the case of defined benefit schemes, the shortfall of the accumulated assets of the pension funds, as compared to the pension entitlements, are recorded as "claims of pension funds on pension managers". As a consequence, pension funds normally have a zero net worth, although as discussed previously, in some countries the responsibility for the shortfall is not always evident, and there may be an alternative accounting. All of this is discussed in more detail in Chapter 9.

Box 3.3. **The role of insurance and pension funds as institutional investors**

Insurance corporations and pension funds have an important role as institutional investors. According to the OECD definition, institutional investors (investment funds, insurance companies and pension funds) are major collectors of savings and suppliers of funds to financial markets. Figure 3.13 offers an overview of total assets held by insurance corporations and pension funds in OECD countries between 2007 and 2016. The share of

Box 3.3. **The role of insurance and pension funds as institutional investors** (cont.)

insurance corporations and pension funds in the assets held by institutional investors increased from slightly more than 60% at the end of 2007 to around 68% at the end of 2010 and 2011. Since then it decreased to 66% at the end of 2016. In terms of percentage of GDP, the OECD average of the accumulated assets of insurance corporations and pension funds increased from 73% at the end of 2007 up to 105% at the end of 2013, with a low of 71% at the end of 2008, right after the economic and financial crisis (see also Keelley, Brian et al., 2010).

Figure 3.13. **Total assets held by insurance corporations and pension funds in OECD countries, 2007-16**
Percentage of GDP and percentage of total assets of institutional investors

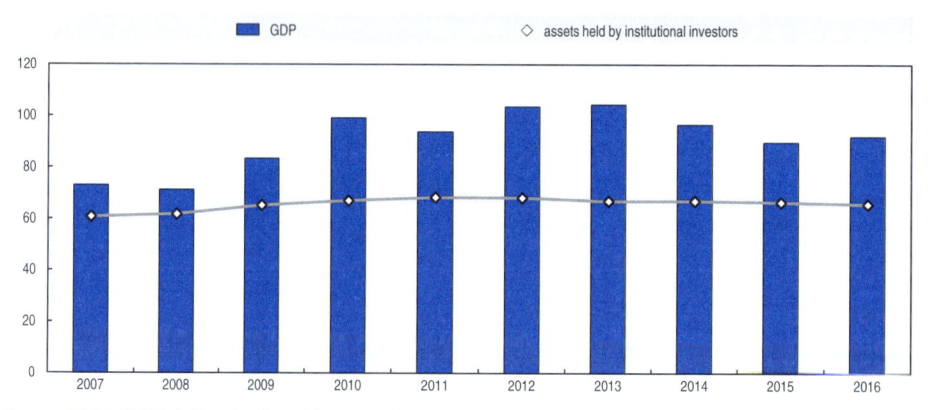

Source: OECD (2017a), "Institutional investors' assets and liabilities", *OECD Institutional Investors Statistics* (database), http://dx.doi.org/10.1787/c4292928-en.

StatLink ⟶ http://dx.doi.org/10.1787/888933588136

The analysis of the composition of insurance corporations and pension funds' investments by instrument in Figure 3.14 shows that the majority of assets consist of debt securities, and shares and other equity. Non-financial assets (e.g. real estate) and loans are less popular investment categories.

Besides having the need to invest contributions or premiums, insurance corporations and pension funds have another very interesting feature: their investments' long-term maturity. Since most of their liabilities have a very long-term maturity, especially in the case of life insurance and pension funds, these institutions tend to match their liabilities' maturity on the assets side. This long term investment has an important role as a counter-cyclical and stabilising factor on the financial markets. Della Croce et al. (2011) identify the special characteristics of these investments as "patient counter-cyclical capital", because these investors typically hold assets for a long period of time or until maturity; "engaged capital" given that they are responsible asset owners, who closely monitor a companies' management; and "productive capital" since their investments drive competitiveness and economic growth.

Box 3.3. **The role of insurance and pension funds as institutional investors** (cont.)

Figure 3.14. **Composition of assets held by insurance corporations and pension funds in OECD countries,* 2007-16**
Trillions of USD

* This figure only includes OECD countries for which data are available for all subsectors and years. Australia, Portugal and the United Kingdom are excluded for the whole period, while some other countries are excluded for part of the period covered.
Source: OECD (2017), "Institutional investors' assets and liabilities", OECD Institutional Investors Statistics (database), http://dx.doi.org/10.1787/c4292928-en.

StatLink ⟶ http://dx.doi.org/10.1787/888933588155

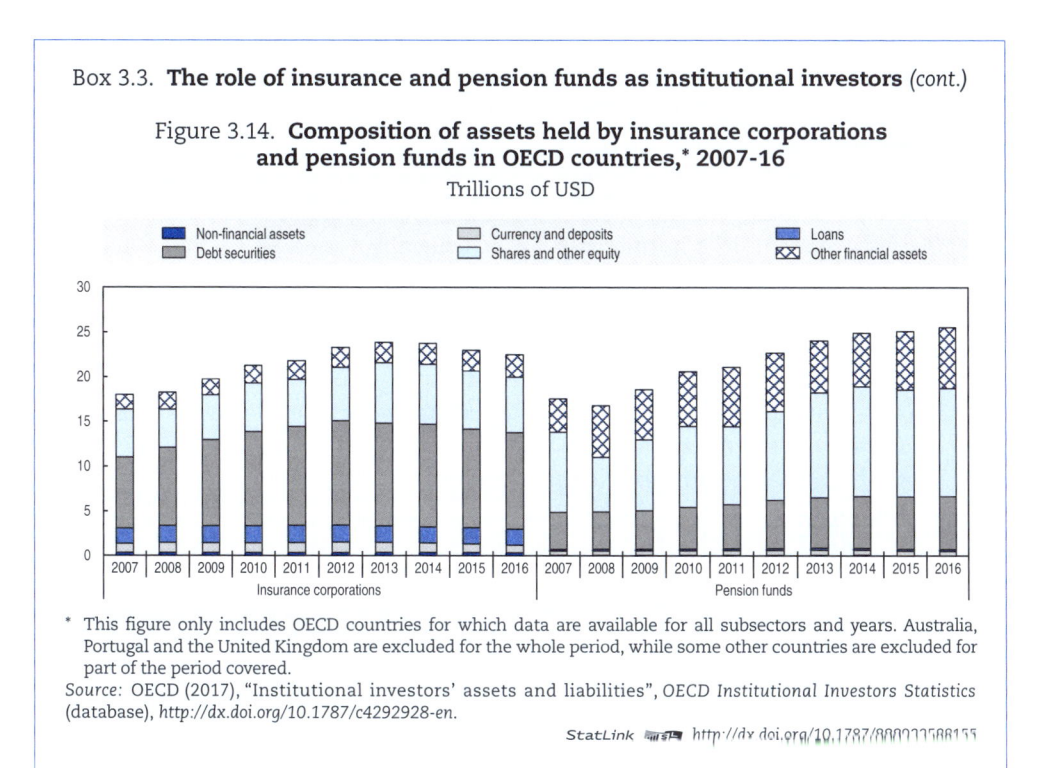

7. Analysing the financial corporation sector

The analysis of the financial sector focuses on the sector's role in channelling funds from savers to investors, and in particular on the efficiency and the resilience with which this central function is performed.

Advantages of a comprehensive presentation of the financial sector

While there has been a long history of comprehensive analysis of the traditional banking sector, the 2007-09 economic and financial crisis has shown that developments in other financial institutions can have large repercussions on banks, financial markets and also the economy as a whole. Given the large number and variety of financial institutions and their interactions, comprehensive coverage is difficult, but missing financial transactions and positions of some institutions may preclude detecting the build-up of problems early enough to attempt corrective action. For instance, the American International Group (AIG) was historically an insurance corporation in the United States, but in the years leading up to the 2007-09 economic and financial crisis it had built up an enormous book of financial derivatives positions, which were not appropriately reflected in financial statistics.

The financial accounts and balance sheets, compiled according to the 2008 SNA, amongst others aim to provide a framework for a comprehensive and consistent coverage of the financial sector. The harmonised classification of financial institutions and financial instruments is essential in that this classification allows combining many different data sources in a single statistical product, and facilitates comparison across the sub-sectors of the financial system on a harmonised basis. Crucially, for some of the actors included in the "other financial institutions" subsector, the financial accounts and balance sheets are, in many countries, the only source of official statistical data. While direct data sources often do not exist for all types of financial institutions, the combination of indirect sources, such as security holdings statistics derived from custodians and counterpart sector information from other statistics, are used by the compilers of financial accounts and balance sheets to close data gaps.

Due to data limitations, the financial accounts and balance sheets may not always allow identifying the precise type of financial actors involved in financial transactions. However, the financial accounts' comprehensive and homogeneous treatment of all financial subsectors and instruments, irrespective of the specific level of subsector detail attainable, still makes them a useful tool for further analysis. For example, it may not be possible to separately identify central counterparties, i.e. institutions that provide clearing and settlement services for trades in foreign exchange, securities, derivatives, etc. However, large amounts of transactions within the subsector "other financial institutions", which correspond to activity in the repurchase agreement market, may be assumed to be associated with one or more central counterparties rather than, for example, a financial auxiliary.

Cross-country comparability

The relative size of the financial sub-sectors varies considerably across countries, as shown in Figure 3.1. A given financial function may be performed by different types of institutions in different countries, depending on regulatory or other national circumstances. Focusing on individual subsectors when comparing a certain part of the financial system across countries can therefore be misleading. For instance, home mortgages may be granted exclusively by banks and retained on their balance sheets in some countries, whereas in other countries non-banks may originate loans and/or banks may predominantly sell them to asset-backed security issuers. In the latter cases, the credit market for residential real estate could be highly misrepresented by focusing solely on banking statistics. Financial accounts and balance sheets therefore facilitate international comparisons because they allow the analyst to cover the whole financial system using a single data source, thereby strengthening the analysis in the presence of country-specific market characteristics.

Aggregate leverage and equity ratios of the financial sector and sub-sectors

Capital and leverage ratios of individual entities or financial groups are core measures used by supervisors of banks and other financial institutions throughout the world. Macro-prudential oversight, in turn, relies upon similar ratios calculated at the aggregate level as part of the toolkit to monitor the strengths and vulnerabilities of the financial system as a whole. The financial accounts and balance sheets often provide the most direct route for the monitoring and analysis of aggregate leverage and equity ratios over time and across countries. Especially for subsectors outside of deposit taking corporations, for which other statistical sources are often inadequate, financial accounts and balance sheets are often the only choice available. Since the aggregate capital position of the financial system may also play an important role in the transmission mechanism of monetary policy, such measures are also of interest to monetary authorities.

A leverage ratio for a sector or a subsector would be typically computed as total debt over total assets; in turn, an equity ratio is usually defined as total liabilities in the form of equity instruments over total assets.[22] Whilst it is possible to compute these ratios for the overall financial system, each sub-sector may have particularities that require some adjustments to these general definitions. For instance, in the Euro Area, the MFI sector includes both deposit taking institutions and money market funds. A question arises as to how to treat the liabilities of money market funds to compute the ratios for the overall MFI sector. Although money market shares may be able to absorb losses, pressure on their value may trigger runs on short-term claims within the financial system (see also Section 4). Consequently it may be preferable to treat them as short-term debt, if one would want to encompass the vulnerability of the financial system to such runs. For insurance corporations and pension funds, unit-linked life insurance technical reserves and defined contribution pension liabilities should not be considered as debt-like obligations in computing leverage, as all the risk associated with the under-performance of the corresponding assets lies with the respective policyholders. In contrast, liabilities derived from defined benefit pensions may be considered as a form of leverage. Finally, non-MMF investment funds (with the notable exception of hedge funds) should generally not be considered to contribute to leverage within the financial system, since their assets are funded by shares and units which are akin to equity.

Financial inter-linkages between sectors

Both academics and policymakers acknowledge the importance of monitoring sectoral balance sheet developments, notwithstanding some neglect prior to the 2007-09 economic and financial crisis. This has spurred the development of financial accounts and balance sheets as a key tool for the analysis of the financial sector. One particular aspect, fundamental to analysing the financial sector using the financial accounts and balance sheets, is the availability of "from-whom-to-whom" (FWTW) information. Financial accounts and balance sheets including such details reveal the financial interlinkages between the financial sector and the other sectors in the domestic economy and the Rest of the World, as well as those among the different financial subsectors.

Perhaps the best known example of the importance of sectoral interlinkages can be found in the Euro Area in the 2009-12 period. Banks in some Euro Area countries were holding increasing amounts of domestic government debt. Doubts about the solvency of these governments eroded the market value of these debt instruments, putting stress on banks' balance sheets. Markets started to question the solvency of the banks as well, hampering their access to funding. Bank distress raised the expectation of a costly government intervention in the financial system, and a feedback between bank and sovereign credit risks (which was termed as a "diabolic loop") ensued. In this episode, standard financial accounts and balance sheets would only have shown that the banking sector was holding increasing amounts of marketable debt. FWTW accounts would have shown the amounts of banks' debt holdings issued by the government sector, thereby revealing the part of the portfolio directly responsible for the "diabolic loop".

Inter-sectoral financial linkages are now considered a fundamental ingredient of policy analysis by central banks and authorities responsible for macro-prudential policy, especially since monetary policy and financial stability are increasingly viewed as mutually interdependent. Networks of linkages at the sectoral or subsectoral level are sufficiently simple to compile and monitor on a regular basis from a set of FWTW financial accounts and balance sheets. Scenarios where a given shock to the financial system is propagated from one sector to another in successive rounds are easily constructed from FWTW data. These scenarios are increasingly used in the construction of stress-test exercises for banks and other financial institutions, as well as for macro-prudential resilience tests of the system as a whole. Additionally, network theory provides synthetic measures that characterise the centrality of a given sector or subsector in the financial system for a particular function, such as financial intermediation, with both macro-prudential and monetary policy applications. These are also easily derived from a system of FWTW accounts.

Key points

- Financial intermediaries play an important role in monetary and economic analysis because of their role in channelling funds from savers to investors. There are many different categories of financial intermediaries: central banks, deposit-taking institutions, money market funds, non-MMF investment funds, insurance corporations, pension funds, and other financial intermediaries.

- Central banks' objectives and functional roles can differ over time and across countries. However, the most common functions of a central bank can be defined as follows: money creation and monetary policy conduction, lender of last resort, bank of the government, and centre of the payment system. Examples of other relevant functions for some central banks are supervision and financial stability functions. Recently, the typical structure of a central bank balance sheet has changed as a result of the monetary policies to avoid deflationary pressures, leading to non-standard measures of purchasing securities.

- Deposit-taking corporations, commonly known as banks, are defined by accepting deposits as their main funding source and are by far the most important type of financial intermediaries in almost any financial system. Deposit-taking corporations are strictly regulated due to the mismatch between their liquid and capital-certain liabilities (deposits), and their more risky and illiquid assets (loans to customers). Deposit-taking corporations are usually the main suppliers of money to the economy, and the main suppliers of credit to households and businesses.

- In the late 20th and early 21st century, new financial institutions came into the market, and new financial products were designed. It can be argued that the new "originate-to-distribute" banking model, and the increased use of securitisations, led to the 2007-09 economic and financial crisis. These changes also led to an increased role for other financial institutions.

- Insurance corporations and pension funds streamline the economy by mitigating social and economic risks, gathering resources from their clients, and having a noteworthy role as institutional investors.

- Financial accounts and balance sheets, compiled according to the 2008 SNA, provide a framework for comprehensive and consistent coverage of the financial sector. The harmonised classification of financial institutions and financial instruments is essential in that this classification allows the combination of many different data sources in a single statistical product, and facilitates comparison across the sub-sectors of the financial system on a harmonised basis. As such, financial accounts and balance sheets, including FWTW information, provide a powerful tool to monitor and analyse risks and vulnerabilities building up in the financial system.

Notes

1. For details on financial corporations and the measurement of the relevant flows and stocks, reference is made to *Financial Production, Flows and Stocks in the System of National Accounts*, United Nations and ECB, 2015; and the special feature "The financial sector in the new national accounts framework" in *Financial Integration in Europe*, ECB, April 2015.

2. See, for example, Colangelo, A. and R. Inklaar (2009), "Measuring the Output of the Banking Sector: Shortcomings of the Current European Methodology and New Perspectives", and M. Niederkorn, "Banking on Lean – A Practicioner's View on Productivity in European Banking", published as Chapters 7 and 5, respectively, in: Balling, M., E. Gnan, F. Lierman and J.-P. Schoder, *Productivity in the Financial Services Sector*, SUERF Study 2009/4, Larcier, Vienna.

3. Derived from a speech by Salvatore Rossi, Senior Deputy Governor of Bank of Italy, on the "Monetary policy and independence of central banks: the experience of the European Central Bank in the global crisis".

4. See, for example, Goodhart (2010) for a good description on the evolution of central bank's role.

5. Investors demand a higher return to hold a riskier asset such as equity than, for instance, bank senior bonds or a deposit. The return for the investor is a cost for the bank. Tax considerations, such as the deductibility of interest expenditure, also play a role in making debt finance more attractive.

6. For more detail on the Basel accords, see *https://www.bis.org/bcbs/index.htm*. It should be noted that under the latest generation of the standards, known as Basel III, requirements on liquidity and leverage have also become part of the standards, in addition to the capital requirements already contemplated in their predecessors, Basel I and Basel II.

7. Currency in circulation represented, for instance, only 9.3% of the broad monetary aggregate M3 in the Euro Area at the end of 2015.

8. Only an intuitive explanation will be offered here. The initial reserve increase leaves banks with a ratio of reserves to deposits above r. As a response, banks increase their lending to restore their ratio to reserves to deposits to r. Why would they increase their lending rather than to accept more deposits? Because it is assumed that depositors were already in equilibrium with respect to their desired money holdings prior to the central bank's intervention. Banks therefore grant credit, thereby creating new deposits. A fraction of the new deposits needs to be added to reserves, so that banks find themselves again with a ratio of reserves to deposits larger than r. As a response, they increase lending again. By iterating this process over and over, one obtains the money multiplier $1/r$.

9. For a non-technical account of this view, see for example, Mc Leay, M., A. Radia and R. Thomas, "Money creation in the modern economy", Bank of England Quarterly Bulletin, 2014 Q1.

10. The financial crisis of 2008 is widely acknowledged to have been followed by such unavailability of bank credit at any price.

11. Prior to the 2007-09 economic and financial crisis, loan securitisation appeared at some point to provide banks with an easy means of obtaining liquidity from their loan portfolios. However, the business model of loan securitisation as it was known then has never been restored, especially with regards easy access to liquidity. For a more detailed discussion of bank securitisation and its role in the financial crisis, see Box 3.2.

12. Long-term debt securities may suffer significant price changes in the short-term due to changes in interest rate expectations and/or the creditworthiness of the issuer. Thus, they may be liquid but they are not capital certain if liquidated before maturity. In that respect, they do not fit the definition of money that can be attributed to banks' short-term deposits. The degree of liquidity varies anyway significantly across different parts of banks' debt portfolios, as well as due to market conditions. Furthermore, large parts of the debt portfolio of banks may be designated for accounting purposes as held to maturity, preventing the liquidation of the holdings until redemption.

13. Derivatives desks in a dealer bank will typically aim to run "matched books" so that their exposure to the underlying risk (say, a change in interest rates) is as close to neutral as possible. This requires them to continuously write off-setting derivatives contracts with other dealers and with end-customers. As a result, the banks housing dealing activities carry large asset and liability positions in derivatives that closely track each other. For instance, in the case of the United Kingdom, financial derivatives represent approximately 30% of total assets and liabilities, and around 10% in France and Germany. In countries where no large dealers are known to operate, in turn, values between 1% to 2% are more common.

14. Large deposits placed by corporations in banks are effectively not insured, making money market funds more attractive from a credit risk perspective due to their diversification without the added cost of having to manage a cash portfolio in-house. Treasurers will also seek to minimise the operational risk that a temporary moratorium on withdrawals may be imposed by supervisory authorities as a protective measure for a bank facing financial difficulties.

15. See, for example, Baba, N., R.N. McCauley and R. Srichander, "US Dollar Money Market Funds and Non-US Banks", BIS *Quarterly Review*, March 2009. For a European perspective, see "Money Market Funds in Europe and Financial Stability", *European Systemic Risk Board Occasional Paper Series* No. 1, June 2012.

16. Other countries where, at the time of writing this publication, OFIs have larger balance sheets than MFIs and ICPFs are Hungary, Ireland, Korea, Luxembourg, and the Netherlands.

17. For a more detailed analysis, see for example "The role of euro area non-monetary financial institutions in financial intermediation", ECB Economic Bulletin, Issue 4/2016.

18. See the Financial Accounts Guide of the Federal Reserve at *www.federalreserve.gov/apps/fof/FOFTables.aspx*.

19. G-20 Data Gaps Initiative (DGI-II), Recommendation II.5 on Shadow Banking: "The G-20 economies to enhance data collection on the shadow banking system by contributing to the Financial Stability Board (FSB) monitoring process, including through the provision of sectoral accounts data. FSB to work on further improvements of the conceptual framework and developing standards and processes for collecting and aggregating consistent data at the global level". (*Sixth Progress Report on the Implementation of the G-20 Data Gaps Initiative*, IMF and FSB, September 2015).

20. Holding companies are defined as units that hold the assets (owning controlling-levels of equity) of a group of subsidiary corporations and whose principal activity is owning the group. They do not provide any other service to the enterprises in which the equity is held, i.e. they do not administer or manage other units (see SNA 2008, paragraph 4.54). If units that hold owning controlling-levels of equity of a group of subsidiary corporations are engaged in the management of the subsidiaries they are classified as "head offices".

21. The Task Force on Head Offices, Holding companies and SPEs, set up under the umbrella of the Inter Secretariat Working Group on National Accounts (ISWGNA) in 2013, concluded that having multiple parents/shareholders is a sufficient qualification for a unit to be treated as a separate institutional unit, and thus not to be consolidated with its owners.

22. The term equity ratio is preferred to "capital ratio" to avoid confusion with supervisory risk-weighted measures of capital adequacy – which are generally not computable at the aggregate level from the financial accounts. An equity ratio computed from the financial accounts measures equity liabilities over total assets, both at market prices. The market price of the equity of financial institutions should in principle price in elements that enhance their loss-absorbing capacity, such as retained earnings or unrealised holding gains on asset portfolios. However, it is the perception of the market about the size of these capital buffers, rather than their regulatory assessment, what drives such a ratio.

References

Baldwin, R. and C. Wyplosz (2006), *The Economics of European Integration* (2nd ed.), McGraw-Hill Education, New York City.

BIS Committee on Payment and Settlement Systems (2003), *The Role of Central Bank Money in Payment Systems*, Bank for International Settlements Press & Communications, Basel, *www.bis.org/cpmi/publ/d55.pdf*.

BoE (2017), *Bankstats (Monetary and Fiscal Statistics)*, Bank of England, London, *www.bankofengland.co.uk/statistics/Pages/bankstats/2017/may.aspx*.

Bordo, M.D. (1990), "The lender of last resort: Alternative views and historical experience", *FRB Richmond Economic Review*, Vol. 76, No. 1, Federal Reserve Board of Richmond, Richmond, pp. 18-29, *www.richmondfed.org/ /media/richmondfedorg/ publications/research/economic_review/1990/pdf/er760103.pdf*.

De Grauwe, P. (2000), *Economics of Monetary Union*, Oxford University Press, Oxford.

Della Croce, R., F. Stewart and J. Yermo (2011), "Promoting Longer-Term Investment by Institutional Investors: Selected Issues and Policies", *OECD Journal: Financial Market Trends*, Vol. 2011/1, OECD Publishing, Paris, *http://dx.doi.org/10.1787/19952872*.

Domanski, D., R. Moessner and W. Nelson (2014), "Central banks as lender of last resort: Experiences during the 2007-10 crisis and lessons for the future", *BIS Papers*, No. 79c, Bank for International Settlements, Basel, *www.bis.org/publ/bppdf/bispap79.pdf*.

ECB (2017), *Eurosystem Consolidated Statements*, European Central Bank, Frankfurt, *https://sdw.ecb.europa.eu/browseTable.do?node=9691294*.

ECB (2017), *Financial Vehicle Corporations*, European Central Bank, Frankfurt, *https://sdw.ecb.europa.eu/browse.do?node=9691119*.

European Union (2012), *Consolidated versions of the Treaty on European Union and the Treaty on the Functioning of the European Union*. European Union, Brussels.

Eurostat (2017), *National Accounts (including GDP)*, Eurostat, Luxembourg, *http://ec.europa.eu/eurostat/web/national-accounts/data/database*.

Goodhart, C.A. (2010), "The changing role of central banks" *BIS Working Papers*, No. 326, Bank for International Settlements, Basel, *www.bis.org/publ/work326.pdf*.

Illing, G. and P. König (2014), "The European Central Bank as lender of last resort", *DIW Economic Bulletin*, German Institute of Economic Research, Berlin, Vol. 9, pp. 16-28, www.diw.de/documents/publikationen/73/diw_01.c.488640.de/diw_econ_bull_2014-09-3.pdf.

Insurance Europe and O. Wyman (2013), *Funding the Future – Insurers' Role as Institutional Investors*, Insurance Europe, Brussels, www.insuranceeurope.eu/funding-future.

Insurance Europe (2014), *Why Insurers Differ from Banks*, Insurance Europe, Brussels, www.insuranceeurope.eu/why-insurers-differ-banks-0.

Keelley, B. and P. Love (2010), "Pensions and the crisis", in *From Crisis to Recovery: The causes, Course and Consequences of the Great Recession*, OECD Publishing, Paris, http://dx.doi.org/10.1787/9789264077072-en.

Kock, M.H. (1982), *A Banca Central*, Banco de Portugal, Lisbon.

Lima, F. and P. David (2011), "*Insurance Companies and Pension Funds: Assessing the Dynamics of their Assets and Liabilities*", Presented at ISI Proceedings – 58th World Statistical Congress, 21 August, Dublin.

OECD (2017a), "Financial Balance Sheets, SNA 2008 (or SNA 1993): Non-consolidated stocks, annual", *OECD National Accounts Statistics* (database), http://dx.doi.org/10.1787/data-00720-en ; and "Financial Balance Sheets, SNA 2008 (or SNA 1993): Consolidated stocks, annual", *OECD National Accounts Statistics* (database), http://dx.doi.org/10.1787/data-00719-en; and "Institutional investors' assets and liabilities", *OECD Institutional Investors Statistics* (database), http://dx.doi.org/10.1787/c4292928-en.

OECD (2017b), *OECD Insurance Statistics*, OECD Publishing, Paris, http://dx.doi.org/10.1787/2307843x.

OECD (2017c), *Institutional Investors*, OECD Publishing, Paris, http://dx.doi.org/10.1787/2225207x.

OECD (2016a), *Life Expectancy at Birth*, OECD Publishing, Paris, http://dx.doi.org/10.1787/health_glance-2015-6-en.

OECD (2016b), *Fertility Rates*, OECD Publishing, Paris, http://dx.doi.org/10.1787/8272fb01-en.

OECD (2015), "Coverage of private pensions", in *OECD, Pensions at a Glance 2015: OECD and G20 Indicators*, OECD Publishing, Paris, http://dx.doi.org/10.1787/19991363.

OECD (2008 and 2009), *Pension Markets in Focus*, OECD Publishing, Paris, www.oecd.org/daf/pensions/pensionmarkets.

Rossi, S. (2014), *Monetary Policy and the Independence of Central Banks: The Experience of the European Central Bank in the Global Crisis*, 19 November, University of Verona, University complex of Vicenza, Vicenza.

US Federal Reserve (2017), *National Accounts*, US Federal Reserve, Washington, DC, www.federalreserve.gov/apps/fof/FOFTables.aspx.

Wintersteller, M. (2013), "Luxembourg's Financial Centre and its Deposits", *Country Focus*, Vol. 10, Issue 9, European Commission, ECFIN, Brussels, http://ec.europa.eu/economy_finance/publications/country_focus/2013/pdf/cf_vol10_issue9_en.pdf.

Chapter 4

Households and their financial behaviour

Michael Andreasch (Oesterreichische Nationalbank)

> This chapter explains the financial behaviour of households as consumers, investors in financial and non-financial assets (dwellings), and owners of unincorporated enterprises. At the aggregate level, households are typically net "savers" and net lenders. This means that they provide funds to other domestic sectors and to non-residents. The creation and the structure of households' financial wealth depends on several factors, such as the level of and change in disposable income and saving, the financial system, market conditions, and regulations related to pensions and taxes. To fully comprehend the relevant data, it is also important to understand the measurement of the relevant statistics, and to clarify what is actually meant with "households". Data sources and compilation routines as well as the statistical standards of the 2008 System of National Accounts (2008 SNA) are addressed in this chapter, with the aim to show which conclusions can be drawn from the data – and which cannot.

The statistical data for Israel are supplied by and under the responsibility of the relevant Israeli authorities. The use of such data by the OECD is without prejudice to the status of the Golan Heights, East Jerusalem and Israeli settlements in the West Bank under the terms of international law.

1. Households as consumers, entrepreneurs, investors and net lenders

Components of GDP, such as final consumption, investment and net exports/imports are seen as the main drivers of economic growth. Households are involved in this process, directly and indirectly, through their final consumption expenditures and through government consumption on behalf of households. Households also act as entrepreneurs by investing in buildings, machinery and equipment related to their business as self-employed workers or sole proprietors. As owners of dwellings they also invest in real estate. All these activities are reflected in the non-financial accounts, which have a direct link with the financial accounts and balance sheets. The sequence of non-financial accounts provides information on saving (i.e., disposable income minus final consumption), which is a key element for the provision of funds. This saving is partly used for investments in non-financial assets. For the remaining part, households are net lenders, which is the case in most OECD countries. In some countries, however, the investments in non-financial assets are larger than saving, and households on an aggregate level need additional funding from other sectors, thus becoming net borrowers. The resulting net lending/borrowing is mirrored in the financial accounts. This parity can be written as follows:

Saving *plus* Net capital transfers *minus* Non-financial investments =
Net lending/borrowing =
Financial investments minus Financing (in the case of households, these are primarily debt liabilities)

After a short discussion of compiling with estimates for the transactions and positions of households, the financial behaviour of households is discussed in much more detail below. However, before doing so, one should note that the term "households" often includes "non-profit institutions serving households (NPISHs)". These institutions consist of, for example, churches or religious societies, social, cultural, recreational or sports clubs, political parties, trade unions, etc. Although culturally important, they are less significant from a purely economic perspective. Usually, little financial information is available on these institutions, which is why they are often grouped together with households.

Measuring transactions and positions of households

From a statistical point of view, it is important to stress that the data on households are often derived from a horizontal balancing procedure, in which the statistics on households are based on the information of counterparty sectors. For example, in the case of debt, the liabilities of households are estimated through the use of information from the creditors. These creditors traditionally consist of domestic banks and other financial institutions, and also the government (granting subsidised loans). This procedure is quite common due to the general lack of timely data with the requested frequency from households themselves. Moreover, results from household surveys often show a lack of coverage, due to, for example, an underrepresentation of the rich and wealthy (as they are less inclined to participate in a survey). As compared to a survey of the average age of people, where missing the extremes will have a negligible impact on the results, missing extremely wealthy people can have a very significant impact on the aggregate results. Therefore, from a statistical perspective, fully capturing the financial and non-financial behaviour of households via surveys is not straightforward, whereas the counterparty information is usually well defined and observed; see further discussion of data sources in the "Going further" section at the end of this chapter.

Role of households

Household behaviour, both financial and non-financial, is a key element of national accounts, due to the role households play in the generation of income and wealth of the economy. One could also say that, ultimately, it's all about households, in the sense that the economy is a means for people (or households) to generate income and well-being.

The financial accounts and balance sheets cover the accumulation of household financial assets and debt as well as the resulting stocks. The household sector simultaneously combines a variety of economic activities: consumers of goods and services; small business entrepreneurs investing in non-financial assets, farmers or other persons running sole proprietorships; stakeholders in companies; owners of dwellings; and finally net lenders or net borrowers. Individuals in the household sector are extremely heterogeneous in terms of the level and structure of (financial and non-financial) wealth and therefore in their (financial) behaviour, which means that monitoring and analysing at the aggregate level only tells part of the story.

Households as consumers

Households have two distinct sources of financing their final consumption expenditures: internal financial sources, which mainly consist of their disposable income (including net capital transfers), and external financial sources, such as consumer loans to supplement their internal sources. How, and how much, households consume critically affects economic growth. The contribution of private consumption to Gross Domestic Product (GDP) ranged between 30% and 70% for OECD countries in the years 2011-15. In the majority of countries, the ratio is close to the mean value of 55% for all OECD countries; see Figure 4.1.

Figure 4.1. **Final consumption of households**
Five-year average, 2011-15; percentage of GDP

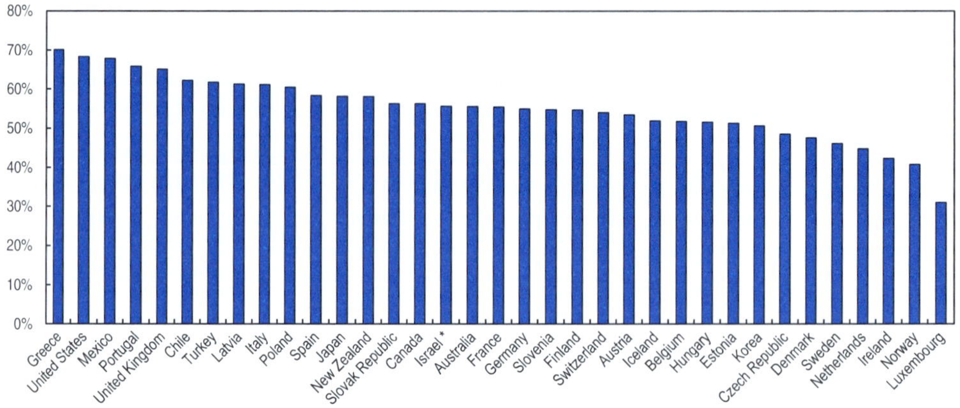

* The statistical data for Israel are supplied by and under the responsibility of the relevant Israeli authorities. The use of such data by the OECD is without prejudice to the status of the Golan Heights, East Jerusalem and Israeli settlements in the Westbank under the terms of international law.
Source: OECD (2017), "Aggregate National Accounts, SNA 2008 (or SNA 1993): Gross domestic product", *OECD National Accounts Statistics* (database), http://dx.doi.org/10.1787/data-00001-en.

StatLink http://dx.doi.org/10.1787/888933588250

In other words, on average, 55 cents of every dollar or euro of total GDP is related to final consumption expenditure of households, such as expenditures on housing (rentals, including imputed rentals for owner-occupied dwellings, water, electricity, gas and other fuels), health, education, furnishing, equipment, food and beverages (including restaurants), etc. In many countries expenditures on health and education are actually done or reimbursed by the government. They are thus part of government consumption expenditure, but in the analysis of the so-called "actual consumption" they are considered as final consumption by households. Most of the funds spent by households are related to consumption of non-durable goods and services. However, consumption also includes expenditures on durable goods, like cars, TVs and computers, unless they are used in the production of goods and services by unincorporated enterprises and self-employed, or they relate to major renovations by owner-occupiers of dwellings.

The most important factor for the analysis of the financial behaviour of households as consumers is the volume of new consumer loans, which are normally granted by banks or other financial institutions. The measurement of new consumer loans is rather challenging, because financial accounts and balance sheets are usually shown on a net basis (deducting down-payments of existing loans from the incurrence of new loans). However, data derived from the ECB interest rate statistics on new loans show that, in the period 2005-15, consumer loans typically account for around 4% of overall consumption in the Euro Area as a whole, with a rather stable pattern over the years. One may assume that most of these consumer loans are related to the purchase of consumer durables such as cars.

Households as investors in financial and non-financial assets (dwellings)

The part of disposable income that is not consumed represents saving. Saving is important for understanding both shorter- and longer-term financial behaviour of households. Saving by households is primarily invested in both financial assets (deposits, securities, pension plans, etc.) and dwellings. Saving may also be used – primarily by self-employed persons – for investments in commercial property, machinery, equipment, etc. needed to set up or extend small businesses. In most countries, the single most important form of household debt relates to mortgage loans for the purchase of dwellings. The development of the debt levels is heavily influenced by the price movements in the housing market.

Figure 4.2 shows household financial investments and non-financial investments of selected OECD countries in the last 20 years. In line with the vulnerabilities after the 2007-09 economic and financial crisis and the low interest rates in the middle of the 2010s, there is a clear shift in preferences from investing in financial assets towards investing in non-financial assets, notably investments in real estate and gold. In 2015, the latest year available, financial investments regain strength, and are almost equal to non-financial investments.

The "life-cycle" and "permanent income" hypothesis, as developed by Franco Modigliani and Milton Friedman, suggests that individuals borrow when they are young (e.g. mortgage loans for the purchase of dwellings, student loans or small business loans), save during the majority of their working lives, and dis-save when they retire, possibly also leaving, in the permanent income hypothesis, bequests to their descendants. In normal circumstances, households as a whole tend to consume less than they earn, thus providing a steady flow of saving to the economy. Economies with few retirees and many young and middle-aged workers will typically save more than economies characterised by a high number of retirees. How demographic trends affect macro-economic developments is discussed in more detail in Chapter 9.

Figure 4.2. **Household financial and non-financial investment of selected OECD countries***

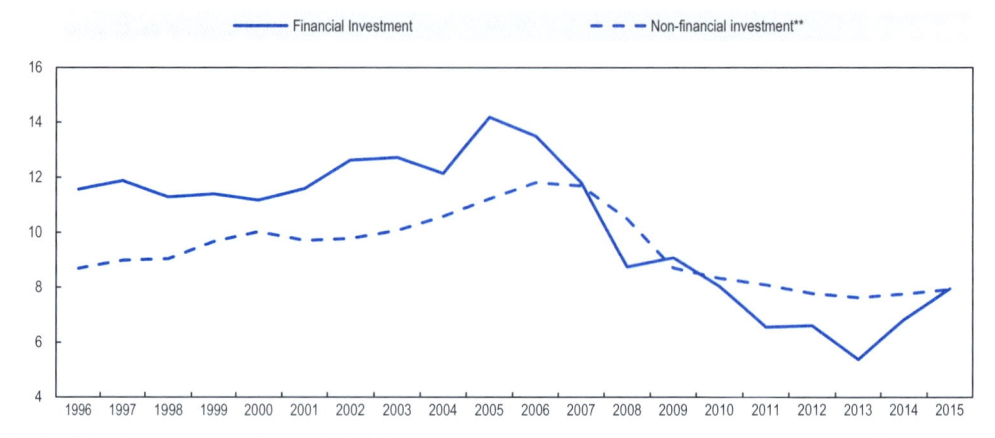

Percentage of household Gross Disposable Income (GDI)

* The following OECD countries are included: Austria, Belgium, Czech Republic, Denmark, Estonia, Finland, France, Germany, Hungary, Ireland, Italy, Netherlands, Norway, Poland, Portugal, Slovak Republic, Slovenia, Spain, Sweden, Switzerland, United Kingdom, United States.
** Non-financial investments refer to gross investments, i.e. not adjusted for consumption of fixed capital (depreciation).
Source: OECD (2017), "Detailed National Accounts, SNA 2008 (or SNA 1993): Non-financial accounts by sectors, annual", *OECD National Accounts Statistics* (database), http://dx.doi.org/10.1787/data-00034-en.

StatLink ⟶ http://dx.doi.org/10.1787/888933588326

Households as entrepreneurs and owners of companies

Before discussing the financial behaviour of households in their role as entrepreneurs, it is key to understand their role in the production of goods and services, as owners of small businesses or as self-employed. On the one hand households can act as entrepreneurs, and invest in non-financial assets related to their business. These investments are reflected in the non-financial accounts, and therefore do not directly affect the understanding of the financial accounts and balance sheets. On the other hand, households can also operate as stakeholders of companies, by making a portfolio investment, through buying shares on organised stock markets, or investing more strategically, such as by acquiring stakes in small and medium-sized enterprises (SMEs). For some countries, equity holdings in SMEs play an important role in the inter-linkage between households and the non-financial corporations' sector, depending on where the enterprises are recorded. For more details on the non-financial corporations sector, see Chapter 5. While the role of households as consumers is rather well defined and traceable in the national accounts data, one usually cannot separately distinguish households as entrepreneurs for the full set of accounts, because their entrepreneurial behaviour is fully intertwined with their behaviour as consumers.

Looking more closely to the sector allocation of SMEs, the 2008 System of National Accounts (2008 SNA) makes a distinction between incorporated and unincorporated enterprises. Enterprises with a separate legal status, which includes relatively small limited liability companies, are always recorded in the corporations sector. On the other hand, an unincorporated enterprise is normally recorded in the household sector, unless the enterprise "… has sufficient information to compile a complete set of accounts and is operated as if it were a separate corporation and whose de facto relationship to its owner is that of a corporation to its shareholders" (SNA 2008, paragraph 4.42). The latter guidance may, however, be implemented quite differently across countries. For example, in the National Income and Production Accounts (NIPA) of the United States, all enterprises, both incorporated and unincorporated, are grouped together in the "business sector". However, for reasons of international comparability, the United States provides data to the OECD in which the enterprises are allocated to the various sectors in line with the international standards.

There are other diverging practices across countries in the allocation of unincorporated enterprises to either the households' or the corporations' sector, but not so extreme as in the case of the US NIPA. In some cases, the diverging practices may be related to the kind of source information that is available for the household sector. As stated before, the compilation of data for the households' sector is often not based on direct observations, but on data from the counterparty sectors, such as the information on lending which may be based on information from banks. In these sources, the delineation of sectors may be different from the one applied in the 2008 SNA. Another point concerns the allocation of family trusts (foundations or funds), which are designed purely to manage the financial and non-financial wealth of very wealthy individuals. If these funds have some form of autonomy, they should be treated as part of the financial corporations' sector in the SNA, but this rule of autonomy may be applied quite differently. Divergences across countries may also be the result of institutional arrangements, such as differences in legislation affecting the economic behaviour of people across countries. They may also be related to differences in the interpretation and the application of international standards by statisticians across the world, especially when it comes to interpreting when the de facto relationship of an unincorporated enterprise is that of a corporation to its shareholders, as discussed above. Some countries apply this criterion very strictly, while others use a looser interpretation. The analysis of the accounts for households in their role as entrepreneur, including the indicators that can be derived from these accounts, therefore needs to be done with some caution, as these divergences may hamper the international comparability of the results.

For example, Figure 4.3 shows the equity holdings of households for a number of OECD countries, as a percentage of their total wealth. The differences are quite startling, ranging from more than 50% in Estonia to next to zero in the

Figure 4.3. **Household wealth in equity, 2015**
Percentage of total financial wealth

[Bar chart showing household wealth in equity as percentage of total financial wealth for various countries, from Estonia (~51%) highest to Slovak Republic (~8%) lowest. Countries in order: Estonia, Finland, Sweden, United States, Hungary, Chile, Belgium, Spain, Denmark, Norway, Italy, Slovenia, Czech Republic, Portugal, Latvia, Austria, France, Poland, Greece, Australia, Canada, Korea, Israel, Ireland, Luxembourg, Switzerland, Japan, Germany, Turkey, United Kingdom, Netherlands, Slovak Republic.]

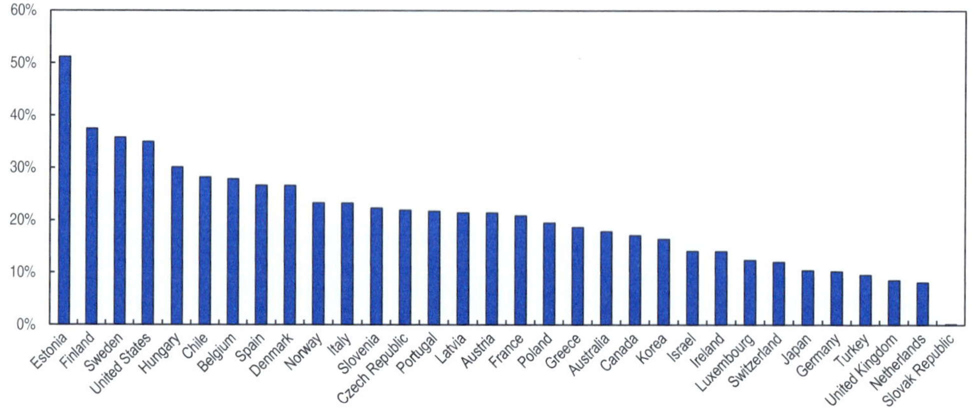

Source: OECD (2017), "Financial Balance Sheets, SNA 2008 (or SNA 1993): Consolidated stocks, annual", *OECD National Accounts Statistics* (database), http://dx.doi.org/10.1787/data-00719-en.

StatLink http://dx.doi.org/10.1787/888933588345

Slovak Republic. This may be related to differences in the prevalence of households to invest in shares and other equity. It may also be related to accumulated pension wealth in some countries that have established large funded pension schemes. However, an important factor can also be related to the recording of a significant number of SMEs as separate entities in the corporations' sector. If this is the case, it automatically leads to an increase of equity wealth, while in the case of consolidation of unincorporated enterprises in the households' sector, no equity is registered. In the latter case, instead of equity, the assets and liabilities of the enterprise are recorded in the accounts of the household sector.

To arrive at a better understanding of the role of households as entrepreneurs, it may be necessary to go back to the survey data, and try to collect information on the transactions and positions that are specifically related to the relevant enterprises. This information could, for example, be derived from integrated household surveys which include income statements and balance sheet data of (unincorporated) enterprises. Tax data may be another source of information, as tax authorities often ask specific questions on the income and wealth related to (unincorporated) SMEs. To better understand the role of households as stakeholders of companies, one may again want to look at more granular data. For example, Magri (2009) has tested for Italy the importance of a household's initial wealth for becoming an entrepreneur. The results showed that the probability of becoming an entrepreneur is positively correlated with a household's initial wealth, but that the effect is also dependent on the size of wealth, with a smaller effect for the richest households.

Households as net lenders or borrowers

Saving plus net receipts of capital transfers minus the investments in non-financial assets represent net lending (or net borrowing), i.e. the residual income that is available for increasing financial wealth. By definition, this residual is equal to the balance of net purchases of financial assets minus the net incurrence of liabilities, although in practice one may observe statistical discrepancies. From a macro-economic viewpoint, households are typically net lenders, i.e. they have a positive net lending/net borrowing, and thus add each year to their net financial wealth. The total stock of wealth, including non-financial assets, is reflected on the balance sheets. Apart from net acquisitions of non-financial assets and the above-mentioned transactions in financial assets and liabilities, the stocks may also be affected by holding gains (or losses) and by other changes in the volume of assets (e.g. catastrophic losses, theft, etc.); see Box 4.1 for a more detailed explanation.

Box 4.1. **Moving from (accumulated) flows to stocks**

As noted in Chapter 1, changes in financial stocks are determined by net purchases of financial assets and by the net incurrence of liabilities or financing. These transactions are recorded in the financial accounts. In addition, stock levels may change as a consequence of flows recorded in the "other changes in assets accounts", which comprise price changes (revaluations) and other changes in volume of assets. The latter are often referred to as stock-flow adjustments. A recap, with a particular focus on aspects relevant for households, is provided in the Table 4.1.

Table 4.1. **Summary of changes in stocks**

$Stocks_{t-1}$	Changes of stocks due to			= $Stocks_t$
	+/-Transactions $_t$	+/-Revaluations $_t$	+/-Other changes in volume $_t$	
	Gross purchases minus gross sales (including realised holdings gains and losses) plus accrued interest (reinvestment of interest until payment)	Changes in the value of stocks due to changes in the exchange rates of foreign currencies; market price changes based on unrealised holding gains and losses including writedowns of tradable securities; changes due to model assumptions (discount rate, etc.), and price changes in unit-linked contracts and defined contribution schemes of individual life insurance and pensions ; all changes due to price and volatility changes of underlying assets in the case of financial derivatives	Changes due to changes in demographic assumptions in the case of insurance and pension schemes *plus* Uncompensated seizures, write-offs of debt, methodological changes	

Box 4.1. **Moving from (accumulated) flows to stocks** *(cont.)*

On average, stock-flow adjustments account for one-third of the total change in financial wealth of households for all OECD countries in the last 20 years. Net purchases thus account for two-thirds of the increase in household financial wealth. However, as Figure 4.4 clearly shows, patterns are quite different across countries. In many countries, the other changes in assets represent more than half of the changes in the value of stocks.

Figure 4.4. **Changes in household financial wealth: contribution of financial transactions versus other changes in assets, 1995-2014**
Percentage of household net wealth at the end of 1995

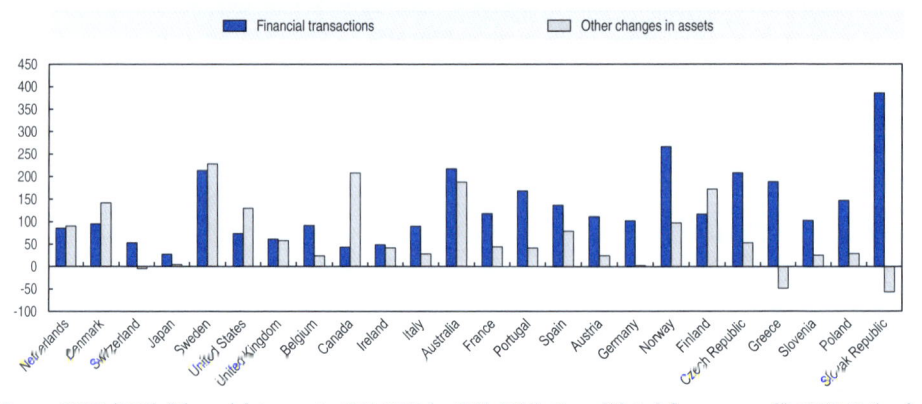

Source: OECD (2017), "Financial Accounts, SNA 2008 (or SNA 1993): Consolidated flows, annual", OECD *National Accounts Statistics* (database), http://dx.doi.org/10.1787/data-00716-en; and "Financial Balance Sheets, SNA 2008 (or SNA 1993): Consolidated stocks, annual", OECD *National Accounts Statistics* (database), http://dx.doi.org/10.1787/data-00719-en.

StatLink ⟶ http://dx.doi.org/10.1787/888933588364

The resources and uses of funds can be analysed by comparing the total financial and non-financial investments with the underlying funding through saving, net capital transfers and borrowing (for households this mainly represents bank loans); this can provide very useful insights. The analysis adds to the understanding of the possible causality between certain types of investments and the sources of funding, i.e. whether or not saving directly influences financial investments or how non-financial investments are financed through internal and/or external funding. Figures 4.5 to 4.7 below illustrate this analysis for three types of countries; i) countries where households show a rather stable net lending situation; ii) countries where households switched from a role as net lenders to a role as net borrowers role and vice versa; and finally iii) countries where households are more or less permanent net borrowers.

In 14 OECD countries,[1] households almost continuously provided funds as net lenders to other sectors in the past 20 years. Generally, net lending as a percentage of gross disposable income (GDI)[2] ranged from close to zero to 10%, with an average of 6%, with the exception of Switzerland, where households showed consistent net lending of more than 10%. However, quite remarkable differences can be observed over time. While households' net lending in Sweden was close to zero in the late 1990s, their net lending increased in recent years to more than 10%. In contrast, the net lending position of Italian households decreased steadily from above 10% in 1995 to 3% in 2013-14. The stocks of accumulated net financial wealth, not taking into account non-financial assets, for these countries ranged from 1.1 to 4.0 times their GDI in 2014. Figure 4.5 illustrates trends in net lending for a selection of these 14 countries.

Figure 4.5. **Net lending for households consistently being net lenders, 1995-2014**
Percentage of GDI (adjusted)

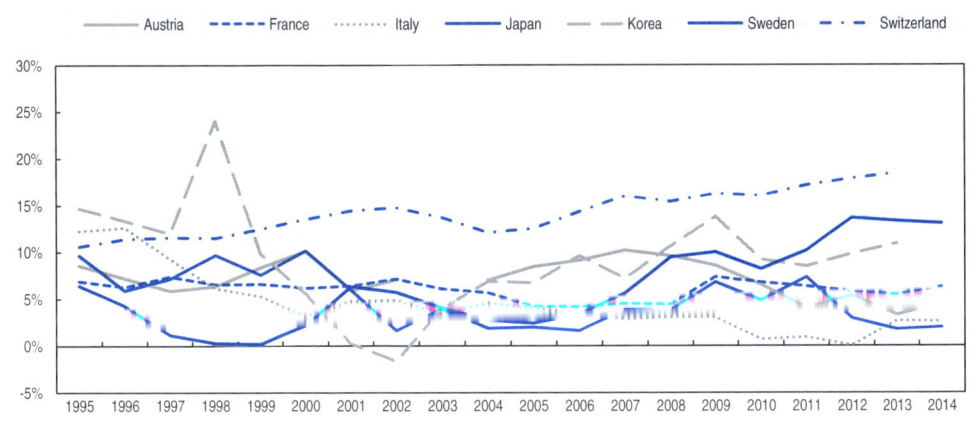

Source: OECD (2017), "Financial Accounts, SNA 2008 (or SNA 1993): Consolidated flows, annual", OECD National Accounts Statistics (database), http://dx.doi.org/10.1787/data-00716-en.

StatLink ⟶ http://dx.doi.org/10.1787/888933588383

In another nine countries,[3] one can observe a shift from households being net lenders to becoming net borrowers, or vice versa. In most of these countries, households were net lenders until the beginning of the 21th century (with the exception of Irish households), and they became net borrowers against the background of the burst of the internet bubble. In most of the countries, the financial position changed again into a net lending position after the 2007-09 economic and financial crisis, partly due to an increase in the saving ratio. For example, in Estonia and Ireland the gross saving ratio was negative until 2007 and became positive from 2008 onwards. Net financial wealth in relation to (adjusted) GDI deviates significantly across these countries, ranging from 0.6 (Norway, Slovak Republic) to 3.1 (the United Kingdom) and 4.0 (the United States). For a further discussion on the impact of financial crises and globalisation on key financial accounts indicators, reference is made to Chapter 10. Figure 4.6 illustrates trends in net lending for a selection of these nine countries.

4. HOUSEHOLDS AND THEIR FINANCIAL BEHAVIOUR

Figure 4.6. **Net lending for households changing from net lenders to net borrowers, and vice versa, 1995-2014**
Percentage of GDI (adjusted)

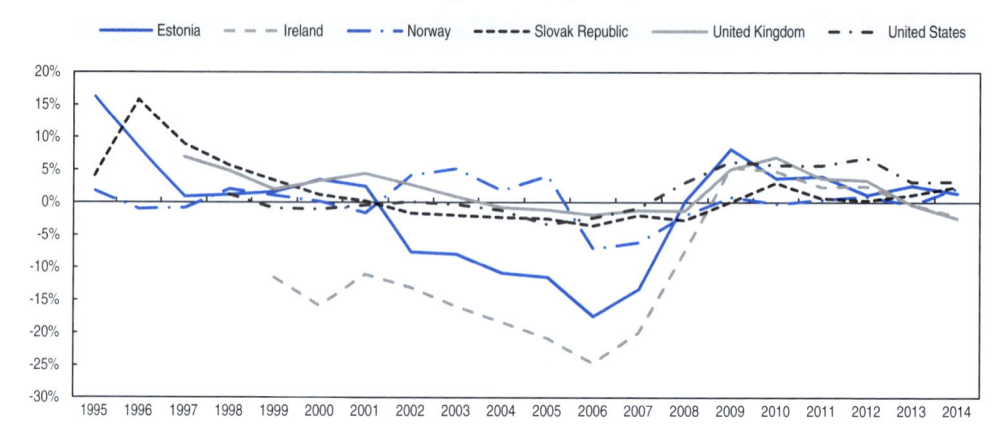

Source: OECD (2017), "Financial Accounts, SNA 2008 (or SNA 1993): Consolidated flows, annual", *OECD National Accounts Statistics* (database), http://dx.doi.org/10.1787/data-00716-en.

StatLink http://dx.doi.org/10.1787/888933588402

Figure 4.7. **Net lending for households as nearly-consistent net borrowers, 1995-2014**
Percentage of GDI (adjusted)

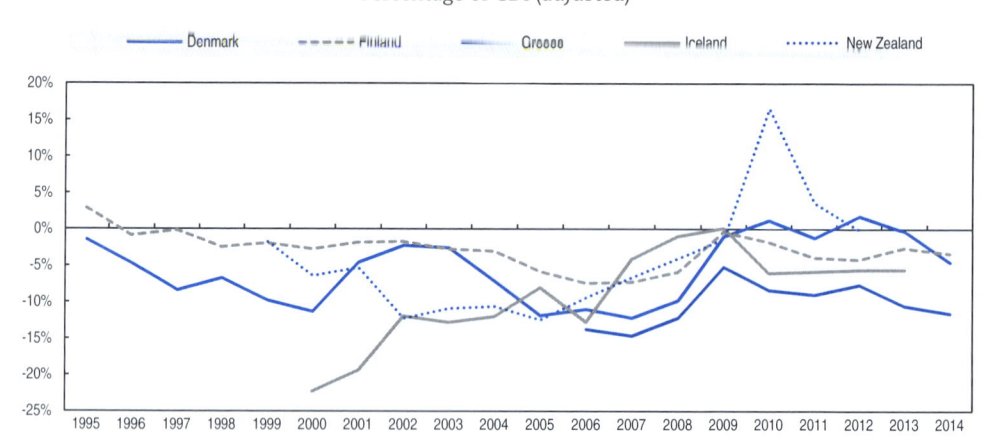

Source: OECD (2017), "Financial Accounts, SNA 2008 (or SNA 1993): Consolidated flows, annual", *OECD National Accounts Statistics* (database), http://dx.doi.org/10.1787/data-00716-en.

StatLink http://dx.doi.org/10.1787/888933588421

Finally, in five countries, including three Northern European countries, households were mainly net borrowers in the last 20 years, with a downward trend since the beginning of the century up until the 2007-09 economic and financial crisis. All these countries had negative saving ratios or saving ratios close to zero, well below the average of OECD countries for the entire period.

Contrary to the households which showed a change in behaviour, they did not increase their saving after the financial crises. The best example to show that nearly permanent net borrowing does not automatically lead to a lower net wealth position is Denmark. Net financial wealth, again excluding non-financial assets, stood at 3.1 times their (adjusted) GDI at the end of 2014. This ratio is above the average value for all OECD countries.

Looking at these developments from the perspective of the counterparty sectors, changes in the financial position of households can also have an impact on the financial position of other economic sectors, as household net lending can be an important source of funding for other domestic sectors or the Rest of the World. On the other hand, if households are in a net borrowing situation, they may become very dependent on funding inflows through the financial system (mainly banks).

2. The interlinkages between income, saving, financial and non-financial investments, and debt

It is evident that the accumulated stock of financial assets can be important for individual well-being, as that stock represents resources available to maintain adequate levels of consumption and welfare, including, for example, after retirement. It also makes households more resilient to deal with misfortune, and thus provides them with more security. Households' financial assets are the result of two factors: the net acquisition of (certain types of) financial instruments from income not spent, and the impact of changes in the prices of the assets accumulated in the past. Overall households are free in their decision whether to invest in financial or non-financial assets. However, two aspects have to be taken into consideration here. First, individual households in countries with a high degree of private (funded) pension schemes are usually obliged to invest in pension plans, typically by building up pension entitlements held with pension funds and insurance corporations (see also Chapter 9). Second, households with outstanding bullet loans will have to invest in repayment vehicles, usually saving deposits, (unit linked) life insurance contracts or equity-oriented investment fund shares.

Looking at national accounts aggregates, the main questions that may arise during the analysis of households' financial investments, borrowing and the accumulation of financial (net) wealth are: "What are the main drivers of the developments in the different components?" and "How are they interlinked?" The following issues may be important in determining the actual financial behaviour of households over time, and allowing us to find explanations for the differences in the level and structure of (financial) wealth and liabilities across countries:

- From a macro-economic viewpoint:
  ❖ the level of and the development in disposable income and saving;

- the arrangements of the financial system (and the direct and indirect participation of households);
- changes in interest rates, and changes in prices on the stock markets and the housing market;
- the presence of funded pension schemes and social security systems;
- investments in and stocks of non-financial wealth (especially housing wealth);
- the tax regime for (the income on) assets and (payments of interest on) debt; and
- various legal aspects, such as foreign exchange liberalisation and credit standards.

● From a microeconomic viewpoint:
- the level of and development in income and wealth of individuals; and
- the impact of the life cycle hypothesis.

Figure 4.8 provides a graphical representation of the financial accounts, and the interconnectedness between the different stages of the sequence of accounts. A distinction is made between i) the direct impact (marked with solid arrows) of certain elements of income, saving, financial and non-financial investments, borrowing, stocks of financial and non-financial assets, and debt; and ii) the analytical interlinkages (marked with dashed arrows) between these components in the sequence of accounts.

In Figure 4.8, the presentation of accounts starts with disposable income. Disposable income is the income available to households to purchase consumer goods and services. It consists of the income received (e.g. compensation of employees, net income from engaging in unincorporated enterprises, interest, dividends, social benefits received, etc.) minus payments (e.g. taxes and social contributions, interest on mortgage loans, etc.). The result of disposable income minus final consumption expenditures, including the addition of the so-called "adjustments for the change in equity of households in pension funds", which corresponds to the financial investments in pension entitlements, represents the saving of households. The saving rate, the total saving as a percentage of disposable income,[4] is a key element in the analysis of the financial behaviour of households.

Saving represents the ability of households to make financial and non-financial investments. Here, it should be made clear that saving, as the term is used in national accounts, is not equivalent to putting additional money on saving deposits, which is only one way of investing money which is available through saving. Saving, including net receipts of capital transfers (like inheritances and large one-off donations between households) and the (net) acquisition of non-financial assets, is part of the so-called "capital account" in the sequence of accounts.

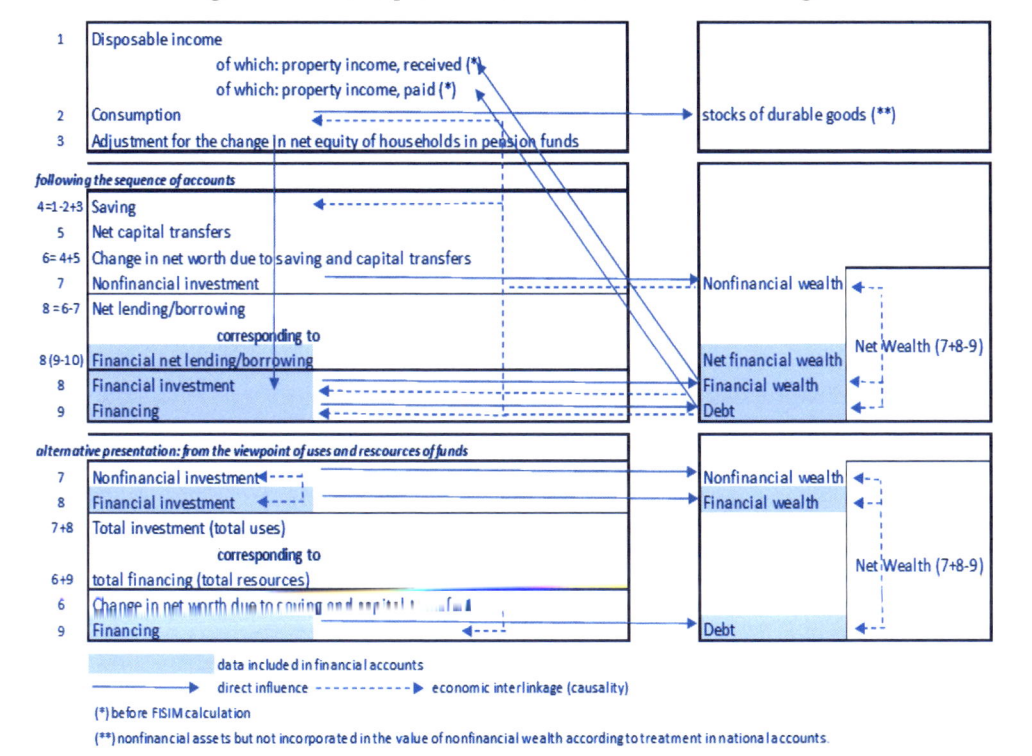

Figure 4.8. **The sequence of accounts and its interlinkages**

1	Disposable income		
	of which: property income, received (*)		
	of which: property income, paid (*)		
2	Consumption		stocks of durable goods (**)
3	Adjustment for the change in net equity of households in pension funds		
following the sequence of accounts			
4=1-2+3	Saving		
5	Net capital transfers		
6= 4+5	Change in net worth due to saving and capital transfers		
7	Nonfinancial investment		Nonfinancial wealth
8 =6-7	Net lending/borrowing		
	corresponding to		Net Wealth (7+8-9)
8 (9-10)	Financial net lending/borrowing		Net financial wealth
8	Financial investment		Financial wealth
9	Financing		Debt
alternative presentation: from the viewpoint of uses and rescources of funds			
7	Nonfinancial investment		Nonfinancial wealth
8	Financial investment		Financial wealth
7+8	Total investment (total uses)		
	corresponding to		Net Wealth (7+8-9)
6+9	total financing (total resources)		
6	Change in net worth due to saving and capital t...		
9	Financing		Debt

data included in financial accounts
→ direct influence ----▶ economic interlinkage (causality)
(*) before FISIM calculation
(**) nonfinancial assets but not incorporated in the value of nonfinancial wealth according to treatment in national accounts.

Financial investments, typically in the form of changes in cash holdings and current accounts, investments in saving deposits, net purchases of bonds, shares and mutual fund shares, and investments in other forms of participation like the holding of equity stakes in limited liability companies, and additional borrowing, usually in the form of loans, are recorded in the financial account. The capital account and the financial account both form part of the so-called "accumulation accounts", i.e. all the accounts which record transactions that have a direct impact on one or more items on the balance sheets. The other set of accounts in the national accounts are the so-called "current accounts", which consist of the production account, the generation and (re)distribution of income accounts, and the use of income account. For more details, see Chapter 1 and the OECD publication "Understanding National Accounts" (2014).

Financial investments on the asset side and changes in borrowing on the liability side are major drivers for the increase or decrease of stocks of financial assets and liabilities. Investments in housing in the form of dwellings (including land) significantly contribute to the change in non-financial assets owned by households. In addition, revaluation effects, and other changes in volume like catastrophic losses and reclassifications, also add to the changes in balance sheet positions. In this respect, it should be noted that national accounts do not consider holding gains (or losses) as part of property income, in contrast to the concept of "yield", which might influence the decision-making process of households in their portfolio allocation. Nevertheless, the levels of both financial assets and debt have an indirect impact on the level of disposable income, due to the fact that property incomes derived from financial assets minus interest paid for debt add to disposable income. All the above details and interlinkages are provided by a full-fledged system of national accounts. More details on the whole sequence of accounts is presented in Annex 2 of the 2008 SNA.

An alternative to the above, more traditional presentation in the form of a sequence of accounts in Figure 4.8, is represented in Figure 4.9. It shows the total "resources and uses of funds". The key difference is that the national account term "saving" is not used. What is presented is an overview of all available (financial) resources: i) internal financing in the form of disposable income, including the adjustment for the change in equity of households in pension entitlements and net capital transfers, and ii) external financing (normally in the form of loans and trade credits, broken down by purpose to reflect the linkage to certain items in the use of funds). These resources are then mirrored by the total uses, broken down into final consumption expenditures and non-financial and financial investments.

Consequently, this type of presentation sums up final consumption (above the line "saving" in Figure 4.8) and non-financial investments (below the line "saving" in Figure 4.8). Both elements are relevant for national accounts in different stages of the sequence of accounts, but the distinction is less relevant for individuals in their economic behaviour. The purchase of a new car (classified as final consumption) is often treated by an individual in much the same manner as the renovation of a dwelling (classified as non-financial investments), using both disposable income and debt financing as the resources for these expenditures.

Regardless of which concept is used, one should realise that there are always limitations to the analysis of the financial behaviour of the household sector. Figure 4.10 illustrates the interconnectedness between disposable income, saving and net financial wealth in a cross-country comparison (Andreasch et al., 2010), by showing data for the savings ratio, the disposable income per capita, and the net financial wealth per capita, as the arithmetic mean for the years 2005-09. The results highlight that there is no such thing as a straightforward link between the saving ratio and net financial wealth.

4. HOUSEHOLDS AND THEIR FINANCIAL BEHAVIOUR

Figure 4.9. **Alternative presentation using total resources and total uses of funds**

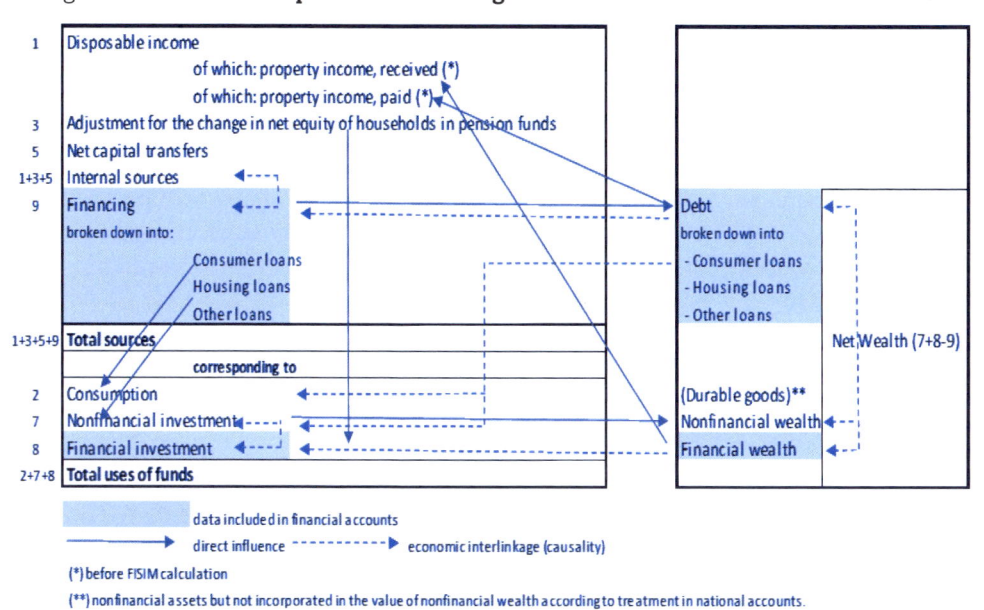

1	Disposable income			
	of which: property income, received (*)			
	of which: property income, paid (*)			
3	Adjustment for the change in net equity of households in pension funds			
5	Net capital transfers			
1+3+5	Internal sources			
9	Financing		Debt	
	broken down into:		broken down into	
	Consumer loans		- Consumer loans	
	Housing loans		- Housing loans	
	Other loans		- Other loans	
1+3+5+9	Total sources			Net Wealth (7+8-9)
	corresponding to			
2	Consumption		(Durable goods)**	
7	Nonfinancial investment		Nonfinancial wealth	
8	Financial investment		Financial wealth	
2+7+8	Total uses of funds			

data included in financial accounts
→ direct influence   ---▶ economic interlinkage (causality)
(*) before FISIM calculation
(**) nonfinancial assets but not incorporated in the value of nonfinancial wealth according to treatment in national accounts.

Figure 4.10. **Savings ratio, disposable income and net financial assets in EU countries**
Per capita, average for 2005-09

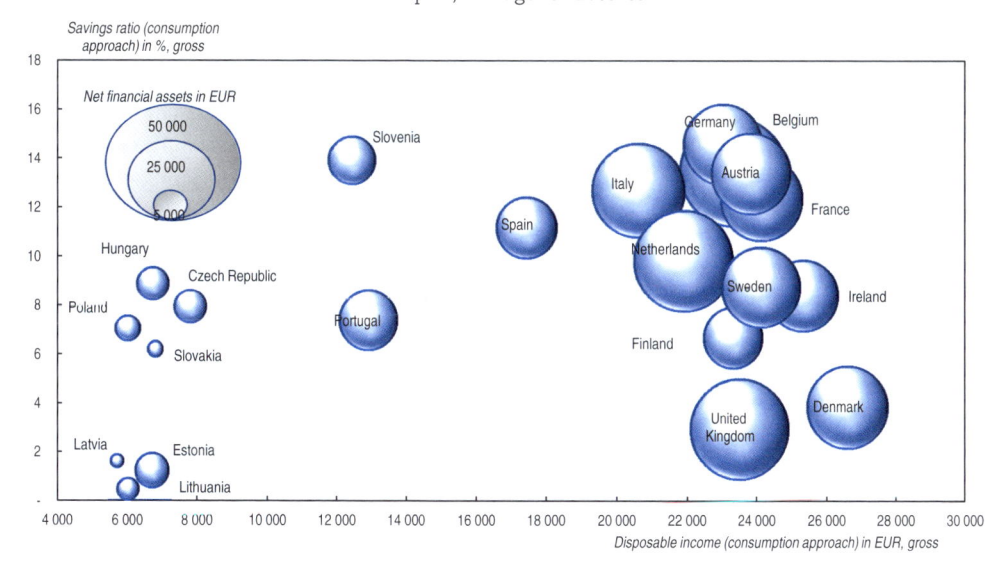

Source: Eurostat (2016), Sector accounts: Households and NPISH (database), http://ec.europa.eu/eurostat/web/sector-accounts/detailed-charts/households-npish.

StatLink ⟶ http://dx.doi.org/10.1787/888933588269

Although the majority of households in this exercise had a disposable income between 20 000 and 26 000 EUR per capita, the savings ratios and the net financial assets are very different across countries.

Furthermore, it is important to look at the linkages between saving and (financial and non-financial) investments, as well as the relationship between internal financing in the form of saving and external financing in the form of loans. There can be a close interaction between (the structure of) financial wealth and the volume of non-financial assets, especially when it comes to housing wealth. The "Three-Equation-Model" (Turk, 2015), for example, evaluates the interaction between house prices, housing stocks and household debt. Moreover, the increase (decrease) of wealth due to the accumulation of assets and holding gains can have a significant impact on household final consumption expenditure, which is a key element in economic growth. Recent studies show a large amount of research and policy analysis on these issues, thus putting even more emphasis on the importance of having high quality data on financial accounts and balance sheets.

The top half of Figure 4.11 illustrates the levels of financial assets of households as a percentage of their (gross) disposable income in OECD countries, while the bottom half shows the composition of the stocks of financial assets. The level of total financial assets diverged strongly across OECD countries. In the Netherlands, the ratio was 6.6 times disposable income in 2014, compared with 1.2 times disposable income in the Slovak Republic. Looking at the composition of financial assets, it can be observed that countries with a high proportion of funded pension schemes and life insurance contracts (including the so-called third pillar pension plans) are usually ranked above the median. In contrast, countries with households which tend to invest a major part of their financial portfolio in currency and deposits tend to rank below the median. In this respect Japan is one of the exceptions. Households in Japan tend to invest every second yen in deposits, but notwithstanding this behaviour their financial wealth to disposable income ratio was 4.4 in 2014, above the median financial assets to disposable income ratio for OECD countries in 2014 (3.6).

Many have researched the impact of the degree of convergence of financial systems across countries, and the relationship between financial systems and the structure of household financial wealth, against the background of a growing liberalisation and globalisation in the 1990s and 2000s. One would expect that globalisation, deregulation, economic integration, and harmonisation of regulations and corporate governance rules would support the harmonisation of financial system characteristics across countries. At a minimum, the increased interest of researchers into these types of issues has raised the question of whether the traditional distinction between the "bank-based" European continental financial system, with its focus on deposits,

4. HOUSEHOLDS AND THEIR FINANCIAL BEHAVIOUR

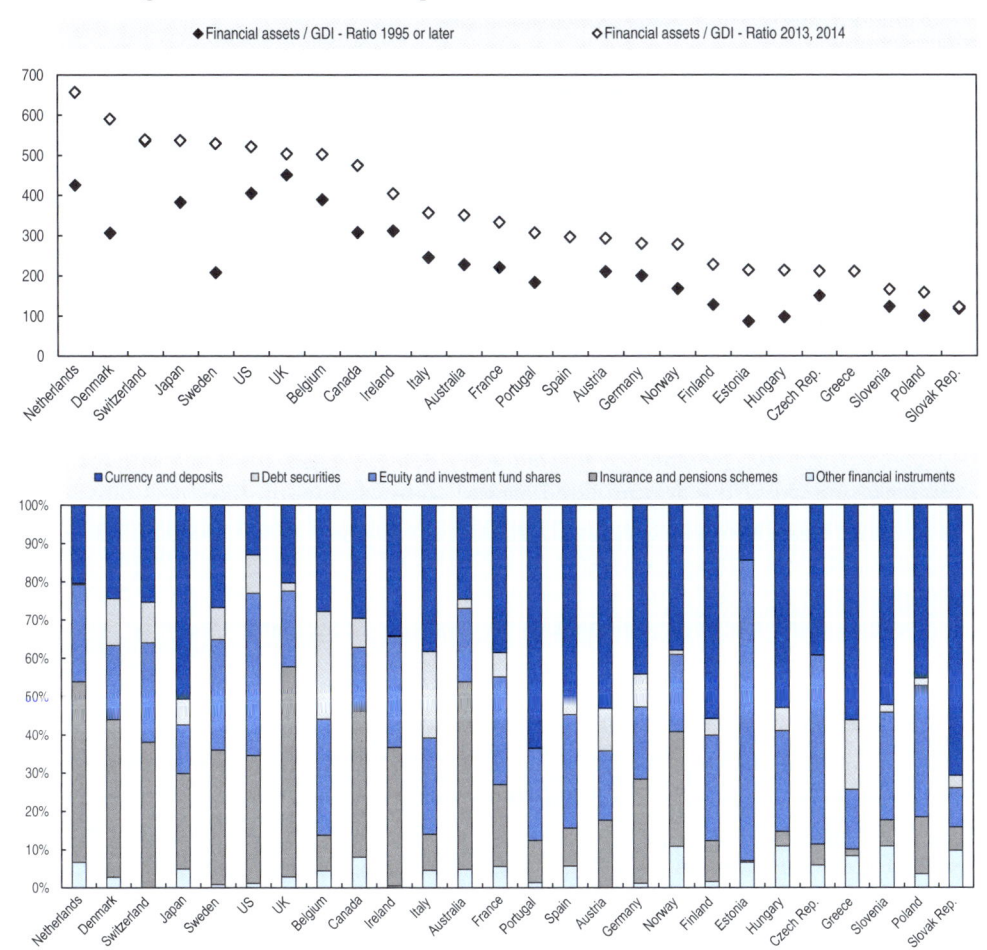

Figure 4.11. **Level and composition of households' financial assets***

* OECD, Canada and Japan according to SNA 93 data. Australia = consolidated data.
Source: OECD (2017), "Financial Balance Sheets, SNA 2008 (or SNA 1993): Non-consolidated stocks, annual", *OECD National Accounts Statistics* (database), http://dx.doi.org/10.1787/data-00720-en.
StatLink ⟶ http://dx.doi.org/10.1787/888933588288

versus the "market-based" Anglo-Saxon financial system, with its focus on shares and other types of equity, is here to stay. In any case, convergence is something that needs to be studied over a longer period of time. De Bonis et al. (2012) analysed the developments across nine OECD countries (Austria, Canada, France, Germany, Italy, Japan, Spain, the United Kingdom and the United States) for the period from 1980 to 2005, and showed that there is certain evidence of international convergence for households' total financial assets, equity components, insurance reserves and pension entitlements, while there are rather mixed results, and often no convergence, for currency, deposits and debt securities. The intensity of bank intermediation, in particular, was quite different across the analysed OECD countries.

De Bonis' analysis of long-term developments can also be decomposed by time periods. In the 1980s, which were characterised by the smooth growth of financial assets against the background of a credit ceiling, high bank reserve requirements and certain limitations to capital movements, constrained the expansion of financial assets in nearly all major OECD countries. This period was followed by the so-called "dot.com" bubble and the subsequent burst at the beginning of the 21st century. The boom resulted in a strong increase in stock market prices of tradable shares and mutual fund shares in households' portfolios. Subsequently, the 2007-09 economic and financial crisis caused financial (net) wealth to contract in the majority of countries. More pronounced effects could be observed in countries with high levels of investments in equity and/or countries in which pension entitlements related to defined contribution pension schemes (where the value of the entitlements has a direct link with the performance of the accumulated assets) were prominent, like the United Kingdom or the United States. The 2007-09 economic and financial crisis exposed the vulnerabilities of the financial situation of banks and other financial institutions, and led to an increase in government debt and a more pronounced focus on private debt. More details on the impact of the crisis are provided in Chapter 10.

Household financial behaviour in an ageing society

Against the background of an ageing population, a key factor driving long-term convergence in financial behaviour may be related to the organisation of employment-related pensions. Continental European countries, which currently primarily run pay-as-you-go social security systems, tend to increase, with the support of government incentives, the establishment and/or growth of the "second pillar" of funded collective pension schemes and the "third pillar" of individual pension arrangements (via life insurance or other forms of saving). Data for OECD countries show that funded pension entitlements in twelve countries account for 90% of total pension fund assets of all OECD countries. Within this group, the United States represents more than half of the pension fund assets of all OECD countries (Van der Wal, 2014).

The changing demographic conditions clearly raise challenges in ensuring the long-term adequacy of retirement benefits as well as questions about the sustainability of future government expenditures on pensions. The transformation from unfunded social security schemes into funded pensions may be accompanied by risk transfers to households, which could increase the vulnerability of the financial wealth of households, especially if the pension entitlements are directly related to the investment returns on accumulated assets. It has been observed, for example, that households' pension entitlements in countries with a focus on funded pension schemes dropped relatively strongly during the 2007-09 economic and financial crisis. This volatility may have a detrimental impact on future final consumption and saving streams, thus affecting the whole economy. Here, it should be noted that the recording and measurement of pension entitlements is not without its own problems, certainly if one would like to compare household wealth across countries. Further explanations are provided in Chapter 9.

More generally, when it comes to preparing for retirement, individuals can earmark nearly all financial instruments (cash, deposits, tradeable securities, and individual and collective pension plans) as well as their housing wealth, in addition to income streams from pay-as-you-go social security systems, to sustain their consumption level after retirement. The pension entitlements that are currently recorded in the system of national accounts only relate to (partially) funded employment-related pension schemes. Furthermore, entitlements from individual life insurance are recorded as "life insurance and annuity entitlements". On the other hand, entitlements that can be derived from pay-as-you-go schemes are not recognised as assets. This clearly hampers international comparability, as households may consider entitlements derived from the latter schemes as strong as the entitlements from funded pension schemes.

According to the requirements of the 2008 SNA, funded pension entitlements are split into defined benefit (DB) schemes and defined contribution (DC) schemes. In DC schemes, the pension entitlements are equal to the assets accumulated through past payments of contributions and investment income earned on the assets (after deduction of the costs of pension funds). The entitlements thus follow closely the market values of the accumulated assets. As pension funds normally apply fair value pricing with little variation in valuation methods across countries, the relevant pension entitlements are comparable across countries offering such a system, like Australia and the United States. In contrast, in the case of DB-systems, such as those in Canada, the Netherlands, Switzerland and the United Kingdom, pension entitlements are based on average wages and the number of years that someone has contributed to the scheme. The entitlements are calculated as the net present value of future benefits, appropriately discounted. However, the methods used to calculate entitlements in the various countries can differ considerably, thus affecting international comparability. For example, the discount rate applied has a significant impact on the level of these entitlements. In some countries this may be a market interest rate, whereas in other countries a long-term interest rate of 3-4% is applied. DB pension schemes may be under- or overfunded, and there is no direct link between the value of pension entitlements and the accumulated assets. It is assumed that the sponsoring employer will take care of the shortfall in funding.

To allow for a better international comparability of pension entitlements, a supplementary table has been developed as part of the 2008 SNA, with the aim of showing a comprehensive picture of all pension schemes, including the contingent entitlements related to pay-as-you-go social security schemes. As discussed earlier, a key question in measuring the level of pension entitlements for DB pension schemes (and, more broadly, pay-as-you-go schemes) is related to the discount rate used to arrive at the current value of future retirement benefits. If countries used the so-called Freiburg model, with the key assumption of a real discount rate of 3% (baseline), the entitlements for unfunded government employees' schemes would increase the assets of households by roughly 50% of GDP, while the entitlements for social security pay-as-you-go schemes would boost the level of assets on average by more than 230% of GDP. At the same time, these pension entitlements would have an equivalent impact on the level of government (contingent) liabilities.

The main counterparties of households

The financial behaviour of households can be monitored by looking at the changes in the types of financial assets they invest in, and the types of debt they incur. But it may also be useful to monitor changes in the debtors of household assets and the creditors of household debt. To be able to apply such an analysis, there is a need to go beyond the traditional financial accounts and balance sheets, and analyse the interlinkages between the various sectors. The 2007-09 economic and financial crisis showed the importance of risks related to the interconnectedness between countries and sectors. As a reaction to this, more countries started compiling from-whom-to-whom (FWTW) matrices, presenting, for each financial instrument, which sector invests in and borrows from which other sector. As discussed in previous chapters, this allows for an assessment of the importance of specific interconnections, e.g. the importance of households investing in bank deposits and bank debt securities for the refinancing position of banks. For illustrative purposes, the results for Austria are shown in Figure 4.12. The thickness and the direction of the arrows indicate the importance of certain creditors for the liability side of the debtors, whereby all financial instruments have been taken together. The size of the circles indicates the importance of financing within the same sector. One of the results that can be derived from Figure 4.12 is that households and non-resident investors are the main financers of the domestic monetary financial institutions (i.e. the traditional banks), with both contributing nearly the same proportion.

A more detailed analysis of household debt

Data derived from the financial accounts and balance sheets can also be used for a more detailed analysis of household debt. This debt mainly consists of loans (often granted by banks and other financial intermediaries) for housing

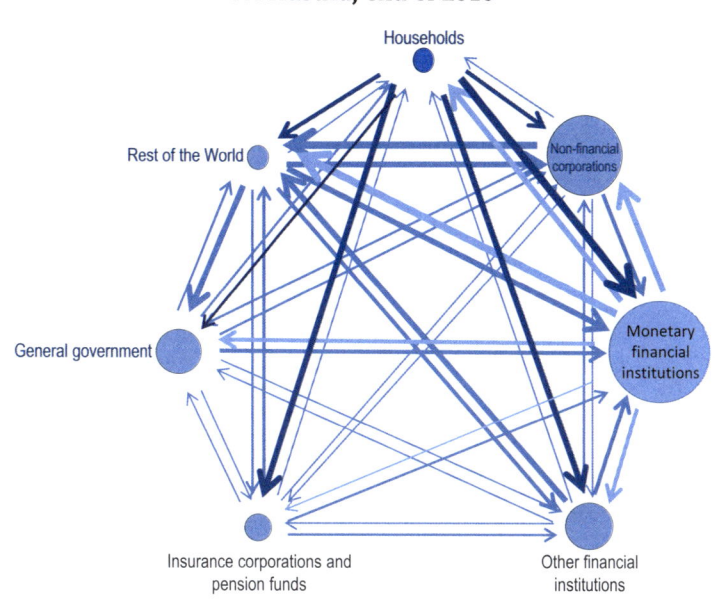

Figure 4.12. **The interconnections between sectors for Austria, end of 2016**

Source: Osterreichische Nationalbank (2017), *National Accounts* (database), www.oenb.at/en/Statistics/Standardized-Tables/financial-accounts.html.

(purchase and renovation), final consumption, and investments in non-residential buildings and equipment (mainly by entrepreneurs as part of the household sector). From the available time series data, it is evident that in OECD countries, on average two-thirds of household debt (ranging from 53% to 83% for individual countries) consist of housing loans. The analyses of household financial behaviour usually look at the household sector as a whole, thus ignoring the fact that not all households are indebted, and also that not all households have housing loans despite owning a dwelling or other kinds of real estate wealth. To arrive at a better understanding of potential risks and vulnerabilities, it is important to have more details on the various subgroups of households, the compilation of which is in a stage of development at the time of writing this book;[5] see also the next section of this chapter.

Figure 4.13 illustrates the indebtedness of households in relation to their GDI in 2014, a common presentation which can also be found in the OECD Dashboard on Households' Economic Well-being.[6] The debt service ratio (defined as the ratio of interest payments plus amortisations to GDI[7]) shows the proportion of the income which cannot be used for consumption. Denmark and the Netherlands show the highest debt levels, which is also driven by tax incentives on mortgage loans. Consequently, the debt service ratio for these countries is the highest amongst the observed OECD countries. Households in Germany, Austria and Italy had debt levels below 90 per cent of GDI, and less than 7 per cent of their GDI "reserved" for debt service.

Figure 4.13. **Debt and debt service ratios of households in OECD countries, 2016**

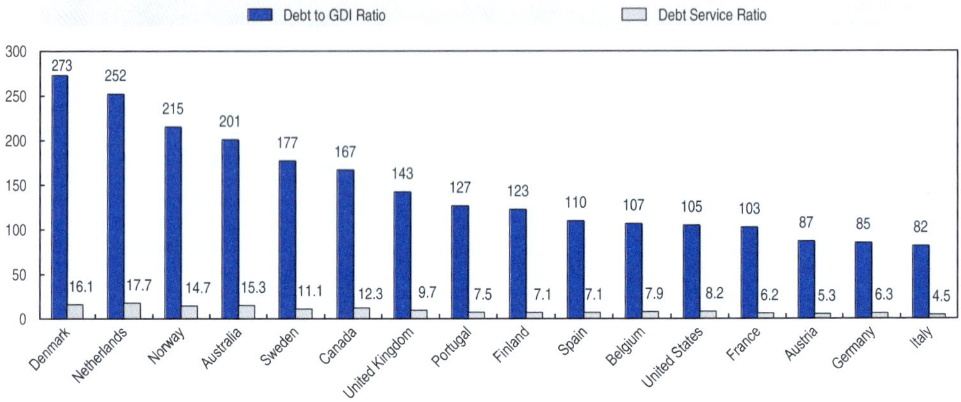

Country	Debt to GDI Ratio	Debt Service Ratio
Denmark	273	16.1
Netherlands	252	17.7
Norway	215	14.7
Australia	201	15.3
Sweden	177	11.1
Canada	167	12.3
United Kingdom	143	9.7
Portugal	127	7.5
Finland	123	7.1
Spain	110	7.1
Belgium	107	7.9
United States	105	8.2
France	103	6.2
Austria	87	5.3
Germany	85	6.3
Italy	82	4.5

Source: OECD (2017), "Financial Balance Sheets, SNA 2008 (or SNA 1993): Non-consolidated stocks, annual", OECD National Accounts Statistics (database), http://dx.doi.org/10.1787/data-00720-en; BIS (2017), Debt Service Ratios (database), www.bis.org/statistics/dsr.htm; and Oesterreichische Nationalbank (2017), National Accounts (database), www.oenb.at/en/Statistics/Standardized-Tables/financial-accounts.html.

StatLink http://dx.doi.org/10.1787/888933588307

The Three Equation Model

The so-called "Three Equation Model", as shown in Figure 4.14, is often used to explain the interlinkage between i) residential investment in housing, ii) house prices, and iii) housing debt, thereby distinguishing between long-run effects and short-run effects.

The 2007-09 economic and financial crisis, including the run-up to this crisis, is a good example of the interactions in the above model. It has clearly shed light on the importance of the relationship between the development of debt and the development of house prices, and subsequently housing wealth. From an analytical point of view, it is worth separating high debt from low debt busts. Research done by the IMF (2012) suggest that housing busts preceded by significant increases of household debt tend to be followed by more severe and longer-lasting declines in household final consumption, and, as a consequence, a fall in GDP and an increase in unemployment. In this respect, one can raise the question whether the larger decline in household spending simply reflects the larger declines in house prices, but the empirical evidence shows that the significant drop in house prices explains at most one quarter of the stronger decline in household consumption. On the contrary, in combination with the pre-bust increase in debt, household deleveraging, i.e.

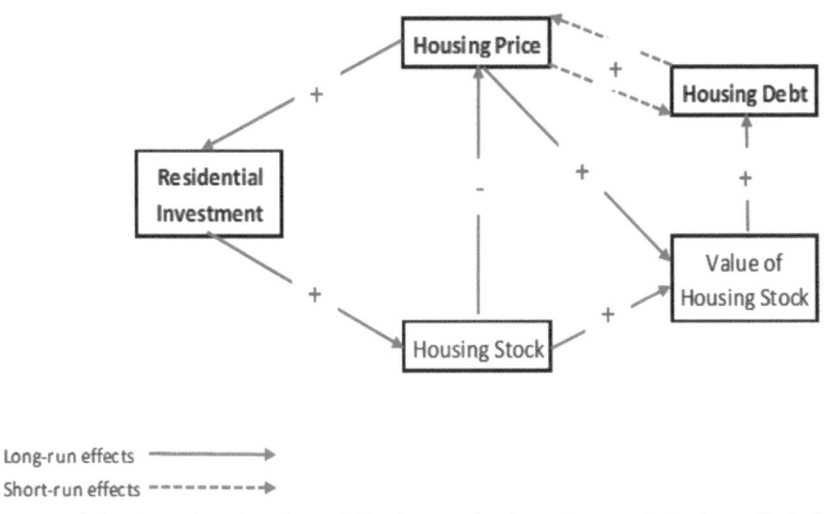

Figure 4.14. **The Three Equation Model for housing and debt**

[Diagram: Residential Investment → (+) Housing Price, (+) Housing Stock; Housing Stock → (+) Value of Housing Stock, (−) Housing Price; Housing Price → (+) Value of Housing Stock, (+) Housing Debt (dashed); Housing Debt → (+) Housing Price (dashed); Value of Housing Stock → (+) Housing Debt]

Long-run effects ⟶
Short-run effects ⇢

Source: Turk (2015), *Housing Price and Household Debt Interactions in Sweden*, www.imf.org/external/pubs/ft/wp/2015/wp15276.pdf.

the wish to run down debt levels, mainly explains the severity of the contraction of household consumption. Moreover, household deleveraging tends to be more pronounced following busts preceded by a larger growth in household debt. Overall, the IMF study concluded that when households accumulate more debt during a boom, the subsequent bust gives rise to a more severe contraction in economic activity.

The above developments are also relevant for the counterpart sectors of household debt. The impact of non-performing loans on the asset side of the creditors, mainly banks, may create spill-over effects to the creditors' liability side. Banks are required to stabilise their own capital reserves, which indirectly also affects the owners of the banks. Based on the approach pursued by Kavonius and Carsten (2009) on the balance sheet interlinkages using FWTW data, Austria has tested equity losses due to non-performing loans of households. The hypothetical transmission of balance sheet shocks in the first ten rounds was simulated assuming a 10% loss on banks' portfolio of loans granted to households. The results for Austria showed that the total losses in the value of equity issued by banks would amount to roughly 16% (Andreasch, 2014). In addition, banks may be affected by the presence of uncertainty among households, which can lead to precautionary saving. Although there is no direct link between saving as a resource of funds, and financial investments as a use of these funds, precautionary saving may increase financial investment in the form of deposits held with banks and consequently influences the role of households as providers of funds to the banking system.

> **Box 4.2. Some indicators from the household sector's financial accounts and balance sheets, used by international organisations**
>
> International organisations use a variety of indicators that can be derived from the financial accounts and balance sheets of households, to make comparisons across countries. In this box, a limited overview is given of such indicator sets.
>
> *Households' Net Financial Wealth Ratio* (used by the OECD, as part of their Household Dashboard): The ratio of financial assets less total debt, as a percentage of Gross Household Disposable Income. When assessing vulnerabilities, one should not only look at gross debt levels, but also at the availability of assets, preferably taking into account both financial and non-financial assets (for households, predominately real estate). One should also be aware of the fact that assets are typically more prone to market price changes than liabilities. For example, for individual households, changes in house prices may easily result in mortgage debt levels which are higher than the value of the underlying dwellings, as a consequence of which the relevant households may end up in a very vulnerable financial situation.
>
> *Households' Indebtedness Ratio* (used by the OECD, as part of their Household Dashboard) and *Gross Debt-to-Income Ratio of Households* (Eurostat Key Indicators): The ratio of total debt (usually determined by loans) to Gross Household Disposable Income. This ratio is often used as an indicator for (changes in) financial vulnerabilities of households; it can also be used to assess debt sustainability.
>
> *Household Debt-to-GDP Ratio* (used by the IMF, as part of their Financial Soundness Indicators (FSI)): The ratio of total household debt (usually determined by loans) to Gross Domestic Product (GDP).
>
> *Household Debt Service Ratio* (used by the BIS): The ratio of interest payments plus amortisation of debt to Gross Household Disposable Income. The debt service ratio provides an indicator for the part of income which needs to be spent on debt and which thus cannot be used for final consumption.
>
> *Household Sector Report* (used by the ECB): The ECB publishes, on a quarterly basis, the Household Sector Report for the Euro Area and for all EU member states. The report contains the following indicators from the financial accounts data:
>
> - Household financing and investment per capita
> - Household investments in financial assets and contribution by components
> - Household saving, non-financial investment, financing and debt
> - Changes to household net worth (financial and non-financial assets minus debt) broken down by flows and other changes in stocks.

In view of the above, the government may intervene to improve the macro-economic situation and decrease vulnerabilities in the financial system by providing temporary fiscal stimulus, automatic support to households through the social safety net, support for household debt restructuring, or assistance to the financial sector. All these interventions have an effect on net lending/net borrowing and will lead, ceteris paribus, to higher government debt, as seen during and after the 2007-09 economic and financial crisis in a number of countries.

3. Distributional aspects of wealth and going beyond households' economic well-being

Linking macro-economic statistics and micro-data on distribution

The data derived from the financial accounts and balance sheets provide powerful information on the financial behaviour of households as a whole, but they do not provide any information on distributional issues. How large is the inequality in the distribution of wealth? Which households actually invest in listed shares during stock exchange booms? Which households ask for loans to invest in real estate? Which households save money for retirement? These are very pertinent questions, not only for economic reasons but also from a well-being perspective. In recent years, more and more work has been done to arrive at distributional information that is consistent with the data from national accounts, by trying to bridge the differences between the macro data from national accounts, and more detailed individual data from surveys (and administrative data) on income, consumption and wealth.

It is important to note that macro and micro wealth data are designed to answer different types of questions about saving and wealth accumulation. Estimates of key macro-economic parameters, such as the marginal effect of income and wealth shocks on consumption (and saving) require high frequency, timely and comprehensive macro data. On the other hand, analyses of individual, more heterogeneous saving and wealth accumulation behaviour due to differences in income, age, personal characteristics and other variables can only be derived from micro-data.

Analysing macro-economic developments in conjunction with the distribution of income and wealth across households shows that an increase of inequality in wealth often occurs in tandem with the increase in income inequality. This is due to the fact that an increase in income for groups at the top of the income distribution results in higher saving, which leads to a further accumulation of wealth. Furthermore, the composition of household balance sheets varies considerably, not only between countries but also between the lower and the upper ends of the wealth distribution. Data for France, Germany, Italy, Spain, the United Kingdom and the United States,[8] for example, highlight that households in the higher wealth quintiles have a higher proportion of equity shares than households in the lower quintiles, while the distribution of real estate across quintiles also differs quite significantly. In the observed countries, these two wealth components also show to be the main drivers behind differentials in the return on assets.

Preferably, one would like to link macro- and micro data on income, consumption and wealth, to arrive at a better understanding of financial behaviour of households, and this behaviour's impact on economic developments. However, the aggregation of individual wealth measures does not sum up to the macro data in national accounts. The reasons for these differences can be split into four groups:

1. differences in the definition of households;
2. differences in the definition of wealth;
3. differences in the valuation of individual portfolio items; and
4. the coverage of the estimates.

Regarding the definition of households, the 2008 SNA defines households as all individuals living in a certain country regardless whether they stay at home, are homeless, or are part of the so called institutionalised population (people hospitalised for longer periods, people living in military institutions, or prisoners). Furthermore, all individuals living in the country for at least one year, irrespective of periods spent abroad of less than one year, are counted as part of the household sector. In contrast, surveys capturing income, consumption and wealth of individuals select a certain sample of families representing the population, usually excluding the homeless and institutionalised population. Empirical data for the Euro Area show that the difference between these two population groupings can amount to up to 5%. Moreover, mainly due to data limitations in the compilation of national accounts, the household sector may include Non-Profit Institutions Serving Households (NPISHs), like churches, trade unions or foundations.

When it comes to the definition of wealth, the classifications and concepts of the various income and wealth items in national accounts are somewhat different from those used in household surveys. Conceptually, micro surveys focus on individual households, and therefore the definition is based on the household point of view, while in national accounts the items are defined at the level of the total economy with a subsequent split into main sectors. One of the examples of this type of divergence – at least in Europe – relates to the definition of business wealth of households managing unincorporated enterprises. In micro surveys, often only the net asset value of the enterprise, i.e. the balance of all financial and non-financial assets less liabilities, is recorded, whereas in national accounts the individual assets and liabilities of the unincorporated enterprise are classified in the relevant categories. In addition, some categories of wealth may not be available in survey based wealth measures, like cash (due to the impossibility of raising the question in an interview) or non-life insurance technical reserves (due to the lack of knowledge of households).

Looking at the valuation of individual portfolio items, one of the differences is related to the valuation of entitlements for retirement. While in micro surveys calculations of the net present value of life insurance contracts and some types of pension plans are made on the basis of premiums and length of the contract, in national accounts the relevant amounts are simply derived from the very detailed estimations of the relevant entitlements by insurance corporations and pension funds. In addition, the valuation of other individual financial instruments may differ. The valuation required by the 2008 SNA follows the market valuation principle as closely as possible. In practice, this is done through the use of centralised information or counterpart information. For example, the valuation of tradeable securities held by households in financial accounts and balance sheets follows the concept of market quotations. Likewise, the main portion of household debt is held as assets by banks and is valued accordingly. Furthermore, in the absence of relevant market price information, equity holdings in limited liability companies are usually valued according to the value of the own funds or book value. In contrast, households may not be in the position to value the assets with the same standards as used for national accounts.

A final point relates to the coverage of the estimates, that is, whether the estimates provide a full and complete picture of the transactions or positions under consideration. The explicit goal of national accounts is to arrive at exhaustive estimates, including hidden and illegal activities. Moreover, the balancing framework of national accounts aims at reaching consistency between all types of assets and the corresponding liabilities for each financial instrument, thus using – when considered appropriate – more reliable counterparty information which tends to lead to a better coverage of the estimates. Moreover, efforts to try to arrive at consistency between non-financial transactions, financial transactions and (changes in) positions on the balance sheets lead to a further improvement of coverage and quality more generally. These considerations do not generally play a role in the survey based compilation of wealth of households. Moreover, the sampling of households usually leads to an underestimation of wealth, even taking into consideration oversampling of certain groups for the improvement of the response rate. It is, for example, of crucial importance to have a good representation of the top 1% of wealthy households, as they have a massive impact on the estimates. However, this would involve the need to include a proper representation in the survey, which is very difficult.

All in all, a naïve comparison, without any adjustments for differences in concepts and methodologies, leads to a lower coverage of financial wealth in survey data, if compared to data derived from financial accounts and balance sheets. These results call for a compilation based on a method in which the definitions and methodologies are aligned as much as possible. Such a comparison is available for the United States for a number of years, showing that survey data actually reports higher figures than the macro data derived from national accounts, mainly in the area of non-financial assets, since 2010. Provisional results show that, after aligning the micro and macro data to the same concepts and methodologies, the results from micro data, as a percentage of macro data, would increase between 10 and 20 percentage points for the majority of Euro Area countries, the ratio of micro data thus amounting to between 40% and 60% of the adjusted financial accounts data.

Beyond financial accounts and balance sheets: households' well-being

The standard national accounts, which are compiled by institutional sector, generate a broad range of indicators for economic well-being, such as household (disposable) income, saving and (financial) wealth. This has also been acknowledged by the so-called "Stiglitz-Sen-Fitoussi Report"[9] by the Commission on the Measurement of Economic Performance and Social Progress. One of the Commission's goals was "… to identify the limits of GDP as an indicator of economic performance and social progress … [and] to assess the feasibility of alternative measurement tools". In its recommendations, the report concludes that, when evaluating material well-being, one should i) look at income and consumption rather than production; ii) emphasise the household perspective; and iii) consider income and consumption jointly with wealth. Other suggestions include iv) to give more prominence to the distribution of income, consumption and wealth; and v) to broaden income measures to non-market activities, such as unpaid housework.

Put differently, these recommendations encourage broadening and deepening the analysis of household behaviour, as noted in the conclusion of the report "… that in the measurement of household welfare all material components should be covered, i.e. consumption, income and wealth, from both the micro as well as the macro perspective". The financial accounts and balance sheets cover the accumulation of household financial wealth and the resulting stocks. Measures of the economic relevance of households include the contribution of household consumption to GDP growth and their share of net lending in the economy, providing funds both as investors and savers to other domestic and external economic sectors.

The measurement of a more encompassing concept of well-being is high on the agenda of the statistical community. The OECD plays a key role in this respect, amid initiatives of the United Nations Economic Commission for Europe (UNECE), the European Commission, and similar initiatives by several advanced and emerging countries. The framework of well-being focuses on the measurement of broader metrics representing the development of well-being of people in each country, in addition to the macro-economic conditions using standard macro-economic performance indicators like GDP. The main goal is to identify the drivers of well-being. Household debt and household (financial) worth are part of this broader set of indicators of well-being.

The indicators used in the context of the broader framework also include material living conditions such as income and wealth, jobs and earnings, and housing. The economic well-being, in the sense of people's command over economic resources, is a multi-dimensional concept whose components (income, consumption and wealth) are separate but interrelated. Looking at these different types of economic resources jointly allows for an improved identification of people in distressed or (dis)advantaged conditions, thus also allowing a better targeting of policies. However, there are numerous other aspects affecting the well-being of people, such as health status, work and life balance, education and skills, social connections, civic engagement and governance, environmental quality, personal security and subjective well-being indicators; see Figure 4.15. A concrete example of such a broader set of indicators trying to capture well-being is the OECD Better Life Index.[10] A dashboard providing a set of more economically oriented indicators can be found in the OECD Dashboard on Households' Economic Well-being.

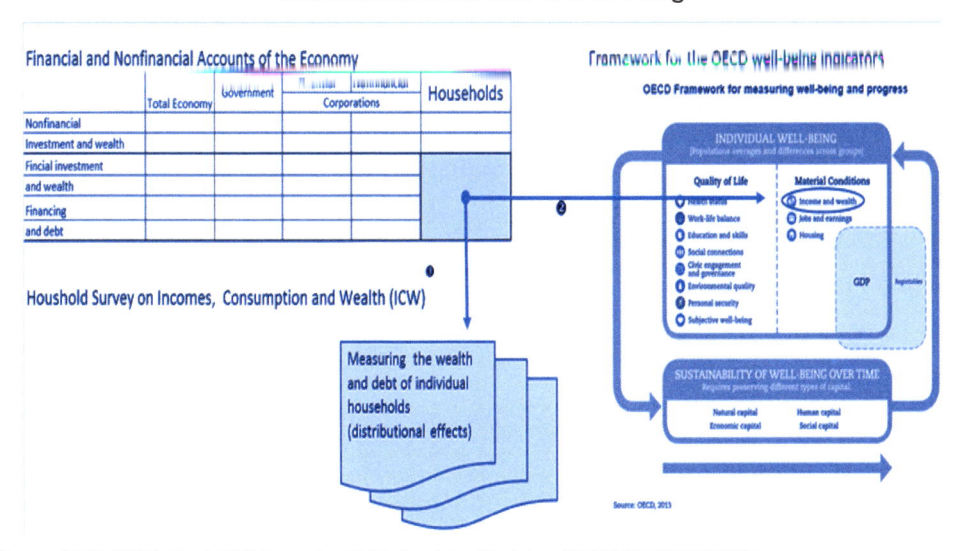

Figure 4.15. **The interrelations between national accounts and broader measures of well-being**

Source: OECD (2013), *How's Life? Measuring Well-being*, http://dx.doi.org/10.1787/9789264201392-en.

Summarising recent developments, it is evident that understanding financial and non-financial behaviour of households has become more important. This leads to a demand for better and more granular statistics on households, which financial accounts and balance sheets can partially help to provide.

4. HOUSEHOLDS AND THEIR FINANCIAL BEHAVIOUR

Key points

- Households act both as an important driver of economic growth, notably in the form of final consumption expenditure, and as a key player in providing funds to other sectors. They also act as producers of goods and services by operating small and medium-serviced enterprises, of which some are incorporated.

- Households in OECD countries partially converged the structure of their asset portfolio, and there is a growing importance in most countries for long-term investments related to pension plans.

- Non-financial wealth, especially in the form of dwellings, has become more important. Often this investment in non-financial wealth is accompanied with a notable increase of household debt, which is now the subject of macro-economic stability analysis, especially after the bubble in house prices and the resulting economic and financial crisis in 2007-09.

- Households in national accounts are grouped together into one "institutional sector", as a consequence of which monitoring and analysis is only possible at the aggregate level. In recent years, there is a growing interest for more detailed analysis for certain subgroupings of households, for which it is necessary to elaborate micro data statistics, trying to align these data to the aggregates from national accounts.

- More generally, it has to be noted that economic indicators only tell a partial story when it comes to the well-being of people. Broader measures have been developed and continue to be improved to capture various (and beyond the economic) elements affecting people's well-being.

Going further

Captured "residually" – Data sources for households in financial accounts and balance sheets

Data on households' financial investments and related financial assets, as well as external financing and related debt, are compiled from a variety of data sources, including balancing procedures using counterparty information. As a consequence, the data are often compiled on a residual basis (often including NPISHs). Table 4.2 gives some indication of the methodologies typically used, but it is important to mention that there are no general rules due to the heterogeneity of data sources and compilation procedures across countries.

Table 4.2. **Summary of data sources for financial instruments**

Financial instrument	Definition	Domestic assets/liabilities	Foreign assets/liabilities
Financial assets			
Currency	Banknotes and coins including silver and gold coins (provided that they can be exchanged for cash at any time). Gold bullions are not included.	Residual item, usually derived from liability side minus holding by domestic financial sector and estimated value for cross-border holdings	Balance of payments statistics (BOP), estimates
Deposits	Current or saving accounts (including saving cards) with domestic and foreign banks, regardless of maturity	Counterpart data from banks	Direct reporting or counterpart statistics from non-resident banks
Debt securities, listed shares, investment fund shares	Debt securities are commercial papers, short-term treasuries, and all kind of bonds (zero-bonds, covered bonds, etc.). Listed shares and investment fund shares are shares which are officially listed on a stock exchange, or traded in any other form of secondary market	Custodian reports or residual compilation based on issuance statistics, statistics on holdings of the financial sector and the government sector, estimates on the split between the holdings of non-financial corporations and those of households, survey data	Direct reporting or transaction-based reporting by banks for BOP statistics
Unlisted shares, other equity	Unlisted shares, or equity issued by limited liability companies	Company register, direct reporting, custodian reporting, residual compilation (see listed shares), survey data	Direct reporting, data derived from Foreign Direct Investment (FDI) statistics, transaction-based reporting by banks for BOP statistics
Life insurance contracts	Actuarial reserves and other technical reserves for entitlements related to individual non-life and life insurance policies	Counterpart data from insurance corporations	Direct reporting, transaction-based reporting by banks for BOP statistics (often based on premiums)
Pension entitlements	Entitlements related to private (funded) pension schemes, provided directly by employers for their employees, or more usually via separated pension funds. Payasyougo systems are not included	Counterpart data from pension funds, banks, insurance corporations and company balance sheet data	Direct reporting, transaction-based reporting by banks for BOP statistics (often based on premiums)
Financial derivatives	Employee stock options offered as part of salaries, tradeable derivatives like options	Custodian reports, direct reporting, data on employee stock options derived from non-financial accounts data, survey data	Direct reporting, transaction-based reporting by banks for BOP statistics
Loans, trade credits	Loans between households, and loans owed by companies with an equity stake of households; trade credits in the form of pre-paid vouchers	Company balance sheet data, survey data	Direct reporting, transaction-based reporting by banks for BOP statistics
Other financial assets	Tax credit, accrued interest on deposits, if not part of the related financial instrument, money in transit	Dependent on national circumstances	Dependent on national circumstances

Table 4.2. **Summary of data sources for financial instruments** (cont.)

Financial instrument	Definition	Domestic assets/liabilities	Foreign assets/liabilities
Liabilities (Debt)			
Loans	Housing loans, consumer loans, and other loans (mainly consisting of loans extended to self-employed individuals and sole proprietorships for investment purposes; loans for debt consolidation, education and retirement investment; and salary advances)	Counterpart data from banks, other financial institutions, government	Direct reporting or counterpart statistics from non-resident banks
Trade credits	Trade credits (difference between delivery and payment) of suppliers for goods and services	Company balance sheet data	BOP-statistics
Pension entitlements	Additional payment liabilities for funded pension schemes by the employees	Counterpart data from pension funds	BOP-statistics
Other	Tax credit, accrued interest on loans, if not part of the related financial instrument loans, money in transit	Dependent on national circumstances	Dependent on national circumstances

Notes

1. These countries comprise Austria, Belgium, Czech Republic, France, Germany, Hungary, Italy, Japan, Korea, Mexico, Portugal, Slovenia, Sweden and Switzerland.
2. Here, gross disposable income refers to "adjusted" disposable income. It thus includes social transfers in kind, i.e. income equivalent to goods and services provided by government for free or at prices that are not economically significant (such as health and education).
3. These countries comprise Estonia, Ireland, Netherlands, Norway, Poland, Slovak Republic, Spain, United Kingdom, and the United States.
4. The recording of pension schemes slightly complicates this calculation. It is necessary to not use disposable income as such, but to add the adjustment for the change in pension entitlements. It is this total figure that should be the denominator in the saving ratio calculation. See Chapter 9 for further details.
5. For more information, see *www.oecd.org/std/na/Measuring-inequality-in-income-and-consumption-in-a-national-accounts-framework.pdf*.
6. See *www.oecd.org/std/na/household-dashboard.htm*.
7. For more details see *www.bis.org/statistics/dsr/dsr_doc.pdf*.
8. Data are derived from the Eurosystem Household Finance and Consumption Survey, data provided by the UK Office of National Statics, Wealth and Assets, and the Survey of Consumer Finances of the US Federal Reserve Board.
9. The Stiglitz-Sen-Fitoussi Report is the closing report of the "Commission on the Measurement of Economic Performance and Social Progress". This commission was set up, at the start of 2000, at the initiative of the French government. The full report is available at the following link: *http://ec.europa.eu/eurostat/documents/118025/118123/Fitoussi+Commission+report*.
10. See *www.oecdbetterlifeindex.org/*.

References

Andreasch, M. (2014), "Analysis of the financial interlinkages of the financial sector in Austria against the background of the recent financial crises", in *A Flow-of-Funds Perspective on the Financial Crisis*, Vol. II, Palgrave Macmillan Studies in Economics and Banking, Basingstoke.

Andreasch, M. et al. (2010), "Investment and financing activities of the institutional sectors of the Austrian economy 2010"in *Sector Accounts in Austria 2010*, Oesterreichische Nationalbank, Vienna, *https://www.oenb.at/dam/jcr.../shst_2010_june_sector_accounts_tcm16-236095.pdf*.

Antoniewicz, R et al. (2005), "Household wealth: Comparing micro and macro data in Cyprus, Canada, Italy and United States", paper prepared for the LWS Construction and Usage of Comparable Microdata on Wealth: The LWS Workshop, Bank of Italy, Perugia, 27-29 January 2005.

BIS (2017), *Debt Service Ratios*, Bank for International Settlements, Basel, *www.bis.org/statistics/dsr.htm*.

Bruno, G. and R. De Bonis (2008), "Do financial systems converge? New evidence from household financial assets in selected OECD countries", *OECD Statistics*

Working Papers, No. 2009/1, OECD Publishing, Paris, http://dx.doi.org/10.1787/224175173554.

Bouis, R. (2015), "Household deleveraging and saving rates: a cross-country analysis", paper prepared for the KDI International Conference on Household Debt from an International Perspective: Issues and Policy Directions, Korea Development Institute, Seoul, 10 July 2015.

Coletta, M., R. De Bonis and S. Piermattei (2014), "The determinants of household debt: A cross-country analysis", Economic Working Papers, No. 989, Bank of Italy, Rome, www.bancaditalia.it/pubblicazioni/temi-discussione/2014/2014-0989/en_tema_989.pdf.

De Bonis, R., D. Fano and T. Sbano (2012), "Household wealth in the main OECD countries from 1980-2011: What do the data tell us?", Questioni di Economia e Finanza (Occasional Papers), No. 160, Bank of Italy, Rome, www.bancaditalia.it/pubblicazioni/qef/2013-0160/QEF_160.pdf.

Domanski, D., M. Scatigna and A. Zabai (2016), "Wealth inequality and monetary policy", BIS Quarterly Review, March, Bank for International Settlements, Basel, www.bis.org/publ/qtrpdf/r_qt1603f.htm.

Eurostat (2016), Sector Accounts: Households and NPISH, Eurostat, Luxembourg, http://ec.europa.eu/eurostat/web/sector-accounts/detailed-charts/households-npish.

Honkkila, J. and I. Kavonius (2013), "Micro and macro analysis on the household income, wealth and saving in the Euro Area", ECB Working Paper Series, No. 1619/November 2013, ECB, Frankfurt, www.ecb.europa.eu/pub/pdf/scpwps/ecbwp1619.pdf.

IMF (2012), "Dealing with household debt" in World Economic Outlook April 2012, IMF, Washington, DC, www.imf.org/external/pubs/ft/weo/2012/01/pdf/c3.pdf.

Kavonius, L. and O. Carsten (2009), "Balance sheet interlinkage and macro-financial risk analysis in the Euro Area", ECB Working Paper Series, No. 1124/December 2009, ECB, Frankfurt, www.ecb.europa.eu/pub/pdf/scpwps/ecbwp1124.pdf?b1f1ab145ac34f5c0ed908641d1e2f9d.

Magri, S. (2009), "Household wealth and entrepreneurship: Is there a link?", Economic Working Papers, No. 719, Bank of Italy, Rome, www.bancaditalia.it/pubblicazioni/temi-discussione/2009/2009-0719/en_tema_719.pdf.

OECD (2017), "Aggregate National Accounts, SNA 2008 (or SNA 1993): Gross domestic product", OECD National Accounts Statistics (database), http://dx.doi.org/10.1787/data-00001-en; and "Detailed National Accounts, SNA 2008 (or SNA 1993): Non-financial accounts by sectors, annual", OECD National Accounts Statistics (database), http://dx.doi.org/10.1787/data-00034-en; and "Financial Accounts, SNA 2008 (or SNA 1993): Consolidated flows, annual", OECD National Accounts Statistics (database), http://dx.doi.org/10.1787/data-00716-en; and "Financial Balance Sheets, SNA 2008 (or SNA 1993): Non-consolidated stocks, annual", OECD National Accounts Statistics (database), http://dx.doi.org/10.1787/data-00720-en.

OECD (2014), Understanding National Accounts, OECD Publishing, Paris, http://dx.doi.org/10.1787/9789264214637-en.

OECD (2013), Framework for Statistics on the Distribution of Household Income, Consumption and Wealth, OECD Publishing, Paris, http://dx.doi.org/10.1787/9789264194830-en.

OeNB (2017), National Accounts, Osterreichische Nationalbank, Vienna, www.oenb.at/en/Statistics/Standardized-Tables/financial-accounts.html.

Turk, R. (2015), "Housing price and household debt interactions in Sweden", *IMF Working Papers, No. 15/276*, IMF, Washington, DC, *www.imf.org/external/pubs/ft/wp/2015/wp15276.pdf*.

Van der Wal, D. (2014), "The measurement of international pension obligations – Have we harmonised enough?", *DNB Working Papers*, No. 424/May 2014, De Nederlandsche Bank, Amsterdam, *www.dnb.nl/binaries/Working%20Paper%20424_tcm46-307802.pdf*.

Chapter 5

The financing of non-financial corporations

James Tebrake (Statistics Canada)
and Patrick O'Hagan (Statistics Canada)

Non-financial corporations are responsible for a large share of the economic activity in most advanced economies. They produce goods and services, they invest, and they employ a large share of a country's labour force. Their importance in the "real" economy is evident in nearly every economic activity. This chapter focuses on non-financial corporations' interactions within the financial system, both as borrowers and as lenders. Their investments of available funds across instruments may provide important insights into their investment strategies and their propensity towards risk. Conversely, different sources of funding for non-financial corporations shed light on their key choices, such as the choice of debt or equity or the mix of long versus short-term debt. This chapter further provides insights on non-financial corporations' balance sheets, and on the indicators that can be derived from them. It also addresses key conceptual and operational issues, such as the differences between the System of National Accounts (SNA) and corporate or business accounting.

The statistical data for Israel are supplied by and under the responsibility of the relevant Israeli authorities. The use of such data by the OECD is without prejudice to the status of the Golan Heights, East Jerusalem and Israeli settlements in the West Bank under the terms of international law.

1. The role of non-financial corporations in the economy and in financial markets

Before we can explore the role of non-financial corporations in the economy and the financial markets, we first need to understand what and who they are. Like most accounting terminology, the generic name "non-financial corporations" does not always encompass the full scope of the subject. Non-financial corporations are incorporated legal entities that largely produce goods and services for the market. The "non-financial" label means that they principally engage in the production of non-financial goods and services, as opposed to financial services. Non-financial corporations therefore encompass many industrial classifications. The "corporations" tag means that these entities come into being by law via incorporation, in many cases authorised by the government. This gives them their own legal status separate from their owners, which limits the liability of the owners in a number of circumstances (e.g. business failure). Their "incorporated" status is also what differentiates these businesses from the unincorporated enterprises and sole proprietorships that are generally part of the household sector discussed in Chapter 4.

Non-financial corporations do not only consist of the large companies and conglomerate firms listed on the stock markets, but may also include smaller unlisted firms with limited liability. This institutional sector includes the enterprises that produce the cars we drive, the televisions we watch, the food we eat and various forms of media that inform and entertain us. They are the enterprises that provide many of us with a pay cheque, and they account for most of the companies in which we invest in order to get our piece of the corporate pie.

Statisticians organise enterprises into sectors based on the predominance of their operations. As said, the commonality of companies in the non-financial corporations sector is that they are separate legal entities and they produce non-financial goods and services. Beyond that the companies can be quite different. The non-financial corporations' sector includes, for example, incorporated energy and resource firms, agriculture, forestry and fishing businesses, manufacturers, companies engaged in distribution of products (wholesalers and retailers), entities engaged in construction and real estate, transportation services, and other non-financial business services (professional, scientific and technical services), as well as information and cultural services.

The three most significant roles of non-financial corporations are as producers of goods and services, as investors in non-financial assets (which leads to the future production of goods and services), and as borrowers in financial markets. The last role implies that they are investment vehicles for the other sectors of the economy such as households and financial corporations. With respect to the latter, it can be added that, in some economies, non-financial corporations have become significant net lenders to other sectors, as their financial position is such that their saving exceeds their need for investments in non-financial assets.

Non-financial corporations' role as producers of goods and services

The sum of non-financial corporations' production is referred to as their output. It is what results from the production of goods and services by combining labour, capital, and intermediate goods and services. Non-financial corporations are the source of much of the world's output and employment. In most countries, non-financial corporations account for over 60% of total output, as can be seen from Table 5.1. This share is fairly consistent from one country to the next. The average share for the OECD countries in the table is almost 70%.

Table 5.1. **Non-financial corporations' output to total output, 2014**

	Non-financial corporations output	Total output	Ratio of non-financial corporations output to total output
	Millions of national currency	Millions of national currency	%
Austria	428 075	609 432	70.2
Czech Republic	7 886 477	10 210 030	77.2
France	2 592 205	3 778 796	68.6
Germany	3 758 273	5 319 338	70.7
Greece	131 812	282 457	46.7
Hungary	49 988 222	66 034 608	75.7
Israel	1 156 763	1 780 896	65.0
Italy	2 049 900	3 063 936	66.9
Netherlands	895 980	1 257 943	71.2
Norway	3 832 918	5 233 258	73.2
Spain	1 367 576	1 926 076	71.0
Sweden	5 132 374	6 965 695	73.7
OECD Average			69.8

Source: OECD (2017), "Detailed National Accounts, SNA 2008 (or SNA 1993): Non-financial accounts by sectors, annual", *OECD National Accounts Statistics* (database), http://dx.doi.org/data-00034-en.
StatLink ⟶ http://dx.doi.org/10.1787/888933589922

Non-financial corporations' role in investment

Investment plays a key role in any economy, ensuring that capital used in the production process to meet the demand for goods and services is in place. In order for non-financial corporations to remain viable, they need to invest in productive assets. Therefore, investment, or gross fixed capital formation (GFCF) as it is called in national accounts terminology, is crucial to non-financial corporations' current and future production. In many economies, non-financial corporations account for the overwhelming share of such investment in non-financial assets. Table 5.2 shows the share of investment of non-financial corporations to total investment for selected OECD countries.

Table 5.2. **Non-financial corporations' gross fixed capital formation to total gross fixed capital formation, 2014**

	Non-financial corporations GFCF	Total GFCF	Ratio of non-financial corporations' GFCF to total GFCF
	Millions of national currency	Millions of national currency	%
Austria	44 854	73 629	60.9
Belgium	56 983	93 326	61.1
Czech Republic	697 371	1 065 464	65.5
Denmark	198 833	370 688	53.6
Estonia	3 183	5 033	63.3
Finland	21 317	42 197	50.5
Hungary	4 184 486	6 971 261	60.0
Ireland	25 378	36 515	69.5
Italy	131 073	267 474	49.3
Japan	67 731 100	107 128 200	63.2
Netherlands	66 033	120 442	54.8
Norway	408 813	733 987	55.7
Portugal	16 082	25 772	62.4
Slovak Republic	9 438	15 766	59.9
Slovenia	3 884	7 324	53.0
United Kingdom	156 717	305 712	51.3
United States	1 644 600	3 378 700	48.7
OECD Average			58.0

Source: OECD (2017), "Detailed National Accounts, SNA 2008 (or SNA 1993): Non-financial accounts by sectors, annual", OECD National Accounts Statistics (database), http://dx.doi.org/10.1787/data-00034-en.
StatLink http://dx.doi.org/10.1787/888933589941

Non-financial corporations' role as an investment vehicle: net borrowing and net lending

Non-financial investment, that is, investments in assets like buildings, machinery and equipment, and software, are the link between the non-financial corporations' "real" accounts (or real activity) and financial accounts (or financial activity). If non-financial corporations are able to generate saving in excess of their non-financial investment needs in a given accounting period, they are known as net lenders or net financial investors. If non-financial corporations are unable to generate saving that match their investment needs in a given accounting period, they are net (financial) borrowers. The relevant balancing item is the net lending/net borrowing position, and is recorded in the capital account. Non-financial investments can be financed in one of two ways, through the use of internal funds (current or retained earnings), or by borrowing funds from other sectors of the economy.

In the event that non-financial corporations require external funds, other sectors must be willing to provide them with funds. This highlights the third important role non-financial corporations play in the economy – an investment vehicle for investors from other sectors. Non-financial corporations offer investors a stake in their earnings (in the form of dividends on equity held) or interest payments on debt. The end result is that claims on non-financial corporations can be found on the balance sheets of other sectors in the economy, such as households, financial corporations and non-residents. The reverse is also true: in the event that non-financial corporations have excess funds they become financial investors and supply these funds to other institutional sectors. In recent years, the latter has been the situation in Canada, the US, and some other countries as well. See also Box 5.1.

Box 5.1. **Non-financial corporations' net lending and investment trends in Canada**

In Canada, as well as in some other OECD countries, the non-financial corporations' sector moved from a net borrowing position to a net lending position around the turn of the 21st century. This structural change fundamentally altered the balance sheets of non-financial corporations, and is an excellent example of the link between the "real" accounts of non-financial corporations and their corresponding financial accounts.

In Canada, corporations began generating large net lending positions since 2000. Corporate earnings have been on a strong upward trend since about 1997 (except for a few interruptions – the high-tech bust in 2001, and the financial crisis in 2008-09). This earnings growth was led by consumer demand and, in many industries, foreign demand (see Figure 5.1).

Clearly, earnings growth has had a major impact on the financial position of non-financial corporations. However, a second significant factor has been lower capital expenditure relative to net operating surplus over the last 17 years (see Figure 5.2).

The above developments suggest a number of things. First, Canadian non-financial corporations have benefitted from generally high commodity prices over the period under consideration – creating a growing gap between the supply of internal funds and the funds required for investment. This has led to a modification in corporate investment behaviour – a shift towards financial investment as a growing use of funds. Notable acquisitions of financial instruments have included both portfolio and inter-company investment. Some of the latter has been directed outside of the country via foreign direct investment, suggesting the increased influence of global production among Canadian multinational enterprises.

5. THE FINANCING OF NON-FINANCIAL CORPORATIONS

Box 5.1. **Non-financial corporations' net lending and investment trends in Canada**
(cont.)

Figure 5.1. **Net lending/net borrowing and net operating surplus of non-financial corporations, Canada**
Millions of CAD

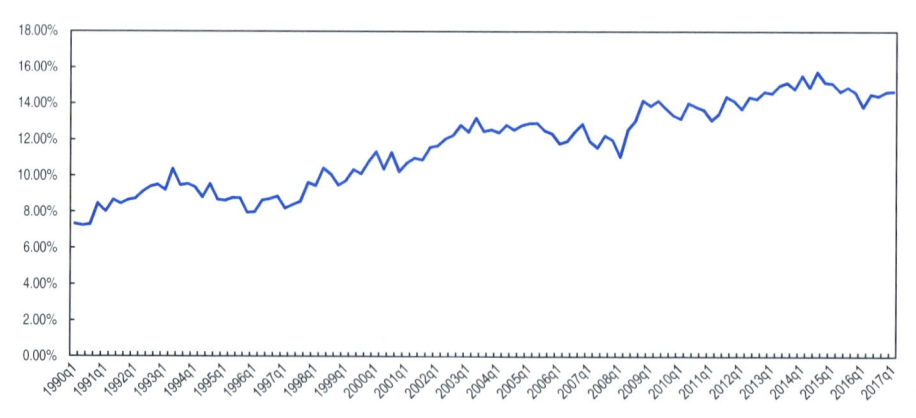

Source: Statistics Canada (2016), Table 380-0076 – Current and capital accounts – Corporations, quarterly (CAD) (database), www5.statcan.gc.ca/cansim/a26?lang=eng&id=3800076.
StatLink http://dx.doi.org/10.1787/888933588440

Figure 5.2. **Net operating surplus and non-financial investments of non-financial corporations, Canada**
Millions of CAD

Source: Statistics Canada (2016), Table 380-0076 – Current and capital accounts – Corporations, quarterly (CAD) (database), www5.statcan.gc.ca/cansim/a26?lang=eng&id=3800076.
StatLink http://dx.doi.org/10.1787/888933588516

> Box 5.1. **Non-financial corporations' net lending and investment trends in Canada**
> (cont.)
>
> Major flows of financial investment have been directed to liquid assets and other portfolio investments since 2000. In particular, currency and bank deposits (domestic and foreign) and various other types of portfolio investments have trended upward since the late 1990s. This development has substantially improved the liquidity position of non-financial corporations. In policy circles, these investments in liquid assets have often been referred to as "dead money" of the non-financial corporations' sector, or funds that could be used for capital expenditure.
>
> Not surprisingly, similar patterns for non-financial corporations have been observed in a number of countries. In the US, this development has been sometimes referred to as the "financialisation" of non-financial corporations – a rise in investment in financial assets along with a decline in accumulation of tangible non-financial assets (see, for example, Davis (2013) and Fano and Trovato [2013]).
>
> The associated issue of "dead money" will be explored in more detail below.

The financial behaviour of non-financial corporations

Thus far it has been established that the national accounts record the role of non-financial corporations as producers of goods and services, investors and net lenders/net borrowers. If the national accounts stopped here, users of macroeconomic statistics would be left with a cliff-hanger, as important questions remain unanswered:

- Where do firms obtain their funds if they need to borrow?
- Where do firms invest their excess funds?
- What tools (or instruments) do firms use to raise funds?
- How do firms raise funds over economic cycles?

These questions are answered by examining the financial accounts and balance sheets of non-financial corporations.

2. Sources and uses of funds for non-financial corporations

A key function of the non-financial corporations' sector financial accounts and balance sheets is to record their financial activity and financial positions. That is, financial accounts and balance sheets show how firms finance investment activities, in particular when their demand for funds exceeds their internally generated source of funds; and in which financial instruments they invest, in particular when their source of internally generated funds is greater than their demand for non-financial investments in the current period.

Put simply, suppose a firm needs USD 1 million to purchase a machine but it has had a bad year for earnings and is just scraping by. The financial accounts and balance sheets record the sources of funds, that is, the firm's borrowing of financial funds, disaggregated by instrument, and who is lending the firm the money needed to purchase the machine. Conversely, suppose the firm had a very successful year and generated a surplus of USD 2 million – the accounts record how it is using the extra USD 1 million in cash (the difference between the USD 2 million surplus and the USD 1 million cost of the machine).

A second key function of the non-financial corporations' financial accounts and balance sheets is to provide insight into the sector's financial management strategy, perceptions of risk and longer term economic outlook. One way to explore both of these functions is to look at the financial accounts from two perspectives: the use of funds and the source of funds.

Investment results from the saving of the non-financial corporations' sector. The latter is the balancing item of the current account (i.e. in 2008 SNA terminology, the combination of the production account and the generation, distribution and use of income accounts). The current account's balance of incomes and expenditures is carried down to the capital account. When non-financial corporations primarily use saving (and other sources of funds) to invest in non-financial assets, they are signalling to the rest of the economy that they believe demand for their goods and services will be sustained, or will increase. They are also implicitly indicating that they expect the return on investment in non-financial assets to be greater than the return they could earn on financial assets. When non-financial corporations primarily use their saving to invest in financial assets (or reduce liabilities), they are in turn signalling to the rest of the economy that they want to strengthen their net financial position, usually in light of projected lower demand for products. The relationship between saving, non-financial investment and financial transactions can vary considerably, even over short periods of time and is an important indicator of economic cycles and growth.

Disregarding net receipts of capital transfers (which are relatively minor in the countries under consideration), Table 5.3 summarises the sources and uses of funds for non-financial corporations in recent years in Canada and the US. A few interesting observations can be gleaned from this table, which compares two closely related economies. First, the components of the sources of funds – both saving and the incurrence of liabilities – tend to be more volatile than those of the uses of funds. Second, the longer-term trend of non-financial corporations towards increased saving has been interrupted in recent years in both countries, most notably in Canada. Third, external sources of funds have picked up over the last three years in both countries, but the uses of funds have not always moved in tandem. This suggests that the economic behaviour of non-financial corporations does not always follow the same pattern. Below is a closer examination of the uses and sources of funds for non-financial corporations.

Table 5.3. **Sources and uses of funds, Canada and the U.S.**
Billions of national currency

	2013	2014	2015	2016
Canada				
Capital Account sources: Internal sources of funds (gross saving)	192.9	201.7	155.9	158.5
Of which: Net saving	20.0	18.8	-38.1	-43.4
Capital Account uses: Non-financial investments	209.5	221.7	221.8	187.4
Financial Account uses: Financial investments	102.7	91.5	101.4	112.8
Financial Account sources: Incurrence of liabilities	118.6	110.8	133.9	246.6
United States				
Capital Account sources: Internal sources of funds (gross saving)	1 873.2	1 919.8	1 882.8	1 849.9
Of which: Net saving	499.3	478.4	342.4	332.5
Capital Account uses: Non-financial investments	1 628.0	1 219.0	1 899.4	1 790.6
Financial Account uses: Financial investments	989.6	927.7	1 451.7	1 204.8
Financial Account sources: Incurrence of liabilities	926.5	1 382.1	1 317.9	1 084.2

Source: Statistics Canada (2017), Table 378-0121 – National Balance Sheet Accounts, quarterly (CAD) (database), www5.statcan.gc.ca/cansim/pick-choisir?lang=eng&p2=33&id=3780121; Statistics Canada (2017), Table 378-0119 – Financial Flow Accounts, quarterly (CAD) (database), www5.statcan.gc.ca/cansim/a26?lang=eng&retrLang=eng&id=3780119&&pattern=&stByVal=1&p1=1&p2=31&tabMode=dataTable&csid=, U.S. Federal Reserve (2017). Financial Accounts of the United States (database), www.federalreserve.gov/apps/fof/FOFTables.aspx.

StatLink http://dx.doi.org/10.1787/888933589960

Uses of funds by non-financial corporations
The acquisition of non-financial assets

As noted above, one of the key uses of funds by non-financial corporations is investment in non-financial assets. In general, non-financial corporations hold a significant amount of an economic territory's non-financial assets such as non-residential buildings and structures, machinery and equipment. Today, investment by non-financial corporations is no longer just about machines and buildings, but also about designs, formulas and software code. Intangible assets, or intellectual property products (IPPs), are becoming increasingly important. Table 5.4 shows the amount of non-financial assets held by the non-financial corporations sector for selected OECD countries compared to the national total of non-financial assets.[1] In many countries the non-financial corporations sector holds a significant portion of the countries' non-financial wealth. Other important categories of non-financial assets are dwellings owned by households, and infrastructure developed by government.

While it is important to measure aggregate investment in non-financial investments, it is equally important to provide details about the type of investments. This detail is important for a number of reasons. Firstly, it provides insight into the evolving production process in the domestic economy. It can also shed light on the composition and industrial-geographical distribution of investment changes over time. In many economies, such changes have been significant over different periods.

Table 5.4. **Non-financial assets held by non-financial corporations, 2014**

	Total non-financial assets	Non-financial assets held by non-financial corporations	Share
	Millions of national currency	Millions of national currency	%
Australia	11 417 000	2 783 000	24
Czech Republic	29 414 466	10 121 474	34
France	13 406 730	4 135 747	31
Japan	2 741 832 900	1 021 332 000	37
United Kingdom	8 517 621	2 097 113	25

Source: OECD (2017), "Detailed National Accounts, SNA 2008 (or SNA 1993): Balance sheets for non-financial assets", *OECD National Accounts Statistics* (database).
StatLink ⟶ http://dx.doi.org/10.1787/888933589979

Secondly, this detail allows aggregate analysis of the duration of fixed assets and the corresponding term structure of the liabilities that may have been incurred to finance the investment. This is essential in terms of the analysis of financial stability. For example, there have been times when non-financial corporations have relied relatively more on either short-term or long-term debt to finance long-term non-financial investment and were seemingly unprepared for unexpected but sustained interest rate developments or abrupt changes in the cost of borrowing.

Thirdly, this detail can shed some light on the sources of funds available to the sector. For example, in some industries and over some periods, investors may be more willing to invest in non-residential structures or machinery and equipment than they would be to invest in intangible assets. In some cases investors may be interested in a stake in the firm's equity if the funds are being used to finance research and development, whereas they prefer debt instruments if the investment is being used to finance the purchase of assets such as buildings and machines.

It is therefore important that the capital and financial accounts and balance sheets of the non-financial corporations sector provide information on the type of non-financial asset investments, and are ideally complemented by a detailed investment account that provides additional industrial, asset and geographic detail.

Financial uses of funds

A second and increasingly important use of funds for non-financial corporations is in the form of financial investments. This is primarily investment in financial assets but it can also relate to liability transactions, such as paying down debt or the buy-back of own shares.

The financial accounts and balance sheets provide a picture of the non-financial corporations' evolving portfolio of financial investments, measuring transactions in financial assets and liabilities by type of instrument. For example, the very different investment patterns over time in the Canadian non-financial corporations' sector are evident from analysing the financial accounts; this is summarised in Table 5.5, with a period of recession in the fourth quarter of 2008 up to the second quarter of 2009.

Table 5.5. **Selected financial asset transactions, Canadian non-financial corporations**
Billions of CAD

	4Q06	1Q07	2Q07	3Q07	4Q07	1Q08	2Q08	3Q08	**4Q08**	**1Q09**	**2Q09**	3Q09	4Q09	...	2Q13	3Q13
Total financial assets	48.6	90.2	48.7	41.0	40.6	58.3	60.2	33.3	**25.7**	**-18.0**	**0.4**	54.3	41.0	...	38.3	22.2
Currency and deposits	10.4	7.2	12.2	16.4	3.5	-21.7	31.2	-5.4	**5.4**	**-9.1**	**12.3**	7.1	8.1	...	10.2	12.8
Short-term paper	-3.3	14.5	-17.0	13.0	-4.9	20.5	-26.7	6.0	**5.1**	**-28.5**	**0.6**	12.4	-5.8	...	1.2	0.6
Bonds and debentures	3.4	4.3	4.1	0	0.5	0.5	0.3	2.0	**1.0**	**-3.6**	**0.5**	-1.0	-.1	...	1.7	0.6
Inter-corporate loans	1.6	5.4	2.2	-0.7	0.8	-.0.4	1.8	2.7	**3.8**	**.2**	**-.6**	-.5	9.5	...	1.3	8.0
Corporate equity	-6.0	66.0	6.5	.9	37.5	30.7	26.3	39.1	**19.6**	**26.6**	**12.5**	16.2	15.1	...	2.7	9.4
Trade accounts receivable	4.3	5.4	0.3	3.0	-.8	7.6	12.1	2.8	**-1.8**	**-18.1**	**-7.3**	0.7	1.8	...	0.6	3.1

Source: Statistics Canada (2017), Table 378-0121 – National Balance Sheet Accounts, quarterly (CAD) (database), www5.statcan.gc.ca/cansim/pick-choisir?lang=eng&p2=33&id=3780121; Statistics Canada (2017), Table 378-0119 – Financial Flow Accounts, quarterly (CAD) (database), www5.statcan.gc.ca/cansim/a26?lang=eng&retrLang=eng&id=3780119&&pattern=&rtByVal=1&p1=1&p2=81&tabMode=dataTable&csid=.

StatLink ꙮ http://dx.doi.org/10.1787/888933589998

In 2008, the sector invested heavily in corporate equity, including inter-company investment. This reflected the surging markets that lasted up to the outset of the global financial crisis. In 2009, investment in equity and investment fund shares decelerated, while investment in currency and deposits increased. In 2013, investment in currency and deposits was again significant, and investment in equity and investment fund shares continued to decline. Clearly, non-financial corporations manage their financial asset portfolio in concert with changes in economic and financial conditions.

More generally, the financial accounts and balance sheets record the financial investment preferences of non-financial corporations, in relation to current economic events, such as earnings, financial market fluctuations and business cycles. Disregarding the settlement of liabilities, they specifically reveal non-financial corporations' choices with respect to the type of financial assets they would like to hold. This is essential in understanding investment patterns and potential risks of non-financial corporations, shedding light on issues such as preferences for short-term versus long-term investment and firms' projections of future demand. Non-financial corporations will invest where the financial return is the highest. For example, if they feel that investing in a machine or a building will bring a significant return to their owners, they will focus on the acquisition of non-financial assets. Conversely, if their expectations about the demand for their goods and services are weak or declining, they may decide that they can earn a higher return (at least temporarily) by directing funds towards financial assets rather than non-financial assets.

In addition to providing insight into the sector's expectations about future growth, the financial account investment flows and balance sheet holdings also provide insight into preferences with respect to the type of financial investments and associated risk. If, in a certain period, non-financial corporations invest heavily in very liquid assets, this provides an indication of their need to access funds in the near term, either due to internal reasons or as a reaction to financial market fluctuations. On the other hand, if non-financial corporations invest primarily in bonds, this provides an indication of their willingness to "tie up" their funds for a longer period of time and their expectations about financial markets. If this investment is focussed in central government securities, corporations are seeking a safe haven for investment, and this detail thus provides information about their current assessment and preferences with respect to risk in their sector, the domestic economy, and the global economy. Needless to say, the "what" non financial corporations invest in provides a significant amount of information about their assessment of risk, their reactions to current economic events and their predictions of future economic conditions. In recent years, non-financial corporations in many countries have increased their investment flows and holdings in liquid assets. When funds are increasingly used to invest in such financial assets, this investment is often referred to as "dead money" – reflecting a perception by some analysts that such funds could be better put to use (see Box 5.2).

In most economies, a notable feature of non-financial corporations is investment in associated corporations. This is accomplished by transferring some of the funds that a non-financial corporation has available in one part of the enterprise group to another part of the enterprise group, either through equity investments or loans and advances. These types of investments can be reflected in the financial accounts (and balance sheets) as an additional breakdown in the equity and investment funds category, as is the case in Canada, where these are called "corporate claims". This detail is important as intercompany investment transactions can be indicative of fixed capital formation in the same industry, in upstream or downstream industries of the enterprise group, and of corporate re-structuring going on in the economy as well as in other economies through foreign direct investment. These flows can often signal times of consolidation through mergers and acquisitions, and expansion through investment in start-ups or affiliates.

Box 5.2. **Dead money in Canada, the US and elsewhere**

In recent years there have been concerns expressed about the large stockpile of liquid assets held by non-financial corporations, sometimes referred to as "dead money". In 2012, the Governor of the Bank of Canada took note of the significant liquidity position of Canadian corporations. He noted that while this reflected prudence on the part of the corporate sector after the financial crisis and recession, the liquidity position also represented funds that could be invested in non-financial assets in order to spur current and future economic growth. More specifically, he noted that "the level of caution could be viewed as excessive … their job is to put money to work".

Similar questions were raised in the US around the same time. As early as 2005, the Governor of the Federal Reserve Board noted: "Although capital investment has been advancing at a reasonably good pace, it has nonetheless lagged the exceptional rise in profits and internal cash flow". In 2013, the Federal Reserve Bank of St Louis emphasised that "US corporations are holding record-high amounts of cash".

Figure 5.3. **Liquid assets of Canadian non-financial corporations**
Percentage of total financial assets

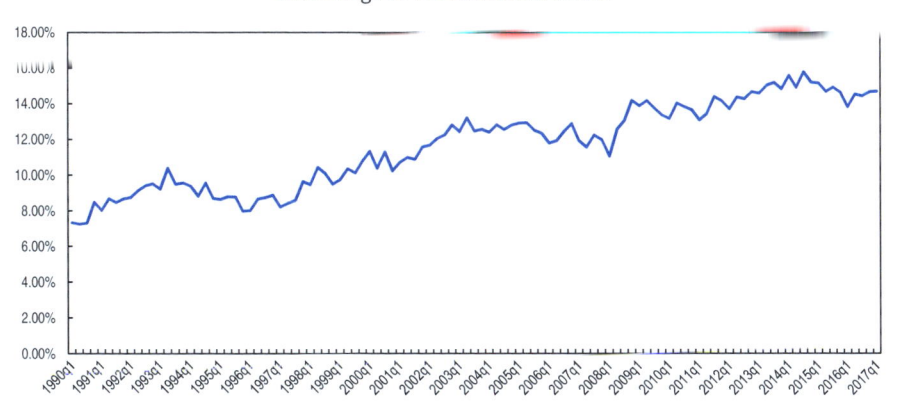

Source: OECD (2017), "Financial Balance Sheets, SNA 2008 (or SNA 1993): Non-consolidated stocks, annual", OECD National Accounts Statistics (database), http://dx.doi.org/10.1787/data-00720-en.
StatLink http://dx.doi.org/10.1787/888933588535

The IMF has recently demonstrated that this increased corporate saving and net lending was the case in a number of G7 and OECD countries (2015). This research into the liquidity of corporations suggested "… that the emergence of the corporate saving glut may be more related to a perceived paucity of profitable (domestic) investment opportunities".

While the inter-company financial investment flows can provide insight into trends over time, there are a number of important questions these data do not address. The first is with whom is this investment being made, and does it represent a vertical investment (supply chain) or a horizontal investment (concentration)? In order to address these questions, users often request that the non-financial corporations' sector financial accounts and balance sheets be sub-sectored into more granular groups, and that these granular groups take the form of a traditional industry-based classification so that they are able to better understand the vertical (within industry) and horizontal (outside of the industry) investment. However, such detail is generally missing from most financial accounts and balance sheets. Furthermore, users are also increasingly interested in whether the inter-company investments are between residents and non-residents. Given the increasingly global nature of enterprises there is a substantial amount of cross-border financial investment taking place, often related to supply chain management. These international flows are specifically captured in the financial accounts with the rest of the world, but also reflected (implicitly, at least) in the financial transactions of the non-financial corporations' sector.

Another use of funds is tied to actively reducing debt loads. In 1981-82, with nominal interest rates at historical highs and in the midst of a six-quarter recession, non-financial corporations in many countries paid off significant portions of both short-term and long term debt. The interest charges associated with their debt levels were becoming unmanageable and, therefore, firms found it more important to reduce their liabilities than to invest in financial assets or non-financial assets. This use of funds contributed significantly to a substantial restructuring of corporations' financial positions, setting the stage for the economic recovery that followed.

Sources of funds for non-financial corporations

As noted earlier in this chapter, non-financial corporations are responsible for a large share of total output, non-financial investments and employment in most economies. As such, they need access to funds in order to finance new initiatives as well as react to changing economic conditions. In developed economies, especially for large corporations, funds are accessed through the capital market (debt and equity), the money market and the business loans market. A key focus of the non-financial corporations' financial accounts and balance sheets is to present the sources of funds available to non-financial corporations. An analysis of these sources of funds reveals a great deal about the overall strategy of firms, as well as how they are reacting to current financial market conditions.

The sources of funds available to non-financial corporations can be illustrated in a number of ways. They can be presented in such a way as to distinguish between internally generated or externally raised funds. In the case of external funds, the accounts reveal whether or not corporations chose to finance their funding needs through borrowing or through the issuance of shares. With respect to debt, the accounts typically articulate whether corporations are issuing short-term or long-term debt. They can also indicate whether the source of funds is domestic or foreign.

Internal sources of funds

As noted above, non-financial corporations exist to generate a return to their owners, whether immediately distributed or not. In the national accounting world this return is measured by the corporate operating surplus. Part of the income generated by a non-financial corporation is used to pay interest to lenders, and to pay corporate taxes. The remainder of the income represents the economic return to the owners. It can be distributed to the owners, or it can be retained within the corporation. The non-distributed portion ends up in the non-financial corporation sector's saving. This saving represents an internal source of funds directly available to a corporation to either invest in non-financial or financial assets, or to reduce debt. Non-financial corporations can also sell assets, most often liquidating financial assets, as a second source of internal funds. However, since it is prudent to retain liquid assets and some financial assets are longer term investments (e.g. inter-company claims), it is common for non-financial corporations to generally raise funds externally.

External sources of funds

In many countries and in most time periods, the internally generated saving of the non-financial corporations' sector are not sufficient to meet non-financial corporations' investment needs; or corporations may decide to divert some of the saving into financial assets. In other words, non-financial corporations generally have a need to raise funds via equity or debt on a regular basis. As such, non-financial corporations must turn to other sectors of the economy in order to secure their required funds for a given accounting period. The ratio of the sources of internal funds (represented by corporate saving, again disregarding the impact of capital transfers), with the total demand for funds on financial markets for Germany and the United States is presented in Figure 5.4. It is clear that, in general, non-financial corporations require more funds than what is internally generated through saving. However, the difference between the two countries presented, Germany and the United States, is quite striking. While the United States' reliance on external funding has been somewhat volatile over the period presented, Germany has been more reliant on internal funding, certainly since 2000.

5. THE FINANCING OF NON-FINANCIAL CORPORATIONS

Figure 5.4. **Internal sources (gross saving) and external sources (change in liabilities) of funds of non-financial corporations in Germany and the United States**
Percentage of gross value added of non-financial corporations

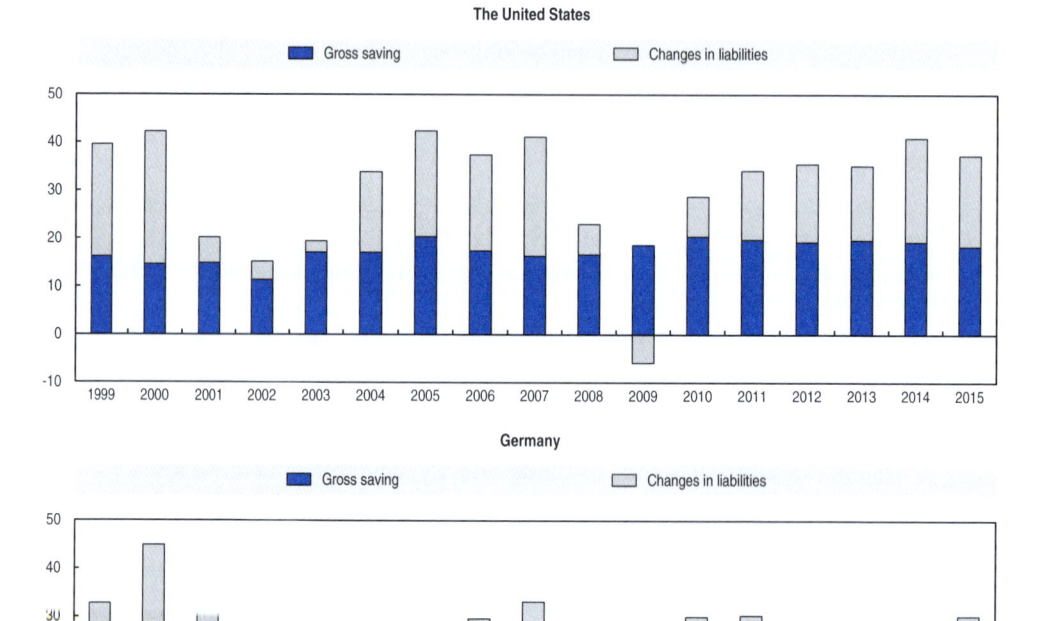

The United States

Germany

Source: OECD (2017), "Detailed National Accounts, SNA 2008 (or SNA 1993): Non-financial accounts by sectors, annual", OECD National Accounts Statistics (database), http://dx.doi.org/10.1787/data-00034-en; and "Financial Accounts, SNA 2008 (or SNA 1993): Non-consolidated flows, annual", OECD National Accounts Statistics (database), http://dx.doi.org/10.1787/data-00718-en.

StatLink ⟶ http://dx.doi.org/10.1787/888933588554

More generally, non-financial corporations have different means to raise external funds. Typically, they borrow from financial corporations, issue debt securities or issue new shares of equity. Their choices provide significant insight into the expectations, behaviour and structure of the corporations. For example, economies where a relatively large proportion of firms are publicly held may engage in more equity financing than in economies where privately held firms are more dominant. This is one material difference between Canada and the US, with the latter having a much higher share of listed firms.

The choice of debt or equity may also be related to the business cycle. In times where stock market prices are low and economic confidence is building –

such as just prior to or the early part of an upturn in a business cycle, when share values typically start to trend up – investors may be more willing to invest in equity than in corporate bonds, and equity financing becomes more attractive to firms. This equity-business cycle relationship can be seen when economic growth is plotted against the net issuance of new equity, with stock markets tending to lead economic growth; see Figure 5.5. On the other hand, in the later stages of a business cycle when share prices are also typically peaking, there may be more of a tendency to increasingly rely on debt as a source of funds, which can lead to financial stability concerns. Generally speaking, in the context of debt issues, a corporation should have enough confidence in the economic conditions so as to not compromise their ability to meet future obligations (including the payment of interest as well as the repayment of debt). In any case, the choice between equity and debt is an important one for non-financial corporations, which is governed by the availability of funds on the financial markets, changes in the financial position, and future prospects, and the choice has varied considerably over time.

Figure 5.5. **Net equity issuance and growth in real GDP, Canadian non-financial corporations**

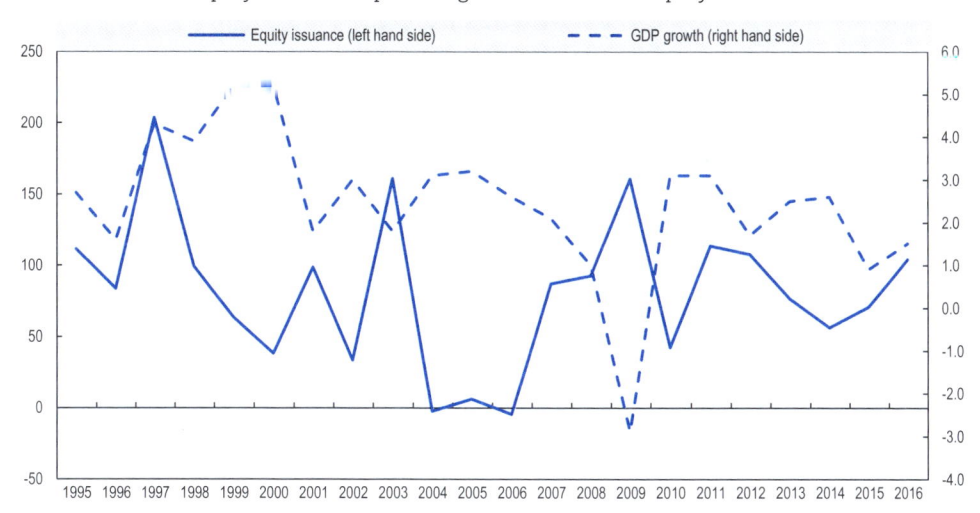

Equity issuance in percentage of total debt and equity issuance

Source: Statistics Canada (2017), *Table 378-0119 – Financial Flow Accounts, quarterly (CAD)* (database), www5.statcan.gc.ca/cansim/a26?lang=eng&retrLang=eng&id=3780119&&pattern=&stByVal=1&p1=1&p2=31&tabMode=dataTable&csid=; Statistics Canada (2017), *Table 380-0064 – Gross domestic product, expenditure-based, quarterly*, www5.statcan.gc.ca/cansim/a26?lang=eng&id=3800064.

StatLink ᠎ http://dx.doi.org/10.1787/888933588573

With respect to debt financing, non-financial corporations also have the choice of short-term or long-term debt. Short-term debt is defined as any debt with a maturity of less than one year at the time of issue, while long-term debt is defined as any debt with a maturity of more than one year. Furthermore, in many economies, only larger firms may have access to the bond market and, especially, the money market. Smaller firms have to rely more heavily on loans from financial corporations to raise funds. The term structure of borrowing in any given period again may reveal a great deal about corporations' expectations regarding future growth and financial conditions such as interest rates. Enterprises tend to issue short-term debt if interest rates are highly volatile, or they expect that interest rates will fall in the near future. Enterprises would tend towards long-term debt when they feel interest rates are stable at an acceptably sustainable level, or if they sense that interest rates may increase in the future. While Canadian corporations' borrowing on money and capital markets trailed off during the last recession, their issues of long-term debt advanced as interest rates reached historic lows after the 2007-09 economic and financial crisis. This is demonstrated in Table 5.6.

Table 5.6. **Debt raised on money and capital markets, Canadian non-financial corporations**
Billions of CAD

	4Q06	1Q07	2Q07	3Q07	4Q07	1Q08	2Q08	3Q08	4Q08	1Q09	2Q09	3Q09	4Q09	...	2Q13	3Q13
Total raised	14.4	8.4	3.7	8.1	1.8	9.4	5.9	3.7	-3.9	3.8	9.4	6.8	-0.3	...	16.0	10.1
Short-term paper	5.5	3.0	-.9	2.9	-0.2	6.9	-1.7	-1.5	-1.9	0	-4.9	-2.1	-7.3	...	4.5	-1.3
Bonds and debentures	8.9	5.4	2.8	5.2	2.0	2.5	7.6	5.2	-2.0	3.8	14.3	8.9	7.0	...	11.5	11.4

Source: Statistics Canada (2017), Table 378-0121 – National Balance Sheet Accounts, quarterly (CAD) (database), www5.statcan.gc.ca/cansim/pick-choisir?lang=eng&p2=33&id=3780121; Statistics Canada (2017), Table 378-0119 – Financial Flow Accounts, quarterly (CAD) (database), www5.statcan.gc.ca/cansim/a26?lang=eng&retrLang=eng&id=3780119&&pattern=&stByVal=1&p1=1&p2=31&tabMode=dataTable&csid=.

StatLink ᛜ http://dx.doi.org/10.1787/888933590017

Short-term versus long-term debt may vary considerably across OECD countries and over time. In Figure 5.6 a striking feature is the strong reliance on short-term debt in some European economies. This situation contrasts with patterns in other European countries such as Finland, Sweden and the United Kingdom, where corporations almost entirely rely on long-term debt.

As with financial investments, information about non-financial corporations' liabilities can also show from whom (at least in part) non-financial corporations receive their funding. An emphasis on from-whom-to-whom information is also a feature of the G-20 Data Gaps Initiative (see Chapter 10). Traditionally, the financial accounts and balance sheets have provided details on the type of financing received by non-financial corporations, but the focus has mainly been on the instruments – debt or equity, long-term or short-term. Increasingly, users are demanding that an additional dimension be added to the financial accounts: "from whom", i.e. from whom are non-financial corporations receiving their funds; from domestic sectors or from foreign sectors; and if funds are from domestic sectors, are the funds coming from other non-financial corporations, banks, institutional investors or other financial corporations. This "from whom" dimension provides additional insight into the economy-wide risk associated with sectoral inter-connectedness.

Figure 5.6. **Loans and debt securities, short-term versus long-term, 2014**
Percentage of total loans and debt securities

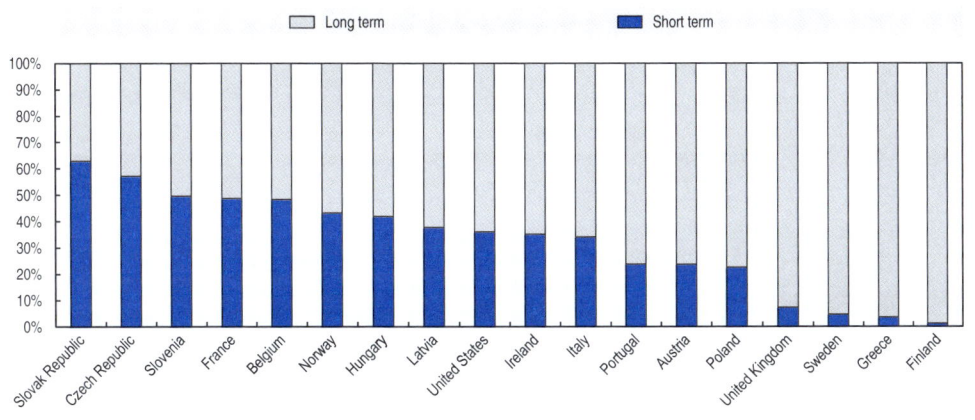

Source: OECD (2017), "Financial Balance Sheets, SNA 2008 (or SNA 1993): Non-consolidated stocks, annual", OECD National Accounts Statistics (database), http://dx.doi.org/10.1787/data-00720-en.

StatLink ᕵᔐ http://dx.doi.org/10.1787/888933588592

Box 5.3. **Data sources and methodology for non-financial corporations**

Data sources for the non-financial corporations' sector vary considerably across countries. The source data are used to estimate financial accounts and balance sheets, as well as other changes in assets accounts. Data quality and asset-liability details may vary across countries, but there are four basic data sources: publicly available corporate balance sheets, survey statistics, tax data, and counterpart information (e.g. banks' deposit liabilities or loan assets) or indirect data (e.g. securities' databases). These are not mutually exclusive sources and most compilers leverage as much information as they can, often using two or more data sources. Integrating these data sources is a further methodological complication as each of these data sources has its own characteristics.

An issue in the compilation of financial accounts and balance sheets concerns the level of consolidation of national accounts data on financial assets and liabilities for non-financial corporations. Depending on the source data, this consolidation can vary considerably across countries. Enterprise-based survey sources tend to present data that are generally consolidated at the enterprise level, i.e., borrowing and lending among related entities would be eliminated. Legal entity-based source data, however, tend to present assets and liabilities in which the borrowing and lending between legal entities belonging to the same enterprise (group) are not cancelled out. As a consequence, total assets and liabilities will be larger in the

Box 5.3. **Data sources and methodology for non-financial corporations** *(cont.)*

latter case than in the former, and may compromise international comparability. Needless to say, it is important to consult any available country metadata in order to properly interpret the financial accounts and balance sheets data for non-financial corporations.

Table 5.7. **Basic sources of data to construct the non-financial corporations' sector**

Data source/general characteristics	Publicly available financial information	Tax data	Survey statistics	Counterpart or indirect data
Frequency	Typically annual although, with the increase in private sector databases, sub-annual information is becoming more common	Annual	Can be designed to be quarterly	Typically quarterly, or higher frequency for some items (securities databases)
Timeliness	Varying lags, from short lags (partial information) to medium and long lags (in excess of one year) for complete financial information; however, with the increase in private sector databases, select information is becoming more timely	Long lag (often in excess of 1-2 years)	Can be designed to have an adequate lag for timely quarterly releases	Typically a short lag
Details	Aggregated, such that limited detailed information may be available	Aggregated, such that limited detailed information may be available	Can be detailed by design	Instrument-specific details
Consolidation	Largely global consolidation for complex MNEs; domestic consolidation for other enterprises (in the case of enterprises consisting of several legal entities possibly only unconsolidated data available). Lack of clearly defined statistical unit	Domestic consolidation, based on legal entities' statistical units	Domestically consolidated enterprises for enterprises consisting of several legal entities; domestic legal entities for simple firms	Reflection of domestically consolidated entities
Coverage	Typically no, as the focus is on relatively large firms	Yes, for legal entities' statistical units	No, is restricted to survey sample	Typically yes for instrument specific details
Cost	Relatively low cost	Relatively low cost, if available	Relatively high cost; concerns about response burden	Relatively low cost

In relation to borrowing from non-residents, there is an additional important dimension: the currency composition of foreign debt, as foreign investors are sometimes unwilling to assume the additional risk (and potential reward) of an appreciation or depreciation of the currency, with respect to the holdings of non-financial corporations' debt. In order to guard against currency fluctuations, non-financial corporations therefore often seek or are required to issue debt in a common currency such as the Euro or the US dollar. For example, in Canada the majority of private corporation bonds held by non-residents have been issued in

US dollars, to "protect" foreign investors against large depreciations of the local currency. As a result, non-financial corporations are exposed to currency risks when raising funds in foreign currency. Specifically, they will have to pay interest and reimburse the principal at whatever exchange rate prevails when these obligations come due. This may lead to increased foreign currency hedging activity on the part of borrowers. It is thus becoming increasingly important that financial accounts provide detail on the currency composition of debt.

3. Capital gains in the non-financial corporations' sector

The previous section discussed the uses and sources of funds of non-financial corporations. Below, the focus changes to the outcome or result of all this activity – namely the stocks of assets and liabilities, or the stocks of wealth. Before one can examine the net worth or net wealth of non-financial corporations, one needs to first examine, in addition to the net purchases of assets and the net incurrence of liabilities, another set of flows to derive a clear picture of the sector's wealth. These flows are comprised of the revaluations of assets and the so-called "other changes in the volume of assets".

Revaluations reflect changes in the price of assets/liabilities during the accounting period, from unrealised gains or losses on those items. Other changes in volume represent changes in assets/liabilities that are not due to financial transactions or revaluations. The latter flows may relate to, for example, discoveries and depletions of subsoil assets, catastrophic losses and uncompensated seizures, as well as adjustments to the value of assets not due to price changes. These two types of other flows are contained in the 2008 SNA "other changes in assets" account.

The "other flows" (revaluations together with the other changes in the volume of assets) have been typically significantly larger than the financial transactions in many developed countries for a number of years, and this has been led by large capital gains and losses. This is the case as relevant financial instruments are measured on a market value basis on the balance sheet account of the national accounts, and the prices of financial assets (and liabilities) can change significantly, given changing market expectations about future returns and risk. By far the largest "other flow" in the accounts of non-financial corporations occurs in corporate equity assets and liabilities. This is generally followed by revaluations of non-financial assets, for example changes in the reproducible costs of fixed assets. Other flows in other financial instruments, such as other accounts payable/receivable, currency and deposits, loans and even bonds, are usually quite small relative to the financial transactions.

The change in the market value of corporate equity provides a good example of the impact of revaluations (see Figure 5.7). Corporate equity has fluctuated significantly over time in Canada, as can be seen from the total change in the liability equity position valued at market prices (blue line). Clearly, these changes have been governed by the other changes in assets account (grey bars), more specifically revaluations. Given the market capitalisation methodology employed to value equity, volume changes are negligible for the corporate equity liability (but can occur as the result of corporate births and deaths). The revaluations, or capital gains and losses, reflect market participants' perceptions of the value of non-financial corporations. While gains have tended to outweigh losses over time, generating an upward trend, the impact of the financial crisis and recession is evident in 2008 and 2009.

Figure 5.7. **Changes in the market value of Canadian non-financial corporations' sector equity – revaluations versus transactions**
Millions of CAD

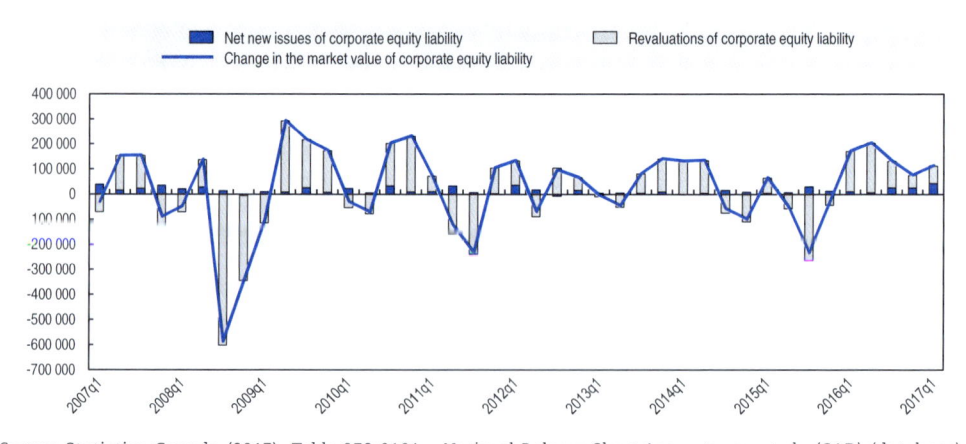

Source: Statistics Canada (2017), Table 378-0121 – National Balance Sheet Accounts, quarterly (CAD) (database), www5.statcan.gc.ca/cansim/pick-choisir?lang=eng&p2=33&id=3780121; Statistics Canada (2017), Table 378-0119 – Financial Flow Accounts, quarterly (CAD) (database), www5.statcan.gc.ca/cansim/a26?lang=eng&retrLang=eng&id=3780119&&pattern=&stByVal=1&p1=1&p2=31&tabMode=dataTable&csid=.

StatLink ᕯᔐ http://dx.doi.org/10.1787/888933588611

4. The financial position of non-financial corporations: balance sheets

As noted before, the ultimate objective of most non-financial corporations is to generate wealth for its owners. If this is indeed the case, the financial accounts for non-financial corporations require a stock dimension – the sum result of all the activity and other changes of non-financial corporations at a point in time. This "sum of activity" is captured in the balance sheets. The balance sheets provide a "picture" at a given point in time of the stock of assets and liabilities of the non-financial corporations sector. They thus measure, at given intervals (quarters, years), the financial health of the sector, or its evolution over time in a time-series format.

The balance sheet account resembles the structure of the capital and financial account. The balance sheet includes the sector's non-financial assets, of which the acquisitions less disposals are recorded in the capital account; the stock of financial assets and liabilities, of which the transactions are recorded in the financial account; and net worth. For non-financial corporations, the balance of assets and liabilities is largely reflected in corporate equity. As we will see later in this section, equity has a particular treatment in the balance sheets of corporations according to the System of National Accounts.

The balance sheet also sheds light on structural changes in the organisation of local and global enterprises as well as on associated wealth and financial stability, and thus on the future operating capacity of non-financial enterprises. It supplements the analysis of production and income generation that can be drawn from the national accounts supply-use tables.[2]

Non-financial assets

For non-financial corporations, non-financial assets typically account for a significant share of total assets. When examining the non-financial assets section of the balance sheet account of the non financial corporations sector, it is important to consider three aspects: coverage, ownership and valuation. In this respect, it could be argued that ensuring complete coverage is the most important consideration in constructing a balance sheet. In many ways, the stock of non-financial assets – or capital base – explains how non-financial corporations go about producing goods and services and generating income for their owners. Produced assets (e.g. structures, machinery and equipment) comprise the principal non-financial assets for the non-financial corporations' sector, followed by land and inventories. If non-financial assets are not fully articulated on the balance sheet, then there is a disconnect between the production of goods and services, the generation of income, and the assets that are used by the sector to produce these goods and services and contribute to net worth changes. This potential disconnect is best illustrated using a few examples.

Currently "branding" does not fall within the asset boundary of national accounts. This means that the development and use of a brand does not find its way onto the national accounts' balance sheets for non-financial corporations. It is widely accepted however, that firms invest in the development of a brand and then use that brand to sell goods and services and earn a return on their investment. Excluding this asset is likely to attribute too much return to other assets that are recorded on the balance sheets. As a result, it is difficult to have a proper understanding of the assets that were used to produce the goods and services of the non-financial corporations sector.

Another asset that is often missing from the balance sheet accounts concerns natural resources. Non-financial corporations in many economies are often granted (for a price) the explicit right to extract natural resources by governments. This right to extract is an asset they acquire in order to produce goods and services. For many non-financial corporations, this is one of the most important assets that they own and exert ownership rights over (i.e. they can sell the asset). However, this asset is often not reflected in the balance sheet of national accounts, mainly because measurement issues related to the delineation and estimation of the reserves (e.g. proven reserves versus probable reserves) and the future income that can be derived from extracting these reserves. The exclusion of natural resources is a significant data gap in some countries that leads to an underestimation of the sector's assets. As a result, the relevance of these accounts and the international comparability of wealth data may be adversely impacted.

The second important aspect that needs to be considered when examining non-financial assets in the balance sheets is the establishment of the owner to which the assets is to be attributed. The purpose of the balance sheets is to provide a current representation of the sector's assets, liabilities, and the balance of these two categories, net worth. Ownership of assets is an important characteristic that needs to be taken into consideration when analysing the balance sheets of non-financial corporations. National accounts distinguish between legal ownership and economic ownership, with a preference for the latter – that is, national accounts allocate assets to the sector of the user (for example, in the case of financial leasing). Therefore, within the balance sheets assets are recorded in the sector that has economic ownership of the asset. In the case of financial leases, a liability (and a corresponding financial asset in the legal owner's sector) is recorded to reflect the "borrowing" of this asset from the legal owner. This approach links the goods and services produced by non-financial corporations and the assets that are used to produce the goods and services.

A final aspect to be considered is the valuation of non-financial assets. As many non-financial assets are not regularly traded on second-hand markets, it is difficult to find appropriate market values for the assets which are in use for a certain period of time. The 2008 SNA therefore uses an alternative method, called the "perpetual inventory method" or the "current replacement cost method" for produced capital assets, which is based on the past accumulation of assets, adjusted for depreciation and price changes. Non-produced assets should be similarly valued at some approximation to market value. More details on this, and other issues concerning the measurement of non-financial assets, are discussed in Chapter 8.

Financial assets

For non-financial corporations, the largest assets tend to be deposits, accounts receivable (mostly intra-sectoral) and inter-company investment. The latter item, which may consist of equity as well as loans, is not separately recorded in standard national accounts presentations, but included under the relevant instruments (equity or loans). It is increasingly important to be able to separate inter-company investment from the individual instruments, especially given the significant growth in recent times of direct investment in subsidiary companies abroad. This is further discussed in the context of globalisation later in this chapter. Furthermore, portfolio investment has also grown in recent years in some western economies, as the growth of companies' earnings has been increasingly directed into liquid assets such as deposits, tradeable shares and debt securities (see Box 5.1) with growing shares in foreign securities. The above factors have, in turn, led to an increase in the share of financial assets to total assets of non-financial corporations in many economies in recent years. This is evident in Table 5.8 with Canadian financial assets gaining ground over Canadian non-financial assets steadily since 2000, growing from 42% to 53% of total assets, interrupted only by the effect of the drop in the value of equity assets in the fourth quarter of 2008. As a result, it has become important to analyse the financial assets of non-financial corporations in terms of instruments held. Table 5.8 also shows the shares of deposits in total financial assets for non-financial corporations for Canada. As can be seen, the share of liquid deposit assets has doubled from 8% to 16% of total financial assets in the 25 years since 1990, with a cyclical increase in liquidity evident in the financial crisis period.

Table 5.8. **Canadian non-financial corporations' holdings of financial assets**
Share of total assets

	1990	1995	2000	2005	2007	2008	2009	2010	2015	2016
Share of financial assets in total assets	0.42	0.39	0.42	0.45	0.52	0.46	0.51	0.49	0.53	0.53
Share of deposits in total financial assets	0.08	0.08	0.11	0.13	0.13	0.15	0.14	0.14	0.16	0.15

Source: Statistics Canada (2017), Table 378-0121 – National Balance Sheet Accounts, quarterly (CAD) (database), www5.statcan.gc.ca/cansim/pick-choisir?lang=eng&p2=33&id=3780121; Statistics Canada (2017), Table 378-0119 – Financial Flow Accounts, quarterly (CAD) (database), www5.statcan.gc.ca/cansim/a26?lang=eng&retrLang=eng&id=3780119&&pattern=&stByVal=1&p1=1&p2=31&tabMode=dataTable&csid=.

StatLink ⟶ http://dx.doi.org/10.1787/888933590036

It is also interesting to analyse the financial assets of non-financial corporations by counterparty, relating investors and borrowers. Increasingly, statistics are becoming available on the counterparty sectors in which the sectors of the economy invest, or from which they borrow, as per the G-20 Data Gaps Initiative (see Box 5.4). The power of the latter detail on "from-whom-to-whom" (FWTW) information for non-financial corporations is best demonstrated using an example. Assume that users are informed that the non-financial corporations' sector holds USD 100 million in financial assets. That single number does not reveal anything about non-financial corporations' risk or their assessment of current economic conditions. Now assume that users are told more specifically that non-financial corporations hold the USD 100 million in currency and deposits. This provides additional information regarding risk (in this case, minimal risk) and indicates that non-financial corporations are probably looking to invest these funds elsewhere in the short to medium term, since they are likely earning a relatively low return. Now assume that users are also told that non-financial corporations hold the currency and deposits, denominated in US Dollars, with a bank in the United States. This information regarding non-financial corporations' financial assets – how much (the value), what type (the instrument) and with whom (the counterparty sector) provides a complete picture that assists in the assessment of the risk and investment patterns of this sector.

Liabilities

Liabilities of non-financial corporations tend to outsize financial assets by a significant margin. The largest liability of non-financial corporations normally consists of equity held by others, though its importance fluctuates over time. This fluctuation reflects changes in the market valuation of equity over time, as well as time-dependent preferences for the use of debt versus equity. Loans, marketable debt instruments (bonds and short-term paper issues outstanding) and accounts payable also tend to be relatively large proportions of total liabilities.

The use of debt securities varies considerably across OECD countries. Figure 5.8 presents the use of debt securities and loans by non-financial corporations for a number of different countries. It shows that the US has the highest proportion of debt securities, which can partially be explained by US non-financial corporations' access to debt markets.

At the same time, the liquidity of non-financial corporations in Canada has also improved in concert with the growth in financial investments in liquid assets. A broad measure related to liquidity looks at liquid assets relative to short-term liabilities and provides a measure of non-financial corporations' ability to meet their short-term debt commitments. Figure 5.9 demonstrates that, in Canada, this ratio fluctuates over time, but the increase in deposits and portfolio investment suggests that liquidity is not currently an issue of concern for the non-financial corporations sector.

Leverage is another measure of the financial health of non-financial corporations. The debt-to-equity ratio is a measure of the non-financial corporations' leverage. Leverage has been on a slight downward trend in

> Box 5.4. **From-whom-to-whom details and the G-20 Data Gaps Initiative**
>
> The importance of measuring the sector inter-connectedness within an economy has been one of the themes of the G-20 Data Gaps Initiative, post-financial crisis. In most affected economies, the rapid transmission of financial instability across inter-sectoral lines in the 2007-09 period underlined vulnerabilities that had not received much attention up to that point. The balance sheet-led financial crisis and recession contributed to an ongoing need to better articulate the assets and liabilities of lenders and borrowers, vis-à-vis different sectors of the economy. This would help users in understanding the inter-relationships and potential proliferation and magnification of risks if major players in one sector experienced economic difficulties.
>
> In short, there is a need to better present financial accounts and balance sheet statistics in terms of interconnections between sectors. This is presented as sectoral details underneath each financial instrument. For example, if a pension funds holds bond assets, then the details on interconnectedness would indicate whether these are bonds of domestic non-financial corporations, financial institutions or governments, or whether these are bonds issued by non-residents. This is known as from-whom-to-whom (FWTW) presentation.
>
> Currently, FWTW information in financial accounts and balance sheets is limited and typically embedded in the type of instrument. For example, the non-financial corporation sector's balance sheets may identify financial investments in non-resident bonds or government bonds; and they may also identify investment in money-market funds or bank deposits (indicating transactions with banks). Such detail begins to provide a picture of "with whom" non-financial corporations are investing. It signals where non-financial corporations feel there is risk and where they sense there is opportunity. The non-financial corporations' financial accounts and balance sheets can, in conjunction with the regional or international accounts, also provide insight on where (which economic territory) non-financial corporations are making their financial investments. As part of the G-20 Data Gaps Initiative (which is discussed in further detail in Chapter 10), it is expected that the FWTW-information will become increasingly available for many countries.

Canada, the United States and other OECD countries over the last 25 years, further underlining the general health of the balance sheets of the enterprises in this sector. Notably, the leverage ratio based on national accounts data is calculated at market value. This makes the ratio sensitive to stock market

5. THE FINANCING OF NON-FINANCIAL CORPORATIONS

swings. Therefore, it is also useful to compile a measure of leverage based on book values or historical cost. Figure 5.10 shows both ratios for Canada. Despite the larger volatility of the national accounts-based ratio, both indicators generally move in concert.

Figure 5.8. **Loans versus debt securities of non-financial corporations, 2015**
Percentage of total loans and debt securities

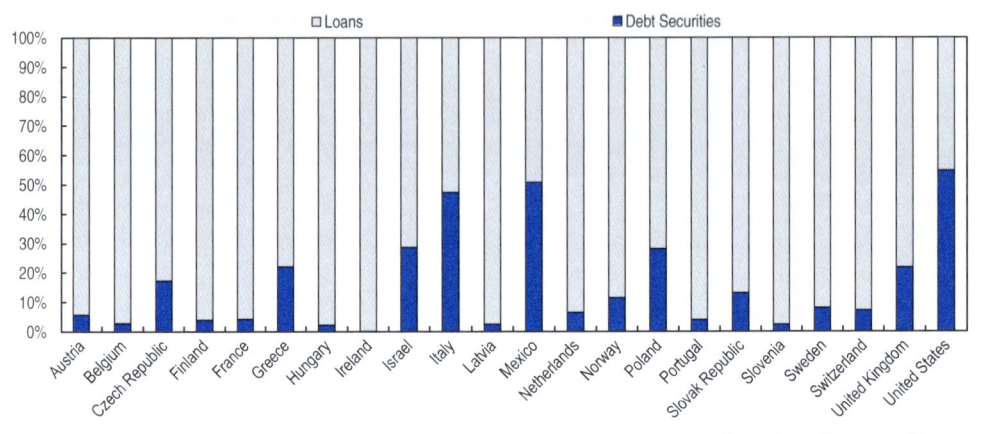

Source: OECD (2017), "Financial Balance Sheets, SNA 2008 (or SNA 1993): Non-consolidated stocks, annual", OECD National Accounts Statistics (database), http://dx.doi.org/10.1787/data-00720-en.
StatLink ⟶ http://dx.doi.org/10.1787/888933588630

Figure 5.9. **Non-financial corporations' liquidity ratio, Canada**
Percentage of liquid assets to short-term liabilities

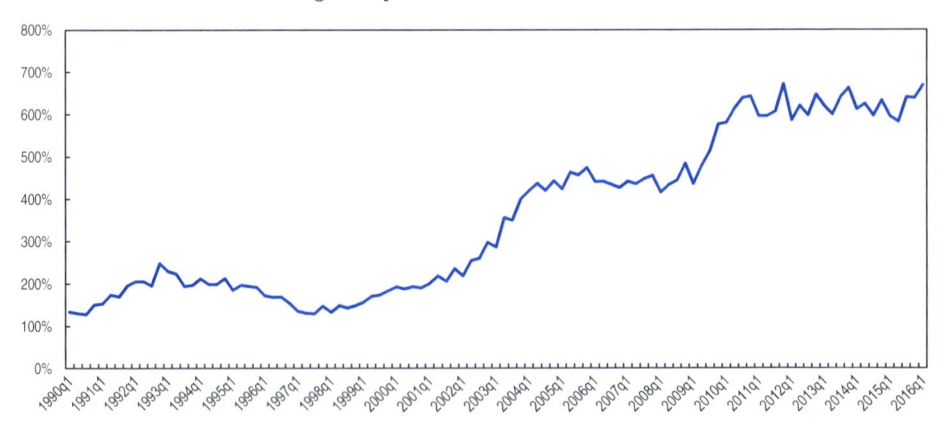

Source: Statistics Canada (2017), Table 378-0121 – National Balance Sheet Accounts, quarterly (CAD) (database), www5.statcan.gc.ca/cansim/pick-choisir?lang=eng&p2=33&id=3780121; Statistics Canada (2017), Table 378-0119 – Financial Flow Accounts, quarterly (CAD) (database), www5.statcan.gc.ca/cansim/a26?lang=eng&retrLang=eng&id=3780119&&pattern=&stByVal=1&p1=1&p2=31&tabMode=dataTable&csid=.
StatLink ⟶ http://dx.doi.org/10.1787/888933588649

Figure 5.10. **Non-financial corporations' leverage, Canada**
Percentage of debt to equity

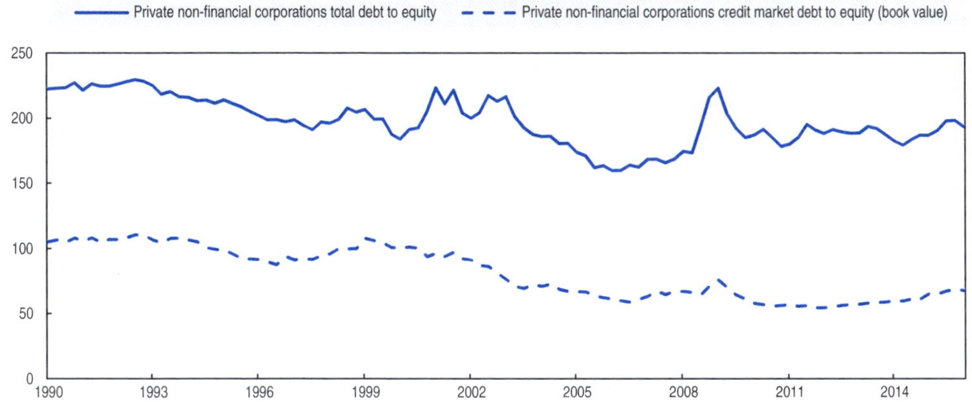

Source: Statistics Canada (2017), *Table 378-0124 – National Balance Sheet Accounts, financial indicators, corporations, quarterly (per cent)* (database),0 www5.statcan.gc.ca/cansim/a26?lang=eng&retrLang=eng&id=3780124&&pattern=&stByVal=1&p1=1&p2=31&tabMode=dataTable&csid=.

StatLink http://dx.doi.org/10.1787/888933588459

Equity and net worth: a key difference between national and corporate accounting

Apart from the valuation and the definition of assets, one of the major differences between business and national accounts accounting relates to the treatment of equity. Differences between national accounts and business accounts are discussed in detail in Box 5.5. Here, we address the differences in defining net worth, net asset value and owners' equity. The basic accounting identity used in business accounting is:

Total assets = Total debt liabilities + Owners' equity

In the system of national accounts, the equity of a corporation, in the sense of shares and other equity valued at market prices, is treated as a liability, hence the accounting identity becomes:

Total assets = Total liabilities (including outstanding equity at market prices) + Net worth (i.e. any remaining residual)

Note that when total assets are equal to total liabilities in the SNA, there is no residual net worth of the non-financial corporations' sector. Furthermore, if stock market prices are particularly high, in view of investors' future profit expectations, then residual net worth may even become negative. This leads to the following three questions:

- *Why is equity treated as a liability in national accounts?* The market value of corporate equity is treated as a liability in the balance sheets (and the financial accounts), because all corporate shares have an external owner. For example, assume that a mutual fund invests in the shares of a non-financial corporation. This investment is a financial asset owned by the mutual fund sector. If the mutual fund holds a financial asset, then there must be a corresponding liability in another sector – in this case, in the non-financial corporations' sector. However, one can also think of the market value of corporate equity (on the liability side of the corporation) as a measure of corporate net worth belonging to shareholders when analysing the non-financial corporations' sector in isolation.

- *Can owners' equity be derived as the net asset value in the system of national accounts?* Yes, it can and some countries (including Canada) release such a supplementary national accounts measure – sometimes referred to as the net asset measure or current value measure of the corporation. It is calculated as total assets *minus* total debt liabilities (i.e. excluding the market value of corporate equity). One would expect that this value is equal or at least close to the market value of the corporate equity liability. However, this is rarely the case, because one amount is based on the value of the shares on the stock market, while the other is based on the intrinsic value of the corporation, i.e. the difference between the assets and the debt liabilities on the balance sheets. The net asset value may also be quite different from the owners' equity according to business accounting. One reason is the divergent valuation practices. For example, in business accounting, non-financial assets are usually valued at historical cost, while the 2008 SNA applies the current replacement cost method. It may also differ due to coverage. For example, some assets are recognised in the national accounts which are not recorded as such in business accounting, such as intellectual property products. On the other hand, in the case of business accounts some provisions for future expenses may be deducted from the owners' equity.

- *Why is there residual corporate net worth in the system of national accounts?* Residual corporate net worth is that part of corporate net worth which is not assigned to another sector as an asset. It can be the result of the methodology employed in recording assets and liabilities in the balance sheets, or it can be related to measurement errors. Measurement errors can arise due to missing or misvalued assets and debt liabilities in the net asset measure of the intrinsic value of the corporation, or any mismeasurement in the calculation of the market value of the outstanding shares (listed and unlisted) in the corporate equity liability measure. In addition, residual corporate net worth may arise due to a "market expectation gap". More specifically, the share prices of corporations reflect the investors' perception about the future earning potential and value of the enterprise. If they are "pricing" the shares higher than the net asset value, it may be an indication of i) excess speculative activity; ii) investors' assessment of assets that are not recorded on the balance sheets; or iii) investors' expectations about future profits which are not reflected in the assets. The reverse can also be the case.

For instance, assume that the non-financial corporations sector's assets for a given country are USD 100 000 and its debt liabilities are USD 90 000. The net asset value of the firm is therefore USD 10 000 (USD 100 000 in assets less USD 90 000 in debt liabilities). Assume that the sector has 1 000 shares outstanding and the current market value (stock market price) of these shares is USD 15 per share. The market value of the firm's equity is USD 15 000 (1 000 shares × USD 15 per share). In national accounts, the difference between the USD 10 000 net asset value (or current value) and the USD 15 000 equity is referred to as the sector's (residual) corporate net worth. In this case, net worth according to national accounts is equal to minus USD 5 000. Figure 5.11 shows these different measures, the net asset value (or current value) and the market value of equity, for non-financial corporations in Canada. While these measures track each other well over time, they are rarely equal, with the difference representing residual corporate net worth.

Figure 5.11. **Net asset value versus equity (market value) for non-financial corporations in Canada**
Millions of CAD

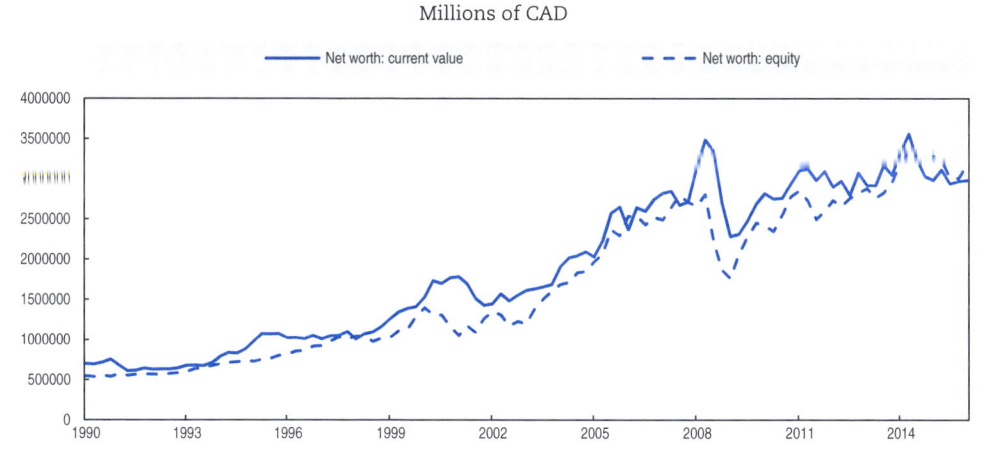

Source: Statistics Canada (2017), Table 378-0121 – National Balance Sheet Accounts, quarterly (CAD) (database), www5.statcan.gc.ca/cansim/pick-choisir?lang=eng&p2=33&id=3780121; Statistics Canada (2017), Table 378-0119 – Financial Flow Accounts, quarterly (CAD) (database), www5.statcan.gc.ca/cansim/a26?lang=eng&retrLang=eng&id=3780119&&pattern=&stByVal=1&p1=1&p2=31&tabMode=dataTable&csid=.

StatLink ᔛ http://dx.doi.org/10.1787/888933588478

In economic theory, putting measurement issues aside, the relationship between the market value of equity to a corporation's net asset value (at current replacement costs) is often referred to as Tobin's q. Tobin's q suggests that the market value of an enterprise should be equal, or close, to its intrinsic value at current values. If Tobin's q is greater than 1 it is reflective of the fact that investors are assigning a premium to something, likely valuing some unmeasured or unrecorded asset of the company, or expecting larger future

5. THE FINANCING OF NON-FINANCIAL CORPORATIONS

profits not reflected in the assets. As can be derived from Figure 5.12, the Tobin's q measure for the non-financial corporations' sector in Canada is quite volatile, with peaks in the dotcom bubble around 2000, and around the Great Recession.

Figure 5.12. **Tobin's q for the non-financial corporations' sector in Canada**

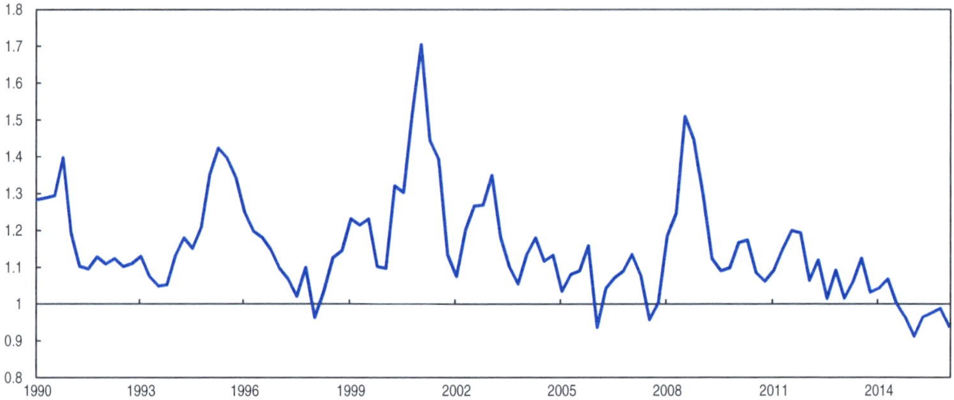

Source: Statistics Canada (2017), Table 378-0121 – National Balance Sheet Accounts, quarterly (CAD) (database), www5.statcan.gc.ca/cansim/pick-choisir?lang=eng&p2=33&id=3780121; Statistics Canada (2017), Table 378-0119 – Financial Flow Accounts, quarterly (CAD) (database), www5.statcan.gc.ca/cansim/a26?lang=eng&retrLang=eng&id=3780119&&pattern=&stByVal=1&p1=1&p2=31&tabMode=dataTable&csid=.

StatLink ⟶ http://dx.doi.org/10.1787/888933588497

Box 5.5. **Key financial indicators of non-financial corporations**

Just like a business's financial statements can be used to derive important financial indicators that speak to the health of the business, the information contained in the national accounts can be used to analyse the overall health of the non-financial corporations' sector. Such ratios can be particularly useful, given the recent emphasis on the financial stability of institutional sectors. Although the level of detail given in sector accounts varies across countries, most compilers should be in a position to produce some of these ratios.

The following list comprises some (but not all) of the informative ratios that can be calculated from the financial accounts and balance sheets, some of which have been used in the main text.

- **Financial assets to non-financial assets ratio:** This ratio provides a broad indication of the structural changes in asset investment, which can be used to assess whether emphasis has shifted towards or against investment in financial assets.

- **Financial asset composition ratios:** The financial assets to non-financial assets ratio can be supplemented by ratios that look at the composition of assets, such as short-term to long-term assets or inter-company investment to other assets. These ratios shed additional light on structural changes (e.g. shifting away from fixed capital formation and into investment in other companies) and/or preferences for liquidity and risk.

Box 5.5. **Key financial indicators of non-financial corporations** (cont.)

- **Liquidity or current ratio (current assets to current liabilities ratio):** This ratio is a measure of the sector's ability to meet its short-term obligations. It may be more useful to exclude other accounts receivable/payable. Excluding inventories (the least liquid current asset) is often referred to as the acid-test ratio.
- **Short-term to long-term debt ratio:** This ratio provides a broad indication of structural changes in liabilities, which can be used to assess whether emphasis has shifted towards short-term or longer-term borrowing.
- **Debt burden (debt service ratio):** This is the ratio of interest (and, optionally, principal) payments to debt. These payments can also be scaled to corporate income. This ratio provides a direct measure of the costs associated with debt, as well as offering a useful supplement to leverage measures. It also provides an indication of vulnerability to interest rate fluctuations.
- **Leverage ratio (debt to equity ratio):** This ratio is a measure of the private non-financial corporations' sector's financial leverage. A higher debt to equity ratio indicates that the sector has been increasing its relative share of debt in external financing (and vice versa). Fluctuations in the market value of equity can also cause changes in this indicator; therefore, this ratio is sometimes calculated using book values.
- **Tobin's q (the ratio of the market value of equity to its net asset value at replacement costs):** This ratio is a measure of any premium (e.g. valuing some unmeasured or unrecorded assets) or discount (expectations of lower returns) investors have assigned to non-financial corporations.
- **Performance ratio (saving or undistributed earnings to equity at book value):** This ratio is a measure of the private non-financial corporations' sector's earning power on shareholders' investment at book value.
- **Return ratio (saving or undistributed earnings to non-financial assets):** This ratio is a measure of the private non-financial corporations' sector's earning power on its non-financial assets, or capital base.
- **Internal to external sources of funds ratio:** This ratio provides an indication of the reliance on funds borrowed or raised externally in relation to saving or own funds. It provides a rough picture of the changing structure of the sources of funds for the non-financial corporations' sector.
- **Saving and/or net lending to GDP ratio:** This ratio provides a broad indication of the role of the non-financial corporations' sector in providing funds for financing investments or in providing funds to the rest of the economy.

5. Globalisation, foreign direct investment and non-financial corporations

Globalisation has become an important feature of the present-day economy. In addition to contributing to growth in foreign trade in goods and services, multinationals are increasingly becoming active in other countries' production processes, with parts of these processes spanning the globe and being allocated to countries on the basis of comparative advantages and cost-effectiveness (including minimisation of the global tax burden).

Foreign direct investment (FDI), both inward and outward, is a useful indicator of a country's level of economic globalisation, allowing some insights into how interrelated economic infrastructure is with the rest of the world. Data on FDI provide information on the first level of connectivity of international inter-corporate relationships, which are closely related to international trade and global production and distribution of goods and services. A more general way of monitoring the impact of globalisation is by compiling non-financial accounts, financial accounts and balance sheets for non-financial corporations broken down by foreign controlled corporations; public corporations (controlled by government); and national private corporations, sometimes part of domestic multinationals. See also Box 5.6.

> **Box 5.6. Foreign control of the Canadian economy – non-financial corporations' sector**
>
> Non-financial corporations account for the bulk of foreign direct investment (FDI) in Canada. The control of employment and capital by foreign non-financial corporations in the Canadian economy is notable, especially in certain industries. For the manufacturing sector alone, these firms contributed 500 000 jobs or one-third of the total employment in the industry in 2013. Wholesale and retail trade sectors contributed 600 000 jobs, accounting for 22% of the total employment in these activities. In fact, non-financial activities account for the lion's share of employment controlled by foreign parents. In manufacturing as well as in mining, quarrying, and oil and gas extraction industries, foreign controlled firms hold significant non-financial assets in Canada.
>
> Of the CAD 1 trillion in revenues generated by foreign-owned Canadian enterprises in 2012, 37% was in the manufacturing sector. The combined wholesale and retail trade sectors followed with a 33% share. Part of this income is related to sales abroad. Foreign controlled corporations tend to be relatively more engaged in international trade, exporting CAD 222.6 billion in 2013, while importing CAD 274.4 billion – representing half of all Canada's goods exports and 58% of all goods imports. While foreign investment contributes significantly to the Canadian economy, there are also certain vulnerabilities with respect to potential production chain interruptions or changes in global production patterns.

> Box 5.6. **Foreign control of the Canadian economy – non-financial corporations' sector** *(cont.)*
>
> On the other side of the ledger are the impacts of direct investment abroad. The focus is again on majority ownership of foreign subsidiaries. Non-financial corporations account for the largest portion of Canadian direct investment abroad, particularly outside of North America and the Caribbean where investment in goods producing industries dominates. In 2013, the activities of foreign manufacturing affiliates were mainly located in the North American and Caribbean regions as well as in Europe. Foreign affiliate sales and employment activity in South and Central America, Asia/Oceania and Africa were concentrated in manufacturing, mining, and oil and gas extraction.
>
> Canadian statistics on activities of foreign affiliates also generate statistics on assets and liabilities, though these are not yet released with respect to outward investment. One of the forthcoming benefits of this information is a broader perspective on foreign exposures of domestic non-financial corporation parents with respect to majority-owned subsidiaries abroad.
>
> More generally, foreign exposures of Canadian non-financial corporations cover any foreign currency denominated assets and liabilities. That includes, among other items, any portfolio investment assets (covered in the portfolio investment survey) and debt issues (covered by other securities databases) as well as direct investment abroad for minority ownership situations (covered in FDI statistics and the direct investment survey). However, for majority-ownership direct investment, domestic parents are exposed to all of the assets and liabilities of these foreign firms. For this reason, they would typically consolidate these firms in their globally consolidated financial statements, whereas in the 2008 SNA the goal is to only record the transactions and positions of the domestic enterprises, including their exposures to foreign affiliates. Therefore, statistics on the assets and liabilities under domestic parents' control would yield more complete information on the foreign exposures of domestic non-financial corporations.

In many economies, a significant portion of FDI takes place in the non-financial corporations' sector. As such, the equity and loans/advances portion of outward FDI are recorded as part of the relevant asset instruments in the domestic non-financial corporations' balance sheets. Moreover, inward FDI is included in the liabilities of non-financial corporations, typically as part of loans and equity. In other words, foreign direct investment flows and stocks are covered, at least implicitly, in the financial accounts of the non-financial corporations sector. The 2008 SNA recommends showing the assets/liabilities related to FDI as additional memorandum items to the standard financial accounts and balance sheets. In order to shed light on the financial position of the sector, the SNA recommendations for the standard tables could be expanded to include additional functional categories or industry details and geographic details forging a stronger link between the sector and international accounts.

More details on FDI of non-financial corporations would lead to a better understanding of the impacts of inward and outward cross-border inter-company investments, either directly or indirectly, on the economic performance of the domestic economy. Clearly, whether a resident multinational chooses to invest in the domestic economy or in another country has a direct impact on the economic growth and employment in the domestic economy. In addition, more detailed data may lead to a better understanding of risks and vulnerabilities of non-financial corporations. Assume, for example, that a company in country A decides to make a loan to an affiliate in country B. In the typical set of accounts for non-financial corporations, this loan would be recorded as a loan asset on the balance sheets of country A. If, as suggested by the 2008 SNA, additional detail was added that recorded the direct investment asset as well as any industry or geographic detail, users would know a lot more about the risk and interconnectedness of the non-financial corporations' balance sheets in country A. We would gain an understanding of the exposure that the non-financial corporations' sector in country A has from its affiliates and investments in other countries.

New types of data on the impact of inward and outward FDI, focussed on the concept of control (more than 50% of voting shares owned), continue to be developed. The OECD Activity of Multinational Enterprises (AMNE) Statistics are part of this work. As can be gleaned from Table 5.9, the share of value added and the level of employment generated by non-financial corporations under foreign control differs across OECD countries, but remains significant.

Table 5.9. **Share of value added in manufacturing generated by foreign controlled firms, selected OECD countries**
Percentage of total value added

	2009	2010	2011	2012	2013	2014
France	0.28	0.28	0.29	0.28	0.27	0.26
Germany	0.23	0.27	0.27	0.22	0.23	0.24
Italy	0.17	0.19	0.19	0.19	0.18	0.19
United Kingdom	0.41	0.44	0.44	0.45	0.45	0.48

Source: OECD (2017), *Measuring Globalisation: Activities of Multinationals 2007*, Volume I, Manufacturing Sector, http://dx.doi.org/10.1787/meas_vol_1-2007-en-fr.

StatLink ᔛ http://dx.doi.org/10.1787/888933590055

Key points

- Developed economies typically have a large and complex set of non-financial corporations engaged in a variety of industries. Non-financial corporations are a subset of the broader corporate sector, which also includes financial corporations. However, the economic and financial activities of non-financial corporations are very different from those of financial corporations. As such, it is important to monitor and understand non-financial corporations' economic behaviour.

- Non-financial corporations own and/or use the bulk of productive non-financial assets in the economy and, as such, contribute significantly to employment, international trade and economic growth.

- They finance their economic activity primarily through undistributed current earnings, or saving, as well as by raising funds through debt or equity. The latter implies a need to generate sufficient future earnings to cover obligations associated with incurring debt, or providing a good return on investments in their equity.

- Non-financial corporations have experienced long and short cycles of relatively high and low leverage. This suggests that monitoring financial stability in this sector might be seen as a priority, in terms of sustainability of economic growth.

- In recent periods, non-financial corporations' financial positions have improved in many economies, reflecting higher holdings of liquid financial assets. Some policy makers have lamented this trend, arguing that these "excess" funds could be put to better use in expanding the productive capital base.

- Both of the above points suggest a need to understand the financial inter-linkages of this sector to other sectors in the economy, by augmenting the financial accounts and balance sheets with details on a from-whom-to-whom basis.

- At the same time, non-financial corporations are heavily engaged in cross-border inter-company investment, either in the form of FDI or in the form of portfolio investment. Increasingly, non-financial corporations have investments in companies abroad and foreign companies have investments in domestic companies. In recent years, the acceleration of FDI flows reflects increased globalisation.

- The latter, in turn, has two implications. First, shifting global production patterns can affect domestic economic growth, employment and trade. Secondly, these patterns can create vulnerabilities, implying a need to better understand the complex international inter connectedness of this sector. This suggests that additional statistical details, for example by breaking down the non-financial corporations' sector into activities by multinational enterprises and other corporations, and improved linkages with international accounts would be useful.

- There are many indicators that can be used to analyse the overall health of the non-financial corporations sector. These indicators are growing in use and importance, given the increased attention that is paid to the financial stability and growth perspectives of non-financial corporations. These indicators include, among other things, financial asset composition ratios, the liquidity ratio, the debt service ratio, Tobin's q, the return ratio, and the saving to GDP ratio.

- While the accounting for non-financial corporations in national accounts is largely similar to the business accounting used in financial reports, there are also some significant differences. The asset boundary, i.e. which non-financial assets are recognised, differs between the two accounting systems, with the 2008 SNA accounting for a somewhat larger set of non-financial assets. Furthermore, equity is presented and classified differently: in business accounting, the fundamental accounting equation is Assets = Liabilities + Owners' Equity, which comprises shares, contributed surplus, retained earnings and reserves (adjusted for provisions). In the national accounts, equity is classified as a liability. There are also differences in valuation and presentation between business financial reports and national accounts.

Going further

National accounting and business financial accounting

There are many similarities between what is presented in national accounts and what is included in business financial reports. This is convenient, as national accounts are largely derived from business financial statements. There are also some important differences.

Presentation

In general the non-financial corporation financial accounts and balance sheets are structurally similar to what you would find in a set of business accounts. Both have an income account, or profit and loss account, but national accounting segments income more finely than business accounting. Similarly, both national accounts and business accounts have an account that relates to capital expenditure. Moreover, the SNA financial account is the equivalent to the business accounting statement of change in financial position. However, the latter also includes revaluations and other changes that are treated as separate accounts in national accounting. The balance sheet is the statement with the largest resemblance between the two bases of accounting. However, even in the balance sheet there remain important differences, especially with respect to the classification and valuation of assets and liabilities.

Valuation of assets and liabilities

At the outset, it should be recognised that, with respect to valuation, business accounting is moving closer to national accounting. The traditional trend in business accounting to rely on book value measures (acquisition cost for assets and issue price for liabilities) and the principle of market valuation in national accounting have resulted in significant differences. The relatively new international business accounting guidelines for corporations, known as the International Financial Reporting Standards (IFRS), recommend more current value accounting for financial instruments as compared to some previous accounting regimes (along with a more comprehensive measure of income). However, this is both a benefit and a challenge for compilers of financial statistics, as companies in the non-financial corporations' sector evolve towards IFRS.

In national accounting, non-financial assets will generally be valued differently from what would be found on a typical non-financial corporation's balance sheet. Estimates of the stocks of non-financial assets themselves along with their depreciation could be substantially different, since the national accounts reflect economic depreciation (rather than tax allowable rates), and use a valuation at current prices (instead of book value, based on historic costs). Even in cases where financial statements move from a book value basis to a more current value basis, the prices and methodology used to determine the current values of both non-financial and financial assets could be quite different from national accounting.

In terms of liabilities, while corporations are moving towards more current valuation for tradeable financial assets, this is not the case for liabilities. This is directly contradictory to national accounting, which applies a market price valuation for tradeable liabilities. The SNA recommends this, because its main purpose is to measure aggregates in industries, sectors and the economy as a whole. In this context, consistency of valuation on both sides of the balance sheet and across all sectors is a requirement related to both the accuracy and relevance of the statistics.

Adjustments to assets-liabilities: provisions

In business accounting charges (expenses) are made against current income for a variety of provisions (e.g. potential asset impairment, deferred income tax, as well as certain environmental liabilities and employee pension obligations). Provisions are amounts set aside for probable but uncertain future asset value losses or future liabilities of an enterprise. The use of provisions is consistent with the principle of accrual accounting, where financial events are recorded on a timely and ongoing basis instead of when the event may be subject to a cash settlement or otherwise final impact on the financial statements. Provisions also give rise to corresponding adjustments on the business balance sheet account: either an asset is reduced in value or a new liability is created, and there are matching appropriations from retained earnings in the equity account such that assets remain equal to liabilities plus equity. In the case of non-performing loans or trade receivables, new provisions are one of the entries (along with recoveries and write-offs) in the allowance for doubtful accounts which is netted against the asset account.

In national accounts provisions, being due to exogenous events with a likely future impact on the business, are not part of income arising from current economic production, and are thus excluded from operating surplus/mixed income (and therefore, saving). Similarly, any provisions based changes to the value of assets or liabilities are not part of transactions in the financial account; rather, to the extent that provisions are known, they should be treated as other changes in the volume of assets. These volume changes would then impact the relevant stocks on the balance sheets, including net worth. However, related to data availability issues, national accountants may or may not record adjustments for these items, as a consequence of which international comparability may be hampered. On the one hand, the allowance for doubtful accounts is typically deducted in relation to impaired loans and accounts receivable (based on the treatment in source data), with the flow (new provisions) accounted for as other changes in the volume of assets. Furthermore, changes in pension obligations on defined benefit plans, due to actuarial revaluations may give rise to changes in the relevant liabilities on the balance sheets. On the other hand, certain environmental liabilities do not necessarily have a counterpart asset in the economy (a 2008 SNA requirement), and are ignored in national accounts. Similarly, deferred income taxes are not treated as liabilities.

Equity and net worth

The different treatment of equity and net worth in business accounting and national accounts has already been discussed earlier in this chapter, at the end of section 4.

Coverage and classification

The national accounts typically have a more complete coverage of assets. Research and development, and other intellectual property products, such as software and databases, mineral exploration, and entertainment, literary and artistic originals, are all recognised and recorded as assets in the system of national accounts, whereas in business accounting expenditures on these categories are often treated as current expenditures, certainly when produced in-house.

There may also be some (usually minor) differences in the way instruments are classified. Instruments such as bonds in business accounts may be classified as currency and deposits in the financial accounts. As another example, corporate financial reports show the components of intercompany investment as separate asset, as opposed to allocating these components with other equity and debt assets on the SNA balance sheet.

Notes

1. It should be noted that here non-financial assets only refer to produced non-financial assets, and do not include so-called "non-produced non-financial assets", such as land and natural resources. Land, in particular, is one of the most important categories of non-financial assets, but few countries have estimates for the total value of land. For more information, refer to Chapter 8.
2. Supply-use tables describe, in detail, the supply of products by domestic industries and by imports, and the use (or demand) of these products for intermediate consumption, final consumption, non-financial investments and exports. The tables also show the production process by domestic industry: which products are produced, and which inputs are used in this process.

References

Fano, D., G. Trovato and L. Paganetto (2013), *Patterns in Financial Flows? A Longer-Term Perspective on Intersectoral Relationships* in Public Debt, Global Governance and Economic Dynamism, Springer Milan, Milano.

Greenspan, A. (2005), *Testimony of Chairman Alan Greenspan: Federal Reserve Board's semiannual Monetary Policy Report to the Congress before the Committee on Banking, Housing, and Urban Affairs*, U.S. Senate, Washington, DC, www.federalreserve.gov/boarddocs/hh/2005/february/testimony.htm.

OECD (2017), "Detailed National Accounts, SNA 2008 (or SNA 1993): Non-financial accounts by sectors, annual", *OECD National Accounts Statistics* (database), http://dx.doi.org/10.1787/data-00034-en; and "Detailed National Accounts, SNA 2008 (or SNA 1993): Balance sheets for non-financial assets", *OECD National Accounts Statistics* (database), http://dx.doi.org/10.1787/data-00368-en; and "Financial Balance Sheets, SNA 2008 (or SNA 1993): Non-consolidated stocks, annual", *OECD National Accounts Statistics* (database), http://dx.doi.org/10.1787/data-00720-en; and OECD (2017), "Financial Accounts, SNA 2008 (or SNA 1993): Non-consolidated flows, annual", *OECD National Accounts Statistics* (database), http://dx.doi.org/10.1787/data-00718-en.

OECD (2017), *Measuring Globalisation: Activities of Multinationals 2007*, Volume I, Manufacturing Sector, http://dx.doi.org/10.1787/meas_vol_1-2007-en-fr.

Sánchez, J.M. and E. Yurdagul (2013), *Why Are Corporations Holding So Much Cash?*, The Regional Economist, Federal Reserve Bank of Saint Louis, Saint Louis, www.stlouisfed.org/ /media/Files/PDFs/publications/pub_assets/pdf/re/2013/a/cash.pdf.

Statistics Canada (2016), *Table 380-0076 – Current and capital accounts – Corporations, quarterly (CAD)* (database), www5.statcan.gc.ca/cansim/a26?lang=eng&id=3800076.

Statistics Canada (2017), *Table 378-0121 – National Balance Sheet Accounts, quarterly (CAD)* (database), www5.statcan.gc.ca/cansim/pick-choisir?lang=eng&p2=33&id= 3780121; and *Table 378-0119 – Financial Flow Accounts, quarterly (CAD)* (database), www5.statcan.gc.ca/cansim/a26?lang=eng&retrLang=eng&id=3780119&&pattern=&stByVal=1&p1=1&p2=31&tabMode=dataTable&csid; and *Table 380-0064 – Gross domestic product, expenditure-based, quarterly*, www5.statcan.gc.ca/cansim/a26?lang=eng&id=3800064; and *Table 378-0124 – National Balance Sheet Accounts, financial indicators, corporations, quarterly (percent)* (database), www5.statcan.gc.ca/cansim/a26?lang=eng&retrLang=eng&id=3780124&&pattern=&stByVal=1&p1=1&p2=31&tabMode=dataTable&csid.

U.S. Federal Reserve (2017), *Financial Accounts of the United States* (database), www.federalreserve.gov/apps/fof/FOFTables.aspx.

Chapter 6

Deficit and debt of general government and public sector

Robert Dippelsman (IMF), Gabriele Semeraro (Banca d'Italia),
João Cadete de Matos (Banco de Portugal), Julia Catz (ECB),
Gabriel Quirós (IMF) and Filipa Lima (Banco de Portugal)

> *Governments play important roles in the economy. In the financial accounts and balance sheets, these include being major borrowers, issuers of securities, and funders of other entities. The chapter first dwells upon the delineation of the general government sector and the public sector, which includes general government and public corporations, both of which have separate economic roles. Governments often have complex structures, which give rise to specific classifications (for example, budgetary and extra-budgetary) and levels (for example, central, state, and local). This chapter also provides more detail on government deficit, financial assets owned by government and the various definitions of government debt, including the pitfalls when comparing such data internationally. It also deals with consolidation issues and some other specifics concerning the valuation of financial assets and liabilities, and the assessment of sustainability of government finance.*

1. Delineating the government sector

Because of its role in providing non-market services (such as education, health care, defence and policing) and redistributing income (via subsidies and social benefits), the general government, or more broadly the public sector, is an important actor in the economy. Governments collect taxes and social contributions to pay for the provision of services and the redistribution of income. As the related amounts are usually substantial and vary over time, general governments also play an important role in the financial markets. Governments may run (temporary) surpluses or deficits, so can function as net lenders or net borrowers in the domestic economy.

General government versus public sector

There is a range of government-related groupings that may meet different needs for analysis. Such groupings include, amongst others, general government, public sector, social security funds, extra-budgetary agencies, the non-financial public sector, and the central government public sector. The most frequently used delineations relate to the general government, the central government, and the public sector, which are discussed in more detail below.

Government entities are grouped in a separate sector, because they differ in economic behaviour as compared to corporations and households. Government entities have policy motivations, such as influencing overall demand or income distribution, rather than maximising income. For example, both private financial corporations and general government may provide loans, but a commercial bank will provide a loan because of factors such as expected return from interest receipts and repayment of principal, while the general government may provide a loan with the objective to encourage a particular industry or to support a particular region. Government entities are significant in any macroeconomic analysis, by virtue of their impact on the whole economy. In addition, fiscal analysis is a field that looks at government in its own right, dealing with issues such as assessment of the effectiveness of government spending and design of tax systems.

The general government consists of institutional units that are non-market producers and that are controlled by the government. A non-market producer charges prices that are not "economically significant" (this term is described in further detail below). Government units are established by political processes and have legislative, judicial, or executive authority over other institutional units within a given area. The principal economic functions of government units are to:

- assume responsibility for the provision of goods and services to the community or individual households primarily on a non-market basis;
- redistribute income and wealth by means of transfers;
- finance their activities primarily out of taxation or other compulsory transfers.

Fundamental to the distinction between general government and corporations is whether or not an entity produces goods or services for the market. Corporations that produce goods and services for the market are included in either the financial corporations' sector or the non-financial corporations' sector, depending on the type of goods and services they produce. Corporations that do not produce goods and services for the market and are controlled by government, are recorded as part of the government. This distinction between market and non-market producers critically depends on whether goods or services are sold at "economically significant prices". The 2008 System of National Accounts (2008 SNA) further defines this criterion as "… prices that have a significant impact on the amounts that producers are willing to supply and on the amounts purchasers wish to buy" (paragraph 22.28). However, this still leaves much room for interpretation, a reason why in the European context a more quantifiable criterion has been agreed. In Europe, the sales of a market producer must cover more than 50% of the production costs (wages and salaries, intermediate consumption and depreciation) and consumers must be free to choose whether to buy and how much to buy on the basis of the prices charged. This criterion is being adopted by countries at an increasing rate.

Government's activities affect the production, income, capital, and financial accounts. For instance, the financial accounts record how a government's deficit (net borrowing) is funded. They also show funding that the government may provide for its public corporations or for the acquisition of financial assets. Governments' funding requirements can affect the availability of funds to other domestic borrowers, or mean that governments must rely on foreign funding. Government debt includes securities, which play a key role as an investment vehicle on financial markets. The level and composition of debt has implications for future fiscal requirements related to interest payments and debt repayments.

The general government is usually broken down into different layers. The 2008 SNA identifies three possible tiers: central government, state government, and local government; as well as an optional fourth tier for having a separate subsector for social security funds. Government functions may be assigned differently across countries. Many countries may not have all levels. The state government, for example, is usually only relevant for large countries with federal constitutions like Germany and the United States, where considerable powers and responsibilities are assigned to state governments. On the other hand, some countries may have defined additional intermediate levels, depending on their national legislative structure, the importance of the various layers of government, and the policy interest for monitoring different layers of government. More generally, it can be noted that the degree of central control over the other levels differs from complete independence to heavy involvement. Finally, social security funds may be treated as a separate subsector or included among the other three subsectors. A majority of countries apply a separate recording of these funds.

The public sector is the most comprehensive government-related category, which cuts across three of the SNA's main institutional sectors, encompassing all government-controlled units, as shown in Table 6.1. In addition to the general government sector, the public sector covers public corporations, which are combined with private sector non-financial and financial corporations in the primary institutional sector classification of the SNA. Public corporations are enterprises controlled by government that produce goods and services for the market. They also include central banks, which are public financial corporations that largely serve public policy functions (discussed in more detail in Chapter 3). Public corporations may vary, from being operated on an almost entirely commercial basis to being significantly involved in quasi-fiscal activities (that is, they carry out government operations at the behest of the government units that control them). The roles of public corporations vary from country to country, but may include serving as an instrument of public (or fiscal) policy for the government, generating profits for general government, protecting key resources, providing competition where barriers to entry may be large, and providing basic services where costs are prohibitive.

Table 6.1. **The public sector and its relation to institutional sectors**

Non-financial corporations	Financial corporations	General governmant	NPISHs	Households
Public Private	Public Private	Public	Private	Private

Examples of public non-financial corporations may include companies involved in public transport, various public utilities, or the exploration of minerals and energy. Whether or not they are actually controlled, or majority owned, by the government very much depends on the ways the economy is organised in a particular country. With the privatisation of many government-owned companies since the early 1980s, many of these corporations have become privately owned and controlled, and have ceased to be public corporations. Public financial corporations typically include the central bank, but may also include other banks, insurance companies, and pension funds.

After the 2007-09 economic and financial crisis for example, governments had to come to the rescue of some very large banks and other financial corporations, some of which were nationalised in the process, becoming completely under the control of government. Public corporations can be major players in financial markets. This is obvious in the case of public financial corporations, but it is also true for public non-financial corporations which may issue substantial amounts of debt securities to cover their investments.

If public corporations cover more than 50%, but less than 100%, of their production costs by sales, such corporations would require additional sources of funding, often from the government, even though they are excluded from the general government sector. When these corporations run ongoing losses or have unsustainable debt liabilities, there can be contagion of funding problems from public corporations to the general government. For that reason, specific information on public corporations is relevant to understand possible implications for general government. See the Government Finance Statistics Manual (GFSM) 2014, paragraph 2.21-2.58, for more details on groupings within the public sector and different analytical uses.

One source of potential confusion in statistical terminology is that "public corporations" in the 2008 SNA are classified as such because of their economic function, i.e. being (non-)market producers, rather than because of their legal status. So, unincorporated entities having sufficient separate status and charging economically significant prices may be considered as public corporations, while heavily loss-making publicly owned corporations with a separate legal status may have prices that are not economically significant, and be included in general government. For example, in some cases, public corporations providing socially beneficial services, such as public transport companies, set prices so low that they are considered as not "economically significant".

A final point in respect of the delineation between public corporations and private corporations concerns the definition of "control". Governments can exercise control through ownership or in other ways, such as through funding. For further details, see paragraphs 4.77-4.80 and 4.92 of the 2008 SNA and Boxes 2.1 and 2.2 of the GFSM 2014. The definition of control has been designed to include government-controlled entities in the public sector, when there is control without ownership. Instead of having a majority ownership, a government may decide to exercise control over some of its entities by, for example, appointing board members who have operational independence.

From the previous discussion, it is clear that the delineation of general government and the public sector is not always straightforward. Issues of identification and sector classification of units are often particularly difficult for governments, because of their complexity and administrative arrangements, control, and pricing strategies. There are often borderline cases which may lead to extensive debate. Therefore, specific manuals have been dedicated to clearly define and delineate the government and the public sector. The GFSM 2014 is a specialised statistical standard for general government and the broader public sector. The GFSM 2014 is harmonised with the 2008 SNA but goes beyond the 2008 SNA in that it provides more breakdowns and additional presentations designed to support fiscal analysis (see Appendix 7 of the GFSM for more details on differences). In the European Union, data for the general government are of very high political relevance, because of the Maastricht criteria for government debt and deficit. According to these criteria, the general government deficit should not exceed 3% of GDP, while gross debt levels should be below 60% of GDP or, if the debt-to-GDP ratio exceeds the 60% limit, the ratio shall, at a minimum, be found to have "sufficiently diminished and must be approaching the reference value at a satisfactory pace". As these numbers depend on the delineation of general government, massive additional jurisprudence has been developed to arrive at internationally comparable standards for defining what belongs to the government and what does not. All of this has been laid down in the Eurostat Manual on Government Deficit and Debt, the latest version of which was published in 2016.

A summary of the criteria used for the delineation of general government and public corporations is presented in Table 6.2.

Table 6.2. **Criteria for classification of units**

	Not economically significant prices (non-market producers)	Economically significant prices (market producers)
Government control	General government	Public corporation, financial or non-financial
Not controlled by government	Non-profit institutions serving households	Private corporation, financial or non-financial

Related to the complex structure of government is the issue of "consolidation." Consolidation is the process of eliminating flows and stocks between units that belong to the same sector or subsector. Data for a consolidated grouping are shown as if that grouping was a single unit. On this issue, the 2008 SNA generally advises that data should be published in unconsolidated form to allow users to make their own choice over whether or not to consolidate, but also recognises the usefulness of consolidation for government data. The unit structure of government can involve a range of administrative and legal arrangements that have varying degrees of "separate" status and that can be somewhat fluid over time and between countries. To remove the effect of flows and stocks within a sector, it is often preferred for government statistics to be prepared on a consolidated basis; this format is also recommended in the GFSM, and in the definition of the Maastricht criteria.

Without consolidation, there may be a ballooning of data, driven by administrative arrangements rather than the underlying economic reality. For instance, funds flowing between different parts of the general government do not change the financial position of the general government as a whole, but will appear to give larger values of revenue and expenditure, and assets and liabilities, in a country where there are a larger number of separate units. It can also be useful to consolidate the data for different levels of government, to avoid double counting the transactions and stocks between these different levels. However, unconsolidated data may also be suitable in some cases; for example, consolidated public sector data would exclude the non-financial public sector's borrowings from public financial corporations, which is useful information. Consolidation is explained in more detail in Section 3 below, and in paragraphs 3.152-3.168 of the GFSM 2014.

Difference between budgetary and statistical presentations

National budgets usually present data in formats that differ from international statistical standards in terms of coverage of units and classifications. These formats often have public prominence because they are used in national political debates and are based on national laws and practices. As a result, almost all countries have two sets of fiscal data – the national format used in the budget and the internationally agreed standard formats of the 2008 SNA and GFSM. The variations in national formats across countries make international comparisons of national budgetary data difficult or invalid. Differences in classifications may mean that terms such as deficit or revenue have different meanings. Similarly, institutional coverage may differ between countries, particularly due to extra-budgetary agencies, which vary significantly in functions, number, and size from country to country. The metadata tables in the IMF's Government Finance Statistics Yearbook identify budgetary and extra-budgetary agencies for each country. Since the scope of the budgetary and extra-budgetary subsectors is based on varying national practices, they do not play a role in the 2008 SNA, but they are both shown in GFSM presentations to allow links to be made with national budgetary data and to monitor the extent to which operations occur outside the budget.

The 2008 SNA and GFSM presentations provide standard classifications that allow consistent treatments for international data comparisons. Nevertheless, even if international standards provide harmonised data, different governmental structures and policies mean that international comparisons should be well-informed. For example, in some countries, a function may be recorded as being undertaken by public corporations, while the same function may be recorded as being undertaken by general government in others, because the strategy for pricing the products differs. Similarly, some functions may be allocated differently between central government and other levels of government.

2. Key financial accounts indicators for general government/public sector

Governments play an important role in financial markets, for example via the issuance of debt securities. These securities often provide a safe haven for investors. Government deficit and debt are therefore extensively monitored and high levels of deficit or debt can raise concerns about the future sustainability of government finance. Can the government raise enough income in the future to finance the debt service (the interest payments and the down payments)? This section discusses the analytical value and policy relevance of a number of indicators than can be derived from the government financial accounts and balance sheets. The following indicators are discussed: net lending/net borrowing, financial assets, gross and net debt, and net financial worth. These indicators allow for detailed analysis of government fiscal performance, understanding of financial (and non-financial) operations undertaken, tracking the evolution of components over time, and understanding how a government finances its deficit.

Net lending/net borrowing

Net lending/net borrowing is the balance of all incomes and expenditures of a government. In addition to current income and expenditure, such as taxes, social contributions and the payments of government employees, net lending/net borrowing also includes capital income and expenditure, mainly consisting of investments in non-financial assets (infrastructure, government offices, computers, etc.). The balance of current income and expenditure is referred to as saving. The GFS includes an additional measure – operating balance, which is equal to the 2008 SNA balancing item "changes in net worth due to saving and capital transfers" (or equivalently, net lending/net borrowing plus net acquisition of non-financial assets).

Net lending/net borrowing, i.e. including all capital income and expenditure, is commonly known as the government deficit (or surplus), or the fiscal balance. In general, governments have tended to be net borrowers, rather than net lenders. If the government runs a deficit, it needs to borrow funds from other sectors. If total income is larger than total expenditures, government has a surplus, and it has funds available to invest in financial assets or to reduce liabilities. These transactions in financial assets and liabilities are recorded in the financial accounts. The financial accounts show the change in the government's net financial worth as a result of the net acquisition of financial assets minus the net incurrence of liabilities. In other words, the financial accounts show the extent to which government is either putting financial funds at the disposal of other sectors or utilising financial funds generated by other sectors, either in the domestic economy or abroad.

Figure 6.1 shows net lending/net borrowing for the G7 countries for the period 2000-17. As noted before, governments in all countries almost consistently run deficits. Exceptions are Canada before the 2007-09 economic and financial crisis and Germany in more recent years. It is also clear that governments were heavily affected by the crisis, with a substantial increase in deficits for all G7 countries.

Figure 6.1. **General government net lending/net borrowing for G7 countries, 2000-17**
Percentage of GDP

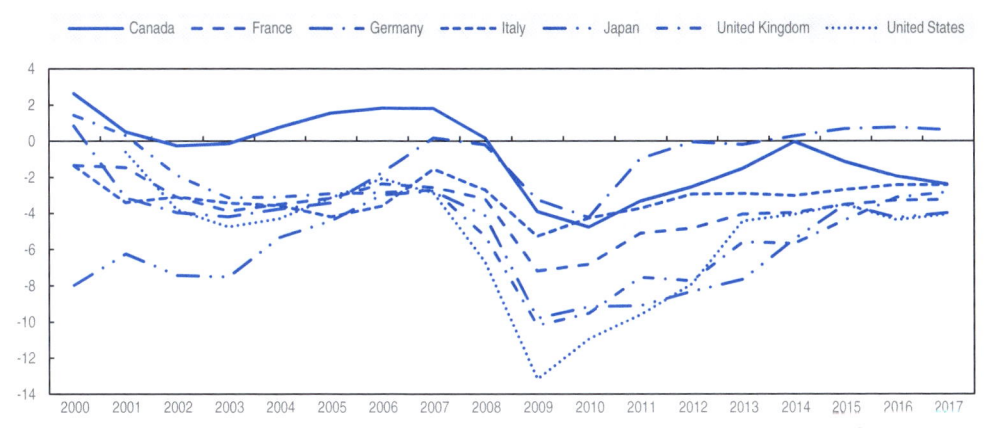

Source: IMF (2017), World Economic Outlook Database, April 2017 (database), www.imf.org/external/pubs/ft/weo/2017/01/weodata/weoselgr.aspx.

StatLink http://dx.doi.org/10.1787/888933588668

Conceptually, the balance of non-financial (current and capital) transactions is equal to the balance of financial transactions as measured in the financial accounts, since a surplus leads to additional funds for investments or reducing debt, whereas a deficit has to be financed. In national accounts, both the balance of non-financial transactions and the balance of financial transactions are therefore referred to as net lending/net borrowing. Although in theory the balancing item from both financial and non-financial accounts should be equal, in practice they often differ. It is common for the non-financial and financial accounts to be compiled independently by different compilers, using different data sources and applying somewhat diverging statistical practices. Sometimes a difference is simply related to the timing of information used to compile the accounts.

The difference between the financial and non-financial accounts is known as the "statistical discrepancy". While discrepancies also arise for other sectors, usually to a much more significant degree, government statistical discrepancies raise special issues, because the more limited number of units makes verification more feasible, and because government financing often has important impacts on the rest of the economy, as a consequence of which much attention is paid to the evolution of the government deficit. The size and bias of the discrepancy may be seen as an indicator of the quality of accounts. Its size in the final estimates of the accounts, after all source information has become available, must be reasonably small, in particular over a longer period of time, if the data are to be considered analytically useful and reliable. In some countries, variables such as other accounts receivable/payable on the financial accounts may be automatically adjusted in such a way to eliminate the statistical discrepancy between the non-financial and financial accounts. This practice ensures that only one figure for government deficit is released by the statistical authorities. In any case, compilers of the non-financial and financial government accounts should discuss and address the possible causes of divergences between the financial and non-financial accounts, and provide an indication to users about the extent of and the reasons for data inconsistencies.

GFSM terminology often refers to "above-the-line" and "below-the-line" transactions. Above-the-line transactions are revenue and expenditure, and correspond to the current and capital accounts of the SNA, while below-the-line transactions cover the financial transactions. Effectively, net lending/net borrowing is the "line" being referred to in the accrual version of the accounts, while it may also refer to the cash surplus/deficit in the "Statement of Sources and Uses of Cash" as defined in the GFSM.

Financial assets

Governments have several reasons to hold financial assets. There may be timing differences between cash receipts (payments) and government revenue (expenditure), as a consequence of which liquidity needs to be managed carefully. Governments may also set aside financial assets, to ensure the payments of future social benefits, such as those related to pensions for government employees or the society at large. They may provide loans to support particular projects for policy purposes (e.g. student loans or loans for social housing). Governments may also provide loans and equity to public corporations. Furthermore, taxes that have been assessed as due to be paid may already be part of government revenue, even though the equivalent cash payments have not yet been received. Such a timing difference is recorded under the financial asset "other accounts receivable". Similarly, unpaid expenses or prepaid revenues are recorded as "other accounts payable", as part of government liabilities. During the 2007-09 economic and financial crisis, governments tended to hold more financial assets. To support financial corporations facing financial problems, they acquired shares in those corporations, they appropriated (bad) debts, and/or they provided loans to those corporations.

Lending for public policy purposes has a different motivation from commercially motivated lending. As such loans have different likelihoods of repayment, it may be worth identifying them separately. GFSM 2014 does indeed recommend separating out these loans. It also provides an "overall fiscal balance" as a supplementary fiscal indicator, where additional policy lending is treated as an expense rather than as a transaction on the financial accounts. See Box 4.1 and paragraph 4.56 of the GFSM 2014 for further information.

Of the eight major 2008 SNA financial instrument categories, there are four main types of assets that are usually held by the general government. The first is equity reflecting the participation of the government in corporations. The second is debt securities, often held by social security funds. The third category relates to currency and deposits. Part of these deposits is held with the central bank. The final category concerns loans made to other countries or domestic corporations. The other types of financial assets – monetary gold and SDRs; insurance, pensions and standardised guarantee schemes; financial derivatives and employee stock options; and other accounts receivable – are usually of lesser significance, although they may be important in particular countries.

Figure 6.2 shows the total of general government financial assets, as a percentage of GDP, for a number of economies. It is clear that there is quite some divergence across countries, with countries within the Euro Area showing relatively high levels of financial assets held by the government, while the United Kingdom and the United States governments own relatively smaller amounts. The increase in the holdings of financial assets by Euro Area governments since 2007 has partly been driven by the support provided to the

Figure 6.2. **Total general government financial assets, 2000-16**
Percentage of GDP

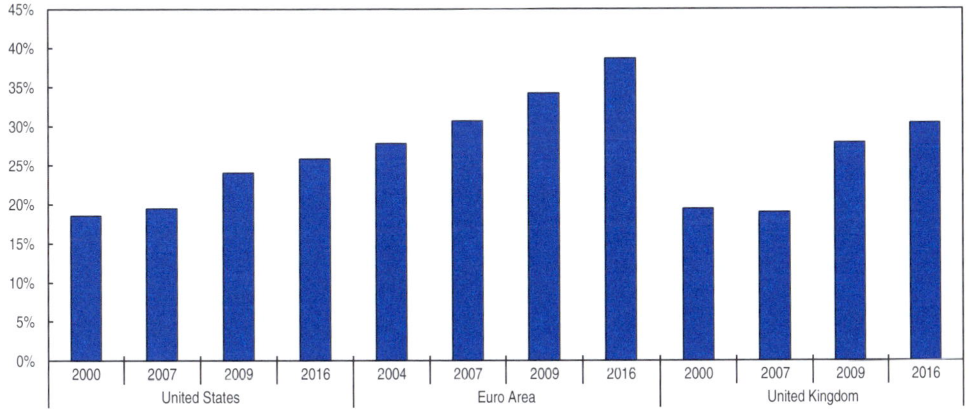

Source: OECD (2017), "Financial Balance Sheets, SNA 2008 (or SNA 1993): Consolidated stocks, annual", *OECD National Accounts Statistics* (database), http://dx.doi.org/10.1787/data-00719-en; and ECB (2017), Statistical Data Warehouse, http://sdw.ecb.europa.eu/browse.do?node=9691262.

StatLink http://dx.doi.org/10.1787/888933588687

financial sector (through, for example, purchases of financial corporations' equity), but also through the (re)classification of financial defeasance structures in the government sector. In the United Kingdom, the increase between 2007 and 2009 was largely driven by support measures to the financial sector.

Figure 6.3 presents the composition of the financial assets held by the United States, the Euro Area and the United Kingdom governments. In the Euro Area and the United Kingdom, the largest share of the financial assets is made up of equity and investment fund shares/units, whereas in the United States the government owns relatively little equities but many more loans and debt securities.

Figure 6.3. **Composition of general government financial assets, by instrument, 2000-16**
Percentage of total financial assets

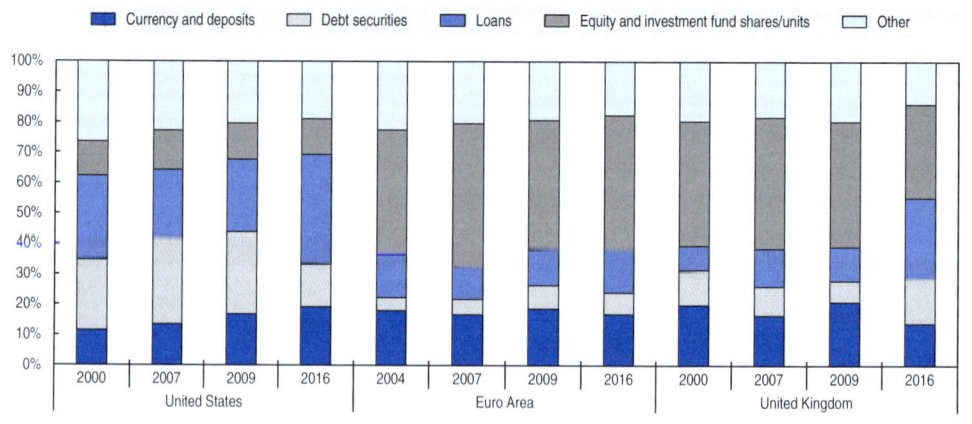

Source: OECD (2017), "Financial Balance Sheets, SNA 2008 (or SNA 1993): Consolidated stocks, annual", OECD National Accounts Statistics (database), http://dx.doi.org/10.1787/data-00719-en; and ECB (2017), Statistical Data Warehouse, http://sdw.ecb.europa.eu/browse.do?node=9691262.

StatLink http://dx.doi.org/10.1787/888933588706

Debt

One of the main indicators of the fiscal sustainability of a country is the country's general government debt, or, more precisely, the general government's debt-to-GDP ratio.[1] There are various ways to define government debt. It is thus important to have a clear picture of how the debt has been defined. First, it is important to know whether the debt data refer to gross government debt, thus taking only liabilities into account, or whether it relates to a measure of net debt, i.e. whether assets owned by the government are also taken into account. Most publications of government debt data concern gross debt. In the SNA, the terms "net financial worth" and "net worth" are wider measures taking into account a wider range of assets and liabilities beyond debt. In this respect, net worth can be considered as the most comprehensive definition, as it includes all assets, non-financial as well as financial, minus all liabilities.

Looking at gross government debt, it is important to know which liabilities are included or excluded. An all-encompassing debt figure would include all liabilities excluding financial derivatives and equity. Equity is not very important for the general government in most countries. However, when analysing the public sector, the equity outstanding can be substantial, because of the inclusion of public corporations in this sector delineation. Financial derivatives are usually also not that significant, partly because only a small number of governments have engaged substantially in financial derivatives.

Government debt according to the "Maastricht", or Excessive Debt Procedure (EDP), definition, as applied within the European Union, only includes the following debt instruments: currency and deposits, debt securities and loans. As shown in Figure 6.4, the difference between an all-encompassing government debt figure and a Maastricht-compliant government debt figure can be quite substantial. The share of debt not included in the European definition adds up to more than 20% of total debt liabilities in the United States, whereas for the Euro Area as a whole, the share ranges between 5 and 10% of total debt. A large part of the other debt liabilities of the US general government (between 17 and 18% in more recent years) relates to the underfunding of pension funds or social security funds for which the government has responsibility. In

Figure 6.4. **Composition of general government (EDP) debt, by instrument, 2000-16**
Percentage of total debt

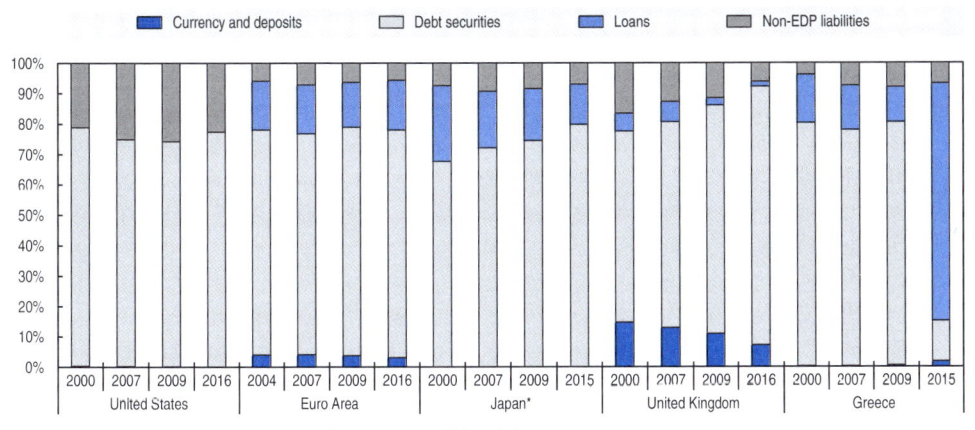

* Japanese data on government debt refer to unconsolidated data.
Source: OECD (2017), "Financial Balance Sheets, SNA 2008 (or SNA 1993): Consolidated stocks, annual", *OECD National Accounts Statistics* (database), http://dx.doi.org/10.1787/data-00719-en; and ECB (2017), Statistical Data Warehouse, http://sdw.ecb.europa.eu/browse.do?node=9691262.

StatLink http://dx.doi.org/10.1787/888933588725

contrast to others, the United States has no loan liabilities, while loan liabilities had become by far the largest component for Greece by 2014, reflecting bailout funding and reduced access to securities markets.

A special case that is important for monitoring and analysing government debt concerns the (non-)recognition and the (non-)recording of pension liabilities and contingent liabilities.[2] In the financial accounts and balance sheets, contingent liabilities related to the payments of future pensions, which are provided by government to large parts of the population, also known as social security pension schemes, are generally not recognised and recorded in the central framework. Furthermore, the 2008 SNA gives some flexibility with regard to the recording of unfunded (or underfunded) government-sponsored employment-related schemes, but – as in the case of social security pension schemes – they are usually only measured and included in supplementary tables.[3] The amounts involved can be enormous, representing much more than the traditional government debt. A further discussion on the recording of pensions can be found in Chapter 9.

It is also clear that the coverage of the government population, or the sector delineation, can have a significant impact on the debt measures, especially when looking at (gross) debt data. Is the data referring to central government, to general government, or the public sector? Or is the data referring to some national classification, such as budgetary government? Therefore, one always has to be aware of the population included, and the definition of debt used.

As an example of the magnitude of the differences that can result depending on which definition and population is used, Table 6.3 shows the impact of using different debt definitions and different populations for the gross government debt of Canada. It shows that, depending on the instrument and institutional coverage adopted, Canada could report "government debt" ranging from 35% to 129% of GDP. This range of values shows how important it is for statisticians and data users to be precise and clear about the definitions and populations used. Moreover, there is the potential for "hidden" liabilities when narrower measures are used, with the consequent inadequate recognition of possible risks and burdens.

In the international context, general government debt is the one that is most frequently used. However, some countries prefer to target a debt variable that not only pertains to the general government sector but also includes the debt of non-financial or all public corporations, as the latter may give rise to potential vulnerabilities for the government. If the public sector also consists of (large) financial corporations, it seems to make more sense to use a net debt concept (see below) for policy analysis, since a large part of the liabilities of these corporations will be offset by the financial assets acquired in the process

Table 6.3. **Consolidated gross government debt for Canada at nominal value, 31 December 2016**

Percentage of GDP

	Central government	General government	Public sector
Narrow*	35.1	77.8	90.9
Wide excl. IPSGS*	39.0	97.2	112.4
Wide*	47.1	114.2	129.4

* The narrow definition covers only currency and deposits, loans, and debt securities. The wide definition includes all debt instruments recognised by the 2008 SNA, excluding financial derivatives. The wide measure excluding IPSGS refers to the wide measure excluding insurance, pensions, and standardised guarantee schemes.

Source: OECD (2017), "Public Sector Debt: Public sector debt – consolidated", *OECD National Accounts Statistics* (database). http://dx.doi.org/10.1787/data-00620-en

StatLink ⟶ http://dx.doi.org/10.1787/888933590074

of financial intermediation. However, gross debt can generally be seen as a more prudent measure of debt, since not all financial assets are liquid.

Another issue that is very relevant for data on gross debt, is whether the results concern consolidated data or non-consolidated data, that is, whether or not liabilities which are owned by other units within the sector under consideration are removed. While the standard presentation in the financial accounts and balance sheets is on a non-consolidated basis, government gross debt indicators usually provide data on a consolidated basis.[4] The introduction already touched upon this issue, and more details are provided below.

A final point on the definition of government debt relates to the valuation of the liabilities. Generally, one can distinguish three types of valuation: market value, nominal value, or face value. Nominal value and face value are quite close to each other. They both refer to the contractually agreed amount that the debtor will have to refund to the creditor at maturity. If the debt is valued at nominal value, it will also include the accrued interest which is not yet paid; this is not included in the case of face value. As such, the nominal value is consistent with the accrual concept for interest income. The market value is the price that someone is prepared to pay for taking over the debt. In the central framework of the SNA, loans – which are usually non-tradeable – are to be valued at nominal value, while tradeable debt securities are valued at market prices. In times of financial crisis, the market value of government debt securities may fall due to perceived declines in creditworthiness of the government, even while the nominal and face values rise. Having said that, the most frequently used debt indicators for government usually apply a nominal valuation for all instruments. As a consequence, even if the population and the debt definition used are exactly the same, the results from the financial accounts and balance sheets, which typically use a valuation at market prices for tradeable instruments, may diverge from published government debt results.

6. DEFICIT AND DEBT OF GENERAL GOVERNMENT AND PUBLIC SECTOR

Disregarding risks of defeasance, bankruptcy of the debtor, and currency developments, differences between the nominal value and the market value are caused by interest rate movements. Assume that one has a debt security of USD 1 000 with a fixed coupon payment of 5% per year. If, following the issuance of this security, the market interest rate changes to 2.5%, it is clear that a potential investor is willing to pay more than USD 1 000 for the existing security which gives him a return of 5% per year. One may thus observe more substantial differences between nominal and market value in the case of quickly changing interest conditions.

Figure 6.5 presents, for a number of economies, gross debt for the general government for the period 2000-17 according to the broadest coverage of instruments (excluding insurance, pensions and standardised guarantee schemes, IPSGS), a key indicator of the financial sustainability of government finance. All tradeable instruments are valued at market prices, while loans, deposits, and other accounts payable, where market prices are not readily observable, are valued at nominal prices. The size of the general government's debt has changed considerably over time. It also differs, even more substantially, across countries. As the figure shows, all G7 countries experienced substantially increasing levels of general government debt during 2008-10, with debt growth levelling off since then in most countries. Only Germany showed a decrease of government debt relative to GDP after the 2007-09 economic and financial crisis. Comparing 2017 government debt as % of GDP to pre-crisis levels, increases were most significant for Japan and the

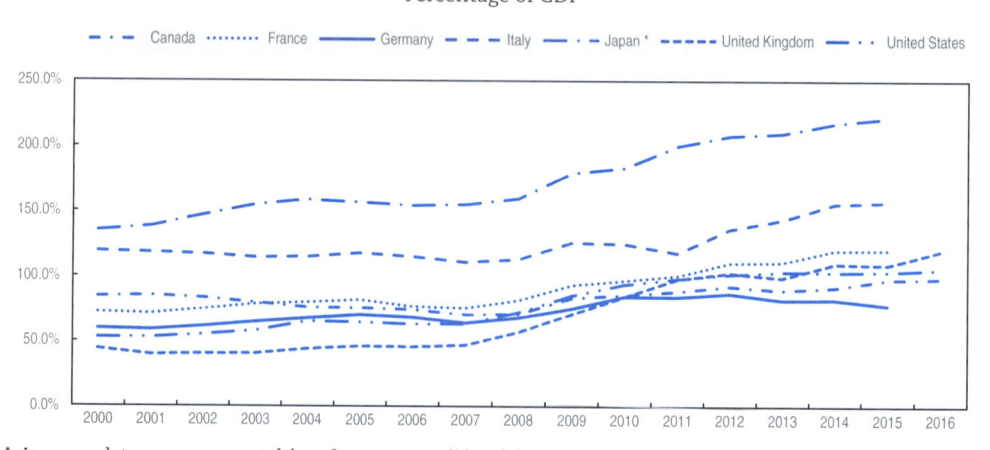

Figure 6.5. **General government gross debt, 2000-17**
Percentage of GDP

* Japanese data on government debt refer to unconsolidated data.
Source: OECD (2017), "Financial Balance Sheets, SNA 2008 (or SNA 1993): Consolidated stocks, annual", *OECD National Accounts Statistics* (database), http://dx.doi.org/10.1787/data-00719-en.

StatLink ⟶ http://dx.doi.org/10.1787/888933588744

United Kingdom, but increases were also substantial in France, Italy and the United States. In respect of the above, it should be noted that Japanese debt is overstated relative to other countries, because they refer to non-consolidated data, and may also include, for example, government bonds held by social security funds.

The difference between the change in debt and the deficit/surplus during a certain period is known as the "deficit-debt adjustment" (DDA) or, more generally, as the "stock-flow adjustment", or, in 2008 SNA terminology, the "other flows" relating to changes in debt. It is widely known that deficits contribute to an increase in (gross) debt levels, while surpluses reduce them. However, the change of government gross debt is also affected by other elements such as non-debt liabilities, the purchase of financial assets, revaluations and other changes in the volume of assets. In formulas, this can be expressed as follows:

(1a) Government surplus = Balance of financial transactions =

= Net purchase of financial assets *minus* Net incurrence of total liabilities

Or:

(1b) Government deficit = Net incurrence of total liabilities *minus* Net purchase of financial assets

Or:

(1c) Net incurrence of total liabilities = Government deficit *plus* Net purchase of financial assets

The total change in stocks of debt liabilities can then be (re-)written as follows:

(2a) Total change in stocks of debt liabilities =

= Net incurrence of debt liabilities *plus* Revaluations of debt liabilities *plus* Other changes in the volume of debt liabilities =

= Net incurrence of total liabilities *minus* Net incurrence of non-debt liabilities *plus* Revaluations of liabilities *plus* Other changes in the volume of liabilities

= Government Deficit *plus* Net purchase of financial assets *minus* Net incurrence of non-debt liabilities *plus* Revaluations of liabilities *plus* Other changes in the volume of liabilities

= Government Deficit *plus* Deficit-Debt Adjustments (DDA)

Or:

(2b) Deficit-Debt Adjustments (DDA) = Net purchase of financial assets *minus* Net incurrence of non-debt liabilities *plus* Revaluations of liabilities *plus* Other changes in the volume of liabilities

As long as the components of the DDA are sound, the difference between the change in debt and deficit is explained and does not raise concerns regarding data quality. In normal circumstances, with debt at nominal value, revaluations and other changes in the volume will be relatively small, and differences in deficit and changes in the stocks of debt liabilities can be explained by net purchases of financial assets. More generally, in statistical terms, DDA is the standard statistical analytical tool to compare flows and stocks which is common to all monetary and financial statistics.

Net (financial) worth/debt

The concepts of net financial debt and net financial worth are closely linked. Net financial debt only pertains to the net positions in debt instruments, whereas net financial worth is defined as the difference between all liabilities and all financial assets. For the general government, which in most countries does not have any equity liabilities, the main difference between these two indicators will concern equity holdings of government. Another difference, which may be more substantial in a limited number of countries, relates to financial derivatives and other accounts receivable/payable. A government's net financial worth changes over time due to transactions (the net impact of which is captured by net lending/net borrowing), revaluations, and other changes in volume (e.g. debt write-offs) of the assets and liabilities included in the definition of net financial worth.

It can be very useful to analyse net financial debt/worth, in addition to gross debt. From a fiscal sustainability point of view, a government owning substantial amounts of financial assets is better off than a government with minor holdings, given that they have similar levels of gross debt. Figure 6.6 shows total liabilities, total financial assets and net financial worth for general government of the United States, the Euro Area, Japan and the United Kingdom. Japanese gross government debt is unconsolidated, as a consequence of which government's net financial worth is better comparable with other countries than their gross debt. For Japan, the United States and the United Kingdom, net financial worth was close to minus 120%, minus 100% and minus 90% of GDP, respectively, whereas for the Euro Area it was around minus 70% of GDP by the end of 2016. However, net financial worth is not negative for all general governments. For Norway, the general government's net financial worth is quite large and positive: almost 295% of GDP by the end of the first quarter of 2017.[5]

Comparison of net financial worth, as can be done using Figure 6.6, is still incomplete in that it does not take into account holdings of non-financial assets. The balance of total assets, financial as well as non-financial, and total liabilities is represented by net worth. For instance, a government owning small values of financial assets but large values of natural resources, like oil or gas, may appear to have low net financial worth and might be perceived by the public as relatively "poor". However, when one takes into account non-financial assets, which include the natural resources mentioned before, this may alter the picture completely. The main reason to exclude non-financial assets from the government's wealth is the unavailability of data on these assets. While the value of "known" natural resources is relatively straightforward to measure if there is a market price for the commodity exploited, the value of non-financial assets in general is quite difficult to estimate due to the absence of markets where the relevant assets are traded. The valuation of these assets therefore usually depends on the accumulation of past investments, appropriately depreciated with assumptions about, for example, asset lives and depreciation patterns that are subject to uncertainty. Furthermore, although it may be possible to readily value some government assets like buildings, they may concern historical buildings that are not likely to be sold, and are unique and irreplaceable, so are difficult to value. Finally, public infrastructure like railway tracks, sewerage systems, infrastructure for utilities, etc. have a high value from the perspective of generating economic benefits for the country, but may not have a commercial value, because the government prohibits the commercial exploitations of these assets. For that reason, its value is also derived on the basis of the depreciation method mentioned before.

Figure 6.6. **Total general government financial assets, liabilities and net financial worth, 2000-16**
Percentage of GDP

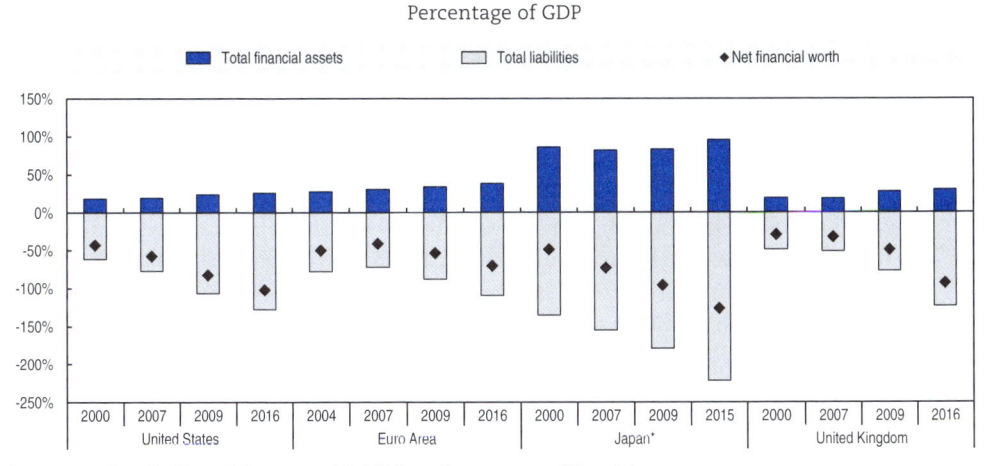

* Japanese data for financial assets and liabilities refer to unconsolidated data.
Source: OECD (2017), "Financial Balance Sheets, SNA 2008 (or SNA 1993): Consolidated stocks, annual", OECD National Accounts Statistics (database), http://dx.doi.org/10.1787/data-00719-en; and ECB (2017), Statistical Data Warehouse (database), http://sdw.ecb.europa.eu/browse.do?node=9691262.

StatLink ⟶ http://dx.doi.org/10.1787/888933588763

> **Box 6.1. The Excessive Deficit Procedure in the European Union**
>
> The Stability and Growth Pact (SGP) is a rule based fiscal framework intended to ensure fiscal discipline in the European Union (EU). The core principle of this Pact is that EU countries should avoid excessive deficits. Hence, the government deficit-to-GDP ratio is allowed to exceed a reference value of 3 per cent of GDP under exceptional circumstances only. The government debt-to-GDP ratio is not allowed to be higher than a reference value of 60 percent of GDP, unless the ratio is sufficiently diminishing and approaching the reference value at a satisfactory pace. These two fiscal indicators, and their reference values of 3 per cent and 60 per cent of GDP, are also the subject of the fiscal convergence criteria for entry to the European Union and to Stage Three of the Economic and Monetary Union (EMU, or Euro Area).
>
> Government debt, also known as "Maastricht debt" or "EDP debt", is defined in the Protocol on the Excessive Deficit Procedure (EDP) annexed to the Maastricht Treaty and in Article 1 (5) of Council Regulation (EC) No. 479/2009 as the total general government gross debt at nominal value outstanding at the end of the year with the following characteristics:
>
> - Sector delineation: EDP debt comprises the (consolidated) liabilities of the general government sector, therefore including all levels of government: central government, local government, social security funds, and when applicable state government. This means that the debt of public corporations (government-controlled units classified in the financial and non-financial corporations' sectors) is excluded from the measurement of government debt in the EU.
>
> - Gross debt: EDP debt is "gross" debt which means that financial assets of general government units are not subtracted in the calculation of government debt.
>
> - Coverage of instruments: EDP debt consists of the following liabilities of general government: currency and deposits, debt securities, and loans, as defined in the 2010 European System of Accounts (ESA 2010). This means that it excludes the remaining financial instruments, namely monetary gold and SDRs; insurance, pensions and standardised guarantee schemes; financial derivatives and employee stock options; and other accounts payable.
>
> - Valuation rules: EDP debt is measured at what it calls "nominal value" and equals the contractually agreed amount that the government will have to refund to creditors at maturity. In the 2008 SNA, GFSM 2014 and Public Sector Debt Statistics: Guide for Compilers and Users 2011, the term "nominal value" is used differently, while the EDP's method of valuation is known as "face value". The latter valuation method means, in particular, that the government debt is not affected by changes in market yields, and excludes unpaid accrued interest. EDP debt is thus measured differently than most government liabilities according to the 2008 SNA, which are recorded at market value.
>
> - Consolidation: EDP debt is consolidated across the general government sector, which implies that government debt instruments held as assets by other general government units are not included in the calculation of government debt.

> Box 6.1. **The Excessive Deficit Procedure in the European Union** (cont.)
>
> All EU countries are legally required to report the breakdown of government debt by instrument and initial maturity to Eurostat, the statistical office of the European Union. Furthermore, the ECB Guideline on Government Finance Statistics (ECB/2014/21) requires all Euro Area national central banks to report additional breakdowns of government debt to the ECB: by residual maturity, by holding sector, and by currency.
>
> Source: Eurostat Manual on Government Deficit and Debt; IMF et al., Public Sector Debt Statistics: Guide for Compilers and Users 2011.

3. Going into more detail

This section discusses some more detailed issues related to government and public sector financial accounts and balance sheets. Subsequently, the following topics are discussed: i) consolidation; ii) some difficult cases potentially affecting the measurement of government deficit and related financial transactions; and iii) valuation and use of financial accounts and stocks. Attention is also paid, in Box 6.2, to the Government Finance Statistics Manual (GFSM) 2014 and how this international standard for government statistics relates to the 2008 SNA.

Consolidation

Similar to business accounting, national accounts and government finance statistics can be presented in a consolidated version, where the accounts for a group of units are reported as if they constitute one single entity. The main concept has been introduced earlier on in this chapter, along with a discussion of consolidation's advantages and disadvantages, in contrast to the 2008 SNA general policy to publish unconsolidated data for all sectors.

Consolidation refers to the elimination, from both assets and liabilities, of financial transactions and positions between units that are grouped together. Consolidation should be applied to financial as well as non-financial accounts: if a bond position between government units is removed from the financial accounts and balance sheets, then the corresponding coupon payments should be deleted from the revenues and expenses of the same units as well.

Consolidation commonly occurs when the accounts of subsectors of general government are combined. Consolidation of the general government sector can be performed by removing financial transactions and positions between units within the same subsector of general government: this is referred to as intra-sectoral (or "within") consolidation. In this case, operations of local government with central government, for example, are not deleted; only the operations between local government entities are. Other methods, often used in national-based publications and primary sources, also require removing of assets and liabilities between different subsectors of government. This process is referred to as inter-sectoral (or "cross") consolidation, and is necessarily more thorough than "within" consolidation; that is, it eliminates more transactions than "within" consolidation. Table 6.4 summarises these two forms of consolidation.

Table 6.4. **Methods of consolidation**

Central government (CG)		Local government (LG)		General government (GG)	
A	L	A	L	A	L
	CG Bonds issued to LG	CG Bond held by LG	LG Bonds issued to non-LG		
	CG Bonds issued to non-government	LG Bonds held by LG		Loans to non-government	Bonds issued to non-government
Loans to non-government			LG Bonds issued to LG		
					Bank loans
Loans to LG			Loans from CG		
			Bank loans		

☐ To be deleted under "within" consolidation

☐ + ☐ To be deleted under "cross" consolidation

It should be noted that cross-consolidation might affect balances at a subsector level, whereas consolidation within subsectors is always neutral: it preserves the balancing items of the unconsolidated accounts, such as net lending/net borrowing and net (financial) worth, while only impacting the magnitude of the aggregate totals. This is shown in Table 6.4 as well, where the consolidating amounts marked in grey on the asset (bonds) and liability (loans) sides of local government do not need to be the same (and neither do the corresponding amounts on the central government balance sheet). Consolidated figures for the balancing items of general government are the same as the unconsolidated numbers, regardless of the method used for its subsectors.[6]

The reasons in favour of consolidation for government statistics are discussed in detail in O'Connor et al. (2004). The main arguments relate to international comparability, i.e. the need to eliminate the distorting effects on aggregates of differing administrative arrangements across countries.

Box 6.2. **Differences and similarities between the SNA 2008 and GFSM 2014, with specific reference to financial accounts and balance sheets**

An alternative version to the 2008 SNA sequence of accounts is the government finance statistics (GFS) presentation. While using definitions and rules that are the same as, or compatible with, the 2008 SNA, the GFS provides a different, but still integrated, picture of the accounts, specifically designed to capture government (or public sector) features. The GFS is less focused on the production of goods and services and the linkages with other sectors, and more focused on both the impact of economic events on the finances of government and – in the opposite direction – the impact of government activities on the economy through taxing, spending, borrowing and lending.

In the 2008 SNA presentation, financial accounts and balance sheets, combined with non-financial accounts, are part of a seven-account sequence that starts with production, and then shows income generation and distribution, use of income for final consumption, and accumulation, focusing on the linkages between sectors of the economy. The GFS presentation starts with a statement of revenue and expense (thus not imputing government output, government consumption, and other items less familiar to policy makers and budgetary accountants), and then presents overviews of transactions in non-financial and financial assets and liabilities. As in the SNA, these transactions and other economic flows are integrated with balance sheets.

Table 6.5 shows three of the four statements recommended by the GFS, showing that all changes in the balance sheets result either from the Statement of Operations, or from the Statement of Other Economic Flows (i.e. revaluations or other changes in volume, not resulting from transactions). In addition, the GFS includes a Statement of Sources and Uses of Cash, to provide key information on liquidity.

Definitions and concepts in the GFS framework are fully compatible with the ones in the 2008 SNA. Technical differences between the 2008 SNA and the GFS Manual include the practices for counterpart entries: similar to business accounting, the GFS is based on double-entry recording, whereas the 2008 SNA is based on quadruple-entry recording, with all transactions recorded from the point of view of all units involved. This kind of difference reflects the fact that the GFS is aimed at providing an exhaustive presentation of a single sector, rather than a picture of the overall economic processes and interactions in the economy. For example, the 2008 SNA partitions interest into a service element and a "pure" interest element, and also partitions the insurance premiums into a service element and the part of the premiums meant to cover the insurance claims. All of this is necessary to measure the output of financial services, but is not relevant to general government revenue or expense and is not observable from government accounts. More information on differences is available in the GFSM 2014, Appendix 7, "GFS and Other Macroeconomic Statistics".

The overviews provided by the GFS add value, because they present information in a way more oriented to the questions of fiscal policy and analysis. In the sequence of tables, the

Box 6.2. **Differences and similarities between the SNA 2008 and GFSM 2014, with specific reference to financial accounts and balance sheets** *(Cont.)*

full reconciliation with the cash-flow statement, an element not relevant to the SNA, marks the policy-oriented nature of the GFS for liquidity management and for identifying payment timing issues.

Table 6.5. **Structure of the GFS presentation**

Stock positions	+	Flows		=	Stock positions
		Transactions	Other economic flows		
Opening Balance Sheet		**Statement of Operations** (Revenue minus Expense) Equals Change in net worth due to transactions (net operating balance)	**Statement of Other Economic Flows** Change in net worth due to other economic flows		**Closing Balance Sheet**
Net worth	+		+	=	Net worth
Equals		Equals	Equals		Equals
Nonfinancial assets	+	Transactions in nonfinancial assets	+ Other economic flows in nonfinancial assets	=	Nonfinancial assets
Plus		Plus	Plus		Plus
Net financial worth	+	Change in net financial worth due to transactions (net lending (+) / net borrowing (−))	+ Change in net financial worth due to other economic flows	=	Net financial worth
Equals		Equals	Equals		Equals
Financial assets	+	Transactions in financial assets	+ Other economic flows in financial assets	=	Financial assets
Minus		Minus	Minus		Minus
Liabilities	+	Transactions in liabilities	+ Other economic flows in liabilities	=	Liabilities

Source: GFSM 2014, Figure 4.9.

Some difficult cases potentially affecting the measurement of government deficit and related financial transactions

In the 2008 SNA and the GFSM 2014, a key role of providing summary information on the overall performance of general government (or the public sector) is played by the main balancing items: the net lending/net borrowing figure and the change in net (financial) worth. The former indicator, commonly known as the "government deficit", is also adopted as a key target for administrative use in the fiscal surveillance of the European Union (see Box 6.1).

Financial accounts and balance sheets for the government sector are based on the same general principles as financial accounts and balance sheets for other sectors in the national accounts framework. In order to properly identify financial instruments, specific provisions may be needed, reflecting that the powers, motivation, and functions of government are sometimes different from those of other sectors. Such special provisions should not be seen as exceptions: they are simply additional rules, able to provide guidance for borderline cases where different 2008 SNA criteria would be appropriate. An important example is provided by the specific provisions for "capital injections", which are payments by the government to public corporations on a large and irregular basis, where formal elements of financial transactions coexist with elements of capital transfers. Of course, both types of transactions are governed by the same principles, but a different classification, depending on whether "capital injections" are deemed to be more similar to financial transactions or capital transfers, would lead to different figures and economic analysis. For these reasons, additional criteria, as developed in the GFSM or the Eurostat Manual on Government Deficit and Debt,[7] are required in order to select the appropriate 2008 SNA treatment. Capital injections are considered to be expenses – rather than financial investments – when they do not result in an effective financial claim on the debtor. This is the case when the purpose of the capitalisation is to cover accumulated past losses, rather than increase the value of government equity (as a normal investor would require).

In order to test whether the government acts similarly to a private investor/shareholder, so that the capital injection can be treated as an increase in equity, the expected return on investment is a crucial factor. A realistic rate of return is indicated by a rate of return that is sufficient to generate dividends or holding gains at a later date and encompasses a claim on the residual value of the corporation. This simple requirement takes into account neither the relationship between risks and rewards, nor the opportunity cost with respect to alternative investments. Nevertheless, it has allowed a number of relevant cases to be ruled out in the past.

More recent experience, notably in the field of government intervention in favour of the banking sector, shows that transfers may often take the form of viable investment (i.e. the government is able, in principle, to generate dividends on its investment), but at out-of-market rates after taking into account risk exposure. Future evolution of the rules, in order to properly partition financial investments and identify transfer components, might imply a major use of instruments taken from financial theory. For example, a standard Capital Asset Pricing Model – CAPM (Bodie et al., 2005)[8] – might be appropriate in deriving a risk-adjusted rate of return, to be compared with average market returns. It should be noted that the complexity of such an approach is exacerbated by the use of the general government as the main target population for indicators on fiscal sustainability. The broader population of the public sector would show balancing items less subject to the impact of borderline transactions, as in this case the relevant transactions would be eliminated upon consolidation if the corporation is or becomes a public corporation, and therefore part of the public sector.

An opposite example, in which the government receives payments, concerns the transfer of pension obligations, which has been observed in several countries. A detailed discussion on pension entitlements is included in Chapter 9. Here, the example is limited to the issue of lump-sum payments related to transfers of pension obligations. A number of governments, in order to facilitate a public corporation's privatisation campaign or new stock market issuance, have "cleaned up" that corporation's balance sheet by assuming that corporation's pension commitments to its employees, receiving in return a lump sum payment corresponding to the financial burden of the future pension payments. The economic substance of this transaction is an equal exchange of cash for the incurrence of an obligation that is a liability. Therefore, the transaction should be treated as a financial transaction and not improve government net lending/net borrowing or net worth. However, depending on the asset boundary, the obligation to pay for future pensions may not appear as a liability on the balance sheet of either of the units transferring or assuming the obligations.

These transactions, owing to their size and relevance for government accounts, had a great influence on the debate on the reform of statistical standards that led to the 2008 SNA, ESA 2010 and GFSM 2014. However, some lack of harmonisation between the SNA, the ESA and GFSM survived in the classification of liabilities to be recorded in the central framework and implicit liabilities which are not recognised in the central framework. In the GFS, pension entitlements of (unfunded) government sponsored, employment-related defined benefit schemes are fully recognised, whereas these schemes are excluded from the central framework of the ESA, and the 2008 SNA provides some flexibility on the treatment of these entitlements. Notwithstanding these differences, the balancing items of government in national accounts can no longer improve as a consequence of pension transfers. Under ESA, the lump sum payment, if not classified as an explicit pension liability, should now be viewed as a prepayment of social contributions for future pension payments and be classified as "other accounts payable" (to the pensioners).[9]

Apart from pension entitlements, the government is particularly likely to be involved in contingent liabilities and in the provision of one-off or standardised guarantees, traditionally not recognised in the national accounts. The international standards for compiling government statistics recognise that some arrangements that are not included as liabilities, such as one-off guarantees and other contingent liabilities, may be analytically important and provide specific guidance for them. For example, the Guide on Public Sector Debt Statistics provides a categorisation and supplementary table for explicit contingent liabilities.

Valuation and use of financial accounts and stocks

Assets and liabilities are valued at market prices in the financial accounts and balance sheets, except for three specific instruments: currency and deposits, loans and other accounts receivable/payable, which are valued at the amount that the debtors are contractually obliged to repay to the creditors, regardless of changes in market prices and rates. Unlike non-financial assets, which for government may include monuments and infrastructure assets that may be difficult to value, financial assets and liabilities are less problematic to value. However, a few exceptions can be observed, including equity stakes in unlisted public corporations, which are without a private equivalent.

An issue of greater interest may instead relate to proper use of financial balance sheets, and to their relationship with fiscal sustainability analysis. The concept of fiscal sustainability concerns a situation in which a government is expected to be able to continue servicing its debts in the long run and to sustain its current spending, tax and other policies, without defaulting on some of its liabilities or promised expenditures, or relying on unrealistically large future corrections to the balance of income and expenditure. One way to express sustainability is by means of a solvency condition in terms of discounted present value of future income and expenditure flows, compared to the current debt, as follows:

$$D_{t_0} - \sum_{t=t_0+1}^{\infty} \frac{PB_t}{(1+r)^{t-t_0}} \leq 0 \qquad (1)$$

Where

D_{t_0} : Debt at time t_0

$PB_t = revenue_t - primary\ expenditure_t = primary\ balance$ at time t where all variables are expressed in GDP terms (D, PB in % of GDP; r is defined as $1 + r = (1 + i)/(1 + y)$, where y is the rate of growth of nominal GDP, and i the nominal interest rate. Primary expenditure excludes interest, which is a useful concept as interest is an outcome of expenditure decisions in previous years.

The above equation illustrates that the discounted value of the total future primary balances should be (at least) equal to the government debt at the starting point t_0. One key issue concerns the stock component (the term "D" in equation (1)), and which debt measure is more adequate to analyse fiscal sustainability: nominal gross debt, debt at market prices in line with the national accounts balance sheets, Maastricht Debt, net (financial) worth, or some other measure.

An alternative characterisation of sustainability was proposed by Buiter (1985), who argued that sustainable fiscal policy should maintain the ratio of net worth to GDP at its current level. Other proposals pointed out the inadequacy of traditional government indicators and put more emphasis on the role of balance sheets and flow of funds, suggesting an extension of coverage for the items included in the accounts (Buiter [1983]; Kotlikoff [1984] and Cadete de Matos et al. [2015]). These proposals recommended including assets as well as liabilities in measures of sustainability (in order to show the total "net worth"). In addition, they proposed that the liability side should comprise implicit entitlements, even though these have a contingent nature.

On the other hand, no clear preference has emerged in relation to which specific rules for the valuation approach should be used in fiscal sustainability analysis. In the specific context of the above equation and its alternative formulations, market valuation might not be helpful. For example, for a government approaching a default situation, debt valued at market prices will automatically decrease, as investors are willing to pay less and less for the relevant debt instruments because of the risk of non-payment. But this phenomenon of decreasing debt at market value does not necessarily signal that the government has a better ability to sustain its current spending in the long run. For this kind of analysis, measures closer to the concept of gross debt at nominal value might provide better information for analysing sustainability.

With this caveat, market valuations – fundamental in the national accounts context – still play an important role in GFS and the 2008 SNA. Data at market value enables a full reconciliation with data from counterparties (which typically value their holdings at market value) and is thus an instrument for cross-checking. It also expresses the cost for terminating units or buying back liabilities, with possible policy relevant implications. Finally, it can be useful in studying the counterparties of government, for example in the analysis of portfolio shifts of investors.

Key Points

- Governments make revenue, expenditure and financing decisions that affect the whole economy. They differ from other units in that they have a public policy motivation. In some cases, the government makes its decisions on spending with the objective of influencing the rest of the economy by reducing or expanding aggregate demand.

- Government deficit is a key variable for analysis because of its need for financing and its contribution to future debt. Government debt may raise particular concerns in relation to financial sustainability – fiscal insolvency has caused a number of financial crises and, unlike business units, expenditures which increase government debt are often related to non-commercial motives, and thus may generate burdens that are passed on to (future) tax paying units. Measures of government debt can vary according to instrument coverage, institutional coverage, valuation, consolidation, and the degree of netting of assets, so these aspects need to be considered in comparisons.

- Governments have complex structures that differ from other entities – budgetary and extra-budgetary components; social security funds; central, state and local levels; and public corporations that have financial implications for government and are motivated to varying degrees by non-commercial motivations. Governments are also able to exercise control over units in more complex ways than in the private sector. The 2008 SNA includes various criteria to identify government control to reflect this.

- Different components of the government may be considered separately for different purposes, such as budgetary central government being the focus of fiscal policy, and local governments being analysed separately to focus on their specialised functions.

- The Government Finance Statistics (GFS) presentation is an alternative version to the 2008 SNA sequence of accounts, specifically designed to capture government (or public sector) features. For example, measures of total revenue and expenditure are key indicators in the GFS, but are not shown in the SNA, where they are spread over several accounts. Definitions and concepts in the GFS framework are almost fully compatible with those in the SNA. However, GFS is more closely related to business accounting, providing a bridge to published national budget accounting data. Furthermore, these issues mainly affect "above-the-line" figures, with financial accounts and balance sheets being the same in the 2008 SNA and the GFSM 2014. The one exception to this is the more inclusive recognition of pension liabilities in the framework for GFS. Pension liabilities have been a particular concern in fiscal risk analysis.

- In addition to recording transactions on an accruals basis, which is in line with the 2008 SNA, the GFS provides an additional Statement of Sources and Uses of Cash. Such a statement, using a cash basis recording, is more in line with the standard practice in many countries' government accounting systems. It also supports management of cash and government budget liquidity.
- In the specific case of government, there are good reasons to deviate from 2008 SNA's general policy to publish unconsolidated data. Consolidation allows analysts to relate government aggregates to the economy as a whole, eliminating the "internal churning" of funds and to compare results across countries, regardless of the degree of centralisation of government functions.
- Another exception from 2008 SNA general policies relates to valuation: nominal value might provide better information with which to assess sustainability. However, market valuation still plays an important role in GFS and the 2008 SNA; for example, market valuation is used for the full reconciliation of balance sheets across the whole economy; to express the cost for terminating units or buying back liabilities, with possible policy relevant implications; and to study the behaviour of the counterparties of government.

Notes

1. Debt sustainability analysis also takes into account maturity, currency composition, off-balance sheet risks such as guarantees, and public corporation debt. See IMF, *Modernizing the Framework for Fiscal Policy and Public Debt Sustainability Analysis*.

2. See Dippelsman et al. (2012) which shows that institutional and instrument coverage of data published as government debt varies widely. For example, some countries include pension liabilities, while in other countries these are recorded in supplementary tables or not at all. It adopts a summary terminology (D1, D2, etc.) to highlight the differences.

3. These supplementary tables only become available at the end of 2017, or in the course of 2018, for OECD-countries.

4. Exceptions of the latter treatment within the OECD are Japan and Korea.

5. *www.ssb.no/en/offogjeld*.

6. For neutrality of consolidation on the GFSM balancing items (including the net operating balance, net lending/net borrowing and net worth, or net debt) for the *aggregate* public sector, see IMF et al. *Public Sector Debt Statistics: Guide for Compilers and Users* 2011, Box 8.1.

7. The Eurostat Manual on Government Deficit and Debt (MGDD) provides very detailed guidance on the recording of specific cases. See *http://ec.europa.eu/eurostat/documents/3859598/7203647/KS-GQ-16-001-EN-N.pdf/5cfae6dd-29d8-4487-80ac-37f76cd1f012*.

8. Bodie, Z., A. Kane and A.J. Marcus (2005), "Investments". McGraw-Hill; see also Chapter 13 in Elton, E.J, M.J. Gruber, S.J. Brown and W.N. Goetzman (2003), "Modern Portfolio Analysis", J. Wiley and Sons.

9. See MGDD 2016, paragraph 20.275. This interpretation would allow to neutralise the effects of pension transfers even when the pension obligations are merged with a *social security scheme*, for which no core-liability is recognized in any statistical standard.

References

Buiter, W.H. (1983), "Measurement of the public sector deficit and its implications for policy evaluation and design." *International Monetary Fund Staff Papers*, Vol. 30, No. 2, (June), International Monetary Fund, Washington, DC, pp. 306-349.

Buiter, W.H. (1985), "A Guide to Public Sector Debt and Deficits", *Economic Policy*, Vol. 1, Oxford University Press, Oxford, pp. 612-35.

Cadete de Matos J., S. Branco and F. Morais (2015), *Conceptual Issues Related to the Definition of Government Debt*, presented at the 60th World Statistics Conference, 26-30 July, Rio de Janeiro.

Dippelsman, R., C. Dziobek and C. Gutierrez (2012), "What lies beneath: The statistical definition of public sector debt. An overview of the coverage of public sector debt for 61 countries", *IMF Staff Discussion Notes*, 12/09, International Monetary Fund, Washington, DC, *www.imf.org/external/pubs/ft/sdn/2012/sdn1209.pdf*.

ECB (2017), *Statistical Data Warehouse*, European Central Bank, Frankfurt, *http://sdw.ecb.europa.eu/browse.do?node=9691262*.

Elton, E.J. et al. (2003), *Modern Portfolio Analysis*, J. Wiley and Sons, Hoboken.

Estrada, M., D. Igan and D. Knight (2014), "Fiscal Risks and Borrowing Costs in State and Local Governments", in *IMF Country Report* No. 14/222, International Monetary Fund, Washington, DC.

European Commission (2014), "Assessing public debt sustainability in EU member states: A guide", *European Economy, Occasional Papers,* No. 200, European Commission, Brussels, http://ec.europa.eu/economy_finance/publications/occasional_paper/2014/pdf/ocp200_en.pdf.

Eurostat, *Manual on Government Deficit and Debt 2016,* Eurostat, Luxembourg, http://ec.europa.eu/eurostat/documents/3859598/7203647/KS-GQ-16-001-EN-N.pdf/5cfae6dd-29d8-4487-80ac-37f76cd1f012.

IMF (2017), *World Economic Outlook Database, April 2017,* International Monetary Fund, Washington, DC, www.imf.org/external/pubs/ft/weo/2017/01/weodata/weoselgr.aspx.

IMF (2011), *Modernizing the Framework for Fiscal Policy and Public Debt Sustainability Analysis,* International Monetary Fund, Washington, DC, www.imf.org/external/np/pp/eng/2011/080511.pdf.

IMF (2002), *Assessing Sustainability,* International Monetary Fund, Washington, DC, www.imf.org/external/np/pdr/sus/2002/eng/052802.pdf.

IMF and other international organizations, *Public Sector Debt Statistics: Guide for Compilers and Users 2011,* International Monetary Fund, Washington, DC, www.tffs.org/pdf/method/2013/psds2013.pdf.

Kotlikoff, L.J. (1984), "Economic Impact of Deficit Financing", *IMF Staff Papers,* Vol. 33, International Monetary Fund, Washington, D.C., pp. 549-581.

O'Connor, L., E. Weisman and T. Wickens (2004), *GFSM 2001 Companion Material, Consolidation of the General Government Sector,* International Monetary Fund, Washington, DC, www.imf.org/external/pubs/ft/gfs/manual/comp.htm.

OECD (2017), "Financial Balance Sheets, SNA 2008 (or SNA 1993): Consolidated stocks, annual", *OECD National Accounts Statistics* (database), http://dx.doi.org/10.1787/data-00719-en; and"Public Sector Debt: Public sector debt – consolidated", *OECD National Accounts Statistics* (database), http://dx.doi.org/10.1787/data-00620-en.

Chapter 7

The financial relationships with the Rest of the World

João Cadete de Matos (Banco de Portugal), Daniele Fano (Fondazione AIB) and Filipa Lima (Banco de Portugal)

> The accounts for the "Rest of the World", which record the transactions and positions of residents of a country with non-residents, are key to understanding many domestic and international economic developments. According to economic literature, the balance of current and capital transactions with the Rest of the World is linked with the growth and international competitiveness of an economy, through the impact of issues such as productivity, costs of production factors, product/market diversification, tariff regimes, development of the financial system, as well as other factors such as the ageing of population, the propensity to save and the trade openness of the country. This chapter discusses the interpretation of persistent imbalances, and its relationship with the international investment position or the indebtedness of a country, including the composition of such foreign exposures. Standard criteria and thresholds to test external debt sustainability are also discussed.

7. THE FINANCIAL RELATIONSHIPS WITH THE REST OF THE WORLD

1. A general overview

References to the position of an economy in its economic relationships with other countries are frequently discussed, and often make the headlines. Prominent examples are: "Is the US current account sustainable? If not, how costly is adjustment likely to be?" (Edwards, 2005); and "German current account surplus to hit record, world's largest in 2016 (Wagner et al., 2017)".

The accounts for the Rest of the World record all transactions and positions between residents and non-residents. This overview of the relationship of one country with the Rest of the World is often referred to as the balance of (external) payments statistics. Within both overviews, the current account balance of a country shows the international balance of its exports and imports of goods and services, and the balance of income transactions (wages and salaries, interest, dividends, taxes, etc.) with the Rest of the World. With respect to the latter, a distinction can be made between primary income and secondary income. Primary income is accrued due to being directly involved in the production process (e.g. the payment of wages and salaries to someone working in one country but living in another country, and vice versa) or due to the ownership of assets (interest, dividends, etc.). Secondary incomes refer to receipts and payments made without receiving something (directly) in return. Examples of the latter are remittances, taxes, social contributions, social benefits, etc. An example of the balance of payments, part of which concerns the current account, is presented in Table 7.1. In addition to the current account, the balance of payments also includes capital and financial transactions.

The current account balance receives (rightly so) great attention from economic analysts. The current account balance is a key indicator that is monitored on a regular basis, giving insight into the economic performance of a country vis-a-vis the Rest of the World. As such, it is also an indicator of the economic constraints and opportunities of a country. Less attention is usually given to how a current account surplus or deficit (positive or negative external saving) is financed. The latter is monitored by analysing the financial accounts and balance sheets. This chapter aims to show that understanding the way a current account surplus or deficit is financed is indeed useful and important.

As discussed in detail in Section 3 below, large and persistent current account deficits, for example deficits caused by having imports which are structurally higher than exports, lead to an increase in foreign debt exposure. To pay for the excess imports, the domestic country will have to borrow money

Table 7.1. **Overview of the accounts for the Rest of the World**

	Credits	Debits	Balance
Current accounts			
Goods and services account			
Goods	462	392	
Services	78	107	
Goods and services (total)	*540*	*499*	*41*
Primary income account			
Compensation of employees	6	2	
Interest	13	21	
Distributed income of corporations	17	17	
Reinvested earnings	14	0	
Primary income (total)	*50*	*40*	*10*
Goods, services and primary income	*590*	*539*	*51*
Secondary income account			
Current taxes on income, wealth, etc.	1	0	
Net non-life insurance premiums	2	11	
Non-life insurance claims	12	3	
Current international transfers	1	31	
Miscellaneous current transfers	1	10	
Secondary income (total)	*17*	*55*	*-38*
Current account balance			*13*
Capital account			
Acquisition or disposals of non-produced assets	0	0	
Capital transfers	1	4	
Capital account balance			*-3*
Net lending (+) or net borrowing (-)			*10*
Financial account (by functional category)			
Direct investment	8	11	
Portfolio investment	18	14	
Financial derivatives (other than reserves) and ESOs	3	0	
Other investment	20	22	
Reserve assets	8		
Total changes in assets or liabilities	*57*	*47*	
Net lending (+) or net borrowing (-)			*10*
Net errors and omissions			*0*

Source: European Commission et al. (2008), *System of National Accounts*, https://unstats.un.org/unsd/nationalaccount/docs/SNA2008.pdf.

StatLink ⟶ http://dx.doi.org/10.1787/888933590093

from other counties. Continuous increases in the level of liabilities may eventually make the international investment position[1] of a country less sustainable, with inevitable economic, political and social consequences (the concept of the international investment position is discussed in more detail later in this chapter). A deficit is not, however, necessarily a negative feature, as will be further discussed in this chapter and in Chapter 10. Some developing countries or some more mature economies may be able to sustain persistent minor current account deficits, as long as the quality of their financing is such that it does not generate instability (see e.g. IMF [2004]). For example, the United States can run persistent deficits because the US Dollar (USD) is generally accepted as the international currency for a significant share of international transactions. As a consequence, non-US residents have quite substantial holdings of USD, which ultimately is a liability of the US Federal Reserve, without any threat to financial stability.

Conversely, current account surpluses are not necessarily benign. Mercantilism was preoccupied with generating surpluses with the Rest of the World, but was rightly criticised as far back as the 18th century for being globally inconsistent. All countries cannot generate surpluses simultaneously. Moreover, if the objective of a surplus is associated with protectionist policies, it may hamper growth. On the other hand, surpluses may contribute to stability by creating a healthy balance sheet position for a country. With that said, abnormally high and persistent surpluses are generally considered a factor of instability. For instance, in EU countries, a current account surplus above 6% will trigger a so-called Macroeconomic Imbalances Procedure,[2] the European Union's surveillance mechanism that aims to identify potential risks, and to prevent and correct harmful macroeconomic imbalances. Excessive surpluses may not only represent a threat to global growth and stability, but they may end up encouraging financial flows towards dubious real and financial investments. They may also lead to international discussions on the fairness of international trade, as a consequence of which partner countries running a persistent deficit may consider protectionist measures to reverse the situation.

Figure 7.1 below shows the current account balance for selected EU countries. It is interesting to see how, following the 2007-09 economic and financial crisis, some imbalances have been narrowing while others have been increasing. Germany's surplus has been increasing steadily, the opposite has happened to the United Kingdom, and Italy and Spain have switched from a deficit to a surplus.

The sections that follow will show how the analysis of the "flip side" of the current account figures, as represented by the financial accounts and balance sheets, may prove to be very useful in uncovering the implications of the excess or lack of national saving implied by current account surpluses or deficits.

2. The balance of payments and its relationship with national accounts

The complete set of transactions with the Rest of the World in the 2008 SNA matches exactly the set of transactions captured in the balance of payments statistics, as defined by the BPM6, although there are some differences in terminology and breakdowns. Box 7.2 explains the similarities

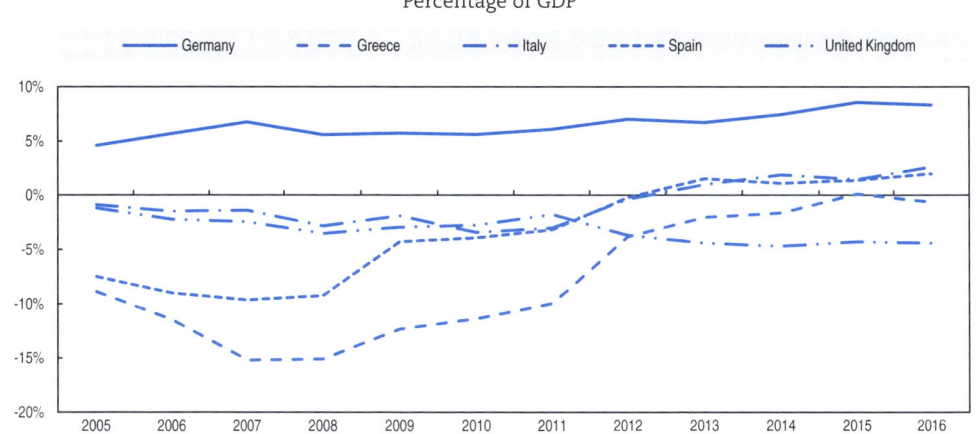

Figure 7.1. **Current account for selected EU countries, 2005-16**
Percentage of GDP

Source: Eurostat (2017), *Balance of Payments Statistics and International Investment Positions* (database), http://ec.europa.eu/eurostat/web/balance-of-payments/data/database.

StatLink http://dx.doi.org/10.1787/888933588782

and differences, as well as statistical discrepancies, with further references to both the 2008 SNA and BPM6. This section aims to help the reader understand the relationship between two key indicators: the current account balance, which is usually directly derived from the balance of payments, and net lending/net borrowing, which is in essence the balance of the current *and* capital accounts and is derived from the Rest of the World financial accounts. Therefore, we start with introducing the capital account.

Introducing the capital account

As shown in Table 7.1, the current account balance is not exactly equal to the balance of international lending or borrowing. To arrive at the net lending/net borrowing figure, capital transactions must be taken into consideration as well. In the context of transactions between residents and non-residents, capital transactions consist of purchases/sales of non-produced non-financial assets and capital transfers. These transactions are usually relatively minor, and therefore it is generally acceptable, with all the necessary caveats, to use the broadly available current account balance as a handy proxy of net lending/net borrowing.

One may wonder why the capital account for the Rest of the World only records the transactions in non produced non-financial assets, and then only part of them. First of all, purchases of newly produced non-financial assets from non-residents, or sales of such assets to non-residents, are recorded as part of imports and exports of goods and services. Furthermore, in the case a non-resident buys a non-financial asset that remains in the country, e.g. a dwelling or a non-residential building, the non-resident is automatically considered as a resident unit for the ownership of the relevant assets, including the related transactions. The purchase is recorded as a financial investment into a "notional unit" when it concerns, for example, a second house, or into an enterprise that uses the assets in the production of goods and services. As a consequence, the transactions in non-financial assets in the Rest of the World accounts are limited to sales and purchases of leases, licenses, etc. The payment for a football player offers a concrete example.

It is useful to consider the sequence of accounts, as presented in Table 7.1, which is drawn from the 2008 SNA. As mentioned previously, the table clarifies how net lending/net borrowing can be derived from the combination of the current account and the capital account. Box 7.1 shows the same logic, but this time in the form of traditional macroeconomic notations. In this theoretical example, the item "Errors and omissions" at the bottom of Table 7.1, which can be calculated as the difference between net lending/net borrowing from the current and capital accounts and the same balancing item from the financial account, is assumed to be equal to zero. It means that the two sets of accounts match perfectly. However, in practice, this usually is not the case; the "Going further" section at the end of this chapter further discusses the "errors and omissions" item.

> **Box 7.1. Saving, investments and the pivotal role of net lending/net borrowing**
>
> It is useful to go through the sequence of accounts, not only by analysing Table 7.1, but also by taking the relevant identities of the national accounts framework as a starting point. In doing so, the first important balancing item in the accounts for the Rest of the World is the external balance on goods and services, also known as the (foreign) trade balance, which shows the difference between the value of exports and the value of imports. The second balancing item of interest is the current account balance, which equals the foreign trade balance plus net receipts of (primary and secondary) income from the Rest of the World.
>
> Foreign trade balance = X − M
>
> Current acount balance = X − M + W
>
> Where:
>
> X = Exports
>
> M = Imports
>
> W = Balance of primary and secondary income transactions with the Rest of the World

> Box 7.1. **Saving, investments and the pivotal role of net lending/net borrowing** *(cont.)*
>
> The current account surplus or deficit also reflects whether a country's investments in non-financial assets are matched with its saving, or, in general terms, if a country's aggregate (internal and external) final demand exceeds domestic production.
>
> (1) $Y = C + I + (X - M)$
>
> (2) $Y + W - C = S = I + (X - M) + W$
>
> (3) $S - I = (X - M) + W$ = Current account balance
>
> Where:
>
> Y = Gross Domestic Product (GDP)
>
> S = Saving
>
> C = Consumption
>
> I = Investment
>
> X – M = External demand
>
> C + I = Internal (or domestic) demand
>
> In order to understand the link between the current account balance and financial transactions, one will have to introduce the capital account, as shown in Table 7.1, to arrive at net lending/net borrowing.
>
> (4) Current account balance + R = (X-M) + W + R = S – I + R
>
> R = Balance of capital transactions with the Rest of the World
>
> As a macroeconomic equilibrium, the balance of equation 4 needs to be financed by external net lending/net borrowing. This financing of the balance of transactions on the current and capital accounts is reflected in the financial account:
>
> (5) $S - I + R = (X - M) + W + R$ = Net lending/net borrowing = NAFA – NIL + net errors and omissions
>
> Where:
>
> NAFA = net acquisition of financial assets
>
> NIL = net incurrence of liabilities

National accounts versus balance of payments

A comparison between Table 7.1 above and Table 7.2 below illustrates how the national accounts and the balance of payments contain the same concepts. They are, however, presented in a slightly different way. Moreover, the terminology differs somewhat. The case of Japan presented in Table 7.2 is interesting in itself. It confirms that the current account is indeed a good proxy of net lending/net borrowing (which, again, represents the combined current and capital accounts). It also highlights the importance of "errors and omissions.

Table 7.2. **Japanese balance of payments standard presentation (simplified), 2016**
Millions of USD

	2016
Current account	187 264.8
Goods and services	40 328.5
Primary income	166 549.6
Secondary income	-19 613.3
Capital account	-6 579.7
Gross disposals of non-produced, non-financial assets, credit	386.7
Gross acquisitions of non-produced, non-financial assets, debit	4 922.4
Capital transfers, credit	108.5
Capital transfers, debit	2 152.6
Current and capital accounts	180 685.1
Financial account	265 378.6
Direct investment	134 749.1
Portfolio investment	274 517.6
Financial derivatives (other than reserves) and employee stock options	-15 815.8
Other investment	-122 741.0
Reserve assets	-5 331.3
Monetary gold	
Special drawing rights	583.2
Reserve position in the IMF	2 890.9
Other reserve assets	-8 805.3
Net errors and omissions	84 693.5

Source: IMF (2017), *Balance of Payments Statistics* (database), www.imf.org/external/datamapper/datasets/BOP.
StatLink ᕮ http://dx.doi.org/10.1787/888933590112

The international investment position

In the end, financial transactions between residents and non-residents, together with revaluations and some other changes in the volume of assets, have an impact on the position towards the Rest of the World, as recorded on the balance sheets. This so-called "international investment position" represents the stocks of external financial assets minus the stocks of external liabilities, and should not be confused with financial transactions.

Transactions in goods and services as well as income and capital transactions are recorded in the current and capital accounts and normally result in a concomitant entry in the financial account. For example, an export of goods will result in an increase in currency holdings, an increase in bank deposits or an increase in trade credits. A transaction may also involve two financial accounts entries, when it concerns a purchase or disposal of a financial asset between a resident and a non-resident. For instance, a foreign government bond may be exchanged for currency and deposits. In other cases, the transaction may involve the creation of a new financial asset and corresponding liability.

As noted, the ownership of stocks of foreign financial assets and liabilities by residents, and the ownership of domestic financial assets and liabilities by non-residents are represented in the international investment position (IIP). The IIP is a key indicator in many financial stability reports. By analysing the IIP together with the current account, one can make a macroeconomic assessment of a country's financial situation, and combine this analysis with other macroeconomic analyses. A strong IIP will help to smooth current account imbalances, whereas a weak IIP, in general, may trigger the need for more drastic structural adjustments. Table 7.3 shows Japan's IIP. It is clear that Japan has a very strong international position, which, coupled with a current account surplus shown above, gives a positive signal for the country.

Table 7.3. **Japanese IIP summary presentation, Q4 2016**

	Q4 2016	
	Millions of USD	% of GDP
Assets	8 586 458.5	174
Direct investment	1 413 767.1	29
Equity and investment fund shares	1 289 032.5	26
Debt instruments	124 721.0	3
Portfolio investment	3 875 436.6	78
Equity and investment fund shares	1 417 739.7	29
Debt instruments	2 457 696.9	50
Financial derivatives (other than reserves) and employee stock options	371 113.0	8
Other investment	1 705 719.2	35
Other equity	71 164.4	1
Debt instruments	1 634 554.8	33
Reserve assets	1 220 414.0	25
Liabilities	5 519 203.4	112
Direct Investment	240 907.5	5
Equity and investment fund shares	198 604.5	4
Debt instruments	42 311.6	1
Portfolio investment	2 729 691.8	55
Equity and investment fund shares	1 508 587.3	31
Debt instruments	1 221 104.5	25
Financial derivatives (other than reserves) and employee stock options	388 407.5	8
Other investment	2 160 188.0	44
Other equity	7 525.7	0
Debt instruments	2 152 662.3	44
Net International Investment Position	**3 067 255.1**	**62**

Source: IMF (2017), Balance of Payments Statistics (database), www.imf.org/external/datamapper/datasets/BOP.
StatLink http://dx.doi.org/10.1787/888933590131

As can be seen in Table 7.3, the Japanese economy has a positive external position with the Rest of the World. More concretely, at the end of 2016, the Japanese net IIP was 62% of GDP. In other words, the financial assets held abroad were higher than the financial assets held by non-residents (liabilities from the Japanese position), and the net amount of assets less liabilities towards the Rest of the World was the equivalent of more than half of the total income generated in Japan in 2016.

> **Box 7.2. IMF Balance of Payments and International Investment Position Statistics versus National Accounts' Rest of the World accounts**
>
> As explained previously, the 2008 SNA governs the presentation of the Rest of the World in national accounts and the BPM6 sets standards for the presentation of the balance of payments statistics.
>
> One would expect that both overviews are consistent with each other. However, there are some differences in terminology and breakdowns between the 2008 SNA and BPM6, but these are generally quite minor. The main differences can be observed in the financial accounts (and balance sheets). While in the 2008 SNA, the traditional financial instruments are distinguished (see Chapter 1), the balance of payments statistics usually apply the breakdown of financial transactions and positions by functional category: direct investment, portfolio investment, financial derivatives (other than reserves) and employee stock options, other investment, and reserve assets.
>
> Other differences, and these can be quite substantial in some countries, may be caused by the balancing, within the national accounts, of the numbers from the balance of payment statistics with the statistics on domestic activities. For each transaction between a resident unit and a non-resident unit, as recorded in the balance of payments, there is a counterpart in the domestic economy. When confronting statistics on domestic sectors with the balance of payments statistics, these transactions and positions, which are derived from a variety of data sources, do not match, and to which adjustments will need to be made. Part of these adjustments may be made to the balance of payments. As a consequence, the balance of payments diverges from the Rest of the World accounts in the national accounts. This also affects the original errors and omissions (discussed in detail in the 'Going further' section at the end of this chapter), which are labelled "statistical discrepancies" in the 2008 SNA. One of the motivations for adjusting the balance of payments data, rather than the source data for domestic activities may actually be related to the adjustment's potential to lower the statistical discrepancies.

In 2016, the strength of the Japanese IIP essentially relied on three particular functional categories:

- direct investment: ownership of foreign enterprises with voting power of more than 10%: these investments usually represent strategic decisions regarding the location of productive activities inside the country or abroad; as such, they often concern long-term investments which are not easily reversed;
- portfolio investment – ownership of tradeable securities: the Japanese economy held a significant amount of foreign debt securities;
- reserve assets: Japanese monetary authorities held an equivalent of one quarter of the GDP in assets denominated in foreign currencies.

3. The underlying components of non-financial and financial accounts

The dynamics of current account deficits/surpluses

As explained in Section 1, the balance of the current and capital accounts comprises both the balance of foreign trade in goods and services and the balance of other income and capital transactions. Typically, an overall deficit coincides with a foreign trade deficit, i.e. when a country imports more goods and services than it exports. By definition, any deficit/surplus on the current and capital accounts is balanced by transactions in financial assets and liabilities in the financial accounts. This identity reflects the double entry bookkeeping system, which also underlies the system of national accounts and the balance of payments system. Any current or capital transaction has to have a matching counterpart in a financial transaction.

Another identity, representing the equivalence of total payments and total receipts for each transaction, is shown in equation 4, in Box 7.1, where the current and capital accounts are expressed as the difference between national saving and investment plus the balance of the external capital account. This equation is basically an alternative presentation of the equivalence of total supply and total use of goods and services, as expressed in equation 1. Unlike closed economies, where investment must always equal saving, open economies may finance a shortage of domestic saving by incurring foreign debt or having non-residents invest, for example, in the equity of domestic corporations. In this perspective, for a given period, a current and capital accounts deficit may be viewed as the domestic country having insufficient national saving to finance the desired level of domestic investment.

Figure 7.2 shows the balance of current and capital accounts for the total of a number of "stressed" EU countries: Greece, Ireland, Italy, Portugal and Spain.

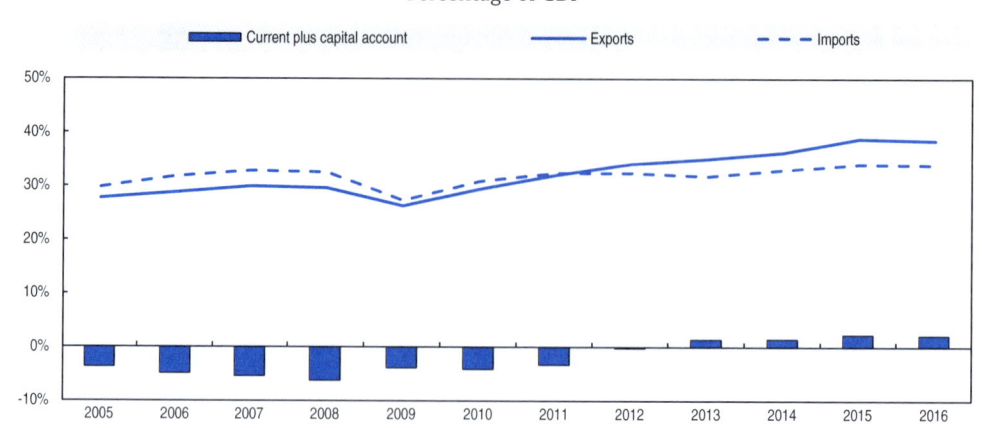

7. THE FINANCIAL RELATIONSHIPS WITH THE REST OF THE WORLD

Figure 7.2. **Balance of payments for selected stressed EU countries,* 2005-16**
Percentage of GDP

* Greece, Ireland, Italy, Portugal and Spain
Source: Eurostat (2017), Balance of Payments Statistics (database), http://ec.europa.eu/eurostat/web/balance-of-payments/data/database; Eurostat (2017), National Accounts Statistics (database), http://ec.europa.eu/eurostat/web/national-accounts/data/database.

StatLink ⟶ http://dx.doi.org/10.1787/888933588839

From 2005 to 2011, these countries had a negative foreign trade balance. From 2013 to 2016, these countries managed, through an internal adjustment process, to turn this deficit into a positive international trade balance. These movements in the performance of exports and imports were also the main drivers of the total balance of the current and capital accounts, or the external net borrowing/net lending figure. Looking at Figure 7.2 in combination with Figure 7.3, which shows the developments in saving and (non-financial) investments, one can easily observe the above discussed macroeconomic identities. Figure 7.3 shows that during the years when the current and capital accounts were negative, domestic investments were larger than domestic saving in the selected EU countries.

As previously mentioned, large and persistent current account deficits may cause external sustainability problems. However they are not, *per se*, necessarily a negative indicator in any economy, and need to be considered along with other macroeconomic indicators such as the growth rates of GDP and investments, as well as export and import fluctuations.[3]

There is also a link between GDP growth and the balance of the current and capital accounts. More specifically, the additional income generated through a growing level of GDP may lead to more demand for goods and services. Some of these goods and services may need to be imported, thus affecting the external goods and services account negatively, *ceteris paribus*. Figure 7.4 illustrates this negative relation between GDP and the current account balance, for the years between 2005 and 2016, for the total of selected stressed EU countries. However,

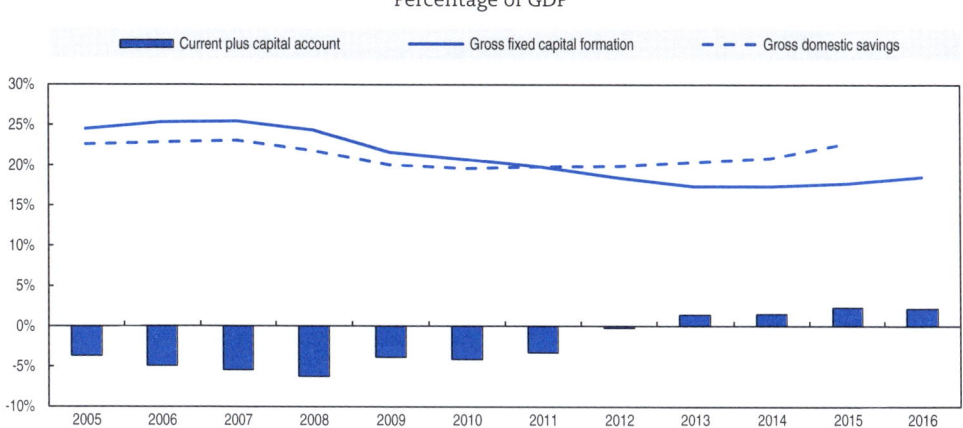

7. THE FINANCIAL RELATIONSHIPS WITH THE REST OF THE WORLD

Figure 7.3. **Savings and investment for selected stressed EU countries,*** 2005-15/16
Percentage of GDP

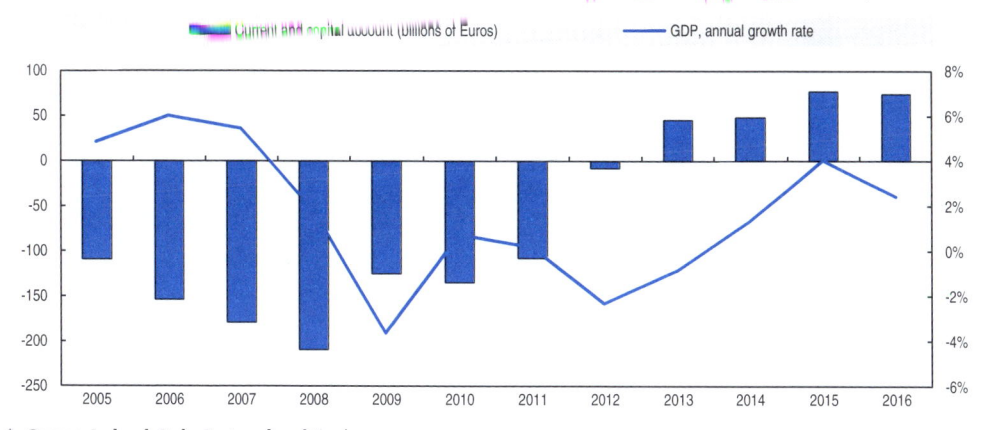

* Greece, Ireland, Italy, Portugal and Spain.
Source: Eurostat (2017), *Balance of Payments Statistics* (database), http://ec.europa.eu/eurostat/web/balance-of-payments/data/database; Eurostat (2017), *National Accounts Statistics* (database), http://ec.europa.eu/eurostat/web/national-accounts/data/database and World Bank (2017), *Gross Domestic Savings* (database), http://data.worldbank.org/indicator/NY.GDS.TOTL.ZS.
StatLink ⟶ http://dx.doi.org/10.1787/888933588858

Figure 7.4. **Current and capital accounts and GDP growth for selected stressed EU countries,*** 2005-16
Billions of EUR (left-hand scale) and GDP annual growth rate (right-hand scale)

* Greece, Ireland, Italy, Portugal and Spain.
Source: Eurostat (2017), *Balance of Payments Statistics* (database), http://ec.europa.eu/eurostat/web/balance-of-payments/data/database; Eurostat (2017), *National Accounts Statistics* (database), http://ec.europa.eu/eurostat/web/national-accounts/data/database.
StatLink ⟶ http://dx.doi.org/10.1787/888933588877

it is also worth mentioning that other factors may also have an impact on the relation between domestic output and the current account balance, thus challenging the negative relationship between GDP and current account balance. For example, the growth of GDP may actually be caused by improved

Current and capital accounts versus financial flows

Figure 7.5 shows, for each year, and for the total of selected stressed EU countries, two different bars: the first shows the main drivers of the balance of the current and capital account (i.e. decomposed into net trade in goods and services, net primary income, and net capital account); and the second shows how the "real" economy is externally financed (foreign direct investment, portfolio investment, other investment and reserve assets).

Figure 7.5. **Current and capital accounts and financial accounts for selected stressed EU countries,* 2005-16**
Billions of EUR

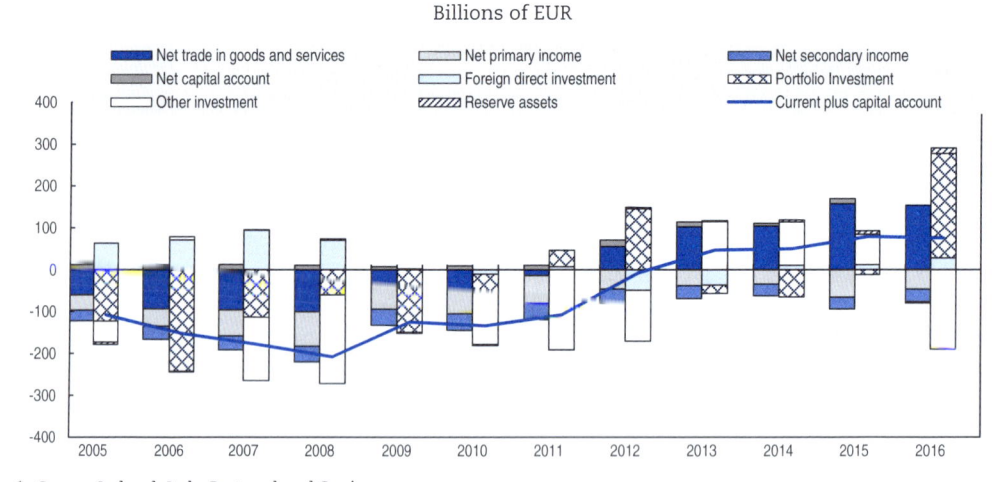

* Greece, Ireland, Italy, Portugal and Spain.
Source: Adapted from Eurostat (2017), *Balance of Payments Statistics and International Investment Positions* (database), http://ec.europa.eu/eurostat/web/balance-of-payments/data/database.

StatLink ⟶ http://dx.doi.org/10.1787/888933588896

As described above, the selected stressed EU countries have experienced an adjustment process between 2005 and 2016, during which they managed to reverse the negative balance of the current and capital accounts into a positive balance. On the "real side" of the economy, in selected countries, the foreign trade in goods and services was clearly the main driver of the evolution of the current and capital accounts. In the 2005-16 time period, income paid by residents to non-residents was always larger than the income received by residents from non-residents.

Deficits on the current and capital accounts need to be financed, whereas surpluses can be used to invest abroad. As noted before, leaving apart statistical discrepancies, the balance of the current and capital accounts is, by definition, equal to the balance of the financial transactions with the Rest of the World. Residents may provide loans to non-residents, and vice versa. They may also purchase foreign debt securities or invest in the equity of non-resident companies, by purchasing shares of a foreign corporation (portfolio investment). An alternative way of investing abroad is to establish a subsidiary enterprise, which is referred to as (foreign) direct investment. Using data from the financial accounts, as also demonstrated in Figure 7.5 above, one can see that in the case of the stressed EU countries, external deficits between 2005 and 2009 were mainly financed through portfolio investments by non-residents, while other investments were generally the main counterpart of the current and capital account balances from 2010 onwards.

The income generated by all these investments, in the form of interest, dividends and reinvested earnings (on foreign direct investment), is an important component of the current and capital accounts. This income is influenced by the stocks of external debt and equity accumulated in the past. In this respect, reinvested earnings are a special category. In the case of foreign direct investment (FDI), the distributed profits of foreign subsidiaries are recorded as investment income. Additionally, the non-distributed profits are considered as payment/receipt of property income, which is subsequently recorded as re-investment in the subsidiary in the financial accounts.

Current and capital accounts sustainability and foreign exposures

Large and persistent current and capital account deficits may constitute a cause for economic concern, particularly when sustainability issues are being raised, questioning the economic prospects of a country. Regardless of the origins, when a country runs current and capital account deficits on a structural basis, it is building up liabilities vis-a-vis the Rest of the World that eventually need to be repaid. Therefore, the country should be able to generate, in the future, sufficient current and capital account surpluses to repay what it has borrowed to finance the current and capital account deficits. In that sense, the extent of the foreign liabilities of a given economy, and their respective servicing costs, may be important aspects to consider when analysing the vulnerabilities of an economy. Whatever the reason behind a current and capital account deficit, high and persistent current account deficits should call for further policy considerations.

When analysing foreign exposures, understanding the composition of the financing is important, as short-term financing is more easily reversed than long-term financing. Similarly, equity financing tends to be more stable than debt-based financing. Particularly, FDI, which is often related to the long-lasting establishment of an enterprise in a country, tends to represent long term investment, whereas other inflows are generally easier to reverse (as in the case of Japan in Table 7.3). Although it may be difficult to state with certainty which components of financing are short- or long-term, some general assumptions can be made. For instance, a current and capital account deficit that is mainly financed by extensive FDI is generally more sustainable than financing through short-term portfolio investments, which may be easily liquidated if the market conditions or expectations change. Moreover, FDI tends to finance long-term investment projects that increase the capital stock of the country and generate revenues required to repay foreign debt in the future. On the other hand, financial sustainability may be seriously threatened if the financing of the external deficit leads to significant losses in official foreign exchange reserves.

Foreign debt exposures

The macroeconomic impact of an increasing foreign or external indebtedness in the case of persistent deficits in the current and capital accounts depends on how the country is using the foreign financing. It also depends on how much a country has borrowed from abroad in the past. External debt requires the payments of principal and/or interest in the future. As such, the liability represents a claim on the resources of the resident's economy. These liabilities may include debt securities, such as bonds, notes and money market instruments, as well as loans, deposits, currency, trade credits and advances owed to non-residents. The debt could be issued with different maturity profiles by different institutional sectors (mainly general government, the non-financial and the financial corporations' sectors). Although not always available, other additional details, such as the geographical breakdown of creditors and debtors and the residual maturity, can be useful to supplement this analysis.

There are a number of valuable methodologies and indicators to measure a key macroeconomic concept like external debt. Overall, they allow for a multi-dimensional approach, making use of several balance of payments items, with their main advantage the possibility to provide a comprehensive measure of external debt consistent across the range of debt instruments, institutional sectors and valuation methods used. Comparisons can be made by focusing on alternatives like gross external debt versus net external debt, external debt vis-a-vis the overall international investment position (IIP), and external debt at nominal value versus external debt at market value. Figure 7.6 illustrates the gross external debt position of the Portuguese general government between Q4 2009 and Q4 2016. Overall, it can be seen that the Portuguese government increased its exposure to the Rest of the World. In the period under analysis, Portuguese gross external debt increased by 33%. The maturity analysis enables the user to understand that this was due to longer term contracts, since short-term debt decreased by 57%.

Gross external debt, at any given time, is the outstanding amount of liabilities of the residents of an economy towards residents of other countries. These debt liabilities, which exclude equity investments of non-residents in the

Figure 7.6. **Portuguese general government gross external debt position by original maturity, 2009-16**
Millions of EUR

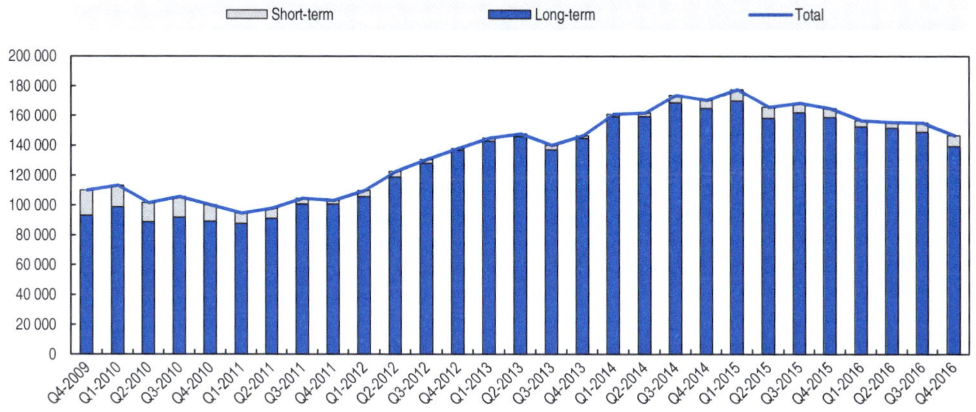

Source: Banco de Portugal (2017): *Balance of payments Statistics* (database), www.bportugal.pt/EstatisticasWeb/(S(d2kqsvm5bxjx3bag2hq5lo55))/DEFAULT.ASPX?Lang=en-GB.

StatLink ⇲ http://dx.doi.org/10.1787/888933588915

domestic economy, only capture one side of an economy's external exposure to international debt markets. Net external debt, which can be obtained by subtracting debt liabilities of non-residents towards residents from gross external debt, captures both sides of external exposure. As such, it can provide additional insights into the sustainability of external debt. The recent massive increase in the use of certain types of financial contracts, such as repurchase agreements, securities lending, collateralised loans and securitisation issues, has driven up gross external debt figures. This is because these instruments simultaneously create new debt positions in both assets and liabilities. As a consequence, net external debt has become more relevant as an indicator of foreign debt exposures.

The analysis of solvency risks related to external debt, which is usually based on net interest payments to the Rest of the World, is inferred from the net external debt concept. In this context, large imbalances in net external debt and large net interest payments generally constitute a credible early warning signal of rising risks concerning the ability of the economy to successfully meet its external financial obligations, particularly in periods of economic distress or in the aftermath of external shocks. Figure 7.7 shows the gap between gross and net external debt for a number of EU countries. From this figure, two clear conclusions can be drawn: i) the level of net external debt is, by definition, lower than that of the gross debt; and ii) some countries become creditors when the net concept is used to measure external debt. The latter relates to, for example, Belgium and Germany.

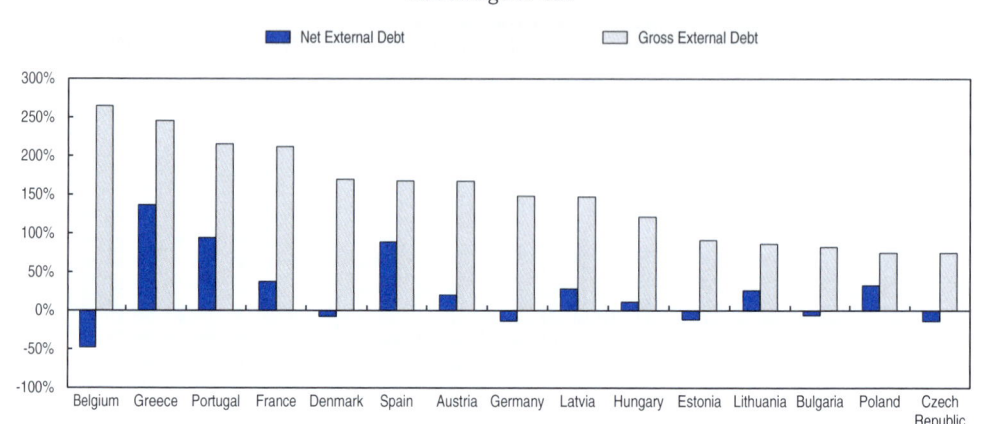

Figure 7.7. **Gross and net external debt for selected EU countries, 31 December 2016**
Percentage of GDP

Source: ECB (2017), *Balance of Payments and Other External Statistics: Gross External Debt* (database), http://sdw.ecb.europa.eu/browse.do?node=9691635; Eurostat (2017): *Net External Debt* (database), http://appsso.eurostat.ec.europa.eu/nui/show.do?dataset=tipsii20&lang=en.

StatLink http://dx.doi.org/10.1787/888933588934

Total international investment position (IIP)

Beyond external debt indicators, other kinds of measures, such as the IIP, can significantly contribute to the analysis of a country's economic performance. The IIP relates to the overall net external financial position of a country. As discussed previously, it measures the sum of all external financial assets (residents' investments in the Rest of the World) minus all external liabilities (non-residents' investments in a country). It thus includes, in addition to the net external debt, the net external position in equity (including FDI), financial derivatives, and other components such as official reserves.

Although the analysis of balance of payments statistics has an important role to play in understanding the sustainability and vulnerability of an economy, IIP data are useful for other purposes as well. According to BPM6, IIP data can be used for:

1. monitoring rates of return of external financial investment;
2. analysing solvency issues, where "assets are insufficient to cover liabilities"; and
3. analysing dependency problems, for example, when the majority of a country's exports are being sold to just one or two countries.

Within the EU context, the IIP is one of the indicators included in the scoreboard of the Macroeconomic Imbalances Procedure, a surveillance mechanism that aims to identify potential risks, and to prevent and correct harmful macroeconomic imbalances in the European Union (as already mentioned above). Figure 7.8 shows the total IIP and the net external debt

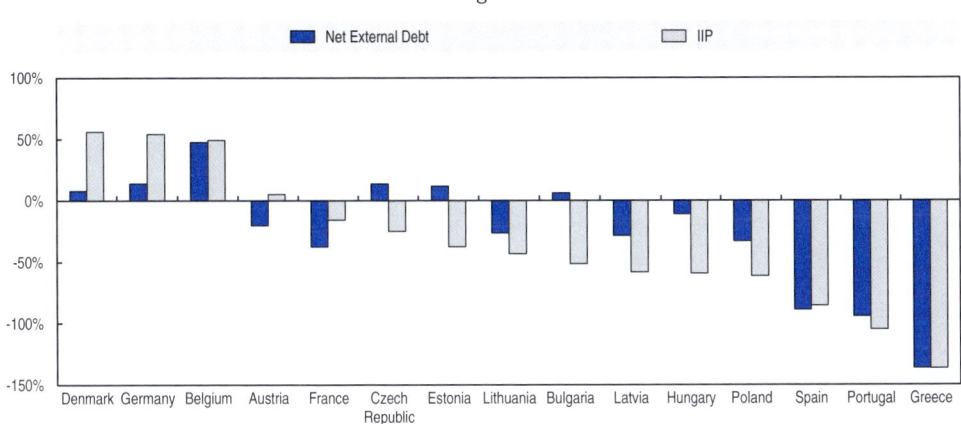

Figure 7.8. **Net external debt* and IIP for selected EU countries, 31 December 2016**
Percentage of GDP

* To ease comparison in this figure, net external debt is represented in negative terms.
Source: Eurostat (2017): Net External Debt (database), http://appsso.eurostat.ec.europa.eu/nui/show.do?dataset=tipsii20&lang=en; ECB (2017): Balance of Payments and International Investment Position (database), http://sdw.ecb.europa.eu/browse.do?node=9688874.

StatLink ⟶ http://dx.doi.org/10.1787/888933588953

position in 2016 for fifteen EU countries. Only Denmark, Germany and Belgium have both external net debt (defined here as assets minus liabilities of residents towards the Rest of the World) and a positive IIP. In this sense, their foreign assets are larger than their liabilities owed towards non-residents. On the other hand, countries like Greece and Portugal have a negative net stock below *minus* 100% of GDP. In practice, that means that, in 2016, both countries owe to non-residents the equivalent of more than one year of value added generated through production (GDP). From Figure 7.8 it is also possible to derive, by the size of the gap between the two bars, the external position of non-debt related instruments. Looking at the difference between the two bars in Figure 7.8, one can observe both positive and negative positions of non-debt related instruments. Denmark and Germany, for example, have substantial non-debt international positions, whilst Eastern European countries typically have negative positions, showing that considerable equity-type investments have been made in these countries.

Specific cases of foreign direct investment

Residence is a key concept, not only when it comes to defining domestic activities, but also when it concerns the definition of external investment positions. In this respect, some issues can arise regarding the inclusion, or exclusion, of some entities to which the application of the concept of residence is not straightforward. Examples include enterprises located in free trade territories or offshore zones, or "Special Purpose Entities" (SPEs). According to the international standards for compiling balance of payments and national accounts, enterprises located in offshore zones should be registered in the economies in which the zones are located, even though such enterprises may belong to non-resident multinational groups. The financial transactions and positions between the enterprise located offshore and the non-resident multinational group to which it belongs constitute a foreign direct investment relationship. Similarly, SPEs are always treated as separate institutional units, if they are resident in another country than that of their owners. A brass plate company, a typical example of an SPE, which has been set up by a non-resident unit to collect worldwide royalties for tax avoidance reasons, is thus also recorded as a foreign direct investment relationship.

As a consequence of the above treatment, the debt issued and registered on the balance sheets of entities legally incorporated or domiciled in an offshore centre is classified as external debt of the economy in which the offshore centre is located. The same is true for SPEs. Any subsequent lending of funds to a non-resident of the economy where the SPE or the offshore is located, e.g. to a parent or subsidiary corporation, is classified as an external asset of the offshore entity. However, as these units do not have substantial economic activities in the country of residence, relevant countries are strongly encouraged by users to separately identify the external positions of these entities, especially when they are significant. Figure 7.9 shows the impact SPEs can have on the interpretation of data on FDI positions for a number of OECD countries. In the Netherlands, for example, the positions of SPEs amount to more than 80% of total FDI. In Hungary, they account for more than 50%. Other countries with substantial positions of SPEs, not presented in Figure 7.9, are Ireland and Luxembourg.

Figure 7.9. **FDI liabilities in OECD selected countries by type of entity, 2015-16**
Percentage of total liabilities

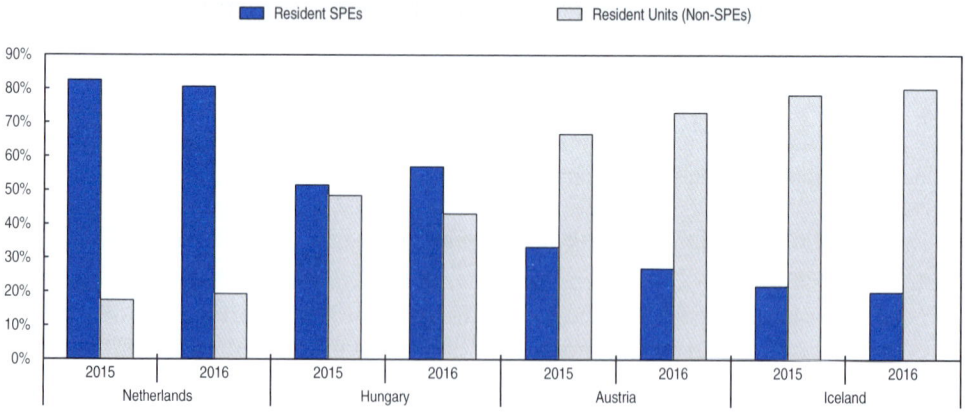

Source: OECD (2017), *OECD Statistics on Measuring Globalisation* (database), https://stats.oecd.org/Index.aspx?DataSetCode=FDI_POS_AGGR.

StatLink http://dx.doi.org/10.1787/888933588972

External debt at nominal value and external debt at market value

International standards encourage the valuation of gross external debt positions at both nominal value and market value. The nominal value of a debt instrument is a measure of value from the viewpoint of the debtor. It reflects the amount that the debtor owes, at any moment in time, to the creditor. This value is typically established with reference to the terms of a contract between the creditor and the debtor. The market value is determined by the prevailing market price, which provides a measure of the opportunity cost to both the creditor and the debtor. As an example of this difference in valuation, consider a country having trouble in settling external imbalances. The measurement of external debt at market value can decrease due to a cut in the government bonds' price, as caused by the perception of an augmented sovereign risk and inherent increase of the risk premium. The latter effect is not observable when analysing the external debt at nominal value.

In addition to transactions in debt instruments, external debt positions can also be affected by non-transaction effects, such as price and exchange rate fluctuations. Figure 7.10 compares, for a number of countries, the change in gross external debt at market value between the end of 2015 and the end of 2016 and the corresponding transactions that occurred during 2016. For some countries, transactions actually show a pattern that is quite different from the change in the position from one year to another. In Estonia and Belgium, the sign is even reversed, meaning that despite of disposals/acquisitions of relevant liabilities the total position at market value has increased/decreased.

Figure 7.10. **Gross external debt change for selected EU countries, 2016**
Percentage of GDP

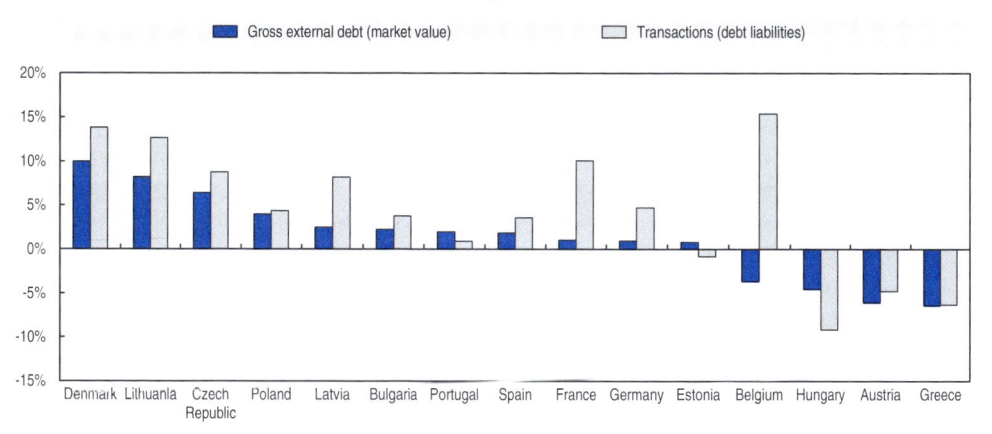

Source: ECB (2017), Balance of Payments and Other External Statistics (database), http://sdw.ecb.europa.eu/browse.do?node=9691635; and Eurostat (2017), National Accounts Statistics (database), http://ec.europa.eu/eurostat/web/national-accounts/data/database.

StatLink ⟶ http://dx.doi.org/10.1787/888933588801

In the case of external debt, the non-transaction flows are mainly linked to earnings/losses caused by exchange rate fluctuations of national domestic currency vis-a-vis other foreign currency in which underlying liabilities are denominated and, in the case of tradeable securities, changes in the price of the relevant liabilities. Other adjustments may include bankruptcies, write-offs and relocations of enterprises (including SPEs) from one country to another.

Maturity mismatch between financial assets and liabilities

Finally, one more important tool in analysing a country's risks and vulnerabilities relates to so-called "balance sheet mismatches". These mismatches can include a mismatch between the maturities of financial assets and the maturities of liabilities, or a mismatch in the currency composition of assets and liabilities. In respect to maturity mismatches, if a country has short-term financial assets and long-term liabilities, the external debt can be considered as more sustainable than if the country had long-term financial assets and short-term liabilities. This maturity mismatch can be analysed by focusing on either original maturity or remaining maturity.

The original maturity, which is typically referenced, enables a user to understand the maturity of the loans initially agreed for the down payment of the loan (also known as the amortisation agenda), as stipulated by the contract. On the other hand, the remaining maturity provides information on the time left for the debt instrument to be completely paid down to the lender. While the original maturity enables analysts to make inferences about the investors' preferences, the residual maturity gives a clearer picture about the time profile of the future responsibilities. Users are increasingly asking for data with maturity breakdowns for both original and remaining maturity for all debt instruments.

Some concluding remarks on sustainability of foreign exposures

In this chapter we have introduced the current and capital accounts and the IIP of a country. We also tried to show that balance of payments figures always need to be put in context. Some economies, be they emerging or already developed, may benefit for a number of years from flows in FDI that may be considered "good liabilities" in that they help develop productivity and competitiveness. The important question is whether the continuation of certain trends is sustainable. Answering this question requires studying the various items of both the balance of payments and the IIP one by one. For example, the balance of goods and services may be rapidly corrected by economic policy measures or financial crises. One key factor is the relationship of debt-creating flows and the sustainability of stocks of debt. Even initially "benign" FDI can turn into a negative, if a financial crisis spurs a wave of international divestments from a country. Moreover, the sustainability of the external debt burden is important to analyse, using external statistics. One should always project different scenarios where the stock of debt can grow exponentially, stabilise or decrease.

The standard criteria to assess the sustainability of an IIP are quite similar to the ones used in the case of domestic public or private debt:

- In an open economy, the discounted value of future (positive) trade balances should be at least equal to the external investment position of the country at a certain point in time. If a country is initially running trade deficits and has a negative external position, i.e. its liabilities towards the Rest of the World are higher than its foreign assets, it needs to run trade surpluses over time to remain solvent.
- Alternative measures, that may be less constraining from a policy point of view, are external debt to exports, debt service to GDP, and debt service to exports.
- Market prices of the value of the external debt of a country may provide another measure of the market perception of the likelihood that a country may not pay in time and in full its external liabilities.

Chapter 10 further analyses the issue of sustainability. Once a problem in relation to the sustainability of a country's external position is assessed, a series of redress policies may need to be put in place, in order to prevent negative external investment positions from "snowballing" (Roubini and Setser, 2004). Such measures may take place on the financial side, for example through rescheduling debt; on the policy side, by improving competitiveness, either through exchange rate adjustments or by a set of macroeconomic measures imposing domestic "austerity"; or through a combination of such measures. On the opposite side, a persistence of current account surpluses for an extended period may also represent an imbalance affecting stability, as explained previously. As Ben Bernanke has noted: "… the gold standard of the 1920s was brought down by the failure of surplus countries to participate equally in the adjustment process" (2015). Policies aimed at increasing domestic demand through investments in infrastructure, raising wages or tax incentives for private domestic investment may be used in such circumstances.

Key points

- The current account balance is a key indicator of a country's position with the Rest of the World. This indicator is usually also a good proxy of net lending/net borrowing, which represents the combination of the current and capital accounts.

- From a pure accounting perspective, the balance of the current and capital account, net lending/net borrowing, is by definition equal to the balance of the financial account. However, in practice there usually are statistical discrepancies or "errors and omissions". When the balancing item of the current and capital account is positive/negative, this means that the Rest of the World is being financed by/is financing the domestic economy.

- The international investment position (IIP) expresses the stocks of financial assets and liabilities of a country vis-a-vis non-resident economies. It results from the accumulation of financial transactions (net purchases of financial assets and net incurrence of liabilities) and other flows (for instance, price changes and exchange rate changes).

- Current account surpluses or deficits need careful interpretation and should never be taken as a "positive" or "negative" in isolation. Key economic and financial factors, such as the rate of growth or the nature and quality of financial flows should be added to the analysis, along with a more thorough analysis of the IIP.

- It is, however, true that persistent deficits may create a situation of disequilibrium and "snowballing" into crises. The level and risk of disequilibria can be assessed and monitored through external statistics, the use of which may help signal risks in a timely manner so as to implement redress policies and avoid crises.

Going further

Net errors and omissions

Net errors and omissions result from the difference between the net lending/net borrowing figure in the financial account and the same balancing item resulting from the current and capital accounts. In the words of the IMF: "… when a resident unit carries out a transaction with a non-resident unit, national compilers are unable to verify independently the counterpart entries in the Rest of the World. As a result, although in principle the balance of payments is balanced, in practice, there may be an imbalance due to shortcomings in source data and compilation … This imbalance, a usual feature of published balance of payments data, is labelled net errors and omissions. The balance of payments manuals have traditionally discussed this item, to emphasise that it should be published explicitly, rather than included indistinguishably in other items and that it should be used to indicate possible sources of mismeasurement".

Balance of payments statistics cover an enormous number of transactions and need to cope with the growing and challenging phenomenon of globalisation. As a result of this inherent complexity, the two recording sides (on the one hand, the "financial" side – the financial account – and, on the other hand, the "real" side – the current and capital accounts) hardly ever match in practice. Imperfect measurements of the balance of the various payments can arise from:

1. Time lags between the recording of payments and the recording of the concomitant receipts (moment of transaction versus moment of payment), and vice versa. These unknown discrepancies mainly arise from differences between when a transaction is entered into the relative accounts of the different parties involved in the transaction and/or incomplete source data, and should not be associated with known trade credits and other accounts receivable/payable;

2. Errors in recorded volumes, stemming from documentation errors and/or from estimation-based records;

3. Incomplete or incoherent coverage of transactions.

The sign (over time) and magnitude of net errors and omissions often has a direct relationship with the quality of balance of payments statistics. Small errors and omissions can also "hide" more significant omissions. The latter is the case when, for instance, there are significant omissions on both sides of the accounts, which cancel each other out and result in an artificially low value for net errors and omissions. Still, significant values of net errors and omissions can tell us something about the imperfections of the compilation procedures and the need for improvements. The dynamics of net errors and omissions may also point economic policy makers to the fact that a part of economic flows which are more difficult to cover (for example, hidden and/or illegal transactions) are missing. This could then lead to changes in the legal framework or to concrete measures to avoid various forms of tax evasion.

Although there is no international consensus on the quantitative limits of net errors and omissions, it is always useful to monitor them and check whether the magnitude is within reasonable and sound thresholds. In fact, over time, one would expect that the accumulated amount of net errors and omissions is more or less balanced, meaning that positive and negative amounts of net errors and omissions cancel each other out. In the case of Portugal, an interval between +/- 3% of the current account turnover is taken as a reference point; see Figure 7.11. It goes without saying that having a positive or negative amount of errors and omissions over longer periods of time may point to a serious quality issue of a more structural nature.

Figure 7.11. **Balance of payments' internal consistency indicator for Portugal, 2006-16**
Millions of EUR

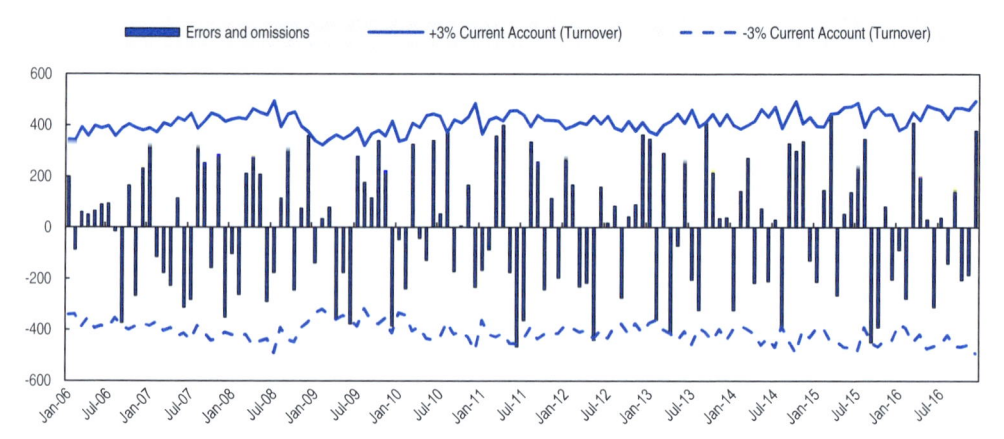

Source: Banco de Portugal (2017): Balance of Payments Statistics (database), www.bportugal.pt/EstatisticasWeb/(S(d2kqsvm5 bxjx3bag2hq5lo55))/DEFAULT.ASPX?Lang=en-GB.

StatLink http://dx.doi.org/10.1787/888933588820

Overall, net errors and omissions are an unavoidable part of the balance of payments compilation procedure, targeted to offset overstatements or understatements of the entries on the two sides of the accounts. Nevertheless, the uncertainty created by net errors and omissions can affect the use and interpretation of the balance of payments itself and the economic and financial statistics that are based on the balance of payments, including the international investment position (IIP). Therefore, despite the difficulties, it is essential to monitor the size and evolution of net errors and omissions over time, in addition to identifying their underlying causes.

Notes

1. The international investment position, according to the definition of BPM6 is equivalent to the balance sheet positions in the 2008 SNA.

2. The European Union's Macroeconomic Imbalances Procedure scoreboard comprises fourteen indicators: current account balance, net international investment position, exports market share, nominal unit labor cost, real effective exchange rates, private sector debt, private sector credit flow, house price index, general government sector debt, unemployment rate, total financial sector liabilities, activity rate, long-term unemployment rate and youth unemployment rate.

3. For a wider discussion on the implications of current account deficits, reference is made to "Judging whether deficits are bad" in: Ghosh, Atish and Ramakrishnan, "Current Account Deficits: Is there a Problem?", International Monetary Fund (2012).

References

Banco de Portugal (2017), *Balance of Payments Statistics*, Banco de Portugal, Lisbon, www.bportugal.pt/EstatisticasWeb/(S(d2kqsvm5bxjx3bag2hq5lo55))/DEFAULT.ASPX?Lang=en-GB.

Bernanke, B. (2015), "Germany's trade surplus is a problem", Brookings Institue blog, www.brookings.edu/blog/ben-bernanke/2015/04/03/germanys-trade-surplus-is-a-problem/.

Edwards, S. (2005), "Is the US current account sustainable? If not, how costly is adjustment likely to be?", *Brookings Papers on Economic Activity*, No. 1/2005, Brookings Instiute, Washington, DC, www.brookings.edu/bpea-articles/is-the-u-s-current-account-deficit-sustainable-if-not-how-costly-is-adjustment-likely-to-be/.

ECB (2017), *Balance of Payments and Other External Statistics*, European Central Bank, Frankfurt, http://sdw.ecb.europa.eu/browse.do?node=9691635.

Eurostat (2017), *Balance of Payments Statistics and International Investment Positions*, Eurostat, Luxembourg, http://ec.europa.eu/eurostat/web/balance-of-payments/data/database.

Eurostat (2017), *National Accounts Statistics* (database), Eurostat, Luxembourg, http://ec.europa.eu/eurostat/web/national-accounts/data/database.

Eurostat (2017), *Net External Debt,* Eurostat, Luxembourg, http://appsso.eurostat.ec.europa.eu/nui/show.do?dataset=tipsii20&lang=en.

IMF (2017), *Balance of Payments Statistics*, International Monetary Fund, Washington, DC, www.imf.org/external/datamapper/datasets/BOP.

IMF (2004), *Assessing Sustainability*, International Monetary Fund, Washington, DC, www.imf.org/external/np/pdr/sus/2002/eng/052802.pdf.

OECD (2017), *OECD Statistics on Measuring Globalisation,* OECD Publishing, Paris, https://stats.oecd.org/Index.aspx?DataSetCode=FDI_POS_AGGR.

Roubini, N. and B. Setser (2004), *The US as Net Debtor: The Sustainability of the US External Imbalances*, NYU Stern School of Business, New York City.

Wagner, R. et al. (2017), "German current account surplus to hit record, world's largest in 2016", *Reuters,* 30 January, www.reuters.com/article/us-germany-economy-trade-idUSKBN15E0W4.

World Bank (2017), *Gross Domestic Savings*, World Bank, Washington, DC, http://data.worldbank.org/indicator/NY.GDS.TOTL.ZS.

Chapter 8

A full accounting for wealth: Including non-financial assets

Peter van de Ven (OECD)

Non-financial assets play a crucial role in economic developments. Investments in these assets provide the fundamentals for the future growth potential of an economy. They can be financed from internal sources, primarily saving, or they may require additional external financing in the form of the incurrence of debt or the issuance of (additional) equity. Accounting for non-financial assets, in addition to the measurement of financial assets and liabilities, is necessary to arrive at a full and complete assessment of stocks/positions, as recorded on a balance sheet. For an economy as a whole, non-financial assets are the most important determinant of net worth, or net wealth, of an economy. This chapter describes the place of non-financial assets in the system of national accounts, and their delineation, ownership and valuation. Attention is also paid to the distribution of non-financial assets and net worth across institutional sectors, and their evolution over time.

1. General introduction to financial and non-financial wealth

The main focus of this publication is on financial accounts and (financial) balance sheets. However, a balance sheet is not complete without also taking into account non-financial assets. In several chapters, e.g. Chapter 4 and Chapter 5, attention has been paid to the link between financial assets (and liabilities) and non-financial assets. This chapter further analyses this link.

The sequence of accounts and the recording of non-financial assets

Stocks and flows of non-financial assets are an indispensable part of the full sequence of accounts, including balance sheets. For each institutional sector, the balance of current incomes and expenditures is labelled "saving". Adding the net receipts of capital transfers (for example, capital taxes, legacies and large gifts, one-off payments to support corporate investments) to saving results in a balancing item which is critical in linking income to the accumulation of assets and liabilities: "change in net worth due to saving and capital transfers".

The latter balancing item is equal to the funds available for investments in non-financial and financial assets. If the change in net worth due to saving and capital transfers is not sufficient for the financing of investments in non-financial assets, the remaining amount of these investments needs to be financed by incurring liabilities. As explained in other parts of this publication, this can be expressed, in line with the sequence of accounts, as follows:

(i) Changes in net worth due to saving and capital transfers *minus* Net purchases of non-financial assets = Net lending/net borrowing

and

(ii) Net lending/net borrowing = Net purchases of financial assets *minus* Net incurrence of liabilities

Combining equations (i) and (ii), one could rewrite this as follows:

(iii) Changes in net worth due to saving and capital transfers = Net purchases of non-financial assets *plus* Net purchases of financial assets *minus* Net incurrence of liabilities

In the system of national accounts, the transactions and balancing items of the first equation are recorded on the so-called capital account, while the items of the second equation are recorded on the financial account. The net purchases of assets, non-financial as well as financial, and the incurrence of liabilities will add to the stock of assets and liabilities recorded on the balance sheets. However, other changes may also lead to increases or decreases of the items on the balance sheets. The first change concerns revaluations due to price changes of assets and liabilities. The second is related to other changes in the volume of assets, such as losses due to catastrophic events, write-downs of loans due to non-payment, seizures, etc. The changes in each item on the balance sheets, non-financial assets as well as financial assets and liabilities, can be written as follows:

(iv) Value at the end of period t = Value at the end of period t-1 *plus* Net transactions in assets and liabilities (recorded on the capital account and the financial account) *plus* Revaluations (recorded on the revaluations account) *plus* Other changes in the volume of assets (recorded on the other changes in the volume of assets accounts)

The balance sheets show, on the left side, the value of non-financial assets (by type of asset) as well as financial assets (by type of instrument); and on the right side, the value of liabilities (also by of type of financial instrument). The balancing item of assets and liabilities is called "net worth" and is also shown on the right side of the balance sheet.

(v) Net worth = Non-financial assets *plus* Financial assets *minus* Liabilities

and

(vi) Net worth at the end of period t = Net worth at the end of period t-1 *plus* Changes in net worth due to saving and capital transfers *plus* Changes in net worth due to revaluations *plus* Changes in net worth due other changes in the volume of assets

The delineation of non-financial assets

When it comes to the delineation of non-financial assets in the system of national accounts, the asset boundary of the 2008 SNA is all-important. In paragraph 3.30, the general definition of an asset is provided: "An asset is a store of value representing a benefit or series of benefits accruing to the economic owner by holding or using the entity over a period of time." A further distinction is made between financial assets and non-financial assets. Financial assets differ from non-financial assets in the sense that in the former case, there is a corresponding financial claim that the creditor has against the debtor. In the system of national accounts, financial assets therefore always have a corresponding liability. On the contrary, there is no such thing as a "non-financial liability".

With the exception of valuables (see below), in the system of national accounts, non-financial assets are explicitly limited to those assets that are used in, or related to, a production process. Consequently, consumer durables, such as cars, kitchen equipment, TVs, computers and mobile phones, etc. that are meant for final consumption purposes by households, are not regarded as assets because the services they provide are not within the production boundary of the 2008 SNA. For economic units producing goods and services, be it corporations, unincorporated enterprises, government units or NPISHs, investments in non-financial assets, such as the purchase of a dwelling or a piece of machinery, are distinguished from "intermediate consumption", i.e. purchases of goods and services which are immediately used up in the production process. Purchases of non-financial assets relate to products which are used over a longer period of time, i.e. more than one year.

Traditionally, the SNA asset boundary only included tangible assets, such as buildings, trucks and machinery. Gradually, this boundary has been extended to include intangible knowledge-based assets that have become increasingly important in production processes. In the 1993 SNA, the definition of non-financial assets was broadened with the inclusion of intangible assets, such as mineral exploration and evaluation, computer software and databases, and entertainment, literary or artistic originals. Mineral exploration and evaluation refers to investment expenditures made on the exploration for and subsequent evaluation of the existence of mineral and energy resources. Software includes the initial development and subsequent extensions of software as well as the acquisition of the right to use this software over a longer period of time. Investments in databases are confined to expenditures on databases which give rise to future benefits, or have a value on the market. Entertainment, literary and artistic originals consist of the original films, sound recordings, manuscripts, tapes, models, etc. They are frequently produced on own account, and subsequently sold outright or by means of licences. The 2008 SNA went one step further, by also considering expenditures on research and development (R&D) as investments in non-financial assets.

Other intangible assets, such as goodwill, marketing assets and contracts, leases and licenses are only recorded when evidenced by an outright purchase. As a consequence, for example, expenditures on advertising to build up a brand are not considered as an investment. An example of these purchased intangible assets concerns the acquisition of a corporation by another corporation, where the payments for the shares that exceed the intrinsic value of the corporation are considered as purchased goodwill. Furthermore, in economics, one often considers "human capital" as one of the main non-financial assets for the future potential of an economy. However, in the 2008 SNA, this is not recorded as an asset, because "it is difficult to envisage "ownership rights" in connection with people, and even if this were sidestepped, the question of valuation is not very tractable" (paragraph 3.48). All in all, the asset boundary is perhaps one of the most disputed issues, not only in national accounts but also in business accounting.

In the SNA, all non-financial assets are recorded as being owned by residents. If a non-resident enterprise owns immobile assets on the territory of the domestic economy, it will be recorded as being "owned" by a resident subsidiary of the enterprise in question. If there is no such resident subsidiary, a "notional resident unit" is imputed which records ownership of the asset; the direct ownership of the asset by the non-resident enterprise is substituted by an ownership of equity in the resident notional unit. A similar treatment is applied when, for example, a non-resident household owns a second home in the domestic economy, and vice versa, when a resident household owns a second home abroad.

A comprehensive balance sheet

Table 8.1 presents the balance sheets for the total of all domestic sectors in Australia and France as a percentage of GDP. A distinction has been made between non-financial assets, financial assets and liabilities, and the balancing item, net worth. In addition, non-financial asset are broken down into produced assets and non-produced assets, a typical breakdown in the system of national accounts. Produced assets are "… non-financial assets that have come into existence as output from production processes that fall within the production boundary of the SNA" (SNA 2008, paragraph 10.9). Buildings, machinery and equipment, infrastructure, inventories, etc. all fall within this class of non-financial assets. On the other hand, non-produced assets mainly consist of natural resources such as land, mineral and energy resources, etc. They are "discovered", not produced by human intervention. Non-produced assets exclude, for example, improvements made to land, which should be classified as produced assets. However, often, it may quite difficult to distinguish the non-produced part of land from the value of land improvements. One may also not

Table 8.1. **A comprehensive balance sheet for Australia and France, 2015**
Percentage of GDP

	Australia		France	
	Non-consolidated*	Consolidated	Non-consolidated	Consolidated
Financial net worth	-58.2	-58.2	-8.5	-8.5
Financial assets	830.9	129.3	1 196.3	295.2
Liabilities (-)	889.1	-187.5	-1 204.9	-303.8
Non-financial assets	715.2	715.2	626.3	626.3
Produced assets	343.9	343.9	355.3	355.3
Non-produced assets	371.3	371.3	271.0	271.0
Total net worth	657.0	657.0	617.7	617.7

* The non-consolidated data for Australia have been compiled by summing up consolidated data for the various (sub)sectors at the most detailed level available.
Source: OECD (2017), "Financial Balance Sheets, SNA 2008 (or SNA 1993): Consolidated stocks, annual", OECD National Accounts Statistics (database), http://dx.doi.org/10.1787/data-00719-en; and "Detailed National Accounts, SNA 2008 (or SNA 1993): Balance sheets for non-financial assets", OECD National Accounts Statistics (database), http://dx.doi.org/10.1787/data-00368-en.

StatLink ⟶ http://dx.doi.org/10.1787/888933590150

have available separate data for land and the buildings or other structures on it. In those cases, the composite asset should be classified in the category representing the greater part of its value.

Financial assets and liabilities are shown on a consolidated as well as a non-consolidated basis. In the former case, all the claims between residents have been eliminated, as a consequence of which only the claims of residents towards non-residents, and vice-versa – on the liability side – the claims of non-residents towards residents, are shown. From this table, one can derive that the total net worth of an economy almost entirely consists of non-financial assets. Actually, in the case of both Australia and France, total net worth is lower than the sum of non-financial assets, because the financial claims of non-residents are higher than the financial claims of residents towards the Rest of the World.

It is clear that one has to take into account non-financial assets to arrive at an appropriate measurement of net worth, or net wealth, of an economy. This is also true for the monitoring of wealth for institutional (sub)sectors, although in this case the imbalance between financial assets and liabilities can have a significantly higher impact on the level of net worth. For example, the non-financial corporations' sector may have substantial amounts of non-financial assets, but these are almost entirely financed by other sectors, either in the form of loans and debt securities or in the form of ownership entitlements (shares and other equity). As a result, net worth is substantially lower than the sum of non-financial assets.

In the remainder of this chapter, Section 2 addresses some of the specificities of recording and measuring non-financial assets in the system of national accounts. Subsequently, Section 3 touches upon the distribution of wealth across institutional sectors. The (de-)accumulation of wealth over time is the topic of Section 4. The chapter concludes with the importance of having more granular breakdowns of the main sectors, by showing an example of the distribution of wealth across various household groups, a topic which nowadays receives increasing attention, not only from a well-being perspective but also from the perspective of economic vulnerabilities and monetary policy.

2. Specificities of non-financial assets, including their measurement

Table 8.2 below shows more details for non-financial assets in France, for a number of years. It shows that in 2016 produced assets represented 56% of total non-financial assets. This share has decreased quite dramatically, as compared to 82% in 1995, almost entirely due to the increasing value of land. Obviously, this is related to the increases of the prices of real estate. As the construction costs of buildings did not change significantly, the increasing real estate prices ended up in the prices of the underlying land. Together, land and buildings, residential as

Table 8.2. **Non-financial assets, by type of asset, France**
Percentage of total non-financial assets

	1995	2000	2005	2010	2015	2016
Produced assets	82.0	73.6	53.0	53.3	56.7	55.8
Fixed assets	75.8	68.2	49.3	49.6	52.9	52.0
Tangible fixed assets	71.8	64.4	46.8	47.2	50.1	49.2
Dwellings	40.4	36.9	27.6	28.4	31.2	30.8
Non-residential buildings	7.4	6.5	4.8	5.2	5.4	5.3
Other structures	15.1	13.2	9.3	8.9	8.8	8.5
Machinery and equipment	8.5	7.5	5.0	4.5	4.6	4.6
Cultivated biological resources	0.5	0.3	0.2	0.2	0.2	0.2
Intellectual property product	4.0	3.8	2.6	2.5	2.8	2.8
Mineral exploration and evaluation	0.0	0.0	0.0	0.0	0.0	0.0
Computer software and database	1.1	1.3	0.9	0.9	1.0	1.1
Entertainment, literary or artistic originals	0.1	0.1	0.0	0.0	0.0	0.0
Research and development	2.8	2.5	1.6	1.5	1.7	1.7
Other Intellectual property product	0.0	0.0	0.0	0.0	0.0	0.0
Inventories	5.2	4.4	2.7	2.7	2.9	2.9
Valuables	1.0	1.1	1.0	1.0	1.0	0.9
Non-produced non-financial assets	18.0	26.4	47.0	46.7	43.3	44.2
Land	16.2	24.6	45.1	44.4	40.5	41.4
Mineral and energy reserves	0.0	0.0	0.0	0.0	0.0	0.0
Non-cultivated biological resources	0.2	0.2	0.1	0.1	0.1	0.1
Intangible non-produced assets	1.6	1.8	1.7	2.2	2.7	2.7

Source: "Detailed National Accounts, SNA 2008 (or SNA 1993): Balance sheets for non-financial assets", OECD National Accounts Statistics (database), http://dx.doi.org/10.1787/data-00368-en.
StatLink http://dx.doi.org/10.1787/888933590169

well as non-residential, represent as much as 77-78% of total non-financial assets in 2016. If one also includes other structures, such as transport infrastructure, sewerage systems and the like, the share becomes 86%. One can also observe that France is a country with hardly any mineral and energy reserves. This is quite different from, for example, Australia where these natural resources represent approximately 10% of non-financial assets.

Looking in more detail at the produced assets in Table 8.2, a classic distinction made in the system of national accounts is the following: i) fixed assets; ii) inventories; and iii) valuables. Fixed assets represent the traditional investments in non-financial assets, which are used in the production of goods and services over a longer period of time. Around 10% of these fixed assets consist of machinery and equipment, while intangible assets represent 5%. The rest constitutes buildings and other structures.

Inventories are goods which are held in storage for sale, use in production or any other use at a later date. Apart from stocks of materials and supplies to be used in the production process, and stocks of finished products for future (re)sale, they also include "work-in-progress". The latter concerns in particular ships, dwellings, complex structures, software, and films, whose production takes more than a year. The part that is finished at the end of the accounting period is recorded on the balance sheet.

Finally, valuables include precious metals and stones, antiques and other art objects, which are not used in the production of goods and services, but are often considered as an alternative investment to shares, debt securities or saving deposits. It is quite complicated to fully capture and appropriately value this category of non-financial assets. One would have to value, for example, the large possessions of museums. This would require complete registers of all holdings, and also detailed market price information, often relating to unique objects. Therefore, very few countries have recordings of these valuables.

More generally, the measurement of non-financial assets is one of the most problematic areas in national accounts. Only a few countries like Australia and France have a fairly complete set of balance sheets, although their statistics also contain information gaps. Most countries within the OECD have estimates for fixed assets, based on the Perpetual Inventory Method (PIM, see below), and for inventories. More problematic is the measurement of non-produced non-financial assets, such as land and mineral and energy resources. However, given the increasing importance attached to balance sheets by policymakers and researchers alike, major efforts are undertaken to close the existing information gaps.

Legal ownership versus economic ownership

Non-financial assets are recorded within the sector which has the "economic ownership" of the relevant asset. Economic ownership can be different from legal ownership, in that it looks at who is entitled to claim the benefits associated with the use of asset, and who runs the associated risks of economic failure. Usually, economic ownership coincides with legal ownership, but there are some notable exceptions. One of these exceptions concerns financial leasing. For example, a bank (the lessor) may purchase an aeroplane and thus become the legal owner of the aeroplane, but then directly pass the economic ownership of the aeroplane to an airline company (the lessee). The airline company accepts all operating risks and also receives the economic benefits from using the aeroplane in the production of air transport services. In return, the airline company pays a periodic fee, representing interest and principal payments, to the bank, thus resembling the repayment of a loan. In this case, the aeroplane is recorded as a non-financial asset of the airline company, while on the liability side a loan from the bank is imputed. Another example is a resource lease, whereby the economic ownership of a natural resource is transferred from, for example, the government to a mining company, in return for a regular agreed payment. However, several criteria have to be considered to evaluate whether or not the economic ownership has actually been transferred in a lease (see SNA 2008, paragraph 17.318).

Sometimes it is quite difficult to give a straightforward answer to the question of economic ownership. An example relates to the allocation of intellectual property products within multinational enterprises. Such intangible assets can be moved quite easily around the world, often for reasons related to the minimisation of the global tax burden. Moreover, the assets and the income derived from them may be routed via "Special Purpose Entities" (see Section 4 of Chapter 3). It then becomes quite complicated to establish the exact location of the ownership of the intellectual property product to the headquarters or the subsidiaries (see UNECE, 2015).

A related but slightly different issue concerns the recording of Public-Private Partnerships (PPPs), which in some countries have become very popular. PPPs relate to the co-operation between the government and the private sector in, for example, constructing and exploiting a piece of transport infrastructure, such as highway or a railway track. Here, the problem is to establish who runs the risks and receives the economic rewards of such a project. If the government is subject to the risks and rewards of the infrastructure, the PPP (and the investment costs of the infrastructure) should be recorded as part of government sector. If the private sector is the economic owner, then the PPP is considered as part of the non-financial corporations' sector. This is a quite important question, as it directly affects the government debt and deficit. Within the European Union, these legal constructions have become very popular, and because of an increased focus, after the introduction of the "Excessive Deficit Procedure" (see Chapter 6), on economic policy indicators such as government debt and deficit, special guidance has been developed for the recording of PPPs; see e.g. Eurostat and EIB (2016).

Valuation of non-financial assets

Paragraph 13.16 of the 2008 SNA states the following: "For the balance sheets to be consistent with the accumulation accounts of the SNA, every item in the balance sheet should be valued as if it were being acquired on the date to which the balance sheet relates." Ideally, observable market prices should be used to value non-financial assets. However, non-financial assets depreciate in value over time due to their use in the production process, and second-hand markets, from which one could derive market prices for assets of different ages, are often non-existent. Exceptions are transport equipment and residential dwellings, in the latter case with the complication that the values do not only relate to the dwelling but also to the land underneath it.

One may argue that special structures and machinery used in the production of goods and services may not bring more than scrap value, if sold on the second-hand market. In this case, preference is given to the value that the asset will bring to the enterprise as a going concern, and not to the value of asset for an enterprise in liquidation. Moreover, some assets, such as roads and railway systems developed by the government, are not for sale and do not have a market value (unless one is allowed to raise fees for the use of them). The same holds for publicly available R&D. Notwithstanding this issue, these infrastructure and R&D assets are valued to represent the economic benefits that these assets bring to the society as a whole.

As a direct valuation based on the observation of market prices in the second-hand market is often not possible, in the system of national accounts, the value of fixed assets is usually estimated using the Perpetual Inventory Method (PIM). Basically, this methodology resembles the current replacement cost method often applied in business accounting. The stock of assets is set equal to the sum of past years' investments. Moreover, the depreciation of the assets is taken into account, to reflect the decrease in value due to the use of the relevant assets. Finally, one of course needs to account for the disposals of the relevant assets, either as a result of a sale or because the asset is scrapped at the end of its economic life-cycle. The goal of the PIM is to arrive at a valuation in current prices. Usually, one typically adjusts the investments in past years by applying an appropriate price index. In contrast, in business accounting, historic prices are typically used, i.e. the price levels for past investments are not (frequently) adjusted.

In some cases, the value of a non-financial asset may be established by estimating the net present value of future returns, appropriately adjusted with a discount rate. This method is typically applied to mineral and energy reserves, where the resource rent per unit of extracted reserves is combined with estimates of the total quantity of the reserves and the extraction pattern. To avoid highly volatile valuations due to quickly changing resource rents as a consequence of changing commodity prices, one usually applies a long-term average of the resource rent. The method may also be useful for, for example, internally generated artistic originals such as book manuscripts and music recordings, for which it may be difficult to find cost-based estimates to apply PIM.

As said before, market prices are only available for the combined value of a dwelling (or the non-residential building) and the land underneath it. One could thus derive the value of land as a residual, by subtracting the value of the dwelling calculated with the PIM from the combined value of the land and the dwelling. This may give rise to implausible, and occasionally negative, results for the value of land. Obviously, in these cases, a re-appraisal of the PIM estimates is needed. One may need to reconsider the assumptions applied for the depreciation patterns or the age-price profiles. An alternative method for measuring land is to measure it directly, via available information on prices per square meter. But here too, one needs to check whether the resulting sum of the buildings and the land is consistent with the market prices of the combined assets.

Figure 8.1 provides an example of the various valuation methods for land in Finland. It compares the direct valuation of land with the residual approach applying an average service life for dwellings of 50 and 60 years, respectively. It shows that the value of land is much more volatile when using the residual approach. The developments in the market prices of dwellings including underlying land are directly reflected in the value of land. An advantage of the residual approach is that the combined value of land and dwellings is based on actual market prices. However, the method is often not applicable for other types of land. For example in the case of non-residential real estate, market prices for the combined value of land and the building located on it may be difficult to find because of the scarcity of transactions and the uniqueness of any objects. More information can be found in Eurostat and OECD (2015).

Figure 8.1. **Land underlying dwellings estimated with direct and residual method, Finland, 1985-2011**
EUR, Billions

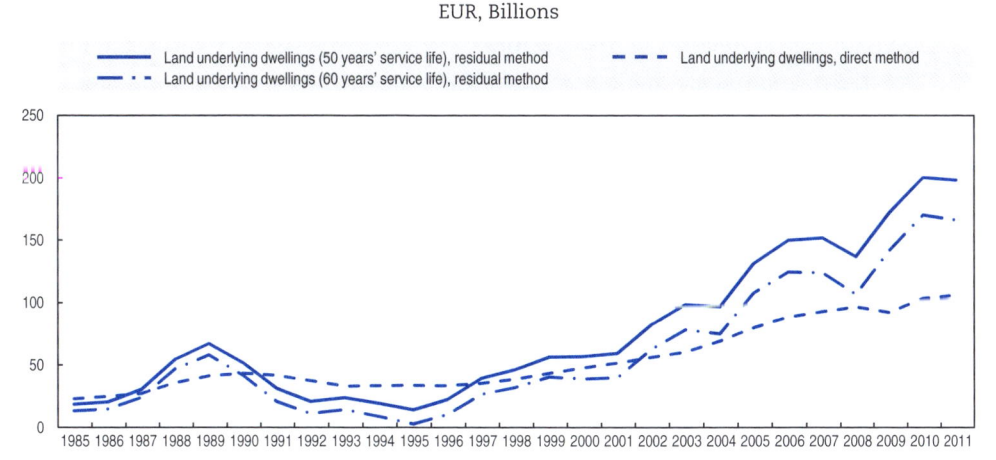

Source: Statistics Finland, National Land Survey of Finland.

StatLink http://dx.doi.org/10.1787/888933588991

Finally, in line with the general rule, inventories are also to be valued at current prices, not historical prices. For finished goods and work-in-progress, this means that they are to be valued at "basic prices", i.e. the prices at which they are sold by the producer excluding taxes (less subsidies) on products. Valuables are also to be valued at current market prices.

3. Who owns wealth: distribution across institutional sectors

As stated in Section 1, in most countries, total domestic net worth is almost equal to the sum of non-financial assets. The only difference between the two concerns the net value of financial assets and liabilities towards the Rest of the World. However, countries with persistent current account surpluses (deficits) with the Rest of the World may have built up large positions of financial assets (liabilities) with non-residents, as a consequence of which total net worth of the domestic economy deviates substantially from total non-financial assets. The most important example is Norway, which has accumulated a net asset position with the Rest of World which amounts to more than 400% of GDP. The Netherlands (90% in 2016) and Germany (42% in 2015) also have significant positive balances with non-residents. On the other hand, Greece, Portugal and Spain have incurred a considerable amount of net liabilities with the Rest of the World, amounting to 135%, 105% and 85% of GDP, respectively, in 2016. However, with the exception of Norway, even in these cases the total value of non-financial assets is much larger that the net position with the Rest of the World. Countries like Italy and Portugal, for which only estimates of fixed assets are available, have non-financial assets in the range of 3.5 times GDP. If estimates on land are also available, such as for Germany, the Netherlands and Norway, the value is in the range of 4.0 to 4.5 times GDP.

Distribution of wealth across sectors

Looking at the distribution of net worth or net wealth across institutional sectors, Figure 8.2 shows the results for France, one of the few countries for which complete balance sheets, including non-produced non-financial assets, are available. The majority of domestic net wealth ends up in the households'

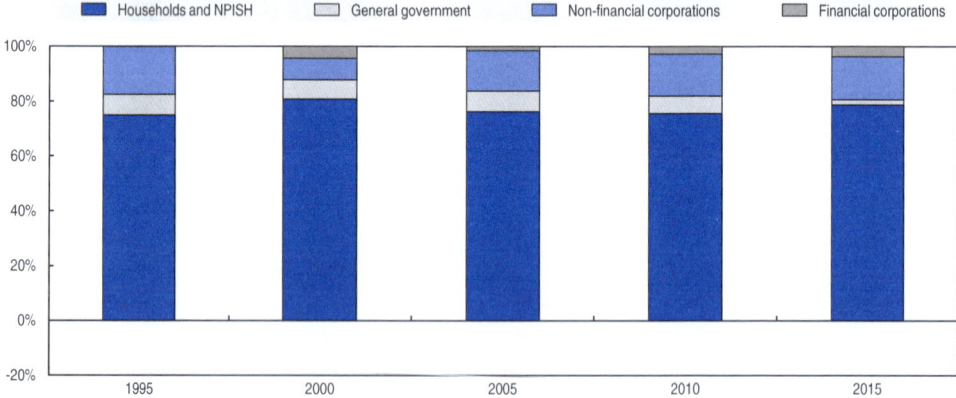

Figure 8.2. **Distribution of net worth across institutional sectors, France**
Percentage of total net worth of the domestic economy

Source: OECD (2017), "Financial Balance Sheets, SNA 2008 (or SNA 1993): Non-consolidated stocks, annual", OECD National Accounts Statistics (database), http://dx.doi.org/10.1787/data-00720-en; and "Detailed National Accounts, SNA 2008 (or SNA 1993): Balance sheets for non-financial assets", OECD National Accounts Statistics (database), http://dx.doi.org/10.1787/data00368-en.

StatLink http://dx.doi.org/10.1787/888933589010

sector. Although government and non-financial corporations own substantial amounts of non-financial assets, their net worth is relatively low, or even negative, because of liabilities in the form of debt securities, loans, and, in the case of non-financial corporations, shares and other equity. Financial corporations, on the other hand, generally own few non-financial assets; for most of the countries, they range from 1% to 3% of total non-financial assets for the economy as a whole.

When it comes to the distribution of net worth across sectors, there may be considerable disparities across countries. In particular, the net worth position of governments with relatively low levels of debt may be quite different from those governments having built up large amounts of debt. The most notable example is again Norway, where government net worth (excluding mineral and energy resources) accounts for almost 3.5 times GDP, equalling around 40% of total domestic net worth.

Non-financial corporations' non-financial assets and net worth

At the sector level, non-financial assets owned by the non-financial corporations' sector almost entirely consist of assets used in the production of goods and services. The total value in Australia and France equals AUD 3 022 billion (183% of GDP) and EUR 4 292 billion (196% of GDP), respectively; see Table 8.3 below. But it has to be acknowledged that Australia, a country with considerable natural resources, does not record any of their mineral and energy reserves on the balance sheets of non-financial corporations, while these assets are negligible for French non-financial corporations.

Moreover, there are significant differences between Australia and France in terms of the shares of the various types of non-financial assets. A striking difference is the share of land in non-financial assets, which in France (32.0%) is almost double the share in Australia (16.1%). On the other hand, buildings other than dwellings account for 53.8% of total non-financial assets in Australia, while this share is only 18.2% in France. Dwellings are also a substantial category in French non-financial corporations, accounting for 15.5% of total non-financial assets. Machinery and equipment and intellectual property products have a share of 21.0% in Australia, and 18.2% in France.

Obviously, the past investments and the resulting capital stocks had to be financed, either by internal funding (gross saving) or by external funding (incurrence of debt or the issuance of new shares and other equity). Looking at net financial worth, the balance of financial assets and liabilities, one can again notice a remarkable difference between Australia and France; see Table 8.4. While Australian non-financial corporations have a negative financial worth of minus 152% of GDP in 2015, leaving them a total net worth of 31% of GDP, the French non-financial corporate sector has a negative financial

8. A FULL ACCOUNTING FOR WEALTH: INCLUDING NON-FINANCIAL ASSETS

Table 8.3. **Non-financial assets of non-financial corporations, by type of asset, Australia and France, 2015**

	Australia		France	
	AUD, billions	% of total non-financial assets	EUR, billions	% of total non-financial assets
Non-financial assets	3 022		4 292	
Produced assets	2 533	83.8	2 594	60.4
Fixed assets	2 392	79.2	2 240	52.2
Tangible fixed assets	2 172	71.9	1 966	45.8
Dwellings	87	2.9	665	15.5
Buildings other than dwellings	1 627	53.8	780	18.2
Non-residential buildings			296	6.9
Other structures			485	11.3
Machinery and equipment	453	15.0	508	11.8
Cultivated biological resources	5	0.2	13	0.3
Intellectual property products	181	6.0	274	6.4
Mineral exploration and evaluation	88	2.9	0	0.0
Computer software and database	21	0.7	117	2.7
Entertainment, literary or artistic originals	3	0.1	5	0.1
Research and development	69	2.3	151	3.5
Other Intellectual property products	0	0.0	0	0.0
Inventories	141	4.7	355	8.3
Valuables	0	0.0	0	0.0
Non-produced non-financial assets	488	16.2	1 698	39.6
Land	485	16.1	1 373	32.0
Mineral and energy reserves	0	0.0	0	0.0
Non-cultivated biological resources	1	0.0	0	0.0
Intangible non-produced assets	2	0.1	325	7.6

Source: OECD (2017), "Detailed National Accounts, SNA 2008 (or SNA 1993): Balance sheets for non-financial assets", OECD National Accounts Statistics (database), http://dx.doi.org/10.1787/data-00368-en.
StatLink ⟶ http://dx.doi.org/10.1787/888933590188

net worth of minus 99% of GDP, resulting in a total net worth of 97% of GDP. In the net worth figure the stock market value of the corporations' equity is included as a liability; therefore, a positive net worth means that the stock market value of the equity issued by non-financial corporations is lower than the intrinsic value (or net asset value), i.e. total assets minus liabilities (excluding equity), of these corporations. One can thus also conclude that the stock market value of Australian corporations' equity is much closer to the intrinsic value of the corporations than in the case of French corporations. The French corporations are either significantly undervalued, or investors have much more confidence in the future earning capacity of Australian corporations. More details on the financing of the non-financial corporations' sector can be found in Chapter 5.

Table 8.4. **Net worth of non-financial corporations, Australia and France**
Percentage of GDP

	1995	2000	2005	2010	2015
Australia					
Non-financial assets	142.2	142.9	152.9	157.7	182.6
Financial net worth	-116.9	-129.5	-150.8	-127.7	-152.1
Net worth	25.3	13.4	2.1	30.0	30.5
France					
Non-financial assets	121.3	130.8	176.8	197.2	195.6
Financial net worth	-55.6	-98.4	-88.6	-97.7	-98.8
Net worth	65.7	32.4	88.2	99.5	96.8

Source: OECD (2017), "Financial Balance Sheets, SNA 2008 (or SNA 1993): Consolidated stocks, annual", OECD National Accounts Statistics (database), http://dx.doi.org/10.1787/data-00719-en; and OECD (2017), "Detailed National Accounts, SNA 2008 (or SNA 1993): Balance sheets for non-financial assets", OECD National Accounts Statistics (database), http://dx.doi.org/10.1787/data-00368-en.

StatLink ⟶ http://dx.doi.org/10.1787/888933590207

General government's non-financial assets

If we now turn to the government sector, Table 8.5 shows that their non-financial assets predominantly consist of land, buildings, and other structures. The latter category includes, amongst others, public infrastructure such as roads, sewerage systems, etc. Intellectual property products, which account for

Table 8.5. **Non-financial assets of the government sector, 2015**

	Australia		France		Germany		United States	
	AUD, billions	Percentage of GDP	EUR, billions	Percentage of GDP	EUR, billions	Percentage of GDP	USD, billions	Percentage of GDP
Total fixed assets	655	39.6	1 156	52.7	1 338	44.1	12 340	68.4
Dwellings	11	0.7	60	2.7	28	0.9	399	2.2
Non-residential buildings	516	31.2	328	14.9	1 139	37.6	5 404	0.0
Other structures*	n.a.	n.a.	612	27.9	n.a.	n.a.	4 425	24.5
Machinery and equipment	100	6.0	68	3.1	93	3.1	972	5.4
Intellectual property products	29	1.8	88	4.0	78	2.6	1 140	6.3
Land	322	19.5	726	33.1	454	15.0	n.a.	n.a.
Other non-produced assets	1 035	62.5	12	0.5	n.a.	n.a.	n.a.	n.a.
Net financial worth	-167	-10.1	-1 659	-75.6	-1 296	-42.7	-18 190	-100.9
excluding pension liabilities	238	14.4	-1 659	-75.6	-1 296	-42.7	-14 221	-78.8
Gross government debt	1 127	68.1	2 639	120.3	2 365	78.0	23 698	131.4
excluding pension liabilities	722	43.6	2 639	120.3	2 365	78.0	19 729	109.4

* For Australia and Germany, other structures are included in non-residential buildings.
Source: OECD (2017), "Financial Balance Sheets, SNA 2008 (or SNA 1993): Consolidated stocks, annual", OECD National Accounts Statistics (database), http://dx.doi.org/10.1787/data-00719-en; and "Detailed National Accounts, SNA 2008 (or SNA 1993): Balance sheets for non-financial assets", OECD National Accounts Statistics (database), http://dx.doi.org/10.1787/data-00368-en.

StatLink ⟶ http://dx.doi.org/10.1787/888933590226

approximately 1.8% of GDP in Germany to as much as 6.3% of GDP in the United States, relate for the main part to public R&D. In resource-rich countries, such as Australia, mineral and energy reserves can also be an important category. In Australia, mineral and energy reserves actually account for more than half of the government's stock of non-financial assets. As noted before, many government assets do not have any value on the market, but their value is still estimated using the PIM, and included in the national accounts because of their benefits for the society as a whole. For Germany and the United States, only data on the stocks of fixed assets and, in case of Germany, also stocks of land are available. Even for countries like Australia and France, who have the most complete set of national accounts data, one can see gaps in the information. For example, no estimates are available for government-owned valuables.

Adding available numbers on governments' non-financial assets to net financial worth, the balance of financial assets and liabilities, one can make an assessment of government's total net worth. It shows that the Australian government has a quite substantial net worth of more than 110% of GDP. If one excludes the pension liabilities, it is even larger: 135% of GDP. For France and Germany, net worth equals 11% and 16% of GDP, respectively. For Germany, no data are available for other non-produced assets, but one may assume that these assets are rather insignificant in the case of Germany. Total net worth of the US government is in negative territory, also when one excludes pension liabilities, but here it has to be noted that no estimates are available for land and other non-produced assets. Including these assets, one may assume that net worth becomes positive.

Households' non-financial assets and related indebtedness

As noted in Chapter 4, households perform a variety of functions in the economy: owners of unincorporated enterprises producing goods and services, owner-occupiers of dwellings, and consumers of goods and services. The first two functions show up in the stocks of non-financial assets as well. Unincorporated enterprises own buildings, machinery and equipment, and other fixed assets to produce the goods and services. However, dwellings and the associated underlying land represent by far the largest share of households' stock of non-financial assets. Households' economic function of being consumers of goods and services is not reflected in the stocks of non-financial assets. As stated before, cars for personal use, equipment used in-house, and other consumer durables are not recorded as investments in non-financial assets, because they are not used in the production of goods and services as defined in the 2008 SNA. As these durable goods also represent a store of value for households, and part of them may be financed through incurring (consumer) debt, the 2008 SNA recommends estimating these durables as a memorandum item, although very few countries produce estimates on these stocks.

8. A FULL ACCOUNTING FOR WEALTH: INCLUDING NON-FINANCIAL ASSETS

Data on non-financial assets, for which loans have been incurred, may be quite relevant to better monitor and analyse household indebtedness. Figure 8.3 shows the evolution of the value of dwellings (including underlying land) and household mortgage debt for four countries. Generally, as expected, the value of the dwellings including underlying land is substantially higher than the related mortgage debt. Looking at the evolution of the value, one can directly observe the impact of the 2007-09 economic and financial crisis, except in Germany where the value shows a continuous moderate upward trend. House prices in the United States have still not recovered from the crisis. When it comes to mortgage debt, one can observe an upward trend in Australia and France, and a negative trend in Germany. In the United States, the crisis clearly reversed the developments in mortgage debt, increasing

Figure 8.3. **Dwellings (including underlying land) versus mortgage loans**

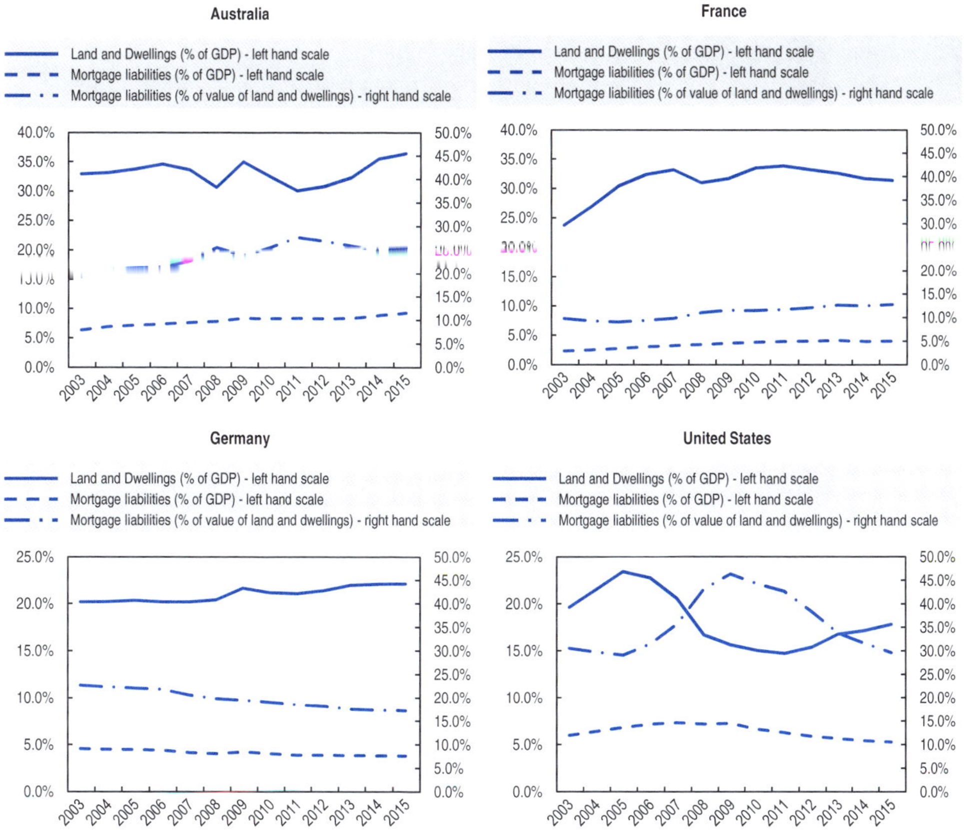

Source: OECD (2017), "Financial Balance Sheets, SNA 2008 (or SNA 1993): Non-consolidated stocks, annual", OECD National Accounts Statistics (database), http://dx.doi.org/10.1787/data-00720-en; and OECD (2017), "Detailed National Accounts, SNA 2008 (or SNA 1993): Households' financial assets and liabilities", OECD National Accounts Statistics (database), http://dx.doi.org/10.1787/8668ceb2-en.

StatLink ⟶ http://dx.doi.org/10.1787/888933589029

before and steadily decreasing after the crisis. Comparing mortgage debt to the value of the dwellings, there are some notable differences across countries. For the United States, mortgage debt as a percentage of the value of the dwellings is consistently 30% or higher, with a strong upward trend to a high of 46% in 2009. At the other side of the spectrum, mortgage debt in France has reached a maximum of 13% in more recent years. Australia showed an upward trend until 2011, reaching the highest level at 28%, after which the debt has been slowly trending downwards in recent years. For Germany, one can see a consistent downward trend to 17% in 2015.

While analysing Figure 8.3, the situation at the macro level may look rather stable and fine, with relatively modest developments in mortgage debt combined with increasing values of real estate, thus suggesting the absence of significant financial risks and vulnerabilities. But this can be quite different at a more granular level, for particular household groups. For example, households having purchased a house at a relatively high price, just before the end of a housing price bubble, may be very vulnerable once house prices start to decrease, and they may end up with a mortgage loan which is substantially higher than the value of their dwelling. Therefore, it is considered very important to have more detailed information on the distribution of wealth across household groups, which is also useful for the analysis of financial stability and monetary policy responses. This information is the topic of Section 5 below.

4. Accumulation and de-accumulation of wealth

Figure 8.4 shows the evolution of total net worth, or net wealth, of France from 1995 to 2015. It shows that total wealth was EUR 13 555 billion in 2015, equivalent to slightly more than EUR 200 000 per capita. Compared with 1995, French wealth almost tripled at the end of 2015. As explained in Section 1, there are four main factors contributing to this evolution: i) net purchases of non-financial assets (adjusted for depreciation of these assets); ii) net purchases of financial assets including net incurrence of liabilities; iii) revaluations of both non-financial and financial assets; and iv) other changes in the volume of assets such as discoveries/depletion of mineral and energy resources, debt write-offs, etc.

Unfortunately, there are no separate data available on the impact of revaluations versus the impact of other changes in the volume of assets. However, as mineral and energy resources are not significant in France, one may assume that the main part of the changes in stocks, which cannot explained by net purchases of assets and net incurrence of liabilities, is driven by revaluations or price changes (and possibly some statistical discrepancies). Using this assumption, one can estimate that net purchases led to an increase of 37% in French net wealth between 1995 and 2015. The rest can be explained by price

Figure 8.4. **Development of net worth in France, 1995-2015**
Year 1995 = 100

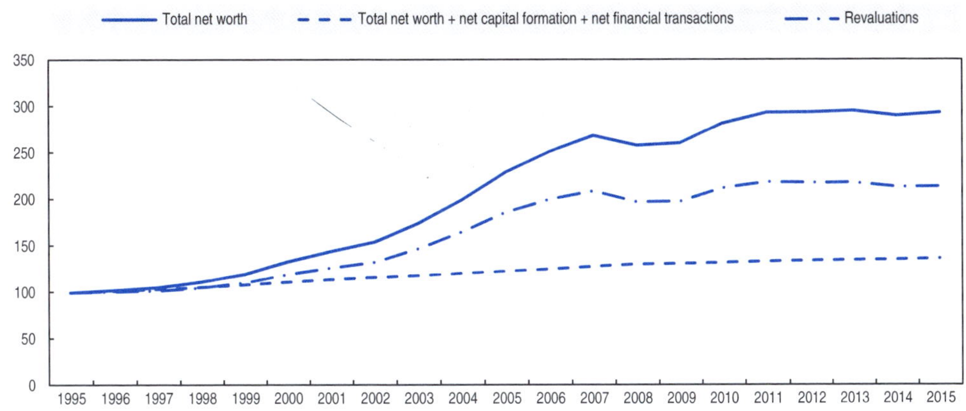

[Figure: Line chart showing Total net worth; Total net worth + net capital formation + net financial transactions; and Revaluations, from 1995 to 2015.]

Source: OECD (2017), "Financial Balance Sheets, SNA 2008 (or SNA 1993): Non-consolidated stocks, annual", *OECD National Accounts Statistics* (database), http://dx.doi.org/10.1787/data-00720-en; and "Financial Accounts, SNA 2008 (or SNA 1993): Non-consolidated flows, annual", *OECD National Accounts Statistics* (database), http://dx.doi.org/10.1787/data-00718-en; and "Detailed National Accounts, SNA 2008 (or SNA 1993): Balance sheets for non-financial assets", *OECD National Accounts Statistics* (database), http://dx.doi.org/10.1787/data-00368-en; and "Detailed National Accounts, SNA 2008 (or SNA 1993): Non-financial accounts by sectors, annual", *OECD National Accounts Statistics* (database), http://dx.doi.org/10.1787/data-00034-en.

StatLink http://dx.doi.org/10.1787/888933589048

movements, which increased by 114%. Looking at the evolution of the total net worth over time, the consistent upward trend was only interrupted by a decrease in 2008, after which the upward trend was continued at a slower pace.

The evolution of the stocks of non-financial assets is an important determinant of the future growth potential of an economy. In this respect, economic analysis often turns to the development of one of the building blocks of these stocks, investments in non-financial assets, over time. This is presented in Figure 8.5, which shows the annual growth of investments in non-financial assets for the OECD as a whole, adjusted for price changes, from 1996 to 2015. One can clearly observe the negative impact of the burst of the dotcom-bubble around 2000, and the massive downturn in non-financial investments during and after the 2007-09 economic and financial crisis. In later years, between 2010 and 2015, investment growth still had not returned to pre-crisis levels.

Turning back to the evolution of net worth in France, more specifically the evolution of revaluations, the 2008 SNA makes a distinction between "neutral" and "real" holding gains and losses. Neutral holding gains and losses consist of revaluations which are consistent with the movements of general inflation, while real holding gains and losses relate to revaluations which are lower or higher than the general inflation. This distinction may be quite relevant for certain non-financial assets such as dwellings and non-residential buildings.

Figure 8.5. **Gross investments in non-financial assets, OECD, 1996-2015**
Annual growth rates in percentage

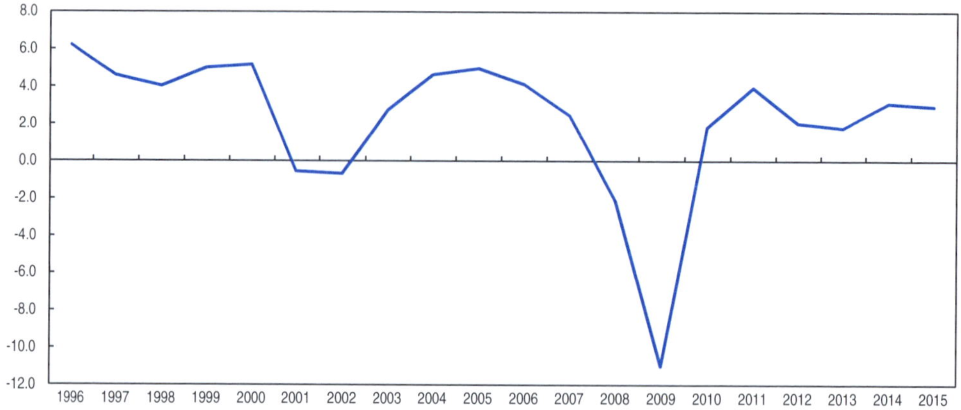

Source: OECD (2017), "Aggregate National Accounts, SNA 2008 (or SNA 1993): Gross domestic product", *OECD National Accounts Statistics* (database), http://dx.doi.org/10.1787/data-00001-en.

StatLink ⮫ http://dx.doi.org/10.1787/888933589067

Again assuming that the other changes in volume of assets (and statistical discrepancies) are relatively small, it shows that the prices of the assets (and liabilities) underlying net worth increased by far more than the general price index: 114% versus 33%. Real holding gains and losses thus amounted to around 60% in the period from 1995 to 2015.

5. Macro and micro: extending the system of national accounts

As noted before, aggregates for the households' sector as a whole may conceal financial risks and vulnerabilities for certain household groups. Inequalities in income and wealth may also have a detrimental impact on the well-being of households. Furthermore, recent research has raised doubts about the presumed positive correlation between income inequality and economic growth. Globalisation and digitalisation have also made policymakers more aware of the growing concerns about the inclusiveness of present-day economic growth, in particular concerns about those left behind. Altogether, major efforts are being made to compile distributional data, which are aligned to the system of national accounts. Amongst others, as part of the G-20 Data Gaps Initiative, the Financial Stability Board (FSB) and the International Monetary Fund (IMF) have included a recommendation on closing this gap in the availability of distributional information.

However, as explained in more detail in Section 3 of Chapter 4, combining micro-data on income, consumption and wealth with the aggregate results on households from the system of national accounts is not a straightforward exercise. Often, large discrepancies between the aggregates from micro-data and national accounts need to be addressed, to arrive at a consistent dataset. Figure 8.6 shows an example, based on the scarce information that is currently available in official statistics. In the Netherlands, 48% of the total household wealth is owned by the top income quintile. In Australia, the same group accounts for 43% of the total. If one compares the average wealth of the fifth income quintile with that of the first income quintile, disparity in the Netherlands is much larger than in Australia: wealthy Dutch households have on average 9.3 times more wealth than the poorest household group, while in Australia the multiple is 5.4. One can also see that wealth inequality is significantly larger for the holdings of financial assets than the inequality for the holdings of non-financial assets.

Figure 8.6. **Wealth inequalities/indebtedness across household groups**
Percentage of household disposable income

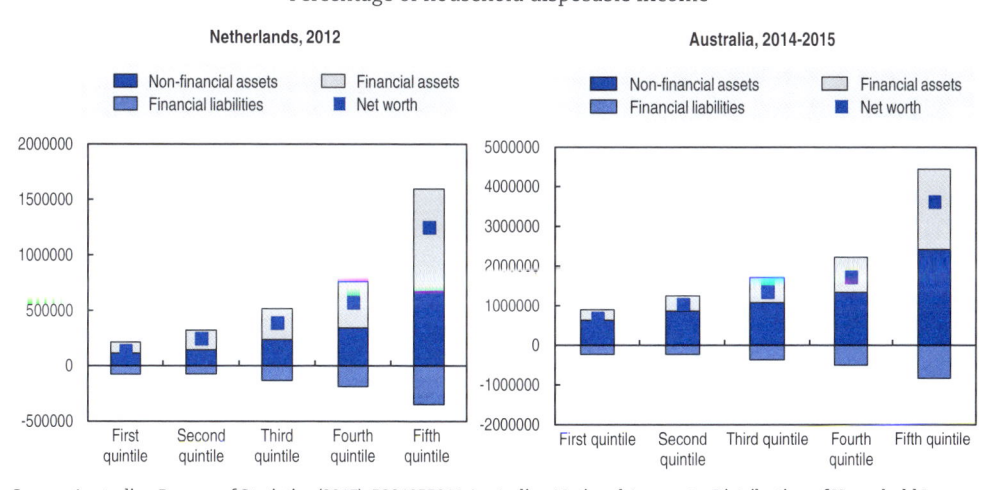

Source: Australian Bureau of Statistics (2017), 5204055011 Australian National Accounts: Distribution of Household Income, Consumption and Wealth, 2003-04 to 2014-15; and Statistics Netherlands (2017), Income distribution of households; National Accounts.

StatLink ⟶ http://dx.doi.org/10.1787/888933589086

Another area of research is related to linking data on the non-financial corporations' sector with more granular data on certain subgroups of corporations. Research questions are, for example, how small and medium sized enterprises are performing as compared to large enterprises, what the impact of foreign-controlled enterprises for the domestic economy is, how large the role of public corporations controlled by government is, etc. These types of questions do not only concern the growth of output, value added and employment for different groupings of enterprises, they also raise issues about the financial health, liquidity, and solvency position, of certain groupings of corporations. Linking data on individual enterprises with national accounts is necessary to make this analysis possible; however, in doing this, one encounters another set of problems, such as the differences between the 2008 SNA and the business accounting standards which are typically applied at the level of individual corporations.

More generally, one can observe a clear user demand for granularity, which requires paying much more attention to the "micro-macro link". Given present-day computing power, this target should be feasible, but it obviously requires time to implement. Nowadays, especially in the area of statistics on financial markets and financial corporations, very detailed micro-datasets have become the starting point for compiling financial accounts and balance sheets. A prime example is the compilation of securities databases, in which one tracks, for each individual security, the issuer and the holder of the security. Such a database would provide an excellent tool for compiling financial accounts and balance sheets, including very detailed from-whom-to-whom information, while it automatically opens the doors for more granular analysis, if needed. As such, the future of national accounts and, more generally, official statistics looks very challenging but also very promising indeed.

Key points

- Investments in and stocks of non-financial assets play a crucial role in the sequence of accounts of the national accounts. A full assessment and analysis of the investment behaviour and the financial funding of these investments is not possible without taking due account of investments in non-financial assets, in addition to the monitoring of financial assets and liabilities.

- Balance sheets are not complete without an appropriate inclusion of stocks of non-financial assets. Notwithstanding their importance for policy analysis and research, the adequate measurement and valuation of non-financial assets poses many problems, and most countries do not yet have a full set of balance sheets in terms of non-financial assets. Many gaps exist, in particular when it comes to the recording of non-produced non-financial assets. However, in recent years much progress has been achieved, and future improvements are expected.

- The most important categories of non-financial assets are related to real estate and other structures including underlying land. It is, therefore, no surprise that the largest part of net worth in a country is owned by households, especially given the fact that households have historically been important providers of financial funds to corporations and government, either directly or indirectly, via the financial system.

- The evolution of non-financial assets, financial assets and liabilities, and their associated balancing item, net worth, is primarily governed by net purchases of assets, including the incurrence of liabilities, and revaluations. Also other changes in the volume of assets, such as losses to catastrophic events, discoveries and depletion of natural resources, write-downs of debt, etc., may affect, to varying degrees depending on a country's circumstances, the stocks recorded on the balance sheets.

- A full understanding and analysis of the financial situation in an economy may require the compilation of more granular statistics, which would be much more detailed than the main sectors that are traditionally distinguished.

References

Australian Bureau of Statistics (2017), 5204055011 Australian National Accounts: Distribution of Household Income, Consumption and Wealth, 2003-04 to 2014-15.

Eurostat and EIB (2016), *Eurostat and European Investment Bank, A Guide to the Statistical Treatment of PPPs*, 2016, www.eib.org/epec/resources/publications/epec_eurostat_guide_ppp.

Eurostat and OECD (2015), *Eurostat and OECD, Eurostat-OECD compilation guide on land estimation*, 2015, http://ec.europa.eu/eurostat/documents/3859598/6893405/KS-GQ-14-012-EN-N.pdf.

UNECE (2015), United Nations Economic Commission for Europe, *Guide to Measuring Global Production*, 2015, www.unece.org/fileadmin/DAM/stats/publications/2015/Guide_to_Measuring_Global_Production__2015_.pdf.

OECD (2017), "Financial Balance Sheets, SNA 2008 (or SNA 1993): Consolidated stocks, annual", *OECD National Accounts Statistics* (database), http://dx.doi.org/10.1787/data-00719-en; and "Financial Balance Sheets, SNA 2008 (or SNA 1993): Non-consolidated stocks, annual", *OECD National Accounts Statistics* (database), http://dx.doi.org/10.1787/data-00720-en; and "Detailed National Accounts, SNA 2008 (or SNA 1993): Balance sheets for non-financial assets", *OECD National Accounts Statistics* (database), http://dx.doi.org/10.1787/data-00368-en; and "Detailed National Accounts, SNA 2008 (or SNA 1993): Households' financial assets and liabilities", *OECD National Accounts Statistics* (database), http://dx.doi.org/10.1787/8668ceb2-en; and "Detailed National Accounts, SNA 2008 (or SNA 1993): Non-financial accounts by sectors, annual", *OECD National Accounts Statistics* (database), http://dx.doi.org/10.1787/data-00034-en; "Financial Accounts, SNA 2008 (or SNA 1993): Consolidated flows, annual", *OECD National Accounts Statistics* (database), http://dx.doi.org/10.1787/data-00716-en; and "Aggregate National Accounts, SNA 2008 (or SNA 1993): Gross domestic product", *OECD National Accounts Statistics* (database), http://dx.doi.org/10.1787/data-00001-en.

Statistics Finland, National Land Survey of Finland.

Statistics Netherlands (2017), Income distribution of households; National Accounts.

Understanding Financial Accounts
© OECD 2017

Chapter 9

Accounting for the financial consequences of demographic changes

Jorrit Zwijnenburg (OECD) and Paul Goebel (Treasury Board of Canada Secretariat)

> *Many OECD countries are facing pronounced demographic changes, primarily in the form of ageing populations. It is therefore important to not only understand these effects, but to also monitor and analyse their impact on macroeconomic developments. This chapter explains the effects that demographic changes may have on the economy. It starts by explaining how households' income, consumption and saving vary across age groups and how demographic changes can affect the saving ratio and the net worth of the household sector as a whole. It then analyses the link between demographic changes and governments' finances and how the sustainability of government finances can be assessed in the light of changing populations. Finally, this chapter discusses the various ways in which pension systems are organised across countries, how they are recorded in the system of national accounts, and how the resulting data can (not) be used to assess their financial sustainability.*

The statistical data for Israel are supplied by and under the responsibility of the relevant Israeli authorities. The use of such data by the OECD is without prejudice to the status of the Golan Heights, East Jerusalem and Israeli settlements in the West Bank under the terms of international law.

1. The effect of demographic changes on household saving and wealth

As saving varies across age groups, demographic changes may affect the saving ratio and the net wealth of the household sector in an economy. This relates to the life-cycle hypothesis by Modigliani and Brumberg (1954), as well as to the permanent income hypothesis formulated by Friedman (1957). The life-cycle hypothesis explains that individuals do not plan their consumption and saving on the basis of their current income, but that they smooth consumption over their life-time on the basis of their lifetime earnings and their initial net worth. Modigliani and Brumberg developed their hypothesis in response to the common understanding in those days that consumption and saving were a function of income and that consumption and saving would increase with income. This was fed by empirical results that the share of consumption in income is lower for higher income households and therefore, saving is positively correlated with income. However, in their hypothesis Modigliani and Brumberg explain that this is not due to a direct link between income and consumption, but merely due to the position of households in their lifecycle. The utility function of an individual consumer is a function of his current and future consumption, and the typical household will try to maximise his utility on the basis of his earnings over his lifetime. Whereas income shows fluctuation over a lifetime, consumption remains relatively stable, as a consequence of which saving fluctuates over time.

Figure 9.1 presents how the life-cycle hypothesis works in theory. Most people borrow during their younger years, when they are studying, in anticipation of future earnings. During their working life, people save to pay off the debt incurred in their youth and to amass funds for retirement. During their retirement, people usually do not earn income from employment and tend to dissave. This pattern of borrowing at a young age and saving up during the active career leads to wealth being accumulated towards retirement age. Saving will be small (or negative) at the start of the career, but will increase towards the retirement age. Consequently, net worth will increase during working life and decrease after retirement.

The permanent income hypothesis, which is closely tied to the life-cycle hypothesis, provides an explanation for levels of consumption for various households. This hypothesis, which was developed by Milton Friedman, states that individuals' consumption will depend on their current income, as well as

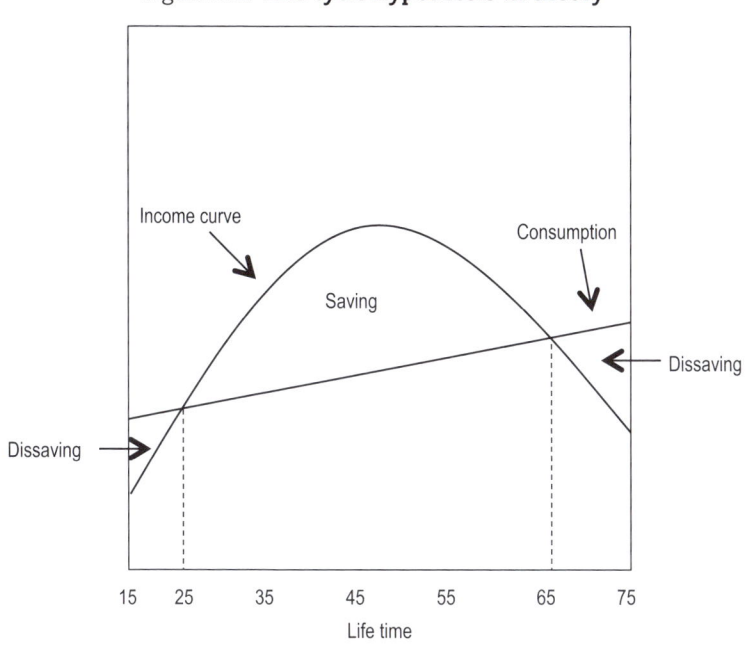

Figure 9.1. **Life cycle hypothesis in theory**

on their expected future income flows. It is the permanent income that determines how much households will consume. The permanent income can be defined as the average of the expected income flows over a lifetime. The hypothesis implies that temporary income shocks will not lead to an increase in consumption, whereas permanent changes in income will. Temporary shocks will only affect saving. Friedman also explains that, as the amount spent on consumption is on average the same fraction of permanent income, the saving rate will not necessarily depend on the level of current income. It will, on the other hand, depend on variables such as the interest rate, degree of uncertainty about future earnings, the length of the retirement period, initial wealth and family size. The main difference between the two models is that the life-cycle hypothesis assumes a finite life-span, whereas the permanent income hypothesis focuses on an infinite life-span. In this respect, the latter also takes into account bequests, which do not play a role in the standard life-cycle hypothesis.

Both theories are supported by empirical evidence. For example, Figure 9.2 presents saving ratios for Australia by age group on the basis of methodology developed by the Expert Group on Disparities within National Accounts (EG DNA) (Zwijnenburg et al., 2017). This Expert Group developed methodology to compile distributional results in line with national accounts totals on the basis

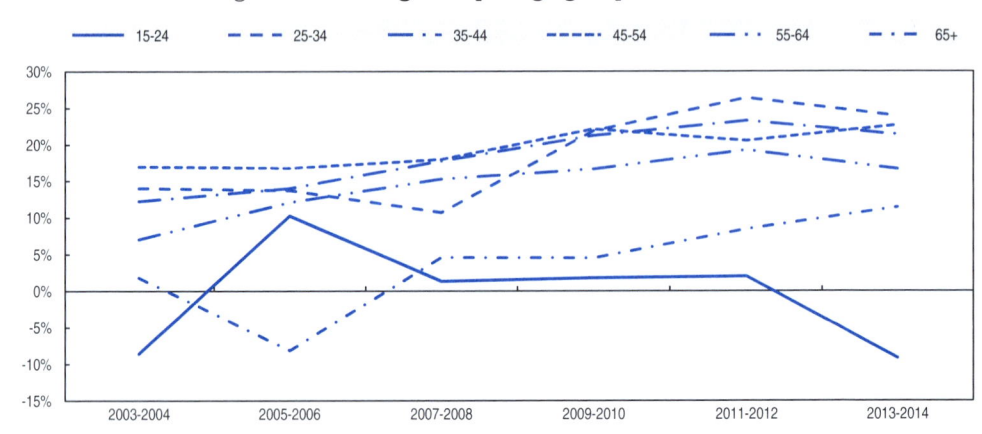

Figure 9.2. **Saving ratio per age group for Australia**

Source: Australian Bureau of Statistics (2015), 5204.0.55.011 – Australian National Accounts: Distribution of Household Income, Consumption and Wealth, 2003-04 to 2014-15 (database), www.abs.gov.au/AUSSTATS/abs@.nsf/DetailsPage/5204.0.55.0112003-04%20to%202014-15?OpenDocument.

StatLink http://dx.doi.org/10.1787/888933589105

of micro-data. As results are aligned with national accounts totals, they can be linked to other macroeconomic aggregates, such as gross domestic product (GDP), household disposable income and household wealth. The results for Australia show that the youngest age group (between 15 and 24) and the oldest age group (65+) have lower or even negative saving ratios, whereas the middle age groups show positive ratios, with ratios varying across age groups.

Both hypotheses also provide a rationale for the variations in net worth, or net wealth, across age groups. Young people will have low or negative net worth as they start their lives, borrowing funds to pay for their consumption. Once they start their working lives, they save up money, which adds to their net wealth. After retirement they will use these assets to pay for their consumption. These hypotheses are also confirmed by empirical results. Figure 9.3 shows the wealth per household according to age group for Australia (for the year 2013/14). It shows that wealth increases up until retirement and that net worth is highest for the pre-retirement age group.

As saving relates to the life-cycle of individuals, the saving ratio and accumulated wealth will differ across age groups. This is why demographic changes will also affect the saving ratio for the household sector as a whole, as well as household wealth. In this respect, Modigliani and Brumberg also developed an aggregated consumption function for a community as a whole and related this to national saving and the accumulation of national wealth, for which Goldsmith (1955) found that it was equal to 4-5 times private income and relatively stable over time. This wealth relates to the sum of saving that has been accrued within an economy as part of individuals' life-cycle patterns. On

Figure 9.3. **Wealth according to age group in Australia, 2013/14**
AUD, millions

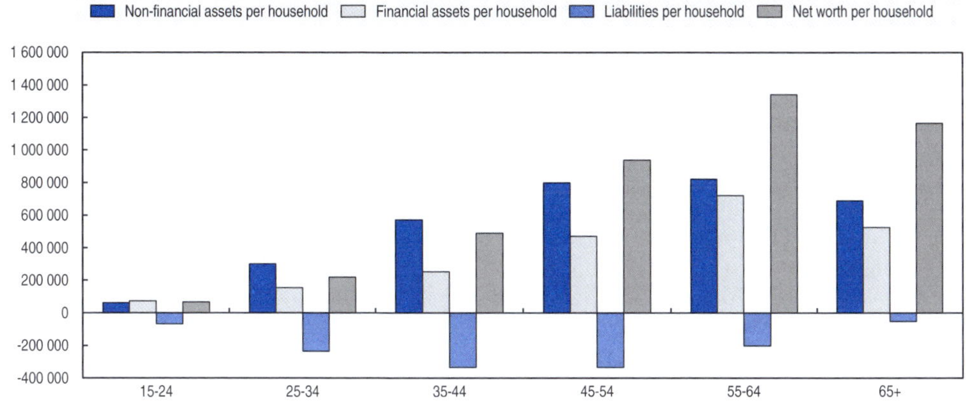

Source: Australian Bureau of Statistics (2015), 5204.0.55.011 – *Australian National Accounts: Distribution of Household Income, Consumption and Wealth, 2003-04 to 2014-15* (database), www.abs.gov.au/AUSSTATS/abs@.nsf/DetailsPage/5204.0.55.0112003-04%20to%202014-15?OpenDocument.

StatLink http://dx.doi.org/10.1787/888933589124

the basis of their life-cycle hypothesis, Modigliani and Brumberg explain that the aggregate saving rate is independent from per capita income, but depends on the level of productivity growth (an increase in productivity growth increases the aggregate saving rate as the income of those who save increases relative to those who dissave), the demographic structure of a society, and life expectancy in relation to the retirement age (see also Jappelli, 2005). This, in turn, will also determine the aggregate wealth-to-income ratio in a country.

In a so-called stationary economy, saving and dissaving will cancel out at the national level, and national wealth will remain at a constant level. Wealth will move across the various age groups over time. People in retirement have large amounts of wealth, part of which is used to supplement lower levels of income and to maintain a certain level of consumption. These funds are usually obtained by the younger working generation, which is saving to pay off debt incurred during youth and to build up wealth for their retirement. However, in the case of changing demographic structures (i.e. a non-stationary economy), the total national wealth will change. For example, in the case of population growth, the number of people saving up for retirement will increase in comparison to the elderly, giving rise to saving exceeding dissaving and therefore an increase in wealth. Other reasons for changes in the saving ratio include changes in productivity growth and changes in life expectancy (relative to the retirement age).

As illustrated above, saving and wealth accumulation are affected by demographic changes. In the case of population growth, the aggregate saving ratio and national wealth will both increase. However, in the case of an ageing society – which many countries will probably have to deal with in the next few decades (see Box 9.1) – dissaving by the elderly may start to exceed the saving of the younger generations, leading to a decrease of the wealth of the household sector as a whole. The latter may affect financial markets as retired people will try to dispose of assets in times of subdued demand for financial investments. Empirical results confirm these findings. Higgins (1998) shows, using data from 100 countries, that national saving is negatively correlated with youth and old-age dependency. Figure 9.4 presents results for Japan, showing the dependency ratio and the saving ratio for the period 1980-2015. Whereas the dependency ratio shows an increase over time, the saving ratio declines over the years. As this may affect macroeconomic developments in various ways, it is thus important to closely monitor these impacts.

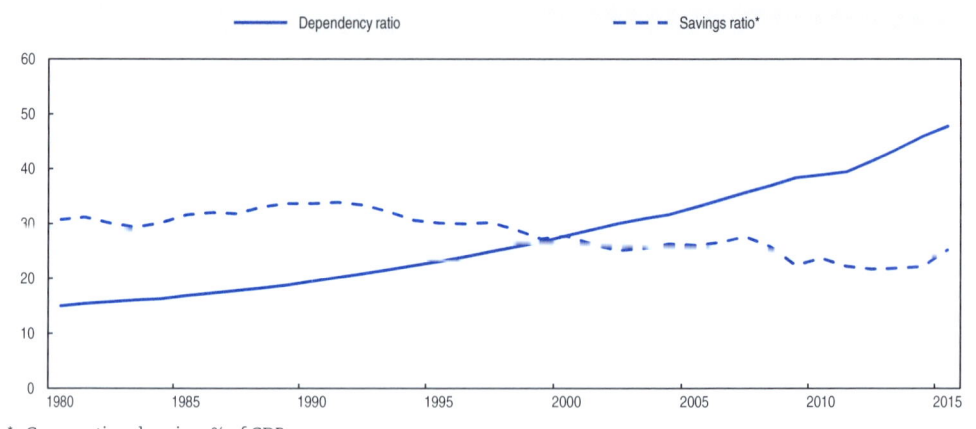

Figure 9.4. **Dependency ratio and saving ratio in Japan**

* Gross national saving, % of GDP.
Source: International Monetary Fund (2016), World Economic Outlook Database: April 2016, www.imf.org/external/pubs/ft/weo/2016/01/weodata/download.aspx and OECD (2017a), "Labour Force Statistics: Population projections", OECD Employment and Labour Market Statistics (database), http://dx.doi.org/10.1787/data-00538-en.

StatLink ᙚᛜ http://dx.doi.org/10.1787/888933589143

Box 9.1. **Demographic changes**

In many countries, the demographic composition of the population is expected to change dramatically over the next few decades. This is due to increasing life expectancy and decreasing fertility rates (UN, 2015). Figure 9.5 shows demographic results for 1950, 2015 and forecasts for 2050 for the total of OECD countries. The figure shows a clear increase in the share of older age groups, not only the total of people in retirement (65+), but also the people in the age group of 85 and older. This is not only caused by increasing life expectancy, but is also related to the impact of the Baby Boom generation currently going into retirement. On the other hand, the figure also shows decreasing shares for younger and middle-aged

> Box 9.1. **Demographic changes** *(cont.)*
>
> groups when comparing with the current phrasing pointing to 'decreasing shares', I think it should be 'when comparing 2050 with 2015', not only related to the growing share of older people, but also caused by lower fertility rates.
>
> Figure 9.5. **Demographic changes for OECD countries, 1950-2050** 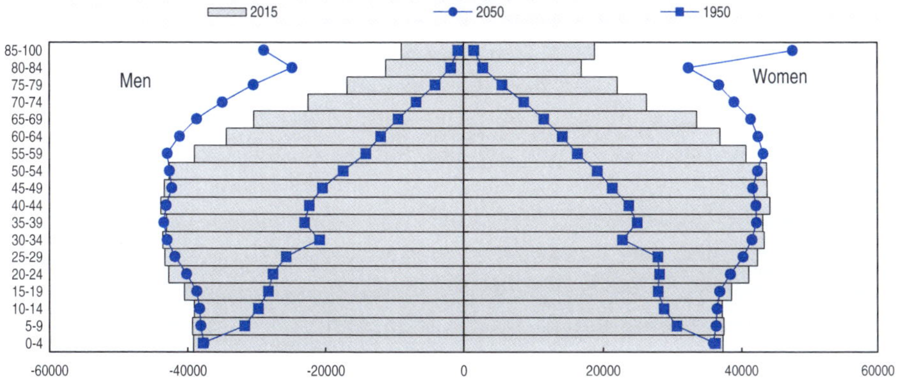
>
> Source: OECD (2017a), "Labour Force Statistics: Population projections", *OECD Employment and Labour Market Statistics* (database), http://dx.doi.org/10.1787/data-00538-en.
>
> StatLink ⟶ http://dx.doi.org/10.1787/888933589162
>
> The demographic changes will lead to changes in the old age dependency ratios, i.e. the ratio of the elderly population (65+) as a percentage of the working population (20-64). In 2015, this ratio was 13.8, but this will increase to 47.1 in 2050. This implies that the future working population will have to provide financial and other care to an increasing number of elderly.

2. Demographic changes and government finances

Ageing societies may also affect government finances, as a significant part of government expenditures is related to age, such as public pensions, health care costs, social housing, and early retirement plans. In a study that was released in 2001, Dang et al. found that for OECD countries between 40 to 60 percent of total public spending consists of expenditure that is sensitive to the age structure of the population. If there is increased life expectancy, the number of retired people will increase and they will claim pension benefits for a longer period of time, thereby increasing pension costs. Furthermore, health care costs, including the costs of retirement homes, are also likely to increase as older people on average, tend to incur greater health care.[1] In addition, costs will also increase for benefits related to early retirement, unemployment and disability, as older people will have to work longer to fund their longer retirements and it may be difficult to help them find appropriate employment. On the other hand, it is expected that costs related to young age, such as education costs and child care, are likely to decrease in an ageing society.

Dang et al. (2001) made projections on changes in age-related spending for the period 2000 to 2050, distinguishing four categories, i.e. old age pensions, early retirement programmes, health care and long-term care, and child/family benefits and educations. Table 9.1 presents the results for 21 OECD countries. The first column of each category shows the expenditure level in 2000 as percentage of GDP. The second columns show the percentage point change for the period between 2000 and 2050. It shows that age-related spending is likely to increase in almost all OECD countries, with Poland as the only exception. Regarding the magnitude of the changes, Norway records the largest change, with a 13.4 percentage point increase. Other countries with large increases are the Netherlands, Canada, Finland, Korea and New Zealand. The underlying components show that old-age pensions as well as health care and long-term care are the main drivers for the increase in old age expenditure.

The 2015 Ageing Report by the European Commission (2015) also confirmed that age-related expenditure is likely to increase in several European countries. The report showed that the age-related expenditure as a percentage of GDP is expected to increase by between 2.5 and 6.8 % of GDP in ten member states (Finland, Austria, Czech Republic, Netherlands, Slovak Republic, Germany, Belgium, Luxemburg, Malta and Slovenia). It also shows that a fall is projected for eight countries (Hungary, Greece, Latvia, France, Denmark, Cyprus[2, 3], Italy and Spain), but that this may be related to reforms that have already been processed or planned.

Government revenues such as taxes and premiums may also be affected by demographic changes, because, in an ageing society, a relatively smaller number of people will pay income taxes and social premiums. The impact of this decrease is, however, expected to be less than the budgetary consequences on the expenditure side (Office for Budget Responsibility (OBR), 2015). An important indicator in this respect is the old age dependency ratio, introduced above, which basically shows how many retirees will need to be supported by the younger population. In the last few decades, the ratio has already showed a sharp increase, and it is expected to increase further in the coming decades. As can be derived from Figure 9.6, the rise is sharpest for Japan with an increase from 10.0 in 1950 to 81.1 in 2050, but for the other countries the increase is also significant.

As the dependency ratio increases, a question arises as to whether government policies are sustainable. Will the government be able to continue its policies without incurring large burdens on future generations by running into structural deficits and concomitant increases of government debt? Many

Table 9.1. **Changes in age-related spending, 2000-50**

	Total age-related spending		Old-age pension		Early-retirement programmes		Health care and long-term care		Child/family benefits and education	
	Level 00	Change 00-50	Level 00	Change 00-50	Level 00	Change 00-50	Level 00	Change 00-50	Level 00	Change 00-50
Australia	16.7	5.6	3.0	1.6	0.9	0.2	6.8	6.2	6.1	-2.3
Austria	10.4	2.3	9.5	2.2	-	-	-	-	-	-
Belgium	22.1	5.2	8.8	3.3	1.1	0.1	6.2	3.0	6.0	-1.3
Canada	17.9	8.7	5.1	5.8	-	-	6.3	4.2	6.4	-1.3
Czech Republic	23.1	6.9	7.8	6.8	1.8	-0.7	7.5	2.0	6.0	-1.2
Denmark	29.3	5.7	6.1	2.7	4.0	0.2	6.6	2.7	6.3	0.0
Finland	19.4	8.5	8.1	4.8	3.1	-0.1	8.1	3.8	-	-
France	-	-	12.1	3.9	-	-	-	-	-	-
Germany	-	-	11.8	5.0	-	-	-	-	-	-
Hungary	7.1	1.6	6.0	1.2	1.2	0.3	-	-	-	-
Italy	-	-	14.2	-0.3	-	-	-	-	-	-
Japan	13.7	3.0	7.9	0.6	-	-	5.8	2.4	-	-
Korea	3.1	8.5	2.1	8.0	0.3	0.0	0.7	0.5	-	-
Netherlands	19.1	9.9	5.2	4.8	1.2	0.4	7.2	4.8	5.4	0.0
New Zealand	18.7	8.4	4.8	5.7	-	-	6.7	4.0	7.2	-1.3
Norway	17.9	13.4	4.9	8.0	2.4	1.6	5.2	3.2	5.5	0.5
Poland	12.2	-2.6	10.8	-2.5	1.4	-0.1	-	-	-	-
Spain	-	-	9.4	8.0	-	-	-	-	-	-
Sweden	20.0	3.2	9.0	1.0	1.9	0.4	8.1	0.2	9.8	-1.2
United Kingdom	15.6	0.2	4.3	-0.7	-	-	5.6	1.7	5.7	-0.9
United States	11.2	5.5	4.4	1.8	0.2	0.3	2.6	4.4	3.9	-1.0
OECD total	16.9	5.5	7.4	3.4	1.6	0.2	6.0	3.3	6.2	-0.9

Based on the assumption of unchanged policy, taking into account legislated but-not-yet implemented reforms.
Source: Dang et al. (2001), *Fiscal Implications of Ageing. Projections of Age-Related Spending*, http://dx.doi.org/10.1787/503643006287.

StatLink http://dx.doi.org/10.1787/888933590245

social programmes run on the basis of intergenerational transfers, whereby the working population pays for the benefits of current pensioners. These programmes are usually set up in such a way that they are sustainable as long as the demographic structure of a society remains generally the same. However, with an ageing society and an increasing dependency ratio, the burden on future generations may increase.

If taxes and social contributions are no longer sufficient to cover the expenses of governments, government deficits will increase. Temporary increases can be endured, but structural high levels of deficits, due to the above demographic shifts, may cause the increases to become unsustainable. Government may need to restore the fiscal balance by either increasing taxation or by cutting expenditures, for example by reducing the benefits of pension schemes for future beneficiaries, or by tightening access to social programmes

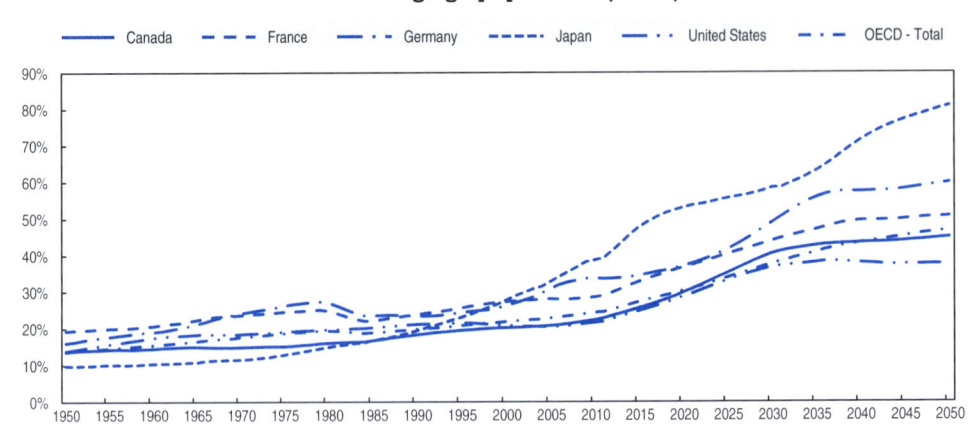

Figure 9.6. **Dependency ratio: population in retirement age (65+) to working age population (20-64)**

Source: OECD (2017a), "Labour Force Statistics: Population projections", *OECD Employment and Labour Market Statistics* (database), http://dx.doi.org/10.1787/data-00538-en.

StatLink http://dx.doi.org/10.1787/888933589181

by changing the eligibility criteria. The longer it takes before action is taken to restore the fiscal balance, the larger the impact on government debt and the larger the burden will be on future generations. Several countries have already pursued such reforms in anticipation of some of the effects of an ageing society.

Governments' balance sheets usually do not reflect the costs related to an ageing society. These costs often concern non-legal obligations that arise from expectations created by past practices, or by current government programmes or promises. These obligations are indirect or contingent, and are not included within the asset boundary of the 2008 System of National Accounts (2008 SNA). To be able to make an assessment of the sustainability of government finance, it is therefore important to have more insight into these types of future obligations. Including them on the balance sheet, if only as a memorandum item, would provide analysts with a more comprehensive overview of government finances.

Another possible way to capture the impact of an ageing society is to use forecasts on government spending and revenues, and combine those forecasts with current government debt levels. For example, calculations by the OBR in the United Kingdom (2015) showed that the projected increase in public spending (excluding interest payments) as a share of GDP will result in public spending gradually exceeding receipts, as a consequence of which the primary balance, i.e. public sector deficit excluding interest payments, will turn negative over time. Consequently, public sector net debt will first drop from 80 % of GDP in 2014-15 to 54 % in the early 2030s (while the primary balance is still positive), after which it will rise again to 87 % of GDP in 2064-2065; see Figure 9.7. The increasing trend is expected to continue from that point onwards. Although these types of calculations have to rely on several (sometimes rather strong assumptions) such projections (with the appropriate caveats and sensitivity analyses) may indeed provide useful insights in sustainability of government finance and the need for any structural reforms.

Figure 9.7. **Projections of public sector primary balance and net debt for the United Kingdom**
Percentage of GDP

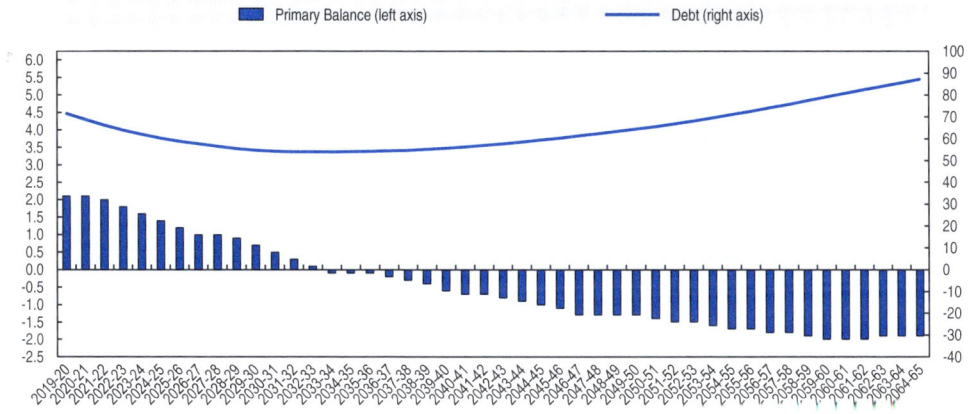

Source: OBR (2015), Fiscal Sustainability Report, http://budgetresponsibility.org.uk/docs/dlm_uploads/49753_OBR-Fiscal-Report-Web-Accessible.pdf.

StatLink ᔕᔕᔕ http://dx.doi.org/10.1787/888933589200

3. Demographic changes and pension schemes

The continuous increase in the dependency ratio has a profound impact on pension schemes, particularly pay-as-you-go pension schemes that rely on workers to pay contributions that fund the benefits of current retirees. For those schemes, an increasing dependency ratio implies that a smaller number of people has to come up with means to fund the benefits of an increasing group of retirees. As many social security pension schemes are pay-as-you-go schemes, many governments have already implemented pension reforms to mitigate the effects of an ageing population and to maintain the financial sustainability of their pension schemes. However, continuing increases in the dependency ratio may require additional measures. On the other hand, funded schemes, in which contributions are used to accumulate funds for the contributor's future retirement benefit payments, may also be affected by demographic changes, particularly in the case of an increase in life expectancy. The accumulated funds may then turn out to be insufficient to cover future benefits, which will have to be paid out for a longer time period than initially foreseen.

Because of the possible impact of an ageing society on the sustainability of pension schemes, pension statistics have received a lot of attention in recent years and are a common topic of discussion among politicians, policy analysts, and the media alike. As different types of schemes may be affected in different ways, this section provides an overview of the various types of schemes, and the calculation and recording of the related entitlements according to the 2008 SNA. This section also explains how the current recording may hamper comparability of pension liabilities and household retirement resources across countries, and how the recording may obscure the possible impact of an ageing society on the sustainability of pension schemes and government finances.

Types of pension schemes

In most countries, there is a variety of pension schemes that collectively ensure a minimum level of income for all retirees while enabling workers to save and invest a portion of their earnings to attain a particular level of income or wealth upon retirement. Pension schemes can be categorised along several different dimensions, including how they are sponsored, how they are funded, and the manner in which they provide benefits.

The first important distinction which is made in the 2008 SNA is between social insurance schemes and individual pension schemes. A social insurance scheme is a scheme where the benefits received are conditional on participation in the scheme, and where at least one of the following three conditions is met: participation in the scheme is obligatory; the scheme is a collective one operated for the benefit of a designated group of workers; or, an employer makes a contribution to the scheme on behalf of an employee (regardless of whether or not the employee makes a contribution). On the other hand, individual pension schemes concern retirement schemes that are taken out by individuals on their own initiative, such as life insurance, and in which there is a direct link between the contributions and the benefits. Social insurance schemes are further subdivided into two categories. The first category concerns social security pension schemes which are schemes that are offered to the population as a whole (or a large segment of the population) and that are imposed and controlled by the government. Pension schemes that are based on an employer-employee relationship, that are part of the conditions of employment, constitute the second type of social insurance schemes. These are known as employment-related or occupational pension schemes. An alternative typology that is frequently used for the breakdown into these three types of pension schemes is the classification into so-called "pillars". In this typology social security pensions constitute the first pillar, employment-related schemes the second pillar, and individual schemes the third pillar.

It is important to note that the distinction between social security and employment-related pension schemes is not the same as classifying schemes as public or private. Pensions are public or private depending on the type of institution that provides the schemes, i.e. the sponsor. Consequently, a public pension scheme can refer to a social security scheme but also to a pension scheme provided by the government to its employees. Conversely, a private pension scheme is a plan provided by an institution outside of the general government sector, although a private employer can still be obliged to contribute to a social security pension scheme as well. In addition, the categorisation of public versus private does not necessarily define the sector in which the liabilities are recorded. Recording will depend on who is responsible for managing the scheme. It may, for example, be the case that a public employment-related pension scheme is managed by a financial corporation, a so-called "autonomous pension fund", in which case the obligations would be recorded in the financial corporations sector. If the government manages the scheme itself, the obligations would be recorded within the government sector.

Pensions can also vary by the manner in which they provide benefits. Most pension schemes take the form of either a defined benefit (DB) or a defined contribution (DC) scheme, although hybrid schemes also occur. In a defined contribution pension scheme, the benefits are determined by the contributions made by the beneficiary and the returns generated from the accumulated funds. In contrast, under a defined benefit pension scheme, the level of benefits payable to each beneficiary is determined by a formula which can include factors such as retirement age, average salary, and years of employment. An important consideration between DB and DC schemes is the assignment of risk. With a defined contribution scheme, the level of benefits payable to beneficiaries is determined by the accumulated funds from past contributions and investment returns, so the pension sponsor and pension manager do not face any risk of insufficient funding. The beneficiaries bear the risk of receiving lower benefits if the pension fund experiences lower investment returns. With a defined benefit scheme, the pension sponsor or pension manager bears the financial risk that contributions and/or investment returns are insufficient to pay for the pre-determined level of benefits. The most common risks are longevity risk, which is the risk that pension beneficiaries will live longer than projected in the calculation of contributions and benefits; and investment risk, which is the risk that the invested funds will not generate an investment return to match the levels projected in the calculation of contributions and benefits. Partly as a consequence of an ageing society, a shift can be observed towards more defined contribution schemes, in which the risk is borne by the covered population.

Pension schemes can also vary by how they are funded. A fully funded pension scheme will have sufficient resources set aside to pay for the benefit entitlements that have accrued to date. A defined contribution pension scheme is by definition fully funded, as the benefit levels are determined by the funding that the scheme has accumulated from past contributions and from investment returns. However, defined benefit pension schemes can operate on a fully funded, partially funded or pay-as-you-go basis. Under a pay-as-you-go pension scheme, no funds are being accumulated; instead, the benefits of current beneficiaries are paid from the contributions of current contributors. A lot of social security schemes are set up in this way, although an increasing number of countries is changing to partially funded schemes, to mitigate part of the impact of an ageing society. Such schemes operate as a hybrid of the two approaches, thus paying for benefits using a mix of both accumulated funding and investment returns from past contributors as well as contributions from current contributors. As was explained before, increasing dependency ratios may particularly affect the sustainability of pay-as-you-go systems and partially funded schemes.

The misalignment between the timing of the premiums and benefits in pay-as-you-go (or partially funded) pension schemes often complicates the assessment of the sustainability of those schemes. As pension obligations are recorded on an accrued-to-date basis, the (implicit) liability is recognised when a worker has provided the relevant service (e.g. a year of employment, including the payment of the required contributions), and thus increases its benefit entitlement. On the other hand, the future contributions that will pay for these benefits will only be recorded once they are actually paid in the future by the then working population. As a result, on an accrued-to-date basis these pension schemes may show significant liabilities without any (or only partially) corresponding assets. That is why for sustainability analyses of pay-as-you-go schemes, future contributions are often also taken into account, to obtain a longer term overview of incoming and outgoing flows. It is understood that this provides a better overview of the sustainability of these schemes (which is discussed later in this chapter).

Table 9.2 provides a summary of the different classifications that can be used to classify pension schemes. As plans can be categorized according to multiple dimensions, the table provides an overview of categories that are not mutually exclusive.

The measurement of pension entitlements

For sustainability analyses and the assessment of the impact of an ageing society, it is important to monitor the value of the pension entitlements for the various types of schemes. In estimating the value of the entitlements, it is necessary to distinguish between defined benefit and defined contribution schemes as their entitlements are measured in different ways. For defined contribution schemes the measurement of the entitlements is relatively straightforward. Since the benefits are determined by the level of funding available at the time of the beneficiary's retirement, the pension liability is simply equal to the accumulated assets in the pension fund. The measurement is more complicated for entitlements of defined benefit schemes, as their

Table 9.2. **Overview of the various classifications of pension schemes**

Distinguishing factor	Types of pension schemes
"Pillars" of pension funding	*Pillar 1: social security*: offered to the population as a whole (or large segments) and imposed and controlled by government *Pillar 2: employment-related*: based on an employer-employee relationship, and part of the conditions of employment *Pillar 3: individual plans*: initiated and funded by individuals, apart from employer or government
Sponsoring institution	*Public sponsorship*: sponsored by the government (for general citizenship or government employees) *Private sponsorship*: sponsored by the private sector
Benefits	*Defined benefit*: benefits determined by a formula which can include retirement age, average salary, years of employment, etc. *Defined contribution*: benefits determined by a past contributions and investment returns on accumulated funds *Hybrid*: benefits partly determined by a formula, and partly by contributions made and their returns
Funding	*Fully funded*: sufficient resources accumulated to pay for accrued-to-date entitlements *Pay-as-you-go*: pension benefits of current retirees are paid for by contributions from current contributors *Partially funded*: benefits are paid for using a mix of accumulated funds and contributions from current contributors

StatLink ᛜ http://dx.doi.org/10.1787/888933590264

benefits are dependent upon a number of future developments not known at the time that the benefit entitlement accrues. Estimates need to be made based on projections of wage growth, expected age of retirement and life expectancy, expected number of years of contributions, and other factors that determine the present value of future cash flows. The total value of pension obligations owed by a pension fund is usually calculated as the net present value of the sum of all estimated pension benefits to be paid in the future to all individuals participating in the scheme.

A simplified representation of the present value of an individual's pension entitlement can be shown as follows:

$$= \sum_{t}^{T} \frac{\text{Pension benefit}_t * \text{Indexation factor}}{(1 + \text{Discount rate}_t)^{(t - \text{Base year})}} * \text{Conditional probability of survival}_t$$

The summation represents the present value of pension benefits for an individual. The summation would begin for the year in which the individual is expected to start receiving pension benefits and end at a year T sufficiently far in the future beyond which the individual is not expected to live (i.e. the conditional probability of survival is close to zero). The future benefits of each year need to be discounted to estimate the value of the pension obligations in the current year (or base year). The total sum of the liabilities associated with the scheme equals the value of the pension entitlements for all participants of the scheme.

As noted before, the value of the pension liability for defined benefit schemes is based on several factors that must be projected far into the future. Future salary and number of years of contributions before retirement will typically determine the amount of the pension benefit. The indexation factor, a method of adjusting future benefits for inflation and/or growth of real income, will likely be based on future inflation or wage growth projections. The conditional probability of survival will be based on future life expectancy. The results of these calculations can be highly sensitive to small changes in some of the factors, particularly the discount rate. For example, Table 9.3 shows the sensitivity of pension liabilities for changes in the discount rate and the real wage growth rate in estimates of the social security pension scheme in Portugal. The calculations were initially performed using a discount rate of 3% and a wage growth rate of 1.5%. Increasing the discount rate to 4% leads to a 14% reduction in the estimated pension liability, while decreasing the discount rate to 2% leads to a 19% increase. An increase in the wage growth rate to 2% leads to a 9% increase in the estimated pension liability, while a decrease in the wage growth rate to 1% leads to a 3% decrease.

Table 9.3. **Sensitivity of the estimates of pension obligations for Portugal**
Percentage change to social security pension liability due to change in wage growth and discount rate

		Discount rate (%)						
		0	1	2	3	4	5	6
Wage growth rate (%)	0	57	28	7	-8	-21	-30	-38
	0.5	64	33	11	-6	-19	-29	-37
	1	71	38	15	-3	-17	-27	-35
	1.5	79	44	19	Base	-14	-25	-34
	2	102	60	31	9	-7	-20	-30
	2.5	113	68	36	13	-5	-18	-28
	3	125	76	42	17	-1	-15	-26
	3.5	153	96	56	27	6	-9	-22
	4	172	109	65	34	11	-6	-19

Source: Kaier and Müller (2013), *New Figures on Unfunded Public Pension Entitlements across Europe – Concept, Results and Applications*, https://static.nzz.ch/files/8/4/6/317-3_1.18125846.pdf.
StatLink http://dx.doi.org/10.1787/888933590283

Using the aforementioned approach to estimate the liabilities of a defined benefit pension scheme, the methodology to conduct these calculations can vary in several ways. The two most notable variations are: i) differences in wage assumptions used to project the level of benefits; and ii) differences in the scope of the population included in the calculations. Regarding the variation in the wage assumptions used to project the level of benefits, the valuation of pension liabilities can vary depending on whether Accrued Benefit Obligations (ABO) or Projected Benefit Obligations (PBO) is applied. Defined benefit pension schemes normally provide a benefit that is based on each member's salary (such as final salary, lifetime average salary, or average salary for a set period of years). As the salary level that will ultimately determine each member's pension benefit is not yet known until they retire, an assumption must be made using either the ABO or PBO method. The ABO method uses each pension member's current salary as the basis for estimating their future benefits, while the PBO method uses a projection of the future salary on which each member's pension benefits would be based at the time of their retirement. For this reason, estimates of pension liabilities based on PBO will be higher than those based on ABO.

Regarding the variation in the scope of the population, some models for calculating pension liabilities use the accrued-to-date method (also known as the closed group without future accruals method), which includes only the benefits that current members (hence, closed group) have earned up to the present period in the calculation. As the 2008 SNA is based on accrued-to-date recording, this is also the underlying principle for calculating pension entitlements in the national accounts. Other models go further by also including future accruals for current members (closed group with future accrual), which means that benefits projected to accrue in the future for current members of the scheme are also included in the calculation. The open group method also includes future pension members in the scope of the calculations (hence, open group), projecting the demographics of future generations of workers, and future labour needs, in order to estimate the benefits of future generations. In this case, the long-term obligations of the pension scheme are estimated by adding projected benefits of future generations to the accrued and projected benefits of current members. Open group estimates of liabilities are normally presented in conjunction with estimates of assets (i.e. projected contributions) in order to view the net asset/liability position of the pension scheme from a long-term perspective.

As an example, Table 9.4 provides the actuarial balance sheet of the Canada Pension Plan (CPP) under each of the three approaches. The CPP is a partially funded, public, defined benefit pension scheme. It started as a pay-as-you-go scheme but was reformed into a partially funded scheme in the 1990s, to cope with the challenges posed by the ageing society. Its current assets of CAD 175 billion are 17.4% of its obligations of CAD 1 trillion, estimated under a closed group (excluding future accruals) basis. However, when the future contributions and benefits of current workers are included in the balance sheet, the CPP has assets amounting to 63.4% of total liabilities. When the contributions and benefits of future generations are included on an open group basis (projecting as far out as 150 years), the pension scheme has assets that are nearly equal to liabilities.

Table 9.4. **Actuarial balance sheet for the Canada Pension Plan at 31 December 2012**

Billions of CAD

	Closed group		Open group
	Excluding future accruals	Including future accruals	Including future accruals
Assets			
Current assets	175	175	175
Future contributions	-	804	2 071
Total assets	175	979	2 246
Liabilities (pension obligations)			
Benefits accrued to date	370	370	370
Benefits accruable due to future contributions	635	1 175	1 885
Total liabilities	1 005	1 545	2 255
Asset excess (shortfall)	-830	-566	-9
Total assets as a percentage of total liabilities	17.40%	63.40%	99.60%

Source: Billig (2016), Compiling the actuarial balance sheet for the Canada Pension Plan – methodological overview, www.osfi-bsif.gc.ca/Eng/Docs/OCA-Assia-Billig-03092016-notes.pdf.

StatLink http://dx.doi.org/10.1787/888933590302

This table provides an example of a partially-funded pension scheme that is financially sustainable in the long-term. While the closed group approaches indicate obligations that are far in excess of assets, they do not capture the pay-as-you-go nature of the pension scheme. The open group approach reflects the concept that future generations of workers will pay contributions that will fund the benefits that current generations of workers have accumulated. This does not mean that the closed group figures are incorrect; they are provided so that users can assess the current state of the pension scheme's finances and identify the implications of pension policy for the current generation of workers.

The closed group without future accruals method is the most suitable approach for estimating the pension obligations that a government has accrued up to the current period, and therefore its results are the most comparable to explicit debt and other stock figures recorded in the financial accounts and balance sheets. Accordingly, this is the method applied for estimating pension entitlements/obligations in the national accounts. However, this approach does not include future accruals, or the future generations that, in a pay-as-you-go scheme, will pay the contributions that will fund the benefits to be paid in the future. As a result, the open group method is best suited to assess the long-term financial sustainability of a pension scheme.

The recording of pension entitlements in the 2008 SNA

The 2008 SNA has particular provisions for recording pension entitlements. Employment-related schemes lead to the accrual of pension entitlements/

obligations under the 2008 SNA, whereas this is not the case for social security pension schemes. The main reason for this distinction is that governments can alter the basis on which the entitlements are determined for social security schemes. However, as the distinction between social security and employment-related pension schemes may not be that straightforward, it is not always clear whether to include entitlements in the central framework of national accounts. As a consequence, the different treatment of these types of schemes may obscure comparisons of pension entitlements and household retirement resources across countries. To ensure comparability, as of the end of 2017 the pension entitlements, transactions and other flows associated with social security and government employee pension schemes are to be recorded in a supplementary table showing the extent of pension schemes included and excluded from the 2008 SNA sequence of accounts.

Table 9.5 summarises the treatment of pension schemes according to the 2008 SNA, based on the pension sponsor and type of pension scheme. Here, as noted above, one should be aware of the fact that in a significant number of countries, the government sponsors a major part of employment-related pension schemes, including those of employees in the private sector. These schemes may be intertwined with the social security schemes, resulting in the absence of any pension obligations in the financial accounts and balance sheets of the central framework of national accounts.

Table 9.5. **The recording of pension schemes based on the sponsor and type of scheme**

Pension sponsor	Type of pension scheme	Recording practice
Non-government	Defined contribution	Central framework
	Defined benefit	Central framework
Government	Defined contribution for government employees	Central framework
	Defined benefit for government employees	Central framework
	Social security	Supplementary table

Pension schemes and the interpretation of government debt

Current practices for recording pension entitlements in the financial accounts and balance sheets can make it difficult to analyse and compare government debt and assess the state of a government's finances. When using data from the financial accounts and balance sheets, users should be aware of these limitations and seek additional information where appropriate. There are two caveats that should be considered. First, the assumptions that are used in estimating the value of pension entitlements can vary from one pension scheme to the next. A change in a key factor such as the discount rate, real wage growth rate, inflation rate or mortality rate can lead to significant changes in the estimated value of entitlements for defined benefit pension schemes. One should thus check for any supplementary information provided with the pension data (e.g. a sensitivity analysis can be especially useful) and be mindful of how differing assumptions can affect the additivity and/or comparability of data.

Second, social security pension schemes are not recorded in the central framework of the national accounts, and neither may any employment-related schemes that are considered to be intertwined with social security. As previously discussed, this is because of the fact that governments can modify the terms, and therefore the value, of the pension entitlements, which makes the associated liability less tangible than a liability stemming from a legal contract. The implication is that when analysing government debt (or the pension entitlements as part of household retirement resources), users should look for any supplementary information on financial obligations pertaining to social benefits in order to verify whether there are any other government-sponsored pension schemes that have not been recorded in the central framework of national accounts.

Table 9.6 demonstrates how different pension arrangements in OECD countries can impact the comparison of government debt recorded in the financial accounts and balance sheets. Column 1 lists the total liabilities of the general government in 2012 as recorded in the central framework of national accounts. Some countries, such as Australia, Canada, Ireland and the United States included the liabilities of unfunded or partially funded defined benefit pension schemes for government employees in their figures for total government liabilities, whereas others did not. To account for this, the unfunded part of the pension liabilities (shown in column 2) is subtracted from total liabilities to provide an adjusted figure in column 3. Even after this adjustment, government debt levels are not fully comparable, because countries with (partially) funded government employee pension schemes and/or (partially) funded social security pension schemes will have accumulated assets. To adjust for this, the accumulated funds of employment-related and social security pension schemes are subtracted from column 3 to provide a fully adjusted figure for government liabilities in column 8. The table shows that these adjustments may lead to significantly different levels of government debt for several countries. For example, the liabilities of the Canadian government drop from 109.7 % of GDP to 38.9 % when adjusting for employment-related and social security funds, and from 129.5 % to 71.8 % for Iceland. Other countries for which the impact is substantial are the United States, Sweden, the Netherlands and Switzerland. Taking into account differences in pension arrangements in ranking countries according to their government debt levels may thus lead to significantly different results.

9. ACCOUNTING FOR THE FINANCIAL CONSEQUENCES OF DEMOGRAPHIC CHANGES

Table 9.6. **Pension systems and their impact on government debt, 2012**

Percentage of GDP

	Total liabilities (1)	Unfunded pension liabilities (2)	Total liabilities excluding unfunded pension liabilities (3 = 1-2)	Accumulated funds related to employment related pension schemes, inside GG (4)	Accumulated funds related to employment related pension schemes, outside GG (5)	Total liabilities, after full adjustment for employment related funds (6 = 3-4-5)	Accumulated funds related to social security pension schemes, inside GG (7)	Total liabilities, after full adjustment for employment related and social security funds (8=6-7)
Australia[1]	57.9	25.8	32.1	5.4	..	..	0.0	..
Austria	86.0	0.0	86.0	0.0	0.0	86.0	0.0	86.0
Belgium	106.4	0.0	106.4	0.0	0.0	106.4	0.0	106.4
Canada	109.7	13.6	96.1	0.0	44.4	51.7	12.8	38.9
Chile	18.6	0.0	18.6	..	..	..	2.2	..
Czech Republic	55.7	0.0	55.7	0.0	0.0	55.7	0.0	55.7
Denmark	59.3	0.0	59.3	0.0	0.0	59.3	0.0	59.3
Estonia	13.3	0.0	13.3	0.0	0.0	13.3	0.0	13.3
Finland	64.0	0.0	64.0	0.0	0.0	64.0	0.0	64.0
France	109.3	0.0	109.3	0.0	0.0	109.3	1.8	107.5
Germany	88.5	0.0	88.5	0.3	0.0	88.2	0.0	88.2
Greece	167.5	0.0	167.5	0.0	0.0	167.5	0.0	167.5
Hungary	90.0	0.0	90.0	0.0	..	..	0.0	..
Iceland	129.5	25.8	103.7	0.0	31.9	71.8	0.0	71.8
Ireland	127.8	0.0	127.8	0.0	0.0	127.8	0.0	127.8
Israel[2]	68.2	0.0	68.2	0.0	..	..	0.0	..
Italy	142.2	0.0	142.2	0.0	0.0	142.2	0.0	142.2
Japan	216.5	0.0	216.5	9.8	..	..	2.2	..

9. ACCOUNTING FOR THE FINANCIAL CONSEQUENCES OF DEMOGRAPHIC CHANGES

Table 9.6. **Pension systems and their impact on government debt, 2012** (cont.)

Percentage of GDP

	Total liabilities (1)	Unfunded pension liabilities (2)	Total liabilities excluding unfunded pension liabilities (3 = 1-2)	Accumulated funds related to employment related pension schemes, inside GG (4)	Accumulated funds related to employment related pension schemes, outside GG (5)	Total liabilities, after full adjustment for employment related funds (6 = 3-4-5)	Accumulated funds related to social security pension schemes, inside GG (7)	Total liabilities, after full adjustment for employment related and social security funds (8=6-7)
Korea	34.8	0.0	34.8	0.0	..	..	0.0	..
Luxembourg	30.2	..	30.2	..	..	..	..	..
Mexico	..	0.0	..	0.0	0.0	..	0.0	..
Netherlands	82.7	0.0	82.7	0.0	47.8	34.9	0.0	34.9
New Zealand	47.6	5.2	42.4	0.0	1.4	41.0	0.0	41.0
Norway	34.7	0.0	34.7	0.0	13.5	21.2	0.0	21.2
Poland	62.3	0.0	62.3	0.0	0.0	62.3	1.0	61.3
Portugal	134.6	0.0	134.6	3.5	0.1	131.2	6.5	124.7
Slovak Republic	56.9	0.0	56.9	0.0	0.0	56.9	0.0	56.9
Slovenia	61.6	0.0	61.6	0.0	0.0	61.6	0.0	61.6
Spain	92.6	0.0	92.6	0.0	0.0	92.6	6.1	86.5
Sweden	49.0	2.3	46.7	0.0	18.9	27.8	27.0	0.8
Switzerland[3]	46.3	0.0	46.3	0.0	31.1	15.2	5.4	9.9
Turkey	..	0.0	..	0.0	0.0	..	0.0	..
United Kingdom	101.6	0.0	101.6	0.0	13.7	87.9	0.0	87.9
United States	122.2	20.1	102.1	0.0	30.0	72.1	0.0	72.1

1. Based on Government Finance Statistics. Data not fully consistent with SNA but the difference in total liabilities excluding unfunded pension liabilities is less than 1% of GDP.
2. The statistical data for Israel are supplied by and under the responsibility of the relevant Israeli authorities. The use of such data by the OECD is without prejudice to the status of the Golan Heights, East Jerusalem and Israeli settlements in the Westbank under the terms of international law.
3. 2011 data for Switzerland.

Source: OECD (2014), OECD Economic Outlook, Volume 2014/1, http://dx.doi.org/10.1787/eco_outlook-v2014-1-en.

StatLink ⟶ http://dx.doi.org/10.1787/888933590340

Retirement resources of households

Notwithstanding the importance of pensions and their financial significance for governments, employers and households, it should be noted that pensions represent only a portion of how households build up resources for retirement. Households accumulate retirement resources through a variety of instruments, including pension entitlements, saving deposits and other investment vehicles, and various non-financial investments such as dwellings. Figure 9.8 displays the level and composition of household assets and liabilities on a per capita basis (in USD) in 2013 for a sample of six countries for which data was available.

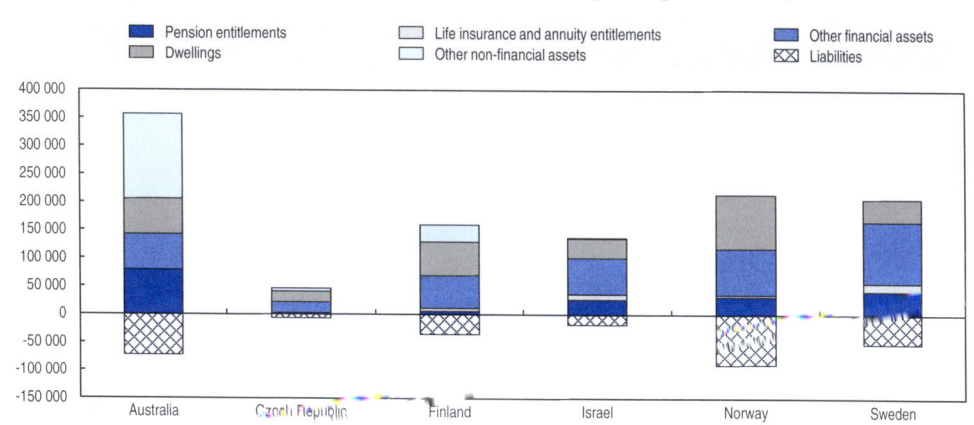

Figure 9.8. **Household assets and liabilities per capita in USD, 2013** *

- Pension entitlements
- Dwellings
- Life insurance and annuity entitlements
- Other non-financial assets
- Other financial assets
- Liabilities

* Data on non-financial assets other than dwellings was not available for Norway and Sweden.
Source: OECD (2017b), "Financial Balance Sheets, SNA 2008 (or SNA 1993): Non-consolidated stocks, annual", OECD National Accounts Statistics (database), http://dx.doi.org/10.1787/data-00720-en; and "Detailed National Accounts, SNA 2008 (or SNA 1993): Balance sheets for non-financial assets", OECD National Accounts Statistics (database), http://dx.doi.org/10.1787/data-00368-en.

StatLink ⟶ http://dx.doi.org/10.1787/888933589219

The figure shows that pension entitlements represent a small portion of a household's total assets. Across the six countries, pension entitlements averaged 12% of total household assets. The share of pension entitlements was the highest in Australia at 22% of household assets, and lowest in the Czech Republic at 3% of household assets. Moreover, life insurance and annuity entitlements only account for a small part of household assets with an average of 3% of total assets across the six countries. Other financial assets (representing holdings in currency and deposits, debt securities, equity and derivatives) averaged 36% of total assets, while dwellings averaged 28%. However, both these other financial assets and the value of the dwellings are normally not dedicated entirely to the purpose of retirement.

It also has to be considered that these household assets do not include entitlements derived from social security pension schemes, as they are not recorded in the central framework of national accounts. As was explained earlier in this chapter, the importance of these types of pension schemes varies across countries. Although the government may alter the benefits from these types of schemes, households usually assume the receipt of some benefits in the future and therefore will regard these entitlements as part of their retirement resources. Therefore, it is also important to look at the relevant amounts from the supplementary table. This will provide a better overview of household retirement resources and lead to better cross-country comparisons.

Key points

- There is empirical evidence that demographic changes affect key economic figures like the saving ratio and net wealth. The monitoring of this phenomenon will become increasingly important with the projected ageing of the population in many countries.
- Demographic changes also affect government finances; an ageing population will lead to increases in pension and health care costs, which will outweigh decreases in costs related to child and family benefits and education.
- Pension schemes will also be affected by an ageing society, with the impact depending on the institutional setup of the schemes. Depending on the scheme, these changes may affect the sustainability of pension funds and government finances, and household retirement resources.
- To have a clear understanding of the consequences of an ageing society for pension systems, it is important to look how the different types of schemes are affected by demographic changes. Financial accounts and balance sheets may provide useful insight in some of these consequences, showing possible changes in entitlements in relation to their accumulated funds. However, users have to be aware that different institutional setups may hamper comparability between schemes and across countries, sometimes requiring additional information to arrive at a comprehensive and comparable overview.
- Sustainability analyses of pension schemes often do not only focus on the accrued-to-date entitlements in relation to the accumulated funds (closed group without future accrual), but also take into account future accruals and contributions by current and future generations (open group approach) to obtain a better overview of their long-term situation. This is particularly important for pay-as-you-go systems, in which accrued benefit entitlements will be paid by future contributions. As this may also affect fiscal sustainability analyses, one has to be aware of how different institutional setups of pension schemes affect results.
- One should also bear in mind that the value of pension entitlements will depend on the benefit formula (i.e. defined contribution schemes in which the entitlements are equal to the accumulated assets in the fund, versus defined benefit schemes in which the entitlements are based on a benefit formula), and for defined benefit schemes also on the underlying assumptions with regard to future wage increases, life expectancy and the discount rate. As these assumptions may significantly affect results, sensitivity analyses may help in providing more insight in the impact of these assumptions and in arriving at more comparable results across countries.

Note

1. Dang et al. (2001) explain that in OECD countries the per capita health care costs for people over 65 are three to five times higher than for those under 65.

2. Note by Turkey: The information in this document with reference to "Cyprus" relates to the southern part of the Island. There is no single authority representing both Turkish and Greek Cypriot people on the Island. Turkey recognises the Turkish Republic of Northern Cyprus (TRNC). Until a lasting and equitable solution is found within the context of the United Nations, Turkey shall preserve its position concerning the "Cyprus issue".

3. Note by all the European Union Member States of the OECD and the European Union: The Republic of Cyprus is recognised by all members of the United Nations with the exception of Turkey. The information in this document relates to the area under the effective control of the Government of the Republic of Cyprus.

References

ABS (2015), 5204.0.55.011 - *Australian National Accounts: Distribution of Household Income, Consumption and Wealth, 2003-04 to 2014-15*, Australian Bureau of Statistics, Canberra, www.abs.gov.au/AUSSTATS/abs@.nsf/DetailsPage/5204.0.55.0112003-04%20to%202014-15?OpenDocument.

Billig, A. (2016), *Compiling the Actuarial Balance Sheet for the Canada Pension Plan – Methodological Overview*, Presentation to the Eurostat/ILO/IMF/OECD Workshop on Pensions, 9 March, Paris, www.osfi-bsif.gc.ca/Eng/Docs/OCA-Assia-Billig-03092016-notes.pdf.

Cecchetti, S.G., M. Mohanty and F. Zampolli (2010), "The future of public debt: prospects and implications", *BIS Working Papers*, No. 300, Bank for International Settlements, Basel, www.bis.org/publ/work300.pdf.

Dang, T., P. Antolín and H. Oxley, (2001), "Fiscal implications of ageing – Projections of age-related spending", *OECD Economics Department Working Papers*, No. 305, OECD Publishing, Paris, http://dx.doi.org/10.1787/503643006287.

Deaton, A. (2005), "Franco Modigliani and the life cycle theory of consumption", *Banca Nazionale del Lavoro Quarterly Review*, Vol. 58, Banca Nazionale del Lavoro, Rome, pp. 91-107.

European Commission (2012), *The 2012 Ageing Report – Economic and budgetary projections for the 27 EU Member States (2010-2060)*, European Union, Brussels, http://ec.europa.eu/economy_finance/publications/european_economy/2012/pdf/ee-2012-2_en.pdf.

European Commission (2015), *The 2015 Ageing Report – Economic and budgetary projections for the 28 EU Member States (2013-2060)*, European Union, Brussels, http://ec.europa.eu/economy_finance/publications/european_economy/2015/pdf/ee3_en.pdf.

Friedman, M. (1957), *A Theory of the Consumption Function*, Princeton University Press, Princeton.

Goldsmith, R. (1955), *A Study of Saving in the United States*, Princeton University Press, Princeton.

Higgins, M. (1998), "Demography, National Savings, and International Cash Flows", *International Economic Review*, Vol. 39, No. 2, Blackwell Publishing, Hoboken, pp. 343-369, http://pages.stern.nyu.edu/dbackus/BCH/capital%20flows/Higgins_IER_98.pdf.

IMF (2016), *World Economic Outlook Database: April 2016*, International Monetary Fund, Washington, DC, www.imf.org/external/pubs/ft/weo/2016/01/weodata/download.aspx.

Jappelli, T. and F. Modigliani (1998), "The age-saving profile and the life-cycle hypothesis", *CSEF Working Papers*, No. 9, Centre for Studies in Economics and Finance, Naples, www.csef.it/WP/wp9.pdf.

Jappelli, T. (2005), "The life-cycle hypothesis, fiscal policy and social security", *Banca Nazionale del Lavoro Quarterly Review*, Vol. 58, Banca Nazionale del Lavoro, Rome, pp. 173-186.

Kaier, K. and C. Müller (2013), "New figures on unfunded public pension entitlements across Europe – concept, results and applications", *Discussion Papers*, No. 52, Forschungs Zentrum Generationen Verträge der Albert-Ludwigs-Universität Freiburg, Freiburg.

Modigliani, F. and R. Brumberg (1954), "Utility analysis and the consumption function: An interpretation of cross-section data", in *Post-Keynesian Economics*, Allen and Unwin, London.

Modigliani, F. (1985), "Life cycle, individual thrift and the wealth of nations", *American Economic Review*, Vol. 76, No. 3, American Economic Association, Pittsburgh, pp. 297-313.

OECD (2017a), "Labour Force Statistics: Population projections", *OECD Employment and Labour Market Statistics* (database), http://dx.doi.org/10.1787/data-00538-en.

OECD (2017b), "Financial Balance Sheets, SNA 2008 (or SNA 1993): Non-consolidated stocks, annual", *OECD National Accounts Statistics* (database), http://dx.doi.org/10.1787/data-00720-en; and "Detailed National Accounts, SNA 2008 (or SNA 1993): Balance sheets for non-financial assets", *OECD National Accounts Statistics* (database), http://dx.doi.org/10.1787/data-00368-en.

OECD (2016), *Focus on Health Spending – Expenditure by disease, age and gender*, OECD Publishing, Paris, www.oecd.org/health/Expenditure-by-disease-age-and-gender-FOCUS-April2016.pdf.

OECD (2014), *OECD Economic Outlook*, Vol. 2014/1, OECD Publishing, Paris, http://dx.doi.org/10.1787/eco_outlook-v2014-1-en.

OECD (2013), "Public spending on health and long-term care: A new set of projections", *OECD Economic Policy Papers*, No. 6, OECD Publishing, Paris, http://dx.doi.org/10.1787/5k44t7jwwr9x-en.

OECD (2001), "Fiscal implications of ageing: projections of age-related spending", in *Economic Outlook 69*, OECD Publishing, Paris, http://dx.doi.org/10.1787/eco_outlook-v2001-1-en.

OBR (2015), *Fiscal Sustainability Report*, Office for Budget Responsibility, London, http://budgetresponsibility.org.uk/docs/dlm_uploads/49753_OBR-Fiscal-Report-Web-Accessible.pdf.

Polackova, H. (1999), "Contingent government liabilities – A hidden fiscal risk", *Finance & Development*, Vol. 36 No. 1, IMF, Washington, DC, www.imf.org/external/pubs/ft/fandd/1999/03/polackov.htm.

UN (2015), *World Population Ageing Report*, United Nations, New York City, www.un.org/en/development/desa/population/publications/pdf/ageing/WPA2015_Report.pdf.

Zwijnenburg, J., S. Bournot and F. Giovanelli, "OECD Expert Group on Disparities in a National Accounts Framework – Results from the 2015 exercise", *OECD Statistics Working Papers*, No. 2016/10, OECD Publishing, Paris, http://dx.doi.org/10.1787/2daa921e-en.

Chapter 10

Globalisation, financial innovation and crises

Bruno Tissot (BIS) and Daniele Fano (Fondazione AIB)

Chapter 10 highlights the usefulness of the framework of financial accounts and balance sheets for understanding financial globalisation, innovation and crises. Developing further on Chapter 7, it provides a more in-depth analysis of countries' fragilities when it comes to financial exposures. The chapter offers a wider perspective on the build-up of financial risks over time and the contributing roles of international finance and globalisation. It shows how the framework of financial accounts and balance sheets can be mobilised to analyse financial crises, drawing in particular on recent episodes of stress and considering the impact of leverage and financial innovation. After underlining the importance of integrating a micro, entity-level perspective in the macro approach of financial accounts and balance sheets, this chapter concludes by reviewing the international efforts undertaken to enhance countries' statistical frameworks in response to the 2007-09 economic and financial crisis.

10. GLOBALISATION, FINANCIAL INNOVATION AND CRISES

1. Introduction

Globalisation and financial innovation are two very different, though intertwined, phenomena. The pendulum towards globalisation has been characterised by specific periods in economic history, with more or less abrupt and prolonged reversals. On the other hand, financial innovation appears to be relentless, though with years of varying acceleration, as driven by the necessities and political impacts of trade and reactions to new regulations and technological opportunities.

The above developments go hand in hand with financial crises. These crises can arise from purely internal (domestic) imbalances, or they can be driven by a combination of internal and external factors. This chapter will start from the latter, as a follow-up to Chapter 7. Countries' fragilities are most apparent when internal sectoral imbalances require external financing from the Rest of the World. The discussion then moves on to show that essentially internal imbalances with no direct impacts on the balance of payments can also lead to major international reactions via financial markets. Leverage and the related successions of booms and busts are often at the heart of the build-up and evolution of crises. The degree of (un)awareness of such imbalances and the reversal of expectations can play a key role as a trigger of crises.

The increased complexity driven by financial innovation, specifically the transition from an "originate-to-hold" banking model to an "originate-to-distribute" banking model, is another challenge of recent years. This shift was made possible by the combined effects of information technology and deregulation. It also led to the emergence of a "shadow banking" sector, which is much less regulated and difficult to capture via statistics. Financial crises have relevant and often long lasting effects on the "real" economy, including economic growth. It is therefore important to closely monitor the information in financial accounts and balance sheets, as they can provide early warnings and forward-looking indicators for policy makers to address possible risks and vulnerabilities.

2. Countries' fragilities and international crises

The external financing of sectoral imbalances

As analysed in Chapter 1, the framework of financial accounts and balance sheets allows for a reconciliation between the "real" economy and its financing, both at the global level and within countries. A key element is the role played by the Rest of the World in acting as a borrower/lender of funds in the case of imbalances in the sum of resident sectors' financing. This feature explains why the globalisation of financial markets has traditionally been seen as a positive way to bridge the gap between saving and investment in specific sectors and countries, leading to better economic outcomes. This has been indeed the reasoning behind development economics: mature economies should generate an excess of saving compared to their investment needs, and this excess of saving should be mirrored by their current account surpluses and therefore by net financial outflows to other countries. In turn these funds should provide finance for more profitable investment in less developed countries where saving is not so abundant, resulting in their progressive "catching up" towards the more advanced countries.

Under this model, the global economy would be characterised by a group of advanced countries with large current account surpluses, while the developing world would have an underlying, or "structural", current account deficit matched by "sustainable" financial inflows. A famous example relates to the British Empire, which benefited from inflows of foreign capital during the initial phase of its industrial revolution in the 18th century and then became progressively a net exporter of capital, financing the expansion of new colonies during the 19th century and up until First World War (Brezis, 1995). As a result, the United Kingdom ran a significant current account surplus from 1850 to 1910, expanding its ownership of foreign assets by providing finance to developing regions, and receiving income in return. In line with this reasoning, countries such as Australia and Canada were considered as able to sustain relatively large current account deficits, because those current account deficits would mirror the high investment opportunities of those "new" countries.

There are, however, three caveats with this development economics approach. One is that the global economy has been characterised by sizeable and lasting exceptions to the situation described above. The United States, for example, though leading the advanced economies in terms of economic productivity, has displayed sizeable and continuous current account deficits over the past few decades. Another exception is that a number of rapidly emerging economies, especially in Asia (e.g. China), have experienced over the past few decades (and especially before the 2007-09 economic and financial crisis, during the 2000s) sizeable current account surpluses and have built very large external reserves, instead of recording current account deficits.

The second caveat is that analysis cannot be limited to the level of the country as a whole: the sectoral counterparts of the Rest of the World financing balance are also very important. Residents have to remunerate (and repay at some point) external financial inflows, which are often denominated in foreign currencies for less advanced economies (the "original sin" view, as put forward by

Eichengreen et al., 2002). The ideal situation is that these flows serve to balance the funding deficits of domestic sectors with the highest investment opportunities and possibilities to generate revenues in foreign currencies – often, the non-financial corporations in the tradeable sector. If, on the contrary, external funding serves to balance the needs of households or the government and is mainly used for current consumption, the situation is more fragile as the future servicing of external liabilities may be harder to ensure. Hence, and as explained in Box 10.1, observers have often focussed on the risks posed by a "twin deficits" situation, when large current account deficits reflect unsustainable government spending and/or disequilibria in the net lending of the private sector.

Box 10.1. **The link between the current account balance and the resident economy**

Looking at the country as a whole, one can compute the aggregate balance of the domestic sectors and derive the flows and positions of the domestic economy with the Rest of the World. In the following, we slightly rewrite equations (1) to (3) in Box 8.1, as follows:

(1') $Y = C_{hh} + C_{gov} + I_{private} + I_{gov} + (X - M)$

Where:

Y = Gross Domestic Product (GDP)

C_{hh}/C_{gov} = Final consumption by households (hh) and government (gov), respectively

$I_{private}/I_{gov}$ = Investments (in non-financial assets) by the private sector (private) and government (gov), respectively

X = Exports

M = Imports

(2') $Y + W - DI_{gov} - C_{hh} = C_{gov} - DI_{gov} + I_{private} + I_{gov} + (X - M) + W$

Where:

W = Balance of primary and secondary income transactions with the Rest of the World

DI_{gov} = Disposable Income of government, i.e. current receipts minus current expenditures (excluding government consumption)

Since $(Y + W - DI_{gov} - C_{hh})$ equals private saving $(S_{private})$, whereas $(DI_{gov} - C_{gov})$ equals government saving (S_{gov}), equation (2') can be rewritten as follows:

(3') $(S_{private} - I_{private}) + (S_{gov} - I_{gov}) = (X - M) + W$

Equation (3') above highlights that the current account balance is equal to the saving minus investments in non-financial assets of the private sector $(S_{private} - I_{private})$ and the government sector $(S_{gov} - I_{gov})$, respectively. For the country as a whole, it is equal to total saving, i.e. public and private saving, minus investments. One immediately sees that if the surplus of saving over investments for the private sector and/or the government declines, then the current account position will diminish as well. In turn, disregarding net capital transactions, the evolution of the current account balance will be reflected in the financial

Box 10.1. **The link between the current account balance and the resident economy**
(cont.)

accounts, since a net current account deficit has to be funded by net financial inflows into the country and/or a variation in its holdings of foreign reserves. Of course, the above assumes that all other things remain equal. In reality, the situation is more complicated because the relevant variables interact. For example, if the government saves less, the deterioration in the country's current account position may be (partially) offset by increasing private saving (if, for example, economic agents are "Ricardian" and anticipate a future increase in taxes).

This simple framework has been often used to explain the features of the global economy in recent decades. One famous example was the twin deficit hypothesis that was put forward to explain the situation of the US economy in the 1980s and 1990s, marked by large government deficits which were mirrored by current account deficits (and net financial inflows into the US economy); see Figure 10.1. However the relationship was not

Figure 10.1. **US current account, saving minus investments of the private sector and government, 1960-2017**
Percentage of GDP

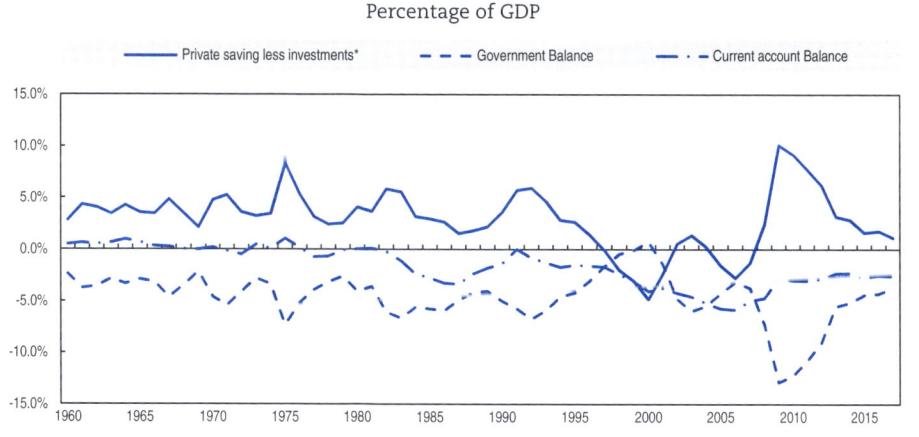

* Private saving less investments is calculated as a residual.
Source: Adapted from OECD (2016), *OECD Economic Outlook, Volume 2016* (database), http://dx.doi.org/10.1787/eco_outlook-v2016-1-en.

StatLink ᎏᏋᎮ http://dx.doi.org/10.1787/888933589238

permanent, and in fact the 2000s were marked by a strong improvement in the government balance, while the current account deficit widened significantly, reflecting a sharp deterioration in the balance of private saving and investments. Another example, this time of a "twin surplus", was the savings glut analysis in the 2000s, whereby the high private savings registered in a number of emerging Asian economies such as China were "matched" by persistently high current account surpluses. These surpluses were mirrored by net financial outflows, mostly invested in advanced economies' assets, resulting in a sharp expansion in the foreign exchange reserves held by emerging Asia.

A last caveat concerns the fact that external balances do not add up at the global level. The reporting of imports and exports do not match across countries; therefore, the sum of all countries' current account positions is not equal to zero as it should be. Indeed, the global economy has been characterised by an annual "current account surplus" of around 300 billion USD on average since the early 2010s, i.e. around 0.4% of world GDP, according to the IMF. By definition, this large statistical discrepancy underscores the uncertainty of any analysis on how domestic imbalances are matched by external financial flows.

Trigger of current account crises

The interrelationship between financial imbalances of domestic sectors and the external position of a country, as analysed above, has put emphasis on the role of international financial flows in triggering episodes of financial stress. Such crises typically occur when investors revise their expectations, leading to a sudden reversal in financial flows and/or a sharp tightening in the country's financing conditions, in turn constraining domestic spending.

Two generations of explanations have been particularly popular to explain this type of foreign exchange-related crises. The first is the balance of payments crisis, as explained by Krugman (1979): if authorities want to maintain an exchange rate that is not deemed sustainable because of weak domestic fundamentals, speculative attacks will eventually exhaust the stock of the country's foreign exchange reserves. Typically, there will be ups and downs in expectations, because speculators' psychology may be subject to reversals, for example in connection with the ability of governments to mobilise alternative funds, such as gold, or following concerted international actions (e.g. IMF programmes). Ultimately, however, the exchange rate may prove unsustainable because of accumulated external imbalances and/or spiralling domestic debt levels, putting into question the ability of the resident sectors to honour their liabilities. Short debt maturity and any foreign currency denomination of domestic debt will exacerbate the problems, since debt burdens would soar in domestic currency terms in case of devaluation. A number of such crises took place in developing regions in the 1980s and 1990s, especially when tighter global monetary conditions and/or weakening currencies exposed the underlying vulnerabilities of these economies and led investors to question the sustainability of their external lending.

Second generation crises, as explained by Obstfeld (1994), rely on the same type of analysis but with the difference that international investors may react to other factors as opposed to just "fundamentals". In particular, even a sound economy may be judged vulnerable because of its exposures to international finance and its inability to face potential shocks. Moreover, investors' expectations can interact with policy makers' behaviour to become self-fulfilling. For instance, even in the absence of imbalances ex ante, the exchange rate may be attacked if market participants believe that – to defend it – the authorities will tighten policy so much that the economy will suffer. Authorities may even not want to resist attacks in the first place, knowing that ultimately they will be defeated. This framework has been used to analyse the speculative attacks on the European Monetary System (EMS) in the early 1990s, especially when the pound sterling had to exit the European Exchange Rate Mechanism on 16 September 1992 (the "black Wednesday").

In both cases, the crisis can be seen as intrinsically linked to the external position of the country. There is little fragility if the domestic funding needs of specific sectors can be covered by savings from other domestic sectors. What matters is the financing of the economy as a whole, and hence its external position vis-à-vis the Rest of the World, both in terms of flows – a too large current account deficit may not be easily financed because of the limited availability of international financing in a specific year – and even more so in terms of stocks. The key element to be considered from a long-term perspective is the accumulation of the external liabilities of the country and (foreign) investors' confidence that they will be repaid (see also Box 10.2). The crisis occurs when these investors take the view that the country as a whole will be unable to service its external debt or to withstand capital outflows. It can break out very suddenly, even if it is the result of imbalances that have been building up for years.

To sum up, international financial flows can be a key trigger of current account crises either because they may lead to the build-up of external imbalances that at some point become unsustainable, or because they provide room for self-fulfilling attacks. As a consequence, the academic and market literature focus largely on "traditional" external indicators for assessing country risks: for instance, current account balances, short-term external funding needs, stocks of foreign exchange reserves (in particular compared to the amounts needed to cover countries' imports), exchange rate positions, etc. Policy recommendations, especially in international fora, have been along similar lines: the focus is to prevent the build-up of current account deficits deemed to be too large, while surplus countries are seen as insulated from financial risks and receive little pressure to adjust. One telling example has been the accumulation of large official foreign exchange reserves after the Asian crisis at the end of the 1990s: this war chest has been widely considered as an effective line of defence against the risk of future episodes of financial stress.

International finance and contagion effects beyond balance of payments crises

The exclusive focus on a country's balance of payments has been questioned over the past few decades, especially in the light of three major

Box 10.2. **Assessing external debt sustainability**

The assessment of the sustainability of the external position of a country can schematically be looked upon from a pure accounting perspective. As shown in Chapter 7, the net foreign liabilities (NFL) of a country are equal to (the inverse of) its net international investment position (IIP), which is the total foreign assets held by its residents minus their total liabilities incurred towards non-residents. One can write the following:

$$-(IIP_{t+1}) = NFL_{t+1} = NFL_t + \Delta NFL_{t+1}$$

where ΔNFL_{t+1} represents the change in the countries' net liabilities occurred in year $t + 1$, which – apart from revaluations, other changes in the volume of assets and liabilities, and some capital transfers – equals the current account balance (CA).

Similarly to public debt sustainability exercises, and defining "GDP_t" as the GDP in nominal terms for year t, "g" as its growth rate (small compared to 1), and "nfl" and "ca" as the NFL/GDP and the CA/GDP ratios respectively, one can arrive at the following equation:

$$nfl_{t+1} * (1+g) = nfl_t + ca_{t+1}$$

Hence, in a steady state, the ratio of net foreign liabilities, as a percentage of GDP, will be stable and equal to "nfl", if:

$$ca = nfl * g$$

The above thus provides a rule of thumb for evaluating whether the current account deficits expected for a country will put its foreign liabilities-to-GDP ratio on an unsustainable path. For instance, if the foreign net liabilities already represent 60% of GDP and the long-term nominal growth rate is 5%, then the country can register a yearly increase in its foreign liabilities – i.e. a permanent current account deficit – representing 3% of GDP, while still keeping a stable net external liabilities-to-GDP ratio, all other things being equal.

However, this simplified approach faces a number of challenges. The first is the adequate measurement of the total assets and liabilities of the country. While this is already far from easy for say the public sector (see Chapter 6), it is even more complicated for the country as a whole. In fact, numbers on IIPs are constantly and sometimes markedly revised, depending on the latest source data collected and/or on the valuation methods applied. Secondly, as noted before, the increase in net liabilities registered by a country in a given year does not solely reflects its current account deficit, but also other items such as capital transfers (e.g. public debt write-off in the case of the poorest countries). Thirdly, revaluations can have a very significant impact, and they can diverge markedly across the components of a country's assets and liabilities. The price of financial instruments (e.g. equity shares versus bonds) may evolve in opposite directions, and their currency composition and hence their valuation in the country's domestic currency may differ substantially.

A telling example is the US IIP, which has deteriorated over the past few decades but much less than what a simple accumulation of US current account deficits would suggest; see Figure 10.2. This in particular reflects valuation effects, especially those stemming from exchange rate movements and the idiosyncratic role played by the US Dollar (USD). US holdings of foreign assets have a relatively diversified currency portfolio, not least because

Box 10.2. **Assessing external debt sustainability** (cont.)

these assets comprise a significant amount of US Foreign Direct Investment (FDI) in a variety of countries. In contrast, the vast majority of US foreign liabilities are denoted in USD, reflecting the primary role played by the USD in international markets as well as the safe haven status of the US economy. As a consequence, when the USD is weakening vis-à-vis other major currencies, the value of US foreign assets in USD goes up, and the US IIP position improves. This effect is amplified over time as, irrespective of the level of the IIP (which is the net difference between assets and liabilities), the stocks of both foreign assets and liabilities have been increasing markedly with economic globalisation. For example, the value of US foreign liabilities now represents almost twice the level of US GDP, and any valuation effect on this large stock of liabilities will thus have a multiplied impact on the comparatively much smaller net IIP position.

In addition, the US situation underlines a number of puzzling elements that relativize any analysis one can make regarding the sustainability of a country's external position (Heath, 2007). The US net primary income balance has remained in positive territory (and slightly higher than the deficit in its secondary income balance), despite the fact that the US IIP is quite negative (around minus 45% of GDP at the end of 2016). This could suggest that a significant stock of US assets abroad, especially intangible assets, are inadequately captured by statistics (the "dark matter hypothesis"; cf. Hausmann and Sturzenegger [2005]). On the other hand, it shows that the income yield on US assets, which are relatively more invested in equity, is much higher that the income yield on US liabilities, which mostly consist of debt instruments. But a rather puzzling element in this respect is that, even for the same kind of investments such as foreign direct investment (FDI), investments in the US persistently earn lower yields than US investments abroad. This can reflect a variety of factors, such as the maturity of the investments, risk appetites, market share strategy, and the impact of tax incentives on the reporting of affiliates' incomes (e.g. intra-firm transfer pricing).

Figure 10.2. **US external position, 1976-2015**
Percentage of GDP

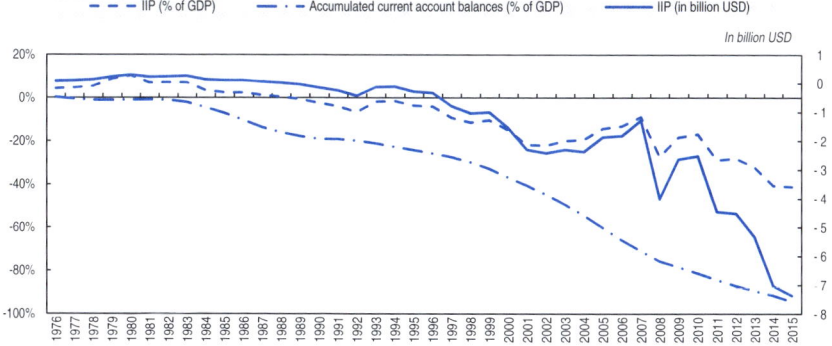

Source: Adapted from IMF (2016), *International Financial Statistics* (database), http://data.imf.org/?sk=5DABAFF2-C5AD-4D27-A175-1253419C02D1.

StatLink ▶ http://dx.doi.org/10.1787/888933589257

episodes. First was the long-lasting financial crisis that hit Japan at the beginning of the 1990s following a period of strong economic performance and large current accounts surpluses. This crisis was not characterised by a sudden reversal in financial flows and sharp exchange rate adjustments, but rather by the prolonged weakness of the Japanese economy following boom years that were driven by excessive risk-taking especially by domestic financial institutions.

Secondly, and similarly, the traditional current account crisis model did not adequately explain the 1997-98 Asian crisis. Some countries in the region did have important fragilities in terms of government deficits and high external debts, as a consequence of which international financial flows suddenly dried up when investors realised that, for example, Thailand's banks and Korean Chaebols had accumulated excessive foreign exchange exposures. However, the root of this crisis was more fundamentally due to excessive domestic lending and a concomitant deterioration in the quality of financial assets, exacerbated by moral hazard problems related to implicit public guarantees. Moreover, tensions that originated in Southeast Asia quickly reverberated in other, a priori unrelated, regions of the world such as Latin America and Russia.

Thirdly, the 2007-09 economic and financial crisis was primarily marked by the collapse of large financial institutions causing systemic, economy-wide disturbances (see Box 10.3). Excessive current account imbalances certainly played an important role for specific countries under attack, such as Iceland, Greece and Spain (which had current account deficits in 2008 of 23%, 14% and 9% of GDP, respectively). Moreover, large financial inflows in the United States facilitated the financing of sizeable current account deficits and in particular contributed to buoyant household spending and the related housing bubble. Yet flows directly related to balance of payments imbalances were only one of the various factors that played a role in the crisis.

Indeed, looking back in history, current account deficits do not necessarily coincide with the build-up of financial imbalances. Some of the most damaging financial crises have occurred in surplus countries – most spectacularly in the United States before the Great Depression of the 1930s (Borio et al., 2014). The exclusive focus on current account imbalances has sometimes even been misleading, as it encouraged pressure on current account surplus countries to expand domestic demand even at times that financial fragilities were building up, as in the case of Japan before the 1990s.

From this perspective, international finance can contribute to financial crises in a broader way than just through the external financing channel. In particular, contagion can arise through perception, spillovers and psychological effects. First, the reversal of investors' perceptions can trigger destabilising

Box 10.3. **The 2007-09 economic and financial crisis and its consequences – Main episodes**

The 2007-09 economic and financial crisis had several phases and led to various periods of financial stress, especially following the contagion to Euro Area sovereign debt in the early 2010s. The following are the main episodes of the crisis (see Carnot et al. [2011] for a more detailed summary of the various events).

The financial boom (first half of the 2000s): threefold rise in US house prices from the mid-1990s to 2006; sharp increase in subprime lending; financial innovation; marked decline in US private savings.

The peak of the bubble (end 2006/May 2007): sudden increase in mortgage delinquency rates; subprime lender bankruptcies; wider spreads on home equity Collateralised Debt Obligations (CDOs); growing signs of volatility in global financial markets.

First stage of the crisis (June 2007/first half 2008): asset-backed securities downgrades by rating agencies; closure of hedge funds and freeze of investment funds; start of the dislocation in interbank money markets; warning of US-related losses by Germany's IKB Deutsche Industriebank AG preceding the first US interest rate cut (17 August 2007); public support for Northern Rock (United Kingdom) and government-sponsored enterprises (United States); co-ordinated action by advanced economies' central banks.

Global loss of confidence (September/October 2008): general shock caused by Lehman Brothers' bankruptcy (15 September 2008); US support for AIG; severe disruptions in interbank money markets and foreign exchange swap markets; co-ordinated set-up of central bank foreign exchange swap lines; US Troubled Asset Relief Program (TARP) to remove bad assets from banks; government interventions to support large banks all over the world; sharp devaluation of the ISK (Icelandic króna), and the IMF programme in Hungary; G7 pledge to take "all necessary steps" and save key banks from collapse (October 2008).

General economic downturn and economic stabilisation (end 2008/end 2009): G20 launch of a far-reaching reform plan for the financial system; bold central bank interventions (Federal Reserve expansion of unconventional policy measures including purchases of US Treasury, ECB purchase of covered bonds); the US Great Recession that began in December 2007 ends in June 2009, and large US financial firms start to repay government aid.

Contagion to sovereigns in the Euro Area (end-2009/2012): lowering of Greece's rating (December 2009); spillovers to Ireland and Portugal (mid-January 2010); sharp rise in the spreads of the Euro Area sovereign debt Credit Default Swaps (CDS); EU/IMF fiscal packages and ECB direct purchases of securities; establishment of European stability mechanisms and reorganisation of the European banking system; implementation of the Basel III framework for banks'

> Box 10.3. **The 2007-09 economic and financial crisis
> and its consequences – Main episodes** *(cont.)*
>
> capital and liquidity; Comprehensive Monetary Easing in Japan (5 October 2010) and Quantitative Easing Part 2 in the United States (3 November 2010); widening of the debt crisis to large Euro Area countries such as Spain and Italy in 2011/12; introduction of the Swiss exchange-rate peg to the Euro (2011); ECB announcement to do "whatever it takes to preserve the Euro" (July 2012); boost for emerging markets provided by very accommodative global financial conditions, with the risk of a build-up in domestic vulnerabilities.
>
> **Progressive calm in global markets (early 2013/2015):** several policy actions in the Euro Area; rescue of Cyprus[1, 2]; termination of the bailout programmes for Ireland, Spain and Portugal; early signals of potential reduction in US monetary stimulus (the summer 2013 "taper tantrum"); ECB introduction of negative interest rates (mid 2014) followed by Switzerland (end 2014); Swiss peg abandoned in 2015; despite renewed Greek concerns in summer 2015, general signs of stabilisation in advanced economies.
>
> **Start of monetary policy normalisation (end 2015/2017):** growing vulnerabilities in emerging market economies following years of rapid credit expansion as well as the combination of an appreciating USD and lower commodity prices since mid-2014; Chinese devaluation in August 2015 and signs of volatility in financial markets; Japan's move to negative interest rates; and further unconventional monetary stimulus by the ECB in the beginning of 2016; first rise in US interest rates since the crisis in December 2015, setting the stage for a gradual withdrawal of the very accommodative global monetary conditions in the course of 2016-17.

financial flows out of a country even if its current account position is balanced. For instance, foreign exchange exposures can be concentrated in a specific sector for which the related currency/maturity mismatches might be hard to deal with – consider the case of foreign-indebted corporates mainly selling their products in domestic markets. There are also limits to how far other agents' foreign assets can be mobilised to "cover" the funding needs of a specific sector. A case in point are official reserves, considered by many observers as useful to protect against potential destabilising financial outflows; yet authorities may be reluctant to use these "war chests" to cover private funding gaps, because of technical challenges (the maturity and currency denomination of the various instruments may differ) as well as moral hazard concerns. Moreover, selling external assets to cover liabilities in times of stress may be difficult in practice, not least due to liquidity issues. From this perspective, looking at external positions on a net terms basis presents the risk of overlooking the underlying fragilities related to the overall stock of assets and liabilities in case of a sudden change in investors' perceptions.

A second important element is due to spillover effects reflecting the impact of so-called "push factors". These push factors are associated with the origins of financial flows, in contrast to the traditional analysis of international crises that focuses on countries' specific fundamentals or "pull factors", associated with the destination of international financial flows. The key idea behind the push factors analysis is that international investors can react irrespective of the idiosyncratic situation of a particular country. Push factors therefore have a lot to do with the state of the global financial system, for instance when there is a general tightening in spreads in international bond markets (see below) or when global portfolios are rebalanced. Contagions across countries will then reflect similar decisions taken by investors on the basis of similar rationales, such as the reliance on specific commodities, the level of trade links and the existence of common exposures to a variety of risks (Tirolle, 2002). However, contagions may also result from more complex elements, such as the impact of random events on global expectations; information biases, for instance when "noisy signals" become the basis of investment decisions; and various cumulative chain reactions, via links in the payment systems, the interbank market, or the complex network of global debtor-creditor relations (Goodhart and Illing, 2002). From this perspective, contagion is purely triggered by the financial context and can arise from the overlapping claims that different regions or sectors have on one another (Allen and Gale, 2007). The global integration of financial markets is likely to have reinforced these dynamics, with growing "common factors" driving financial flows, risk premiums and asset prices all together.

Yet a third, related element is the role played by psychological factors, which can be instrumental in triggering contagion effects across sectors and borders. In fact, there is significant evidence that market participants tend to behave in a correlated manner, with typical herd behaviour (e.g. buying when prices go up), collective irrational enthusiasm for the latest trends (e.g. the Dutch tulip mania of the 17th century), and the importance of moral hazard issues (e.g. the incentive for economic agents to take excessive risks as they anticipate that in case of problems they will benefit from public support). A recent example was the general complacency during the US house price boom in the 2000s, characterised by weak lending standards and lenient underwriting practices. As argued by Robert Shiller (2008), the over-valuation of real estate in those circumstances was brought on by a "contagion of bad thinking". Americans as a whole became convinced that fundamentals driving the real estate market, such as personal income, the cost of building and the ratio of home values to rent, no longer mattered.

All the contagion effects above may be particularly powerful for emerging markets that are often considered as part of the same asset class: as a result, any country-specific shock can lead to a general modification of investors' portfolio allocation, impacting other countries irrespective of their own economic situation. But contagion effects are not confined to the developing world. The 1982 Latin American debt crisis led to significant problems in the US banking system. Similarly, tensions that originated in the US subprime markets during the 2000s quickly reverberated in the global financial system, in particular in Europe, after the 2007-09 economic and financial crisis.

3. Assessing the build-up of financial risks in a globalised world

Sovereign debt, banking crises, and the impact of globalisation

Traditionally, a financial crisis used to be associated with sovereign default, with government unable to repay its debt. In closed economies, the way out of such crises was by finding a possibility of repudiating or rescheduling the obligations of the government vis-à-vis its resident investors. However, in modern history sovereign debt crises have typically occurred with a significant part of the public debt held by non-resident investors. Indeed, globalisation has allowed investors to diversify their portfolios across countries, reducing home bias. From this perspective, episodes of financial stress have increasingly entailed an external component, as they involve foreign creditors at least to some extent. In case of a sovereign default, international investors, for instance, have to collectively agree on a rescheduling of the government debt – as is done in the context of the Paris Club for public sector creditors or of the London Club for commercial banks. All in all, external current account crises and sovereign debt crises are often mixed.

Sovereign debt crises are also tightly intertwined with another type of crisis referred to as a "banking crisis" (see IMF, 2015). The reason is that banks usually have large holdings of domestic government debt securities in their books, so any concern about the position of the government can quickly adversely affect banks' balance sheets. Conversely, governments are seen as exposed to any failure of their domestic banks, either because of formal commitments (deposit insurance schemes) or because of investors' perception that they would offer support in case of stress. Laeven and Valencia (2013) estimate that around 40% of crises are "pure currency crises", 10% are "pure debt crises", and 30% are "pure banking crises", the rest being "twin crises" and "triplet crises". Obviously, such classifications can be quite arbitrary, depending in particular on the various thresholds applied. But they nevertheless underline the sheer diversity of the episodes of stress that can occur and the importance of their financial stability dimension.

Globalisation is likely to have reinforced these interactions. Empirical evidence shows that government debt as well as banking crises are particularly severe when they involve foreign funding. Moreover, economic development has led to a sharp expansion of the financial liabilities incurred by all sectors, including private sectors. Indeed, one can distinguish three forces that have driven the expansion of international financial links with the globalisation of economic activity (BIS, 2017c): one was the need to finance the expansion in cross-border trade (that is, to deal with the settlement of trade transactions); the second was the financing arrangements related to the fragmentation of production across countries in global value chains (GVCs); and a third was the increasing need for managing balance sheet positions at a global level. As a result, financial openness has substantially outpaced real trade openness since the late 1980s, especially for advanced economies. One implication is that financial fragilities can occur in different regions and various sectors of the economy (e.g. the government, financial corporations, households, non-financial corporations) and have system-wide consequences, leading to financial instability.

A framework for assessing the build-up of vulnerabilities during financial cycles

Whatever the characteristics of financial stress episodes, a key element to consider is the role played by the financial cycle (BIS, 2015a). The financial cycle is defined as a succession of long-lasting episodes of financial booms and busts, and characterised by a much wider amplitude and length compared to "traditional" business cycles; see Figure 10.3 for the US case. Needless to say, the financial accounts framework is a key instrument to assess this financial cycle in general and the episodes of crises in particular, because it is a useful tool to capture the evolution of leverage by economic sector (Dembiermont et al., 2013).

The upward phase of the financial cycle starts with a boom in credit and asset prices. As a result, private sector debt-to-GDP ratios rise sharply, supporting spending and output. Excessively favourable financial conditions are instrumental in driving these boom episodes. They often take the form of very low credit spreads and volatility, aggressive risk-taking among investors, and interest rates that are well below their "equilibrium" levels. Another common feature is "liquidity illusion", as market liquidity often appears ample in boom times, before vanishing quickly during episodes of stress. A key issue is that these financial forces can be self-amplifying, with a feedback loop between overly optimistic perceptions of risk and value, on the one hand, and weak financing constraints, on the other hand. The financial system is thus said to be "pro-cyclical" – this refers to the progressive build-up of financial fragility and how aggregate risk evolves over time (Crockett, 2000). An important driver of this pro-cyclicality is that higher asset prices boost the value of collaterals, making borrowing easier and supporting leverage-financed spending – one will often refer to positive "wealth" effects in this context, which can be very powerful, in particular when they concern the impact of housing valuations on household spending.[3]

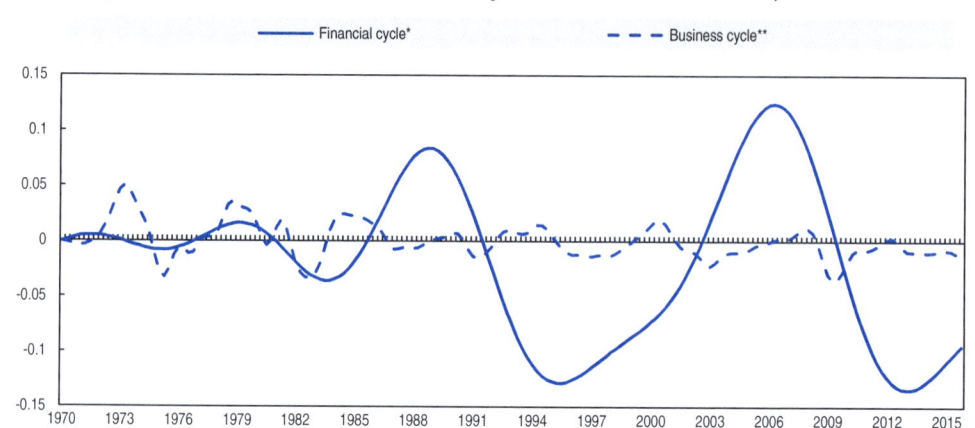

Figure 10.3. **Financial and business cycles in the United States, 1970-2016**

* The financial cycle as measured by frequency-based (bandpass) filters capturing medium-term cycles in real credit, the credit-to-GDP ratio and real house prices.
** The business cycle as measured by a frequency-based (bandpass) filter capturing fluctuations in real GDP over a period from one to eight years.
Source: Adapted from Drehmann et al. (2012), "Characterising the financial cycle: don't lose sight of the medium term!", www.bis.org/publ/work380.htm.

StatLink ⟶ http://dx.doi.org/10.1787/888933589276

The process, however, goes into reverse as increased leverage gradually leads to a negative drag on disposable income from increasing debt service burdens. At some point, investors start to realise that balance sheets have become excessively overstretched and that financial imbalances cannot be sustained any more. This turning point – also called a "Minsky moment" (Minsky, 1982) – can be quite rapid, as it depends on the change in perceptions of the accumulated fragilities. The ensuing financial bust is precipitated by a general deleveraging and sharp corrections in asset prices. This, in turn, makes borrowing more difficult and further depresses demand, reinforcing pressures on asset prices: the downward phase of the financial cycle is therefore also very pro-cyclical. In the end, demand takes significant time to normalise because of the lagged impact of accumulated debt and of the necessity to repair balance sheets.

Apart from its pro-cyclicality, systemic risk has a second, "cross-sectional" dimension. This relates to how financial risk is distributed within the system at a given point in time. It explains why an apparently idiosyncratic shock, instead of being limited to the failure of an individual firm, can propagate itself within the entire financial system, both within a country and across borders. Such a system-wide propagation can result from two main aspects (Caruana, 2010).

First of all, economic agents' balance sheets are interconnected, so that a shock hitting one institution can quickly spread to the other connected institutions that are otherwise sound. This raises the risk of "bank-run" type episodes, when suspicions about the soundness of a counterparty can quickly spill over and lead to the paralysis of the financial system. The Herstatt German bank was a good example of that mechanism. When this bank had to suddenly stop its operations in 1974, some of its counterparties had already undertaken transactions with it and were unable to collect their payments.

A second aspect of the "cross-sectional" dimension of systemic risk is that non-directly connected institutions can be affected by the same shock because of their common exposures, for example if they are similarly exposed to a specific asset class, such as the US housing subprime mortgage loans in the 2000s. A variety of financial factors, such as asset prices, market liquidity and funding conditions, can drive such common exposures effects. One irony is that efforts to reduce bilateral interconnections may lead market participants to diversify their activities so much that, ultimately, they display a more homogeneous profile and become more exposed to the risk of common exposures.

International finance adding fuel to the fire?

International finance has largely contributed to the development of these two key aspects of the financial system, that is, the pro-cyclicality of systemic risk and the importance of system-wide common exposures/interlinkages. In fact, it is no coincidence that the amplitude and length of financial cycles seem to have increased considerably since the financial liberalisation undertaken in the 1970s. This has generated a so-called "excess financial elasticity" in the global system (BIS, 2015a), for three main reasons.

First, there has been the growing importance for domestic economies of global financial flows, which can move freely across currencies and borders (Heath, 2015). In particular, the financial liberalisation initiated in the 1980s has made funding easier and cheaper[4] to obtain for a wider range of borrowers. For example, emerging market economies are nowadays much more integrated into the global financial system than ever before. The result, however, is that financial interconnections have increased across countries, facilitating the propagation of systemic risk around the globe. Looking at the 28 major financial centres (including China) representing over 80% of global GDP, the Financial Stability Board (FSB) estimates that total financial assets represented USD 321 trillion in 2016, i.e. about five times total GDP (FSB, 2017).

Two important financial intermediation phases have been particularly powerful in the recent decades. The first phase was mainly characterised in the second half of the 20th century by the expansion of cross-border operations of internationally active commercial banks. The international banking statistics (IBS) collected by the Bank for International Settlements (BIS) show that the outstanding amount of banks' global cross-border claims has steadily increased, from about 5 trillion USD in the mid-1970s to around 30 trillion USD in the late 2000s, after which the outstanding amount has roughly stabilised around the latter level and actually declined as a share of global GDP (BIS, 2015b). The second phase has entailed a shift from bank lending to market finance, with the sharp expansion of international debt securities issued by financial and non-financial corporations. This reflects, in particular, the increased debt issuance by emerging market borrowers in advanced economies and/or offshore centres, either directly or through their controlled affiliates. The outstanding amount of international debt securities, as estimated by the BIS, now represents more than 20 trillion USD, compared to just 5 trillion at the beginning of the 2000s. A telling example of this globalisation of financial markets is China, which by the mid-2010s had become the world's 8th largest borrower in terms of cross-border bank claims and the 11th largest borrower as measured by the issuance of international debt securities by its nationals.

Secondly, financial systems worldwide have changed markedly and have become extremely diversified in terms of actors and products, allowing for a greater interaction with the "real economy". Housing finance has in particular evolved dramatically, through the development of securitisation and the increased ability to take credit by pledging home equity as collateral. Another key factor has been the deepening of bond markets, facilitating firms' access to capital market funding and widening the investor base. Yet another important aspect has been financial innovation with the development of new instruments, complex financial engineering and the diversification of the credit intermediation chain that is no longer limited to "traditional" banking financial intermediaries (see below).

Thirdly, the globalisation of the financial system has heightened the likelihood for financial imbalances to occur simultaneously across countries due to the common influence of global factors. This highlights the powerful role played by "global liquidity", a concept that can be understood as the degree of ease of financing in global financial markets. Credit is obviously among the key indicators to be considered for estimating this global liquidity. In particular, the BIS has constructed three indicators of global liquidity by drawing on national data and its own international banking and financial statistics: banks' international claims, banks' total claims on the private non-financial sectors, and total credit by currency of denomination. The concept of "global liquidity" refers to a property of the system as a whole, resulting from the global interaction of private investors, financial institutions and monetary authorities, which in turn is setting the tone in countries' domestic credit and market liquidity conditions. A key element supporting these transmission mechanisms is the role played by international funding currencies, which are increasingly used outside the issuing country's borders (McCauley et al., 2015). For example, the USD-denominated debt of non-bank borrowers that are not US residents has steadily increased in recent years, to around 10 trillion USD; see Figure 10.4.

As a consequence, US monetary conditions are increasingly affecting borrowers located outside the US economy. Another important channel is the role of exchange rate policies, explicit or implicit. For instance, if the US financing conditions are accommodative, other countries may be tempted to reduce their interest rate differentials vis-à-vis the US to avoid an excessive appreciation of their own currencies. By importing de facto the US monetary stance irrespective of the situation of their economies, these countries run the risk of having inadequate domestic financial conditions, leading to the subsequent build-up of financial vulnerabilities.

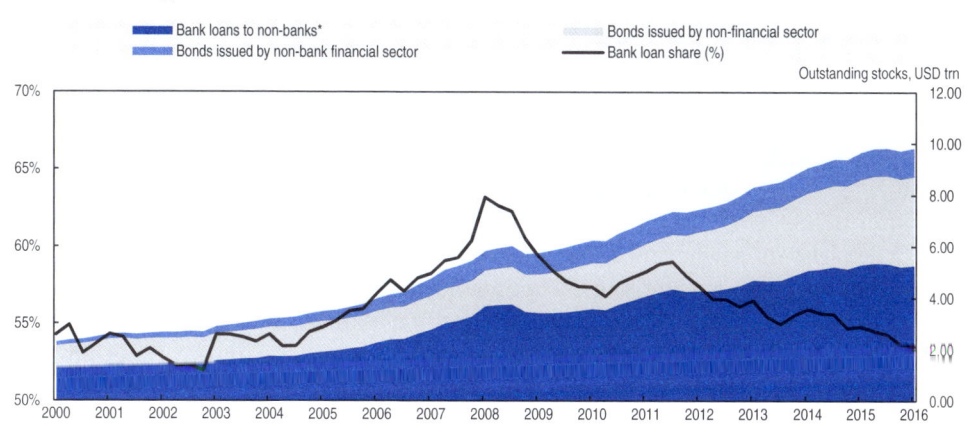

Figure 10.4. **USD credit to non-banks outside the United States**

* Bank loans include cross-border and locally extended loans to non-banks outside the United States. For China, locally extended loans are derived from national data on total local lending in foreign currencies on the assumption that 80% are denominated in USD. For other non-BIS reporting countries, local USD loans to non-banks are proxied by all BIS reporting banks' gross cross-border USD loans to banks in the country. Bonds issued by US national non-bank financial sector entities resident in the Cayman Islands have been excluded.

Source: BIS (2017a), *Locational Banking Statistics* (database), www.bis.org/statistics/bankstats.htm?m=6%7C31%7C69; IMF (2017), *International Financial Statistics* (database), http://data.imf.org/?sk=5DABAFF2-C5AD-4D27-A175-1253419C02D1; Thomson Reuters (2017), *DataStream* (database), https://financial.thomsonreuters.com/en/products/tools-applications/trading-investment-tools/datastream-macroeconomic-analysis.html.

StatLink ⟶ http://dx.doi.org/10.1787/888933589295

What are the implications of financial globalisation for systemic risk? As regards its system-wide dimension, the development of international finance is likely to have multiplied the potential channels allowing for contagion effects. The enormous expansion of investment funds means that portfolio reallocations at the global level can lead to large swings in asset prices across borders. The role of large and complex financial institutions operating globally has also reinforced these effects. The result is that global financial conditions can easily pass through to domestic economies in a simultaneous way and trigger seemingly unrelated domestic financial fragilities.

As regards the pro-cyclical dimension of systemic risk, external sources of credit expansion, especially in foreign currency, appear to be playing a key role in encouraging procyclicality as they often provide the marginal source of funding feeding episodes of financial booms. As can be seen in Figure 10.5, growth in international bank credit to both banks and non-bank borrowers has tended to be very strong in the upward phase of the financial cycle (for instance during the 2000s), characterised by buoyant financial conditions and subdued volatility in markets (here measured through the VIX Index, a barometer of investor sentiment and market volatility derived from stock option prices). Episodes of financial stress such as in 2008-09, on the contrary, are characterised by a surge in volatility and the drying up of international bank credit. The high procyclicality of international financing flows may explain why attention has focused so much on external positions to explain financial crises. As financial booms often involve excessive spending, the fact that cheap external funding is available can facilitate and exacerbate the build-up of domestic fragilities. In other words, international finance can add fuel to the fire. One telling example is the evolution of the US housing boom prior to the 2007-09 economic and financial crisis, characterised by a decline in households' saving and an increase in residential investment (Palumbo and Parker, 2009). As a result, the US household sector moved from a net lending position in the 1990s to a net borrowing position in the 2000s, with a very large expansion of its liabilities (mainly mortgage debt). This was mostly financed by a sharp expansion in the net lending provided by the Rest of the World.

Figure 10.5. **The relationship between financial markets volatility and international bank credit, 1978-2016**

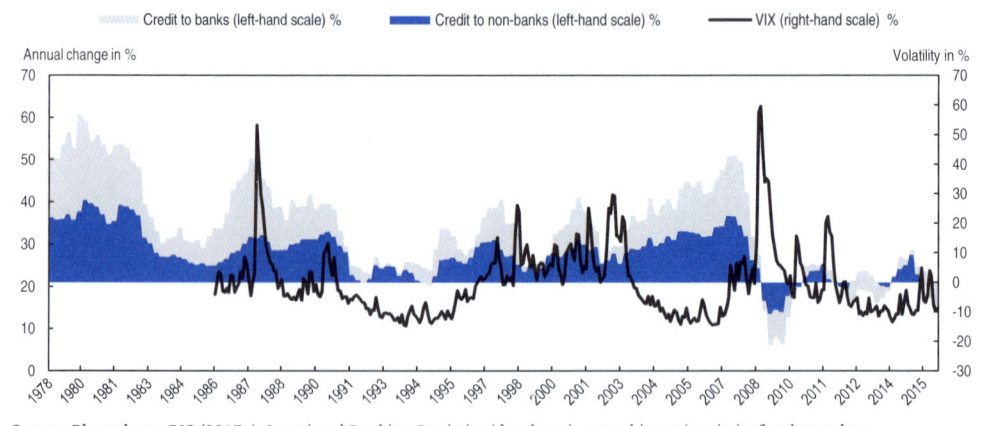

Source: Bloomberg, BIS (2017a), *Locational Banking Statistics* (database), www.bis.org/statistics/bankstats.htm.

StatLink http://dx.doi.org/10.1787/888933589314

4. Analysing the impacts of leverage and financial innovation on economic growth and policy

The central role played by leverage

Debt has a central role in the build-up of crises, and the ability to reduce leverage has a central role in ending crises. Certainly, the level of necessary debt reduction after a boom can differ significantly, both across sectors and times. But a general feature is that the longer deleveraging is postponed, the more difficulties the economy faces to return to a steady-state growth path. From this perspective, gaining time and postponing necessary adjustments often has to be paid back in terms of a longer period of sub-par growth and more persistent financial fragilities.

As regards the non-financial private sector, a common pattern is that its debt as a percentage of GDP expands rapidly in the boom years preceding a financial crisis. This trend quickly reverses after the bust as balance sheets have to be repaired. Yet the rhythm of this deleveraging can vary markedly, depending in particular on policy incentives to ensure that debt is repaid by debtors and/or written off by creditors. To favour private debt reduction once the crisis hits, it is usually necessary to proceed to a full restructuring of the financial sector itself. The key is to make lenders recognise the true quality of their assets, restructure their accumulated stocks of "bad debts", and raise adequate capital to cover the resulting losses. This often requires strong public interventions to guarantee deposits (partially to avoid bank runs and panic reactions), to close the weakest institutions, and to force the other institutions to clean their books – often by providing public support like guarantees, purchases of illiquid assets, provision of direct loans, recapitalisation of ailing institutions (and even nationalisation, at least temporarily), or the setting up of ad hoc public-guaranteed defeasance structures tasked to take over impaired assets.

Turning to the public sector, its financial position usually deteriorates sharply after the bust and for several years in crisis-hit economies. This reflects the strain on public finances that comes from bailing out the financial system, as well as the effect of lower economic growth and increasing unemployment on the income and expenditure of government. This can lead to a fast and protracted expansion of government debt-to-GDP ratios, which can in turn bring its own risks in terms of financial stability. Examples of the latter are the long-lasting difficulties experienced by a number of Euro Area countries in the early 2010s that had let their public debt soar after the 2007-09 economic and financial crisis. The reason is that sound public finances are a key factor anchoring the stability of the financial system and the economy as a whole, not least due to the benchmark role played by the yields on government debt securities for most financial market prices. Hence, there is a clear trade-off between the need for some government support to accompany the deleveraging of the private sector, and the necessity to preserve the credibility of fiscal authorities.

At the level of the economy as a whole, the picture after a financial crisis will depend on the combination of private (usually down) and public (usually up) leverage patterns. In aggregate, total debt may remain quite high even many years after the bust. However, history shows that different scenarios can happen (Dembiermont et al., 2015). A widely recognised example of successful deleveraging occurred in a number of Nordic countries that saw a collapse in their banking systems in the early 1990s. In both Finland and Sweden, private sector debt came down quickly after the crisis, reflecting strong policy actions. This was accompanied by a sharp deterioration in government accounts. However, this situation was temporary and the public debt trajectory was able to correct downwards rapidly once most of the deleveraging of the private sector had been completed.

A rather opposite example relates to the situation in Japan at the beginning of the 1990s. Private sector deleveraging was quite muted after the collapse of the asset price bubble, and was mainly concentrated in the non-financial corporate sector. Household debt as a percentage of GDP continued to rise slightly several years after the crisis and was not corrected afterwards. The restructuring of the financial system was delayed over a long period of time, with banks continuing to keep a large amount of bad debts in their books. Japan's public debt rose, though less rapidly initially than it did in the Nordic cases, reflecting the slower repairing of banks' balance sheets. But in the end, the government debt position worsened over a much longer period of time and ended up at a much larger level.

Turning now to the last economic and financial crisis in 2007-09, the picture is still relatively mixed. Almost ten years after the bust, overall debt reduction seems to have only just started; see Figure 10.6. Total debt in the non-financial sector of the advanced economies affected by the crisis has expanded significantly since 2007, by about 35 percentage points of GDP. There are certainly important differences between countries, with, for example, a somewhat quicker pay-down of debt in the United States and the United Kingdom. In aggregate, however, the debt dynamics of the advanced economies have resembled more the pattern of those of Japan than of the Nordic countries in the early 1990s. Aggregate private debt has barely stabilised since the 2007-09 economic and financial crisis, let alone started to be corrected downwards, even in the corporate sector. And government debt has continued to rise steadily, in a manner reminiscent of Japan's trend deterioration in the 1990s, and unlike the large but temporary deterioration followed by a rapid improvement in fiscal positions experienced by the Nordic states during the same period.

Figure 10.6. **Private and public debt patterns before and after the 2007-09 economic and financial crisis, 2002-15**
2002 = 100

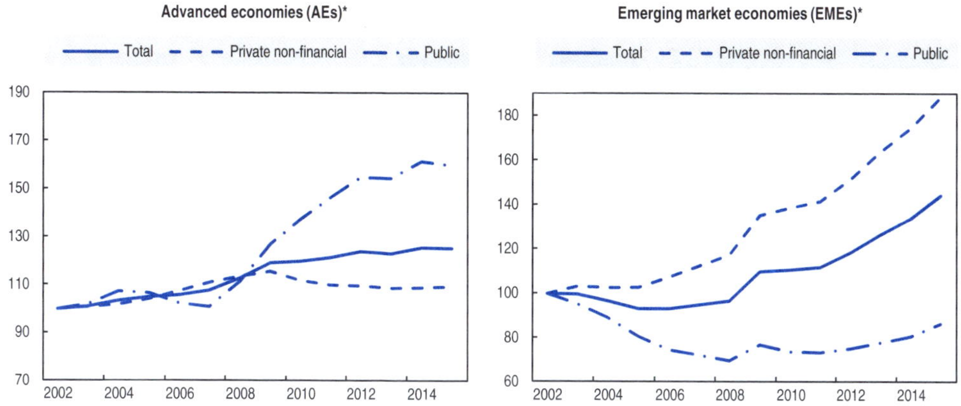

* Regional aggregates calculated by using PPP weights; valuation at market prices, except EMEs' public debt in nominal terms.
Source: Adapted from BIS (2017b), *Credit to the Non-financial Sector* (database), www.bis.org/statistics/totcredit.htm?m= 6%7C326.

StatLink http://dx.doi.org/10.1787/888933589333

Financial innovation and the need to address complexity

The 2007-09 economic and financial crisis underscored the importance of innovation in the financial system, which is constantly and rapidly evolving in ways that are difficult to follow, especially for policy makers. The first important development from this perspective has been the banks' move from their traditional "originate-to-hold" intermediation model towards the "originate-to-distribute" model, in which banks resell loans via securitisation (this is also discussed in Chapter 3).

Adrian and Shin (2013) define the traditional "originate-to-hold" model as a "short intermediation chain", with the stylised representation pertaining to the mortgage market presented in Figure 10.7 (left panel). To put it simply, the bank is directly intermediating between the households who have deposits and those who need to borrow to buy a house. A similar stylised diagram underlines the "long intermediation chain" for the "originate to distribute" model (right panel). In that case, creditors place their savings in some investment funds, which in turn invest in commercial banks. Such investments can have a very short-term nature, as households are typically able to withdraw their savings from institutions such as money market funds quite easily. The system thus leads to significant maturity transformation, as banks invest their short-term funds in structures of composite (and often complex) financial products (asset backed securities, or ABSs) issued by the ABS issuers repackaging individual mortgage loans.

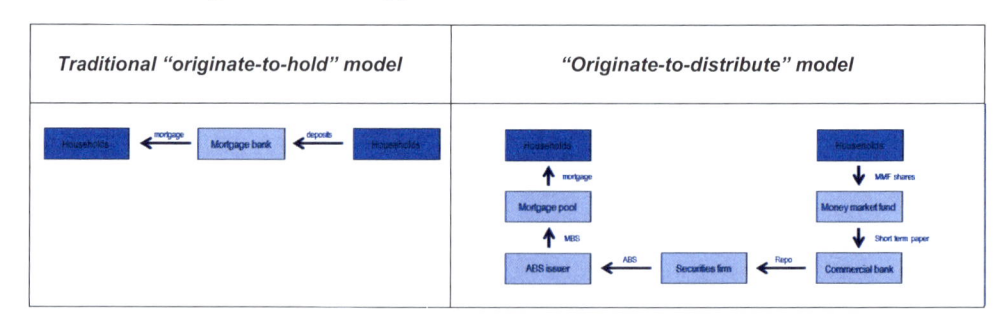

Figure 10.7. **Two types of financial intermediation chains**

Traditional "originate-to-hold" model	"Originate-to-distribute" model
Households ← mortgage ← Mortgage bank ← deposits ← Households	Households → mortgage → Mortgage pool → MBS → ABS issuer ← ABS ← Securities firm ← Repo ← Commercial bank → Short term paper → Money market fund → MMF shares → Households

Source: Adrian and Shin (2010), "The changing nature of financial intermediation and the financial crisis of 2007-09".

It has been claimed that this new, long intermediation chain presents several advantages: for example, securitisation may enable dispersion of credit risk (since the investor is exposed to the risks of several mortgages bundled in a specific ABS product) and promote more efficient maturity transformation (since the short-term deposits by creditor households are at the end funding long-term loans for mortgage borrowers). However, as highlighted by Adrian and Shin (2010), the evidence observed during the 2007-09 economic and financial crisis points the other way. Firstly, instead of mixing the risk profiles of various assets they held, investors were able to buy specific high-yielding "tranches" whose credit quality was concentrated on highly indebted agents, for example, US households with low credit ratings borrowing in "subprime markets". Secondly, the length and complexity of the originate-to-distribute chain led to a sharp disconnection between the perceived quality of the ABS products and the value of the underlying mortgages. And thirdly, financial intermediaries were more intertwined than expected, especially as the process relied on unsustainable maturity transformation (i.e., investors were forced to sell their ABS products when they faced a drying up in their short-term financing, triggering a downward spiral of asset prices). This in fact reflected investors' "liquidity illusion" before the crisis, when they (wrongly) thought that the complex assets were liquid and could be easily exchanged; as it turned out, these assets could only be sold with large discounts.

The expansion of leverage, combined with banks' move to the new originate-to-distribute model, has favoured the expansion of "shadow banking" entities. This category comprises all entities outside the regulated banking system that perform core banking functions and are therefore very active in providing leverage-based maturity and liquidity transformation (Kodres, 2013). As seen in Chapter 3, the framework of financial accounts and balance sheets can be mobilised to track these entities which are outside the "traditional" area covering banks, insurers, pension funds, etc. Although in practice the identification of these entities may be challenging and differs across countries, it is estimated that the total assets of the "other financial intermediaries" (OFIs) sector represented USD 92 trillion in 2016 for the major jurisdictions analysed by the FSB. This represented 29% of global financial assets (estimated at USD 321 trillion), compared to 42% for "traditional" banks, 7% for central banks, 9% for pension funds and 9% for insurance corporations (FSB, 2017).

Another, more pertinent, measure of the shadow banking sector has been developed by the FSB. This measure only includes the non-bank financial entities that are considered by authorities to be involved in credit intermediation where risks for financial stability may occur. This "narrow measure" of shadow banking is estimated to represent, in terms of the value of assets, around one-third of the OFIs' size in 2016; that is, USD 34 trillion and 69% of the GDP of the 27 major advanced and emerging economies covered by the FSB (China being excluded from this narrow measure).

To conduct such an exercise, the FSB schematically differentiates five main types of economic functions performed by shadow banks (FSB, 2017). The first is the management of client cash pools, by, for example, real estate investment funds which pool investors' funds to purchase assets and have features that make them susceptible to runs. A second is the provision of loans dependent on short-term funding by, for example, so-called finance companies that issue commercial paper and use the proceeds to extend credit to households. A third is the intermediation of market activities, realised through short-term funding and/or the secured funding of client assets, performed by, for example, broker dealers. A fourth is the facilitation of credit creation, by, for example, credit insurance companies and financial guarantors. And a fifth is credit intermediation based on securitisation and funding of financial entities, by securitisation vehicles such as Special Purpose Vehicles (SPVs).

The developments in non-bank credit intermediation, as analysed above, would have been impossible without the major advances in information technology and the financial innovations observed in recent decades. Computers not only store and process vast amounts of information, they also make it possible to "slice and dice" portfolios and to transfer them more easily from one entity to another. Technology and financial innovation have therefore spurred an increase in the number of entities participating in financial transactions and multiplied the links that connect them in ever broader networks.

In any case, the old-fashioned assumption that there are specific sectors specialised in lending to distinct borrowing sectors is not relevant anymore. For instance, most deposit-taking institutions now act as both lenders and borrowers. Combined with the growing importance of the less regulated area of shadow banks, this has led to an increasingly opaque and complex network of interconnected financial relationships across a wide range of institutions, markets and instruments. In turn, the interactions between the financial sphere and the real economy have become more diversified, more complex to analyse, and presumably also more conducive to financial risk-taking by various agents. Needless to say, this reinforces the usefulness of having comprehensive financial accounts and balance sheets that facilitate the measurement and understanding of such interactions.

This is particularly important since increased complexity and global interconnectedness in financial markets can generate strong co-movements in crisis periods which in turn make systemic crises more probable. As pointed out in Haldane (2009), "… the past twenty years have resulted in a financial system with high and rising degrees of interconnection, a long-tailed degree distribution and small world properties. That is an unholy trinity. From a stability perspective, it translates into a robust-yet-fragile system, susceptible to a loss of confidence in the key financial hubs and with rapid international transmission of disturbances".

Indeed, the challenges that increased complexity raises are enormous. The 2007-09 economic and financial crisis highlighted the difficulties of the determination of appropriate market prices, suggesting that the efficient market hypothesis cannot be respected since prices are not able to reflect the vast and complex amount of information to be considered. It also underscored the weakness of the traditional national accounts frameworks that rely on the representative agent model, which considers identically all decision-makers of a certain type (for example, the typical consumer), at least at the aggregate level. In reality, a key component of financial exposures is counterparty risk, implying that the impact of an exposure to a group of heterogeneous agents is not the same as the sum of the individual exposures to them. Furthermore, it highlighted the importance of non-linear dynamics, with sudden shifts in the state of the economy leading to opposite outcomes, and of extreme events. Complexity may furthermore prevent clear and transparent information, thus undermining trust and creating obstacles to the normal flow of transactions. This is precisely what happened in 2008 when the interbank market froze because many of the major banks refused to lend to each other in the absence of information on the true quality and value of their assets. This was a key issue because of the role played by trust in financial markets, in which various parties – e.g. financial institutions, households, and corporations – have to agree on reciprocal commitments with current as well as future implications.

Looking ahead, while some observers think that globalisation may already have peaked,[5] information technology and ensuing financial innovation have probably still a very long way to go. This suggests a potential for further complexity in financial intermediation patterns, with radically new and unpredictable stress scenarios. On the other hand, the recent recognition of the need to regulate and streamline the financial sector may well end up delivering more simplicity and transparency. New financial technology, or "Fintech", may also lead to a revolution in the ways financial services are provided to agents in the real economy (Wolf, 2016).

Impact of financial crises on growth

A major lesson of history is that the collapse of financial cycles usually causes devastating and long-lasting economic damage – much more pronounced compared to "traditional" business cycles recessions. The bursting of the booms is often characterised by deep recessions, weak subsequent recoveries (i.e. lower post-recession growth rates) and permanent losses in terms of potential output. This was clearly true in the 2007-09 economic and financial crisis, echoing what had been observed during the Great Depression in the United States at the end of the 1920s, as well as the financial crisis in Japan in the 1990s. According to the OECD, potential GDP for the OECD area is currently increasing by around 1.5% per year, compared to 2% on average in the 2000s. In parallel, the rate of accumulation of productive capital stock has weakened significantly in major advanced economies.

The reason behind the relatively high damages caused by financial busts is due to the long-lasting consequences of the fragilities developed during their preceding boom phases. The financial sector is usually broken by the impact of collapsing asset prices and high defaults, implying that it is no more in position to play its role to intermediate savings among economic agents. Households and/or corporations are usually left with large debt overhangs and asset quality problems after the bust, constraining their spending. Government finances are also in a poor state, limiting the room for any stimulus. All these elements explain why post financial busts' cyclical recoveries are usually weak.

Perhaps more importantly, the financial cycle can adversely interact with long-term growth prospects. Easing financing conditions in boom years often lead to long-lasting resource misallocations, in both capital and labour (BIS, 2015a). The reason is that resources tend to be diverted to the parts of the economy that are boosted by credit expansion, and not necessarily in those areas which are the most productive. This results in a long-lasting drag on the long-term factors driving economic growth. For instance, credit booms associated with buoyant housing prices are often characterised with sizeable resource shifts from tradeable to non-tradeable sectors, such as real estate and the construction industry. It is only after the boom that one realises that the investments made were diverted to non-productive assets, lowering long-term productivity prospects. Moreover, balance sheets have to be repaired after the bust, limiting the supply of finance to new investments and constraining capital accumulation down the road. Furthermore, as workers become redundant – especially in the previously booming, low-productivity sectors – they are unable to shift easily to other areas, leading to a long-lasting increase in structural unemployment and/or a fall in participation rates. The combination of all these elements explains why potential growth patterns are usually much weaker after the crisis, compared to the pre-crisis economic performance, which had been artificially inflated by the unsustainable credit-based expansion.

Policy implications

From the above, one may wonder about the implications of financial crises for the conduct of government policies. A key implication is the long-lasting consequences of the bust on the state of government finance. This was particularly true after the 2007-09 economic and financial crisis: government debt in advanced economies expanded markedly after 2007, from 75% of GDP for the OECD economies as a whole to 115% in 2015. Yet this deterioration was not unprecedented: fiscal positions had indeed also worsened significantly after the Japanese financial crisis in the 1990s as well as after the Asian crisis.

Interestingly, deterioration in fiscal positions is often less affected by government interventions to rescue the financial system than by the indirect impact of adverse developments in economic activity (i.e. lower economic growth and increasing unemployment). One recent example is related to the impact of the 2007-09 economic and financial crisis in the Euro Area. It is estimated that from 2008 to 2014, the accumulated gross costs for supporting the financial sector, as triggered by the crisis, amounted to about 8% of GDP – and almost half of that has already been recovered (ECB, 2015). There were certainly significant disparities across countries, with costs estimated at around 20% of GDP for Ireland, Greece and Cyprus.[6] But the main message is that these "direct" costs accounted for a very small part (one fifth) of the overall increase in government debt registered during the same period for the Euro Area as a whole.

This recent example is apparently confirmed by more general studies looking at various episodes of financial crises. For instance, a recent report by the IMF (2015) recognises that a comprehensive indicator of the impact of banking crises on public finances is the change in gross public debt, but it can be useful to clearly distinguish between the "direct" and the "indirect" fiscal costs – see Table 10.1.

Moreover, the IMF study also shows that, based on a panel of banking crises observed between 1970 and 2011, the overall median increase in government debt and in the direct fiscal costs associated with banking crises were about 12% of GDP and 7% of GDP, respectively. Again, there is significant variety across countries. For example, it is estimated that the direct fiscal costs

Table 10.1. **Fiscal Cost of Banking Crises**

Type of Fiscal Costs	Examples
Direct	• Bank recapitalisations • Asset purchases • Calls on government guarantees • Depositor payouts • Central bank recapitalisation
Indirect	• Revenue effect from lower growth and the decline in asset prices • Expenditure effect from automatic stabilisers • Discretionary fiscal policy (revenue and expenditure) in response to increasing economic slack • Mark effects on borrowing costs • Effects through exchange rate changes

Source: IMF (2015), "From banking to sovereign stress: implications for public debt", www.imf.org/external/np/pp/eng/2014/122214.pdf.

of the 1997 Indonesian crisis amounted to more than 50% of GDP, and accounted for almost the entire change in the government debt observed there. In contrast, the direct cost (less than 20% of GDP) of the 1997 Japanese crisis represented only about one-third of the change in public debt. Similarly, in the Nordic countries the 1991 crisis' direct costs represented only about 5 to 10% of GDP, a very small impact compared to the change in public debt incurred by their governments at that time (see also Honohan and Klingebiel, 2003). Needless to say, it is important to emphasise the sheer uncertainty related to the measurement of government interventions in the case of a crisis, not least due to the lack of transparent information as well as the usage of "creative accounting".[7]

Perhaps a more peculiar feature of the 2007-09 economic and financial crisis was the impact on monetary policy. First, central banks in major advanced economies lowered their policy rates close to zero, and some of them even decided to set negative interest rates. For the OECD as a whole, short-term interest rates have stayed at very low levels since the crisis – the unweighted average short-term interest rate was close to 0% in 2015, down from 3½% in 2007 in the G3 (i.e. United States, Euro Area and Japan). This extreme degree of monetary accommodation was accompanied by very low market interest rates along the entire yield curves: G3 long-term interest rates averaged around 1% in 2015, compared to 3½% in 2007. Secondly, the crisis had a very large impact on central banks' balance sheets following their decisions to embark in large-scale non-conventional policies. In fact, the amount of total central bank assets has grown from less than 10 trillion USD at the beginning of the 2007-09 economic and financial crisis to almost 25 trillion in 2017 – with the balance sheets of the central banks of the United States, the Euro Area and Japan representing around 25%, 40% and 90% of GDP, respectively (see Figure 10.8).

A third key lesson from past financial crises is the recognition of the importance for public policies to deal with the pro-cyclicality of the financial

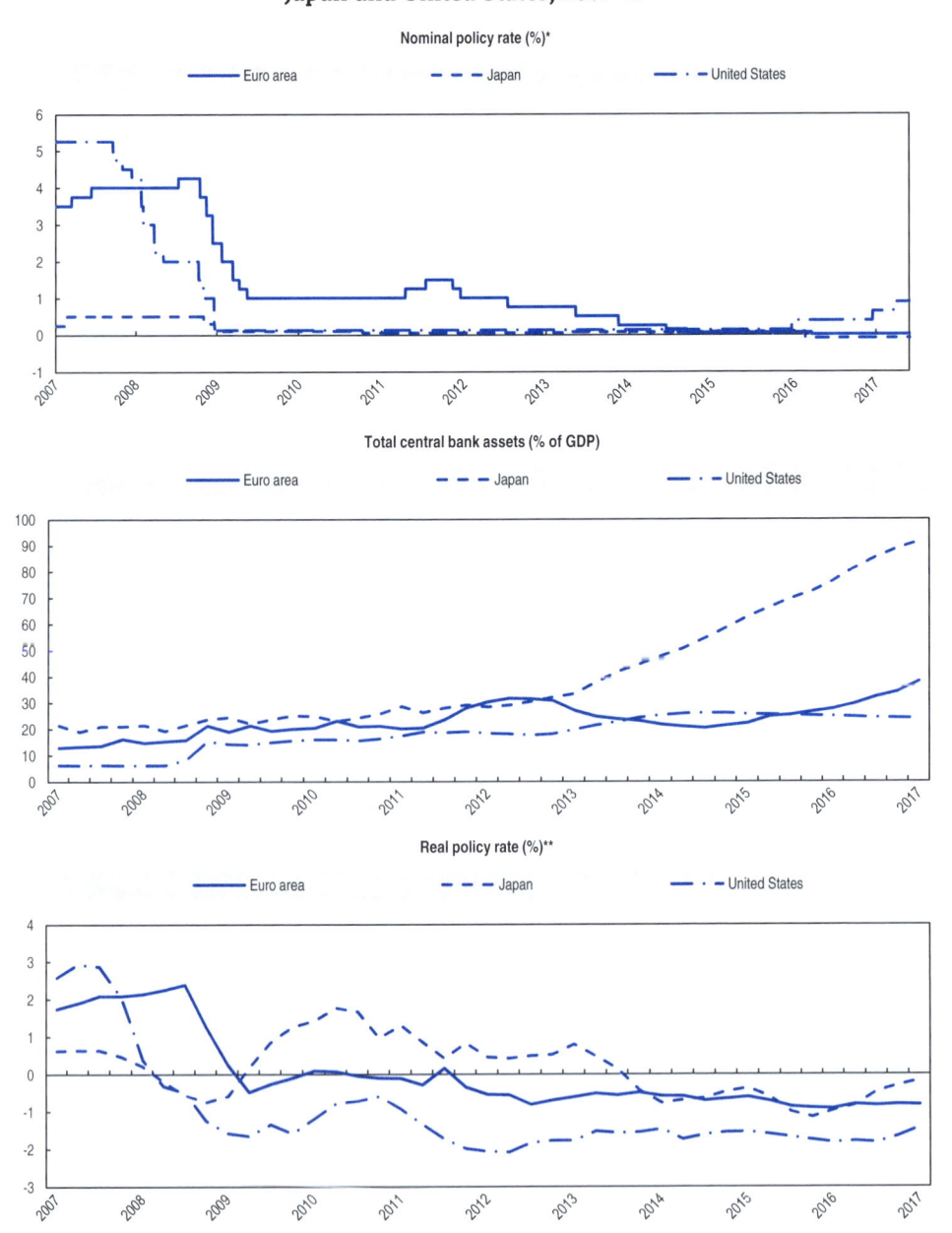

10. GLOBALISATION, FINANCIAL INNOVATION AND CRISES

Figure 10.8. **Policy rates and central bank assets: Euro Area, Japan and United States, 2007-17**

* Policy rate or closest alternative.
** Nominal policy rate less inflation excluding food and energy; for Japan, also adjusted for a consumption tax hike adjustment for 2014 and 2015.
Source: BIS (2017c), 87th Annual Report 1 April 2016-31 March 2017, www.bis.org/publ/arpdf/ar2017e.pdf.
StatLink ⟶ http://dx.doi.org/10.1787/888933589352

system and the need to constrain upfront the build-up of financial vulnerabilities. Fiscal policies should be more prudent in boom years: government accounts are artificially flattered by strong leverage-based growth which cannot be sustained; and the ex-ante build-up of some room to manoeuvre might prove useful once the bust occurs and balance sheets have to be repaired. Turning to monetary policy, authorities should better integrate in their framework the adverse effects of booming asset prices and excessive leverage, even if inflation appears well controlled. Lastly, the supervision of financial corporations should have a systemic or "macro-prudential" orientation. Indeed, since the 2007-09 economic and financial crisis, a number of ambitious macro-prudential frameworks have been implemented with the aim of i) strengthening the resilience of the financial system; and ii) mitigating financial booms and thereby the subsequent busts. These frameworks rely on a wide range of instruments, such as maximum loan-to-value or debt-to-income ratios, adjustments to capital requirements and through-the-cycle provisioning rules (Gadanecz and Jayaram, 2016).

5. Integrating micro information in the financial accounts perspective

The legacy of the 2007-09 economic and financial crisis: greater institution-level supervisory requirements

The 2007-09 economic and financial crisis has triggered a swift and ambitious set of reforms to strengthen the global financial system, with a primary focus on individual financial institutions. This means that the "macro-based" framework of financial accounts and balance sheets needs to be complemented with an institution-based approach to allow for a comprehensive analysis of the financial system. This is particularly true for banking entities. The Basel Committee on Banking Supervision (BCBS), which is hosted by the BIS and represents national banking supervisors, has developed a comprehensive Basel III Framework in recent years (BCBS, 2011).[8] The aim is to improve the banking sector's ability to absorb shocks arising from financial and economic stress; enhance risk management and governance; and strengthen banks' transparency and disclosures. In doing so, the Framework has both a micro and a macro perspective. At the bank-level, stricter micro-prudential regulation aims to raise the resilience of individual institutions to periods of stress. At the macro level, a macro-prudential overlay aims to address system-wide risks that can build up across the financial sector at a point in time as well as the pro-cyclical amplification of these risks over time. These two micro and macro perspectives to supervision are complementary, as greater resilience at the individual bank level reduces the risk of system-wide shocks.

The Basel III Framework has several aspects to improve the strength of the entire banking sector (see a summary in Table 10.2). Its key element is the

Table 10.2. **Basel Committee on Banking Supervision reforms Basel III**

Basel III capital and liquidity standard	Requirement*	Description
Minimum capital requirement	Minimum equity of 4.5% of risk-weighted assets (RWAs)	Requires banks to have minimum level of equity in relation to their assets; based on a risk-based approach: a bank's capital requirement depends on weights reflecting the riskiness of its assets
Capital conservation buffer	Equity of 2.5%	Limits a bank's discretionary distributions when the buffer is not complete
Counter-cyclical buffer	Equity range of 0-2.5%	Needs to be established during times of rapid credit growth to limit the build-up of financial fragilities
Capital loss absorption at the point of non-viability	Prudential treatment of a bank's total loss-absorbing capacity (TLAC), considering in particular the liabilities issued by other G-SIBs	Aims to reduce the risk of contagion within the financial system should a G-SIB enter resolution
Non-risk based leverage ratio	Test minimum requirement of 3% for the ratio of Capital-to-Exposure measure	Ensures a minimum amount of regulatory capital in relation to a bank's balance sheet size (including off-balance sheet exposures); serves as a backstop to risk-based capital requirement
Loss absorbency requirements	Equity range of 1% to 2.5%, depending on systemic importance	Apply to systemic banks, which need to have more capital compared to a non-systemic bank with the same exposures
Liquidity coverage ratio (LCR)	Minimum requirement of a 100% threshold	Minimum liquid assets to withstand a 30-day stressed funding scenario
Net stable funding ratio (NSFR)	Ratio of available-to-required amount of stable funding ≥ 100%	Longer-term structural ratio designed to address liquidity mismatches

* For the precise definitions related to this table, especially regarding the concepts of equity and assets considered, see: www.bis.org/bcbs/basel3/b3summarytable.pdf; for the phase-in arrangements of Basel III capital and liquidity requirements (including the exact dates for introducing the minimum standards that have yet to be calibrated), see www.bis.org/bcbs/basel3/basel3_phase_in_arrangements.pdf.

minimum capital requirement which constitutes Pillar 1 of the Framework. A bank should have a minimum level of equity defined in relation to its assets, based on a risk-based approach. The level of capital required depends on "weights" reflecting the nature of the risks of the respective assets; for instance, a mortgage loan guaranteed by the value of the housing collateral would be considered as safer than an uncollateralised loan, so the risk weight for the first type of loans would be lower, all other things being equal. This is complemented by a clause to ensure that specific capital instruments can be written off or converted to common equity, if the bank is judged to be non-viable. An example of such a capital instrument is contingent convertible bonds, or "CoCos", which can be converted from debt obligations to equity, if needed. In addition, a capital conservation buffer is added to the capital requirement with the effect of limiting a bank's discretionary distributions (that is, reducing the possibility of paying dividends) when the capital set aside for this buffer is not sufficient. Furthermore, a counter-cyclical buffer has to be set up at time of rapid credit growth to limit the build-up of financial fragilities (that is, more capital would be required during the upward phase of the credit cycle). All these capital requirements are reinforced by rules regarding the supervisory requirements related to specific risks, for instance those related to the holding of (complex) securitised products. Moreover, a non-risk based leverage ratio serves as a backstop to the risk-based capital requirement, to ensure a minimum amount of regulatory capital in relation to the balance sheet size of a given bank. Furthermore, specific additional loss absorbency requirements are set for "systemic" banks, which would need to have more capital compared to a non-systemic bank with the same exposures. There are also regulatory measures related to liquidity, with requirements for banks to have minimum high quality assets in case of stress, a "liquidity coverage ratio", and a "net stable funding ratio" to address liquidity mismatches.

The above liquidity and capital requirements are supplemented by a wide range of actions that supervisors may request when reviewing banks' risk management (this supervisory review constitutes Pillar 2 of the Framework), as well as specific disclosure requirements to be fulfilled by the institutions themselves in order to enhance market discipline (Pillar 3). In particular, the framework provides incentives for banks to assess the implications of "extreme" events. In this respect, "stress testing" has become an important risk management tool for banks in the Basel capital and liquidity frameworks. It supplements other risk management approaches and measures, and aims to provide an indication of how much capital might be needed to absorb losses should large shocks occur. Supervisors in many jurisdictions have been increasingly supporting the use of such stress tests since the 2007-09 economic and financial crisis.

Supervisory requirements are also progressively developed for other type of financial institutions, such as insurance companies. Here again the approach tries to combine micro-level requirements and the due consideration of macro, system-wide risks. One difficulty, however, is in developing a "common" approach for dealing with institutions that belong to different sectors and which have different business models and risk profiles, e.g. commercial banks, asset managers, insurance companies, central counterparties (CCPs)[9], etc. Another difficulty is the fact that a number of financial intermediaries are much less regulated or are imperfectly captured by the statistical apparatus. Even large non-financial corporations can play a key role in financial markets, for instance when acting as counterparts to financial systemic institutions. Another issue is the need for cross-border and cross-sector co-operation so as to properly regulate large financial institutions that operate across borders and sectors.

The impact of globalisation and the need for corporate group-level information

In addition to the impact of the 2007-09 economic and financial crisis with respect to national financial corporations, the growing globalisation of economic activity beyond and across national borders has also raised the need for data at the level of global entities. This primarily reflects the development of multinational enterprises (MNEs) and their large cross-border activities, for instance in terms of foreign direct investment (FDI). One issue is that internationally operating companies contribute to a growing part of countries' exports and imports of goods and services. This reflects the increasing opportunities to organise production chains globally, leading to a rise in cross-border flows exchanged within the same conglomerate. In addition, international companies behave globally, as they "…allocate resources, price intra-company transactions, and bill transactions in a manner that is designed to reduce their global tax burden. As a result, national accounts measures based on MNEs' business records may not accurately reflect the underlying behaviour of the real economy in the countries where they operate" (United Nations Economic Commission for Europe, 2011). A case in point is that the financing of investments may be completely disconnected from the country in which these investments are actually made, reflecting decisions made by head offices based on group-level factors (e.g. strategy, cost of financing, risk appetite). In addition, the difficulty in identifying the allocation of output and value added attributable to a particular national economy can distort the related measures of economic activity in the national accounts and balance of payment statistics. An example of the latter is the extraordinary economic growth of 26.3% registered for Ireland in 2016, which was mainly driven by the relocation of intellectual property products and related economic activities.

From this perspective, globalisation is changing the nature of the statistical information that is necessary to monitor economic developments. The growing role played by large and complex internationally-active institutions emphasises the importance of focussing on the global economy as a whole, which cannot be solely analysed through aggregated, country-based statistics. A significant part of corporations' domestic activities are now governed by parent companies located abroad, rather than by the (resident) reporting institutional units. Symmetrically, residents' actions are increasingly influencing the actions of other "controlled" agents located in other sectors and/or countries.

The issue is that the controlling and controlled units forming a corporate group usually belong to different economies and different sectors. Therefore, the aggregation of group-level information cannot be consistent with the traditional residency-based framework of the national accounts. This framework records assets and liabilities of the economic units that are resident in a specific economic territory, information that is progressively losing its relevance in the era of globalisation. It is necessary to capture the claims and liabilities of groups' affiliates that can have an important impact at the level of the parent company, since the parent company is accountable for the business of all the entities under its control and ultimately bears the related risks. That requires consolidated group-level, risk-based data, an approach which is often described as "nationality-based". The information of the various institutional units belonging to a group characterised by a specific "nationality" has to be consolidated independently of the residency of each of these units (Inter-Agency Group on Economic and Financial Statistics, 2015).

In order to construct such nationality-based statistics, one needs to access granular, institution-level data. A number of data sets have been developed along these lines. The BIS consolidated International Banking Statistics (IBS) comprise data on internationally active banks' foreign claims broken down by nationality of the reporting parent banks at the top level of consolidation, and by country of residence of the counterparties. They build on measures used by banks in their internal risk management systems and are broadly consistent with the consolidation scope followed by banking supervisors. In particular, one part of the IBS is presented on an ultimate risk basis, i.e. claims are attributed to the country where the final counterparty resides (taking account of risk transfer mechanisms such as guarantees). For simplicity's sake, the nationality concept is not only applied here at the reporting bank group level but also at the level of the counterparties of the reporting bank, as a consequence of which the positions of each initial (immediate) borrower are reassessed to take into account the transfer of risks to the ultimate borrower.

With regard to non-financial corporations, the OECD has been developing a framework to harmonise and integrate the statistics on FDI and multinational enterprises. The aim is to also have financial measures consolidated at the group level. This is done by netting investments between the affiliates of a group from the group's total assets. This not only removes funds that go into and out of affiliates simultaneously (so-called "funds-in-transit"), but also eliminates funds that are invested by one affiliate in another affiliate on behalf of the same controlling entity ("round-tripping"). The objective is to show the assets controlled by corporate parent entities in each country in aggregate, and stripped of intra-firm positions between their affiliates.

How can micro-data help?

The impact of globalisation and the development of institution-level supervisory requirements call for mobilising new types of information. Certainly, the "macro" lens of the financial accounts and balance sheets has proved particularly useful to analyse the financial system and its interactions with the real economy. Yet globalisation and the supervisory responses to the 2007-09 economic and financial crisis call for developing new statistical frameworks to adequately combine micro- and macro-level information. The need, as summarised by Borio (2013), is to have "good information about the system as a whole and the individual institutions within it – that is, we need to see the forest as well as the trees within it". From this perspective, micro-data can add significant value to the macro-framework of financial accounts and balance sheets.

A key objective is to include granular information that is relevant from a macro perspective. Aggregated data is not enough since financial fragilities can arise at the level of specific institutions (e.g. Lehman Brothers), financial market segments (e.g. derivatives) or instruments (e.g. US subprime mortgage loans), and may have implications for the financial system as a whole. Such micro-level information can have a systemic importance but be masked by "traditional" macro, aggregated indicators. Hence, when assessing financial stability fragilities, it is essential to understand what lies behind the macro level. Countrywide indicators can reflect the homogeneous situation of a group of economic agents or, on the contrary, the combination of idiosyncratic positions. Non-linearity effects mean that, on average, the implication of an aggregate number will differ from the implication of the sum of individual situations. Actual exposures at the micro-level are hard to capture in the aggregated national accounts framework, because sectoral aggregation can mask specific situations that matter for assessing systemic risk, such as heterogeneous business models across specific financial institutions (especially the degree of leveraged financial intermediation they provide), the complexity of the balance sheet, maturity and liquidity mismatches, type (and riskiness) of financial instruments, exposure diversification and importance of counterparty risk, degree of guarantees (collaterals), and impact of potential correction in asset values.

Three main contributions of micro-data have been highlighted in this context and are relevant to enhance the financial accounts framework. A first and primary contribution is to further enhance the quality of macro statistics: the objective is to use the richness of granular data sources to enhance the accuracy and details of "traditional" macro statistics. Some countries have even launched interesting initiatives to base the entire compilation of their financial accounts and balance sheets on exhaustive micro-datasets, and there is a growing policy awareness of the richness of existing administrative datasets that could be better mobilised.[10] A second contribution relates to having an improved understanding of the distribution of economic indicators; to judge, for instance, how aggregated figures for the banking sector may cover a wide range of situations depending on particular sub-groups that may have very large exposures compared to average positions in the sector ("fat tails"). A third contribution of micro-data relates to economic understanding: micro statistics can trigger a paradigm shift in the knowledge frontier by highlighting the usefulness of having different frameworks for analysing the functioning of the economy. As noted above, of particular interest is the possibility provided by institution-level data to analyse the actions of multinational groups and compute "macro" aggregates that are not solely based on the residency basis but also on a nationality basis.

6. Addressing the information gaps highlighted by the 2007-09 economic and financial crisis

The detailed monitoring of global systemically important institutions (G-SIFIs)

Micro-data are not only useful to enrich the financial accounts framework, but they can also be an important source of complementary information, for two reasons. One is the need to look at "pure" micro information to assess the situation of a specific institution or market, e.g. the balance sheet composition of a large bank considered as having (global) systemic importance. As of November 2016, 30 financial institutions were identified by the BCBS and the FSB as Global Systemically Important Banks (G-SIBs), which had to meet additional requirements to hold additional capital (see Table 10.3). According to estimates by Berger et al. (2015), the G-SIBs account for around half of all the publicly traded bank assets worldwide.

A second contribution is related to policy assessment. Micro information can be instrumental in tracking individual responses to public policy decisions and, in turn, the overall impact of these policies, especially for financial markets. This dimension has become particularly relevant with the increase in supervisory requirements initiated in response to the 2007-09 economic and financial crisis. Financial supervisors have indeed been at the forefront of the initiatives to collect institution-level information to address systemic risk in their own jurisdictions. At the global level, a number of actions have been initiated in particular to collect internationally comparable institution-level data that could be shared for analysis to the various authorities (see also Box 10.4). The focus has been on having information for consolidated financial conglomerates, i.e. the headquarters and their affiliates, irrespective of the location of the residency of these affiliates. This has called for specific arrangements to ensure international co-operation and data sharing.

Three important channels have been highlighted in this endeavour. The first relates to governance. Because of confidentiality, the data to be collected have to be closely monitored by the senior authorities supervising the major financial centres, who decide to share institution-level information deemed relevant for the stability of the global financial system. Strict procedures have to be set up to ensure the accuracy, confidentiality, completeness and timeliness of these statistics, which could have the potential to move prices in financial markets if they were disclosed. A second issue is comparability. A particular effort has been made to coordinate banks' compliance with reporting guidelines so as to achieve international comparability. One problem, however, is that accounting standards continue to differ across regions; while some convergence is being called for by the international community, the concrete application of these standards in each domestic jurisdiction is often judgement-based and may still leave substantial room for differences across countries. A third issue concerns how to collect consistent group-level information when the group is made of various entities located in different countries, acting in different sectors, and using various legal structures. All of this puts a premium on developing some kind of identifier to avoid double counting.

Table 10.3. **Allocation of the Global Systemically Important Banks and required levels of additional capital buffers (as of November 2016)**

Bucket	G-SIB in alphabetical order within each bucket
5 (3.5%)	(Empty)
4 (2.5%)	Citigroup JP Morgan Chase
3 (2.0%)	Bank of America BNP Parisbas Deutsche Bank HSBC
2 (1.5%)	Barclays Credit Suisse Goldman Sachs Industrial and Commercial Bank of China Limited Mitsubishi UFJ FG Wells Fargo
1 (1.0%)	Agricultural Bank of China Bank of China Bank of New York Mellon China Construction Bank Groupe BPCE Groupe Crédit Agricole ING Bank Mizuho FG Morgan Stanley Nordea Royal Bank of Scotland Santander Société Générale Standard Chartered State Street Sumitomo Mitsui FG UBS Unicredit Group

Note: The bucket approach is defined in BCBS (2013); numbers in parentheses are the required level of additional common equity loss absorbency as a percentage of risk-weighted assets that applies to each G-SIB; see Box 10.4 and www.fsb.org/wp-content/uploads/2016-list-of-global-systemically-important-banks-G-SIBs.pdf.

StatLink http://dx.doi.org/10.1787/888933590359

The latter challenge is indeed common for all global data collections involving institution-level data. A particular initiative endorsed by global authorities since the 2007-09 economic and financial crisis has been the requirement that market participants be identified by the recently introduced

> Box 10.4. **The collection of data on global systemically important institutions in the BIS-hosted International Data Hub**
>
> At the international level, the collection of micro-data for global systemic institutions has been promoted by the Financial Stability Board (FSB), and is being conducted with the operational support of the International Data Hub (IDH) set by the BIS (see FSB [2011] for the initial overview of this project).
>
> Actual data have started to be collected for a subset of the global systemically important banks (G-SIBs) that have been characterised as having "systemic importance" by the FSB and the Basel Committee on Banking Supervision (see BCBS, 2013). The data encompass a variety of micro indicators – based on banks' assets (exposures), liabilities (funding), and off-balance sheet figures (contingent positions) – aiming at assessing interlinkages among the institutions surveyed as well as with their key counterparties ("network effects"), and the concentration of these institutions in specific sectors and markets ("size effects"), with various frequencies.
>
> In terms of analytics, the value of different combinations of these micro-data will depend on circumstances, e.g. the need for monitoring a single institution, or the exposures of a number of institutions to a given counterparty or risk factor, etc. Making sense of the data and presenting them in a synthetic way requires the development of ad hoc analytical tools and metrics to capture "micro specific" situations that are of system-wide relevance. For instance, the purpose of the IDH data collection is not to simply consolidate the micro-data collected and analyse the aggregated situation of all G-SIBs taken together; it is rather to filter the (large) amount of data available and extract the specific information deemed important for macro financial stability analyses at a specific point of time.
>
> The set-up of the Hub was organised along three phases. Phase I, started in 2013, involved the collection of simple I-I ("Institution-to-Institution") bilateral data to measure the G-SIBs' exposures to their major counterparts; for example, the claims of Bank X on Bank Y. It also comprised I-A ("Institution-to-Aggregate") data to assess the concentration of the exposures of G-SIBs to specific sectors and markets; for example, the claims of Bank X on the resident non-financial sector in country A. These latter I-A data are in fact the institution-level data underlying the Consolidated Banking Statistics (CBS) collected by the BIS; for instance, the data reported by Bank X in the example above will be a subset of the CBS for the claims of all banks headquartered in Bank X's country on the non-financial sector in country A. The I-A data collected by the IDH have progressively become more detailed, in parallel with the implementation of the enhancements of the CBS. In particular, more granular information has been made available in terms of instrument and counterparty sector breakdowns.
>
> Phase II, launched in 2014, again focused on I-I bilateral data, but this time on the largest funding providers (bank and non-banks) of individual banks, as well as on their funding structures (e.g. the use of wholesale funding). With the decision to start implementing Phase III in 2015, additional I-A information covering reporting banks' consolidated balance sheet will be provided after 2017, with cross-breakdowns by counterparty country and sector, and by instrument, currency and maturity.

Legal Entity Identifier (LEI). The LEI is a 20-digit reference code to uniquely identify legally distinct entities that engage in financial transactions. As of 2017, around 500 000 active entities from almost all countries in the world had obtained LEIs from the around 30 operational LEI issuers. Work is ongoing to develop principles and standards for facilitating the identification of parent relationships between entities using LEIs. Certainly, there are many difficulties, including the ability to share granular data and the need to collect and make sense of very large amounts of information. But the aim is to allow for the consolidation of institution-level data using different perimeters. This work will also be facilitated by further progress expected in the standardisation of reporting financial operations – including the definition of a unique transaction identifier (UTI) and unique product identifier (UPI).

The G20 Data Gaps Initiative

While this was not, by far, the main cause of the 2007-09 economic and financial crisis, public authorities have realised that important information had been missing on the financial system, and that further statistics are needed. Therefore, a key element of the policy response after the crisis was to enhance the availability of financial statistics. In 2009, the International Monetary Fund (IMF) and the Financial Stability Board (FSB) issued *The Financial Crisis and Information Gaps* report to explore information gaps and provide appropriate proposals for strengthening data collection (IMF and FSB, 2009). This initial Data Gaps Initiative (DGI-I), endorsed by the G-20, comprised 20 recommendations focussing on three key statistical domains: i) the build-up of risks in the financial sector; ii) international financial network connections; and iii) vulnerabilities to shocks. One part of these recommendations aimed at developing the relevant conceptual and statistical frameworks; a second part was focussed on extending, developing and improving existing statistics.

From the onset, this effort was clearly inserted within the general framework of financial accounts and balance sheets. Indeed, a key objective was to develop "integrated sectoral financial accounts", so as to complete the traditional national accounts framework by presenting information on financial flows and positions. In particular, recommendation #15 of the first DGI Initiative invited international organisations to "develop a strategy to promote the compilation and dissemination of the balance sheet approach (BSA), flow of funds, and sectoral data more generally". In this context, the challenge posed by the lack of data was clearly recognised, especially for households and non-financial corporations. To this end it was also recommended that "data on non-bank financial institutions should be a particular priority".

This initial phase of the DGI highlighted the limited availability of reliable and timely statistical data in various domains. Moreover, it also showed that imperfect statistical harmonisation at the international level challenges the collection of comparable data across jurisdictions, in particular at the entity level. To address these challenges, the international community decided to launch in 2016 the second phase of the DGI (DGI-2) in order to implement "the regular collection and dissemination of comparable, timely, integrated, high quality, and standardized statistics for policy use" over the next five years (IMF and FSB, 2015). Three main areas were identified as a priority: i) the monitoring of risks in the financial sector; ii) the assessment of interlinkages (in terms of vulnerabilities, interconnections and spillovers); and iii) the adequate communication of official statistics (see the "Going further" section at the end of this chapter for the precise list of recommendations). The collection of more granular data was recognised as of particular importance so as to "help straddle the divide between micro and macro analysis".

As with the first phase, the second phase entails considerations that are specifically targeted to financial accounts and balance sheets, with two particular areas of action (Heath and Bese Goksu, 2016). One recommendation is related to the shadow banking sector, whose monitoring can be greatly enhanced through the provision of sectoral accounts data. A second recommendation is a more general one, to "Compile and disseminate, on a quarterly and annual frequency, sectoral accounts flows and balance sheet data, based on the internationally agreed template, including (...) other (nonbank) financial corporations sector, and develop from-whom to-whom matrices for both transactions and stocks to support balance sheet analysis."

Key points

- Countries' fragilities have been traditionally related to the external financing of sectoral imbalances. However, the build-up of domestic financial imbalances and consequent international contagion can be quite independent from current account deficits.

- Since the 2007-09 economic and financial crisis, attention has increasingly focussed on the risks posed by the functioning of the financial system, and in particular on the risk of systemic crises resulting from its pro cyclicality and interconnectedness. While international finance can exacerbate such systemic risks, greater attention needs to be devoted to balance sheet positions and in particular to the developments in credit observed during financial cycles' booms, often characterised by rapid financial innovation.

- A key policy response after the 2007-09 economic and financial crisis was to strengthen the capacity of the financial system to withstand episodes of financial stress; in particular, financial institutions are being asked to set up higher and better-quality capital buffers.

- The conceptual framework of the macro financial accounts and balance sheets is instrumental to address these issues; yet it can be usefully complemented by the collection of micro-data, especially to properly monitor and regulate global systemically important institutions.

- Such statistical efforts are being pursued in the context of the Data Gaps Initiative, supported by the major international organisations and endorsed by the G-20, in order to address the information gaps highlighted by the 2007-09 economic and financial crisis.

Going further

Recommendations of the DGI-2

The 2007-09 economic and financial crisis revealed some gaps in the availability of key information for policy making and for the timely assessment of risks across countries. Given that the G-20 economies are among the world's largest advanced and emerging economies, representing about 85 percent of global GDP, it was considered important to close the most important data gaps for these economies. In 2009, the IMF and the FSB consulted widely with users, and the data gaps identified through this consultation process resulted in 20 recommendations for the improvement of statistics: the G-20 Data Gaps Initiative (DGI). These recommendations included in the DGI were subsequently endorsed by the Finance Ministers and Central Bank Governors of the G-20 economies. The main message was the need to strengthen the analytical and conceptual framework for financial stability analysis and global monitoring of financial stability risks. In addition, the evidence of increasingly global financial transmission mechanisms and strong feedbacks between the financial sector and the real economy were considered very important topics for further investigation.

In 2015, another round of consultations with users resulted in a slightly revised set of 20 recommendations, referred to as the second phase of the G-20 Data Gaps Initiative (DGI-2). While the same range of recommendations is maintained in DGI-2, the focus has shifted to more specific objectives with the intention of compiling and disseminating increasingly consistent datasets across the G-20 economies. More and more, the templates for compiling and collecting internationally comparable macroeconomic statistics, as agreed under the umbrella of the DGI, have become a worldwide standard going beyond the G-20 economies.

The 20 recommendations of the DGI-2 are listed below. For more details, refer to IMF and FSB (2015).

1. *Monitoring and Reporting*: Staffs of the FSB and IMF report back to G-20 Finance Ministers and Central Bank Governors by June 2010 on progress, with a concrete plan of action, including a timetable, to address each of the outstanding recommendations. Therefore, staffs of FSB and IMF to provide updates on progress once a year. Financial stability experts, statisticians, and supervisors should work together to ensure that the program is successfully implemented.

2. *Financial Soundness Indicators*: The G-20 economies to report the seven Financial Soundness Indicators (FSIs) expected from SDDS Plus adherent economies, on a quarterly frequency. G-20 economies are encouraged to report the core and expanded lists of FSIs, with a particular focus on other (non-bank) financial corporations. The IMF to coordinate the work and monitor progress.

3. *Concentration and Distribution Measures (CDM)*: The IMF to investigate the possibility of regular collection of CDMs for FSIs. G-20 economies to support the work of the IMF.

4. *Data for Global Systemically Important Financial Institutions*: The G-20 economies to support the International Data Hub at the BIS to ensure the regular collection and appropriate sharing of data about global systemically important banks (G-SIBs). In addition, the FSB, in close consultation with the IMF and relevant supervisory and standard setting bodies, to investigate the possibility of a common data template for global systemically important non-bank financial institutions starting with insurance companies. This work will be undertaken by a working group comprised of representatives from FSB member jurisdictions, relevant international agencies, supervisory and standard setting bodies, and will take due account of the confidentiality and legal issues.

5. *Shadow Banking*: The G-20 economies to enhance data collection on the shadow banking system by contributing to the FSB monitoring process, including through the provision of sectoral accounts data. FSB to work on further improvements of the conceptual framework and developing standards and processes for collecting and aggregating consistent data at the global level.

6. *Derivatives*: BIS to review the derivatives data collected for the International Banking Statistics (IBS) and the semi-annual over-the-counter (OTC) derivatives statistics survey, and the FSB, in line with its 2014 feasibility study on approaches to aggregate OTC derivatives data, to investigate the legal, regulatory, governance, technological, and cost issues that would support a future FSB decision on the potential development of a mechanism to aggregate and share at global level OTC derivatives data from Trade Repositories (TR). The G-20 economies to support this work as appropriate.

7. *Securities Statistics*: G-20 economies to provide on a quarterly frequency debt securities issuance data to the BIS consistent with the Handbook on Security Statistics (HSS) starting with sector, currency, type of interest rate, original maturity and, if feasible, market of issuance. Reporting of holdings of debt securities and the sectoral from-whom-to-whom data prescribed for SDDS Plus adherent economies would be a longer term objective. BIS, with the assistance of the Working Group on Securities Databases, to monitor regular collection and consistency of debt securities data.

8. *Sectoral Accounts*: The G-20 economies to compile and disseminate, on a quarterly and annual frequency, sectoral accounts flows and balance sheet data, based on the internationally agreed template, including data for the other (non-bank) financial corporations sector, and develop from-whom-to-whom matrices for both transactions and stocks to support balance sheet

analysis. The IAG, in collaboration with the Inter-Secretariat Working Group on National Accounts (ISWGNA), to encourage and monitor the progress by G-20 economies.

9. *Household Distributional Information*: The IAG, in close collaboration with the G-20 economies, to encourage the production and dissemination of distributional information on income, consumption, saving, and wealth, for the household sector. The OECD to coordinate the work in close co-operation with Eurostat and ECB.

10. *International Investment Position (IIP)*: The G-20 economies to provide quarterly IIP data to the IMF, consistent with the Balance of Payments and International Investment Position Manual, sixth edition (BPM6), and including the enhancements such as the currency composition and separate identification of other (non-bank) financial corporations, introduced in that Manual. IMF to monitor reporting and the consistency of IIP data, and consider separate identification of nonfinancial corporations, in collaboration with IMF Committee on Balance of Payments Statistics (BOPCOM).

11. *International Banking Statistics (IBS)*: G-20 economies to provide enhanced BIS international banking statistics. BIS to work with all reporting countries to close gaps in the reporting of IBS, to review options for improving the consistency between the consolidated IBS and supervisory data, and to support efforts to make data more widely available.

12. *Coordinated Portfolio Investment Survey (CPIS)*: G-20 economies to provide, on a semi-annual frequency, data for the IMF CPIS, including the sector of holder table and, preferably, also the sector of non-resident issuer table. IMF to monitor the regular reporting and consistency of data, to continue to improve the coverage of significant financial centres, and to investigate the possibility of quarterly reporting.

13. *Coordinated Direct Investment Survey (CDIS)*: G-20 economies to participate in and improve their reporting of the IMF CDIS, both inward and outward direct investment. IMF to monitor the progress.

14. *Cross-Border Exposures of Nonbank Corporations*: The IAG to improve the consistency and dissemination of data on non-bank corporations' cross-border exposures, including those through foreign affiliates and intra-group funding, to better analyse the risks and vulnerabilities arising from such exposures, including foreign currency mismatches. The work will draw on existing data collections by the BIS and IMF, and on the development of the OECD framework for foreign direct investment. The G-20 economies to support the work of the IAG.

15. *Government Finance Statistics*: The G-20 economies to disseminate quarterly general government data consistent with the Government Finance

Statistics Manual 2014 (GFSM 2014). Adoption of accrual accounting by the G-20 economies is encouraged. The IMF to monitor the regular reporting and dissemination of timely, comparable, and high-quality government finance data.

16. *Public Sector Debt Statistics*: The G-20 economies to provide comprehensive general government debt data with broad instrument coverage to the World Bank/IMF/OECD Public Sector Debt Statistics Database. The World Bank to coordinate the work.

17. *Residential Property Prices*: The G-20 economies to publish residential property price indices consistent with the Handbook on Residential Property Price Indices (RPPI) and supply these data to the relevant international organizations, including the BIS, Eurostat, and OECD. The IAG in collaboration with the Inter-Secretariat Working Group on Price Statistics (IWGPS) to work on a set of common headline residential property price indices; encouraging the production of long time series; developing a list of other housing-related indicators; and disseminating the headline residential property price data via the PGI website.

18. *Commercial Property Prices*: The IAG in collaboration with the Inter-Secretariat Working Group on Price Statistics to enhance the methodological guidance on the compilation of Commercial Property Price Indices (CPPI) and encourage dissemination of data on commercial property prices via the BIS website.

19. *International Data Co-operation and Communication*: The IAG to foster improved international data co-operation among international organizations and support timely standardized transmission of data through internationally agreed formats (e.g., SDMX), to reduce the burden on reporting economies, and promote outreach to users. The IAG to continue to work with G-20 economies to present timely, consistent national data on the PGI website and on the websites of participating international organizations.

20. *Promotion of Data Sharing by G-20 Economies*: The IAG and G-20 economies to promote and encourage the exchange of data and metadata among and within G-20 economies, and with international agencies, to improve the quality (e.g. consistency) of data, and availability for policy use. The G-20 economies are also encouraged to increase the sharing and accessibility of granular data, if needed by revisiting existing confidentiality constraints.

Notes

1. Note by Turkey: The information in this document with reference to "Cyprus" relates to the southern part of the Island. There is no single authority representing both Turkish and Greek Cypriot people on the Island. Turkey recognises the Turkish Republic of Northern Cyprus (TRNC). Until a lasting and equitable solution is found within the context of the United Nations, Turkey shall preserve its position concerning the "Cyprus issue".

2. Note by all the European Union Member States of the OECD and the European Union: The Republic of Cyprus is recognised by all members of the United Nations with the exception of Turkey. The information in this document relates to the area under the effective control of the Government of the Republic of Cyprus.

3. See Debelle (2004) for a general discussion of the impact of housing equity in advanced economies.

4. That finance has become easier to access for a wider range of borrowers is not disputed and has indeed been a key factor explaining the growing importance of finance in recent decades ("financial deepening") in the global economy. Whether finance has become cheaper has been questioned by those that have highlighted the fact that financial intermediation margins have remained high. Wolf (2016) reports that the unit cost of US financial intermediation seems to have been unchanged over the last century, a sign of steady rent-extraction by banks. However, the fact that a wider range of (lower quality) borrowers has gained access to finance may be compatible with this findings. Moreover, the risk free interest rate has steadily declined in the past decades (Turner, 2013), suggesting that total finance costs for borrowers has come down too.

5. This remains a debated issue; see BIS (2017c) for a review of the various arguments.

6. See footnotes 1 and 2.

7. One issue relates to the recording of government liabilities related to the creation of so-called "financial defeasance structures" to manage the "non-performing" assets of distressed institutions, especially as regards the perimeter of the government sector and the treatment of contingent liabilities (see in particular Ynesta et al. [2013]).

8. See BCBS's Basel III overview table on *www.bis.org/bcbs/basel3/b3summarytable.pdf*.

9. A central counterparty (CCP) is a "financial institution that provides clearing and settlement services for trades in foreign exchange, securities, options and derivative contracts." These institutions are an increasingly important part of the financial system, particularly following post-crisis reforms to mandate central clearing of standardised over-the-counter derivatives contracts through CCPs (see BCBS et al, 2017).

10. Cf. the recommendation to "*Remove obstacles to the greater use of public sector administrative data for statistical purposes*" in the recently conducted independent review of UK economic statistics (Bean, 2015).

References

Adrian, T. and H.S. Shin (2010), "The changing nature of financial intermediation and the financial crisis of 2007-09", *Annual Review of Economics*, Vol. 2, Annual Reviews, Palo Alto, pp. 603-618.

Allen, F. and D. Gale (2007), *Understanding Financial Crises*, Oxford University Press, Oxford.

BCBS (2013), *Global Systemically Important Banks: Updated Assessment Methodology and the Higher Loss Absorbency Requirement, July*, Basel Committee on Banking Supervision, www.bis.org/publ/bcbs255.pdf.

BCBS (2011), *Basel III: A Global Regulatory Framework for More Resilient Banks and Banking Systems – revised version, June*, Basel Committee on Banking Supervision, Basel, www.bis.org/publ/bcbs189.pdf.

Basel Committee on Banking Supervision, Committee on Payments and Market Infrastructure, Financial Stability Board and International Organization of Securities Commissioners (2017), *Analysis of Central Clearing Interdependencies, July*, Basel Committee on Banking Supervision, Basel, www.bis.org/cpmi/publ/d164.pdf.

Bean, C. (2015), *Independent Review of UK Economic Statistics: Interim Report, December*, UK Government, London, www.gov.uk/government/uploads/system/uploads/attachment_data/file/481452/Bean_review__Interim_Report_web.pdf.

Berger, A., P. Molyneux and J. Wilson (2015), *The Oxford Handbook of Banking, Second Edition*, Oxford University Press, Oxford.

BIS (2017a), *Locational Banking Statistics*, Bank for International Settlements, Basel, www.bis.org/statistics/bankstats.htmB.

BIS (2017b), *Credit to the Non-financial Sector*, Bank for International Settlements, Basel, www.bis.org/statistics/totcredit.htm?m=6%7C326.

BIS (2017c), *87th Annual Report 1 April 2016-31 March 2017*, Bank for International Settlements, Basel, www.bis.org/publ/arpdf/ar2017e.pdf.

BIS (2015a), *85th Annual Report 1 April 2014-31 March 2015*, Bank for International Settlements, Basel, www.bis.org/publ/arpdf/ar2015_ec.pdf.

BIS (2015b), "Enhanced data to analyse international banking", *BIS Quarterly Review*, September, Bank for International Settlements, Basel, www.bis.org/publ/qtrpdf/r_qt1509f.htm.

Borio, C. (2013), "The Great Financial Crisis: setting priorities for new statistics", *BIS Working Papers*, No. 408, Bank for International Settlements, Basel, www.bis.org/publ/work408.pdf.

Borio, C., H. James and H.S. Shin (2014), "The international monetary and financial system: A capital account historical perspective", *BIS Working Papers*, No. 457, Bank for International Settlements, Basel, www.bis.org/publ/work457.pdf.

Brezis, E. (1995), "Foreign capital flows in the century of Britain's industrial revolution: new estimates, controlled conjectures", in *Economic History Review, XLVIII, I*, Economic History Society, Hoboken, pp. 46-67.

Carnot, N., V. Koen and B. Tissot (2011), *Economic Forecasting and Policy, 2nd edition*, Palgrave Macmillan, Basingstoke.

Caruana, J. (2010), *Systemic Risk: How to Deal With it?*, Bank for International Settlements, Basel, www.bis.org/publ/othp08.htm.

Crockett, A. (2000) *Marrying the Micro- and Macroprudential Dimensions of Financial Stability*, Speech to the Eleventh International Conference of Banking Supervisors, 21 September, Basel, www.bis.org/speeches/sp000921.htm.

Debelle, G. (2004), "Household debt and the macroeconomy", *BIS Quarterly Review*, March, Bank for International Settlements, Basel, www.bis.org/publ/qtrpdf/r_qt0403e.pdf.

Dembiermont, C., M. Drehmann and S. Muksakunratana (2013), "How much does the private sector really borrow – a new database for total credit to the private non-financial sector", *BIS Quarterly Review*, March, Bank for International Settlements, Basel, pp. 65-81, *www.bis.org/publ/qtrpdf/r_qt1303h.pdf*.

Dembiermont, C., M. Scatigna, R. Szemere and B. Tissot (2015), "A new database on general government debt", *BIS Quarterly Review*, September, Bank for International Settlements, Basel, pp 69-87, *www.bis.org/publ/qtrpdf/r_qt1509g.pdf*.

Drehmann, M., C. Borio and K. Tsatsaronis (2012), "Characterising the financial cycle: don't lose sight of the medium term!", *BIS Working Papers*, No. 380, Bank for International Settlements, Basel, *www.bis.org/publ/work380.pdf*.

Eichengreen, B., R. Hausmann and U. Panizza (2002), *Original Sin: The Pain, the Mystery and the Road to Redemption*, Presented to the Conference Currency and Maturity Matchmaking: Redeeming Debt from Original Sin, 21 November, Inter-American Development Bank, Washington, DC.

ECB (2015), "The fiscal impact of financial sector support during the crisis", *ECB Economic Bulletin*, Issue 6/2015, European Central Bank, Frankfurt, *www.ecb.europa.eu/pub/pdf/other/eb201506_article02.en.pdf?fadae43a45a35a30cd17d3213277042d*.

FSB (2017), *Global Shadow Banking Monitoring Report 2016*, Financial Stability Board, Basel, *www.fsb.org/wp-content/uploads/global-shadow-banking-monitoring-report-2016.pdf*.

FSB (2011), "Understanding financial linkages: a common data template for global systemically important banks", *FSB Consultation Papers*, Financial Stability Board, Basel, *www.fsb.org/wp-content/uploads/r_111006.pdf*.

Gadanecz, B. and K. Jayaram (2016), *Macroprudential Policy Frameworks, Instruments and Indicators: A Review*, IFC Bulletin No. 41, May, *www.bis.org/ifc/publ/ifcb41c_rh.pdf*.

Goodhart, C. and G. Illing (2002), *Financial Crises, Contagion and the Lender of Last Resort, a Reader*, Oxford University Press, Oxford.

Haldane, A. (2009), *Rethinking the Financial Network*, speech at the Financial Student Association, Amsterdam, 28 April.

Hausmann, R. and F. Sturzenegger (2005), "Global imbalances or bad accounting? The missing dark matter in the wealth of nations", *Centre for International Development at Harvard University Working Papers*, No. 124.

Heath, A. (2007), "What explains the US net income balance?", *BIS Working Papers*, No. 223, Bank for International Settlements, Basel, *www.bis.org/publ/work223.pdf*.

Heath, R. (2015), "What has capital flow liberalization meant for economic and financial statistics?", *IMF Working Papers*, No. 15/88, International Monetary Fund, Washington, DC, *www.imf.org/external/pubs/ft/wp/2015/wp1588.pdf*.

Heath, R. and E. Bese Goksu (2016), "G-20 Data Gaps Initiative II: Meeting the policy challenge", *IMF Working Papers*, No. 16/43, *www.imf.org/en/Publications/WP/Issues/2016/12/31/G-20-Data-Gaps-Initiative-II-Meeting-the-Policy-Challenge-43760*.

Honohan, P. and D. Klingebiel (2003), "The fiscal cost implications of an accommodating approach to banking crises", *Journal of Banking and Finance*, Vol. 27, Elsevier, Amsterdam, pp. 1539-60.

Inter-Agency Group on Economic and Financial Statistics (2015), "Consolidation and corporate groups: An overview of methodological and practical issues", *IAG reference document*, Bank for International Statistics, Basel, *www.bis.org/ifc/publ/iagrefdoc-oct15.pdf*.

IMF (2016), *International Financial Statistics*, International Monetary Fund, Washington, DC, http://data.imf.org/?sk=5DABAFF2-C5AD-4D27-A175-1253419C02D1.

IMF (2015), "From banking to sovereign stress: implications for public debt", *IMF Policy Papers*, March, International Monetary Fund, Washington, DC, www.imf.org/en/Publications/Policy-Papers/Issues/2016/12/31/From-Banking-to-Sovereign-Stress-Implications-For-Public-Debt-PP4940.

IMF and FSB (2015), *The Financial Crisis and Information Gaps – Sixth Implementation Progress Report of the G20 Data Gaps Initiative*, Financial Stability Board, Basel, www.imf.org/external/np/g20/pdf/2015/6thprogressrep.pdf.

IMF and FSB (2009), *The Financial Crisis and Information Gaps*, Financial Stability Board, Basel, www.imf.org/external/np/g20/pdf/102909.pdf.

Kodres, L. (2013), "What is shadow banking?" *Finance & Development*, Vol. 50, No. 2, International Monetary Fund, Washington, DC, www.imf.org/external/pubs/ft/fandd/2013/06/pdf/basics.pdf.

Krugman, P. (1979), "A model of balance-of-payments crises", *Journal of Money, Credit and Banking*, Vol. 11, No. 3, Wiley, Columbus.

Laeven L. and F. Valencia (2013), "Systemic banking crises database", *IMF Economic Review*, Vol. 61, No. 2, International Monetary Fund, Washington, DC, www.imf.org/en/Publications/WP/Issues/2016/12/31/Systemic-Banking-Crises-Database-An-Update-26015.

McCauley, R., P. McGuire and V. Sushko (2015), "Global dollar credit: Links to US monetary policy and leverage", *BIS Working Papers*, No. 483, Bank for International Settlements, Basel, www.bis.org/publ/work483.pdf.

Minsky, H. (1982), "Can 'It' happen again?", in *Essays on Instability and Finance*, M.E. Sharpe, Armonk.

Obstfeld, M. (1994), "The logic of currency crises", *NBER Working Papers*, No. 4640, National Bureau of Economic Research, Cambridge, www.nber.org/papers/w4640.pdf.

OECD (2016), *OECD Economic Outlook, Volume 2016*, OECD Publishing, Paris, http://dx.doi.org/10.1787/eco_outlook-v2016-1-en.

Palumbo, M. and J. Parker (2009), "The integrated financial and real system of national accounts for the United States: Does it presage the financial crisis?", *NBER Working Papers*, No. 14663, National Bureau of Economic Research, Cambridge, www.nber.org/papers/w14663.pdf.

Shiller, R. (2008), *The Subprime Solution*, Princeton University Press, Princeton.

Tirole, J. (2002), *Financial Crises, Liquidity and the International Monetary System*, Princeton University Press, Princeton.

Turner, P. (2013), "Benign neglect of the long-term interest rate", *BIS Working Papers*, No. 403, Bank for International Settlements, Basel, www.bis.org/publ/work403.pdf.

United Nations Economic Commission for Europe (2011), *The Impact of Globalization on National Accounts*, United Nations, Geneva, www.unece.org/fileadmin/DAM/stats/groups/wggna/Guide_on_Impact_of_globalization_on_national_accounts_FINAL21122011.pdf.

Wolf, M. (2016), "Good news – fintech could disrupt finance", *The Financial Times*, 8 March, www.ft.com/content/425cb3ca-e480-11e5-a09b-1f8b0d268c39.

Ynesta, I. et al. (2013), *Government Finance Indicators: Truth and Myth*, presented at the Working Party on Financial Statistics, 30 September-1 October, OECD, Paris, https://one.oecd.org/document/COM/STD/DAF(2013)16/en/pdf.

Chapter 11

Financial accounts uses

Riccardo De Bonis (Banca d'Italia), Celestino Girón (ECB),
Luigi Infante (Banca d'Italia) and Gabriel Quirós (IMF)

> This chapter takes the perspective of users of the macro framework of financial accounts and balance sheets. Different frequencies, quarterly versus annually, may be more or less appropriate depending on the questions raised by these users. Thus, portfolio shifts may be better captured through quarterly financial accounts and balance sheets, whereas annual data may provide more accurate information for structural types of analysis. The interest in financial accounts and balance sheets is also a function of specific events and times. Undoubtedly, the 2007-09 economic and financial crisis has increased the demand for financial accounts and balance sheets, both from a general macroeconomic point of view, and from the perspective of financial stability analysis and monetary policy. This chapter highlights the latter use of financial accounts and balance sheets for policy purposes, and also discusses the use of financial statistics by famous economists, from the early 1950s to today.

1. Annual versus quarterly financial accounts and balance sheets

Financial accounts and balance sheets have traditionally been published on an annual basis, reflecting to a large extent the complexity of their compilation process. In order to get a comprehensive and fully integrated set of information on financial flows and positions across economic sectors, various statistical sources, often designed for different purposes and not necessarily sharing common methodological standards, have to be used and combined. Under these circumstances, the compilation of the accounts is a time consuming exercise of data confrontation and reconciliation, which requires expertise in both national accounts and in financial reporting. Moreover, the absence of high frequency data for some of the sectors and the poor timeliness of some of the data sources can make the compilation of quarterly financial accounts a very challenging endeavour.

However, the financial accounts and balance sheets describe financial phenomena where frequency and timeliness in the provision of statistics are particularly crucial. There is a need for timely and frequent data in financial accounts for many reasons, including the instability of financing conditions, the rapid changes of portfolio compositions and asset prices. As annual financial accounts and balance sheets lack the required periodicity and timeliness, quarterly accounts have been developed to better meet user demands. They provide the framework for detailed, timely analysis of financing developments, enabling users to pinpoint changes in the sources of finance and in financial wealth of the various sectors in the economy. Quarterly accounts also provide insight into changes in liquidity, solvency, and exposures to certain types of risks. For example, quarterly accounts facilitate the monitoring of shifts between intermediated financing and market financing, and between different types of intermediaries within the former. This provides valuable information on the effects monetary policy decisions have, such as how the so-called "unconventional measures" of central banks influence the financial conditions of borrowers.

Furthermore, quarterly financial accounts and balance sheets can show whether movements in money holding are related to portfolio shifts, or they may offer insights into the impact of such shifts on price developments. Similarly, the accounts allow for monitoring the cross-institutional sector dimension of monetary developments and their implication on balance sheets. Through the quarterly accounts, one can also relate financing developments to investment trends, both within sectors and across sectors, in particular if the quarterly accounts can be combined with high frequency data on developments in saving and investments in non-financial assets. Overall changes in wealth can then be analysed at quarterly frequency, both in terms of their determinants and components, which can also serve as platforms for modelling, forecasting and simulation tools that link the financial and non-financial spheres, borrowers, lenders and intermediaries.

Annual accounts as an intermediate step towards quarterly accounts

Timely quarterly financial accounts and balance sheets have been relied upon increasingly frequently by users in policy and research work, examples of which are presented in Boxes 11.1 and 11.2. Nonetheless, although they are not well suited for analysing business cycles, annual accounts still provide very valuable information on balance sheet positions, financial investments and financing, e.g. for structural analysis.

Box 11.1. Uses of financial accounts and balance sheets in the Euro Area: households

As already discussed in Chapter 4, financial accounts and balance sheets serve as a platform for integrating financial information that otherwise would only be accessible via various statistical products which may follow different classifications, valuation techniques and recording conventions. In this box, two examples are provided of uses of financial accounts and balance sheets for the analysis of the households' economic behaviour. They are based on the Euro Area Accounts (EAA), compiled and published on a quarterly basis by the ECB and Eurostat.

Figure 11.1 shows the dynamics of the financial portfolio of households in the Euro Area. To achieve this comprehensive representation, the compilers have put together monetary statistics, securities holdings statistics, insurance statistics, investment funds statistics, balance of payments data, and statistics on corporate balance sheets, all integrated in the institutional sector accounts framework.

The encompassing picture allows analysts, for example, to disentangle shifts in the portfolio of households. Over the period 2002-16, deposits and insurance technical reserves have been driving the dynamics of financial investment, but their roles in the different parts of the cycle have varied considerably. The large increases in financial investment during the boom prior to 2007, mirroring mainly the buoyant household disposable income, materialised in increases of deposits and insurance technical reserves, in line with the traditional household portfolio composition that favours these two asset categories. However, the downturn in household income as of 2007 and the associated decreases in financial investment initially mainly affected insurance technical reserves, while deposits continued to accelerate up to 2009, due to a portfolio shift away from investment funds. The latter trend reversed in 2013, as the recovery in financial investments again favoured investment funds, thus meeting an economy that has progressively moved towards a less banking intensive and

Box 11.1. **Uses of financial accounts and balance sheets in the Euro Area: households** (cont.)

Figure 11.1. **Financial investments of households in the Euro Area, 2002-17**
Annual percentage changes; contributions in percentage points

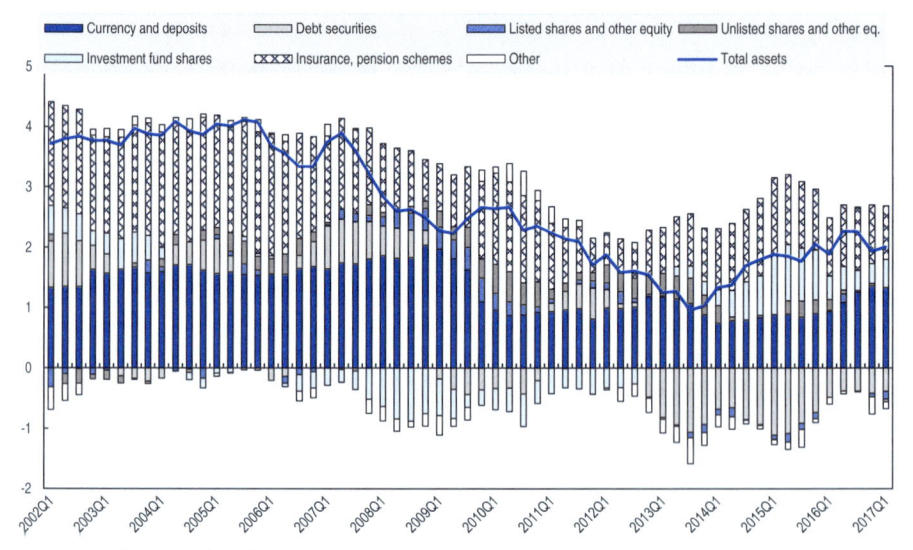

Source: ECB and Eurostat (2017).

StatLink http://dx.doi.org/10.1787/888933589371

more market based financing stance. By contrast, direct exposure to securities, as opposed to indirect exposure via investment funds, has declined, as households moved away from government securities in the aftermath of the government debt crisis.

Figure 11.2 shows the accumulation of households' net assets (including both financial and non-financial assets), or net worth. The changes in net worth are broken down into the following categories: net purchases of assets (in the figure referred to as financial investment); (minus) net incurrence of liabilities other changes in financial assets and liabilities, among which revaluations (other changes, financial); net purchases of non-financial assets (non-financial investment); and other changes in non-financial assets (other changes, non-financial). Finally, the figure also shows the total change in net worth which is due to transactions in financial as well as non-financial assets and liabilities. The latter item corresponds to saving (together with net capital transfers and the statistical discrepancy between financial and non-financial accounts), and is shown with a negative sign as it constitutes, together with the incurrence in liabilities, the source of financing for the accumulation of assets.

Figure 11.2 illustrates the possibility of combining financial and non-financial accounts in a single analytical space, in this case aimed at understanding the accumulation of net

Box 11.1. **Uses of financial accounts and balance sheets in the Euro Area: households** (cont.)

Figure 11.2. **Accumulation of households' net assets: changes in household net worth, 2002-17**
EUR per capita; changes over four quarters

Source: ECB and Eurostat (2017).

StatLink http://dx.doi.org/10.1787/888933589409

assets, or net worth, by households. The dynamics of net worth is clearly dominated by changes in asset prices (and other non-transaction related changes in assets), in particular of non-financial assets. Moreover, both financial and non-financial asset price changes tended to move in tandem, except for the period 2002-03, which is dominated by equity price falls in the wake of the bursting of the dot-com bubble, concerns about corporate governance and the geopolitical uncertainty in the aftermath of 11 September 2001; and the period 2012-14, when financial wealth recovered faster from the downturn after the 2007-09 economic and financial crisis, partially as a result of the implementation of unconventional monetary policy measures by the ECB, while non-financial assets only started to increase after 2014, thus showing a longer reaction time lag.

All in all, saving shows a relatively modest contribution to the accumulation of net worth, as compared to the other changes in assets. The first years after the 2007-09 economic and financial crisis, saving showed an increase as a precautionary reaction, then it decreased following subdued income growth, and finally, since 2014, it started to increase modestly, as both income recovery and precautionary behaviour converged, thus contributing to a stronger net asset accumulation.

At the same time, there is no fundamental methodological dichotomy between annual and quarterly accounts. They simply represent two stages in the development of the same statistical product determined by available data sources and statistical capacity. In this respect, the compilation of annual accounts provides valuable insights for developing quarterly statistics. On the basis of their experience with the annual data, compilers gain understanding of the sources available and the integration challenges. Thus, the experience with annual accounts helps statisticians to familiarise themselves with the adjustments required to align each of the sources with the national accounts standards, or the needs for the estimation of items not sufficiently covered by available sources.

Importantly, differences in methodological standards which led to resource intensive adjustments of source statistics are becoming less relevant, facilitating the compilation of quartrely accounts. A major milestone in this respect has been the efforts undertaken by the international statistical community to align the latest international standards for compiling national accounts, the 2008 System of National Accounts (2008 SNA), with the latest standards for balance of payments, the Balance of Payments and International Investment Position Manual (BPM6). This has removed what has traditionally been a major source of discrepancy, as the balance of payments is one of the most important sources used to compile financial accounts and balance sheets.[1] Moreover, high frequency financial statistics in certain jurisdictions are increasingly being aligned with the standards for the institutional sector accounts. This is, for example, the case in the European Union, where recent updates of the regulatory framework for the compilation of statistics on balance sheets for Monetary Financial Institutions, Financial Vehicle Corporations, Investment Funds and Insurance Corporations are aligned, to the extent possible, with the European System of Accounts (ESA) 2010, the adaptation of the 2008 SNA in the European context.

At the same time, new high frequency financial data are becoming available, extending good periodicity to other areas that in the past required the use of "quarterisation techniques". In particular, the availability of micro-databases in the areas of securities and loans have increased the ability to produce highly reliable and frequent data covering the non-financial sectors.

Moreover, the development of sophisticated analytical technologies supporting multi-dimensional data has also enabled the complex geometry of financial accounts, in particular in from-whom-to-whom data, to be compiled more easily with a higher periodicity. Similarly, methodological and technological developments now enable much faster and efficient algorithms for balancing the data, which also contributes to the feasibility of timely quarterly financial accounts.

It should be reiterated that the financial accounts are a single entity, for which the quarterly and annual accounts are just two representations of the same system, only different in terms of periodicity. In this they do not depart from non-financial, current and capital, sector accounts, for which quarterly and annual accounts also co-exist. However, in some countries there may be a difference between the two cases. In non-financial sector accounts, the availability and/or the quality of quarterly source statistics can be quite problematic, as a consequence of which the quarterly accounts are often constructed using indicators to extract quarterly patterns out of the annual accounts; this is due to the fact that the statistical basis for high quality non-financial accounts is usually of annual frequency. In financial accounts and balance sheets, however, the compilation objective is to develop a high quality quarterly statistical basis and appropriate methods on which the compilation of the accounts can be based. This is unavoidable if the intention is capturing financial developments, which are by nature of higher frequency. The annual financial accounts and balance sheets then just become a "by-product" of the quarterly accounts (rather than the latter being an extension of the former), by using temporal aggregation of quarters.

A clear example of published quarterly financial accounts and balance sheets that has followed the above two-stage development pattern can be found in the quarterly Euro Area Accounts (EAA), jointly published by the ECB and Eurostat. The project started back in 2005[2] by combining Euro Area financial statistics (or building blocks) and nationally available financial accounts and balance sheets. The project required the development of quarterly national accounts in a number of countries to be successful at the Euro Area level, which was achieved in 2007. Meanwhile, the institutions developed and published annual accounts, which served to help them gain experience in data completion and adjustment, confrontation and reconciliation. The interim experience with annual accounts was particularly useful for better understanding the implications of integrating financial and non-financial accounts, which is pursued in EAA for most institutional sectors.

The 2007-09 economic and financial crisis and the increased need for quarterly accounts

In the years following the onset of the global economic and financial crisis in 2007, the financial markets have shown declines in the value of assets, large financial transactions, disorderly balance sheet restructuring, shifts in portfolios, and adjustments to saving, financing and intermediation patterns. The crisis has taken various forms, and has impacted many areas, from the housing markets to the sustainability of government finances. Sharp financial movements initiated by non-bank intermediaries resulted in large banking crises intertwined with government debt crises. Imbalances moved swiftly across sectors and countries. Balance sheet configurations were suddenly at the centre of political concerns, including the relationship between them and the non-financial economy.

Understanding the intricate relationships between these events required, in principle, undertaking the challenging task of pooling and analysing economic and financial data with different methodological backgrounds. Moreover, traditional analysis often lacked comprehensive and methodologically consistent tools to help make sense of the various messages embedded in this multiplicity of data. Financial accounts and balance sheets, in particular if integrated with non-financial sector accounts, may fill this gap and provide useful insights for the analysis.

For example, the financing patterns of non-financial corporations are a major topic that financial accounts and balance sheets can shed light on. The run-up to the 2007-09 economic and financial crisis saw an increase in financing channels other than traditional banking loans. The phenomenon took different shapes, but in the Euro Area securitised loans were the most prominent; see Chapter 3 and the discussion on the "originate-to-distribute" model. More generally, one can also monitor from the financial accounts and balance sheets developments in the "shadow banking" sector. i.e. high-leverage institutions providing finance and performing bank-like intermediation without formally being banks (without being subjected to bank regulations). Financial accounts and balance sheets thus allow a user to see the developments of shadow banking in conjunction with banking and in relation to the overall sources of corporations' financing, see Box 11.2.

Box 11.2. **Uses of financial accounts and balance sheets in the Euro Area: non-financial corporations and financial institutions**

Chapter 5 discusses non-financial corporations in detail. Figure 11.3 presents the total financing of non-financial corporations in the Euro Area, broken down by financial instrument, to show changes in financing patterns over the last 15 years. The Euro Area non-financial corporations have been very dependent on bank financing (MFI loans) up to the start of the 2007-09 economic and financial crisis, especially from 2005 onwards, when the last financing boom period started. As a consequence, the crisis manifested itself in the Euro Area with a sharp decline in bank financing, also accompanied in the first two years by a fall in trade credits, both reflections of the sudden decline in economic activity.

The continued downturn in financing in the subsequent years was also characterised by very low bank financing, reflecting the severe banking crisis in many countries, but, as opposed to the previous period, this was partially offset by more buoyant financing via the issuance of debt securities and inter-company financing (trade credits and intercompany loans). This seems to indicate a gradual structural change in the sources of financing in the Euro Area towards more market-based funding, as opposed to bank financing, also considering that loans granted by Other Financial Institutions (OFIs) and non-residents may cover funding from securitisation companies and the issuance of securities via captive institutions.

11. FINANCIAL ACCOUNTS USES

Box 11.2. **Uses of financial accounts and balance sheets in the Euro Area: non-financial corporations and financial institutions** *(cont.)*

The figure also illustrates the possibility of presenting financial accounts and balance sheets together with other information that may shed light on, or supplement, the analysis of financing trends. In this case, the cost of borrowing is shown to pinpoint periods where, for various reasons related to the monetary policy stance, it was not fully following the same pattern as financing. This happened, for example, from 2003 to mid-2005, from 2010 to 2012, and notably since 2014 with the clear decoupling of the two series.

Figure 11.3. **External financing of non-financial corporations in the Euro Area, 2002-17**
Four quarter sum in % of total liabilities

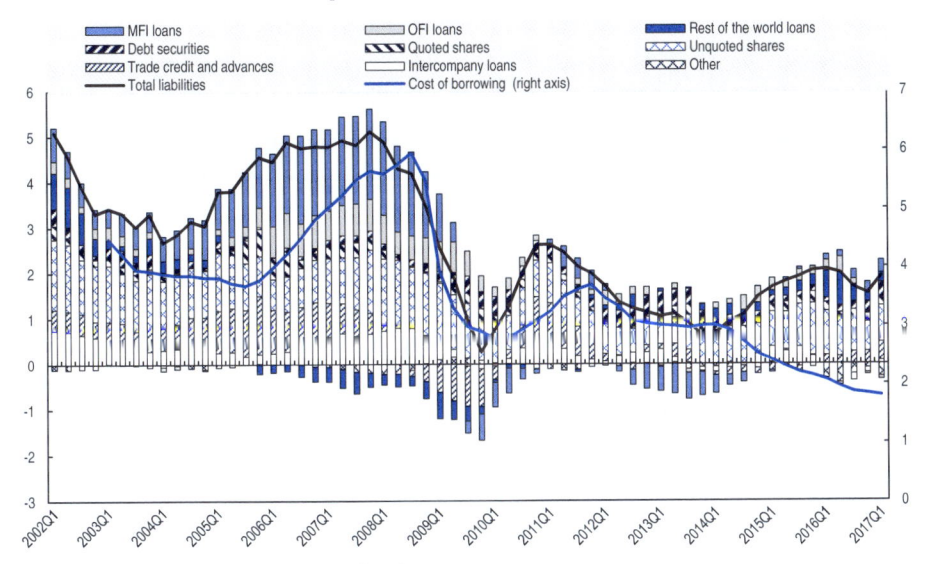

- MFI loans
- Debt securities
- Trade credit and advances
- Total liabilities
- OFI loans
- Quoted shares
- Intercompany loans
- Cost of borrowing (right axis)
- Rest of the world loans
- Unquoted shares
- Other

Source: ECB and Eurostat (2017), EAA; ECB (2017), *MFI Interest Rates*.

StatLink ⟹ http://dx.doi.org/10.1787/888933589428

Figure 11.4 presents the capital position of the financial corporations' sector in the Euro Area, providing a macroeconomic perspective of the sector exposure to excess leverage. Three measures are provided. The headline indicator "net assets to assets ratio" (or capital ratio) shows the net assets (difference between total assets and total liabilities, the latter excluding equity) as a percentage of total assets, and provides a measure of (the inverse of) leverage in terms of national accounts concepts. The dynamics of this ratio, however, do not only reflect the active efforts by the financial system to build up capital buffers, as – following 2008 SNA valuation criteria – the ratio is also affected by asset price changes. As an alternative, the "notional net assets to assets ratio" (or notional capital ratio) is presented, which is calculated like the headline ratio, but with stocks/positions valued at historical acquisition costs (notional stocks), so that asset price changes do not affect the ratio.

Box 11.2. **Uses of financial accounts and balance sheets in the Euro Area: non-financial corporations and financial institutions** (cont.)

The period from 2003 to 2007 reflects the different dynamics of the two ratios, as the headline ratio was increasing on the back of strong asset price increases, while the notional ratio was decreasing, leading to a concomitant decrease of capital reserves relative to assets. More generally, the notional ratio shows the different dynamics of leverage before and after the 2007-09 economic and financial crisis. The ratio decreases very rapidly during the boom period up to the end of 2008, as a consequence of a large increase in lending that was not matched by a similar increase in precautionary capital buffers. This changed sharply after 2008, when the trend reversed and capital was built up more rapidly than lending as a result of a combination of precautionary reactions, more stringent regulatory requirements and government interventions.

Figure 11.4 is completed with the "equity to assets ratio", calculated as the quotient of equity liabilities at market value to assets at market value. Compared to the headline indicator, it shows whether the market perception of the capital stance is larger or smaller than what can be derived from the net assets of the sector. As such, the difference between the two ratios is nothing but a measure of "Tobin's q". Figure 11.4 shows a clear change in the relation between the ratios (i.e. in the market perception of the capital position relative to the value of net assets) before and after the start of the 2007-09 economic and financial crisis, with the equity ratio being larger than the net assets to assets ratio before 2008 (Tobin's q being larger than 1), and being smaller after 2008 (q lower than 1).

Figure 11.4. **Capital position of the financial corporations' sector (excluding investment funds) in the Euro Area, 1999-2017**

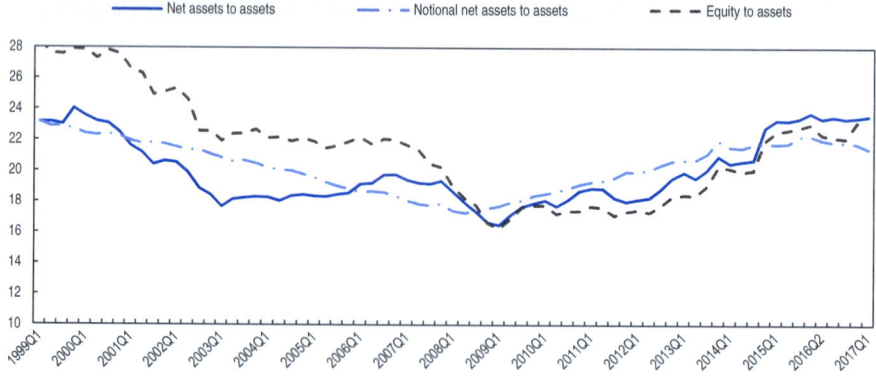

Note: Equity comprises listed and unlisted shares and other equity. Net assets is the difference between assets and liabilities, the latter excluding equity. All assets and liabilities are valued at market value. The "notional net assets to assets" ratio is calculated on the basis of net assets and assets excluding changes in prices of assets and liabilities. Interbank deposits and Eurosystem financing are netted out from assets and liabilities.
Source: ECB and Eurostat (2017).

StatLink http://dx.doi.org/10.1787/888933589447

After the start of the crisis, the extraordinary balance sheet constraints faced by Monetary Financial Institutions (MFIs) also fostered alternative sources of financing. Apart from shadow banking, market financing via bonds became relevant in areas where it was not prevalent before, such as in the Euro Area; see also Box 11.2. This shift in composition and relevance, visible through the analysis of financial accounts and balance sheets, impacted monetary policy decisions aimed at restoring the credit financing channels through the so-called "unconventional measures". Again, financial accounts facilitated the identification of the type of instruments and institutions that, if targeted, could have a stronger impact on the access to financing by non-financial corporations.

"From-whom-to-whom" breakdowns and network analysis tools

"From-whom-to-whom" (FWTW) breakdowns (see Chapter 2), whose importance had already been highlighted as far back as 1968 by Brainard and Tobin, are attracting increasing interest among analysts. Counterpart sector information is key to understanding financing and investment flows, by supporting analysis on which sectors are financing which other sectors. Using tools of network analysis, these inter-sector relationships can be identified as direct or as indirect (those that go from ultimate lenders to ultimate borrowers via intermediaries), thus also facilitating the monitoring of the role of the various sectors in the intermediation function. The FWTW presentations constitute the ultimate tool for a true "flow-of-funds" analysis.

Similarly, a FWTW presentation of balance sheets provides information on inter-sector exposures. This tool can better answer questions such as which sectors would be more affected by a decline in asset prices of equity and debt instruments issued by a given sector. Network theory can be applied to disentangle how shocks in asset prices impact across sectors, how leverage rebalancing effects would travel in the network, or which sectors are the most vulnerable and interconnected. Financial stability analysis, from a macro perspective, benefits enormously from the availability of counterpart sector information.

The more granular the sector breakdown, the more useful the analytical possibilities brought by FWTW information become. In particular, having rich subsector details for financial institutions is a prerequisite for a high quality financial stability analysis of vulnerabilities, contagion and propagation chains. Similarly, further breakdowns of the non-financial sectors (for instance, disaggregating households by income or wealth quintiles, or non-financial corporations by size or balance sheet structure) would enhance the information content for the analysis of exposures. In other words, the richer, the more complex and the more representative the networks in the FWTW matrices are, the more can be obtained from network analysis applied to them.

Further exploitation of micro-data and distributional household accounts

The availability of source data for compiling granular breakdowns might be rather limited for some sectors, in particular for the non-financial sectors. However, by combining information from core financial accounts and balance sheets with micro-data (including survey data and administrative registers), one could still infer FWTW matrices with high granularity. Generally, further work in the area of combining macro- and micro-data to enhance the macro analysis is very high on the agenda of financial accounts compilers. For example, in the aftermath of the 2007-09 economic and financial crisis, a significant amount of work has been done, and is still ongoing, to compile very detailed data on the issuances and holdings of securities. Another line of work in integrating macro and micro information relates to information on the distribution of income, consumption, saving and wealth across households. The increasing inequality in income and wealth in modern economies has not only become a matter of social and political importance, but also of high relevance for monetary and financial stability policy. Financial and non-financial sector accounts, by providing key indicators for the households sector, offer the possibility of linking national accounts with micro-data on income and wealth of households. While sector accounts offer detailed and complete information on the "average" household in an economy, households surveys and administrative data (e.g., from tax authorities) have the potential to provide key distributional information that could be mapped with the aggregate information in the traditional system of national accounts. For more information on the complexities of this micro-macro linking, refer to Zwijnenburg et al. (2016).

2. The use of financial accounts to assess financial stability

As discussed extensively in Chapter 10, financial accounts and balance sheets play a key role in financial stability analysis. This analysis focuses on the assessment of risks that represent a potential threat for the financial system. The evaluation encompasses either risks originated within the financial system, such as liquidity and market risks which spread through financial intermediaries, or risks from outside the financial system, mainly from macroeconomic conditions such as business cycle conditions, developments in non-financial sectors' debt levels, and international imbalances (Bardsen et al., 2006). Financial accounts and balance sheets are instrumental in detecting imbalances and thus offering important insights into mismatches that may lead to significant rebalancing by corporations and households. Sectoral indicators built on financial accounts are relevant for policy purposes, such as the so-called "Macroeconomic Imbalances Procedure" (MIP) in Europe, and the so-called "IMF Balance Sheet Approach".

The EU Macroeconomic Imbalances Procedure

To improve governance, the European Union adopted a surveillance procedure in 2011 to detect and correct macroeconomic imbalances. This Macroeconomic Imbalance Procedure (MIP) has an alert mechanism, in which a scoreboard of indicators monitors country risks in a more systematic way. The scoreboard contains indicators that are able to capture both internal and external imbalances of countries, including countries' competitiveness. The indicators are used as an initial screening tool for the alert mechanism report (AMR). For each of the indicators, a threshold is defined which is to be considered as indicative, and countries reporting values beyond this threshold are not considered automatically vulnerable. The assessment of countries is based on an "economic reading" of the scoreboard, which also takes into account other relevant economic information.

With respect to financial accounts and balance sheets the MIP scoreboard covers, for example, private sector debt, private sector credit flow, and total liabilities of the financial sector. The presence of stock and flow indicators makes it possible to capture short-term deteriorations as well as longer term accumulations of imbalances (European Union, 2012). Figure 11.5 summarises

Figure 11.5. **MIP: Private sector debt (consolidated) in European countries,* 2011 and 2015**
Percentage of GDP

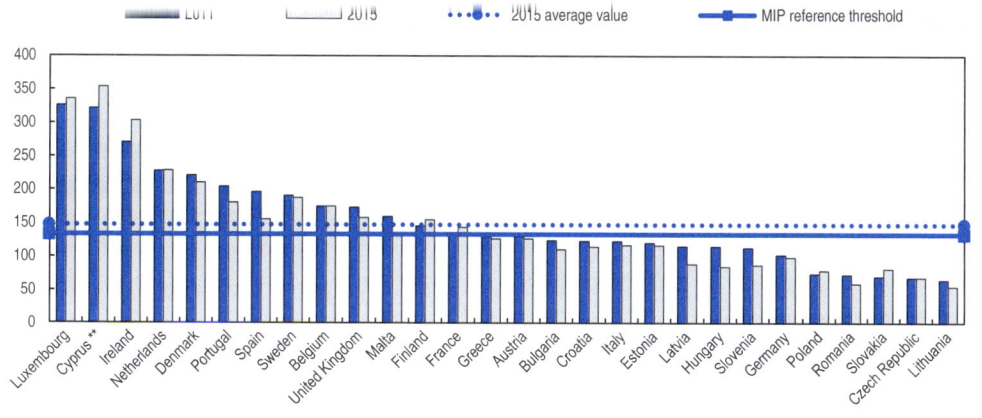

* The private sector refers to non-financial corporation and household sectors. Countries are decreasingly ordered according to 2011 debt ratio.
** Note by Turkey: The information in this document with reference to "Cyprus" relates to the southern part of the Island. There is no single authority representing both Turkish and Greek Cypriot people on the Island. Turkey recognises the Turkish Republic of Northern Cyprus (TRNC). Until a lasting and equitable solution is found within the context of the United Nations, Turkey shall preserve its position concerning the "Cyprus issue".
Note by all the European Union Member States of the OECD and the European Union: The Republic of Cyprus is recognised by all members of the United Nations with the exception of Turkey. The information in this document relates to the area under the effective control of the Government of the Republic of Cyprus.
Source: Eurostat (2017b), *Macroeconomic Imbalance Procedure Indicators* (database), http://ec.europa.eu/eurostat/web/macroeconomic-imbalances-procedure.

StatLink https://dx.doi.org/10.1787/888933589466

the MIP private sector debt indicator, based on financial accounts and balance sheets, for European countries. At the end of 2015, the average debt was about 150 per cent of GDP, slightly larger than the MIP reference threshold. The heterogeneity of the debt indicator plotted in the figure may reflect country-specific factors; for example, in Ireland and Luxembourg, the high presence of multinational enterprises contributes to the high ranking.

Figure 11.5 shows that 16, out of 28, European countries recorded a debt ratio below the reference threshold in 2015, while ten countries showed a debt ratio increase, as compared to the level at the end of 2011. The contribution of new transactions to the debt developments since 2011 can be assessed in Figure 11.6. Between 2012 and 2015, repayments were larger than the incurrence of new debt in fewer than half of countries (in the figure presented as negative flows). Only three countries exceeded the reference threshold in 2012, and only one country exceeded the threshold in 2014 and 2015.

Figure 11.6. **MIP Private sector credit flow (consolidated) in European countries,* 2012-15**
Percentage of GDP

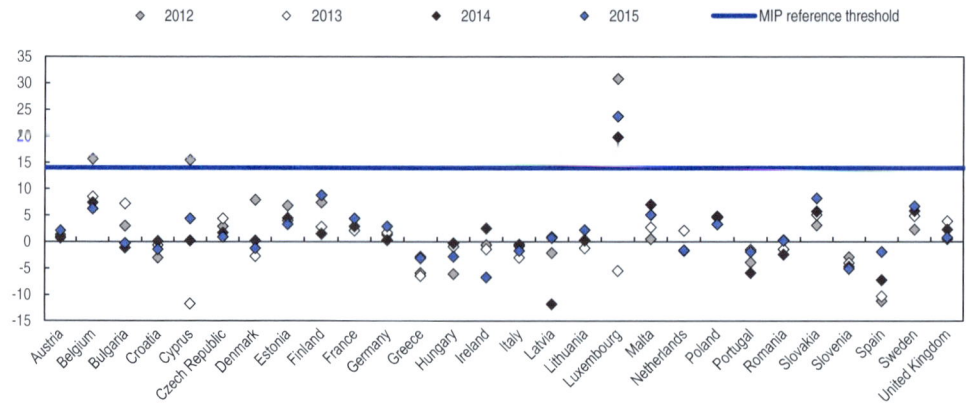

* The private sector refers to non-financial corporations, households, and non-profit institutions serving households.
Source: Eurostat (2017b), *Macroeconomic Imbalance Procedure Indicators* (database), http://ec.europa.eu/eurostat/web/macroeconomic-imbalances-procedure.

StatLink http://dx.doi.org/10.1787/888933589485

The analysis of financial stability in the IMF Balance Sheet Approach

Analyses of determinants of financial and currency crises, which have hit many economies since the 1970s, focus on different variables. The first models, typically referred to as first generation models and developed by Krugman (1979) and Flood and Garber (1984), emphasise the role of fundamentals in generating crises: fiscal budget, foreign trade deficits, inflation, interest rates, etc. The deterioration of these variables can give rise to imbalances with the pegged exchange rate to which the central bank is committed. These imbalances may be overlooked if central banks have large stocks of foreign reserves, but when reserves are low, or are perceived as low by the market, a speculative attack on the currency could be triggered. In line with the prediction of these models, the 1992-93 speculative attacks to the exchange rate mechanism (ERM) of the European Monetary System have been attributed to inadequate monetary and fiscal policies (BIS, 1993). The Mexican crisis in 1994-95 shared some similarities to the ERM dysfunction. In the midst of severe political instability, the government adopted a relaxed monetary and fiscal discipline in the run-up to the presidential election. As a consequence, foreign capital inflows reduced along with foreign exchange reserves, and the government was finally unable to roll over the dollar-denominated short-term debt (Krugman, 2010). This situation led the Mexican authorities to depreciate the peso.

Not all economists agreed with these interpretations. Empirical evidence by Eichengreen et al. (1995) shows that, while some speculative attacks are preceded by rapid growth of money and inflation, other attacks cannot be explained very well by imbalances, but seem more in line with a story of self-fulfilling crises, where sudden change in market participants' sentiment plays a crucial role. The second-generation models developed by Obstfeld (1994) hold this view.

The debate about the role of fundamentals led in 1989 to the proposal of the so-called "Washington consensus" among US economic officials, the International Monetary Fund and the World Bank (Williamson, 2004). Based on the experience of Latin America economies during the 1980s, the Washington consensus document discussed economic policy instruments that are perceived as important for sustaining growth in developing countries. The list of ten policy prescriptions addressed topics related to fiscal discipline, public expenditure priorities, tax reform, interest rates, exchange rates, trade liberalisation, foreign direct investment, privatisation, deregulation, and property rights. In line with this policy agenda, strong privatisation, deregulation and trade liberalisation were prescribed and followed in Latin America and Eastern Europe. However, growth was below expectations. Similarly, the take-off in Sub-Saharan Africa revealed disappointing results, despite significant policy reform (Rodrik, 2006).

While the first two generations of models seem to fit many crisis stories up to the mid-1990s, they fail to explain the disruption in the major Asian economies in the late 1990s. The Asian crisis of 1997-98 (a "new-style" crisis as labelled by Dornbusch [2002]) shifted attention to other directions. The third generation of models highlighted the presence of currency mismatches in corporations' and banks' balance sheets, in particular where banks borrowed in foreign currency and lent in local currency. As a consequence, financial shocks were amplified and spread to other sectors and economies, even in the presence of a sound fiscal situation and a sustainable external deficit. The key lessons learned were that the economy should be seen as a network of sectors where interactions could lead to a potential contagion of shocks. Due to the removal of capital restrictions and increased globalisation, economies had become more interconnected, with shocks not being restricted to a single sector or country, but having possible spill-over effects, which leads to more systemic risk.

After the Asian crisis, the IMF fostered the foundation of a new approach to country surveillance beyond monitoring inflation, public sector and balance of payments imbalances. This new strategy, implying a critique of the Washington consensus strategy,[3] was called the Balance Sheet Approach (BSA). It was proposed by Allen et al. (2002), as a complement to the flow analysis. The BSA focuses on stock variables and the analysis of a wider range of sectors (central bank, other depository corporations, other financial corporations, general government, non-financial corporations, other resident sectors, and non-residents). It is evident that such an analysis can only be based on the availability of balance sheets for each of the sectors, including FWTW information. The agreed scheme, as presented in Table 11.1, looks like the traditional financial accounts and balance sheets, but adapted to take into account inter-sectoral assets and liabilities, in the same vein as the FWTW version of the financial accounts and balance sheets. The information that can be derived from this table only relates to the overall position of the sectors, i.e. total assets and total liabilities, with a breakdown by currency. In addition, one can derive information on the counterpart sector, in particular whether there are large exposures toward the Rest of the World, which generally plays an important role during the build-up of a crisis. The matrix was and is considered as a starting point to investigate the presence of risks and to evaluate the potential transmission channels of shocks.

Within the BSA framework, the analysis focuses on four different risks (Allen et al., 2002):

- "maturity mismatch", typically related to balance sheets where long-term assets coexist with short-term liabilities;
- "currency mismatch", in the presence of liabilities denominated in foreign currencies;
- capital structure, looking at the debt exposures compared to equity; and
- solvency, analysing whether assets are able to cover all liabilities.

Key indicators to unveil potential vulnerabilities are the "net financial position" (or net financial worth) of sectors, along with the "net foreign currency position" (defined as the difference between assets and liabilities denominated in foreign currencies) and "net short-term position" (defined as the difference between short-term assets and short-term liabilities). Large negative foreign currency positions may signal a sectoral vulnerability to exchange rate variations, in particular in the case of high short-term debt which may be difficult to roll over. Large negative net financial positions may be correlated to solvency problems, and a high leverage can exacerbate the vulnerability of a

Table 11.1. **Balance sheet matrix***

	Government		Central Bank		Other depository corp.		Other financ. Corp.		Non-financial sector		Households		Non-residents		Total	
	A	L	A	L	A	L	A	L	A	L	A	L	A	L	A	L
Government																
Total																
in domestic currency																
in foreign currency																
Central Bank																
Total																
in domestic currency																
in foreign currency																
Other depository corp.																
Total																
in domestic currency																
in foreign currency																
Other financ. Corp.																
Total																
in domestic currency																
in foreign currency																
Non-financial sector																
Total																
in domestic currency																
in foreign currency																
Households																
Total																
in domestic currency																
in foreign currency																
Non-residents																
Total																
in domestic currency																
in foreign currency																
Total																
in domestic currency																
in foreign currency																

* A: Assets; L: Liabilities.
Source: IMF (2015), *Balance Sheet Analysis in Fund Surveillance*, www.imf.org/external/np/pp/eng/2015/061215.pdf.

sector. Finally, short-term liabilities highlight, for example, a sector's (in)ability to withstand rises in the interest rate.

Prior to the 2007-09 economic and financial crisis, the IMF only complemented the more traditional flow based indicators with balance sheet analysis for a few economies (IMF, 2015), in particular for transition countries like Estonia, Latvia, and South Africa. Advanced countries were considered to be in sound condition and less exposed to the above mentioned risks and vulnerabilities, although some sectoral vulnerabilities were highlighted. For example, the IMF (2002) strongly emphasised the high indebtedness of non-financial corporations in the United States. After the global financial crisis the IMF increased the use of the balance sheet analysis in its surveillance, and at the same time launched different initiatives to enhance the availability of data.

The G-20 Data Gaps Initiative (see Chapter 10) and the IMF's Special Data Dissemination Standard Plus addressed the issue of data shortage and made further recommendations to enhance data availability. New initiatives aim at recovering currency breakdown, remaining maturity[4], off-balance sheet items (contingent assets and liabilities), and bilateral counterparty statistics to track sectoral interlinkages. In the same vein, Palumbo and Parker (2009) discussed the importance of having a more detailed classification of assets which separates out structured financial products, along with the need to have a more detailed representation of financial intermediaries, which allows users to analyse which intermediaries are more exposed to leverage.

> Box 11.3. **The balance sheet approach in Thailand**
>
> During the first half of the 1990s, Thailand was a starring economy part of the so called "Asian miracle", thanks to the liberalisation of financial markets and the reduction of foreign trade barriers. Driven by exports and the inflow of large amounts of foreign capital, the economy experienced an accelerated GDP growth along with a strong increase in investments. Notwithstanding this background, Thailand was one of the Asian economies hit in the late 1990s by the severe Asian crisis.
>
> By using balance sheets, it is possible to analyse and assess whether imbalances were at work before the crisis unfolded. At the end of 1996, non-financial corporations and banks showed a high short-term debt denominated in foreign currency, which posed risks in case of exchange rate depreciation (Dawson, 2004). Non-financial corporations had raised foreign currency debt provided by domestic banks, thus increasing sectoral linkages (Allen et al. 2002). While foreign exchange reserves increased coherently with the large country imports, the foreign exchange reserves looked inadequate to the risks posed by the amounts of foreign short-term debt. Banks were also suffering a maturity mismatch in their balance sheets, with short-term assets unable to cover short-term liabilities.
>
> The flow analysis also highlighted weakness in the current account. Due to lower competitiveness, exports decreased in 1996, in turn provoking a deficit of the current account. This fragile outlook was perceived by international lenders as a very risky and vulnerable situation, mainly because the foreign currency denominated short-term debt was not matched by the country's foreign exchange reserves. As a consequence, lenders decided to reduce their exposures. In 1997 the Thailand currency (baht) underwent a speculative attack which led to an exhaustion of international reserves and to a devaluation of around 30 per cent. This triggered the crisis, with foreign lenders refusing to roll over the Thai debt.

Detecting imbalances through the financial accounts and balance sheets

Chapter 10 discussed how the 2007-09 economic and financial crisis drew new attention to balance sheets and to their interplay with financial flows. Important questions have been analysed through financial accounts statistics: leverage cycles, intermediation chains, interactions between the real economy and financial systems, etc. (Winkler et al. [2014]). Some research using these statistics showed how the potential signs of weakness could have been detected, at least partly, before the outbreak of the crisis.

Focusing on the financial structure of the G7 plus some small European countries (Greece, Ireland, the Netherlands and Portugal), Infante et al. (2012) ran a simple exercise by comparing gross and net positions of each institutional sector between two periods: the average financial stocks between 1997 and 1999 (a period with relatively balanced financial positions) and the financial stocks at the end of 2007, before the inception of the crisis, when the imbalances may have reached their peak. The first pattern that emerged revealed intense international integration[5] between the 1990s and 2007. Thanks to the removal of capital controls, low interest rates, rapid liquidity and credit expansion, showing favourable global financial conditions, all countries increased their assets and liabilities with the Rest of the World; see Figures 11.7 to 11.9.

While well-developed and open global financial systems may allow for the optimal allocation of capital and diversification of risks, higher levels of asset and liability positions have been shown to increase exposure to valuation gains or losses and increase financial stability risks. Furthermore, the foreign currency denomination of liabilities along with a large presence of debt, as explained in the previous section, may increase the fragility of the country in case of currency devaluation. Figure 11.7 to 11.9 also shows that internationalisation is usually more intense in small countries than in large countries: the average stocks of the Rest of the World's assets as a percentage of GDP moved from 3.5 to 6 times GDP between 1997-99 and 2007 (with Ireland reaching a peak in 2007 equal to 13 times the GDP), while the liability side changed from 3.4 to 5.8 times GDP. Looking at the domestic sector, the imbalances were mainly accumulating in the balance sheets of households. In banking and other financial sectors, the net positions were rather balanced. However, the composition of assets and liabilities hid some important vulnerabilities, in particular related to the use of leverage and the characteristics of debt. Intermediaries employed short-term debt (i.e. interbank loans) to widen their balance sheets (which raised maturity mismatches) and, in many cases, relied on foreign capital.

The domestic financial developments can be associated with the sustained international financial integration, and the size of financial systems was found to be positively correlated to the external financial positions (Lane and Milesi-Ferretti, 2008). This interplay between the financial system and international

Figure 11.7. **Financial accounts and balance sheets: Large Euro Area countries**

Absolute changes of stock values between the average of 1997-99 and 2007; in percentage points of GDP

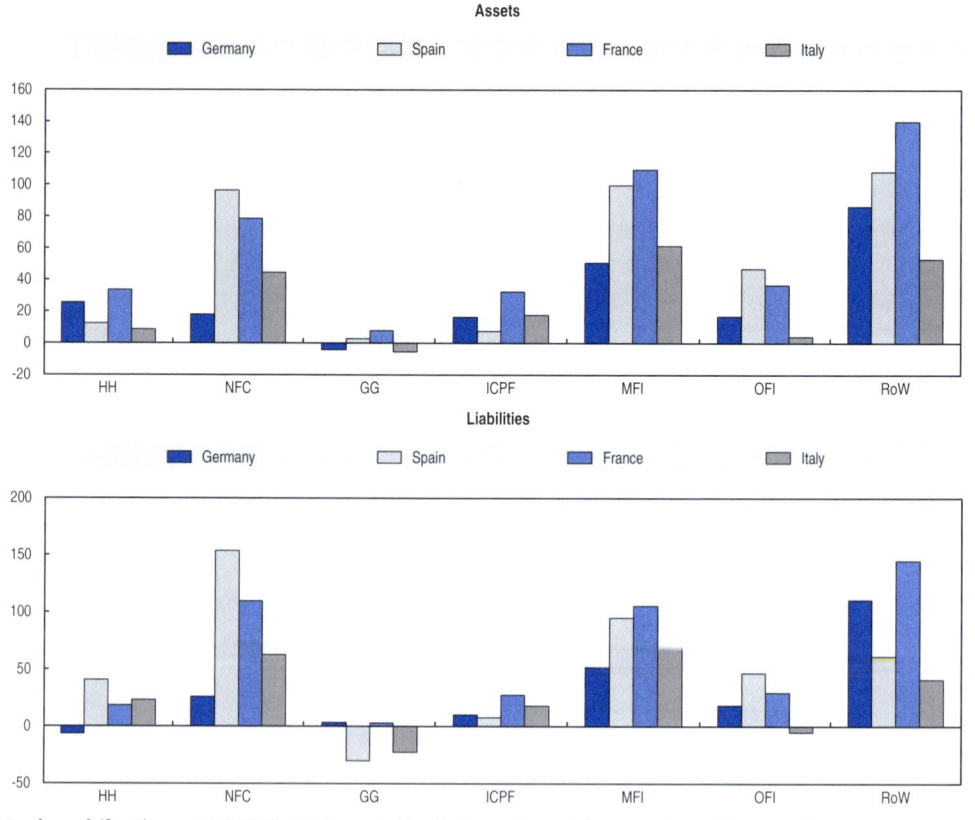

Map legend (for Figures 11.7-11.9): HH: households; NFC: non-financial corporations; GG: general government; ICPF: insurance corporations and pension funds; MFI: monetary financial institutions; OFI: other financial intermediaries; RoW: Rest of the World.
Source: Source (for Figures 11.7-11.9): Infante et al. (2012). 'Imbalances in Household, Firm, Public and Foreign Sector Balance Sheets in the 2000s : A Case of "I Told You So?"'

StatLink http://dx.doi.org/10.1787/888933589504

capital flows led to an increase of credit growth, thus raising the likelihood of a crisis outbreak (Mendoza and Terrones [2008]; Schularick and Taylor [2012]). In presence of open financial systems, domestic banks managed to enhance their funding opportunities thanks to the possibility of collecting financial resources from foreign depositors or from international interbank counterparties. The latter opportunities allowed banks to increase their non-monetary liabilities (i.e. wholesale funding), and to grant credit beyond collected deposits. The dynamics of loan growth showed a decoupling from money growth (Schularick and Taylor [2012]). Lane and McQuade (2013) also emphasised that the domestic credit growth was strongly correlated with international capital flows; the correlation involved only debt flows and not equity instruments.

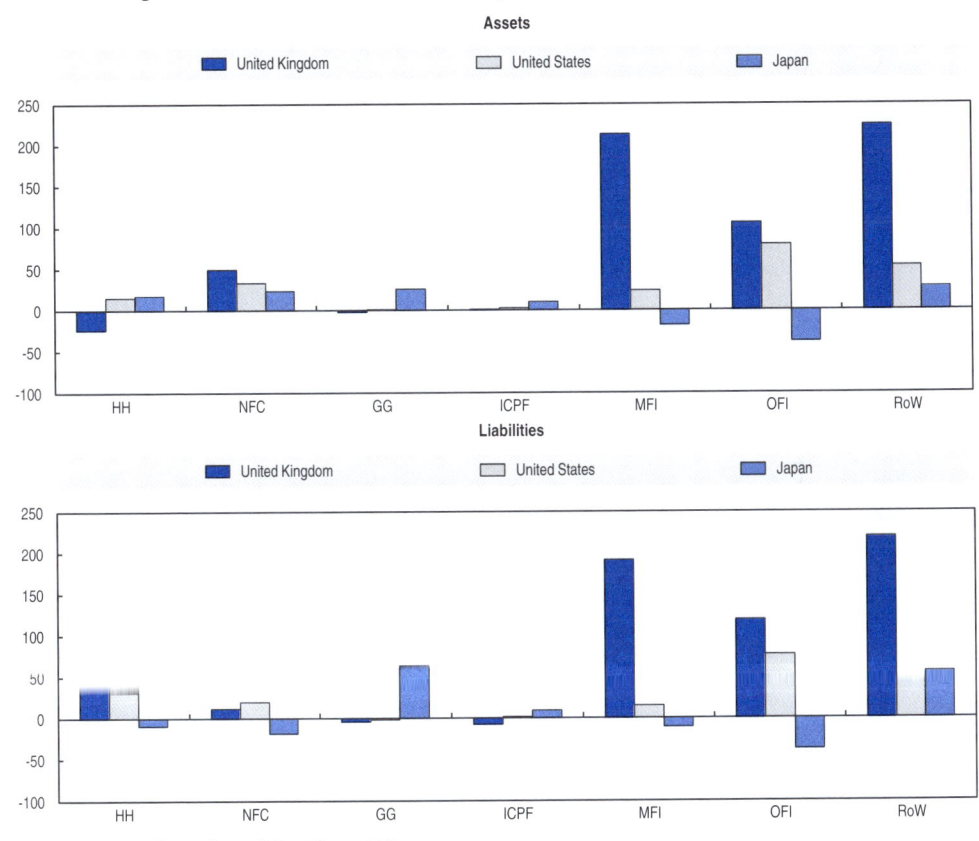

Figure 11.8. **Financial accounts and balance sheets: Large non-Euro Area countries**
Absolute changes of stock values between the average of 1997-1999 and 2007; percentage points of GDP

Source: Source and map legend: See Figure 11.7.

StatLink ⋑ http://dx.doi.org/10.1787/888933589523

Leverage has been an important factor in explaining the build-up of mismatches and financial instability. Adrian and Shin (2008) documented how financial intermediaries exploited the asset price booms to expand the size of their balance sheets, through actively managing leverage, while a symmetric strategy was adopted during downturns in order to shrink the balance sheets. Any increase in asset prices, with liabilities valued at their nominal values, automatically raised the value of the assets of financial intermediaries, and consequently the market value of their equity (defined as total assets minus total debt liabilities), resulting in a reduction of leverage. Contrary to the evidence for other sectors, financial intermediaries reacted to this by restoring leverage to at least its previous level by increasing liabilities (mainly using repurchase agreements), which in turn were employed in new market claims, for instance the acquisition of new securities or the supply of loans.

11. FINANCIAL ACCOUNTS USES

Figure 11.9. **Financial accounts and balance sheets: small Euro Area countries**
Absolute changes of stock values between the average of 1997-99 and 2007; percentage points of GDP

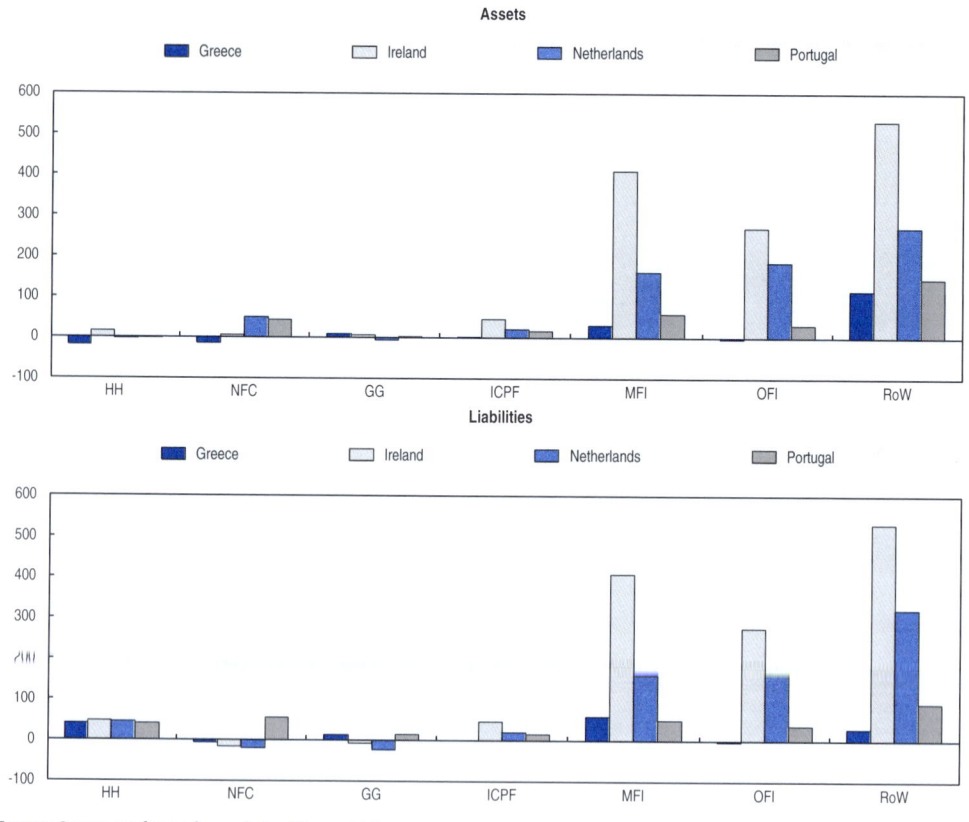

Source: Source and map legend: See Figure 11.7.

StatLink http://dx.doi.org/10.1787/888933589542

Through the US financial accounts and balance sheets, Adrian and Shin (2008) produced evidence of a pro-cyclical use of leverage by showing the co-movement of assets and liabilities for both the banking sector and the security brokers and dealers. During the expansionary phase, the growth of assets was matched with an increase in liabilities, in order to restore the leverage ratio, while during the downturns the reduction in the value of assets was followed by a reduction in liabilities. The pro-cyclicality was more pronounced for security brokers and dealers than for the banking sector, due to the differences in the composition of the balance sheets of the two classes of intermediaries. Banks hold a large amount of loans that are recorded in the financial balance sheets at book value, while security brokers and dealers hold, for instance, securities reported in the balance sheets at market value, which are therefore more vulnerable to developments in market prices.

Based on the data from the institutional sector accounts, Girón and Mongelluzzo (2014) also verified the impact of the use of leverage by monetary financial institutions on credit developments. The authors focused not only on the balance sheets (outstanding positions) of monetary financial institutions, but also on the net acquisitions of assets (financial transactions), to disentangle changes in leverage due to asset price movements (defined by authors as automatic reaction of leverage) and those due to deliberate decisions to increase positions through net acquisitions of assets (active leverage). They confirmed leverage pro-cyclicality for six out of ten European countries (Belgium, France, Germany, Italy, the Netherlands, and Spain). Moreover, before 2008, the growth in the provision of credit on the assets side, with the ensuing enlargement of the balance sheets, could not be associated with a proportional increase in the banks' own equity, but was instead boosted by inordinate growth of liabilities and therefore by an increase of leverage.

The increase of leverage in the financial sector did not only translate into an increase of loans to households and non-financial corporations, but to some extent also led to the growth in the size of lending/borrowing within the financial intermediation system itself. Using financial accounts and balance sheets from 1995 to 2007, Bartiloro and di Iasio (2012) proved that financial innovations introduced by banks, mainly in funding activities, did not result in a significant improvement of non-financial corporations' financial conditions. Changes in intermediation activity only led to an increased interconnectedness within the financial system. The authors reported a low ratio of deposits to liabilities in the United States' financial sectors (19 per cent), compared to higher percentages in Italy and Spain (respectively 42 and 56 per cent). At the same time, data showed a larger use of short-term loans, which was at the heart of the increased interconnections within the financial system. Moreover, to complement deposits with short-term funding in the wholesale credit market, banks benefited from loan securitisation which helped them to recover liquidity from illiquid assets (i.e. mortgages). Securitisation contributed to the relaxation of banks' reliance on the savings of non-financial sectors, and the building up of linkages within financial systems.

Based on US financial accounts and balance sheets, Adrian and Shin (2009) added evidence on the deep transformation in the financial system. Securitisation was intensively used by banks, increasing their interconnections with the financial markets for debt securities. Starting from the 1980s, bank loans, mainly mortgages, were transformed into securities and sold to investors, a process that mirrored the very large growth of security brokers and dealers' assets, or more generally the assets of the other financial intermediaries. Banks originated loans and distributed them to the market with the aim to reduce lending risk by spreading it among a large number of agents, in this case the holders of the securitised loans. This mechanism explained, at least partly, the increase of subprime mortgages. Figure 11.10 shows the evolution of assets of other financial intermediaries (excluding investment funds) in the United States, the Euro Area and the United Kingdom during the last two decades; in all these economies the assets show a strong positive trend. Between 1995 and 2007 the sector in the United States grew almost 300%, while in the other countries the growth was even more pronounced (around 600% in the Euro Area[6] and almost 700% in the United Kingdom).

Figure 11.10. **Other financial intermediaries**[1, 2]
(total assets; billions of USD)

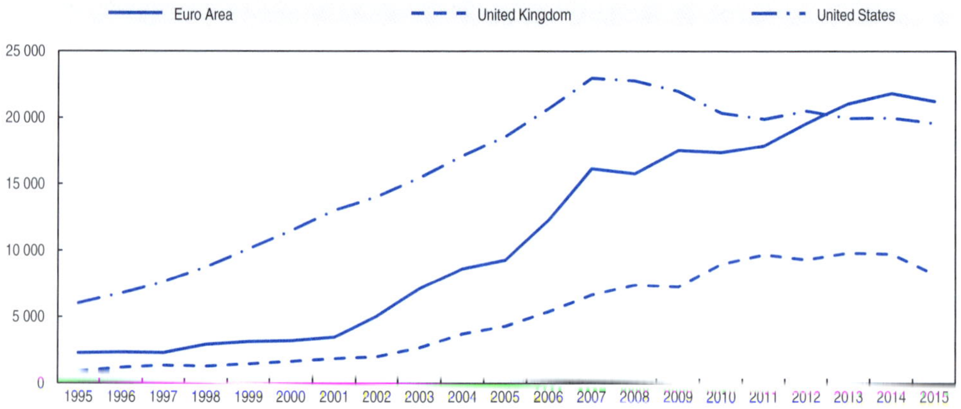

1. Euro Area contains Austria, Belgium, Estonia, Finland, France, Germany, Greece, Ireland, Italy, Luxembourg, the Netherlands, Portugal, Slovak Republic, Slovenia and Spain. For some countries time series are not complete, German data are reported from 1999, for Ireland and Slovenia data starts from 2001, finally the first observation for Luxembourg is 2002.
2. For comparability across countries, the sector includes other financial intermediaries (excluding non-MMF investment funds and insurance corporation and pension funds), financial auxiliaries, captive financial institutions and money lenders.

Source: OECD (2017), "Financial Balance Sheets, SNA 2008 (or SNA 1993): Non-consolidated stocks, annual", *OECD National Accounts Statistics* (database), http://dx.doi.org/10.1787/data-00720-en.

StatLink http://dx.doi.org/10.1787/888933589390

Rebalancing mismatches after the 2007-09 economic and financial crisis

The 2007-09 economic and financial crisis was triggered by sectoral imbalances and evolved into a balance sheet recession. The recovery relied on re-balancing the mismatches. Within Euro Area countries, the correction of the macroeconomic imbalances started in the period between 2008 and 2010. Measures were directed to the recapitalisation of financial institutions to assure a proper functioning of the financial system, and to the consolidation of government finances along with the adoption of structural reforms. Adjustments took place in countries with foreign trade deficits (Greece, Spain, Portugal and Ireland), mainly through a compression of domestic demand (ECB, 2012). Non-financial corporations and households consequently increased their saving rates, to reduce their debt. Corporate debt was reduced in Spain, while it remained stable in Greece and Portugal. Also in the United States, households increased their saving, jointly with a moderation of consumption and a lowering of residential investments which had peaked during the years before the crisis. Uncertainty on future conditions affected the US corporate sector, which reacted by augmenting the retained earnings and reducing their debt exposure.

To offset the impact of the crisis and to support private demand, the governments adopted counter-cyclical measures which, together with the financial support to the financial system, resulted in a worsening of government debt. Although Koo (2011), for example, considered these measures as insufficient to compensate for the decline in aggregate demand, after the sovereign debt crisis, governments of the Euro Area countries started to rebalance their balance sheets.

He et al. (2010) analysed balance sheet adjustments by quantifying how sectors in the United States dealt with securitised assets (i.e. mortgage backed securities and other asset-backed securities) when the crisis started. Between the second quarter of 2007 and the second quarter of 2009, the problems in the repo markets, in particular the rise in (agreed) write-offs on debt and the worsening of credit conditions started to affect non-bank financial intermediaries which in turn started to deleverage. Mortgage backed securities had to be transferred to the government sector, which played a pivotal role in the adjustment of the whole financial sector. In addition to buying securities, the government indirectly helped the banking sector by offering guarantees. Banks were mainly financed through government-backed debt, while the Treasury also purchased preferred shares and various hybrid debt instruments. Contrary to other financial intermediaries' balance sheets, banks increased the acquisition of securitised assets, resulting in a further increase in leverage[7]. Leverage was almost doubled as compared to normal periods, showing that not all sectors deleveraged in the same way. According to this view, leverage was re-distributed across the financial intermediaries. A possible explanation for this banking behaviour is that commercial banks still had access to stable funding, while other financial intermediaries were mainly funded through repos.

The policy use of sectoral indicators

The increased understanding of the causes of the 2007-09 economic and financial crisis pushed policy makers to increase the monitoring of financial flows and positions, with the aim of detecting potential misalignments and designing measures to intervene. For years, economists focused on price variables as sufficient indicators of market equilibrium, neglecting the potential information contained in the financial transactions and positions of sectors (Visco [2012]). In 2009, the IMF and the Financial Stability Board (FSB) recommended a number of improvements in statistics to strengthen economic analysis and policy. The recommendations of the G20 Data Gaps Initiative (DGI) (see Chapter 10) stressed the relevance of monitoring the risks in the financial sectors, the (inter)national financial linkages, and the potential vulnerabilities of domestic sectors through financial accounts and balance sheets data and other comparable financial statistics. The communication of official statistics was also considered as an important area of improvement.

Several countries produce a financial stability review through which the developments of risks in financial systems and the sectoral exposure are assessed, along with their ability to withstand shocks.[8] Heath (2013) mentions the key role that institutional sector accounts play in the analysis of macroeconomic conditions and the development of macro policies. The recent compilation of FWTW statistics was also considered relevant to demonstrate the linkages with other domestic sectors and their exposures towards the Rest of the World. The analysis of links within the financial system is at the heart of the shadow banking statistics, whose implementation represents one of the goals of the second phase of the G20 DGI launched in September 2015. The DGI fosters the regular collection and dissemination of reliable statistics for policy use and addresses the need for more granular data to enhance the analysis of vulnerabilities and possible spill-over effects.

The dissemination and improved communication of statistical information is considered as a priority for closing the statistical data gaps and therefore improving the functioning of markets (Heath, 2013). This was supported, amongst others, by the IMF Special Data Dissemination Standard Plus. With respect to pre-existing categories of statistics, starting from 2012 the IMF Executive Board also approved a further enhancement of data that includes references to the measurement of government debt and financial balance sheets more generally.

The crisis fallout in Europe showed different degrees of resilience across countries, in particular within the Euro Area, due to differences in the level of internal macroeconomic imbalances. A thorough analysis of the origins of the imbalances (different trends in competitiveness, heterogeneity in fiscal positions, the flow of capital from northern to southern countries, and so on) pointed to weaknesses in economic governance. As discussed previously, the EU Macroeconomic Imbalances Procedure provides a surveillance programme to detect and correct macroeconomic imbalances by relying on a scoreboard of indicators that monitor country risks in a systematic way, which are based on information in national accounts. The use of financial accounts and balance sheets, and more generally indicators based on national accounts, thereby assures consistency across indicators along with comparability across countries, thanks to the common methodology applied.

3. Uses of financial accounts and balance sheets in economic research

Financial accounts were first modelled by Morris A. Copeland who published in 1952 "A Study of Moneyflows in the United States" (see De Bonis and Gigliobianco [2012] for a full narration). Copeland collaborated with economists and statisticians at the Federal Reserve and the National Bureau of Economic Research. In 1955 the Federal Reserve produced the first version of what they referred to as the annual "flow of funds". Quarterly flow of funds were published for the first time in 1959 in the Federal Reserve Bulletin. With the regular publication by the Federal Reserve, financial accounts and balance sheets became an established tool of economic analysis. In the 1960s other countries started to set up the collection of financial accounts on a regular basis. As such financial accounts became part of a triad that also included (non-financial) national accounts and input-output tables (Klein [2003]).

Money demand, asset portfolios, and econometric models: Tobin's contribution

In his Nobel Memorial Lecture held in 1981, James Tobin spoke on "Money and finance in the macroeconomic process". Tobin's goal was to summarise a system of simultaneous equations, or a model of general equilibrium interdependence, where the relationships between variables describe the national economy. In his lecture Tobin presented two tables. The first referred to the "flow of funds" matrix in the United States for eleven assets and nine sectors in 1979. In the second table the data were further aggregated into four sectors and four assets. Then Tobin presented a model of the determination of output and prices in the short-run. Among the main features of the model were typical characteristics of financial accounts and balance sheets, such as the presence of different assets, the consideration of both flows and stocks, the modelling of both monetary policy operations and other financial operations, the sources of new supplies of private wealth, and household demand for asset accumulation.

Of course, the interest of Tobin for flow of funds was not new. While Keynes had put emphasis on income and interest rates as the main determinants of money demand, Tobin progressed to explain the demand for financial assets, where the latter are chosen according to their risk-return profile, in the general framework of portfolio choice theory. As wealth does not only consist of money but also includes other financial assets and non-financial assets, Tobin looked at the way economic agents distribute wealth across financial and non-financial assets.

Brainard and Tobin (1968) proposed an econometric model based on interrelated financial markets for assets and liabilities. Prices, interest rates and quantities in the financial system both influence and are influenced by the real economy. A large amount of research followed, by, amongst others, scholars belonging to the so-called Yale School. Econometric models were also developed by national central banks. For instance, the 1986 version of the Bank of Italy Quarterly Econometric Model contained a complete description of the links between saving, non-financial investments and financial flows[9].

The fall of financial accounts and balance sheets and the work of Godley

In the 1960s and the 1970s financial accounts were at the centre of economic analysis. From the mid-1980s until the 2007-09 economic and financial crisis, interest in financial accounts and balance sheets more or less vanished, for a number of reasons: a growing focus on the micro-economic foundations of macroeconomics; the increasing role of monetary and credit aggregates for the conduct of monetary policy that implied a lower focus on the entire financial system; trust in the self-correcting market mechanism through price adjustments, while considering quantities – both flows and stocks – less important; the rational expectation critique of Keynesian models; a growing inclination among economists to separate monetary and real phenomena; and the problems of achieving full international harmonisation of statistics until the introduction of the 1993 System of National Accounts (SNA93).

In contrast, Wynne Godley never abandoned the idea that economic models should be founded on flows and stocks, and developed consistent models of the US economy and other countries. In his approach, modern economies have an institutional structure comprising (non-financial) enterprises, banks, governments and households. The evolution of economies through time is dependent on the way these agents take decisions and interact with one another (Godley and Lavoie [2007]). At the beginning of each period stock variables in an economy – i.e. all physical stocks together with financial assets and liabilities – offer a summary of the past evolution. Transactions between the different institutional sectors then take place: final consumption, non-financial investments, government expenditures, the payment of taxes and the generation of profits, and the purchases and sales of financial assets and liabilities. These transactions move the stock variables from their state at the beginning of each period to their state at the end, to which holding gains and losses will have to be added. In their book Godley and Lavoie start from a simple model with one asset, money, and one country. They then make the model more complex by adding portfolio choices, bonds, holding gains, and the open economy.

Godley and Lavoie recognised that their model – sometimes labelled as the New Cambridge School – shared some features with the tradition of Tobin and the Yale School: the tracking of stocks; the existence of several assets and rates of return; the modelling of financial and monetary policy constraints;

and the importance of agents' budget constraints. The Yale school and the New Cambridge school are in agreement on the importance of consistent accounting, consistent stock-flow analysis and consistent constraints on behavioural relationships. Godley and Lavoie also emphasised how their models are distinct from those of Tobin. For example, they provide a clearer description of the dynamics of the economy, while Tobin put more emphasis on one-period models; market clearing through prices only occurs in some specific financial markets, and changes in quantities rather than in prices keep the economy in equilibrium; and institutions are not intermediaries acting on behalf of individuals.

Comparing financial systems and building balance sheets: Goldsmith's contribution

Goldsmith dedicated his research programme to the building of national and sector balance sheets, following the scientific advice of Hicks (1935) – who suggested that "We shall have to draw up a sort of generalized balance sheet, suitable for all individuals and institutions" – and presenting in Goldsmith (1985) a reconstruction of the national balance sheets of twenty countries from 1688 to 1978. When Modigliani and Brumberg first "invented" the life-cycle model, they cross-checked their intuition with Goldsmith's figures (see Modigliani [1999] and Fano [2011]).

Goldsmith's work has been a precursor of comparative economics: countries differ because their financial systems differ. In his interest for the quantitative comparison of financial structures, Goldsmith introduced the financial interrelations ratio (FIR), the ratio of gross financial assets to non-financial (real) wealth. FIR measures the weight of the financial system with respect to the real economy. The ratio depends directly on the amount of liabilities issued in the period and the change in the value of the stock of outstanding liabilities. The FIR is also dependent on the inverse of the ratio of non-financial wealth to GDP (see Bartiloro et al. [2005] for a breakdown of FIR into its components).

FIR generally increases with time because the growth of financial assets tends to be faster than that of real wealth. According to Goldsmith, the process stops when FIR reaches the value of 1 or 1.5; thereafter the ratio stabilises. Goldsmith reached this conclusion looking at long time series, but did not provide a theoretical explanation of this tendency. When FIR increases, the financial structure becomes more complex. For instance the stock exchange becomes more important and non-bank intermediaries start to develop. In arriving at this conclusion, Goldsmith already intuited the importance of what we today call the shadow banking system and its role in increasing FIR. There is a positive correlation between per capita GDP and the size of financial systems but the causality nexus is difficult to ascertain.

Goldsmith also introduced the financial intermediation ratio (FIN), with the goal to analyse the degree of "institutionalisation" of a country's financial structure and the role played by intermediaries. There are different definitions of FIN (see Goldsmith [1969], chapter 6). One can look for instance at the ratio between the liabilities of financial corporations – the central bank, commercial banks, other financial intermediaries and insurance companies and pension funds – and the total financial liabilities in a country. FIN is high in countries like the United Kingdom, Canada, Japan, the United States and Germany; see Table 11.2. Countries like Italy and Spain are characterised by lower levels of FIN, where financial intermediation is less developed with respect to the assets of the other institutional sectors. The financial intermediation ratio can also be calculated for banks alone, so as to better understand the role they play in different economies.

Table 11.2. **Financial liabilities of financial corporations as a ratio of total financial liabilities, 2015**

Canada	0.46
France	0.40
Germany	0.44
Italy	0.38
Japan	0.45
Spain	0.37
United Kingdom	0.52
United States	0.44

Source: OECD (2017), "Financial Balance Sheets, SNA 2008 (or SNA 1993): Non-consolidated stocks, annual", *OECD National Accounts Statistics* (database), http://dx.doi.org/10.1787/data-00720-en.
StatLink ⇒ http://dx.doi.org/10.1787/888933590378

The literature on finance and growth, still at the centre of the debate, often starts with Goldsmith's research on the correlation between economic development and the size of the financial system. Many scholars supported the view that the causality nexus goes from developments in the financial markets to economic growth (see, for instance, Demirguc-Kunt and Levine [2001]). Other economists, however, were of the opinion that "finance follows", or that the impact of financial developments on economic growth has been overemphasised. Following the 2007-09 economic and financial crisis, sceptical views became more common, arguing that finance has a non-linear effect on growth. Despite the differences in interpretations and results, all scholars paid tribute to Goldsmith's measurement of financial system dimensions.

How Thomas Piketty studied the wealth/income ratios

Piketty underlined the importance of household wealth to income ratios in developed countries with his publicly acclaimed *Capital in the Twenty-First Century* (2014). Building time series exploiting the availability of financial accounts and balance sheets, including statistics on non-financial assets, he showed that the ratio of total household net wealth to GDP has risen from 2-3 times in 1950 to 4-6 times today. Piketty started his analysis with the dynamics of the wealth to income ratio in France and the United Kingdom, the two countries for which the longest time series are available. He shows that in both countries the ratio has followed a U-curve since 1700, and that it is nowadays at the same level as three centuries ago. Over the same period, wealth has also undergone a metamorphosis, with a sharp relative decline in wealth of land, replaced by the value of dwellings (even if the increase in the value of dwellings can often be associated with the value of the underlying land). Net foreign assets, i.e. the difference between assets and liabilities with non-residents, have always been minor, in spite of the two countries' colonial empires. Since the 1980s, privatisations have reduced government owned assets and increased private wealth in both countries.

In Germany and the United States the dynamics of the wealth to income ratio were quite different. Since the late nineteenth century, the so-called Gilded Age, Germany has always had less private wealth than France and Britain, despite relatively high household savings rates since World War II, for two reasons. First, house prices in Germany are lower than in France and Britain, in part due to the relatively low demand for owner-occupied dwellings (as compared to other countries), and market flooding of low-value houses following the national reunification in 1989. Second, the value of corporate equity in Germany is relatively low, due to the impact of the so-called "Rhenish capitalism", where the involvement of banks is crucial and the stock exchange is underdeveloped. Wealth has also been consistently lower in the United States as compared to France or the United Kingdom; in the United States, houses have historically been cheap by international standards due to abundant availability of land. The United States' net foreign assets too have always been negligible, as the country was never a colonial power.

Since 1870 the wealth to income ratio in Europe has always been higher than in the United States, except between 1920 and 1980. Between 1915 and 1950, wealth in Germany, France and the United Kingdom was destroyed by war, by the reduction in net foreign assets, and by low saving. After 1950, private wealth did not expand significantly, reflecting the slow rise in asset prices until 1980, as a consequence of strong public intervention. Private wealth in these rich countries amounted to between 2 and 3.5 times GDP in 1970. On the contrary, since 1980, the ratio rose quickly in all countries. In 2013, it was higher in Spain, Italy, France and the United Kingdom than in the United States, Canada, and Germany; see Table 11.3. The rise in the ratios, disregarding short-term fluctuations, is also related to the jump in the prices of dwellings and shares, which had moved relatively slowly in the decades following 1945, because of rent control and financial regulation.

Table 11.3. **Household wealth: ratios to GDP, 2013**

	Total Assets	Non-financial Assets	Net Financial Assets
Canada	3.9	2.0	1.9
France	4.9	3.4	1.5
Germany	3.6	2.4	1.2
Italy	5.5	3.7	1.8
Japan	4.9	2.2	2.7
Spain*	5.1	4.0	1.1
United Kingdom	4.9	2.8	2.1
United States*	4.1	1.0	3.1

* For Spain and the United States, non-financial assets consist of dwellings only.
Source: OECD (2017), "Financial Balance Sheets, SNA 2008 (or SNA 1993): Non-consolidated stocks, annual", OECD National Accounts Statistics (database), http://dx.doi.org/10.1787/data-00720-en; and "Detailed National Accounts, SNA 2008 (or SNA 1993): Balance sheets for non-financial assets", OECD National Accounts Statistics (database), http://dx.doi.org/10.1787/data-00368-en.
StatLink ⟶ http://dx.doi.org/10.1787/888933590397

According to Piketty, the increase in the wealth to income ratios is not only explained by the increase of the numerator, but also by the low GDP growth rate, first and foremost due to low population growth in advanced countries. Piketty expects a further decrease in GDP growth, thus remaining rather pessimistic about the potential of population growth and technical progress to replicate the "golden age of growth" from 1950 to 1980. This forecast is akin to the secular stagnation hypothesis put forward by Summers (2014). A further finding, developed by Piketty and Zucman (2014), is that the increase in wealth to income ratios is more related to the accumulation of past saving than to increases in the prices of non-financial and financial assets owned by households. This finding is not that straightforward in view of the real estate and stock market bubbles in the 1980s/1990s as well as in the twenty-first century. Moreover capitalist economies differ from one another, because households choose to invest in different types of financial assets (De Bonis and Pozzolo, 2012). In some countries the composition of financial assets is tilted towards listed shares and insurance/pension instruments (such as in the United States and the United Kingdom), while in other countries bank deposits and debt securities are more popular (such as in Italy and Japan). Since the 1970s, households have generally increased the share of investments in the stock market, either directly or indirectly via investment funds, and – with the exception of Japan – decreased their investments in bank deposits (De Bonis, Fano and Sbano, 2013).

Piketty (2013) builds upon the work of Goldsmith (1985), by reconstructing balance sheets for a number of countries. As an annex to his successful book, Piketty also made available another 900 pages of statistical time series and methodological discussion on income, wealth and other macroeconomic variables for eight countries: the United States, Japan, Germany, the United

Kingdom, France, Italy, Canada and Australia (see *http://piketty.pse.ens.fr/files/ PikettyZucman2013Appendix.pdf*). Some scholars have argued that a good part of the increase in the wealth to income ratio depends on trends in real estate investments and house prices. The problem is the difficulty of establishing a common methodology that allows for the measurement and international comparison of countries' shares of increases in wealth that are due to saving, to higher prices of financial assets, and to higher house prices. There is no doubt whatsoever that wealth has increased significantly, particularly in developed countries, but we still do not have a consensus on the determinants. Econometric analysis is often hampered by problems with clearly distinguishing the causal nexus of wealth and other macroeconomic and institutional variables, such as saving, unemployment, interest rates, social expenditures, taxation, and the age composition of population.

The reassessment of interactions between the real economy and the financial sector

More generally, the interactions between the financial sector and the real economy were already studied before the 2007-09 economic and financial crisis. There are different strands of literature, such as the study of the correlation between money, credit and nominal national income; the analysis of the non-monetary effects of the banking crises in the propagation of the Great Depression; the research into the bank lending channel and the subsequent declinations of the bank capital channel and the liquidity channel, which stress that capital and liquidity matter for credit supply; and the "financial accelerator" approach (Bernanke et al., 1996).

Most of the previous contributions told a partial story, and their results have not been well incorporated in macro-econometric models. These models sometimes emphasised only the demand for credit without taking into account the supply side of credit. The amount of IMF research on macro-financial linkages was quite limited; even by the end of 2008 the research efforts in this area were insufficient. However, after the 2007-09 economic and financial crisis, the importance of such interactions is now well-acknowledged and at the centre of economic research.

De Bonis et al. (2014) estimated the determinants of investments in machinery and other equipment, residential investments and final consumption expenditure for the United States and a sample of Euro Area countries, focusing on the impact of credit on these categories of spending. The main results were that, in the United States, credit to enterprises has a positive impact on investments in machinery and equipment, and that consumer credit and mortgage loans are positively associated with final consumption, the latter through the mortgage equity withdrawal mechanism (i.e., the possibilities of consumers to borrow additional funds against the increased market value of their dwellings). In the Euro Area, the authors found a similar positive link between loans and investments (in both machinery and equipment and residential buildings). However, the correlation between consumer credit/mortgage loans and final consumption was shown to be weaker than in the US case, probably because household debt is smaller in the Euro Area than in the United States and mortgage equity withdrawal is less common.

One of the most promising recent uses of financial accounts and balance sheets in econometric models can be found in Duca and Muellbauer (2014). The authors first present a credit-augmented life cycle consumption function, where household wealth and credit constraints play a key role. Final consumption is not only linked to income and interest rates, but also to net liquid assets, illiquid financial assets, and housing assets. In doing so, the authors place the consumption function into a larger system of equations, taking into account the conditions of the consumer credit and of housing credit markets. They also show how financial innovations – such as the mortgage equity withdrawal – and loan availability influence consumption. Duca and Muellbauer conclude that economists should build macro-financial models for some key sectors – such as non-financial corporations and households – that incorporate financial linkages in a tractable way. This will address some of the criticism on the Tobin-Bainard and Godley's approaches as being too complex and difficult to manage for policy making purposes; see, for instance, Goodhart's review (2008) of Godley and Lavoie (2007).

It can be concluded that analysing the impact of financial frictions on the real economy is not an easy task. While during recessions there is no doubt that bank credit and other forms of finance matter, the same result is more difficult to observe in "normal times". Indeed, the empirical estimation of macro models based on financial accounts and balance sheets, including all kinds of financial interactions, remains a challenge.

Key points

- In recent years, there has been a return of interest in financial accounts and balance sheets. Economists and policymakers are increasingly interested in the type of analysis that can be done with (quarterly) financial accounts and balance sheets, FWTW breakdowns, network analysis tools, the reconciliation of macroeconomic data with micro statistics, including the compilation of distributional information.

- Crises manifested in different ways during recent decades, forcing economists to adapt their models to detect vulnerabilities. The Asian crisis at the end of 1990s emphasised the role of sectoral connections and the need to complement the usual analysis based on the flows in the national accounts with the study of balance sheets. The imbalances that were at the heart of the 2007-09 economic and financial crisis could have been detected, at least partly, through the lens of financial accounts and balance sheets. On the other hand, some transformations of the financial systems, such as the shadow banking system, hindered a complete assessment of the economy with the available statistics.

- The use of leverage was likely one of the most important causes of imbalances, mainly in the financial sector. During asset price booms, financial intermediaries increased their leverage to enlarge the balance sheet, whilst an opposite strategy was adopted when prices decreased. This pro-cyclical behaviour contributed to intensifying the financial market fluctuations.

- The strong use of securitisation contributed to changing the model of financial intermediation. Banks originated loans and distributed them to the market through other financial intermediaries, which was reflected in the sustained growth of non-bank intermediary balance sheets.

- During the years preceding the 2007-09 economic and financial crisis, one of the key mistakes was to think that tracking financial quantities was not important (see e.g. Visco [2012]). Popular pre-crisis econometric models excluded banking and finance, taking as a given that finance and asset prices were a mere by-product of the real economy (Muellbauer [2016]). The 2007-09 economic and financial crisis showed that financial flows and stocks do matter.

- The study on the interactions between the real economy and the financial sector, the evolution of the wealth to income ratios, the analysis of wealth composition and the interdependence between households, corporations and financial intermediaries are nowadays at the centre of analysis, with a renewed interest in financial accounts and balance sheets.

Notes

1. However, even though the two international standards are almost fully consistent, in practice discrepancies still exist between balance of payments and financial accounts for the Rest of the World sector. This is mainly due to the fact that financial accounts integrate the balance of payments data with other statistical sources on domestic sources. As a consequence, the data from balance of payments might be adjusted to ensure consistency. Balance of payments statistics are to a certain extent also the result of integrating various underlying statistics, but usually not to such an extent as the financial accounts and balance sheets (for good reasons, as balance of payments only refer to flows and positions of residents vis-à-vis non-residents). Nevertheless, there is work in progress in various fora, in particular in the European Union context, to reduce the existing differences.

2. Partial, non-integrated, series of the financial accounts and balance sheets for the non-financial sectors had been published by the ECB since 2002 ("Table of Financing and Investment").

3. Before this crisis, the analysis was mainly based on risks deriving from flow variables, while stock variables or stock-based indicators were deemed only to be relevant for public sector debt or foreign debt (IMF, 2015).

4. In the 2008 SNA, the standard breakdown of maturity refers to the original maturity.

5. During this paragraph, the term "integration" is used to describe a situation of a country's openness to both the liberalisation of international trade (elimination or reduction of foreign trade barriers) and international capital flows. Following financial integration, the accumulation of larger stocks of foreign assets and liabilities is clearly visible in many countries (Lane and Milesi-Ferretti, 2008).

6. For the Euro Area the percentage can be overstated since not all countries reported data in 1995.

7. He et al. (2010) estimated an increase in banking leverage, during the period studied, from 10 to between 20 and 32.

8. IMF has been publishing a Global Financial Stability Report since 2002.

9. On the different approaches for modelling the monetary and financial sectors in econometric models, see Ando and Modigliani (1975) including the replies by Tobin and Smith in the same volume.

References

Adrian, T. and H.S. Shin (2008), "Liquidity, monetary policy, and financial cycles", *Federal Reserve Bank of New York, Current Issues in Economics and Finance*, Vol. 14, Federal Reserve Bank of New York, New York City, www.newyorkfed.org/medialibrary/media/research/current_issues/ci14-1.pdf.

Adrian, T. and H.S. Shin (2009), "The shadow banking system: Implications for financial regulation", *Federal Reserve Bank of New York Staff Reports*, No. 382, Federal Reserve Bank of New York, New York City, www.newyorkfed.org/medialibrary/media/research/staff_reports/sr382.pdf.

Allen, M. et al. (2002), "A balance sheet approach to financial crisis", *IMF Working Papers*, No. 210, International Monetary Fund, Washington, DC, www.imf.org/en/Publications/WP/Issues/2016/12/30/A-Balance-Sheet-Approach-to-Financial-Crisis-16167.

Ando, A. and F. Modigliani (1975), "Some reflections on describing structures of financial sectors", in *The Brookings Model: Perspective and Recent Developments*, North-Holland, New York City.

Bardsen, G., K. Lindquist and D.P. Tsomocos (2006), "Evaluation of macroeconomic models for financial stability analysis", *Norwegian University Working Papers*, No. 4 Norwegian University, Trondheim, http://static.norges-bank.no/globalassets/upload/import/publikasjoner/arbeidsnotater/pdf/arb-2006-01.pdf?v=03/09/2017122307&ft=.pdf.

Bartiloro, L. and G. di Iasio (2012) "Financial sector dynamics and firms' capital structure", in *The Financial Systems of Industrial Countries*, Springer, New York City.

Bartiloro, L. et al. (2006), *The Financial Structures of the Leading Industrial Countries: A Medium-term Analysis*, presented at the Bank of Italy Financial Accounts: History, Methods, the Case of Italy and International Comparisons Conference, 1-2 December, Perugia.

Bernanke, B.S., M. Gertler and S. Gilchrist (1996), "The financial accelerator and the flight to quality", *Review of Economics and Statistics*, Vol. 78, MIT Press, Boston, pp. 1-15.

BIS (1993), *63rd Annual Report*, Bank for International Settlements, Basel, www.bis.org/publ/arpdf/archive/ar1993_en.pdf.

Brainard, W.C. and J. Tobin (1968), "Pitfalls in financial model building", *American Economic Review*, 58 (2), American Economic Association, Nashville, pp. 99-122.

Copeland, M. (1952), *A Study of Moneyflows in the United States*, National Bureau for Economic Research, New York.

Dawson, J.C. (2004), "The Asian crisis and flow-of-funds analysis", *Review of Income and Wealth*, Vol. 50, Wiley, Hoboken, pp. 243-260.

De Bonis, R. and A. Gigliobianco (2012), "The origins of financial accounts in the United States and Italy: Copeland, Baffi and the institutions", in *The Financial Systems of Industrial Countries. Evidence from Financial Accounts*, Springer, New York City.

De Bonis, R. and A. F. Pozzolo (2012), (edited by), "The Financial Systems of Industrial Countries. Evidence from Financial Accounts", Springer, New York City.

De Bonis, R., D. Fano and T. Sbano (2013), "Household aggregate wealth in the main OECD countries from 1980 to 2011: what do the data tell us?", *Bank of Italy Occasional Papers*, No. 160, www.bancaditalia.it/pubblicazioni/qef/2013-0160/QEF_160.pdf?language_id=1.

De Bonis, R., L. Infante and F. Paternò (2014), "Determinants and consequences of credit tightening: An analysis of the United States and the Euro Area", in *A Flow-of-Funds Perspective on the Financial Crisis, Vol. I*, Palgrave Macmillan, Basingstoke.

Duca, J. and J. Muellbauer (2014), "Tobin lives: Integrating evolving credit market architecture into flow of funds based macro-models", in *A Flow-of-Funds Perspective on the Financial Crisis, Vol. II*, Palgrave Macmillan, Basingstoke.

Demirguc-Kunt, A. and R. Levine (eds.) (2001), *Financial Structure and Economic Growth: A Cross-Country Comparisons of Banks, Markets and Development*, MIT Press, Boston.

Dornbusch, R. (2002), "A primer on emerging-market crisis", in *Preventing Currency Crisis in Emerging Markets*, University of Chicago Press, Chicago.

ECB (2017), *MFI Interest Rates*, www.ecb.europa.eu/stats/financial_markets_and_interest_rates/bank_interest_rates/mfi_interest_rates/html/index.en.html.

ECB (2012), "Comparing the recent financial crisis in the United States and the Euro Area with the experience of Japan in the 1990s", *Monthly Bulletin*, Vol. 95, European

Central Bank, Frankfurt, www.ecb.europa.eu/pub/pdf/other/art2_mb201205en_pp95-112en.pdf?25ffe7781f62867f24bf043a9ff82e57.

Eichengreen, B., A.K. Rose and C. Wyplosz (1995), "Exchange market mayhem: The antecedents and aftermath of speculative attacks", *Economic Policy*, Vol. 10, Issue 21, Oxford University Publishing, Oxford.

European Union (2012), "Scoreboard for the surveillance of macroeconomic imbalances", *Occasional Papers*, No. 92, https://ec.europa.eu/info/sites/info/files/swp_scoreboard_08_11_2011_en.pdf.

ECB and Eurostat (2017), *Euro Area Accounts (EAA)*, http://ec.europa.eu/eurostat/web/national-accounts/data/database, www.ecb.europa.eu/stats/macroeconomic_and_sectoral/sector_accounts/html/index.en.html.

Eurostat (2017b), *Macroeconomic Imbalance Procedure Indicators*, Eurostat, Luxembourg, http://ec.europa.eu/eurostat/web/macroeconomic-imbalances-procedure.

Fano, D. (2011), *Financial Accounts in the System of National Accounts and in the Current Economy: An Introduction*, UniversItalia, Rome.

Flood, R. and P. Garber (1984), "Collapsing exchange rate regime: Some linear examples", *Journal of International Economics*, Vol. 17, Elsevier, Amsterdam, p. 1-13.

Girón, C. and S. Mongelluzzo (2014), "Bank leverage and the credit cycle in the Euro Area: A Bayesian semi-parametric approach", in *A Flow-of-Funds Perspective on the Financial Crisis*, Vol. 1, Palgrave McMillan, Basingstoke.

Godley, W. and M. Lavoie (2007), *Monetary Economics: An Integrated Approach to Money, Credit, Income, Production and Wealth*, Palgrave MacMillan, Basingstoke.

Goldsmith, R.W. (1969), *Financial Structure and Development*, Yale University Press, New Haven.

Goldsmith, R.W. (1985), *Comparative National Balance Sheets, A Study of Twenty Countries 1688-1978*, The University of Chicago Press, Chicago.

Goodhart, C. (2008), "Review of Godley and Lavoie (2007)", *Economica*, November, Wiley, Hoboken, pp. 798-99.

He, Z., I.G. Khang and A. Krishamurthy (2010), "Balance sheet adjustments in the 2008 crisis", *NBER Working Papers*, No. 15919, National Bureau of Economic Research, Cambridge, www.nber.org/papers/w15919.pdf.

Heath, R. (2013), "Why are the G-20 Data Gaps Initiative and the SDDS Plus relevant for financial stability analysis?", *IMF Working Papers*, No. 13/6, International Monetary Fund, Washington, DC.

Hicks, J.R. (1935), "A suggestion for simplifying the theory of money", Economica, Vol. 2, No. 5, Wiley, Hoboken, pp. 1-19.

Infante, L., A.F. Pozzolo and R. Tedeschi (2012), "Imbalances in household, firm, public and foreign sector balance sheets in the 2000s: A case of "I told you so"?, in *The Financial Systems of Industrial Countries*, Springer, New York City.

IMF (2015), "Balance sheet analysis in fund surveillance", *IMF Policy Papers*, www.imf.org/external/np/pp/eng/2015/061215.pdf.

IMF (2002)," United States: selected issues", *IMF Country Report No. 02/165*

Klein, L.R. (2003), "Some potential linkages for input-output analysis with flow-of-funds", *Economic Systems Research*, Vol. 15, September, Taylor & Francis, Oxford, pp. 269-277.

Koo, R.C. (2011), "The world in balance sheet recession: causes, cure, and politics", *Real-World Economics Review*, No. 58, World Economics Association, Bristol.

Krugman, P. (2010), Crises, unpublished, *www.princeton.edu/ pkrugman/CRISES.pdf*.

Krugman, P. (1979), "A model of balance-of-payment crises", *Journal of Money Credit and Banking* Vol. 11, Wiley, Hoboken, p. 311-325.

Lane, P.R. and P. McQuade (2006), "Domestic credit growth and international capital flows", ECB Working Paper Series, No. 1566, *www.ecb.europa.eu/pub/pdf/scpwps/ ecbwp1566.pdf?c15c44c01379f3346ad1511091ea6149*.

Lane, P.R. and G.M. Milesi-Ferretti (2012), "The external wealth of nations mark II: Revised and extended estimates of foreign assets and liabilities, 1970-2004", IMF Working Papers, No. 69, International Monetary Fund, Washington, DC, *www.imf.org/external/ pubs/ft/wp/2006/wp0669.pdf*.

Mendoza, E.G. and M.E. Terrones (2008), "An anatomy of credit booms: Evidence from macro aggregates and micro-data", NBER Working Papers, No. 14049, National Bureau of Economic Research, Cambridge, *www.nber.org/papers/w14049.pdf*.

Modigliani, F. (1999), *Memorie di un Economista*, Laterza, Bari.

Muellbauer, J. (2016), "Macroeconomics and consumption: why central bank models failed and how to repair them", *Vox.eu*, 21 December, *http://voxeu.org/article/why-central-bank-models-failed-and-how-repair-them*.

Obstfeld, M. (1994), "The logic of currency crises", NBER Working Papers, No. 4640, National Bureau of Economic Research, Cambridge, *www.nber.org/papers/w4640.pdf*.

OECD (2017), "Financial Balance Sheets, SNA 2008 (or SNA 1993): Non-consolidated stocks, annual", *OECD National Accounts Statistics* (database), *http://dx.doi.org/10.1787/ data-00720-en*; and "Detailed National Accounts, SNA 2008 (or SNA 1993): Balance sheets for non-financial assets", *OECD National Accounts Statistics* (database), *http:// dx.doi.org/10.1787/data-00368-en*.

Palumbo, M.G. and J.A. Parker (2009), "The integrated financial and real system of national accounts for the United States: does it presage the financial crisis?", *American Economic Review: papers and proceedings*, Vol. 99, No. 2, pp. 80-86.

Piketty, T. (2014), *Capital in the 21st Century*, Harvard University Press, Cambridge.

Piketty, T. and G. Zucman (2014), "Capital is back: Wealth-income ratios in rich countries 1700-2010", *Quarterly Economic Journal*, Vol. 129, No. 3, Oxford University Press, Oxford, pp. 1155-1210.

Rodrik, D. (2006), "Goodbye Washington consensus, Hello Washington confusion? A review of the World Bank's economic growth in the 1990s: learning from a decade of reform", *Journal of Economic Literature*, Vol. 44, No. 4, American Economic Association, Nashville, pp. 973-987.

Schularick, M. and A.M. Taylor (2012), "Credit booms gone bust: monetary policy, leverage cycle and financial crises, 1870-2008", *American Economic Review*, Vol. 102, No. 2, American Economic Association, Nashville, pp. 1029-1061.

Summers, L.H. (2014), "U.S. economic prospects: secular stagnation, hysteresis, and the zero lower bound", *Business Economics*, Vol. 49, No. 2, Springer, New York City, pp. 65-73.

Visco, I. (2012), "Foreword" in *The Financial Systems of Industrial Countries*, Springer, New York City.

Williamson, J. (2004), *The Washington Consensus as Policy Prescription for Development*, speech in the Practitioner of Development series, 13 January, World Bank, Washington, DC.

Winkler, A., A. van Riet and P. Bull (2014), *A Flow-of-Funds Perspective on the Financial Crisis: Introduction and Overview*, Vol. 1, Palgrave McMillan, Basingstoke.

Zwijnenburg, J., S. Bournot and F. Giovannelli (2016), "OECD Expert Group on Disparities in a National Accounts Framework – results from the 2015 exercise", *OECD Working Papers*, No. 76, *http://dx.doi.org/10.1787/2daa921e-en*.

ORGANISATION FOR ECONOMIC CO-OPERATION AND DEVELOPMENT

The OECD is a unique forum where governments work together to address the economic, social and environmental challenges of globalisation. The OECD is also at the forefront of efforts to understand and to help governments respond to new developments and concerns, such as corporate governance, the information economy and the challenges of an ageing population. The Organisation provides a setting where governments can compare policy experiences, seek answers to common problems, identify good practice and work to co-ordinate domestic and international policies.

The OECD member countries are: Australia, Austria, Belgium, Canada, Chile, the Czech Republic, Denmark, Estonia, Finland, France, Germany, Greece, Hungary, Iceland, Ireland, Israel, Italy, Japan, Korea, Latvia, Luxembourg, Mexico, the Netherlands, New Zealand, Norway, Poland, Portugal, the Slovak Republic, Slovenia, Spain, Sweden, Switzerland, Turkey, the United Kingdom and the United States. The European Union takes part in the work of the OECD.

OECD Publishing disseminates widely the results of the Organisation's statistics gathering and research on economic, social and environmental issues, as well as the conventions, guidelines and standards agreed by its members.

OECD PUBLISHING, 2, rue André-Pascal, 75775 PARIS CEDEX 16
(30 2017 06 1 P) ISBN 978-92-64-28125-7 – 2017